SOCIOLOGY
Understanding Social Behavior

Alan P. Bates / Joseph Julian

University of Nebraska

SOCIOLOGY
Understanding Social Behavior

HOUGHTON MIFFLIN COMPANY · BOSTON

Atlanta · Dallas · Geneva, Illinois · Hopewell, New Jersey · Palo Alto · London

Printed in the U.S.A.
Library of Congress Catalog Card Number: 74-11712
ISBN: 0-395-18652-8

Contents

Preface

Our aim in writing this text has been to present a clear overview of the sociological perspective in a way that will relate practically to the everyday experiences of students. Given the breadth and complexity of the field and the intellectual controversies within it, this is no easy task. Yet we are convinced that contemporary sociology contains ideas that belong in every good liberal education. Thus the student who takes only one course in sociology will meet some of the most important of these ideas. Students who pursue the discipline more thoroughly will have a foundation that will not betray them.

Keeping the student reader in mind, we have used as little technical jargon as possible and have kept to a minimum the theoretical aspects of the presentation (concepts, competing theories, etc.). The work is theoretically eclectic. In our view, the divisions among sociologists can probably be better explored after the introductory course, even though there are references to such controversies in this book. Our strategy is to introduce students to the essential sociological viewpoint. Experience indicates that this by itself is a challenging job.

ORGANIZATION

A few words about the book's organization seem appropriate. The first four chapters, comprising Part One, present core ideas and concepts that appear repeatedly in subsequent chapters. Thus, while it would be feasible to change the order in which Chapters 5 through 16 are considered, students should be familiar with the first four chapters before undertaking any of the others. In these four chapters the basic viewpoints of sociology and social psychology are set forth, and key concepts like culture, socialization, interaction, values, norms, roles, and groups are given extended treatment.

Beyond Chapter 3 the book represents, to a degree, a progression from small to large social units. For example, Chapter 4 deals with very small units, that is, with what is sometimes called "microsociology." Beginning with such small units may help the newcomer to sociology, for they are simpler and closer to everyday experience. Part Two, "Social Units and Processes," covers a wide variety of what might be termed "middle-range" phenomena. Many of these topics, however, resist being forced into a size progression. Communities, for example, range from tiny hamlets to giant metropolises, and—as a class of social units—are not inherently larger or smaller than, say, occupations or complex organizations. The size principle appears a little more clearly in Part Three, "Social Institutions." If institutions are conceived as elements of culture (as is the case here), then they are among the very largest subparts of a society's culture. Finally, Part Four, "The Sociological Perspective," discusses society, an entity that includes all the diverse phenomena considered earlier and the largest unit considered in this book.

SPECIAL FEATURES A number of special or unusual features of the book ought to be mentioned. For example, each chapter contains a section on practicing the sociological perspective. It is one thing to gain an intellectual insight from the pages of a book, and quite another to apply that insight to the disorderly world of everyday experience. So, we have provided many suggestions to help the reader move back and forth between idea and specific social reality.

Many have noted the strong pragmatic theme in American culture, the tendency to ask of anything: what is it good for? While the main emphasis in this book is on sociology as a field of basic knowledge, a section of each chapter discusses some practical implications of this knowledge for the solution of social problems. And almost every chapter contains still another special section, one focused on social change. This section, a natural outgrowth of the chapter's analysis of the order and predictability in social life, sets social structure into motion and shows how order itself always changes its character through time.

Throughout, there are innumerable references to the experiences college students are likely to have. Making the fundamental ideas of sociology applicable to personal experience seems important. At the same time, not all of these fundamental ideas can be simply illustrated from the experiences of young adults. Hence, we have also taken examples from areas far removed from students' experience. In doing so, we have made a serious effort to choose examples that are interesting and important. Athough we have attended to the siren song of "relevance," we have not allowed it to drown out other important considerations.

ACKNOWLEDGMENTS

Although the authors are responsible for what is written here, the fact remains that the book would not exist were it not for the direct and indirect assistance of many people. Obviously, we stand on the shoulders of those who, in one way or another, were our mentors through long years of study and teaching. In terms of this particular enterprise, Ernest Q. Campbell gave searching criticism and advice in the earlier versions of the manuscript. At a later stage, Norman W. Storer was an invaluable critic of the entire work. The influence of these distinguished sociologists is present at a great many points. We are also indebted to many others for criticisms of particular sections at various stages in the development of the book. Among those who read portions of the manuscript and offered many valued suggestions are Clyde Nunn, Tom Bates, Elaine Hess, and Susan Jacobs. Our colleague Nicholas Babchuk was of great assistance in one particular chapter. We also appreciate the efforts of the many people at Houghton Mifflin who have made this book possible.

Finally, thanks to our wives, Elsie Bates (who did considerable manuscript typing) and Lynn Julian. Quite simply, the book could not have been done without their forbearance during what must often have seemed interminable periods of sequestered preoccupation with writing and rewriting.

ALAN P. BATES
JOSEPH JULIAN

PART 1
Some Fundamental Ideas

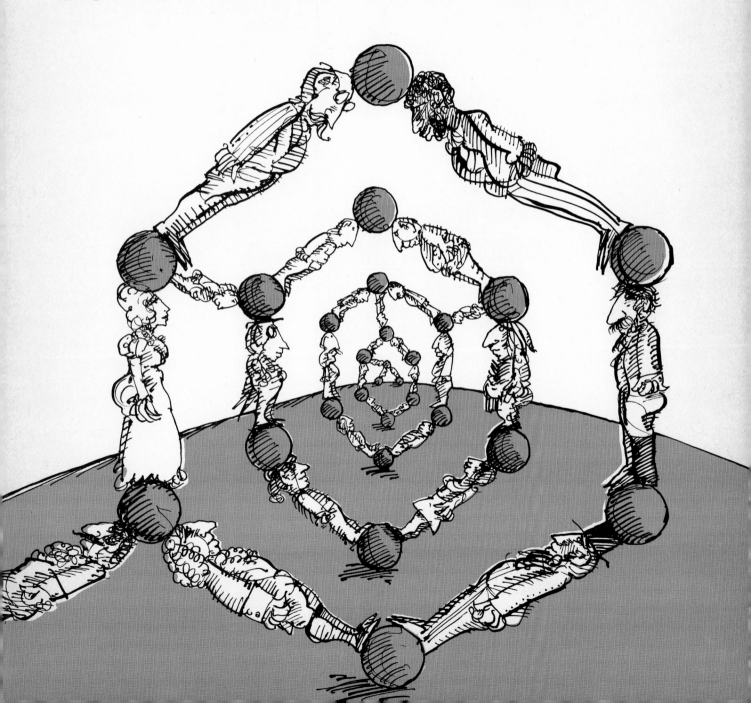

The four chapters of Part One are the foundation on which this book rests. The central task of Chapter 1 is to introduce the sociological perspective as a way of thinking about human behavior and to compare it with other more familiar perspectives—biological, psychological, and moral. Since American sociology is heavily influenced by social psychological thought, social psychology is also introduced as a perspective and is distinguished from sociology.

The concept of culture is treated in Chapter 2. Culture, man's social heritage, is as essential to human life as is the physical heritage transmitted through the germ plasm. A grasp of the culture concept is indispensable for the analysis of all forms of social behavior.

Chapter 3 presents the book's most continuous and extended treatment of social psychology. Having to do with relationships between the individual, on the one hand, and social behavior and culture, on the other, social psychology contains ideas that are implicit or explicit in most of the rest of the book. We have chosen socialization as a kind of master social psychological process around which to organize our discussion of social psychology.

Chapter 4 begins with the most microscopic level of behavior so far as sociology is concerned: the situation in which a single act of one person affects (and is affected by) a single act of another person. Proceeding from this point to an analysis of social interaction and communication, it arrives at the formal concept of group, which is treated in considerable detail. The reader who masters these four chapters will find them very helpful in understanding all that follows.

Sociology and the Sociological Perspective

Only in man has life on earth become aware of self. The creature who calls himself *Homo sapiens* occupies a lonely eminence, for he alone can contemplate himself and ponder the nature of the world and his place in it. For thousands of years, man has gazed inward at himself and outward at the universe; on its countless adventures, his probing mind has experienced wonder, fear, and hope.

Man remembers his experiences, thoughts, and feelings. He has used them to produce religion, art, technology, and science—and societies to shelter these and many other creations. But though these ceaseless journeys of the mind and heart have immeasurably enlarged man's knowledge, he finds himself asking more questions than ever before. He has amassed knowledge surpassing the imagination of his forebears but does not rest content. Man is uneasy, struggling with problems that present knowledge cannot solve. Curiosity and need impel him into a little-known future, save that it will be very different from the present.

There are many who say that what man still knows least about is man himself. Measured against the long history of human intellect, the study of man through the social sciences is still in its infancy. Of course men have observed social behavior and thought seriously about it for centuries. Many of the deepest insights produced by art, philosophy, and literature are the product of this observation and thought. But systematic intellectual disciplines, designed to study human nature and behavior on a scientific basis of empirical observation, are of recent birth. It was not until the nineteenth century that disciplined scholarship, in-

We shall study human societies in this book, and human societies, while having some things in common, also vary tremendously. Some, for instance, are technologically much simpler than others (though not necessarily simpler in other ways). These illustrations suggest something of the range of complexity in technological means. All societies must survive in a natural environment. Not so in modern urban societies, which bring important and sometimes destructive changes to the environment upon which they depend. Here we see Peruvian Indians, the Ginza, a main shopping street in Tokyo, Japan, an Ethiopian farmer, and an expressway in the United States.

cluding the method of knowing called science, was seriously applied to human social behavior. As organized sciences, psychology, sociology, and anthropology are not much more than a hundred years old. Yet in this short time they have permanently altered man's views of himself and given him rudimentary but already powerful new tools for coping with his universe.

Only a newborn infant looks at the world with completely naive eyes. The limitations of the human senses are such that we can perceive and respond to only a fraction of the stimuli that impinge upon them at any given time. Thus, in order to survive, we learn quite early to select which stimuli to respond to and which to ignore. Once developed and supported by habit, these characteristic ways of responding tend to be perpetuated unless something new changes or adds to them. The full story of how selectivity evolves demands a long account of learning, perception, and socialization, and cannot be undertaken here. We shall use the term *perspective* to denote a thought-structure that consists of a few basic assumptions; these express a conception of what the world, or some important part of it, is "really like," and how it "really works." The characteristic of perspectives most important here is that they work as major organizers in the selection of responses within the individual. Because a perspective provides a mental picture of reality, a person who accepts it finds that it suggests many specific attitudes and actions.

We all acquire a number of perspectives on the world, and among the most important are those on human behavior. Mere living raises a thousand questions about people. What makes an occupation satisfying over a lifetime? Why hasn't war been abolished? Why is there conflict between the generations? What makes for a successful marriage? Our complex world could not function if we had to treat each of these questions separately; usually, we relate such questions to some broad perspective whose assumptions about reality furnish guidelines for our behavior.

These perspectives, or world views, originate with society; the individual does not manufacture his own, though he may have the illusion that he does. Every society makes available to its members a number of perspectives on reality. They may be very ancient, or quite recent. The individual may modify them slightly, but he does not invent them. A simple, homogeneous society has few perspectives, and the individual may know and accept all of them as guides to conduct. In our complex, pluralistic society it is probably impossible even to be aware of all the available perspectives. And no one could accept all of them, since they sometimes offer not only different but incompatible views of reality.

Most people acquire fewer new perspectives as they grow older—not only because of lowered capacity to learn, but because familiar world views block out new ones. Old perspectives have at least the virtue of comfort; it takes real effort to learn new ones. People often cling to old orientations toward reality, even when they demonstrably don't work. The mentally ill are not alone in holding tenaciously to notions of reality which are unrealistic or even harmful.

Our pictures of reality are not always conscious and rational. We begin to acquire them in childhood; as time goes by, we get so used to them that we scarcely know they are there. Sometimes perspectives are formed quite deliberately, intellectualized, scrutinized, and adopted by large numbers of people—for example, those based on Oriental world views employed by some segments of contemporary youth culture. But usually perspectives thoroughly learned are applied with little reflection. A look at several familiar nonsociological concepts of human behavior should help us to grasp the sociological perspective. Sociology's special viewpoint is sometimes confused with these other concepts. Learning what sociology is *not* concerned with will be of assistance when we turn to the central concerns of our field.

THE BIOLOGICAL PERSPECTIVE   This outlook locates the causes of human behavior in the structures and processes of the body. Whatever else people may be, they are certainly physical organisms. Always present and functioning, the body makes possible every act the individual performs. Some kinds of behavior are very closely linked to organic states. Alcohol in the bloodstream slows reflexes. Adrenalin, released into the blood supply of a person who is angry or afraid, makes possible extraordinary outputs of energy. People must eat (almost anything if necessary) in order to survive. But there are limits to what the body can do. The recent remarkable improvement in the speed at which men have run the mile does not lead to the hope that future athletes will finish in less than four seconds rather than four minutes.

Limitations of the Biological Perspective   Consider the last two illustrations again. The need for nourishment accounts neither for the wide variety of foods nor for the customary frequency with which we eat—not to mention the complicated behavior which so often accompanies refueling the body. The ultimate limits to unaided human speed (as yet unknown) do not explain the fierce competition to reach those limits. To take another example, the biological mating which occurs everywhere fails to account for a particular family institution, for changes in the family system of a society, or for variations among different family systems. As Burgess and Locke succinctly put it, "The animal mates, but man marries" (1945:6).

The biological perspective has contributed immensely to our knowledge of human behavior. A widely appreciated example is modern medicine, a technology largely based on a biological model. On the other hand, the human biological makeup *permits* an enormous variety in behavior which it does not specifically *determine,* and it is often hard to assess the role of organic versus nonorganic factors. This has been the case, for instance, in seeking the causes of a serious mental illness, schizophrenia. Experts have also long disagreed about the relative contribution of biological and nonbiological causes to alcoholism.

The general public has often used the biological perspective naively, and stretched its ability to "explain" behavior far beyond its capacity. For some behavior, organic explanations simply won't do. Why did Jesus freaks appear on the American scene in the late sixties and early seventies? Why was student activism at a high point about 1970 and why did it then decline? Why are so many of society's most virulent social problems now centered in the inner city? Biology cannot answer these questions, not because it is wrong but because it deals with other things.

THE PSYCHOLOGICAL PERSPECTIVE Psychology looks for the causes of behavior in properties of the mind or personality; it deals with the individual. Take intelligence, for example. Despite difficulties with the concept, psychologists agree that there is an inherited capacity to learn, and that it varies widely from one person to another. Thus if one explains the performance of a brilliant student by unusually high intelligence, one is using the psychological perspective. Or imagine a college student who is bored with his courses and whose grades reflect his indifference. Then one term he takes a course in English poetry, and suddenly he becomes enormously enthusiastic. The student goes on to additional poetry courses and the quality of his work in other areas improves too. Observing all this, we say that he became motivated to study hard only after he found a course that really appealed to his interests. Where we attribute a change in behavior to the arousal of certain psychological states in the student, we employ a psychological perspective.

Informal psychological perspectives are used almost constantly as people meet and respond to one another and seek to make sense out of their encounters. The unfailing friendliness of an acquaintance is explained as gregariousness, that is, the psychological quality of liking to be with people and behaving accordingly. In popular psychology the word *personality* is invoked over and over again: people act as they do because of the personalities they have.

Americans probably employ some kind of psychological perspective for their explanations of behavior more often than they use any other. This is not surprising since the authority of traditional theological and moral orientations has declined. Meanwhile, for many people the world has become large, perplexing, and unmanageable. They need a clear and *authoritative* point of view to help them make sense out of confusing, even inexplicable, conduct. Science has great prestige in contemporary culture; psychology lends its prestige as a science to the popular use of psychological perspectives.

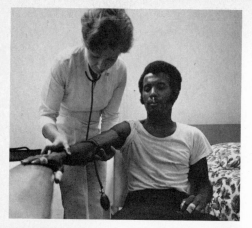

Each of these three different perspectives—biological, psychological, and moral—is concerned with part, but only part, of the human story.

Limitations of the Psychological Perspective The need for a trusted explanation of conduct has led to such a vogue for the psychological perspective that oversimplification and even misrepresentation are common in popular psychology. The public is bombarded with advertisements for books, correspondence courses, and lectures by self-styled psychologists who promise to "unlock the hidden powers within you" and to enable you to secure spectacular success in business, friendship, and love.

On a more sophisticated plane, psychoanalysis in several versions has become for many a kind of magic for understanding and solving human problems. Psychoanalytical orientations have a major and legitimate role in applied psychology, casework, and medical practice. But educated laymen sometimes use them in dubious and uncritical ways. Psychoanalysis has penetrated the intellectual life of the United States to a remarkable extent. Its influence can be traced in novels, poetry, biography, drama, literary criticism, and history, and it has had a good deal of impact on the social sciences (Hall and Lindzey, 1968).

Another popular psychological perspective has grown out of psychological testing and is based on the *trait theory* of personality.[1] Its main assumption is that everyone has a spectrum of behavioral tendencies which can be measured to predict behavior. This proposition is seductive in a society of mass education and massive organizations employing thousands of people. No doubt every reader of this book has had his characteristics "tested" many times. In recent years, overenthusiastic users without proper training have brought down considerable criticism on this approach (Hoffman, 1964).

Yet the psychological perspective is often appropriate. Here is a rough rule of thumb: it is useful whenever we are trying to understand the *individual*—how he perceives, learns, feels, and acts—and the effects of other people on him. Inclusive as this view is, it cannot explain a great deal of important human behavior. It tells us nothing, for example, about why there has been a rapid growth in the past century toward complex, centralized, and bureaucratic social organization in the United States and other technologically advanced societies. And this change in the human landscape has made a profound impact on almost every aspect of life.

THE MORAL PERSPECTIVE Among many other orientations is the moral perspective, which furnishes an interesting contrast. It is concerned not only with what the world is, as are both the biological and the psychological perspectives, but also with what it *should* be, which is ordinarily not a concern of the other two models. To observe the world from a moral perspective is to see human conduct in terms of values, and to make judgments about it. Actions are *good* or *bad*, either intrinsically or because of their

---

[1] The reader should understand that no attempt is made here to review all the important psychological schools of thought.

consequences. People have the ability, inborn or learned, to tell good from evil, and they are constantly tempted to choose evil. Criteria for conduct are described by more or less fixed rules, which come from divine authority, from government, or from a moral conviction that things ought to be done in some ways rather than others. Characteristic of the moral perspective is a comparison between what people ought to do and what they actually do.

As in the sciences, distinctions are made between specialists and lay users of the same moral perspectives. Here the theologian and the philosopher are the "experts" who apply disciplined scholarship to an analysis of the world in moral terms. While the layman's ideas are often nourished by the specialist, they are usually formed and applied in a somewhat haphazard way.

Relevance of the Moral Perspective Knowing when any major perspective on human experience is appropriate is a real problem. It is often very hard to tell which perspective applies or when more than one may bear on a situation. Difficulties of this kind are among the things that make human experience complicated. It is not easy to be sure when a moral perspective is called for or when it may have dire results. Still, it is possible to set up rough guidelines. Following are three pairs of circumstances. In each case ask: is it appropriate to respond with moral judgments to this situation?

I. A. A fierce argument between two men leads to violence and one man kills the other.
    B. In strictest confidence a person gives a close friend information which, if divulged, would be highly damaging. The friend "leaks" the information.

Nearly everyone, we think you will agree, would feel it appropriate to condemn both these behaviors morally.

II. A. A married woman who is pregnant seeks an abortion on the grounds that she and her husband already have all the children they can provide for.
     B. A scientist engages in research which he knows is designed to develop new means of biological warfare.

Some people would condemn both these behaviors on moral grounds and others would not. Even within a single society there is often considerable disagreement on the criteria for moral judgments.

III. A. Are individuals working alone, or several individuals working together, better at solving abstract problems?
      B. Why are most large cities in this country having serious financial problems?

You will probably agree that in dealing with questions like these a moral perspective simply has no relevance.

These cases do not probe very deeply into the complexities of the moral perspective. But they do show two interesting things. First, the relevance of moral judgments is obvious in some instances and problematic in others, depending on which of several moral contexts is invoked. Second, the moral perspective is not relevant in determining questions of fact, as in the last pair of examples. There may be moral implications in a set of facts, but one does not discover facts by moralizing.

NEED FOR SEVERAL PERSPECTIVES The world of man is complex beyond the compass of *any* one view of it. Hence different perspectives on the human scene often report different findings on the same behavior. Some are sensitive to aspects of behavior which others do not record at all. Since no perspective can include everything men want to know about themselves, it follows that none—and there are many we have not discussed—is superior to the others in all circumstances. For men living in advanced societies the problem is not how to choose one "correct" perspective so as to discard the others; rather, it is to know which is *most applicable* in given circumstances. Nothing in human conduct violates the laws of physics, but these laws are irrelevant if we want to understand why the civil rights movement of the sixties occurred when it did rather than at some other time. The biological model is valuable, but it does not show why so many great composers of the eighteenth and nineteenth centuries were German.

As we suggested earlier, people tend to prefer the perspectives most familiar to them, most deeply built into their habits—even when they are unaware of them as distinctive intellectual orientations. But today more than ever we need the clearest possible grasp of alternative concepts of reality.

SOCIOLOGY'S SPECIAL PERSPECTIVE Our path toward the first major objective of this book has been roundabout, but we are now ready to introduce the sociological perspective. A short definition will serve as a start. *Sociology is the study of patterned social behavior, its antecedents, and its consequences. Social behavior* exists whenever the behavior of one person affects and is affected by that of one or more other persons. Social behavior is patterned when the conduct of two or more persons toward each other has some degree of predictability, that is, when in given circumstances it tends to occur again and again. *Antecedents* are the host of factors that precede and sometimes bring about and explain *patterned* social behavior. *Consequences* are events that occur at least partly because of patterned social behavior.

There are many definitions of sociology, and sociologists disagree about which is best. But any sociologist will find a world of meaning in the definition above. To the beginner, however, it may seem deceptively simple. Our next task, then, is to build bridges from this definition to the happenings it denotes. Like every perspective, that of sociology concentrates upon certain aspects of human behavior and ignores others. What does the sociological eye pick out from all there is to see? Let us look at a few examples.

Identifying a Sociological Reality   The circles in Figure 1-1 represent five people who have spent twenty hours together (in one-hour sessions) solving a series of problems. While they worked, a record was kept of every instance in which each person communicated to every other. The lines and bars connecting the circles symbolize this record. The thickness of the bars is directly proportional to the number of communications between any two persons over the twenty hours.

This is a very simple sociological picture. The bars reveal the frequency with which people spoke to one another but nothing about what was said. Notice that communication is not equally distributed among the group members, but that there seems to be some pattern in the picture. Person A communicated more with the other members than did anyone else. The pattern appears to center on A as though A were the hub of some portion of a wheel. *This network of communication is a sociological reality.* The circles represent people, but reveal nothing about them. We don't know whether they are male or female, old or young. The circles simply designate points of origin and destination for communications. Because so much that ordinarily engages our attention when we observe people *has been left out,* the eye moves to the pattern of bars connecting the five points. We "see" the network of communication channels—a pattern not present when the group began. At the end of the first session it was hard to see any significant departure from randomness (chance) in the exchanges. The pattern appeared gradually.

Games played in teams furnish interesting examples of sociological forms. People often think of a football coach as a kind of applied psychologist, and he is. A coach must motivate his players under varying conditions of stress. But a coach is also an applied sociologist, even though he may never have thought of himself that way. A football team is more than a collection of physically fit young men who are willing and able to perform various athletic feats; a football game is more than a violent struggle between opposing mobs. The offensive team is a highly organized social group with a complex division of labor. Every man has a specific set of jobs to do, each interdependent with others. The totality of these tasks is a cunning plan, which unfolds through time toward the objective of moving a ball across a goal line. The defensive unit is organized with equal complexity to prevent the plan from succeeding. The game is a formal, almost ritualized social conflict enacted according to a rigid set of rules. The coach *must* see the whole thing as an elaborately organized social happening. On offense, he must attempt to disorganize the unfolding *pattern* of the enemy's defense, while maintaining intact the *pattern* of his

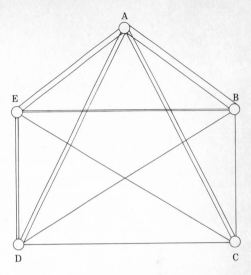

FIGURE 1-1   COMMUNICATIONS NETWORK

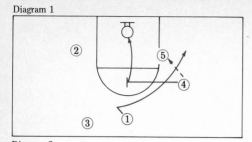

Diagram 1

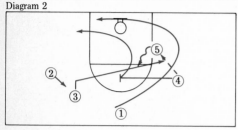

Diagram 2

FIGURE 1-2 DIAGONAL SCREENING OFFENSE: FORWARD TO LOW POST

The diagonal offense is a semi-control offense which involves a great deal of screening and movement. . . . It is an offense designed to capitalize on the mistakes of the defense. . . . If your guards and forwards are good ball handlers and shooters, then the diagonal offense would be an excellent offense since they interchange position frequently.

Any time the forward 4 passes to the low post 5, he screens for the nearest man, which is 1 in this case. Player 1 becomes the first cutter going over the top of the center and 4 the screener is the second cutter going to the basket after executing a reverse pivot on the screen and roll (Diagram 2). If neither of these men are open, then they should clear out under the basket. This will give 5 an opportunity to go one on one. If he doesn't have this opportunity, then he should take a slide dribble to meet 3 who becomes the third cutter. The cutter shooting the jump shot should shoot over the post man. Any time the post man hands off to a cutter, he should roll to the basket. [Quoted from Joe Cipriano, Bill Harrell, and Glenn Potter, Nebraska Basketball (Lincoln, Nebraska: University Extension Division, University of Nebraska, 1968), p. 19.]

own offensive plays. As a strategist, a football coach is a clear illustration of the applied sociologist.

Now look carefully at Figure 1-2, together with the commentary. The figures are "pictures" of a basketball play, and the commentary is quoted from the book in which the diagrams of the play appear. The pictures show only one team in a game situation, but the descriptions of the play, properly understood, assume the presence of the other team since they suggest a sequence of actions to be taken if any one action should be inhibited by the opposition. Read the description of the diagonal screening offense and study the diagram of the play as you do so. Your object is not to become an instant expert in basketball strategy, but to see these hypothetical events as sociological in nature. The play consists of an interdependent set of units or incidents of behavior, each leading to the next through time. *This developing pattern of interdependence is sociological.* Notice that no reference is made to the unique personalities of the players. In other settings these might be crucial. Here they are essentially irrelevant; all that need be assumed about a player is that *he understands the pattern and can execute his part of it.*

There is a significant difference between this sociological picture and that in Figure 1-1. The latter represents a record of *past* behavior linking a number of people. Figure 1-2, however, contains a set of instructions for coordinating the *present* or *future* behavior of a number of people. Sociologists (and anthropologists, among others) apply the word *culture* to this latter sort of phenomenon; it denotes more than a "set of instructions" for behavior, although this is one of its central meanings. As we shall see, sociologists are interested in culture as well as in patterns of actual social behavior.

Figure 1-3 is another sociological picture; it is of a type of organization often called a bureaucracy. While Figure 1-1 pictures social patterns derived from observing the actual conduct of people in each other's presence, Figure 1-2 is a script that tells people how to behave. Figure 1-3 differs from both. Assume that it is an organization chart of some industrial firm. Such charts represent some *part* of a real social organization, but never all of it. They do not show the many informal social relationships that are always present in large organizations. The chart is also an idealized picture in that it shows the official, legal division of labor, the hierarchy of authority, and the flow of communication regardless of whether or not the facts fully conform to the model.

Miller and Form's comments on Figure 1-3 are entirely sociological. Again, no personal characteristics of individuals are given, nor are they needed for an understanding of what is being portrayed. Observe that the pattern need not be threatened if any particular individual leaves, so long as he is replaced or his jobs are redistributed.

You have now viewed several pictures of sociological reality. They symbolize patterns of social behavior and come about as

FIGURE 1-3   LINE ORGANIZATION SHOWN AS A STRAIGHT LINE AND
AS A PYRAMID

*As suggested, bureaucracy is simply a hierarchical arrange-
ment of unit organizations. It is, or should be, an orderly
arrangement of units based on division of function and authority. This means that a bureaucracy is an organization or a
society of unequals. The basic inequalities are exemplified in
the* supervisory hierarchy, *which forms a pyramid of authority.
The hierarchy may be visualized as several layers of authority.
At the top is the president, who has greatest power. His subor-
dinates are the managers, division chiefs, department chiefs,
foremen, and workers, in that order. Although variations exist
in the names given to offices in the layers, everywhere the
structure is coordinated by a series of superior-subordinate or
man-boss relations. In such a structure the man on the top presumably directs and controls the entire organization. Ex-
cepting him and the workers in the lowest layer, everybody in
between reports to a boss and is in turn a boss over several
other people. Thus the big boss* looks down *the supervisory
structure, the workers fret about the bosses* above *them, and
division chiefs, department heads, superintendents and
managers worry* both *about their bosses and about those whom
they boss. Each rank is responsible for doing a specific job and
is accountable to someone who wants it done. [Quoted from
Delber C. Miller and William H. Form,* Industrial Sociology, The
Sociology of Work Organization, *2nd ed. (New York: Harper and
Row, 1964), pp. 124–125.]*

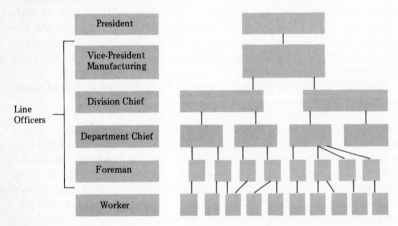

close as possible to pointing at samples of what the sociologist
looks for in human behavior. These illustrations should help you
to grasp the generalized perspective of the sociologist, but their
very specificity can be misleading. After all, there are millions of
possible examples, each differing to some extent from all others.

The Search for Pattern   Sociology examines the behavior of people, looking for evidence of pattern in that part of behavior which

Examine these pictures and see if you can find a pattern of social behavior that is common to all three. Sociologists study the basic patterns that underlie the endless diversity of social behavior.

constitutes interdependence among individuals. It describes the nature and characteristics of orderliness in social behavior and how changes take place in the patterns themselves. Evidence that human social behavior does form patterns exists on every hand. The sociologist finds it in things as large as a nation and as small as a pair of lovers, as diverse as the structure of an American city and the civil rights movement, as conventional as the middle-class suburbs, and as unconventional as life in a hippie commune. Wherever people engage in social behavior, that behavior comes in time to have pattern and predictability, and it is this that the sociologist wants to understand.

It is not the endless diversity of social behavior that most interests him, though this profusion has its attractions. One value of sociological study is awareness of the numerous meaningful social worlds man has constructed, and recognition that his familiar world is neither the best nor the only one possible. But beyond the fascinations of variety and novelty lies the fundamental goal of sociological analysis. Inkeles expressed sociology's primary concern when he said that it is "the study of those aspects of social life which are present in all social forms" (1964:16). Not every sociologist would agree with Inkeles, but his words describe the present discussion, which puts the case for the part of sociology's orientation that is not shared with any other field.

Sociology, seeking generalized, abstract—and therefore broadly applicable—accounts of human social behavior, takes its place among the generalizing disciplines and sciences. Like botany, it is not interested in how one leaf differs from all others, but in what all have in common. Sociology does not deal with the unique family unit, but with family units in general. It cares little about the influence and authority of one particular John Smith; but it wants very much to understand why influence and authority are unequally distributed.

The Search for Antecedents We have said that sociology deals not only with patterned social behavior but also with its antecedents and consequences. A sociologist examining the ways in which children are reared in America will focus on patterned relationships with parents, from the time children are born until they leave home. He will also study recurring patterns between children and other adults such as schoolteachers, and relationships among children themselves.

But he will probably want to go beyond the patterns of current American child-rearing to find how this complex of social relationships came about. Knowing that child-rearing practices have changed a great deal in recent decades he will ask how and why. What factors and forces were antecedent to the present situation? Our sociologist will almost surely find that the industrialization and urbanization of this country set in motion a chain of cause and effect that transformed child-rearing. Parents became far less sure of what to do and showed their uncertainty by an increasing reliance on "experts" and by giving children more freedom from their control.

The Prediction of Consequence Our sociologist may also wish to predict possible consequences of the social patterns he is studying. Will current "permissive" child-rearing techniques (coupled with great affluence) reduce the desire of future Americans to strive for success in life? This motive has played an important role in our rapid technological advance. Even though the sociologist cannot know what will happen, he may assess the probable influence of child-rearing practices on what could become a major change in American values.

The time span covered by a sociological study may have something to do with what is seen as cause and effect. Industrialization and urbanization have had a *continuing* series of effects on child-rearing. One early result of reliance on experts was emphasis on strict scheduling of the child's training, popular in the twenties and thirties. In part, the current "child-centered family" is a reaction against this rigidity. So, if we took a short view we

A Note on the History of Sociology

Compared to the physical sciences and the long record of philosophical interest in the nature of society, sociology is quite a young discipline. It did not appear at any single point in time, but emerged gradually in the eighteenth and nineteenth centuries. Auguste Comte, a French scholar who worked during the first half of the nineteenth century, coined the word *sociology*, visualized it as a science, and attempted to establish its foundations.

Even as Comte wrote, the Industrial Revolution, which was to have such momentous consequences for all of mankind, was getting under way. At once it began to produce a sequence of social problems that has not ended to this day. In the same period the theory of evolution as formulated by Darwin was having a tremendous impact on the intellectual life of the Western world. The social theorists who followed Comte came to terms in their own ways with these developments. Herbert Spencer and Karl Marx are other writers who made major contributions to the thought of this period—Spencer by popularizing the ideas of science and Marx by fathering a new concept of political economy.

Seldom did these thinkers engage directly in the gathering and analysis of empirical data, which has since come to characterize the social sciences. This trend appeared toward the close of the nineteenth century. Scholars in Germany, Italy, France, England, and the United States identified themselves as sociologists and began to visualize sociology as an empirical science. The work of some of these sociological pioneers, men like Max Weber, Ferdinand Tonnies, Georg Simmel, Emile Durkheim, William Graham Sumner, and Lester Ward, is still influential in contemporary sociology. The research tools and the financial resources available to these scholars were primitive and inadequate by present standards. Nevertheless, today's sociologists stand on the shoulders of these predecessors.

In the early decades of the twentieth century the new discipline grew most rapidly in the United States, spreading from the Midwest till it found a place in the curriculum of nearly every campus in the country. Almost from the beginning, some sociologists saw the field as a detached, ethically neutral scientific study of social behavior, while others saw it as a weapon in the struggle to relieve the social problems of industrial civilization. This difference of emphasis has continued into the present period, with considerable fluctuation from time to time in the relative dominance of the one view or the other. Since World War II there has been considerable strengthening of the position that sociology (and sociologists) should participate rather directly in the reform and reconstruction of society. Yet not all sociologists agree by any means.

Most popular views on what it means to live in a big city instead of a small town are based on folklore and "common sense." For instance, one view holds that the city, as compared with the village, is rampant with all kinds of social evils. It might also seem that life in the small community pictured here (with the factory well in the background) is more relaxed and pleasant than the harried tempo of the urban scene. In fact, though, cities have so recently become the dominant community form that there is much we don't really know about their effects on human experience.

could say that current practices were "caused" by the immediately preceding era. But it is just as accurate to say that *both* philosophies of child-rearing are products of urbanization and industrialization, a historical trend of more than a century.

Developing the Sociological Perspective You have now glimpsed the core of the sociological vision, but your view of it may be sharpened by a few additional observations. Both society and sociology are products of the human mind and expressions of human nature. Sociology says: "here is another way to view the human scene." To take this view does not change man. It does not make him any more or any less human. The sociological model is neither better nor worse than others. It is different, and that difference is what we have tried to show so far.

Now and then, probably everybody behaves like an applied sociologist without knowing it. After all, the reality sociologists study is ever present, and *must* be dealt with somehow. What is new about sociology is not its subject matter; that has always been with us. But only recently has this reality been sorted out from other aspects of human behavior, identified, and given distinctive intellectual form and expression. One great promise of this field is that, as our understanding increases, we will be able to deal with the sociological aspects of human behavior with ever-increasing effectiveness.

Helping someone else to understand the sociological viewpoint can be difficult because most of us do not make its acquaintance until quite late—we do not grow up learning this perspective in a thousand ways and situations, as we learn the psychological, biological, and moral orientations. These more familiar outlooks, useful as they are, get in the way of our sensing and suitably responding to those elements in a situation which are sociological in nature.

Communication is made harder because sociology gives familiar words such as *group* or *society* restricted and special though often more precise meanings. So a layman may wrongly believe that he is using such a word in the same way the sociologist does. There are other terms whose special meaning originated in sociology and later entered popular speech where their usage broadened and diffused. Examples are *in-group, primary group,* and *power structure.*

As one begins to understand and use the sociological perspective, he soon sees that there is much we do not know about human behavior from this point of view. Even the professional sociologist feels that his discipline is much closer to the beginning than to the end of its quest. So he is likely to be skeptical about claims that practical common sense can tell us all we need to know.

As an example, countless Americans are convinced that simple common sense indicates that persons who commit crimes should be sent to prison. It seems self-evident that criminals should be punished so that they will not commit more crimes. Yet we have known for decades that a person imprisoned for committing a crime is in fact unlikely to be deterred from further criminal acts. In fact, many are *more* likely to engage in crime after a term in prison. The sociologist who studies criminal behavior has long since abandoned the erroneous assumptions of common-sense knowledge about the problem of crime. He recognizes that the problem is very much more complicated than it seems to be in popular thinking. And while he has already accumulated much tested information on this topic, he knows that much more needs to be discovered before we can confidently adopt policies that will achieve the desired results.

The sociologist is likely to feel that below the smooth, familiar surface of the social world lie new classes of facts and novel, even startling, insights and discoveries, all of which can revolutionize our view of man.

We believe that sociologists should first and foremost seek to build an ever-growing body of reliable knowledge about human social behavior, employing the best available methods of disinterested scholarship. The accumulating results of such research and theorizing are what we mean by "basic" sociology. This position does not deny that rigid objectivity is often impossible in sociological research. Yet not to take this position is to imply that sociology is only another ideology, less admirable than most because of its hollow pretensions to impartiality. The effort to seek truth, no matter what the obstacles, is a tradition too hard-won to be lightly abandoned, even in an age when contending social philosophies seem to demand choosing sides on every occasion. A black or white sociology, a communist or a capitalist sociology, is a social science that in our opinion is not worth much.

"BASIC" AND "APPLIED" SOCIOLOGY

The main reason for developing the best possible basic sociology is its potential usefulness in human affairs. Efforts to spell out this utility are what we mean by "applied" sociology. Any sociologist knows that he cannot yet predict the certain outcomes of alternative courses of action. Nor can he generate social technologies comparable in power and reliability to those which pour forth from the more mature physical sciences. He knows that most aspects of sociological knowledge have implications for social practice, though often not yet ferreted out and made available to the persons who might use them. However tentative, however inadequate in a world anxious for immediate solutions to fearful problems, sociology can suggest which avenues to explore and which to ignore as a waste of time and resources.

The practical utilization of sociology can often help in the further development of basic knowledge; the relation between the two levels is not a one-way street (Gouldner and Miller, 1965). Referring again to the problem of crime control, the emergence of better understanding at a theoretical level depends considerably on the testing of such theories in actual crime control situations. Though not all sociologists agree, we think it possible to insist on a distinction between basic and applied sociological knowledge, and we believe that the integrity of the first can be defended while simultaneously seeking to expand the practical use of such knowledge.

SOCIOLOGY AND THE OTHER SOCIAL SCIENCES

The social sciences are alike in their application of disciplined scholarship to the study of man's behavior. The historical circumstances of their development differ, however, and they differ in degree of specialization, in the aspects of behavior emphasized, and often in characteristic techniques for gathering and analyzing knowledge.

Economics, compared with sociology, is a comparatively specialized field. Its concern is with the production, distribution, and consumption of goods and services. This does not mean that an economist will ignore noneconomic events, for example, a political revolution. But insofar as he takes account of such events he does so in order to discern their impact on the behavior that most concerns him. Rather similarly, political science specializes in one main arena of social behavior—power, and in particular, power as it relates to the governmental system of a society. Another social science, anthropology, has long had an unusually close relationship to sociology. This satement holds true for at least one part of the field, cultural anthropology, though other branches are related more closely to the biological than the social sciences. In recent years it has become difficult to find any important distinction between cultural anthropology and sociology. Earlier, cultural anthropologists were likely to do research in relatively primitive, isolated societies, while sociologists mainly studied modern, complex societies.

THE BREADTH OF THE SOCIOLOGICAL PERSPECTIVE Among the social sciences, sociology and cultural anthropology are unusually broad in perspective. Sociology's concern with "those aspects of social life which are present in all social forms" embraces *every* social setting, whereas most related fields have a restricted range of settings. Incidentally, nobody ever sat down and divided human behavior neatly into different compartments and assigned each compartment to a new social science; the development of these fields was more haphazard than that. The boundaries between the disciplines are typically vague: almost all the social sciences get outside their "own" and into "somebody else's" with great frequency. As these disciplines continue to develop, the arbitrariness of existing boundaries becomes ever more evident. Everywhere work done in one discipline is understood and used in others. Surely this is as it should be.

Part 1 / Some Fundamental Ideas

SOCIAL PSYCHOLOGY, A HYBRID DISCIPLINE   There is one other discipline, social psychology, and we will now turn to it in somewhat more detail for a special reason. While economics is mostly developed by economists, and political science by political scientists, social psychology evolved and grows out of the common concerns of psychology and sociology. It is truly a hybrid field.

The first two texts in social psychology were published, quite independently of each other, in 1908. One was by a distinguished sociologist, E. A. Ross, the other by an equally distinguished psychologist, W. McDougall. This coincidence was a historical accident, but a happy and appropriate one, for social psychology has been shared by its two parent disciplines ever since, showing all the vigor so often associated with hybrids. A large number of sociologists work comfortably within social psychology's perspective. Hence, a brief sketch of its intellectual orientation will round out this purview of sociological investigation.

Like its parent disciplines, social psychology is large, has many subfields, and is rapidly changing, but its basic approach can be put simply. *It is the study of social and cultural influences on the individual, and of individual influence on social behavior and culture.* It always involves the behavior or psychological organization of the single person, and so differs from sociology. And it always incorporates social or cultural variables in its formulations, which is not necessarily true in other regions of psychology.

Because American sociology is and always has been deeply influenced by social psychology, this perspective will appear in every chapter of this book, even those that conform most closely to the strict sociological model. Chapter 2 is devoted entirely to some important ideas of modern social psychology.

Differences Between Sociology and Social Psychology   In studies of suicide rates classified by age, sex, marital or economic status, and other factors (Gibbs, 1966), the observed rate differences are assumed to be produced by social and cultural factors related to stress. In other words, the likelihood that any given person will take his own life is shown to be related to social experiences that vary in the amount of stress. Psychological variables are not ordinarily used in such researches. But a study that sought to determine whether certain psychological traits predisposed persons to take their own lives when faced with stress would be social psychological. Research into the relationship between the organization and the efficiency of groups would be sociological. But studies to see whether individuals work better in isolation or in social settings would be social psychological. Research on the way racial stereotypes are distributed in a large population would be sociological. But a study of the process by which individuals learn such stereotypes would be social psychological.

Even after pondering these examples you may feel that the distinction is none too clear. And one who reads extensively in either sociology or social psychology will find that the boundary line between the two is often blurred. For example, most social psychology texts contain some material (particularly on the organization of groups) that is really sociological in the strictest sense. Scholars in these fields often are not careful about telling readers when they shift from one perspective to the other. If you have trouble here, there is no need for special concern. The most important point in this chapter is that patterned social behavior is the core subject matter of sociology.

In Chapter 2 we review some important ideas drawn from social psychology, ideas which will be helpful as (beginning in Chapter 3) we take up subjects that are more sociological in nature.

Practicing the Sociological Perspective

Acquiring the sociological perspective will make the rest of this book more interesting and significant to you. What is more important, the sociological orientation will be useful to you throughout life. Long after most of this book has been forgotton, long after many of its facts are obsolete and the incomplete theories in it have been modified or abandoned, you may continue to use this way of thinking. It will not go out of date. With it you may become your own sociological analyst.

We have begun with the sociological perspective in the hope that you will *practice* it as you read the later chapters. For one thing is certain: the beginner in sociology should start at once to practice its perspective. New insight must be buttressed by new habits, or it will be undermined by old ones.

But practice should go beyond this book, and it should begin the day you read this chapter for the first time. Perhaps later today you will walk into a classroom. If so, deliberately inhibit the automatic and habitual tendency to view the scene in psychological terms. Screen out the familiar personalities. Turn a deaf ear to the usual content of what is being said and why. Think of what is happening as an ebb and flow of communication, which moves back and forth among the persons who "send" and "receive" it. Can you visualize the pattern of communication flow? Could you sketch it on paper? How many things can you discern about it without referring to the physical or psychological characteristics of the people involved? Ask yourself what *ideas* shared by students and teacher give pattern and direction to the *actual* behavior you see from moment to moment. Could you write down the ideas you think are shared by all persons interacting with one another that define how a student behaves and how a college professor behaves? Where do you think these ideas came from? How old are they? What keeps them alive and able to influence what people do?

The fact that these two widely known public personages were having some kind of argument here might have prevented their listeners from attending to the issues being argued. When personalities overshadow issues in social conflict, it becomes harder to seek and find rational solutions to complicated problems.

Analyzing arguments gives excellent practice in the sociological perspective. At first this may not seem true because disputes often arouse strong emotions, which tempt us to see them as arising from unreasonable or unlovable qualities in the other person. If this happens it can be very hard to resolve effectively the issue originally in dispute. To focus on personalities may be to miss the real cause of the problem, which sometimes lies in an aspect of the social situation in which both parties are involved.

We can see the truth of this in collective bargaining, where union and management representatives dispute over wages, working conditions, and other matters. True, people are involved in these situations, and so personal hostilities may be aroused. But two points of view on how workers should be rewarded are really at stake, views represented by two persons at different locations in the same organization. Effectiveness on both sides of the bargaining table depends on the ability to use those strategies that serve what is really at stake. Personal antagonisms interfere with this process. Perhaps you have noticed that although attorneys on opposite sides of a case may seem hostile to one another, they will go out for lunch amicably after the case is over. They employ the appearance of hostility as a tool in what is really a highly organized process of social conflict.

Think of other kinds of disputes you know about. For practice, assume that the personal qualities and motives of the persons involved *have nothing whatever to do with the dispute.* Instead, assume that the behavior arises from something in the social organization of the situation. In other words, add sociological explanations to the more personalistic explanations you already use. They will not always be superior, but sometimes the evidence will better support them than psychological or moralistic interpretations. You will then be able to cope much more effectively with many conflict situations.

Sociological analysis of small and intimate groups and relationships is useful and is something we can all do. The beginner may find it hard, though, to visualize close personal relationships in sociological terms. Let's assume that you are in love with someone and engaged to be married. Perhaps no experience in your life has been so intensely personal, so infused with emotion. The relationship between the two of you is so private and important that it seems unique. Surely it is free from the impersonal influences of society and culture! Still, look up de Rougemont's classic study of romantic love (1940) and learn how this particular "style" of heterosexual love developed centuries ago in Europe and how it is found in some societies but not in others, so that one does not love this way unless one's society carries this alternative within it. Probably the two of you have discussed your future marriage, anticipating the "roles" you will play with each other and with children, relatives, and friends. Where do you think those roles come from? *They did not originate with you!* In short, think about your love affair in sociological terms.

It is common for college students to return home during holidays to find that their relationships with their parents have changed in subtle ways. Sometimes this causes uneasiness and guilt. One may find it hard to communicate with parents about new experiences or ideas encountered at college. Suppose this has happened to you. Try to account for the stiffness, the certain reserve in the relationship, entirely in sociological terms. Do this and you will find that a meaningful interpretation is possible which ignores completely the personalities of the people concerned and even the particular issue which may have given rise to the tension.

A great deal of practice in sociological analysis is needed to get the hang of it, but the effort will be richly repaid. Little by little, as you increase your grasp of sociological concepts, you will learn to separate patterns of social behavior from other aspects of people. Your response to that fascinating creature, man, will thus be permanently broadened in variety and flexibility.

Culture: The Humanizing Agent

In this chapter we focus on something that cannot be seen, heard, smelled, touched, or tasted, yet has been in continuous existence for hundreds of thousands of years. It is very real, and so important that without it human societies, human existence, would be quite impossible. It is *culture*.

If, by some unknown means, the existing culture of mankind was wiped out—yet leaving the human species biologically intact —it would result in a catastrophe at least as great as any nuclear holocaust. Surrounded by the magnificent technology of modern civilization, men would have lost all knowledge of even the simplest means of survival. In a short time virtually the entire species would disappear forever. To understand why this would be so, and to understand in other ways the great significance of human culture, we need to gain a secure understanding of this concept.

An old but still used definition of culture as a concept in social science was formulated in 1871 by the English anthropologist E.B. Tylor. *"Culture is that complex whole which includes knowledge, belief, art, morals, law, custom, and any other capabilities and habits acquired by man as a member of society"* (1871:1). Culture is *everything* that people have learned and preserved from past collective experience. Some things in culture are thousands of years old (the idea of the wheel and the use of fire), and other things are very new (laser-beam technology). The volume and

THE CULTURE CONCEPT

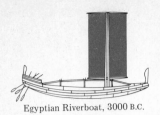

Egyptian Riverboat, 3000 B.C.

Carrack, 1400

Clipper Ship, 1850

FIGURE 2-1
*Over the centuries, the primitive sail be-
came an effective tool in man's discovery
and increasing mastery of his world. Each
improvement—in size, shape, and number
of sails on a ship—was refined and handed
down to later societies. The Egyptian riverboat (3000 B.C.) is the earliest known
sailing ship; the carrack (1400), a European merchant ship, used the square sail of
the Egyptian ship but added more of them
and had a stronger hull. The clipper ship
(1850), the high point of sail power and
speed, had numerous sails of various sizes
and shapes and a sleek hull.*

complexity of culture grow with time, even though some parts of
it are lost or discarded. Thus contemporary artisans in stained
glass cannot duplicate the formulas that produced the magnificent colors of the windows in medieval cathedrals.

CULTURE IS LEARNED Culture can only be preserved from the
past and transmitted into the future by learning. It cannot be
transmitted biologically through the germ plasm. Thus individuals in all societies spend many years learning the necessary
minimum of the cultural heritage. When we go to school we learn
some aspects of the culture, but this is only a small part of the
process. We learn culture from our parents, from the mass media,
from agemates at all times of life, and from many other sources.
A grade school child learns arithmetic in school, but he learns to
play games that are centuries old from his playmates, even though
he has no idea that these games have been passed along by
countless generations of children. An American who smokes
cigarettes may have no notion that the first people to smoke tobacco were American Indians from whom the habit (in various
forms) traveled around the world, or that cigarettes were introduced to the United States by English soldiers who picked up
the practice from their Turkish allies in the Crimean War (Linton,
1936:334).

The culture of a group, an organization, or an entire society is
not a disorderly collection of customs. There is always some degree of organization, some sense in which it fits together as a
whole. Kluckhohn and Kelly use the phrase "design for living" to
suggest this quality: *"A culture is a historically derived system of
explicit and implicit designs for living, which tends to be shared
by all or specially designated members of a group"* (1944:84). Of
course there are variations—some of them dramatic—among the
cultures of different societies. But all men belong to the same
biological species, and all face some of the same problems of survival in the environment; hence there are underlying similarities
in all cultures, too.

THE IMPORTANCE OF CULTURE Most of us take the existence of
culture wholly for granted. While this is understandable, since we
are immersed in culture from birth onward, it does blind us to the
overwhelming importance of culture for human life. It is hard
even to imagine what life would be like without culture. If each
new generation had to solve even the most elementary problems
of existence all over again, human life would remain incon-
ceivably primitive forever. Culture provides a summation and dis-
tillation of past experience that is an *indispensable* foundation for
living in the present and developing in the future. When we view
man comparatively, in relation to other forms of life, culture is
seen to be his chief means of survival and adaptation—a statement which can not be made of any other species.

Fundamentally, culture consists of *shared ideas*. If we looked

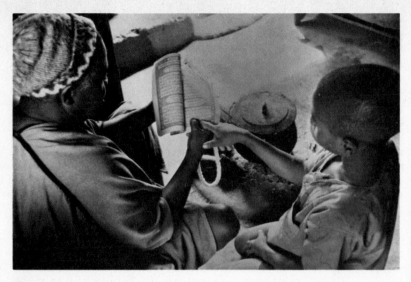

There is only one way to acquire culture: it must be learned. While animals know how to do certain things instinctively, humans must be taught. Kittens, for example, know instinctively how to wash themselves, but children must be instructed. Of course, culture includes much more than such basic activities. Here, a child is being taught the Koran, the "design for living" of Moslem societies, by an adult.

at just one person at a time, we would say that culture is located in his mind; it is what he has learned in society. Every individual lives in a social world, and that world as a whole contains in the minds of all its members the entire social heritage we call culture. A society's fund of shared ideas includes all the varieties of knowledge, religious and other beliefs, social rules from the most important to the most trivial, customs, myths, every conception of art and beauty, and many other things as well.

CULTURE AND SOCIAL BEHAVIOR

We have just said that culture is shared ideas. By contrast, social behavior is what people actually do in their contacts with one another. A considerable part of culture is ideas that bear directly or indirectly on behavior. For instance, custom decrees that people be considerate to the handicapped. It is the behavior-directed part of culture that concerns us most at the moment. But it should be understood that many other parts of culture are not directly connected with social behavior, for example, the technological knowledge that permits the transplantation of a human heart from one body to another.

Paintings in a museum, a symphony orchestra, books in a library, these things are what many people mean by culture. But as we use the term, these are only expressions of culture, for culture is not objects but shared ideas.

THE INTERDEPENDENCE OF CULTURE AND SOCIAL BEHAVIOR Culture largely controls and guides social behavior, yet culture can be sustained and kept alive only by social behavior, and behavior often alters culture. By our definition of sociology, culture is at once an antecedent ~~and a consequent of social behavior~~.

We see many people sitting in long rows facing a man who stands in front of them at a slightly higher level. He speaks, and they all bow their heads. It is, of course, a church service and the people are praying in response to a signal from the minister. Each person in this example of social behavior knows how to behave and can predict the behavior of the others, because all are guided by mutually understood cultural prescriptions that tell them what to do. On the other hand, a Protestant who attended a Catholic service might find himself confused by the different cultural definitions of appropriate behavior during prayer. In this instance, we see culture as *antecedent* to social behavior. In much this same way, virtually all social interaction takes place in relation to cultural understandings that exist before the behavior itself. Without these guidelines, human social behavior would be chaotic. Indeed, society at any level would be impossible.

While culture continually influences social behavior, culture itself would quickly disappear if it were not constantly reinforced by social behavior. We are not propounding a riddle. Remember that culture is ideas shared by a number of people in contact with one another. The "proof" that the ideas exist and are shared is that real behavior is modified by them. Without the sustaining effect of behavior, culture would be forgotten or would be only a memory, having little effect on current experience.

Custom once prescribed that when a well-bred man was introduced to a lady he bowed from his waist and perhaps lightly kissed her extended hand. The culture which decreed this little episode is now dead. The gesture is a kind of cultural fossil. Thousands of American towns and cities a few decades ago had laws which forbade going to movies on Sunday. These laws (a part of culture) often remained on the books long after they were disregarded in practice. As culture, they ceased to exist because they no longer influenced people's actual behavior. On the other hand, every time a teacher assigns work and a student does the work, this interaction reaffirms and sustains the part of culture that defines the relation between teachers and students.

THE IMPERFECT FIT BETWEEN CULTURE AND SOCIAL BEHAVIOR Culture never completely controls social behavior and this fact greatly affects the relationship between the two. It may be helpful here to think of this connection as a little like the relationship between the script of a play or the score of a symphony and its live performance. Without script or score there could be no performance, but every performance of a given work differs from every other. So is it likely to be with culture and social behavior.

Misunderstandings and Acceptable Alteratives   There are many reasons why culture and social behavior don't exactly coincide. Meanings (including culture) are defined and transferred in social behavior, a process that depends on symbolic tools, especially language. This is a delicate, subtle process in which there are many possibilities for misunderstandings and mistakes. Have you ever had this kind of a conversation with an instructor?

STUDENT: "It seems to me that I answered the question very well."
INSTRUCTOR: "But you didn't answer the question I asked. What you said was good, but it wasn't what I asked for."
STUDENT: "I thought you wanted us to. . . ."

In this case the behavioral prescription was misunderstood and the behavior therefore failed to conform to the demand.

Frequently, culture permits a wide range of possible behaviors, *any* of which will be seen as meeting the cultural guideline. At a party that is to begin at nine in the evening, guests may arrive a little before and considerably after that hour without arousing resentment, that is, without violating that part of culture which prescribes courtesy in interpersonal relationships. In other words, social behavior often departs from cultural prescriptions because the latter are not clearly understood or because the prescriptions are not so rigid as they first appear.

A common cultural fossil. This custom was originally intended to protect women from mud splashed by horses from unpaved streets.

Individual Differences in Capacities to Conform   Individuals engaged in interaction differ in their *capacities* to conform to what culture requires. A student with good verbal skills will find it easy to satisfy an English instructor's standards for a theme, while another student who can't write a coherent paragraph may try just as hard yet be unable to do an acceptable job. Individuals also vary in their *desire* to realize cultural guidelines. A famous American economist, John R. Commons, came close to flunking out of college because he refused to work hard in courses that didn't interest him. Finally, the circumstances of social interaction often affect the degree to which it can be controlled by culture. When a Jewish man marries a Protestant woman, the cultures of the two religious groups prescribe different ceremonies. Obviously there is no way the two can marry without violating at least one set of cultural directions.

Cultural Changes Caused by Behavior   Because there is never a perfect fit between culture and social behavior, changes in culture arise out of the inevitable departures of actual behavior from what culture prescribes. Given enough time, culture *always* changes for this reason. Here our analogy between culture and a play or symphony breaks down. No matter how many interpretations of Shakespeare's Hamlet different actors give, the script of the play remains unchanged. But culture is altered in the very process of being enacted. Little by little, the culture that prescribes relationships between teachers and students, husbands and wives, employers and employees is changed as particular people depart in greater or lesser degree from the original prescriptions. This is true because culture is ideas in the heads of the same people who make culture manifest in their relations with each other. Just as we can say that their social behavior is influenced by the ideas in their heads, so we can say that the ideas in their heads are modified by their experience in acting out these ideas in particular circumstances. So we can readily see that culture is not only an antecedent of social behavior but also a consequent. The two aspects of human experience are inseparable.

To summarize, when we observe ongoing social behavior, we can be sure it is being influenced somehow by the shared understandings we call culture. Culture furnishes an indispensable script to human actors, without which their efforts to coordinate behavior in pursuit of valued ends would surely fail. In their encounters with each other, people sustain the culture which is carried in their heads. But in these encounters they cannot exactly replicate the culture for many reasons and so they also change the culture, sometimes slowly and sometimes suddenly.

Students of culture have developed a considerable vocabulary of terms. We now consider three of these: *value, norm,* and *role,* because they are especially useful in understanding the relationship between culture and social behavior.

VALUES In her book *Life Among the Giants,* Leontine Young constructs this conversation between a father and a daughter (1966:35):

At the dinner table Mary reaches for the bread and Father tells her mildly, "Don't grab at the table. Ask for what you want." So Mary says, "Give me the bread." Father replies, "Say please." Mary says, "Please give me the bread."

A few minutes later Father says, "Pass me the bread." Mary, who knows an opportunity when she sees one, answers firmly, "Say please." Father gives her an irritated glare and barks, "Don't be impertinent." A moment or so later he turns to the dinner guest and murmurs politely, "Mrs. Brown, would you pass me the cream, please?"

By coffee time Father has forgotton the small incident and wonders why Mary is aggrieved. "What does get into children?" he mutters to himself.

Underlying the father's orders to ask for the bread and to "say please" is a *value.* It could be put like this: good manners are important. This value *justifies* what he says to his daughter. On this occasion he does not express the value directly; we must infer it from what he does say. But there is more to the episode. The father violates the very value he has just called to Mary's attention. When she calls him on this he reprimands her, and we get a glimpse of how difficult and subtle it can be to learn culture. For what is Mary to think? Apparently, the value of good manners applies differently to adults and to children. If we chided her father for his inconsistency, perhaps he would fall back on another value: it is bad for children to be impertinent to adults. But we can't blame Mary for being confused and resentful.

An elementary but significant fact about people is that they do not and cannot remain indifferent to what goes on about them. They always have preferences for some things, ideas, and experiences over others. A process of evaluation comes into play whenever a person (or group) confronts a range of alternatives. Alternatives are viewed selectively in the sense that some are valued more than others. Values, therefore, are *"those conceptions of desirable states of affairs that are utilized as criteria for preference or choice or as justifications for proposed or actual behavior"* (Williams, 1970:442).

VALUE HIERARCHIES Of course all values are not of equal importance. In most nations the value of loyalty to country is so great that it justifies sending some members of society to certain death on the battlefield. Generally, the most important values are those that are accepted as being vital to the survival and well-being of a group (organization, society) and of the individual. But evaluation also goes on in matters as trivial as hamburger with catsup versus one without. Any time people engage in frequent interaction there will be some, though never complete, agreement on the relative importance of those values which bear on their mutual relations. In such situations we may speak of a *hierarchy* of values, ranked at least roughly from the most to the least important. And we may generally assume that when two values conflict (when both cannot be realized) the more important will take precedence.

The Board of Directors of the United Fund in a certain city is trying to allocate available resources among many agencies. Youth-oriented groups are asking an increase over last year to combat juvenile delinquency. Mental health agencies need staff to do the job assigned to them. The aged are increasing and agencies helping them need more money. Community centers in decaying neighborhoods urgently need more financial assistance, and casework agencies serving troubled families are losing staff because salaries are falling behind. There is just not enough money to meet all these very legitimate needs; some will have to be deferred or even abandoned completely. Faced with this situation the directors must make difficult choices. What they finally do will largely represent their hierarchy of values: the most important thing (as they see it) will be taken care of first, and so on.

Hierarchies of values are seldom reflected precisely in behavior. People cannot always behave rationally, nor can they always agree on the hierarchy. And they sometimes lack the information to order their choices reasonably. Consider the agonizing disagreements among Americans in the 1960s about the allocation of national resources to national ends (values). There was the war in Vietnam and space exploration. There were the crushing domestic problems of the inner cities, of poverty, of race, of education, of overpopulation, and so on. Figure 2-2 indicates some of

FIGURE 2-2 UNITED STATES BUDGET, 1973
The percentage of money allocated to different areas of the national budget is one indication of the hierarchy of values within the United States. [Source: Executive Office of the President, Office of Management and Budget, *The United States Budget in Brief* (Washington, D.C.: Superintendent of Documents, U.S. Government Printing Office, 1974) p. 48.]

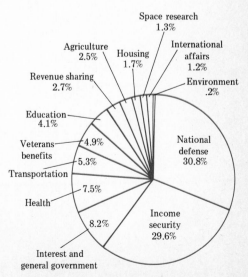

Space research 1.3%

Agriculture 2.5% Housing 1.7% International affairs 1.2%

Revenue sharing 2.7% Environment .2%

Education 4.1%

National defense 30.8%

Veterans benefits 4.9%

Transportation 5.3%

Health 7.5%

Income security 29.6%

8.2%

Interest and general government

the priorities within the United States. For years, Americans have been locked in controversy about which values take priority when the satisfaction of one prevents adequate realization of another. Yet there is always *some* order of values in social situations, large and small. As choice is inevitable in the original selection of some values over others, there is some agreement on which of the accepted ones are most and which are least important.

VALUES AND SOCIAL BEHAVIOR As with other elements of culture, values are both antecedents and consequences of social behavior. Existing values guide interacting people in the selection of alternative courses of action, and they explain and justify the choices made. In choosing their leaders, Americans today take for granted the values of representative and democratic government. The actual social machinery for selecting leaders is, on the whole, remarkably consistent with these values. It seems strange now to realize that the founding fathers who drew up the Constitution in Philadelphia were by no means in such agreement. There was some sentiment for a monarchy, and many viewed the values of democracy with overt suspicion.

At any given time, the values affecting social conduct may vary greatly in age. Their origins may be lost in antiquity or known only to a few scholars. People may act as if such values had always been, had some mysterious life of their own, existed in the nature of the universe, or had some extra-human source. They seem just to be there, unchanging and unquestioned. When they are also important, such values can inspire respect, awe, wonder, and even veneration. Such are the values of family relationships and religious faith. Other values operating at a given time may be of much more recent origin. For instance, the disapproval of discrimination based on sex has become important only recently in the United States.

Whether ancient or modern in origin, values have social significance in the present only if they actually influence the course of ongoing social behavior. The pending constitutional amendment which outlaws unequal treatment based on sex testifies to the value placed on sex equality, but it will be meaningless unless it is obeyed. All values, no matter how old, *originate* and are maintained in social exchanges. Life always presents people with many choices and limited resources for exploring them. Values help them make choices and allocate resources. Where existing values do not perform this function, people will modify them or create new ones. Specifically, as meanings are communicated in social behavior, any of three things may happen:

1. People quickly find that existing values are adequate to the situation. It is simply a question of acting by them. For instance, a social club has "always" elected a president, vice president, and treasurer once a year by secret ballot. As election time approaches members find that they still like the values un-

Part 1 / Some Fundamental Ideas

derlying these procedures, so their behavior is routine and predictable. The old values are reinforced and validated by current social behavior.

2. Social behavior shows that the old values are being questioned. Nobody wants to replace them entirely, but some feel the need for change. As time passes and various changes are considered, the end result may be some modification. A very old value in our civilization says, in effect: a person who deliberately kills someone else should forfeit his own life. But the practice of capital punishment has come under increasing attack in recent years. Many states have virtually eliminated it and substituted long imprisonment. In effect, the prescription of severe punishment for first degree murder is retained, but that part of the value which called for the death penalty is eliminated.

3. As meanings are exchanged in social situations, it becomes clear either that the old values are no longer accepted, or that there are no acceptable values appropriate to the situation. In either case, new values must be created out of social behavior. The values present in a social situation are often "hidden," for they are so taken for granted that they do not need to be explicitly stated. They may be given direct expression only on ceremonial occasions, if ever. Value positions come to the fore, however, when existing values are challenged. A new situation, or the need to make an especially important decision, may challenge existing values or may point out the absence of needed values.

CREATION OF NEW VALUES   When new values must be created, the exchange of meanings is likely to touch on everything that relates to the shared interests of the participants. Members reveal their

The practice of busing schoolchildren to different parts of town as a strategy in equalizing educational opportunity arouses and sharpens value conflicts among Americans. Some strongly favor busing; others strongly oppose it. Can you think of hidden values that may be involved in this controversy, and what do you think is the relationship between these values and the behavior shown here?

own dispositions as alternative value positions are considered. Sometimes quite suddenly, but often so slowly that participants are scarcely aware of it, choices are made and communicated back and forth. A choice becomes a collective value as members realize that they are now conducting themselves in such a way as to support the choice. A new value has come into existence.

Most of us have been present when people were hammering out new values. We can watch and take part as traditionalists argue for the good old ways with innovators who want something different. We can see the weighing of different possibilities and the attempts to spell out the consequences of differing choices. The more heated the discussion, the more likely people will reveal their convictions and try to get others to adopt their values. At other times the whole thing may proceed more quietly. People may with little fuss simply adopt makeshift rules for conducting their affairs. But any principles for guiding social behavior have value *implications.* Simply to adopt them is to accept tacitly the values they reflect. Only later may the members see that the values underlying their improvised rules have come to mean a lot to them.

Look around you for situations in which values are created. Suppose your student government is being severely criticized by students. There is even talk of abolishing it or of setting up a rival organization. The rationale for all this is that the existing government is based on unacceptable values. If you listen to conversations on the controversy, you are sure to hear statements of value positions. In the exchange you will see people striving for some consensus on what values should underlie student organization. Something like this has gone on throughout history when values are created. Some we still live by took form thousands of years ago in a process very like the one which at this moment is forging still others at many places in society.

NORMS   Values and norms are so closely related that it has been hard to discuss one without reference to the other. Values are conceptions of desired conditions which have implications for behavior. Our values are expressions of what we like or want, and if we can we behave in ways that will realize them. But values do not tell us *how to behave in any specific way;* they tell us where to go but not how to get there. They specify the ends we seek but not the means for achieving these ends. A person may believe in generosity, but this does not specifically require him to contribute a particular sum to the local United Fund. A citizen of the United States who believes in democratic values does not get from this belief a clear picture of just how he is obligated to support these values by particular kinds of behavior, other than voting.

Values furnish the objects, explanations, and justifications of behavior. Norms specify the kinds of behavior appropriate or required to realize values. They spell out the meaning of values in concrete situations. *"A norm is a rule that is widely accepted in a social situation, specifying behavior that is appropriate or required of designated persons"* (Bates, 1967). We can illustrate the connections between values, norms, and social behavior.

VALUE: Telling the truth is good.

RELATED NORM (in a particular family): When the children ask questions they should be answered truthfully, even if it is difficult or embarrassing to do so.

SOCIAL BEHAVIOR: A four-year-old child asks his mother where babies come from and she answers truthfully, allowing for his capacity to comprehend.

VALUE: Equal opportunity is a good thing.

RELATED NORM: Employers should not discriminate against job applicants on the basis of race, religion, or sex.

SOCIAL BEHAVIOR: An employer hires a black woman because she has the best qualifications for the job, even though several white persons have also applied.

From these illustrations you can see that, compared with norms, values tend to be quite general or abstract. They have wide applicability to many different situations. The value of truth will come into play in hundreds of diverse settings, and the same is true for the value of equal opportunity. Norms tie values to particular kinds of behavior in specific situations where people are engaged in social interaction.

THE EMERGENCE OF NORMS   In the broadest sense, norms evolve because of the real problems that arise when two or more persons try to realize values in ways based on their interdependence. To succeed they *must* coordinate their behavior. Choices *must* be made among the possible kinds of behavior which might be effective. Sustained uncertainty about how to act can be agonizing and destructive. If choices have to be made about every new episode in social interaction, the need to cooperate becomes impossibly complex. Norms do not solve all problems of social interaction, for the individual or the group, but they answer many recurring questions about who should do what, how, and when. When a group has evolved a norm, each member pays a kind of price: he gives up some individual freedom of choice. What each person (and the group) gets in return is collaboration toward common ends, and a saving of time, energy, and other resources.

As with values, some norms are very old, while others are of recent origin. The injunction to "honor thy father and thy mother" has existed in most of the world for more than two thousand years. The norms governing the behavior of airplane pilots approaching head-on are only a few decades old. And just as with values, norms both guide social behavior and are themselves created and sustained by it. Whenever a social act begins, what happens either confirms the existing norms or reveals the need for new ones.

Imagine a simple, familiar situation: a committee formed to

carry out a definite job but with no instructions on how to organize to do the job. The members decide that one person should be designated leader. This can be done in several ways. A personality test could be given to see who is the best potential leader. Volunteers could be called for. A leader could be chosen by lot. The leadership could be rotated, each member taking his turn. Members could even engage in physical combat to see who won. Suppose that two persons are nominated, and one is elected by secret ballot. Probably this method will be proposed almost immediately, and it will be clear from the discussion that all consider it the best way. At this point it will be established that a norm exists in the group: a leader *should* be chosen by election. The norm is borrowed from the culture of democratic behavior, but it is nonetheless freshly adopted by this particular group. Next time the problem arises in this group, the norm will be applied without question.

NORMATIVE CONTROL OF SOCIAL BEHAVIOR We said earlier that culture never wholly controls social interaction and gave some reasons why. Norms are part of culture, and here we refer to several of their attributes that influence the *degree* to which social behavior is a response to their influence. In doing this we are treating an aspect of conformity and deviance in human behavior, a topic treated extensively in Chapter 11. Everyone has experienced the social rules we call norms. Everyone obeys such rules much of the time and violates them sometimes. Many factors determine the conditions under which people obey or disobey norms. Our focus now is on those *characteristics of norms* which increase or decrease their control over social interaction. Four such characteristics are mentioned below.

Consensus The degree to which applicable norms are agreed upon by all concerned can vary greatly. Early in this century the great French sociologist Durkheim used the word *anomie* to refer to normless social situations, those in which agreement on social rules would be at or near zero. Anomie may be found in new groups which have not had time to establish agreement on rules of interaction. In other situations there *once* was high consensus on norms, but now there is no feeling that all participants are guided by the same rules. In many American families today (as contrasted with a few decades ago) the parents may be at odds with each other or simply lack confidence in appropriate rules for parent-child relations. The children, in turn, may not agree with either parent, or with each other. Because norms are vital in coordinating interpersonal behavior toward realizing common values, any situation near anomie has problems. A basic assumption is that the greater the consensus about norms, the more likely it is that social interaction will be guided by them.

It does not follow that there is any "best" degree of consensus on norms. People can tolerate considerable variation in agreement.

Social interaction in extreme hazard—for example, an infantry platoon under fire in wartime—requires more consensus about norms than a group of friends on a picnic. Probably an optimum level of consensus could be defined for any particular condition.

Relative Importance　We have said that the values in social behavior are generally arranged in a hierarchy of importance. So are the norms associated with values. In most circles, though not all, the value of human life is greater than the value of property: the norm against murder is more compelling than that against theft. The norm prescribing loyalty to a group and its members is among the most universal and powerful of norms. A norm indicating that a napkin should be placed in the lap, not tied around the neck, is trivial. Other things being equal, the more important a norm is to those in social interaction, the more likely it is that behavior will conform to it.

Norm Conflict　Some norms are compatible with others, while some are in conflict. By compatible we mean that adherence to one norm will not interfere with adherence to others in the same setting. For example, the expression of love between husband and wife doesn't normally conflict with their expression of love toward their children. On the other hand, when behavior along one norm crosses behavior along others morally, logically, even physically there is conflict. A famous case of such conflict was Robert E. Lee, who at the outbreak of the American Civil War debated loyalty to his country against that to his native state. He cast his lot with Virginia and contributed mightily to the cause of the Confederacy. Had he stayed with the Union, the course of the war might have been changed. Clashing norms pull people different ways. Obedience to one norm can mean automatic disobedience to another. Personal costs of norm conflict include anxiety, doubt, confusion, and guilt. Social costs include reduced effectiveness of associated persons in reaching goals. Generally speaking, the presence of incompatible norms reduces the influence of norms upon the behavior of interacting people.

Norm conflict is so personally distressing and socially inefficient that people try to eliminate it. But this is often difficult in societies like that of the United States. Such societies contain so many diverse ways of life and are changing so rapidly in poorly coordinated ways that norm conflict is one of their prominent sociological features. Americans constantly find themselves in situations where obedience to one norm raises problems with others. People are taught *both* to love one another as brothers, and to compete fiercely in a struggle for individual success. Citizens are supposed to obey the law, *but* it is sometimes appropriate to break the law, especially if you don't get caught. It isn't whether you win or lose but how you play the game, *but* winning is all-important. Women should have the same right to develop their capacities as men do, *but* being a homemaker is the proper

Norm conflict among Americans is illustrated by the controversy over abortion. While some do not hold strong views on the issue, millions of citizens hold to bitterly conflicting normative views. The values which underlie the conflict make the issue extremely difficult to resolve, for to be morally right by one point of view is automatically to be morally wrong by the other.

way of life for a woman. Such incompatibilities rise in small settings like families and groups of friends, and also permeate the life of the nation as a whole. Most Americans probably believe sincerely in equality of opportunity for all, yet large numbers of people have not only practiced but advocated less than equal opportunity for some citizens because of race, religion, or sex. This single inconsistency has caused huge social costs and incalculable personal suffering.

Norm Appropriateness Norms, you will recall, are specifications for the behavior needed to realize values. In general, when people are guided by the norms that they espouse, values are realized to a satisfying degree. But this is not always true. Sometimes norms call for behavior which is very inefficient in reaching desired goals. In religion, tenacious adherence to traditional norms of behavior may reduce the popularity of a church which wishes to grow. In education, outworn methods often weaken teaching. A business firm whose goal is profit may decline because, under changed conditions, its management cannot give up old and familiar ways. Elmo Roper in 1969 questioned the explanations offered by railroad management for the sharp decline in passenger traffic. According to him, "Over the last few decades . . . railroad management has consistently resisted change, held back on innovations, and has viewed new transportation developments as threats rather than opportunities."

Norms ultimately cease to work when circumstances change and people fail to adapt. Emotional loyalty to the old ways of doing things is often strong. It can blind people to the fact that their norms are outmoded, even in the face of powerful evidence. Nevertheless, inappropriate norms lead to progressively greater frustration, because they are ineffective in attaining goals. Continued failure becomes demoralizing, and people lose their commitment to the common enterprise. If this process is not reversed by a better adjustment between values and norms, it may end in the death of the association between interacting persons.

Our brief consideration of four characteristics of norms gives further insight into why culture (in this case values and norms) never rigidly controls the actual behavior of people in social interaction. The chances that all four of these characteristics will have maximum potential for behavior control in any particular situation are small. By empirically investigating such characteristics as these four, the sociologist has a basis for understanding the degree to which culture controls behavior under varying circumstances. He knows that while culture always molds actual social behavior, the interesting questions are: to what degree does it do so, and under what specific conditions?

ROLE What does the word *father* mean to you? Very likely the first thing it calls to your mind is your own father. The word denotes a

Part 1 / Some Fundamental Ideas

person. The picture evoked will probably include his personal appearance. It will also include some of your memories of how this particular man has interacted with you over the years. And surely the word will arouse feelings, out of your own highly individual experience with your father. These may include love and respect, but there may also be resentment or antagonism.

Your personal reaction to one man does not keep you from realizing that *father* also refers to an entire class of similar relationships which link the behavior of millions of pairs of older and younger persons. These innumerable people differ from each other in hundreds of ways. Nearly all of them are unknown to you. Yet the social exchanges which spell out a relationship have marked similarities, and you unquestioningly identify these similarities with the word *father.*

There are many nouns which, like father, don't define a person so much as they define a set of activities involving someone in social contact with other persons. For example, read the definition of the term *foreman,* from *The U.S. Dictionary of Occupational Titles.* Terms like *father* and *foreman,* then, are sometimes used to denote particular individuals (My father; Jack is the foreman). They also denote anyone who engages in certain kinds of behavior which involves interaction with other people (fathers in general; all foremen).

The specific and generic usages do not conflict. When the word *father* brings your own father to mind, you are thinking of one instance of a much larger class. Any particular father-child relationship will have some unique characteristics and some universal ones. Nouns of the kind we are discussing are handy labels which may denote particular persons or whole classes of persons, but always in some way imply actions linking people in social relationships.

Foreman

Supervises and coordinates activities of workers engaged in one or more occupations: Studies production schedules and estimates man-hour requirements for completion of job assignment. Interprets company policies to workers and enforces safety regulations. Interprets specifications, blueprints, and job orders to workers, and assigns duties. Establishes or adjusts work procedures to meet production schedules, using knowledge of capacities of machines and equipment. Recommends measures to improve production methods, equipment performance, and quality of product, and suggests changes in working conditions and use of equipment to increase efficiency of shop, department, or work crew. Analyzes and resolves work problems, or assists workers in solving work problems. Initiates or suggests plans to motivate workers to achieve work goals. Recommends or initiates personnel actions, such as promotions, transfers, discharges, and disciplinary measures. . . .

Source: Dictionary of Occupational Titles Vol. 1, 1965, pp. 294–295, published by the United States Department of Labor. The description continues at some length. The thousands of job titles described in the volume from which this passage comes are, in effect, role descriptions.

These actors are performing roles defined in the script of a play. All of us perform roles in everyday life, and the roles we act out are contained in the script called "culture."

ROLE AND ROLE PERFORMANCE   Without using the term directly we have been discussing *role*, a central concept in sociology and social psychology. Corresponding to the distinction between culture and actual social behavior which has been discussed in connection with norms we shall define two closely related terms (Bates and Cloyd, 1956). Role is a component of culture. *A role is a pattern of behavior prescribed by one (or more) members of a group for one (or more) other members.* To say that the behavior is prescribed means that it is in some sense obligatory; the person is supposed to behave this way. *The actual behavior of a member for whom a role is prescribed is termed role performance.*[1]

The word *group* itself should be defined, and we will treat it at length in Chapter 4. For the moment it will be assumed that there is sufficient agreement as to its meaning. The reference to pattern indicates that the separate acts which constitute a role or role performance are not independent of each other but are meaningfully interconnected. Sociologists are likely to say that they are "functionally related." *Each act makes some contribution to the entity which is the role, and this contribution is its function.* The role of a committee chairman, for example, includes many acts. He may need to set times for meetings, notify members, call meetings to order, prepare and work through an agenda, see that decisions are made, and make arrangements for following through on decisions. Because each of these separate acts is functionally related to the others and to the role as a whole, it is hard to think of them independently of each other. Obviously, they go together to make a pattern.

The definitions state that a single role may be associated with more than one member of a group. For instance, in a college class there are many people, but only two roles: *teacher* and *student*. The role of teacher is typically performed by only one person, the role of student by many.

Finally, the definition implies that a role may not be associated with a given person by all other members of the group. The students in a college class may have more than one role for their teacher. Some may prescribe for him a rather traditional, authoritarian pattern of behavior, while others prescribe a democratic, nondirective pattern. Two roles would exist for this teacher. While it is more typical that in any particular group each person has only one role which is defined with considerable agreement by the other members, exceptions are not rare, and present interesting problems in role analysis. For example, is there more than one role for the students in a class?

---

[1] The term *role* has been defined in many different, frequently overlapping ways. The definitions given here lie well enough within the main tradition of role analysis to be useful. The most comprehensive modern source for reviewing the theoretical and research literature of this field is Biddle and Thomas (1966). Among briefer, easier accounts, that of Yinger (1965:98–138) is particularly recommended.

Part 1 / Some Fundamental Ideas

NORMS AS COMPONENTS OF ROLES It is important to understand how role and role performance relate to norms and social behavior. Remember that a norm is a social rule for the behavior of one or more members of a social system. A norm defines one kind of behavior within a role. Norms are components of roles. Each kind of behavior in a role is defined by a norm. A role incorporates several, sometimes many, norms. It is also more complex than a norm because, as indicated by the notion of pattern, there is functional interdependence among its parts.

ROLE PERFORMANCE AND SOCIAL BEHAVIOR How is role performance related to social behavior? Remember that role performance is how a person *actually* behaves, as compared with role, which defines appropriate or required behavior. Social behavior is reciprocal, linked behavior between two or more persons. An act of one individual is both a response and a stimulus to the behavior of another. With these ideas in mind, two things become evident. First, a role performance exists in social behavior. Second, a role performance is an incomplete part of any episode of social behavior. One person's role performance is how he acts in relation to others, but it does not include their role performances. A complete episode of social behavior includes the interdependent role performances of all involved. If we extract in sequence the behavior of just one person, we will have that person's role performance. But to do so we must break down the total sequence of social behavior involving two or more persons. Figure 2-3 shows some of the relationships among values, norms, roles, and role performances in a two-person group.

The Invisibility of Roles As with norms, roles are not often explicitly spelled out in interaction settings; you can see this for yourself in the next group setting you enter. What is directly visible is people interacting; you see them doing and saying things which certainly are interconnected. But you can't see *role,* and this may

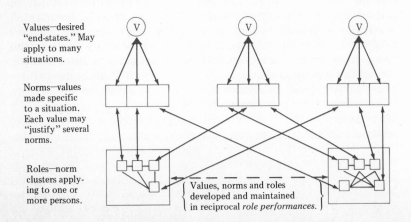

Values—desired "end-states." May apply to many situations.

Norms—values made specific to a situation. Each value may "justify" several norms.

Roles—norm clusters applying to one or more persons.

Values, norms and roles developed and maintained in reciprocal *role performances.*

FIGURE 2-3 VALUES, NORMS, AND ROLES IN A TWO-PERSON GROUP

make role seem a rather shadowy concept. Now and then, in certain circumstances, roles or parts of roles are made explicit. One such situation occurs when newly organized groups need to define roles, and people discuss the question "Who is going to do what?" Gradually, the collective decisions on this question acquire normative elements that transform them into feelings that "X *should* do this" and "A *should* do that."

Another situation which often elicits definite role prescriptions is the failure of a person to deliver an adequate role performance in the eyes of those observing him. The others will show their disapproval and may directly remind the offender of the role prescription being violated. When the Supreme Court overturns a decision of a lower court on the grounds that in the original trial the behavior (role performance) of the judge or the prosecuting attorney was improper, the Court is saying that a role prescription has been violated.

Usually, however, roles are invisible because interacting persons don't need to spell them out. They are pretty much understood and taken for granted, so much so that people may not think about them much even when performing them. Attention focuses on what is happening at the moment. The ways in which that activity is influenced by roles are not in the forefront of attention. Role performances, on the other hand, are visible and manifest in social behavior.

Role and role performance are important sociological concepts not only because they describe important patterns in social behavior, but because the relationship between the two is thought to be an important source of the order we see in social behavior. The part of culture we call *role* is an important influence on the part of social behavior we call *role performance,* and vice versa. People behave as they do toward one another partly because they share ideas on how they *ought* to behave. But it is also true that their shared ideas about interpersonal behavior are influenced by the experience of putting those ideas into practice.

INDEPENDENCE OF ROLES   To sensitize oneself to the presence of roles that cannot be directly seen in operation, it is helpful to think about the distinction between roles and persons. Consider the fact that some roles are very much older than any living person. The roles called sister, leader, and friend are as old as human society, although they are given somewhat different content in the culture of particular societies. Some other very old roles are boss, priest, and patient. By contrast, roles like policeman, scientist, and bureaucrat are much newer, while others such as astronaut and women's libber evolved only yesterday. Such roles exist independently of the particular persons who perform them; it is what is meant when we say that roles are part of culture. The need for distinguishing between person and role is dramatically illustrated in the disturbing news story "Sanity in Bedlam" (p. 42). It suggests that, regardless of the actual psychological characteristics of in-

Part 1 / Some Fundamental Ideas

dividuals, persons who are committed to mental hospitals are assigned a social role (mentally ill person), and the distinction between role and person may be overlooked even by professional clinicians.

Jerome Beatty, Jr., (1969) once reported an amusing anecdote about a child's confusion between person and role. It involved a man who had flown during World War II and continued private flying later. As the man tells it:

Last week-end I asked my six-year-old daughter if she would like to go up for a flight. She had been on commercial airlines a few times when we went to see her grandparents. She said, "Oh, yes, when can we go?"

My wife said, "Be careful!" I took my daughter out to a local airport and rented a twin-engine job. I strapped her in, pushed the starter button, and began to warm up. She yelled, "Where's the pilot?" I replied that I was. She looked at me for a moment and started screaming and trying to unfasten her seat belt. She continued to scream even after I turned off the engines—and that was that. A kid certainly knows how to hurt a guy.

While *roles* may be distinguished from the *persons* who perform them, *role performances* may not. Role performances exist *only* in the actual behavior of particular people in particular circumstances of time and place. Every time you interact as a student with a professor you produce a concrete manifestation of the student role. And because no two people are alike and the circumstances surrounding two performances of the same role are never identical, role performances never exactly duplicate the related roles. Every person has a repertoire of role performances, one for every setting in which people expect him to interact with them in a role that has been prescribed.

CHANGE AND STABILITY

Sociocultural change is so important that it will get special consideration in each of the chapters that follow.[2] In periods when, by present standards, societies changed slowly, people often believed that they didn't change at all. The very idea of change was somewhat unfamiliar. Today it is no longer possible to believe in an unchanging social world. Indeed, it may seem sometimes that there is nothing but change.

Sociologically speaking, stability and change are not absolutely different, mutually exclusive states. The surface of the earth provides a parallel to what we mean. From the brief perspective of a human life span, the earth appears stable and unchanging. But we know from geological evidence that the surface is constantly changing. Mountains rise where once there were seas and the continents drift to different locations. Stability and change in the surface of the earth are therefore *relative* to the time intervals from which geologic features are observed. As the interval in-

---

[2] The word *sociocultural* is a convenient way to refer to *both* the cultural and the "actual behavior" aspects of a social situation. We will use it often from now on.

Sanity in Bedlam

The plight of the normal person who finds himself committed to a mental institution and unable to convince anyone he is not insane is a standard plot for horror fiction. But in a remarkable study last week, Dr. David L. Rosenhan, professor of psychology and law at Stanford University, and seven associates reported just such a nightmare in real life. To find out how well psychiatric professionals can distinguish the normal from the sick, they had themselves committed to mental institutions. Their experiment, reported in the journal Science, clearly showed that once inside the hospital walls, everyone is judged insane.

The "pseudopatients," five men and three women, included three psychologists, a pediatrician, a psychiatrist, a painter and a housewife, all of whom were certifiably sane. In the course of the three-year study, the volunteers spent an average of nineteen days in a dozen institutions, private and public, in New York, California, Pennsylvania, Oregon and Delaware. Each pseudopatient told admitting doctors that he kept hearing voices that said words like "empty," "hollow" and "void," suggesting that the patient found his life meaningless and futile. But beyond falsifying their names and occupations, all the volunteers described their life histories as they actually were. In so doing, they gave the doctors every chance to discern the truth. "I couldn't believe we wouldn't be found out," Rosenhan told NEWSWEEK's Gerald Lubenow. But they weren't. At eleven hospitals the pseudopatients were promptly diagnosed as schizophrenic and, at the twelfth, as manic-depressive.

As soon as they had gained admission, the volunteers studiously resumed normal behavior. They denied hearing voices and worked hard to convince staff members that they ought to be released. But such efforts were to no avail; doctors and nurses interpreted everything the pseudopatients did in terms of the original diagnosis. When some of the volunteers went about taking notes, the hospital staff made such entries in their records as "patient engages in writing behavior." The only people who realized that the experimenters were normal were some of the patients. "You're not crazy," said one patient. "You're a journalist or a professor. You're checking up on the hospital."

During a psychiatric interview, a pseudopatient noted that he was closer to his mother as a small child, but as he grew up, became more attached to his father. Although this was a perfectly normal alteration of identity figures, it was taken by the psychiatrist as evidence of "unstable relationships in childhood." The hospital, Rosenhan concluded, distorts the perception of behavior. "In a psychiatric hospital," he says, "the place is more important than the person. If you're a patient you must be crazy."

Rosenhan and his colleagues were not exposed to the squalor and degradation of any modern snake pits, but they did witness incidents of abuse and brutality. One patient was beaten for approaching an attendant and saying "I like you."

All this, the Stanford psychologist points out, is part of a pervasive depersonalization and helplessness that afflicts patients in a mental hospital. The experimenters found much additional evidence that the staff didn't regard the patients as people, or even in some cases, acknowledge that they existed. On one occasion, a nurse casually opened her blouse to adjust her brassiere in the midst of a ward full of men. "One did not have the sense she was being seductive," said Rosenhan. "She just didn't notice us."

From their fellow patients, the volunteers quickly learned that they were caught up in a kind of Catch-22 paradox. "Never tell a doctor that you're well," said one patient. "He won't believe you. That's called a 'flight into health.' Tell him you're still sick, but you're feeling a lot better. That's called insight." "You've got to be sick and acknowledge that you're sick," says Rosenhan, "to be considered well enough to be released."

As it was, it took up to 52 days for the volunteers to get out of the hospital, even though most had been admitted voluntarily and the law in many states makes discharge mandatory on request in such instances on 72 hours' notice. Three of the volunteers finally walked out of the hospital. The other nine were ultimately discharged, but with the stigma of the diagnosis "schizophrenia in remission."

Rosenhan bears no ill will against the doctors and nurses who run the institutions he and his associates saw. The staffers' behavior and perceptions, he feels, were controlled by the situation, not by personal malice or stupidity. Perhaps, he hopes, alternate forms of therapy, such as community mental health centers and crisis intervention will increasingly replace the hospital in the treatment of mental illness.

Source: Newsweek, January 29, 1973. Copyright Newsweek, Inc. 1973 reprinted by permission.

creases we realize that change never altogether ceases, though it may be faster at some times than others.

It is the same with human social behavior, whether we are concerned with huge entities like whole societies, which last for many centuries, or small, short-lived groups. A sociocultural pattern can *seem* completely stable because the time interval is too short to reveal the extremely small changes that are nevertheless going on.

Perceptions of stability and change are also relative to different *rates* of change in different social patterns. Consider two cars traveling side by side at 60 miles per hour; neither is moving at all, *in relation to the other*. But if one is moving at 60 miles per hour and the other at 80 miles per hour, the latter moves past the former at 20 miles per hour, yet both are actually moving at much higher speeds. A ranching family remote in the Rockies may see no change at all in the patterns of their life compared to the fantastic changes they see in the urban parts of the country. Yet their patterns are changing too. The relations between husband and wife and between parents and children alter steadily with time. When we speak of the present as an era of great social change, the statement's meaning lies mostly in comparison with past epochs with less rapid change, or with other parts of the present world in which change is less than in ours.

PATTERNS AND CHANGE If all social behavior changes through time, slow or fast, how may we speak of patterns of social behavior, which are the subject matter of sociology? Essentially, the answer is that *as time passes,* we observe that people behave toward one another in *substantially* the same ways, over and over again. You are probably reading this book in connection with a college course. Observe that no two sessions of your class are exactly alike. In fact, your class almost certainly changes in a fairly orderly way as the term proceeds. Yet each session is recognizably like the earlier ones, and we can rather confidently predict that the pattern will continue as long as the class meets. In other words, socially patterned behavior (and its associated culture) have stability that is *relative*. Society and all its parts consist of this *comparative* regularity and persistence through time. Social patterns are both manifested and changed through time, and the sociologist is interested both in the details of sociocultural patterns and the processes through which they are altered.

Popular discussions of current social change usually center on massive or dramatic tendencies in society, like the industrial revolution, urbanization, and crime. But as sociologists, we cannot ignore change at the microsociological level. In fact, even the largest currents of social change have their effects on this level, and in turn depend on correlated changes of a microsociological nature. Again and again we shall return to the topic of sociocultural change. Here, we shall confine ourselves to elaborating what has already been said about the implications for change in the relationship between culture and actual social conduct.

TENSION AND CHANGE We have indicated that culture channels, modifies, and constrains actual behavior, that people engage in social behavior in patterns which approximate the "designs for living" provided by culture. And we have insisted that while this is true, actual social behavior never exactly coincides with culture's designs. There is always a certain *tension* between culture and actual behavior. Culture is the "normal," the "should," even the "must" in man's collective conduct. Each person in a social drama reminds the others and is reminded by them that some kinds of behavior are acceptable and others are not. Often real penalties are paid by the individual who does not heed this process of defining what should be done. Nevertheless, departures from culturally prescribed patterns are inevitable, and we have earlier reviewed some of the reasons why.

This tension between culture and social behavior is inherent in all social life. It has existed ever since humans began to develop culture. We cannot speak for other species, but for man the need to evolve culture and then to *obey* its strictures creates frustration for individuals; this is one price we pay for the efficiencies of social living. We feel stress as a consequence of the strain between culture and actual behavior. This stress is often manageable; in growing up we learn various ways of coping with it. But it is always a potential source of social change, particularly when it increases with time.

While we can't be sure, this young soldier's display of a "peace signal," widely popular during the Vietnam war, may reflect tension between his military role and his disagreement with the war. The strains that develop in the relationship between culture and actual situations in which people are caught up is an enduring source of social change.

Tension-Management Theory Wilbert Moore (1963:70–82) has developed this view into a kind of "tension-management" theory of social change, applicable to both large- and small-scale settings. Those points in a social situation where tension is greatest and where it is increasing are the places to look for potential change. People behave in ways intended to lessen the tension built into patterned behavior, and in the process change not only the social pattern but the culture which underlies it.

Once sensitized to it we can see this process at many points in society. A major example comes from the American labor movement in this century. For the first few decades labor unions had to battle for recognition and acceptance by employers and government. As a result, the norms comprising the roles of early labor leaders called for aggressiveness and a willingness to engage in physical combat and to be imprisoned for the cause if necessary. Many tough, combative men rose to power in those days. In the thirties and forties, however, the battle for recognition was won; government, both federal and local, guaranteed the right of workers to organize and to bargain collectively with their employers. Important changes soon took place in the actual behavior linking employers and employees and involving issues over pay and working conditions. Conflict between the two groups didn't

The role of leader in the early years of the American labor movement required very different personal qualities than in later years when both government and business accepted the idea that labor would have a piece of the action. The changes were so great that it was hard for particular individuals to be leaders in both eras. Here we see Alexander Berkman of the Industrial Workers of the World addressing a crowd during the early days of the labor movement. More recently, at a steel contract signing in 1960 are (from left to right) R. Heath Larry, United States Steel (almost cut off); John Morse, Bethlehem Steel; R. Conrad Cooper, United States Steel and chief industry negotiator; David McDonald, steelworkers president; and Arthur Goldberg, union counsel.

disappear, but it no longer resembled warfare. It was governed by new, binding norms on both sides. Labor leaders now sat as equals with employers at the bargaining table. The diplomatic arts of argument, persuasion, and compromise became more and more important. The changed situation called for men who looked and in many ways acted like business leaders, who worked in attractive offices, lived in suburbia, and took part in civic enterprises. In a word, the character of the *role* was altered as the social exchanges between labor and management changed. As old leaders retired or died, new sorts of men took over. Some, like Walter Reuther of the United Auto Workers, could span both periods, adjusting their role performances to the new situation. Others were unable to make the change and ran into difficulties.

PRACTICAL IMPLICATIONS OF THE CULTURE CONCEPT

As one begins to understand the culture concept and its many ramifications it can become an illuminating practical aid to the understanding of human behavior. To see how, it helps to put aside our usual interpretations of behavior in biological, psychological, and moral terms (see Chapter 1). Useful as these are, they get in the way of thinking in cultural terms.

INTERPRETING THE BEHAVIOR OF OTHERS What interpretations would you make if told about a man who married his sister, an-

Culture: The Humanizing Agent

The portrayals above are familiar ones, but do they accurately reflect these cultural groups? What do you really know about them? Is it possible that you have only a restricted stereotypical picture of such persons, one that is provided by your own cultural background? If you do not understand how the world looks to these people from their cultural perspective, how can you be fair in dealing with them?

other who belched loudly and deliberately after dinner, and a third who found the highest religious experience in handling live poisonous snakes? To the first, your reaction might be indignation at an outrageously immoral act. The person who belches is simply a boor, and the snake handler might strike you as mentally ill. Yet in ancient Egypt the culture surrounding royalty prescribed the marriage of brothers and sisters. In some parts of the Orient, belching expresses appreciation of a fine meal. And a snake-handling Protestant sect exists at present in the United States.

We know that one factor in producing the patterns in visible social behavior is the invisible culture people carry in their heads. It is culture which gives meaning to behavior. If we don't know the culture we can't understand the behavior, and so reach erroneous interpretations which can lead to inappropriate and ineffective responses on our part.

So in understanding human behavior (especially when it is different from our own) nothing helps more than understanding the culture underlying it. This was never understood by the European nations at the time when they established their overseas colonial empires. They attributed the strange behavior of the native inhabitants to ignorance or immorality, and mostly to inferiority. *Ethnocentrism,* the assumption that one's own society and culture are superior to all others, is an ancient and abiding sin. One wonders how different history might have been if the colonizers had tried to understand and appreciate other cultures.

CULTURAL ANALYSIS IN FAMILIAR SETTINGS Whenever you meet people whose background differs from your own (and this happens often in a heterogeneous society like the United States) your ability to behave effectively requires a real effort to understand just how their culture defines the world and its meanings in ways that differ from your own.

Consider a college senior caught cheating on a vital exam, failed in the course, and barred from graduation. His dismayed and bewildered parents grope for understanding. It seems at first glance a simple case of moral failure. Cheating is wrong, says a familiar norm. The young man cheated; he is punished by the college authorities. This is all. But, is it? The parents are inclined to agree, but they also ask if some quirk in their son's psychology could make him behave so irresponsibly.

As it happens, the crucial facts in this incident will never be seen except from a sociological perspective. This student cheated not for lack of moral standards, not because he is mixed up psychologically, but because a different norm in a group of students with whom he constantly interacts *prescribes* cheating in certain circumstances. And for him, this norm is more important than the one which prohibits such behavior. In many student groups the "wrongness" of cheating is easily rationalized away. Grades don't really reflect what you learn, and anyway, everybody does it.

Neither parents nor college authorities, if offered this explanation, have to accept it or act on it. They may persist in regarding the incident *only* as a case of delinquency or of psychological malfunction. But if they really want to know why it occurred and why cheating is common on that campus, if they really wish to reduce it in the future, they will have to attack the problem at its most important source. There are innumerable times when the power to act effectively is rooted in the ability to explain behavior through the relationship between norms and related behavior.

Application in a Legal Setting   Understanding culture can be of practical value in almost any setting. We cite just one more example. Attorneys have long been concerned with the selection of persons to serve on juries, for it is well known that various characteristics of jurors can affect the outcome of a trial, quite apart from the evidence. While most trial lawyers have their own ideas about selecting jurors, social scientists also can give good advice.

In fact, a number of social scientists (Schulman et al., 1973) conducted research on how to advise defense counsel on selecting jurors for the trial of the "Harrisburg Seven" in 1972. The defendants were anti-Vietnam war protestors, and the federal government had indicted them for alleged crimes committed in their antiwar activities. The social scientists interviewed a random sample of the population around Harrisburg, Pennsylvania, and compared them with the panel from which jurors would be chosen; characteristics included age, sex, education, occupation and race. The researchers also sampled attitudes potentially related to issues that would appear in the trial. Since we know attitudes derive from sociocultural experience and background, it is at this point that the social scientists made indirect use of the culture concept.

The relationships discovered between backgrounds and trial-related attitudes turned up some very useful clues to selecting jurors.

We discovered, for example, that religion was significantly related to all the attitudes that concerned us. We therefore recommended that the lawyers should ask prospective jurors about religion, which they had been reluctant to do; and that certain religious categories—e.g., Episcopalians, Presbyterians, Methodists, and fundamentalists—were "bad" enough from our point of view to warrant exclusion from the jury unless there were strong reasons to the contrary. (The "better" religions were Catholic, Brethren, and Lutheran.) (1973:40.)

In the end, the prosecution was unable to convince the jury and the case ended in a mistrial on ten out of twelve counts. Analysis strongly suggested that the use of the social science evidence used by defense lawyers in choosing the jury played a significant part in this outcome.

After the conflict between Indians and the federal government at Wounded Knee, South Dakota, in 1973, Indian leaders smoked the pipe of peace with an assistant United States attorney general, marking the end of the episode. To American Indians, smoking tobacco was more than a simple pleasure, for it was intertwined with important ceremonial occasions.

Practicing the Sociological Perspective

For the beginner, the great difficulty in understanding the concept of culture—and more specific terms like value, norm, and role—is that culture is invisible. It is, as we have said, ideas carried around in people's heads. This difficulty is acute in small-scale social settings because here we are vividly aware of the personal characteristics of individuals, and this interferes with our view of culture as shared ideas which are molding the behavior of us all. In larger settings it is easier to disregard the purely personal aspects of social interaction and see the effects of the invisible but powerful ideas we call culture. We often must *infer* these ideas from the behavior we can see, though sometimes values and norms will be openly expressed. Here is an observation which may help. If you regularly attend a church, attend a service of another kind of church, one as different from your own as possible. If you do not belong to any church, attend services at two quite different churches not more than a week apart. Your task is to identify some of the *norms* which operate in the two church situations. What you can directly observe is *behavior* in two different religious settings. This behavior may include a few direct verbalizations of norms. If so, note them down. In other instances, you will have to infer that certain norms exist because the behavior of the people suggests them even though the norms are never explicitly stated. Write these inferred norms down too. Then compare the two lists of norms, one for each church. You will have a partial accounting of the different religious *cultures* which underlie the different behavior in the two churches.

Almost certainly there are foreign students on your campus, plunged into a new cultural setting in an American college. A few may be suffering *culture shock,* acute anxiety caused by the endless strain of adapting to an unfamiliar culture. These few cannot continue in this environment unless they can learn the new cultural definitions of appropriate behavior. Think what it means to learn new values, norms, and roles each day. If you can imagine yourself in their situation, you will get a fresh insight into the critical importance of culture.

Perhaps you can help a few of these foreign students in this way. Let them know that you have at least some notion of the task they face. And ask them to tell you something about their culture. Be a good listener. Ask questions and show appreciation of a culture which certainly means a lot to them. Remember that a foreigner must always be sounding out unfamiliar situations and will sometimes feel inadequate in them. Give him a chance to be the expert and to explain how things are done back home. If you do a good job, you will genuinely widen your own perspective on the cultures people have devised to meet their needs.

Socialization: The Link Between Society and the Individual

3

To his most famous and enigmatic painting, Gauguin appended the words "Where Did We Come From? What Are We? Where Are We Going?" The artist gave no answers. There are no final or complete answers to such questions. Yet they are asked by thoughtful people in every generation. Some of the most enduring riddles arise from the relationship between a single human being and the organized social world. To what extent is each of us formed and controlled by society? Is society necessarily an oppressor of the individual? Is it possible for an individual to live apart from society? Does society really amount to anything more than a collection of separate individuals?

When approached from the perspective of the social sciences, such questions lie in the special domain of social psychology. The object of inquiry here is not the separate organism, treated as if it did or could exist apart from a sociocultural environment. Nor is it society, analyzed in a way which excludes the full psychological reality of any living person. The focus is upon the *strands of interdependence* linking every living man, woman, and child with the social structures and cultural traditions which have been painfully built and rebuilt through the centuries.

One chapter is too short a space for a systematic survey of social psychology. Instead, we shall treat a number of topics of special interest to sociological students of social psychology, and we shall group them together as aspects of a process called *socialization*. Consistent with the viewpoints of Clausen (1968:3), Elkin (1960:3–6), and many others, we see socialization as a kind of master process in human development. It continues throughout the human life span, and at every point in it involves contact between society and the individual.

All students of socialization are concerned with the process (events linked through time) whereby individuals acquire capacities permitting them to take part in organized social life. Socialization is a process with two sides. From one side it is a series of developments within the individual; from the other it comprises the social arrangements which produce changes in the individual. The first of these conceptions is embodied in the following definition (Elkin, 1960:4). Socialization is "*the process by which someone learns the ways of a given society or social group so that he can function within it.*" The following definition stresses social arrangements (Aberle, 1961:387). "*Socialization consists of those patterns of action or aspects of action which inculcate in individuals the skills (including knowledge), motives and attitudes necessary for the performance of present or anticipated roles.*" Zigler and Child (1969:474) have still another definition, one which better serves our purposes here because it incorporates both aspects of the process. "*Socialization is a broad term for the whole process by which an individual develops, through transactions with other people, his specific patterns of socially relevant behavior and experience.*"

LEARNING SOCIAL ROLES   The term *socialization* is sometimes applied only to the childhood years. Here it denotes any situation at any time of life where a person is engaged in socially relevant learning. It would include all the following: a small boy learning the male sex role, a college student training for biochemistry, a young married couple learning to be parents, a young adult becoming an active member of the Democratic party organization in his community, a recently promoted production worker in a factory learning a supervisory role, a widow learning to live without her husband, and an old couple entering a retirement home.

One good way to give an overview of socialization is to link it to the human life span, showing how the need for role-learning arises at every age. We shall not follow this procedure for several reasons. Some age-related aspects of socialization will be discussed in later chapters (Chapter 12 on the family, Chapter 8 on occupations, and Chapter 13 on education). Moreover, theory and research on socialization are not yet well distributed over the life span: most of it deals with the earlier years. Studies of socialization in adulthood, though rapidly increasing, remain comparatively scarce. The comments of Inkeles, a leading student of socialization, suggest why there is an urgent need for study of the process across the entire life span.

Inevitably we change as we move through life. These changes lead to experiences that are new for us. Hence, the need for socialization rises over and over again, from our earliest to our latest years.

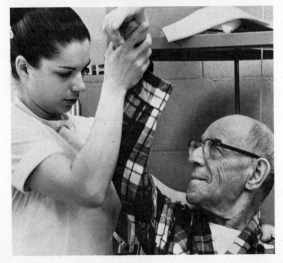

By the age of four the brain may have attained 90 percent of its potential weight, but at that age the individual, as a member of society, has probably acquired not much more than 10 percent of the repertoire of social roles he will later play in life. We can be easily misled by the assertion that in the development of our general intelligence, 50 percent takes place between conception and age 4, and 30 percent more between ages 4 and 8. Social development, admittedly harder to measure, must be recognized as mainly occurring at later ages. A child may at age 11 know 50 percent of all the words he will know, but so far as other forms of socially relevant knowledge are concerned, virtually all of his learning and development are still ahead of him (1969:630).

The human infant, "muling and puking in the nurse's arms," as Shakespeare put it, knows nothing and doesn't even know that he knows nothing. Weak and helpless, he gives not the slightest sign of his slumbering potential. In a few short years he may advance the frontiers of human knowledge, set foot upon Mars, coldbloodedly murder an innocent person, or become a modern saint, but now he neither knows nor cares what lies ahead. From his parents he has received a body which is enough like all human bodies to admit him to the broad arena of human possibilities— and different enough from all other bodies to contain a degree of uniqueness in his potential. His society gives him claim to a set of future experiences which will interact with his biological makeup to determine what he becomes. Neither set of factors exclusively controls the outcome. No biological starting point guarantees that the child will finally become a businessman or an attorney. No set of sociocultural influences can make him a creative mathematician if his inherited intelligence is too low. What is involved in this complicated drama of confrontation between individual and society?

SOCIALIZATION INPUTS Every time an individual enters a situation that has socialization possibilities for him, two sets of variables come into play. One set is sociocultural; the other is comprised of his own existing characteristics. The interaction and interpenetration of the two sets of variables will determine the outcomes of the situation for the person and for society.

SOCIOCULTURAL FACTORS When we are born, we find society already there. We meet it in a small group called the family, the first of a long sequence of groups and larger organizations extending throughout our lives. Figure 3-1 shows some of the ways in which the family helps to introduce the individual to various elements of the society. And, in a sense, society (in the form of all these groups and organizations) is ready for us. Society is thousands of years old: one human life can scarcely span a century. Therefore, because society can only be carried on by living people, the appearance of each one of us on the scene is, so to speak, expected and prepared for in advance.

Part 1 / Some Fundamental Ideas

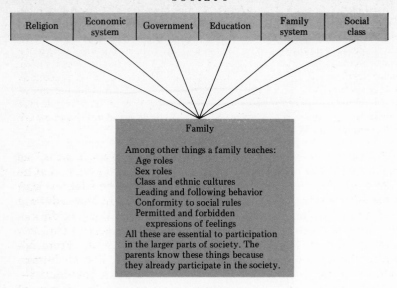

SOCIETY

Religion	Economic system	Government	Education	Family system	Social class

Family

Among other things a family teaches:
  Age roles
  Sex roles
  Class and ethnic cultures
  Leading and following behavior
  Conformity to social rules
  Permitted and forbidden
    expressions of feelings
All these are essential to participation
in the larger parts of society. The
parents know these things because
they already participate in the society.

FIGURE 3-1 THE ROLE OF THE FAMILY AS A VITAL SOCIALIZING AGENT FOR SOCIETY

Longevity and Member Replacement   Think of the Roman Catholic church in this connection. As an organization and a religious subculture it has had a continuous existence for almost two thousand years. Think of the millions of persons, dead and forgotten, who for a brief time kept this part of society alive, just as living Roman Catholics do today. Generations flow through such an organization, leaving it intact. To survive so long, the church has had to devote great care to socializing new recruits, whether by birth into already Catholic families, or by conversion of those who began life outside the church. It is interesting to note that this need for organizational continuity arose only *after* the belief of some very early Christians that Jesus would return to the world in their lifetime proved to be false.

The church's problem of recruiting and replacing members is shared by all social units, large and small, if they are to survive. A college that took in no freshmen would go out of existence in four years. Every social unit that receives new members undertakes to socialize them. They must be taught the culture of the group or organization, assigned a location in its structure, and a corresponding role to perform. From birth onward, society's units are prepared for us.

Social settings vary a great deal in the degree to which socialization is central to their normal operation. Socialization is the primary goal of schools and colleges; it is an equally important, if not primary, aim of the family. There are innumerable other scenes in which socialization is a deliberate and important means to a higher end, for example, on-the-job training in industry.

A lot of socialization takes place informally, without anyone paying much attention to the process. Each generation of college students accepts the current definition of appropriate clothing, scarcely aware, perhaps, that over a few years substantial changes occur in what is appropriate. These two photographs show college clothing styles in the 1950s and the 1970s.

There are also many situations in which the training of newcomers is not often thought about, but occurs as an unintended by-product. College students quickly learn the slang in vogue among their peers. They do so in a process so informal that most of the time neither party is aware of the process going on. From now on we will sometimes refer to a person being socialized as a "neophyte" or "socializee." Individuals engaged in socializing others will frequently be called "socializing agents," or, more briefly, "agents."

In general, the *content* of socialization consists of the values, norms, and roles indigenous to a particular social setting, together with the knowledge and skills needed to produce satisfactory role performance. This is what must be transmitted. There is of course great variation in the specifics found in different situations. Obviously the culture and job skills acquired by an auto mechanic are very different from those studied by a person headed for the ministry. But both processes include the transmission of culture and the knowledge required in the particular social setting.

The Role of Neophyte Faced with the eternal necessity of socializing newcomers, people in groups and organizations have been inventive in devising ways to accomplish the task. Dozens of educational philosophies and technologies have been devised and tried. Despite the bewildering variety, a few generalizations about socialization and its strategies can be made that apply very widely. Look at the following list of nouns.

greenhorn	apprentice	recruit
tenderfoot	learner	bride
beginner	novice	probationer
pledge	swab	plebe

These are twelve different ways of naming essentially the same thing: the *role of neophyte.* It is a universal role because the problem of socializing newcomers is universal. And it is a genuine role because, like any other, it is comprised of more or less specific behavioral prescriptions for the guidance of any person assigned to the role. Sometimes the role of neophyte is defined with great detail and clarity, as in the case of apprentices in craft labor unions in the United States. At the other extreme, in informal groups, the role of newcomer may be very transitory and ill-defined, consisting of little more than the realization that it will take him a while to get adjusted to the group. But the newcomer role is still there.

In all cases the role includes the recognition that the newcomer must for a while be permitted to make mistakes without being punished for them. This is because he cannot yet know the culture of the social unit he has joined. Tolerance for the failures of the beginner is thus part of the role. But the reciprocal of this tolerance is the expectation that he will work at learning the culture of the unit, including his part in it. In short, the role is a temporary one, temporarily privileged. The newcomer is expected to work himself out of it in due course.

Sanctions Every social unit has at its disposal both rewards (positive sanctions) and punishments (negative sanctions) for securing compliance of members to behavioral prescriptions. And these sanctions will be used in dealing with neophytes. Rank within the group is one resource which can be used as a sanction, since most members value high rank more than low. Although the relationship between rank and conformity to role prescriptions is not simple, Homans (1950) and others have shown that in some circumstances rank is a consequence of how well a member's role performance adheres to his role. In many groups and organizations, though not all, the member starts low in rank. Occasionally newcomers are reminded explicitly of their unworthiness to be fully privileged members, as in the traditional hazing of pledges in college fraternities. But there is the hope of privileges and higher rank to be *earned* if the neophyte works at learning the group's ways. Higher rank may be marked by explicit things such as a pay raise or a new title, but it can also be expressed more subtly— a smile or a friendly word—telling the neophyte that he has passed the tests and is fully accepted as an insider. The normal operation of the group structure is seen as an interlocking set of roles and role performances, and it is adapted to the socialization of new members by the use of a neophyte role. The new member's gradually improved performance in this role results in his socialization.

THE BEGINNER'S CHARACTERISTICS Socialization begins almost at the moment of birth. What does the human infant bring to its first socialization encounters? Detailed comment on man's biological equipment is outside the purview of sociology. But intelligence, sex, sexual maturation, body type, rate of physical aging, and the life span are all partly or wholly controlled by genetic factors. None of these is more important than the phenomenal *capacity to learn* possessed by the normal human infant.

Taken altogether, these biological structures and capacities differ from one individual to another, and in all cases they set very broad limits on what can happen to a particular infant in his later years. Simply to be born male, or female, is to be virtually guaranteed some kind of learning experiences and forbidden others. Tall stature in the male is all but essential if the individual is to succeed at professional basketball. On the other hand, in World War II there was an unusual demand for dwarfs who could work in airplane factories in confined spaces inside aircraft hulls.

Despite the continuing modification of "original equipment" by socialization, the individual remains a unique biopsychological entity with a unique personal history. To each new socialization encounter he brings his own needs and perspectives which are not quite like those of anyone else. In other words, the beginner can

Here is a socializing encounter between a mother and child, obviously one involving feeling on both sides. How may parents themselves be changed as a result of having to socialize a child?

never be a passive object manipulated by socializing agents. It is true that he is changed by experience in socialization, but it is also true that the socialization setting is changed. Neither the person nor the social unit is ever quite the same after a particular sequence in socialization. Parents as well as children are changed by the socializing experience.

Or consider the relationships between a college and a single student. To the student, the flow of influence may seem one-sided. A college or university is massive indeed compared to a single student. It may seem impossible that a single new student could possibly affect the college, a socialization setting with many agents. Yet this is not so. Students are an important channel through which changes taking place in the surrounding society make their way into the college. The very fact that new students are continually entering the system guarantees that the nature of student and faculty roles, and the tasks undertaken over four years, are bound to change. Every student modifies the total system, even if only in a small way. A few years ago, small groups of students were able to bring about important changes on particular campuses in the space of a single academic year.

SOCIALIZATION OUTCOMES
FOR THE INDIVIDUAL

The consequences of socialization for the individual often seem quite trivial in the short run but overwhelmingly important in the long run. Because a child tidies up his room as directed, he gets to stay up late to watch a TV program. In a high-delinquency area, a child adept at learning to shoplift earns friendly acceptance in a peer group of delinquents. A young woman who has worked hard at mastering the traditional female role is rewarded with lavish attention from men and several offers of marriage. Another young woman who has long wanted to be a lawyer is admitted to the bar after meeting all requirements for practicing law in her state. One young man learns to view life as a never-ending competitive struggle for success, and uses everything in his life as a weapon. Another sees life as a set of opportunities for growth through love and service to others. One person learns to hate himself, and finally commits suicide. Another learns such passionate self-love that he becomes socially dangerous, and is committed to a mental hospital.

An individual's psychological organization is formed gradually out of the interchanges of socialization. Each new experience in socialization deposits a more or less enduring residue. Out of wholly biological beginnings the *person* emerges, changes, and grows. Psychological structures of several kinds arise in the individual through interaction between biological characteristics and a sequence of social situations. Much of social psychology is concerned with the study of these biosocial structures. Since we must be selective, we shall restrict our attention here to two cases: motives (especially for achievement) and self-awareness.

TABLE 3-1 SOCIALIZATION: INDIVIDUAL DEMANDS AND SOCIAL DEMANDS OVER A LIFETIME

INDIVIDUAL DEMANDS		SOCIAL DEMANDS
	Birth	
Feed me, cuddle me, take care of me		Learn how to speak, control bodily elimination, obey your parents
I want to play with the kids		Learn the rules of the peer group and obey them, otherwise you can't play with us
I want to know how to read		Go to school, study, obey the teacher, learn the student role
I want both boys and girls to like me		Learn the sex roles
I want to be free to do what I like		Sorry, but that isn't always allowed. Learn to like what you have to do. You may rock the boat a little, but be careful
I want a good job		Choose one, go to school, study hard, cultivate those who can help you
I want to marry		Get acquainted with the opposite sex, learn the rules of the dating game, commit yourself to another
I want to be a good parent		Talk with other parents, read books on the subject, spend time with your child, learn parental roles
I want to get ahead		Do what is expected of you in your occupation. Work hard, obey the rules, be seen with the right people
I want to be a good citizen		Vote, keep up on the issues, support worthy causes, join civic organizations
I want to enjoy myself		Play games with other people, buy luxuries, indulge yourself
I want security		Work hard, save, invest
I want to be needed		Be active in organizations, join hobby groups
I don't want to be lonely		Join a club, visit your children, enter a retirement home
	Death	

NEEDS, MOTIVES, AND ACHIEVEMENT MOTIVATION   We have already suggested that learning the ways of society is society's price for supporting the individual in reaching his own goals. For example, society says in effect: "You spend several years learning the law and how it operates, and you will be permitted to practice law, something you have wanted as a career." But society's influence goes beyond instruction in *how* to achieve personal goals. It also is a major determinant of *what* goals the individual will seek to realize. It is almost as though a bargain were struck between society and the individual in the socialization process. In learning and conforming to social demands the individual gives up some of what he wants and some of the ways he would like to satisfy his needs. In return he gains social support in gratifying his desires. Society owes him this support. From the individual, society receives a role performance enabling society itself to continue in existence. Table 3-1 shows some of these individual and social demands throughout the life span.

  At birth, human needs are comparatively simple, undifferentiated, and biological. There is little difference between the needs of one infant and those of any other. But through its agents of socialization, society at once begins the long process of teaching the child *both* what to strive for, and what procedures to follow. Hence with the passage of time, people no longer want pretty much the same things. Rather, one man thirsts for wealth and doesn't care how he gets it. Another hungers for power over others and satisfies this need in any way he can. A third has a passion for social justice. A fourth asks for nothing more than to go on playing the juvenile role indefinitely.

Motives In psychology and social psychology, what we have been referring to as goals and needs are frequently referred to as *motives*. Broadly defined, motive denotes "activation from within the organism" (Munn, Fernald, and Fernald, 1969:367). "A motive arouses and directs the organism." Motive (and motivation) "refer to such inner conditions as physiological states, attitudes, values, and interests." The original inner conditions that activate human organisms are physiological. But the immense human capacity for learning, and the predominantly social character of the human environment, insure that motives will evolve under the strong influence of the socialization process. Each person possesses a repertoire of very stable motives, which are for him one of the important outcomes of socialization experience.

Motivation for achievement is an important and interesting aspect of the whole subject of motivation. At present it is receiving a good deal of vigorous theorizing and research. Our brief discussion of it is intended as an illustration of the larger field of socialized motives. Putting aside certain difficulties in defining achievement motivation, we shall consider it here as *effort directed toward the achievement of standards of excellence* (McClelland, Atkinson et al., 1953).

Acquiring Motivation for Achievement Much is now known about the conditions under which a child will develop a relatively strong or weak need for achievement. One of the classic researches in the field, by Rosen (1959:47–60), illustrates the work that has been done to uncover the determinants of different levels of achievement motivation seen as an outcome of socialization.

Rosen's subjects were 427 mother-son pairs living in four northeastern states and chosen to represent six racial or ethnic classifications: French-Canadian, Italian, Greek, Jewish, Negro, and white Protestant. All the sons and most of the mothers were native-born Americans. Each boy was privately interviewed and measured for achievement motivation. The test used was a projective type in which the subject tells an imagined story about each of several ambiguous pictures shown to him. Long experience with the test had produced objective methods of identifying the imagery contained in the stories. Each mother was also interviewed in private, and asked several questions relating to her own achievement, her value orientations, and her aspirations for her son, as well as a number of other matters.

Think about this picture in relation to the point that society has much to do with the goals we seek and the means by which we seek them. In such settings as this, millions of American children encounter society and learn of its possibilities for them. What difference would it have made if these children had grown up in a suburban or some other environment?

Rosen's analysis of existing evidence had led him to believe that Protestants, Jews, and Greeks stress achievement training of their children more than do the other groups in the study. He thought that Italians and French-Canadians would rank lowest in this trait. So he hypothesized that the achievement scores, grouped by racial and ethnic categories, would show differences consistent with his assumptions about the training the sons had received. His data supported his hypothesis.

The value orientations of the mothers, and their expressed aspirations (both educational and vocational) for their sons, while not consistent in every detail, also strongly supported his basic assumption. In other words, sons with strong motives to achieve were extremely likely to have mothers oriented toward high achievement for their children. Rosen also analyzed his data by social classes and found a high correlation: the higher the class, the higher the aspiration and motivation, and vice versa. The ethnic and class factors operated somewhat independently of one another. So far we should find nothing particularly mysterious about these findings. They demonstrate that different subcultures in a society actually do have different values, norms, and role prescriptions. When introduced into relationships between neophytes and socializing agents, these do produce characteristic differences in achievement motivation.

While such findings are no longer surprising to a social psychologist, they have great import for the individual. In a society which places great emphasis on striving for achievement, the level of achievement *motive* a person acquires in early training can have a great deal to do with the degree to which he *actually* achieves excellence in later life. One does not need to assume a one-to-one correspondence between achievement motive and actual achievement to accept some validity in such a statement. And the evidence shows clearly that how much achievement motive one has depends to a considerable extent upon who one's parents were and what their location in society happened to be.

THE SELF Who are you, reading this page? What are you? Where are *you* located? In your head, or your heart, or where? Are *you* more present in your eyes, or the sound of your voice, or the touch of your hand? Where were *you* when you were still in your mother's body? We speak here of self-consciousness, the *experience* of a personal identity apart from the rest of the world and from other persons. This selfhood is as real as anything we know. We believe that we exist because, metaphorically speaking, we can observe ourselves existing. When we use words like *I, me, myself,* and *my* there is no doubt in our minds about what the words denote. But even though this sense of identity has such overwhelming authenticity for most of us, when we begin to reflect seriously on its character some rather puzzling questions arise.

For instance, if you try to remember as far back in your life as you can, you will soon discover that ultimately all direct memory of a separate identity disappears. Try it. We should warn you that there is some basis for confusion here, because sometimes what we believe to be remembered experiences are really memories of later accounts of those experiences by older members of our family. Still, try it. You are sure to find that your recall of early life fades out and finally disappears. In other words, there is no self-awareness in the newborn child, and for a considerable time afterward. Why is this, and how does self-consciousness emerge?

Or take the matter of the location of selfhood, about which we have already questioned you. You probably have not thought much about where your self resides, although it is probable that there is some sense, however unspecific, that the home of your self is your body. And it may be that, for you, the self is associated more with some parts of the body than others. Over the centuries people have often believed that the soul, spirit, or self (not the same conceptions but with meanings that have often overlapped) does have a definite location, perhaps in the brain, heart, lungs, or spleen. The seventeenth-century French philosopher Descartes thought that the soul was centered in the pineal gland. Actually,

Rembrandt's self-portrait is one of the masterpieces of Western art. The more you study this painting the more you find in it. The features bear the stamp of the events of a long life. In fact, a good deal of the portrait's power derives from the temptation to speculate about the man behind the face. Yet, even though Rembrandt is making a statement about himself in the painting, his nature can never be fully revealed in this way. What was Rembrandt really like? What were his self-conception, his values and attitudes, his views of man, God, and the universe? As a person formed out of the complex interplay between biological heritage and society, Rembrandt must remain mostly hidden to the eye. Yet, for us as for Rembrandt, the body and the self do have an intimate relationship.

Part 1 / Some Fundamental Ideas

there is no specific physiological site where the human self "lives." Selfhood invariably involves the body, but is not to be equated with the body. What does this mean? If the self is not present at birth though the body is, if it entails bodily awareness but is more than that, what then is the self?

Nature of Selfhood Our observations about the nature of the self and its development in the individual derive from such pioneer thinkers in this area as James (1890), Cooley (1902) and Mead (1934). Although their ideas were expressed in different ways, all believed that selfhood develops gradually in the child as a consequence of repeated social interchanges with persons who enter into role-defined relationships with him. They saw these interchanges as indispensable to the acquisition of identity. It scarcely seems possible that personal identity can be an outcome of a social process, yet the evidence is very strong that this is the case.

From many acceptable definitions of the self we choose that of Newcomb (1950:328): *"Self . . . refers to the individual as perceived by that individual in a socially determined frame of reference."* The self so defined is made up of what the psychologist calls *cognitions*. It is the manner in which a person perceives himself. The person becomes "an object to himself," as Mead put it, and there is no fundamental difference in this perceptual process from the manner in which any other object is perceived. The self is an organized set of responses the person makes to himself as a stimulus object. It includes all the answers a person would give to the question "Who am I?"

How does a person become an object to himself? How does the self come into being? According to Cooley, Mead, and other such thinkers, and the research of psychologists like Piaget (1952), self-awareness emerges gradually after birth. Only little by little does a child learn to distinguish itself from other significant objects in the environment. But it is necessary to the development of self-consciousness that there be other objects to which the child has some kind of relationship. Only by becoming aware of such other objects and his relationship to them can the child progressively become aware of himself and the fact that he is separate from these other things, persons, and events. We are referring here to the "socially determined frame of reference" mentioned in Newcomb's definition of the self. More specifically, the relationships between a child and its parents are organized by roles from the time the child is born. This is the socially determined frame of reference within which awareness of separate identity first appears and begins to grow.

Role-Taking and the Self Within the role-defined relationships of infancy and childhood the self emerges gradually as the child learns to *assume the perspective of other role players toward himself.* The process of imaginatively projecting oneself into the

Sex roles are defined by culture and learned through socialization. They are not specifically ordained by nature. In our illustrations, the little boys playing "pregnant mothers" and the girl playing with trucks are experimenting in ways that depart from cultural stereotypes in this society. They remind us that sex roles could be far more flexible than they actually are likely to be at any particular point in a society's history.

role perspective of another is called *role-taking*. By "taking" the role of another person who has a relationship with him (father, mother, and so forth) the child can see himself as he appears, or as the child supposes he appears, to that other person.

Thus a father in teaching his four-year-old daughter to play the first few bars of "Three Blind Mice" on her toy piano held her hand and guided her fingers to strike each note with the comment, "Now you hit this one, then this one, then this one, and so forth." This little interact had occurred only a few times when he later observed his daughter to be holding her right hand with her left hand and guiding her index finger while telling herself, "Now you hit this one, then this one, and so forth." She was not yet striking the correct notes in the correct sequence, but she was producing a substantial portion of the father's role, as well as of her own in the little interact (Cottrell, 1969:544).

A young child's attempts to project itself into the role of another are often entertaining to adults simply because it cannot do so except in a very fragmentary way. Role-taking is a complex skill and requires incessant practice for years before it is developed to a level needed for living in a complex adult world. Actually, some children are much better at it than others, and considerable differences are found at every age level. Perhaps you have sensed the skill with which some persons know how others think and feel, and you may have met people who seem extraordinarily insensitive. In both cases your impressions probably reflect real differences in role-taking skill. There are also extreme distortions of role-taking capacity, as in paranoid disorders, where the victim develops a set of erroneous assumptions that various persons have hostile attitudes toward him. Such persons are unable to interpret the role performances of others accurately.

Interesting light on the evolution of self-awareness through role-taking is furnished by the work of Kuhn and associates (1954), who developed a test for getting at the content of self-images. Widely used, it is called the Twenty Statements Test (TST). Persons taking it simply respond twenty times in succession to the question "Who am I?" Researchers have found that the most common initial responses to this question *are the names of roles the respondent plays*. A man might answer: I am a man, a husband, an engineer, a Presbyterian. Later responses are more likely to include personal qualities (I am bright, friendly, insecure). Evidence of this sort, for adults, suggests vividly how over the years personal identity comes to be intimately associated with roles which themselves were learned by role-taking.

Role-Taking Skill While our main attention here is upon the function of role-taking in the development of the self, it should be noted that role-taking is a skill required for normal participation in social behavior throughout life.

We are saying that in order to perform one role a person must be able to adopt the role *perspective* of other roles that are complementary to the role to be performed. A good way in which to see

Part 1 / Some Fundamental Ideas

the point is presented by any familiar team game, such as base-ball. A person playing the role of batter cannot adequately per-form the role (which is defined in the rules of the game) unless he can assume the perspective of the pitcher and other players *toward him.* "What will they do if I bat the ball?" "If I swing at the ball and miss?" What is clear in the relative simplicity of baseball is equally true, though much more complex, in the give-and-take of everyday life. Role-taking is essential to social behav-ior. The self, in a sense, is a product of long-continued role-taking and role-playing. Learning the sex roles current in one's society is one of the more important sources of selfhood. The quo-tation from Betty and Theodore Roszak's book *Masculine and Feminine* suggests that traditional definitions of what it means to be masculine and feminine may have destructive effects for the self and for the individual's love relations with persons of the op-posite sex. After reading their words, see if you agree.

He Is Playing Masculine. She Is Playing Feminine.

He is playing masculine because she is playing feminine. She is playing feminine because he is playing masculine.

He is playing the kind of man that she thinks the kind of woman she is playing ought to admire. She is playing the kind of woman that he thinks the kind of man he is playing ought to desire.

If he were not playing masculine, he might well be more feminine than she is—except when she is playing very feminine. If she were not playing feminine, she might well be more masculine than he is—except when he is playing very masculine.

So he plays harder. And she plays . . . softer.

He wants to make sure that she could never be more masculine than he. She wants to make sure that he could never be more feminine than she. He therefore seeks to destroy the femininity in himself. She therefore seeks to destroy the masculinity in herself.

She is supposed to admire him for the masculinity in him that she fears in herself. He is supposed to desire her for the femininity in her that he despises in himself.

He desires her for her femininity which is his femin-inity, but which he can never lay claim to. She admires him for his masculinity which is her masculinity, but which she can never lay claim to. Since he may only love his own femininity in her, he envies her her femininity. Since she may only love her own masculinity in him, she envies him his masculinity.

The envy poisons their love.

He, coveting her unattainable femininity, decides to punish her. She, coveting his unattainable masculinity, decides to punish him. He denigrates her femininity— which he is supposed to desire and which he really envies—and becomes more aggressively masculine. She feigns disgust at his masculinity—which she is supposed to admire and which she really envies—and becomes more fastidiously feminine. He is becoming less and less what he wants to be. She is becoming less and less what she wants to be. But now he is more manly than ever, and she is more womanly than ever.

Her femininity, growing more dependently supine, be-comes contemptible. His masculinity, growing more op-pressively domineering, becomes intolerable. At last she loathes what she has helped his masculinity to become. At last he loathes what he has helped her femininity to become.

So far, it has all been symmetrical. But we have left one thing out.

The world belongs to what his masculinity has become.

The reward for what his masculinity has become is power. The reward for what her femininity has become is only the security which his power can bestow upon her. If he were to yield to what her femininity has become, he would be yielding to contemptible incompetence. If she were to acquire what his masculinity has become, she would participate in intolerable coerciveness.

She is stifling under the triviality of her femininity. The world is groaning beneath the terrors of his masculinity.

He is playing masculine. She is playing feminine.

How do we call off the game?

Source: Betty and Theodore Roszak (eds.), *Masculine and Feminine* (New York: Harper, 1970).

Responsibility for Role-Taking It may be objected that an infant or a very young child cannot voluntarily participate in a role-defined relationship, for this would seem to require prior knowledge of the culture of the group in which the roles occur. The difficulty disappears when we realize that parental and child roles are designed to take the child's helplessness and ignorance into account, to reduce them *gradually,* and thus eventually to make possible the child's voluntary and responsible participation in role-defined behavior.

A young mother in a maternity ward was spanking and scolding her newborn baby. When a nurse was asked about this behavior, she responded in exasperation: "Is she doing that again? She punishes the baby if it won't eat as it should; says she's going to start it off right." The mother's behavior was bizarre because she assumed that a two-day-old infant can *knowingly* and *willfully* disobey. Intuitively, most of us recognize that intentional behavior occurs only in a creature which has a self, and we are at least dimly aware that a newborn baby doesn't yet have a self which can be held responsible.

Resource Mediators A child enters into the long, subtle process of role-taking because, as Whiting and Whiting (1960) point out, other persons are *resource mediators.* That is, the child can attain desired satisfactions only through the mediation of older persons. A parent will sometimes withhold resources from the child as a socializing strategy. "If you want ice cream, you'll have to eat the rest of your dinner first." The child realizes that the parent has more effective resource control than he has and begins to identify with the parent. While we must not overintellectualize this process, it is much as though the child said to himself, "If I do as mother does, if I become mother, then I will have her wonderful powers." Thus, the child is motivated to take the role of mother toward himself, with all that implies for awareness of himself as an object.

As the self-image comes into existence, and from then on throughout life, it plays a significant part in determining an individual's behavior. Norms, values, and role prescriptions once external are now taken into the person, and in somewhat modified form are related to his sense of identity. Now they are *his.* If one thinks of a person's actual behavior—including his role performances—as a set of dependent variables, and sociocultural forces outside him as independent variables, then the self-concept operates as an *intervening* variable. That is, external social pressures are monitored by the self. Their influence on conduct is filtered through self-consciousness, which may accept, reject, or modify them. Figure 3-2 illustrates the relationship of these variables.

Role Definition and Stable Identity A study by Schwartz, Fearn, and Stryker (1966:300–305) conveys something of the flavor of

FIGURE 3-2 THE SELF AS AN INTERVENING FACTOR IN BEHAVIOR

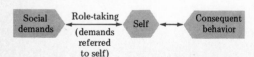

Social demands → Role-taking (demands referred to self) → Self ↔ Consequent behavior

Part 1 / Some Fundamental Ideas

research now being done in this field. The subjects were emotionally disturbed children, twelve to thirteen years old, who were patients in two Canadian institutions. Assuming that all human beings desire a stable self, the investigators reasoned that the role of "disturbed child" can provide an important reference point for the formation of a stable identity. Thus disturbed children who feel most strongly committed to such a role should have more positive feelings about themselves than those not so strongly committed to the role. They also reasoned that children most committed to the role should reveal less "variability in self-meanings," that is, more stable identities, than children less committed. Therapists evaluated the chances of these children for recovery, and the researchers assumed that children rated as having a poor chance for recovery would have relatively strong commitments to the role of disturbed child, and vice versa.

The children responded to ten pairs of evaluative items, such as *cruel-kind, bad-good, unimportant-important, beautiful-ugly.* For each pair they were asked how they felt about themselves, how they thought they were seen by their mothers, how they thought they were seen by their fathers, and how they thought they were seen by their therapists.

The children whose prognosis for recovery was poor had slightly more positive self-meanings than children whose chances for recovery were good. Furthermore the former revealed more stable identities (as measured by lower intra-individual variability in self-meanings) than those with favorable prognoses. The children's self-descriptions on these paired items were compared with the views of themselves they attributed to their parents, their best friends, and their therapists. Again the correlation was the same. In terms of our broad discussion of the nature of the self, it can be said that the "good prognosis" children did not see in the presumed attitudes of others toward them a clear-cut definition of themselves as disturbed children. They were not yet fully committed to this role, and so they were still open to influences from important people which would permit self-definitions omitting the idea of being disturbed. But the "poor prognosis" children revealed a very close correspondence between their own self-ratings and the views they thought others had of them. Rightly or wrongly, they saw social confirmation of their own commitment to the disturbed role.

For the "poor prognosis" children, a vicious circle seems to have developed. Yet, for the children themselves, the situation is livable. They achieved a stable and (they think) socially validated identity, and consequently have more favorable self-meanings. The children with better chances of recovery are more anxious about their identities. While this anxiety can be used in therapy, it leaves the children both more uncertain of who they are and slightly less satisfied with their self-images, at least for the present.

At first glance these findings may seem strangely topsy-turvy. Surely the more emotionally disturbed child is less likely to have either an acceptable or a stable identity! Yet from the standpoint that selfhood is grounded in role-defined relationships with others, the results make perfectly good sense. Cohen (1966:5–14) argues that much the same process takes place in persons who seek to establish personal identity in a process of progressive commitment to deviant behavior of several kinds. All this strongly suggests that the acquisition of selfhood takes a similar course among normal, deviant, and emotionally disturbed children, if by "similar course" we mean the underlying *process of interaction between the individual and available role models.*

SOCIETY'S STAKE
IN SOCIALIZATION

Plainly, socialization has fateful consequences for the individual. A person is literally formed in thousands of interchanges between the original bundle of strictly biological potentialities and the initially external world of organized society. Social psychologists are interested in the interpenetration of two systems, the personal and the social. This fusion, which is illustrated in Figure 3-3, is what Berger (1963) means when he speaks of "man in society" and "society in man." Every newborn child has an immense personal stake in the socialization experiences which lie in wait for him. Society has life and death stakes in the same process, and that is the theme to which we now briefly return.

CULTURAL SURVIVAL The most important function of socialization for society is the provision of persons adequately prepared to perform roles in all the interlocking social systems, large and small, which comprise a society. True enough. But this generalization is so broad as to conceal the details and problems which make the actual situation in any society very complex.

Every human society, if it is to endure, must be reproduced not

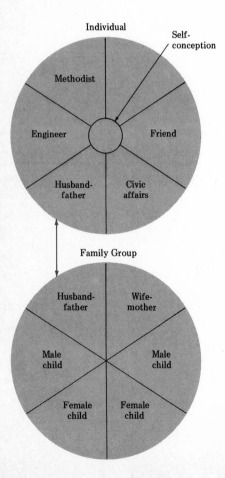

FIGURE 3-3 INTERPENETRATION OF INDIVIDUAL AND GROUP
The diagram illustrates the interpenetration of individual and group in terms of the role concept. The two diagrams are very much alike, as you see. Each suggests a cluster of related roles, but the relationship among the roles has a different basis in the two cases. In the individual diagram the cluster holds together because one person plays all the roles. In the group diagram the roles form a pattern because each is literally defined in terms of the others. Another difference between the two role clusters is that in the individual pattern self-consciousness is present, a self-concept that attempts to order the relationships among the roles. Groups, as such, do not have self-consciousness. Despite these differences, the diagrams illustrate that part of what we call a person is made up of internalized roles, and at the same time groups also may be described as constellations of roles. Individuals and groups are distinct entities, yet each enters deeply into the nature of the other.

Part 1 / Some Fundamental Ideas

only biologically, but socially and culturally as well. A substantial part of its total resources must be devoted to maintaining its way of life, and this requires an elaborate and expensive process of socializing the endless stream of biological newcomers. A society's way of life includes many things, such as religion, technical knowledge for securing the basic necessities, the values and norms surrounding kinship, the governance of people in the society, and protection from external foes. The preservation, practice, and transmission of these essentials takes time, energy, and resources, which must be diverted from biological reproduction. Consequently, fertility (the actual reproductive performance) is always less than fecundity (the maximum biological reproductive performance) (Davis, 1949:551–94). No society can afford a birth rate at the maximum biological level. Births simply must be reduced enough to maintain culture, which entails the socialization of the young.

It must not be supposed that effective reduction of fertility only appeared with that marvel of the modern age, the pill. Davis (1949:557–61) shows how a wide variety of cultural rules in different societies, most of them not *designed* to reduce fertility, have this result. There are, for instance, numerous taboos on associations between males and females, thus reducing opportunities for procreation. The celibate orders of the Roman Catholic clergy are an example. Just as common are a variety of proscriptions on sexual intercourse, such as minimum ages for marriage, and norms forbidding premarital and extramarital sexual contacts. Abortion and infanticide are also found in many societies, and so are many specific contraceptive techniques which have some measurable effect in reducing conception from what it would otherwise be.

The costs and complexity of socialization are greatly increased in societies undergoing rapid change. Since much of the world today is changing rapidly, we give the matter special attention here.

SOCIALIZATION AND SOCIAL CHANGE

When the rate of change in a society is high, roles and role clusters once well adapted to conditions are forced into continuous alteration and adjustment. Some roles, like Pullman car porter, livery stable operator, and nursemaid, decline or disappear altogether, and may do so in a very few years. Completely new roles emerge, such as astronaut or computer programmer. When this happens, traditional ways of socializing newcomers to become effective role performers in society are called into question.

In societies like the United States there is constant strain from the partial obsolescence of existing arrangements for recruiting and training individuals to perform needed roles. Socialization requirements to some extent outrun the means for fulfilling them. As Inkeles says, "An outstanding example would be the shift

This dignified gentleman is Mr. H. B. Sweatt, tin peddler in New Hampshire during the early 1900s. He performed a role that has now entirely disappeared. How many other such roles can you name?

in the modern Euro-American nations from a predominantly rural resident, agriculturally employed labor force to an overwhelmingly urban resident, industrially employed population" (1969:616). The consequences of this strain for society can be serious. In Inkeles' words, "The society or major institutional units within it, may find the discharge of their social responsibility for production, security, governance of whatever, impaired by the inadequate role performance of the individuals they have recruited or have had assigned to them" (1969:616).

An example of what Inkeles is talking about is the need in capitalist industrialized societies for many people high in achievement motivation. In the more advanced countries there now appears to be a fairly good balance between supply and demand for this characteristic, with some conspicuous exceptions. Industrialization has been under way for more than a century, and socialization has had time to adjust. According to the German social scientist Max Weber, religion played a significant historical part in this development. In his famous study *The Protestant Ethic and the Spirit of Capitalism* (1930), Weber contended that there were psychological consequences of the theological shift in Protestantism toward self-reliance and away from dependence upon an institutionalized church. Many of the characteristics of the good Protestant child, as implied in Weber's discussion, would fit a description of what might here be called a person high in achievement motivation.

At present, developing countries in Asia, Latin America, and Africa are strenuously trying to industrialize and to do so at a speed that is historically unprecedented. McClelland (1961) and others, reasoning along lines suggested by Weber, argue that an essential requirement of this development is the socialization of the achievement motive to a much higher degree than has been true for these countries in the past. In other words, many societies are today setting forth on a course of social change which requires not only massive inputs of capital, technological knowledge, and other such familiar elements, but also a vast increase in the development of certain psychological characteristics in their citizens.

The need for speed itself creates problems, not just for the society but for individuals with other values and beliefs. Consider the man who deeply believes that once his minimum material requirements are met he need not strive for more. How does a society convince him that he should bring up his child to serve a different set of values demanding lifelong hard work, thrift, and the deferral of present satisfactions to obtain greater ones later?

CHANGES IN TRADITIONAL VALUES   Recent experience in such affluent societies as the United States suggests that some of the traditional values and attitudes essential in the early stages of capitalist economies may later have much less significance. The incredible productivity of the American economy *now* seems to require a population oriented to ever-increasing consumption and conditioned to accept the rapid obsolescence of material goods. Today's citizen is urged to spend his resources at least as much as he is urged to save them. Rapid shifts of this kind, brought on by changes in the economy, can cause conflict between generations. Many parents want their children to have a higher standard of living but find it hard to adjust to the casualness with which their offspring take such bounty for granted.

SOCIALIZATION AND CHANGE FROM SOCIETY'S STANDPOINT Because culture is transmitted by learning, changing societies must see that socialization effectively passes new cultural elements onto newcomers. In urban-industrial societies more and more resources must be devoted to socialization. Each generation finds a larger proportion of the population in school and staying there longer. (A more detailed and factual analysis of the educational institution is presented in Chapter 13.) Adult education becomes more familiar as people sense that almost throughout life people need organized training. In earlier societies it was unthinkable that a man's vocational skills could be outdated during his lifetime. Today the experience is commonplace. The knowledge explosion, along with its attendant technological applications, now confronts society with a very large new problem whose outlines few, other than specialists, have yet discerned. It is the problem of how this huge volume of new culture is to be assimilated and transmitted. Traditional agencies and techniques of socialization strain under the growing burden. Industrialized societies face major and continuous overhaul of their formal socialization machinery for a long time to come.

Often it is not only new information that needs to be taught; new attitudes, values, roles, and even new distributions of personality traits may be called for. New occupations and professions spring into being. New ways of looking at man and his environment may be urgently needed. For example, man must soon learn attitudes of greater responsibility for his natural environment and its resources, if human society is to continue. In sum, the current rate of change constantly generates problems arising from the gap between what society needs from socialization and the character of the existing procedures at any particular time. The latter tend always to be somewhat obsolescent.

SOCIALIZATION AND CHANGE FROM THE STANDPOINT OF NEOPHYTES Beginners too face a much more complicated situation when society is swiftly changing than when it is comparatively stable. Earlier we spoke of the bargain between the individual and society entered into via socialization. In a period of massive social change society may alter the original terms of the bargain many times, and without the consent of the neophyte. Some of the moral standards a person acquires in the family into which he was born may be successfully challenged by subsequent groups, thereby presenting him with painful moral conflicts. In our time

In the many developing countries that wish to industrialize, more is involved than simply shifting from old technologies to new ones. Old values may have to give way to others, and motives and goals that once would have been scorned may have to be given heavy emphasis.

"SORRY, TODAY IT'S ONLY BLUE-EYED GRANDMOTHERS WITH ODD-NUMBER LICENSE PLATES . . . TOMORROW IT'S BLONDE TEACHERS UNDER 25 WITH EVEN NUMBERS."

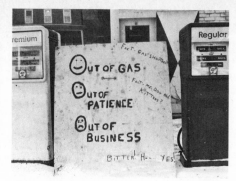

Most Americans have been brought up to take unlimited sup-plies of raw materials, energy, and food completely for granted. The shortages that surfaced in 1973 and 1974 brought personal frustration to many, and substantial economic dislocations, es-pecially in certain parts of the country. These events posed another challenge to existing socialization practices. Are these practices growing dangerously obsolete in an increasingly crowded world whose resources are not unlimited?

the content of masculine and feminine roles is changing con-siderably. People trained to one conception of sex-linked behavior may be deeply troubled by changes that occur a few years later, as when middle-aged and older people find it difficult or impossible to accept the vogue for long hair on men.

Married couples reared to find large families desirable now en-counter efforts to convince them that to help curb the population explosion, they have a duty to rear small families. Young males, and to a lesser extent females, are told that they must choose and learn an occupation. For the male there is no more fateful deci-sion. But society presents him with an incredible variety of oc-cupations from which to choose, and often no adequate basis on which to make so important a choice. Changes in the occupa-tional structure during each person's lifetime may make the initial choice a bad one, but the individual has no control over such developments and little ability to foresee them.

Our intent is not to argue that swift social change makes sociali-zation miserable for beginners. It may do so sometimes, but there is also a stimulating variety and challenge to existence in such periods. The real point is that the learning of attitudes, values, and roles becomes much more complex and takes on a tentative, problematic quality. If not at first, the beginner ultimately real-izes that he lives in a social world which is liable at any time to change the rules on him—all of which strongly suggests that psy-chological adaptability is one of the most useful traits a person can have in this kind of world.

Part 1 / Some Fundamental Ideas

SOCIALIZATION AND CHANGE FROM THE STANDPOINT OF SOCIALIZING AGENTS Socializing agents also face problems generated by social change. Schools, for example, face the problem of how to organize to turn out graduates who are not only up-to-date now, but equipped to *remain* so. What kinds of knowledge, skills, and attitudes will be needed ten or twenty years after a student graduates, and what kinds will be disappearing? How can the schools preserve a common core of liberal education in a time when knowledge becomes ever more specialized? A teacher's career spans perhaps thirty-five years. How can a teacher in a scientific field keep properly tooled for his job over so long a period when scientific knowledge is accumulating so rapidly? Such queries only highlight the many problems facing educators for which traditional educational procedures no longer provide good enough answers.

When we speak of those who socialize others as "agents," we should realize that they not only act on behalf of society but also on behalf of the individuals they are training. This often leads to perplexities and poignant dilemmas, and nowhere is this better seen than in the tasks faced by parents in a period of rapid change. Most parents want their children to lead personally satisfying lives and to do so in ways that are approved by society. How to accomplish this when society is undergoing swift transformation is a problem. The knowledge that parents acquired in their earlier years may now prove inadequate to rearing their own children. Parents look ahead to the *future adult* their child will be. But what kind of society will their children live in? What kind of skills and personality attributes will then be valuable for their children?

Some of the answers to such questions must remain unknown. So some parents cling to traditional conceptions of parental roles. Others, aware that society is changing and uncertain of guidelines, try to anticipate what the requirements of a society in change will be as they impinge on their own children. Such parents, as LeVine (1969:515–17) has suggested, are likely to turn away from traditional or religious conceptions of parental roles to the authority of science. They are likely "to *rationalize* the process of socialization by consciously gearing both its ends and means to information feedback from a changing environment." But the strategy is complex and often frustrating. The advice of experts often changes, since scientific knowledge has by no means reached the stage where it can serve as an infallible guide to parents trying to raise their children in a society which goes on changing, even during the short years when their task is under way.

SOCIALIZATION AS A CAUSE OF CHANGE The problems faced by society, by neophytes, and by socializing agents during rapid change can be seen as *consequences* of such change. But it needs to be pointed out that socialization also plays an *active* part in changing society. How can this be so? For one thing, socialization is an indispensable means for consolidating desirable changes and seeing to it that they are not lost. The new idea, the new technique, will be conserved by being taught to the young. But the matter goes much further than this. Especially in the realm of scholarly and scientific knowledge (and the dozens of applied technologies based on such knowledge) socialization assures that *still more knowledge, still more advanced techniques,* will be produced in the future. In short, socialization in contemporary industrialized societies (and particularly in certain aspects of those societies) is not only a conservative but also an innovating force. The college student who learns the scientific method from his mentors is being socialized in a procedure *designed* to produce change. It follows that under some conditions socializing agents are also *agents of change.* In really modern schools, for example, teachers in many subject areas are not just conservators of past achievements but instigators of new ones that will be brought into being by their students.

People growing up in our society today are *trained to expect change.* The very pervasiveness of this anticipation encourages further alterations of society. In dozens of ways and in hundreds of settings, training content directly or implicitly defines our society as a changing one. This definition becomes a subtle but significant change-producing aspect of socialization. In a very stable society socialization acts mainly to retard change. But when a society has become adjusted to a high rate of change, socialization helps to maintain and even to accelerate the process. Imagine a heavy metal wheel motionless on a level surface. Considerable effort is required to start the wheel rolling. Once under way, however, even small applications of energy are enough to keep it moving. Although much more complicated, the situation we are describing may be linked to this mechanical example.

SOME IMPLICATIONS OF
SOCIALIZATION FOR
EVERYDAY LIFE

Modern social psychology sees man as a deeply social creature; yet he is not social at birth. The outlines of society are not imprinted in his genetic inheritance, awaiting only the right environmental cues to make their appearance, as is the case with the other social animals known to biological science. No social knowledge or skill sleeps in the newborn baby. All that is there is the capacity for *learning* these things, if—and only if—society presents him with the appropriate socialization settings. When we look at the thing we call *society,* we see at once that its existence requires the continuous presence of living beings. Nevertheless, it is something different from any particular person. Something of society must be introduced into each new biological recruit in order that the whole body of biological newcomers can make possible its own continuation.

Part 1 / Some Fundamental Ideas

IMPACT OF SOCIETY ON THE INDIVIDUAL   To say that society is *in man* is to make an abstract statement, but one which refers to very specific things in each person's experience. It means that most of the things an individual wants he has learned to want from society including such things as dietary preferences, taste in clothing, particular kinds of experience with the opposite sex, education, standard of living, and recreational activities. Nearly all his values and beliefs are taken from a society where they had existed before he became aware of them. His fate in life is not entirely his to control, for society defines what alternatives are open to him in the first place, then gives each individual strong pushes toward some alternatives and away from others. Even his conception of who he is and his entire personality are deeply marked by social experience.

The evidence from the study of socialization and from all social psychology on this point leads inexorably to the conclusion that the individual *cannot escape from society for society is within each person.* Rebelling against society is not escaping from it. Neither the hermit in his wilderness, the revolutionary striving to destroy the existing social order, nor the hippie turned off by the central social values of society can manage it. Short of death, or perhaps the last stages of schizophrenia, there is no way to drop out completely.

BIOLOGICAL FACTORS   To insist on the strong social component in man's nature is not to argue that the character of the individual is wholly social. Person and society are two things, irrevocably interdependent but not the same. True, they are so intimately related that it is quite proper to say that both are different aspects of a larger whole: the entire human experience. Yet one should not lose sight of the differences between the two. Profoundly social as the individual is, he is also biological, and there are limits to what society can do to mold him through socialization. Dependent upon the flow of socialized individuals as society is, it nevertheless has characteristics, a history, and differences from other societies which cannot be understood only by reference to the attributes of its members.

No social psychologist would deny that every person is to some degree unique, and that this uniqueness, while partly derived from the socialization process itself, is also due to the biological features of the individual. *These biological characteristics simultaneously make possible the molding, formative influence of society, and insure that some part of each human being will evade the full control of social forces.* Social psychologists would agree with the statement that, even if we knew every last detail of the social forces impinging on a given person over his past life, we still could not predict his future actions with complete accuracy.

SENSE OF KINSHIP   If some readers are unhappy with our emphasis on the social nature of man, we point out that there may be

How many specific things can you find in this photograph that suggest the members of this commune still depend in direct or indirect ways on the larger society, which they reject?

The boys cooking over a picnic fire and the jungle dwellers preparing a meal live in almost totally different social worlds. Yet they are linked with each other and with men across the centuries by the idea of preparing food over a fire (an element of culture).

aspects of this view which they have overlooked. For one thing, it makes very clear the kinship of each person with countless millions of others. We recognize this relatedness in the biological sphere. Everyone knows that we are physically descended from those who lived before us and that we are the ancestors of others who will live thousands of years from now. But this knowledge seems remote and impersonal to most Americans. In a different way the great religions of the world stress the brotherhood of man, past, present, and future. For many people the religious vision of the relationships and reciprocal responsibilities joining men is familiar and meaningful. The same message also comes in a less familiar guise from the social sciences, particularly from sociology, anthropology, and social psychology. In the process of socialization each human child is brought into contact with human experiences that were lived, socially organized, and passed along by men and women who have been dead for many centuries. Not just their germ plasm but also their thoughts, their dreams, and all their reactions to human existence live on in today's society, coming anew to consciousness in each person. When the child grows up he may be able to find deep satisfaction in the knowledge that he is an indispensable link in passing on mankind's great heritage to generations yet unborn.

UNDERSTANDING THE SOCIAL NATURE OF BEHAVIOR   Once a person has recognized the case for the social nature of man, many specific insights and implications are likely to manifest themselves in time. Here are some. Few men ever rise above the behavior standards of their past, present, or future group memberships. If you wish to know what a man's standards really are, even if he will not tell you, or in spite of what he tells you, look at the groups he identifies with. Do not expect a boy whose chief affiliation is a delinquent gang to accept the values of a Boy Scout troop, simply because you think he should. Many people express views which are simply contradictory, not because they are stupid, but because they have internalized conflicting values and norms from different groups. In such societies as ours this is a common phenomenon. You may even be guilty of it yourself!

Occasionally we are distressed by someone who appears to have a self-image which is grossly distorted, either better or worse than others think warranted. Such distortions are not due to innate perversity, but to a socialization history which has permitted the development of an inappropriate view of self. Once in existence, a self-image tends to be quite resistant to change.

Practicing the Social Psychological Perspective

To practice the social psychological perspective is to sensitize oneself to the countless ways in which the inner life is bound to the life of society in all its manifestations. It is to increase one's awareness of the ceaseless interdependence at even the deepest levels between the human psyche and the group. We suggest a few simple things you can do, and hope they will suggest others which you will devise for yourself.

To begin with, look about you for situations in which socialization is going on. They are not hard to find. Any situation in which a person is learning (and being taught) the ways of the group will do. Some situations, such as college classrooms, are too obvious. Search for those in which the process is more subtle and may even be a minor aspect of the total situation. Who is being socialized? Who are the socializing agents? What techniques do they use? What rewards do you see for the neophyte making good progress? What penalties for the slow or reluctant learner?

Ask yourself: "Who am I?" Do it seriously. Put other things aside for a time and ask the question sincerely. Write down as many answers as occur to you in five minutes. Do the same thing with a few other persons. Do you see any connection between this chapter and the answers you get about the self-concept? Do any of the answers imply *relationships* with other people? Does your list contain what might be called qualities of a person? If so, do any of these qualities suggest interpersonal experience?

Here is a little exercise which may, depending somewhat on circumstances, illustrate the notion of changes in socialization with the passage of time. First ask yourself what your attitudes are toward the use of marijuana. Viewing yourself as the socializee, next attempt as carefully as possible to identify the socializing agents who transmitted these attitudes to you. When you have gone as far as you can, ask several people of your parents' generation about their attitudes toward using marijuana. As diplomatically as you can, try to learn the identity of the socializing agents in their experience. Does comparing your answers with theirs give you new insight into the difficulties of socialization in a period of rapid social change?

4

Interaction, Roles, and Groups

A thousand bricks can make a wall. Four walls make a good start toward a house. A few score houses make a neighborhood. A number of neighborhoods, plus a business section and a few shopping centers, can make a town or a city. What are the bricks of society, the smallest units which are organized into the progressively larger and more complex entities that construct man's social worlds? In this chapter we shall be concerned with some of society's smallest parts. This is where society is always very close to each of us. While very large units in society—government, great corporations and associations of all kinds—have characteristics of their own, they also incorporate large numbers of the kinds of bricks we shall discuss here.

INTERACTS AND SOCIAL INTERACTION

In 1969, an unusual workshop on crime and correction brought together a number of convicts, lawyers, judges, prosecutors, policemen, prison officials, state legislators and others (Hammer, 1969). The conference was held at St. John's College in Annapolis. At one point a number of the nonconvicts attending the conference were processed into state prisons in the normal way, and the officials processing them as new inmates were not in on the secret. One of these "inmates" was actually a judge who had sentenced many men to this very prison. When he left his cell for lunch a guard who was in on the experiment planted a knife in his cell. It was discovered and the judge was thrown into solitary confinement in the hole. Shortly thereafter he was ordered before a disciplinary board whose members had not been informed of the experiment.

IDENTIFYING INTERACTS   In a moment we shall use the conversation that followed to illustrate what are probably the tiniest of social units. We shall call them *interacts* (Wieck, 1968). *An interact consists of a single action by one or more persons and the response it elicits in one or more others.*

We return to the judge, who "was dressed in prison slacks and shirt, white socks without shoes; his hair was tousled, his face distraught. The board chairman asked 'Do you know why you're here?' 'They told me you found a knife in my cell.'" This is a single interact, initiated by the board chairman and completed by the judge. One item of information is asked for and received. Quite often interacts occur as small, isolated episodes of behavior. More often, however, they are linked together in sequences or chains. While this particular interact could stand alone, it suggests that there will be further developments, as proves to be the case.

1. "That's right. Can you tell us how it (the knife) got there?"
2. "No. I can't think how."
3. "Did you bring it in with you?"
4. "No. Somebody must have put it there."
5. "When did you get here?"
6. "This morning."
7. "Do you know anybody in here?"
8. "No."
9. "Does anybody in here have anything against you?"
10. "No."
11. "Then why would somebody have planted a knife in your cell?"

There are ten interacts in this chain of eleven statements.

Interact 1:   statements 1 and 2
Interact 2:   statements 2 and 3
Interact 3:   statements 3 and 4
Interact 4:   statements 4 and 5
Interact 5:   statements 5 and 6
Interact 6:   statements 6 and 7
Interact 7:   statements 7 and 8
Interact 8:   statements 8 and 9
Interact 9:   statements 9 and 10
Interact 10: statements 10 and 11

In this sequence the *second* part of each interact becomes the *first* part of the next. Each statement, except the first and the last, enters into two interacts. Thus while each interact, taken alone, has some meaning for the people involved, that meaning is enlarged and undergoes linked sequence with other units of the same kind. Sometimes just one interact says it all. "Do you take this woman to be your lawful wedded wife?" "I do." But much more frequently these tiny units are found together in chains of varying length and complexity. In the brief interchange between the judge and the disciplinary board, what began as a simple request for information ended with the judge (who was innocent of the charge) being sentenced to thirty days of solitary confinement in the hole. Small as it is, this episode—itself comprised of smaller episodes—gives an inkling of how larger social patterns are built out of the very smallest units found in society.

Even though each of us takes part in countless thousands of interacts, we are unlikely to think of this activity as social in nature, because more familiar habits of thought—essentially the psychological perspective—get in the way. We see two or more individuals behaving, but we do not focus on the *connectedness* of their behavior. The notion of interact shows us that the behavior of person B would not have occurred without the behavior of person A. In the interchange between the judge and the disciplinary board no single statement, considered in isolation, makes much sense. Not until it is linked to prior and subsequent statements *by other people* does it contain substantial meaning. Interacts link the behavior of two or more persons. On the smallest possible scale, this is the essence of the social element in human experience.

Interacts are not always as simple as the ones above. For example, in a single conversational statement a person may convey a number of meanings and the person addressed may respond to all or only to some of them. Mary says, "It's such a beautiful day (message one). I'd like to take a bike ride with you (message two), but I have an awful headache" (message three). John replies, "I'm sorry about your headache." John's reply is to the third message in Mary's statement and completes a single interact. He ignores messages one and two, and so interacts do not occur in those instances. If he had replied to all three messages, three interacts would have resulted from the single exchange.

Interacts also become more complicated when more than two people are involved. In a committee meeting the chairperson says, "I suppose we'd better quit now." One member responds, "Yes." But another says, "Let's keep going for a while." Here each response joins with the chairman's remark to form a separate interact and we have two. Or think of a political rally attended by several thousand people. A speaker shouts, "And I say that the future of this country depends on the outcome of the next election!" Thousands shout and applaud in approval. Here a single remark triggers the simultaneous formation of thousands of interacts, one for each person in the audience who claps or shouts in response to the words of the speaker. When we focus not on a single interact but on many linked in sequences, as in our sample conversation above, it is customary to speak of *social interaction*.

INTERPRETATION AND MEANING We must look deeper into what happens in interacts and social interaction in order to know something of what goes on in each participating individual that makes

Part 1 / Some Fundamental Ideas

this interchange possible and gives it direction. When one person acts in the presence of another, that act is subjected to interpretation before it is responded to. In a single interact, what happens is not: *act → response*. More accurately, it is: *act → interpretation → response* (Blumer, 1962). When a person interprets the act of another he seeks the meaning of that act. Only after he has found such a meaning can he respond to it appropriately. Go back to the conversation between the judge and the chairman of the disciplinary board. Clearly the latter believes the prisoner to be lying. The *meaning* of the prisoner's answers is that he is attempting to conceal his association with a confederate who has given him the knife. The disciplinary board's interpretation of the judge's remarks happens to be incorrect, as we know. But it is on the basis of this interpretation and assignment of meaning that the judge receives a heavy penalty.

We must go still further. The *meaning* of anything (an object, event, person, experience) resides in how people behave in particular situations with respect to that object, event, person or experience. It is important to think carefully about this, for we may seem to be violating common sense about meanings. The Simpsons have $700 in their savings account. The *meaning* of that money is what they can do with it. They are not wealthy and when they spend $500 for a new color TV it is a big event in their financial life—big because it eliminates other possible uses of this money. To a millionaire, the meaning of $700 would be quite different. Spending $500 on a TV set would be a trivial matter. In other words, the meaning of money is not inherent in the money itself but in how much it can do for people, and that varies with circumstances.

To one person the meaning of a recording of a Beethoven symphony is that it should be avoided because the music is boring. To another, it is something to be turned down low as a soothing background for conversation. A lover of classical music turns up the volume and listens carefully. Perhaps he claims that the other two people don't understand the real meaning of the music. From our perspective, we observe that the same object is assigned different meanings by different people. The meaning of the object resides in people's response to it, not in the object itself.

Social interaction, then, requires an interpretive process in which the behavior of another is assigned meaning before it is responded to. But meanings are not haphazard and erratic. They arise in particular situations which ordinarily are in some degree familiar to the persons involved because they have had previous experience with such situations. The Simpsons understand one another in their discussion of their savings account and the purchase of the TV set because they have many times faced the problem of how to get the most from their scarce resources.

LANGUAGE AND SOCIAL INTERACTION Communication among human beings is made possible by mutually understood symbols

In both of these pictures people are carrying loads on their backs, but the meaning of this activity is different in these two situations. The purpose of the activity and the social setting in which it is performed determine its significance.

which represent the experiences, objects, ideas, and feelings to which meanings become attached. Language is the most vital of the symbolic tools used by man. Because of language, interacting persons can organize past, present, and even future experience to bear on a present situation in which it is necessary to assign meanings in social interaction.

Here are two students talking to one another:

PHIL: I don't think I'll take that exam today.
STEVE: You ought to. You nearly flunked the last one.
PHIL: But I haven't studied enough to do any better.
STEVE: You keep this up and you're going to flunk a course you need in order to graduate.

In this episode, language brings *past* and *future* into *present* interaction between two persons. While language is crucial in social interaction men also commonly employ other forms of symbolic behavior. Mathematics and the Western system of musical notation are highly formalized examples. More relevant to our discussion of everyday interaction are the many fragmentary, informal symbolic devices people use to *supplement* language: gestures (waving and shaking hands), bodily postures, facial expressions, and tones of voice.

Nonverbal Communication Goffman (1967) among others has shown how such nonverbal symbols greatly complicate the assignment of meaning through the use of language. The *meaning* transmitted in social interaction is by no means always exactly what the *words* employed would seem to convey. We suggest that in the exchange between Phil and Steve, part of the meaning conveyed is Steve's disapproval of Phil. If we could see Steve as he talks we could probably get some evidence of this meaning in his facial expression and tone of voice.

For his play *Strange Interlude,* Eugene O'Neill invented a dramatic device which is related to our point. He had his characters speak aloud their thoughts as well as the words they actually say to each other. In this way the audience directly observes the inner process of assigning meaning to behavior in interaction, a process which is not directly and completely audible (or visible) in actual social interaction.

In our daily contacts, nonverbal behavior partially bridges the gap between inner interpretation and verbal communication. Once you become sensitized to the nonverbal symbols people employ in interaction you will see how vital a role they play. Take the words: "Hey, I see you've changed the way you fix your hair." Depending on the nonverbal cues which accompany this statement, the meaning may be flattering, humiliating, or anything in between. In the unending search for meaning in social interchange, people become amazingly sensitive to both verbal and nonverbal indicators.

Part 1 / Some Fundamental Ideas

Here are four examples of nonverbal symbolic behavior. Is the meaning of all four clear to you? Note that, unlike mathematics, languages, and other symbolic systems, these symbols can convey their meaning alone, apart from other symbols.

In Chapter 2 we introduced the concepts of role and role performance. While we first mentioned them in our discussion of culture, they also belong here in a treatment of microsociological units.

GROUP

ROLES AND ROLE PERFORMANCES AS MICROSOCIOLOGICAL UNITS

You will recall that *roles* are units of culture, while *role performances* are patterns of actual behavior. A role is a pattern of several norms which, in turn, are related to values. A role performance involves participation in thousands of interacts and many long and short sequences of interaction. Thus a role performance is a larger, more inclusive unit than an interact. It is expressed in interaction.

Some care is needed to keep these concepts clearly distinguished. A role performance is the behavior of a single person. Thus it can never contain completed interacts, because interacts involve communication between at least two persons. A conversation between two people, for instance, involves two role performances and many interacts. These are formed as social interaction

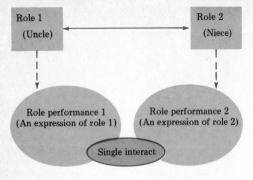

FIGURE 4-1 ROLES, ROLE PERFORMANCES, AND INTERACTS

proceeds. Each role performance provides segments of interacts, but interacts as units require the interaction of two or more role performances. The diagram in Figure 4-1 illustrates this interaction.

Neither roles nor role performances occur in isolation from reciprocal roles and role performances. Try to imagine a mother without imagining a child, a leader without a follower, a friend without another friend, or a lawyer without clients. Roles occur in clusters. The role of mother is a set of specifications for interacting with someone performing the role of child. The role performance of a mother is her actual behavior in relation to the behavior of her child. This intrinsic interdependence of roles (and of role performances) brings us to the concept of *group*.

DEFINING GROUP *A group exists when social interaction among two or more persons both sustains and is guided by shared values and by interlocking roles and role performances.* This definition identifies two closely related aspects of a group: group culture, values, and roles for achieving values; and social interaction in the form of interdependent role performances. These two aspects of a group are closely related. Each springs from and influences the other in ways that were discussed in Chapter 2.

Consider a family group: it will have values held by all, not merely by one member. Perhaps all are working together toward an unusually attractive vacation. Each member has a role inseparable from the family role system. Husband-father implies wife-mother and child; brother implies sister; each role implies all the others. Some parts of these roles are many centuries old. Others are quite new and reflect the adjustment of families to an urban-industrial society. A few are peculiar to this particular family. Each member also engages in role performances which will be compared by other family members with their particular roles. Each person's role performance is a part of the social interaction that links each to all and all to each.

Not all the social patterns studied by sociologists are groups. Our definition, for example, excludes situations where social interaction is too brief to be related to existing cultural forms or to produce new ones. It also excludes certain units in which there is no direct social interaction among members. General Motors is a single organization, but not a group; there is no direct social interaction between its president and the newest apprentice machinist.

The word *group* is sometimes applied to what sociologists prefer to call *aggregates* or *social categories*. These are collections of persons with one or more common characteristics: all female college freshmen in the United States, all families with incomes of less than $10,000 a year, all individuals holding jobs by political appointment, all males over six feet tall on a particular campus. Such aggregates and social categories as these are definitely not

A number of people in close proximity don't necessarily form a group, for the latter requires social interaction that manifests itself in roles and role performances. The aircraft crew probably illustrates a true group, though we can't be certain. The people on the sidewalk are probably not a group, and the people having their picture taken may be a close-knit group but may also be strangers.

groups as the term is used in this book. As Gibb (1969:206) puts it: "It is true, of course, that the aggregate would disappear if all the units were taken away, but no unit of the aggregate is changed by its nearness to other units."

GROUP BOUNDARIES Groups have boundaries. This may seem self-evident, but in practice the location of boundaries may be surprisingly uncertain. Let us return to the family. Taken as a whole, a family is a single group. But do not the husband and wife sometimes constitute a group? Suppose there are three children. May they not also sometimes be a group? The term *subgroup* is often used in such circumstances.

Again, most of us have attended social events—say, large parties—where many people come together to enjoy one another's company. Typically on such occasions people form temporary groupings which break up and reform into new clusters. Now, most of these units fall short of meeting all the requirements of the group as we define it. It wouldn't be far amiss to call them "quasi-groups." Some may evolve into fully developed groups, while most probably will not. Just where we draw a boundary line around a system of social interaction and call it a group will depend somewhat on our purpose at the moment. What we decide to call a single group may include several subgroups or quasi-groups.

Locating Group Boundaries Yet group boundaries can be determined with considerable precision, as implied in our definition of a group. For one thing, boundaries are set by frequency of interaction. In effect, this means that social interaction will take place more often *among* group members than between members and *other* persons present. Boundaries may be set by finding the number of interacting persons whose behavior toward one another is affected by the same set of values. Finally, boundaries may be located by discovering the number of persons whose interpersonal behavior is guided by a single set of interdependent roles.

PRIMARY GROUPS AND SECONDARY GROUPS

Obviously, there are many kinds of groups, and it isn't surprising that sociologists have ways of classifying and distinguishing among them. Groups may be classified by size, longevity, kinds of members, functions they perform for their members or for society, complexity of organization, and in many other ways. We shall consider only one distinction, that between primary and secondary groups.

Think of the closest, most intimate friendship you have. You and your friend presumably feel great affection for each other. You would do a lot for your friend and "take a lot" from him or her. The chances are that you do many kinds of things together, as many as you can. No one can take the place of your friend. This is a unique relationship, and it probably took a while to develop fully. Contrast this two-member group with another, which includes you and a bank teller, on a particular day in your bank. You greet one another, perhaps exchange a comment on the weather, and he cashes your check. You take your money and leave. That is all. The first of these is a *primary,* the other a *secondary,* group.

This distinction has existed in sociological thinking ever since a pioneer sociologist and social psychologist, Charles Horton Cooley, introduced the concept of primary group over a half century ago (1909:23). The following definitions paraphrase those given by Bates and Babchuck (1961:185), and avoid certain problems found in Cooley's original and better known definition. *A primary group is one in which members are predisposed to enter into a wide range of activities with each other, and their emotions toward one another are both strong and much more positive than negative. By contrast, a secondary group is one in which members are predisposed to enter into only a narrow range of activities. The emotional quality of relationships is not of central importance. Instead, relationships tend to be contractual with an emphasis on rights and obligations of each to the others.*

Primary and secondary groups are not mutually exclusive, rather they differ less in kind than degree. One group may be more primary than a second, but less so than a third. The emphasis in these definitions is on the orientation of members to one

Part 1 / Some Fundamental Ideas

another. It is their attitudes toward sharing activities and toward defining rights and obligations, and their feelings toward one another that are the basis of distinction. Almost any kind of group may have primary or secondary characteristics. Most families (but not all), most friendship groups, and most peer groups are high in primary qualities. Most employer-employee groups (but not all), most teacher-student groups, and most leader-follower relationships are high in secondary characteristics.

PRIMARY GROUP RELATIONSHIPS   It is in primary group settings that people have their most emotionally intense interpersonal experiences. Roles in such groups are not treated lightly, and role performances are often infused with strong feeling. We begin life in a primary group, the family. The relationships formed there are the first we know, and the most vital in the formation of our personalities. As infants and children in the family we develop the deep-seated need for primary relationships with others which will accompany most of us for the rest of our lives. The poet Robert Frost wrote,

Home is the place where, when you have to go there,
They have to take you in.

It is the place where, in spite of everything, you are a person of unique value simply because you are you. Even after we leave our parents' homes, we need and seek other associations with something of the same full personal acceptance and mutual loyalty and support.

Have you ever felt really homesick? If so, you have experienced one of the psychological effects of being cut off from the accustomed support of a primary group. Homesickness disappears only when at least the beginnings of new primary associations are established. Long and severe isolation from primary group experience can have serious effects. Sociologists and psychologists agree that primary contact is vital for mental and social health.

Primary Group and Survival   Several studies of soldiers in combat situations show the profound importance of primary groups to the individual. Shils and Janowitz (1948), dealing with German soldiers in World War II, and Moskos (1967), studying American G.I.s in Vietnam, agree that soldiers are not sustained in an important way by patriotism or the political purposes of war. What lets them endure the terrible pressures of ground combat is the support of and loyalty to a small group of buddies, a primary group. In the struggle to stay alive, this group is what men count on. Who will support you when the chips are down? The best answers you can give to that question represent the strongest primary associations you have.

Sociologists have suggested that as societies become larger, more urbanized, and more industrialized, primary group experience declines relative to secondary group experience. More

Which of these pictures represents primary groups, which secondary? Could any of the groups be either primary or secondary?

and more of one's total group contacts are weak in primary qualities. Contrast a small village, in which most of the inhabitants spend their whole lives, with a great metropolis where people have many fleeting, segmented encounters with strangers. It has often been said that a big city can be the loneliest place in the world. The stranger in the city, and many a permanent resident, has little or nothing but secondary contacts to sustain him.

Further, our lives are increasingly compassed by the impersonal, massive boundaries of the big complex organizations characteristic of industrialized societies (see Chapter 9). What American has not felt that he is "just a number" in some impersonal organization, or raged at petty bureaucratic rules which seemed to him to make no sense?

Sociologists hold that primary groups are not only vital to the well-being of individuals, but are important in linking the individual to the values and roles of the larger aspects of society. But sociologists are not in full agreement as to whether the decline in primary contacts has reached a dangerous point. The support of a primary group makes it possible for combat soldiers to serve the political ends of the state, even though they are not motivated by such ends. On the other hand, fewer than 54 percent of eligible voters bothered to vote in the 1972 presidential election. Clearly the primary groups in which Americans live do a poor job of motivating people to perform a critical act of citizenship in a democratic society.

One thing is sure: people continue to form primary groups spontaneously, even in the largest cities and the biggest organizations. While the organization charts of big corporations, government agencies, and universities never show it, their very nature breeds countless primary groups in which people band together for a more personal social experience, and often for protection against rules and regulations which seem ridiculous or oppressive. Workers, pressured by management to become ever more productive, informally establish and enforce upper limits on production.

SECONDARY GROUP EXPERIENCE   Secondary groups are radically different in their emotional quality. Many ask little in the way of emotional commitment and offer little personalized support. Often the concern of the individual is that there be a kind of even exchange. In return for a certain amount of labor, the worker receives a certain amount of pay. In return for the payment of taxes, the citizen receives certain services. Such relationships are reasonably satisfactory as long as people feel that they have gotten about as much as they have given. Feeling, if it is strong, is likely to be negative, and aroused by the belief that there has *not* been an even exchange, that the product or service was not as represented. Such group experiences need not be frustrating, so long as the terms of association are understood by all, and so long as people can count on more primary groups to supply other kinds of satisfactions not limited by contract.

One unfortunate aspect of group life is the attempt to build group loyalty by excluding other groups of people or by invoking real or imagined enemies. If we want to know what one group is really like, the last place for reliable information is among people for whom this is an out-group.

IN-GROUPS AND OUT-GROUPS You have often heard people say, "You're either for us or against us." "United we stand, divided we fall." "America, love it or leave it." "We're number one." All such statements are expressions of *in-group* attitudes. Conversely, you hear, "Down with Tech." "We don't want any hippies in this town." "The equal rights for women amendment to the Constitution is a subtle, sinister communistic tactic to demoralize and destroy the family unit."[1] Such statements express attitudes toward out-groups. When the members of a group feel loyal to one another and to the group, that group is an in-group for its members. When members of an in-group view another group with such feelings as competitiveness, fear, or hostility, that other group is an out-group.

Effects of Group Identification In-groups and out-groups really exist only in relation to each other. The "we-feeling" of in-group membership implies a "they-feeling" toward one or more out-groups. It is perhaps strange that positive identification with one group is so often accompanied by dislike of some other. Such we-they orientations may be very weak; members may scarcely be aware of them. But they may also be intense, like the attitudes of many black and white Americans toward each other. Sad to say, one age-old way to strengthen loyalty to the in-group has been to raise the specter of the frightening, dangerous, or perhaps just peculiar out-group. On a very large scale, the intense patriotism found on the home front in some wars is a by-product of fear and hatred of the enemy.

The in-group out-group distinction has led to many ironies produced by historical change. In World War II Germany, Italy, and Japan were out-groups for Americans. They were the hated

---

[1] This and similar statements were commonly found in letters to state legislatures in a 1972–1973 campaign to prevent state ratification of the equal rights amendment. The campaign was supported by the "Stop ERA Committee" and related groups.

Interaction, Roles, and Groups

enemy about whom almost anything bad could be believed. Today they are staunch friends and allies, part of a very large in-group out-group orientation which pits the non-Communist against the Communist world.

GROUP STRUCTURE Have you ever noticed that in classrooms where the instructor does not assign seats, after a while students will occupy the same seats every day? People spontaneously develop an ordered way of relating to one another in a particular space. We have referred many times to *social patterns*, and our use of the term *pattern* is deliberately very broad. It denotes any and all kinds of observed regularity in human social behavior. Social patterns include such different things as the variation in suicide rates by age and sex, and the tendency for group interaction networks to center on a leader.

SOCIAL STRUCTURE We shall now begin to use a closely related but narrower term, *social structure*. Structure denotes particular aspects of orderliness (patterning) found in groups or larger entities such as organizations which may engage thousands of people. So we could use structure in discussing the reciprocal roles in a two-member group, or in the chain of command in the United States Department of Justice. We use it for features of complete social entities, but not for social patterns seen apart from any complete social unit. Thus we do not speak of structure when referring to the fact that suicide rates go up with age and are higher among men than women.

Structure relates to the way parts are arranged to form a larger whole. A chair has four legs, a seat and a back, assembled to produce a recognizable unit. The parts of a group are not so obvious. But in general, we are dealing with group structure whenever we consider the ways in which interaction among members and between parts of the group culture (values, norms, and roles) exhibits order over time. Two ways in which sociologists think about group structure follow.

STRUCTURE IN SOCIAL INTERACTION Put yourself into a room where people around a table are talking about a matter of common interest. You can see that they are concentrating on the subject matter of the conversation, or perhaps on one or more aspects of the persons present. For example, A may be asking himself: "Why did B just say that? What is his motive?" You, however, ignore what is said and why it may be said. You are looking for evidence of order, design—in short, structure—in the flow of interaction.

Do you see signs that the talk appears to flow toward or away from some persons in particular? Do some people appear to ask an unusual number of questions? Do others supply an unusual number of answers? Do you notice any changes in the rate of social interaction, perhaps sudden bursts or lulls? Does the flow of talk seem to be related to any changes in the overall tone of the group? Perhaps there are times when tension or uneasiness appears to be mounting, and others when there is a sudden release of tension expressed in joking and laughing. These are simple things which can be informally observed and which suggest that interaction may exhibit regularities often not recognized by group members.

Because really detailed and accurate records of social interaction are hard to make under natural or field conditions, much of the research on structure in interaction has been done with contrived laboratory groups. One widely known research tradition stems from the work of Bales (1950), who developed a theory and related observational and recording method called *Interaction Process Analysis*. The focus is on problem-solving groups, and much of the research uses laboratory groups which meet for a few sessions under controlled conditions.

Problem-Solving Groups Problem-solving groups are a common experience. Many small groups have, at least broadly, a common task to perform: students studying for an exam, committees, workgroups of all kinds, meetings of small organizations. As Bales sees it, a group with a task to perform faces a number of difficulties which must be solved if it is to get the job done and have reasonably harmonious relationships among its members. These difficulties are of two types: one arises from the members' need to complete the task before them; the other stems from the need to maintain satisfying personal relationships.

To put it differently, the members must work at the task if it is to be done. But they cannot work well if they can't get along. Most people have known groups in which there was so much antagonism that the work suffered. There are also times when members enjoy one another's company so much that the work suffers. The set of problems having to do with the group task is called the *task area* (or *instrumental* area). The set of problems concerning the personal relationships of members is called the *social-emotional* (or *expressive*) area.

The two kinds of problems are interdependent. Overlong concentration on the task, for instance, can become frustrating. Members grow weary. Feelings are hurt in arguments. Tensions rise and relationships are strained. Eventually, unless interaction switches to the expressive area, completion of the group's task may be threatened. It seems reasonable to assume that after a long period of hard work the group will begin to engage in social-emotional behavior. When it does, tensions are relieved. Members are reminded that, after all, it is important to get along with one another as well as to get the job done. But if too much time is spent this way, the need will be felt to return to the task which is the group's main reason for existence.

In the first of these pictures, long concentration in the task area is producing signs of weariness and tension in the members. In the second photo, members are shifting to expressive behavior and relieving tension. Problem-solving groups typically alternate between these two emphases.

Bales theorized that strains arising from overconcentration in one area will be relieved by switching interaction to the other, and that groups go through characteristic sequences of such alternations. If sequences of this sort can be observed in many different groups, we have evidence for structure in interaction, that is, persistent patterning or regularity.

Studying Social Interaction in Experimental Groups To see how Bales approached the study of this and other kinds of structure in social interaction we need to know something of his technique for recording interaction while it was going on. At this point you should carefully study Figure 4-2.

The Bales technique provides that every act of a group member can be placed in one of his twelve categories of behavioral meaning. For instance, suppose Mary says, "I'm not doing any good here." And Phyllis replies, "I think you're doing a very good job." Mary's remark would be coded in Category 11 (shows tension, asks for help, withdraws out of field). Phyllis's rejoinder would be coded in Category 1 (shows solidarity, raises other's status, gives help, reward). The twelve categories in Figure 4-2 were developed to reflect different kinds of task behavior and social-emotional behavior. The categories were made broad enough so that the behavior of people in different kinds of groups could be put into comparable classifications, thus permitting the discovery of patterns which might otherwise be hidden by the surface differences between groups.

In practice, social interaction is observed by persons trained in a

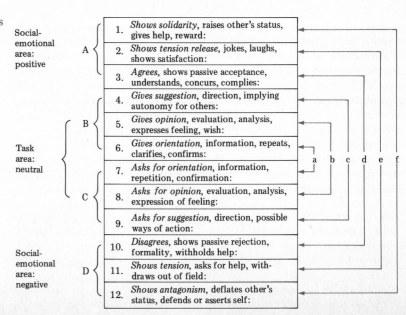

FIGURE 4-2   BALES INTERACTION CATEGORIES

[Source: Robert F. Bales, *Interaction Process Analysis* (Cambridge, Mass.: Addison-Wesley, 1950), p. 9.]

KEY:

a. Problems of communication
b. Problems of evaluation
c. Problems of control
d. Problems of decision
e. Problems of tension reduction
f. Problems of reintegration

A.   Positive reactions
B.   Attempted answers
C.   Questions
D.   Negative reactions

Social-emotional area: positive

A
1. *Shows solidarity*, raises other's status, gives help, reward:
2. *Shows tension release*, jokes, laughs, shows satisfaction:
3. *Agrees*, shows passive acceptance, understands, concurs, complies:

Task area: neutral

B
4. *Gives suggestion*, direction, implying autonomy for others:
5. *Gives opinion*, evaluation, analysis, expresses feeling, wish:
6. *Gives orientation*, information, repeats, clarifies, confirms:

C
7. *Asks for orientation*, information, repetition, confirmation:
8. *Asks for opinion*, evaluation, analysis, expression of feeling:
9. *Asks for suggestion*, direction, possible ways of action:

Social-emotional area: negative

D
10. *Disagrees*, shows passive rejection, formality, withholds help:
11. *Shows tension*, asks for help, withdraws out of field:
12. *Shows antagonism*, deflates other's status, defends or asserts self:

a b c d e f

Part 1 / Some Fundamental Ideas

method which breaks down interaction into very small units of meaning. The observer records each unit in terms of (a) who does (says) something, (b) whom the behavior is directed toward, and (c) its content category among the twelve categories in Figure 4-2. The entry is made on a moving tape attached to a clock mechanism, so that the time sequence is also noted. A single meeting of a small group may produce thousands of units, each classified by origin, destination, and category of meaning, all in the order in which they occurred. Such a record can be compared with others to search for recurring patterns in the interactional flow.[2]

Bales and his associates (1965), and later other investigators, have produced substantial evidence that interaction in problem-solving groups does in fact reflect the two kinds of difficulties mentioned above. It does show tendencies toward a balance or equilibrium between the task and the social-emotional aspects of group activity. This appears from the analysis of changes over time in a group meeting. It shows when the total amount of interaction in a group session is distributed into the twelve content categories. And it shows when the total amount of interaction for a group session is distributed among the members of a group.

While these patterns may vary somewhat from one group to another, they are in general quite predictable. In other words, sociologists appear to have identified one kind of structure in social interaction. This structure is a regularity which arises out of the common dilemmas faced by people in problem-solving groups as they seek to master a task and still preserve their interpersonal ties. And it is a structure which may be wholly invisible to people in the group.

ROLES AND ROLE PERFORMANCES AS STRUCTURE The Bales approach to the analysis of social interaction does not directly use the concepts of role and role performance. Given our definition of group it would appear that evidences of group structure might also be discovered in the notion that a group is a set of roles and role performances. Notice that the interaction studied by the use of the Bales method is also a set of interlocking role performances. Perhaps a bridge can be built from the patterning revealed by the Bales technique and that perceived in roles and role performances. It may be that other invisible structures have a significant relationship to the roles of which members are more likely to be aware.

Interaction and Role Emergence Earlier we suggested that social interaction is influenced by culture and also produces culture. If norms and roles do not exist when people begin to interact, they will soon be developed. Some understanding of how roles evolve

---

[2] In fact, such records can be kept permanently and used over and over again by different researchers who wish to study interaction in order to test quite different ideas.

out of interaction in newly formed groups has been gained through research by Slater (1955:300–310) which used the Bales method, among others, to secure information from twenty problem-solving groups studied in the laboratory. Each group met for four sessions. At the end of each session, the subjects answered the following questions in writing:

a. Who contributed the best ideas for solving the problem? Please rank the members in order. *Include yourself.*
b. Who did the most to guide the discussion and keep it moving effectively? Please rank the members in order. *Include yourself.*
c. How well did you personally like each of the other members? Rate each member on a scale from 0 to 7, where zero means "I feel perfectly neutral toward him," and seven means "I like him very much."

At the end of the fourth session an additional question was added:

d. Considering all the sessions, which member of the group would you say stood out most definitely as a leader in the discussion? How would you rank the others? *Include yourself.*

From the replies, each member was given an average rank-order on each question, based on the ratings each received from his fellows. Analysis of these ratings and rank-orders revealed that two kinds of specialists emerged. One was called the "Best-liked man," the other the "Idea-man." This means that as time went by there was *increasing agreement* that one person had the best ideas for working on the group problem while another person was liked the best by the others. You have probably noticed that these two specialists suggest the basic distinction between the task and social-emotional areas of interaction. Certain members were outstanding in one of these areas, but not in both. Further evidence of this distinction was furnished by the Bales interaction records, which showed that "Idea-men tend to specialize in active problem-solving attempts, and Best-liked men in more reactive, less task-oriented behavior" (Slater: 306).

There was a complementary relationship between the two specialists in that both performed important functions useful to the whole group. In view of this, it is interesting to note that in the main, each type of specialist *liked the other* better than did other persons in the group. It is almost as if each recognized and appreciated, at least intuitively, the reciprocal nature of their contributions to effective group performance.

Slater was studying newly formed groups which lasted for only four meetings. Therefore, we cannot assume that the groups lasted long enough for roles and role performances to develop fully. More specifically, the task and social-emotional specialist designations do not refer directly to role performances. Remember, these specialists were picked by composite ratings of members on how well each person had performed in matters important to the group. Such ratings might reflect role performances if we knew that roles were, in fact, present. What is more likely is that we are seeing signs of the gradual emergence of roles and role performances.

One kind of evidence is of particular interest in this matter. Slater computed the percentage of cases in each of the four meetings in which the top member on ideas was also the top member in being liked. At the end of the first meeting, the same individual held both top positions 56.5 percent of the time. At the end of the fourth meeting this was true only 8.5 percent of the time. In other words, with each successive meeting, each type of specialized behavior became more clearly identified with just one person.

We may be quite sure that this trend coordinates with the gradual evolution and clarification of roles and role performances. Every new group must "grow" its own values, norms, and roles to some extent. When the group is of a familiar type, the culture of familiar models is adapted to the new situation. But even then the suitability of known roles must be verified in the new situation, members of the present group must be sorted out and fitted into the appropriate roles, and role performances must be developed and tested. It is a process which takes some time. Anyone can informally watch this process at work in newly formed groups.

Parsons and Zelditch (1955) speculated that the tendency in such laboratory groups to seek a satisfactory balance between the task and social-emotional areas, and the tendency for individuals to specialize in these different activities, may also be seen in the characteristic roles and role performances of groups far removed from experimental settings. More specifically, might the father and mother roles in the family represent this kind of differentiation? Zelditch tested the idea with anthropological evidence from fifty-six different societies. Although not all the data were consistent, he found strong evidence that the husband-father is the task specialist and the wife-mother the social-emotional specialist. Levinger (1964), working with a small sample of American middle-class families, supported the Zelditch findings when children were present, but not with respect to the marriage pair per se. Levinger attributes this to the unusual importance of social-emotional qualities in American marriage, and also to the notion that in two-member groups, social-emotional specialization serves no purpose in maintaining the group. Here is an instance of how ideas about group functioning developed in controlled laboratory situations may lead to further understanding of groups occurring under natural conditions in society.

Groups, Roles, and Individuals Slater's work deals with a specialized aspect of roles as group structure. In more general terms, it should be understood that a set of interdependent roles and role performances *is* a structure, as we implied earlier. When a group is visualized as a set of roles and role performances, each role and role performance is a component of the structure, and the ways in which they are interdependent make up the whole which is the group.

What we are saying may be clarified by examining Figure 4-3, which represents a small part of a family structure visualized as role performances. It depicts a few fragments of role performance in a typical family. Think of the familiar names father, mother, and child not as denoting complete persons but as the *locations of reciprocal rights and obligations*. To find sample elements of father's role performance with respect to mother and child, locate husband-father in the left-hand column, then read to the right. The diagonal arrows linking compartments call attention to the reciprocal character of the role performances. Figure 4-3 helps to clarify the distinction between what is social structure linking these people and what is something else (personality, or behavior which is not group-related).

CONTINGENT FACTORS IN GROUP BEHAVIOR

Have you ever wondered how people's behavior in groups might be affected by their relationship to each other in space? The traditional classroom arranges people in parallel rows, all facing the same direction, with the teacher in front, facing the class. Would classroom behavior change if the people were arranged in a

FIGURE 4-3 SAMPLE COMPONENTS OF ROLE PERFORMANCE IN A FAMILY

Role Performance of: With respect to →	Husband — Father	Wife — Mother	Child
Husband — Father		1. Financially supports 2. Offers affection 3. Accepts affection 4. Takes wife out socially	1. Financially supports 2. Instructs child 3. Plays with child 4. Offers affection 5. Accepts affection
Wife — Mother	1a. Accepts financial support 2a. Accepts affection 3a. Offers affection 4a. Does housekeeping 5a. Looks nice when taken out		1. Instructs child 2. Comforts child when unhappy 3. Offers affection 4. Accepts affection
Child	1a. Accepts financial support 2a. Accepts instruction 3a. Plays with father 4a. Accepts affection 5a. Offers affection	1a. Accepts instruction 2a. Accepts comfort 3a. Accepts affection 4a. Offers affection	

Part 1 / Some Fundamental Ideas

circle? The distribution of group behavior in physical space is an example of what we mean by contingent factors, that is, conditions not actually part of the group but which accompany group phenomena. Another such factor is the size of the group. What happens to behavior as a group gets bigger?

SPATIAL ARRANGEMENT How would you feel if, in performing a marriage ceremony, a minister insisted on standing no more than twelve inches away from the bride and groom? What would you think if a man proposing marriage stood thirty-five feet away across a large room? Such behavior would seem decidedly odd. And this fact suggests that there may be widespread norms which specify appropriate distances between people engaged in particular kinds of social interaction. Among others, Hall (1966) and Sommer (1961, 1962) found evidence that such norms do exist. Baxter studied the distances between members of pre-existing two-member groups in natural settings (1970). One of his findings was that Mexican subjects came closer together in conversation than black or white Americans. Relatively close proximity among people reared in Mediterranean cultures has been reported by other investigators. That is, preferred distances for the same kind of interaction appear to differ between very broad cultural settings.

Think about what these two kinds of classroom arrangements mean for the reciprocal roles of teacher and pupil. What different kinds of information or teaching are likely to take place in these settings?

Function and Spatial Arrangement In a rather different vein, Batchelor and Goethals (1972) investigated the idea that the function of a group would influence the way its members arranged themselves in space. They formed eight-member experimental groups, all of which met in a large room at different times. Half the groups were to discuss and collectively reach a solution to a problem presented to them. In the other groups, each individual had to report his own solution to the same problem; there was no group decision. Members of both types of groups were free (using folding chairs) to sit anywhere in the room. In general, not only did the collective decision group members sit closer to one another than members of the individual decision groups, but there was far less variation in their seating patterns. Referring to earlier studies of seating arrangements in discussion groups, Hare and Bales (1963:480) report that

communication networks are *implicit* in the seating arrangements of discussion groups and that these implicit networks also affect the interaction pattern. Steinzor found that individuals seated in a circle tended to talk more to group members opposite them than to those next to them. The studies by Sommer and by Strodbeck and Hook both report that leaders are more likely to choose a position at the end of a rectangular table. Further, subjects who sit at the corners of a rectangular table tend to contribute least to the discussion. Thus we find that not only does seating position influence the amount of interaction a person will give and receive, but also that persons who might be inclined to dominate the discussion choose the more "central" seats.

Hall (1966) indicates that the amount and kind of information available at different distances between people is also important in spatial arrangements. He distinguishes distances between interacting persons as intimate (full contact to eighteen inches), casual-personal (eighteen to forty-eight inches), social-consultative (four feet to twelve feet), and public (twelve feet to maximum carrying distance of the voice) (Wieck, 1968:389). In Hall's view, the boundary lines between these distance categories are set by changes in the kinds of information available.

As persons move closer to or farther from someone else, variables such as these change: clarity of facial detail, possibility of touch, loudness of voice, area of sharp vision, prominence of heat and odor cues, ability to see eyes and mouth in one glance, area covered by peripheral vision (person only or person-in-setting), amount of sensory input, and visual distortion of facial features. At each of the boundary points, several of these cues change (Wieck, 1968:389–90).

While many problems concerning the relation between space and group behavior remain to be solved, enough has been done to indicate that this is a promising area for research. In passing, we might note that this kind of study could be termed "micro-ecology."[3]

GROUP SIZE Recent research indicates that even in small groups, behavior reflects size variations in specific and measurable ways. One way to grasp the significance of size is to consider what happens to the number of pair relationships as the number of group members increases. A two-person group has one pair relationship to maintain; a three-person group has three. As the number of members increases the number of possible pair relationships goes up at a faster rate. This number can be computed for a group of any size by the formula:

$$\text{pair relationships} = \frac{n(n-1)}{2},$$

where n is the number of persons in the group. For example, while a three-person group has only three possible pair relationships, a fifteen-member group has one hundred and five. Sub-groupings involving more than two members also increase rapidly with growth in size.

As size increases, and the structure of the group becomes more complicated, there is more elaboration of norms, more development of cliques and possibly of factions, and less satisfaction to members (Thomas and Fink, 1963:371–84). The tendency to-

---

[3] In the recent upsurge of interest in preserving the physical environment the scientific meaning of the word *ecology* has been altered. In science, the term refers to the study of relationships between organisms and their environment. Current popular usage almost equates ecology with the cause of saving the environment.

ward less personal relations as size increases begins even in small, face-to-face groups.

Special Features of Two-Member Groups   A number of conditions are associated with certain group sizes. Consider that if either member leaves a two-person group, the group disappears. Also unique to the two-person group is that, in decision-making, the only possible majority is unanimity. Bales and Borgatta (1965:501–2) produce evidence from interaction analysis that two-person groups show high rates of tension (Category 11 in the twelve-category scheme), but low rates of disagreement (Category 10) and antagonism (Category 12). Such data suggest that members of two-person groups are aware of the precarious nature of an association which ends if one withdraws. The situation is an inherent cause of anxiety. For these reasons members of such groups are relatively careful about showing hostility or other negative reactions to one another.

Groups of Odd and Even Numbers   A special characteristic of three-person groups is a tendency for two of the members to form a coalition that isolates or controls the third. A considerable body of research has explored this tendency under varying conditions (Collins and Raven, 1969:127–37). Differences between groups with even and odd numbers of members have also been studied. Groups with even numbers (2, 4, 6, 8) can split evenly in decision-making, whereas groups with odd numbers (3, 5, 7, 9) cannot. By interaction analysis, Bales and Borgatta (1965) showed that— excluding the special case of two-person groups—those with even numbers rank high in disagreement (Category 10) and antagonism (Category 12) and low in asking for suggestions (Category 9). These findings appear consistent with the consequences of deadlocks between equal numbers. When such a split occurs, each person has as many allies as any other and may hope to win a majority eventually. Conditions generally favor extended efforts to achieve a majority and therefore the hostility which can result from protracted disagreement.

Without knowing any more than you see here, which of these committees do you think would, over time, have the greater difficulty in making decisions? Why?

The stability of group structure is only relative. Even in the short run, minute changes take place each time a social pattern is repeated. In the long run, major structural changes cannot be avoided. Human social life occurs in patterns, but the patterns are always changing. Social structure and social change are two sides of the same coin. The sources of change may be located either inside, within a group, or outside, in the group's environment.

INTERNAL SOURCES OF CHANGE IN GROUPS   It is rather arbitrary to locate a source of change as being either inside or outside a group.

GROUPS AND SOCIAL CHANGE

To illustrate the point, take the fact that the popularity of skiing has been increasing rapidly all over the country for several decades. Then imagine a group of friends who have shared their recreational activities for years, and have recently, as a group, begun to take up skiing. Shall we say that this change in activity is caused by internal factors such as boredom of the members with what they have been doing? Or shall we say that the change came about because of a national shift in recreational preferences which is merely reflected in this group of friends? Both interpretations have merit, and this would be true of many situations where we were trying to decide whether the source of a change was outside or inside a particular group. Hence our classification of sources is to a considerable extent a matter of convenience in presentation.

Roles, Role Performances and Change We have already pointed out (Chapter 2) that role performances always depart somewhat from roles, and that the relationship between them is a potential source of change. But we can say that change due to internal causes will be minimal when members are satisfied with the degree to which role performances adhere to roles in their group. In such cases the inherent strain between what is and what ought to be is stabilized. Simply stated, these are groups where everything is going well. People are satisfied with the way they are organized to serve the purposes of the group, and generally feel that everyone is pulling his weight.

But such balanced states between role and role performance are easily disturbed. Indeed, groups cannot avoid facing this situation from time to time. What happens when such a disturbance occurs? Often, the first response is to try to restore the original relationship between role and role performance. Pressures will be brought to bear upon deviating members to restore their former performances. But this doesn't always work. In attempts to reduce the tension caused by behavioral deviation from group roles, the roles themselves may have to be changed. No group can survive a state of affairs in which role and role performance no longer have a meaningful relationship. If we think of group culture as a guidance system for actual interpersonal behavior, and see that it is not guiding anything, we are facing an impossible situation. In short, the inherent strain between roles and role performances always, sooner or later, produces changes in both.

Role Conflict Another situation likely to produce change is role conflict. Like norm conflict, this condition exists whenever the performance of one role in a group interferes in some way (physically, morally, or otherwise) with the performance of another role or roles. An important controversy in the early seventies that illustrates role conflict was whether journalists could legally be forced to reveal sources of information. In effect, the agreement of a journalist that he will not disclose the identity of an informant is a mutually accepted role prescription and often a condition for obtaining information. On the other hand, before a grand jury or a judge, the journalist may be subjected to an incompatible demand, from his role as citizen: that he name his informants, The two roles are indeed hard to reconcile; some journalists went to jail rather than comply with the orders of courts or grand juries.

Role conflicts arise in hundreds of less dramatic situations, and everyone faces them from time to time. Husbands and wives differ on whose duty it is to punish their children for misbehavior. Students and teachers disagree on what each may rightfully expect from the other.

Role conflicts are not only personally distressing; they interfere with the performance of groups. They are an inner source of tension which is likely to produce change in the structure of groups. Members may try to alter roles in ways which, in effect, *compromise* the conflict. They may resolve the conflict by *eliminating* one conflicting set of role prescriptions. Or they may try to *ignore* the conflict, isolating it in some way so that it does as little damage as possible (Gross, McEachern and Mason, 1957). But some kind or degree of change in roles and role performances is virtually certain.

Change in Individuals Within a Group Individuals and groups, we have said, are not the same, but are indispensable to each other. An important change in a group will have at least some effect on its members. And change in the individuals who belong to it will ultimately change a group. The role a person plays in one group is only one among his many roles. He has a different role in each group to which he belongs. The individual, trying to maintain consistency and well-being in all the roles he plays, may easily introduce changes into his role in any of the groups he belongs to. Change is as inevitable for the individual as it is for the group. For any single group, this is an internal factor certain to produce change over time.

There are many ways to show how this is true. One example is the changes that take place in the members of every family. Family sociologists often speak of the family life cycle, by which they mean the total duration of a family group from the time it is formed by marriage until the last child has left and one of the parents dies. Every family goes through stages related to the advancing ages of its members. Thus the roles of parent and child alter radically from the time the child is born to the time when the parents are in their eighties and the child is in its sixties. It is not uncommon to find a kind of role-reversal in the latter period, with the child acting in some ways like a protective parent, and the parent somewhat like a dependent child. A person's movement from one age level to the next invariably has implications for the social structure of the various groups to which he belongs.

Alexander Solzhenitsyn, great Russian novelist, now living in exile in Switzerland. Two of his roles were literary artist and Soviet citizen. His devotion to truth as a literary artist led to his denunciation in 1974 by the Russian government as dangerous to the Soviet system. To serve one role was to violate another.

Member Replacement Groups that last for considerable periods sooner or later face the problem of replacing members who leave. Every time an old member leaves and a new one enters the scene, a source of change has been introduced into the group. For instance, President Nixon appointed several new justices to the Supreme Court in his first term, all of whom were viewed as being more conservatively inclined than the previous Court. While many aspects of the Court's structure were unaffected by the new members, it is generally agreed that its decisions became more conservative.

EFFECTS OF ENVIRONMENT Every group functions in an environment which challenges its well-being and even its survival. Changes in the environment are a major source of internal changes in group structure. Some parts of the environment are physical. For example, a professor and his students would like to have informal class sessions with a good deal of discussion, but the seats in their classroom are fixed to the floor in traditional rows. If they can transfer to a room in which flexible seating is possible, even so simple an environmental change may bring about measurable differences in the degree to which interaction is distributed among all present.

More important, probably, is the social and cultural environment of a given group. In America, countless small groups exist within large, complex organizations. A single corporation may be made up of thousands of face-to-face groups. A product change or a change in production methods may force changes in many of these groups. It is true that groups often resist changes demanded by the larger organization. Sometimes orders from above are effectively nullified by group action from below. This is one reason why, after a different political party has taken over control of elective offices, the day-to-day operations of government may change very little. Civil service employees, operating essentially in small groups, can weaken and deflect changes called for by political leaders. But even the effort to resist changes from outside the group may lead to changes within the group.

Culture is another external source of change for groups. How many college friendships have disintegrated when the group environment was changed from the college campus to the culturally more complex world of full adulthood. Such groups continue only if members succeed in modifying old roles to make them more appropriate to the new environment and at the same time retain adequate satisfaction. Grown children often feel much closer to friends made in later life than to their own brothers and sisters with whom they shared the culture of the parental family. This is not so much because the siblings have themselves changed as because their most meaningful role performances are no longer anchored in the same culture.

We know also that the characteristic roles of husband-father, wife-mother, and child have undergone major changes in the United States in the last few generations. These changes did not originate inside individual family units, but reflect the tremendous changes that have followed from the industrialization of society. Many American colleges and universities were established in the eighteenth and nineteenth centuries. While they have had a continuous existence, they have changed immensely in these years. And this change reflects profound alterations in society at large more than within the colleges themselves.

The sociology of small groups has several uses directly based on scholarly work in the field. Other types of practice illustrate the principles of group sociology but probably were not deliberately based on them. And with this aspect of sociology as with all others, one of the most valuable applications is the influence of understanding on a student's intellectual resources and thus on his capacities for effective action in group settings. We try to learn about groups because the evidence indicates that groups are one of the vital resources for understanding why people behave as they do.

THE PRACTICAL VALUE OF GROUP SOCIOLOGY

GROUP THERAPIES   The term *group therapy* can refer to a variety of techniques and approaches used along with or instead of other clinical methods for treating the adjustment problems of individuals. We shall mention only two such techniques, the first of which is interesting because it makes calculated use of the notion of role. Developed by Moreno (1953), it is employed in some mental hospitals and clinics and is usually called *psychodrama*. In a psychodrama, a patient acts out key roles in his own life experience under the direction of a psychiatrist or other clinician before a small audience. Other important figures in his life's drama are often represented by staff members or by other patients. In effect, the patient engages in role performances during which he reveals his understanding (or misunderstanding) of his role requirements in the significant groups to which he belongs. His performance may be interrupted, discussed, and started again, perhaps with changes of scene. By this process the patient begins to stand apart from the social relationships that play a part in his troubles, to see them and his feelings about them more objectively, and hence to gain insight that may help him work out his problems.

Also interesting are several amateur group therapies. First and best known of these is Alcoholics Anonymous. Others have since been modeled on this precedent, for example, an organization called Synanon (Yablonsky, 1962) which is concerned with the rehabilitation of drug addicts. Most such groups carefully avoid the control of medical, psychological, or other clinical professionals. Part of their appeal is that the only criterion for mem-

Group therapy can be used in dealing with a variety of individual adjustment problems. Group support helps to reinforce improved or changed behavior, as in this exercise class. Such behavior might be more difficult to accomplish on an individual basis.

bership is that a person has a problem, such as compulsive drinking, which he cannot control and which has had devastating consequences for him. An in-group is created at once by this means. Only "we" really understand what it is like to suffer this problem; therefore only "we" can help one another. And we do this by wholeheartedly accepting the group's values and norms.

Most people who join such groups have known progressive deterioration of their own role performance in "respectable" society. The new group accepts them without judgment or qualification, assigns them a role that permits self-respect in spite of their problem, and provides group support in maintaining it. There are also techniques for reinforcing group values and securing conformity. Since backsliding is always possible, there are ways of keeping an erring member in the group rather than rejecting him, as most groups usually do. These groups become more interesting as one reflects that they are made up of people whose past experience seriously disables them in interpersonal behavior. Whatever their rationale and ideology, all group therapies are based on two sound premises. First, roles and role performance are important points of origin for many unmanageable psychological problems. Second, role-defined relationships can be used both as ways to self-insight and as sources of healing.

SENSITIVITY TRAINING *Sensitivity training, T-groups,* and *encounter groups* are a related cluster of group techniques that have received a great deal of attention in recent years. Back (1971) identifies three main centers which have contributed to this development. One is the National Training Laboratory (NTL), which reflects the influence of Kurt Lewin and some of his students. Lewin was an imaginative social scientist concerned both with social psychological problems and with the functioning of groups. The T-groups associated with the NTL view work mainly to improve the functioning of specific groups.

Every weekend innumerable workshops, encounter, and T-groups are conducted by more or less reputable organizations and individuals. Business firms send their executives and employees to various programs, in their own plants as well as at special retreats: college and church groups have programs varying from short demonstrations to training programs lasting several weeks (Back, 1971:133).

Another center is the Tavistock Institute in London. While Tavistock is more psychoanalytical than sociological, their programs, like those of NTL, are intended for the improvement of groups. A third center developed in California, and influenced by humanistic psychologists and by Oriental religious concepts, uses encounter groups not so much to improve groups as to enhance the sensitivity and spontaneity of the individual. The same is true of Esalen, a later California-based development. With the exception of Esalen, there has been considerable contact among these different centers.

In one way or another, all these developments are responses to certain qualities in our society. There is much in American society that inhibits people from spontaneous expression, that makes them deny their deepest feelings, and that keeps them from entering into really significant relationships with each other. In a different vein, it is often felt that we need to learn how to release the potential effectiveness of face-to-face groups within larger organizations. The mere possibility of having a vital new experience seems to be one justification for encounter groups, so that they have created a new form of middle-class recreation. "Esalen was a place where educated middle-class adults came in the summer to get out of The Rut and wiggle their fannies a bit" (Wolfe, 1968:119). Whatever the particular rationale, it would seem that sensitivity training speaks to real and previously unmet needs in many people. The remarkable growth in popularity of these various techniques attests to that.

On the other hand, the ease with which sensitivity training may be arranged by enthusiastic but untrained people has revealed genuine dangers. One serious possibility is mentioned by Back (1971:136).

There is some common agreement that individuals who are currently disturbed should not participate in sensitivity training, but little effort has been made to screen applicants to these sessions. A more subtle disturbing effect arises from the fact that the length of the sensitivity workshop is predetermined. The participant is left at some stage of disturbance, insight, or incipient change, to fend for himself as best he can. Sensitivity training leaders do not take any professional responsibility beyond the actual sessions.

On the whole, it appears that current efforts to improve the quality of experience in groups show possibilities for the application of basic knowledge in this area. Moreover, much can be done at little cost.

Practicing the Sociological Perspective

Tape record a few minutes of a conversation and assign a letter or number to each speaker. Play the tape through, recording a sequence of interacts much as we did early in this chapter. You will probably find that not all the conversation can be coded into interacts, for we often send out messages which are not responded to. Remember, an interact occurs only when the behavior of at least two people is known to have been linked for a moment. Examine the probable meanings of single interacts, then see if you can grasp how these meanings are extended, because the single interact is linked to a series so that the meaning of a whole episode of interaction is somewhat different from the meanings of its parts taken separately.

Organize a game of charades for its value in sensitizing you to the role of language in the transfer of meaning between people in social interaction. The point of charades is getting around difficulties which arise when specific meanings must be communicated *nonverbally*. Remember that in playing the game a member of your team is given a verbal statement by the opposite team. Your teammate must perform actions before you which will allow you to identify the original statement. Imagine how it would be if all communication required such a struggle to transfer meanings. At the same time, charades demonstrate that nonverbal transfer of meaning does take place. They remind us that despite the comparative efficiency of verbal communication, nonverbal cues play an important supplemental part in the communicative process.

Often the boundaries of groups are obvious. But the boundaries of subgroups are much less evident. Try locating the boundaries of subgroups within larger groups you can observe. Remember that as the size of a group increases the number of *potential* subgroups increases rapidly. Locate three or more groups of quite different sizes. Calculate the potential number of two-member subgroups for each size of group. Then try to determine how many of these arithmetically possible subgroups actually exist. What is the proportion of actual to possible subgroups in each case? Does the proportion decline as main groups get larger?

Choose a group to which you belong and which may at least in some ways be a problem-solving group. First, identify behavior that you would classify as either task behavior or social-emotional behavior. Next, try to name one person whom you think stands out as a task specialist and another as a social-emotional specialist. Acts which directly or indirectly seem to lead toward goals important to group members are task behavior. Acts which express positive feeling toward the group and its members, which accept and support others, and which relieve tension among members, indicate social-emotional behavior.

PART 2
Social Units and Processes

The chapters in Part Two treat a rather wide range of social phenomena, which are larger and more complicated than those discussed in Part One. Most are also somewhat more removed from individual awareness and immediate interpersonal experience. Yet these structures and processes have powerful effects on everyone, for they define the boundaries of possibility for individual lives.

Every one of the units treated here contains large numbers of the interacts, norms, values, roles, and groups analyzed in Part One. As an illustration, even a small community (Chapter 5) organizes millions of interacts, hundreds of roles, and scores of groups into a complex, inclusive whole.

In a rough way the topics considered in Part Two may be thought of as "middle-range" phenomena. They are both bigger than the units analyzed in Part One and smaller than those introduced in Parts Three (social institutions) and Four (societies). On the other hand, *within* Part Two the chapters are not presented in order of size.

One should also be aware that the aspects of society considered in Part Two are overlapping in several ways. For instance, a single complex organization (Chapter 9) may contain many occupations (Chapter 8). Then too, occupations play a significant part in social stratification (Chapter 6). Social deviance (Chapter 11) occurs in all of the other units under discussion and the same is true of collective behavior (Chapter 10).

Communities

5

The complex activities of man are not evenly distributed across the space men occupy. They concentrate and cluster, and the most general term for these clusters is *community*. This chapter is about communities, which are among the oldest natural social units in human experience. The stress will be on urban communities, because cities are rapidly becoming the dominant form throughout the world.

Community is another of those terms which sociology has taken over from everyday speech and which is therefore variable and ambiguous in meaning. It often refers to a number of persons with similar opinions or interests, as in terms like community of opinion and business community. It may signify common ownership as in the notion of community property. Even when it is restricted to some geographically based grouping, questions of boundary are hard to resolve. Is a single suburb of a large city a community? How about the center of the city? Where are the boundaries of a city as a community? At the legal limits? Beyond? If beyond, where does the urban community come to an end in the surrounding hinterland?

Community and urban sociology are long-established specialties in sociology, but to this day definition plagues the field. So we must be somewhat arbitrary in adopting a single definition for use

THE CONCEPT OF COMMUNITY

Four communities in recognizably different cultural settings: a jungle community located in the Alto Beni district of Bolivia; the Eskimo village of Gambell on St. Lawrence Island in Alaska; the Pueblo community located in what is now Taos, New Mexico; and the California boom town Placeville-Hangtown in the early 1900s. Each of these settings fits our definition of a community because they occupy a distinct land area and have, or had, an interdependent, culturally specified way of life.

in this chapter. Yet our definition is consonant with many that prevail and it will be of use in developing a number of points we make later.

A *community is a durable, geographically located social form. It is both a place and an interdependent, culturally specified way of life for its inhabitants. They know that their lives are bounded by the community and respond accordingly.* This definition says that a community is a distinct and comparatively autonomous social unit occupying a particular land area. Within it, inhabitants live, or are capable of living, complete lives. St. Louis, then, is a community. But what some call the financial community located in St. Louis would not meet our definition. Our notion of community thus has a psychological dimension. Inhabitants are aware of the community's important role in their lives and they respond by some identification with it. One says, "I love this town. My friends and relatives live here and my best memories are here." Another says, "I don't particularly like the place. But it's where I live and I doubt I'll ever leave it." These two comments differ in enthusiasm, but both recognize a community as a *place which encompasses human lives.*

SMALL AND LARGE COMMUNITIES As we define community the term is broad enough to include small villages and the largest cities, and also such varied forms as medieval monasteries and modern communes located in rural or remote regions. But more than size distinguishes small from large communities.

Gemeinschaft and Gesellschaft The German scholar Tönnies (1887) described two kinds of society, to which he attached the names *Gemeinschaft* and *Gesellschaft*. People are born into a Gemeinschaft, feel they belong to it, are attached to it by strong emotional ties. It is simply there, the unquestioned setting for their entire lives. One might almost say that the relationships between members of a Gemeinschaft have a quality like that between kinfolk. By contrast, in a Gesellschaft people *decide* to enter into relationships with others and do so in the pursuit of their own interests. That is, many social bonds are both voluntary and contractual. The voluntary association, one whose members *choose* to join it, is characteristic of the Gesellschaft. (We shall have more to say about voluntary associations in Chapter 8.) In effect, people enter into relationships because they expect to derive some advantage from them, while in the Gemeinschaft relationships are predestined and in the very nature of the social world as the individual understands it.

The qualities of Gemeinschaft are much more frequently found in small towns and villages, and the qualities of Gesellschaft are especially prominent in large cities. To put it differently, a city is not a big village. The qualities of human relationships are different in communities which differ greatly in size. In a village it is possible to know all or nearly all the residents, to know them very well, and to know them for long periods of time, something that is impossible in the city. A person who seriously tried to convert all the transitory relationships of the city dweller into the intimate relationships possible in a hamlet might well go mad. The city dweller is constantly stimulated by contacts with people most of whom are strangers or nearly strangers. He *must* maintain substantial psychological distance from most of these people, and this condition is conducive to the formation of relationships on a fleeting, contractual basis. You do something for me and I'll do something for you—no more and no less.

Population Density Just as the sheer size of a community has important effects on social relationships, so does the density with which people are concentrated in a given land area. Consider this statement of Hauser (1963:4):

Let us consider the differences in potential social interaction in a community with a fixed land area but varying population density. Let the land area be that which lies within a circle with a ten-mile radius, namely, 314 square miles. In such an area the size of the population under different density conditions is shown below.

Population Density (Population per Square Mile)	Number of Persons Circle of Ten-mile Radius
1	314
50	15,700
8,000	2,512,000
17,000	5,338,000
25,000	7,850,000

The density of one person per square mile is not too far from the density of the United States when occupied by the Indians. The density of 50 is approximately that of the United States today, and also of the world as a whole. The density of 8,000, in round numbers, was that of central cities in metropolitan areas in 1950, the density figure of 17,000 was that of Chicago in 1950, and the 25,000 density figure that of New York.

An increase in community size is associated with an increase in population density. What happens when, as in the case of New York, a person moving about within a ten-mile radius has the potential for nearly eight million social contacts? One consequence is an intensification of the Gesellschaft qualities already noted for an increase in community size alone. Another is an increase in the competition for scarce land. Land values rise sharply; one consequence in the United States was the development of the skyscraper. There are also other effects, as yet imperfectly understood, of extremely high density upon human relationships. For instance, what does it do to the relations among people when whole families must live in one or two small rooms? In short, as the size of a community and the density of its population increase, important changes appear in social relationships.

DEPENDENCE OF VILLAGES UPON AGRICULTURE As we define the term, communities are thousands of years older than written history. The village accompanied man's invention of agriculture. Before that, except for fishing villages, the nomadic life imposed by hunting and food-gathering prevented the growth of settled communities. The village, particularly the agricultural village, is the kind of community in which most men have lived till very recent times (Greer, 1955:45). Thousands of years ago, the spreading success of village communities based on agriculture permitted the production of food surpluses which in turn made the development of cities possible in many parts of the world. As Greer says,

A city is a concentration of population in a space so small that it cannot produce its own necessities; instead, the city exports certain goods (military power, manufactures, credit, administrative order) and imports its food and raw materials from the open country, or hinterland. Such concentrations can therefore occur only when there are many agricultural villages, since it is upon the surplus production of the peasants that the urban population is supported (1955:46).

THE DEVELOPMENT OF CITIES

The earliest cities rose along the banks of the Euphrates and Nile rivers perhaps five thousand years ago. Somewhat later, important cities came into being at many points around the Mediterranean basin, in other parts of Europe and Africa, and in India and in China, long before the modern era. There were large urban centers in what are now Mexico, Central America, and Peru many centuries before Europeans arrived. When Cortez marched down the Valley of Mexico in 1519 to the Aztec capitol Tenochtitlan (now Mexico City) he found a city of some three hundred thousand inhabitants, five times the size of London at that time.

The earliest cities were small by modern standards. Estimates based on archeological evidence suggest that many had populations of five to fifteen thousand (Davis, 1955:431). The great Egyptian capitol of Thebes probably had fewer than a quarter of a million inhabitants at most (Davis, 1955:431). At its height, Athens had from one hundred twenty to one hundred eighty thousand and was about the size of Lincoln, Nebraska, today (Davis, 1955:432). Rome and Constantinople were by far the largest cities of the ancient world with several hundred thousand people each. After their decline no European cities approached their size until the nineteenth century. All the old cities of Europe were quite small through the long centuries. In 1377 London had only about 30,000 inhabitants (Davis, 1955:432).

RATE OF GROWTH Not only were the early cities small; they also contained tiny proportions of the total population, probably not more than one or two percent. They were isolated urban islands in lands which remained overwhelmingly agrarian. Then about one hundred seventy years ago urbanization really began to gather momentum as a result of a huge expansion of world trade and, a bit later, the industrial revolution. Trade increased the size of city hinterlands, especially those along major trade routes, and industrial growth quickened the demand for labor. At the same time the world's population began to grow rapidly. According to Matras (1973: 84–85), world population, estimated at 906 million in 1800, had increased to more than three and a half billion in 1970. This is rapid indeed, for it is an increase of 350 percent. But in the same period, cities of one hundred thousand or more increased

A surviving fragment of a Roman city at Sahbreta near Tripoli, Libya. While cities of all periods have some characteristics in common, such as crowding and intricate street patterns, those of ancient times were urban islands in an agrarian sea, a condition that no longer holds.

1370 percent (from 1.7 to 23.3 percent of world population in 1970).

One thing these figures tell us is that in the modern world cities have absorbed and provided livelihoods for much of the dramatic increase in world population. This is most true in the most industrialized parts of the world and much less true of the least industrialized parts. For instance, the proportion of people living in cities of one hundred thousand or more in 1970 was 57.6 percent in North America, but only 11.5 percent in Africa. On the other hand, recent rates of increase in urban population have been slowing down in older industrial nations. You may be surprised to know that in the United States the highest *rate* of urbanization occurred between 1861 and 1891. It is the industrially underdeveloped nations that have the highest rates of urbanization today.

Because cities concentrate large numbers of specialized and often culturally diverse people in small areas with high rates of social interaction, they have always been centers of innovation and change as well as seats of power. They are where the action is, where history is made. They have both shaped and expressed the most characteristic features of their societies.

CITIES IN THE UNITED STATES

In its brief history, the United States has been transformed from an almost completely agrarian society to one that is dominantly urban. This trend continues today. The first ten-year national census (provided for in the Constitution) was taken in 1790. In every succeeding decade the proportion of urban to total population has increased. Cold statistics testify to a profound and astonishingly rapid transformation whose ramifications touch every aspect of national life.

URBAN GROWTH   The figures in this section come from the federal census, a priceless repository of social bookkeeping. In order to understand them, one needs to know the definition of *urban* used by the Bureau of the Census. This agency applies the term to places having twenty-five hundred or more inhabitants, including densely settled fringe areas outside the legal boundaries of urban communities. Small definitional changes made in 1950 and 1960 slightly increased the proportion of the population regarded as urban. This effect is identified as "added by current urban definition" in Figure 5-1. The graph in Figure 5-1 records the growth of the American population beginning with the initial census in 1790, and distinguishes between rural and urban inhabitants. Notice that for many decades the *absolute size* of the rural population increased, though at a less rapid *rate* than the urban population. In other words, since the first census rural residents have constituted a declining proportion of the total. In 1790, 95 percent of the population was rural, but in 1970 it was only 26.5 percent. The trend is also evident for occupations. In the early nineteenth century about three out of four workers were employed in agriculture, but in 1972 only 3.6 percent were so employed. (See Chapter 8 for additional information on the occupations of Americans.) In 1790 New York was already the largest American city, yet had fewer than fifty thousand inhabitants. In 1970 there were 156 cities of one hundred thousand or more.

For most of our history, the rural-urban migration has been one of the main ways in which cities have grown; others are immigration from abroad and surplus of births over deaths. Rural-urban migration has now gone so far that there is little distance left for it to travel. "Families now remaining on farms are too few to contribute any major numbers of maturing youth to urban residence and nonagricultural occupations" (Taeuber, 1964:111–12).

SUBURBAN GROWTH   The statistics of urban growth are complicated by the fact that cities have increasingly expanded beyond their official boundaries. In most parts of the country the procedures for setting these boundaries are controlled by state legislatures; thus the statistics for central cities do not reflect total urban aggregation, since expanding suburbs are actually tied to the central city in many ways. Recognizing this distinction between the *legal entity* of the city and the *social reality* of the metropolitan community, the Bureau of the Census in recent decades has recorded data separately for the two.

The census term for the metropolitan community is "Standard Metropolitan Statistical Area," which we abbreviate to SMSA. An SMSA consists of a central city containing fifty thousand or more inhabitants together with the surrounding and contiguous area which is socially and economically integrated with the central city. In 1970, 243 such communities contained 68.6 percent of the population!

For several decades the urban population *outside* the central cities—that is, in the suburbs—has been increasing faster than the population of the central cities themselves. In 1970 the two figures were seventy-five million and sixty-four million. The movement to suburbia was so strong that by 1960 several large central cities had actually lost population while the SMSAs of which they were a part showed substantial increases. And this trend was accelerating, for by 1970, thirteen of the twenty-five largest central cities lost population. Detroit's population decreased by 10 percent, Pittsburgh's by 15.2 percent, Cleveland's by 15.6 percent, and St. Louis's by 19.0 percent. If data had been collected only for central cities, it would appear that the trend toward urbanization might soon be reversed. But the evidence for SMSAs makes it certain that this is definitely not occurring.

URBAN PHYSICAL STRUCTURE   We need to consider what else—besides growth—has been happening to cities, in order to gain deeper insight into the urbanization of America. Thus we shall consider urban structure. The activities of urban residents have

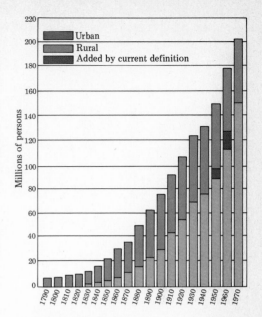

FIGURE 5-1   URBAN AND RURAL POPULATION: 1790 TO 1970

[Source: Irene B. Taeuber, "Population and Society," in R. E. L. Faris (Ed.), *Handbook of Modern Sociology*, © 1964 by Rand McNally and Company, Chicago, Figure 3, p. 110, "Urban and Rural Population: 1790 to 1960." Reprinted by permission of Rand McNally College Publishing Company. (Slightly revised and brought forward to 1970.)]

never been scattered randomly in the geographical space occupied by a city. The many differences among people, their interests, and their activities are reflected in urban spatial structure, the physical pattern of different but related parts. While a few American cities were planned in advance, far more do not represent the deliberate application of human intelligence to this problem. Most cities are visible products of impersonal economic and sociocultural forces.

The first large American cities appeared during the industrial revolution. These were quite different urban physical structures than those industrialized European cities which were already of good size when the industrial revolution began. The many similarities among American cities do not exist because they were decreed by some governmental body; they exist because of similar social forces operating in the same era.

There is a highly skilled profession called city planning, and most American cities have permanent planning bodies. Yet these are recent innovations which have not yet achieved a high level of control over current city structure, and which had no bearing on the long period before serious efforts at planning were begun.

Impact of the Railroad The use of steam power in transportation and manufacturing in the nineteenth century was an enormous stimulus to urbanism and to the shape of cities. Steam had one particularly significant characteristic for manufacturing: it was not an easily transportable source of power. Factories had to be built at or near the plants which produced the power, and while the railroad—the chief use of steam in transportation—was effective in linking communities, it did not further internal movement within cities.

As a result, new cities grew along railway lines or at their terminals and became highly compact in space. Most workers in the new factories had to live nearby; they had to get to work on foot or by horse-drawn vehicles. The stores and shops they used had to be crowded into the same areas, and only the more affluent people could sometimes afford to live further away. The situation, as Greer puts it (1961:632), "led to the construction of multi-storied factories and warehouses, row-houses without yards, and many-storied tenements and apartment houses. Railroad commutation, practical when stops are few and far between, made possible the commuter suburbs of the upper classes."

The pattern of high density in the central city with a lower concentration in a closely surrounding ring of suburbs was loosened somewhat by the electric streetcar. This effect was apparent at the margins of the community. More people could live further away from work. Trolley lines radiated outward from the center, and along them to the fringe the suburbs grew, like beads on a string. This faster and more flexible system also helped further to

The availability of water power for use in mills and factories was once important to the location of American cities. Steam power, including rail transportation, had a tremendous impact on urbanization in the early period of industrialization. Note, in the photo top right, the close proximity of residences and factories. Later, streetcars permitted a loosening of urban structure and the development of suburbs lying at some distance from the city center. The automobile brought an explosion outward of city structure with major traffic arteries making possible a radical decentralization both of residences and places of business. The last process has not yet run its course.

develop the urban center, since it was easy to get to and from downtown even as the city as a whole was rapidly growing. *As the city center became more crowded, competition for scarce space led to spectacular increases in land value and intensity of land use.* The skyscraper was the dramatic answer.

This powerful centralizing movement and the competition for favorable location at the center produced the characteristic form of American cities before the automobile. A vigorous school of urban sociology at the University of Chicago in the nineteen twenties explored and mapped this structure, using Chicago itself as their field of research, and drawing concepts from plant and animal ecology (Park, Burgess and McKenzie, 1925). Later studies found a similar pattern in many American cities. This work was an early and major contribution to human ecology, long before ecology in its broadest outlines became an area of general concern.

THE CONCENTRIC ZONAL STRUCTURE   Park and his colleagues described the structure of the city as a series of concentric zones surrounding the center (see *A* in Figure 5-2). In each zone is a similar type of land use. In the center is the business district, with retail stores, wholesalers, banks, hotels, theaters, newspapers, business offices, railroad stations, often warehouses and factories, and the hub of the city's transportation network. Each working day a tide of people sweeps into this central zone from outlying areas, and each evening it sweeps out again. A smaller tide rises in the evening as residents enter the district for entertainment. Only a few people, mostly transients in hotels, live there.

The next zone is the zone of transition. In order to grasp the special meaning of *transition* here, you must recall that these young industrial cities were constantly growing out from the center. As the intensity of land use in the central zone increased, the zone itself encroached on the surrounding area, once filled with the residences of working people. Hence around each urban center is a ring into which the business district is slowly moving.

Because of this anticipated movement, land values in the zone of transition are high and continually rising, even though the buildings there are old and decaying. Landowners will not replace them with new homes because they anticipate selling the land for different and more profitable uses. Yet by crowding many people into these old buildings, even at fairly low rents, and by investing as little as possible in repair and maintenance, the land can be made to turn a considerable profit while awaiting its transition to new uses connected with the central business district.

This is the classic pattern of growth for the American urban slum. The slums may include a number of ethnically or racially homogeneous areas which have come to be known as ghettos. Many of the ghettos in large cities have been inhabited by wave after ethnic wave, each new group replacing the old as the latter gradually improves its lot and moves to better areas farther out. Recently, with the slowing of immigration from abroad and the movement of American blacks out of the rural South into the cities, the ghettos have become predominantly black. Racial discrimination has made it much more difficult for these Americans to move out of the slums. Besides slums, the zone of transition contains warehouses, light industries, vice districts, and often an area of homeless, transient men called skid row.

Next comes the zone of workingmen's homes, with low to medium rents and prices. Here are aging single family residences and inexpensive apartment houses. Here immigrants fleeing the zone of transition often find their next homes. Distances to the center of the city are still short.

The next outer concentric ring, also residential, is mainly middle class. The proportions of single family residences and of home ownership are high. Apartment houses are of distinctly better quality. At its outer edges this zone merges into a commuter's zone; some of it is outside the corporate limits of the city. Land use is less intensive and more scattered. Originally, it was the home of the most affluent, who could afford the relatively high costs in time and money of living so far from the city center.

Since the whole city is expanding outward, all zones except the inmost are, in a way, zones of transition. If we project the pattern over a long enough period of time, it is clear that every zone is constantly moving out through the next one, and that the commuter's zone is pushing ever farther into the countryside. The concentric pattern of any particular city, however, should be seen as only an approximation. Sometimes it has been interrupted by natural features. Occasionally, because of strong local traditions, the character of an area remained unaltered far longer than the usual succession of changes would allow. Firey (1947) has shown how this factor operated in the preservation of an upper-class residential district in Boston called Beacon Hill.

THE SECTOR STRUCTURE The concentric picture of urban physical structure fitted American cities until the automobile; it brought major changes which led to other attempts to find patterns typical of large numbers of cities. Like the concentric, Hoyt's formulation (1939) recognized growth outward from a center, but saw it as taking place in *sectors* of similar land use (*B* in Figure 5-2). That is to say, high status residential areas often move outward to and beyond the margin of the city without leaving the sectors in which they originated. Low-rent districts also may extend all the way from the center to the periphery, moving out within the same axial lines, somewhat like a slice of pie. Hoyt dealt only with residential areas, using studies of residential rent distributions in 142 cities, which enabled him to offer considerable evidence for his generalizations.

Up to a point, Park, Hoyt, and other students of urban structure were all correct. Even today, evidence of both concentric rings and fanlike sectors can be seen in most American cities. A continuing problem in all efforts to find a *general pattern* is the constant change through which communities have been going. Even

A. Concentric Zone Theory
1. Central business district
2. Zone in transition
3. Zone of workingmen's homes
4. Residential zone
5. Commuter zone

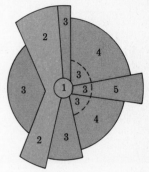

B. Sector Theory
1. Central business district
2. Wholesale, light manufacturing
3. Low-class residential
4. Medium-class residential
5. High-class residential

FIGURE 5-2 THEORIES OF URBAN GROWTH

[Sources: Concentric zone theory reprinted from Ernest W. Burgess, "The Growth of the City: An Introduction to a Research Project," in *The City*, by Robert E. Park, Ernest W. Burgess, and Roderick D. McKenzie (Chicago: University of Chicago Press, 1925). Introduction © 1967 by The University of Chicago. All rights reserved. Sector theory from Homer Hoyt, *The Structure and Growth of Residential Neighborhoods in American Cities* (Washington, D.C.: Federal Housing Administration, 1939); drawing reprinted from "The Nature of Cities" by Chauncy D. Harris and Edward L. Ullman in volume no. 242 of THE ANNALS of the American Academy of Political and Social Science. All rights reserved.]

Typical land uses by zone. Skyscrapers in the central zone show the intensive land utilization forced by very high land prices. Tenements in the transitional zone also occupy expensive land, but you wouldn't know it to look at the dilapidated structures. A bit further out, row houses are characteristic of the workingmen's zone. Then come middle-class homes and a high proportion of home ownership. Finally, farthest out from the center are the homes of the upper middle class and the wealthy.

as Park's Chicago group was mapping the concentric zones of the railway era, the city was reacting to the impact of the automobile. A city like Los Angeles, whose explosive growth came after the automobile era had begun, is structurally different from other large cities because it had not become large when steam was dominant.

In short, since they have grown during industrialization, American cities have never shown a stable and unchanging pattern. Yet streets and buildings are enduring enough so that many structural forms developed in an earlier era survive into a later one. New patterns are imposed on older ones already solidly in existence. We can see this whole process at work in the profound and continuing impact of the automobile.

AMERICAN CITIES IN THE AUTOMOBILE AGE   For a time, the speed and flexibility of transportation by private car increased the density of city centers even more, because it was possible to come into the central core from a larger surrounding area. But the auto was also the key in what became a powerful *decentralizing* trend. Not just the wealthy, but middle- and working-class families also could now live in the suburbs. Figure 5-3 on population distribution in three cities shows that in the thirties, auto transportation had already loosened the density of the *total* urban aggregation. The process has continued more strongly ever since. A larger and larger proportion of the total population resides farther and farther from the dense urban core.

The increasing use of electricity for industrial power made possible industrial parks in suburban areas. Highways were built *around* the cities and the traffic on these now is often as heavy as on the roads headed for the center. Huge shopping centers rise where roads moving toward the urban core intersect others which ring the city. An increasing proportion of Americans do most of their working, playing and shopping in these suburban subcenters. Many suburbanites seldom visit the central city to which they think of themselves as belonging.

CITY AND METROPOLITAN COMMUNITY   The distinction between city and SMSA is partly legal. A city's boundaries are geographically precise and set by law. It is a legal entity with taxing and other powers delegated to it by state legislatures. The boundaries of a metropolitan district, however, have no important legal recognition and are impossible to define exactly, since these boundaries can be determined by many possible criteria. Such criteria include the area within which most workers commute for employment to the central city, the area within which department stores deliver, and the areas served by wholesale establishments and utilities in the central city.

Such methods of delimiting the metropolitan community indicate that the SMSA *is* the modern American urban community. Though legally distinct, the city and the dependent area outside its borders are not sociologically distinct. The suburbs are linked to the central cities in many ways. Nevertheless the legal distinction has grave consequences for the total urban complex.

In some parts of the country the boundaries of metropolitan communities grow together and merge. The term *megalopolis* is sometimes applied to these supercommunities made up of strings or clusters of SMSAs, each with its central city. It is in such gigantic urban complexes that most future Americans are destined to live out their lives.

FIGURE 5-3 GROWTH OF THREE AMERICAN
CITIES

[Source: From *New City Patterns* by S. E. Sanders and A. J.
Rabuck © 1946 by Litton Educational Publishing. Reprinted by permission of Van Nostrand Reinhold Company.]

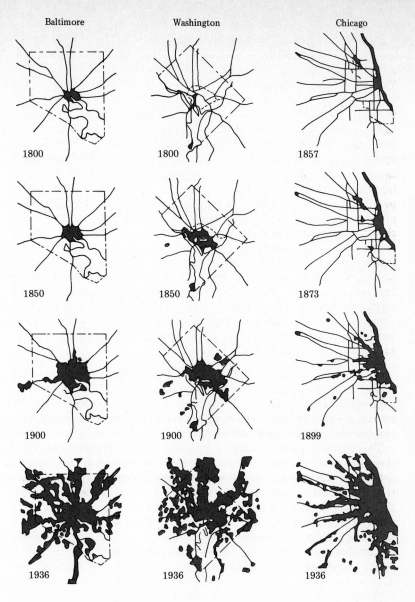

Baltimore — Washington — Chicago

1800 — 1800 — 1857

1850 — 1850 — 1873

1900 — 1900 — 1899

1936 — 1936 — 1936

THE COSTS OF URBAN
STRUCTURAL CHANGE

Many of our most serious problems, most resistant to solution,
arise from increasing urbanism, and not a few of these come from
the physical changes we have described.

URBAN TRANSPORTATION In American cities, the steam age produced a structure ill-adapted to the efficient circulation of people
and goods in the present auto-dominated period. Our central cities
are choking on their traffic. Public transportation struggles to sur-

vive at the moment when it most needs to expand. Buses, subways, streetcars, commuter trains, and other means (some only on the drawing boards) can carry more passengers with far less congestion and environmental pollution than private cars. Yet the latter continue to handle a larger and larger part of the load. People continue to prefer the relative speed and convenience of autos and scorn the deterioration of public transportation, which gets worse through their insistence on using their own cars. Traffic in central Philadelphia now moves at about the speed it did with horse-drawn vehicles. The problems of transportation become more urgent with each year. It is true that selfishness, stupidity, and lack of foresight have allowed the traffic problem to become worse than was necessary and have hindered efforts to improve it. But it is also true that we really did not have the means to foresee what the changing industrial and transportation technologies would do. The situation was novel in human history because the technology was novel. The interaction of technological innovations with existing social and cultural forces created a problem. Belatedly, we are beginning to focus our collective energies, intelligence, and resources on it. In 1970, Congress passed legislation setting up a ten-billion-dollar twelve-year program not only to rescue foundering mass transit programs but also to research and develop new ones.

THE FINANCIAL CRISIS OF THE CITIES Another problem arising from the legal separateness of the central city and its surrounding metropolitan area is that many people outside the city use its streets and municipal services, but are free, or nearly free, of the tax burden which makes these possible.

The problem is deepened by another trend. In recent decades, movement to the urban fringes outside the central cities has been especially high among relatively affluent Americans. This means that residents of central cities are, comparatively speaking, less able to bear urban costs than those who have left. The trend is especially visible with respect to race. As we show in Chapter 7, black Americans, because of systematic discrimination, are economically disadvantaged. And blacks make up a growing proportion of the population of central cities. Table 5-1, which shows the

TABLE 5-1 PROPORTIONS OF AMERICANS LIVING IN CENTRAL CITIES AND URBAN FRINGE AREAS, BY RACE, 1950–1970

		WHITE	NEGRO AND OTHER
1950	Central city	31.1	39.2
	Urban fringe	14.7	6.1
1960	Central city	30.0	50.5
	Urban fringe	22.8	8.4
1970	Central city	27.9	56.5
	Urban fringe	28.9	12.3

Source: Compiled from the Statistical Abstract of the United States, 1973, Table 16, p. 16.

proportions of all white and nonwhite Americans residing in central cities and in urban fringe areas over a twenty-year period, illustrates our point. Note especially the rapid growth in the proportion of whites residing outside central cities and the growth of nonwhites inside central cities.

The Agony of the Commuter

In retrospect, it is becoming clear that Doomsday for the American urban commuter—be he a shipping clerk on the Boston subway or a vice president sweating out a morning traffic snarl in St. Louis—is not so much an event as a state of being. Just this past year, portents of doom seemed to arrive with the morning mail. New York's once superior subway system, after thirty years of systematic neglect, succumbed in quick succession to a series of equipment breakdowns, power failures and frightening mid-tunnel stalls; in May, it suffered its first fatal crash in forty-two years. In the fiscal year ending in June, eight privately owned bus systems—in cities as disparate as Baltimore, Minneapolis–St. Paul, Salt Lake City and Santa Cruz, Calif.—just plain collapsed and had to be taken over by the cities, with Federal help. And suddenly last summer, the Penn Central Transportation Co., the largest railroad in the country and carrier of 140,000 commuters a day, turned bottom up and slid into the biggest bankruptcy in history.

The message is a hard one to miss. The Eastern Seaboard's increasingly tatterdemalion commuter system of public highways, private autos, capitalist railroads, semisocialist subways and buses can no longer handle the job of getting people to work and back. At the same time, the cities are learning to their distress that they cannot even keep the present subway and bus lines running without huge infusions of state and Federal money. In one of those frightening epiphanies not unlike the recent dawning of awareness of air and water pollution, the nation seems to be snapping awake to the danger that anyone who can't walk to work in the morning may just be too far away.

In most cases, even the attempt to get there is hateful. Traffic in central Philadelphia moves at 12 miles an hour, the same speed achieved by horsedrawn carriages 100 years ago. Commuters on Long Island, enraged by slave-ship crowding, lack of heat, air conditioning and plumbing, by no-show trains, maddening and unexplained delays and genuine physical danger from brokendown equipment, have banded into angry commuter groups whose members have sometimes elected to go to jail rather than pay the fare.

The urban transit mess is so bad, and the costs of long-term neglect are getting so huge and so obvious, that complex rescue operations have been forced on the reluctant Federal and state governments—and indirectly on industry.

Even the optimists—including President Nixon, who signed the pioneering mass-transit bill last October—do not believe that the crisis will get much better in less than five years. Expanding city boundaries and the flight to the suburbs have created millions of new commuters. Eighteen million persons ride the nation's mass transit each day, and perhaps 50 million more drive off to work in their cars, of which there are now 80 million (twice as many as in 1950) parked expectantly in and around the major cities. The explosion of people and vehicles is getting relentlessly worse. . . .

Nationwide, thirteen commuter lines have abandoned service since 1950. Buses have picked up some of the overflow, but the great majority of suburban jobholders now get to the city and back in their autos. Some 343,000 cars creep into downtown San Francisco every workday and 600,000 vehicles into Manhattan. About 160,000 autos a day crunch into downtown Boston, which has off-street parking spaces for 28,000. Strangulating to the city, poisonous to the atmosphere, offensive to the nervous sytem, ruinous to the billfold, the commuter automobile is a bright purple urban disaster—and naturally the cities have done everything they know how to encourage it.

Pushed by lobbyists, the cities in their ignorance have acquiesced—usually with enthusiasm—to state and Federal programs aimed at shooting superhighways into the heart of every urban center. This means draining off passengers from the railroads to pile more cars into cities that have no room for them, but the cities still cry drunkenly for ever stronger wine.

Source: Condensed from *Newsweek*, January 18, 1971. Copyright Newsweek Inc. 1971, reprinted by permission.

Caught between inadequate revenues and the demand for services, most large cities in the United States are in chronic financial crisis, and the situation worsens with the steady rise of material and labor costs. In recent years, unionization has made much progress among city employees such as policemen, firemen, teachers, and others; their steady pressures for improved pay and working conditions have deepened financial emergencies. In the winter of 1970–1971, New York faced the nightmare possibility of simultaneous strikes by its policemen, firemen, and sanitation workers. And in fact a wildcat strike of 80 percent of its uniformed policemen did take place. In 1970 a strike of Philadelphia's schoolteachers closed the schools for weeks and the Philadelphia AFL-CIO threatened to call a twenty-four-hour work stoppage of its 325,000 members. Quite apart from the merits involved in particular conflicts of this kind, city budgets continue to grow faster than city income.

It seems obvious that many aspects of the problem would be relieved if the legal boundaries of the central city and the standard metropolitan area were made to coincide. The entire urban community would then have a better tax base and greater freedom to enact policies in the interests of the whole complex. It may be obvious, but this course of action has so far been successfully evaded in most big urban communities. Suburbanites resist being absorbed by cities, and have found ready allies in state legislatures which, at least until recently, have been rurally dominated. Moreover, suburbs often fight even the piecemeal annexation of land by the city, which is the way boundaries are usually expanded.

In effect, suburbanites want to have their cake and eat it too. They wish to make their living in the city and use its facilities, but not pay a share of its taxes. The position is understandable, viewed from the standpoint of the citizen whose means are always less than he would like; from the standpoint of the overall problems of the larger community, their resistance has hindered the solution of some very difficult problems.

So great is the financial predicament of cities that they have turned increasingly to the federal government in recent years. Through a variety of programs having to do with welfare, crime control, transportation, Model Cities, and others, more and more federal dollars flowed to the cities until the budgetary cutbacks and reallocations announced by the national administration early in 1973. At no time has enough money been available to enable cities to remain financially solvent and to cope with their myriad social problems. Every year, some cities have to curtail or eliminate vital programs.

SLUMS AND SOCIAL COSTS   As we saw, slums are typically located in the zone of transition, immediately outside the core of the city, and are the historic place of settlement of immigrants. Yet despite crowding and the poor physical condition of the dwellings, not

Cities epitomize in intensified form not only the best but the worst characteristics of a society; the latter are suggested here: vice districts, maddening traffic jams, breakdown of city services, street crime. The people who work in the city use its streets and depend for protection on its police force and on other services, but many do not live in the city and therefore do not contribute to the financial costs of these services. How can the cities stay financially solvent under these conditions, which are becoming intolerably costly? Yet it is difficult to assign blame for these things; nobody wants them to exist. But who will assume responsibility for bringing these consequences of urban development under control?

all slum neighborhoods are socially demoralized. Over long periods, such areas sometimes retain great stability and social solidarity by almost any measure. Fried and Gleicher (1961) studied a largely Italian working-class slum in Boston and discovered that residential mobility within the area was very low and that 75 percent of the residents liked it as a place to live. People who lived in this slum were caught up in a myriad of social relationships beyond the family that tied them to the area and within which they experienced a valued sense of belonging.

One senses from such studies a warmer and more cohesive

neighborliness than is usual in middle-class neighborhoods. In the latter, the strongest identification is often with the dwelling itself rather than with the neighbors, and privacy is one of the values with which the dwelling is invested, for it protects one from others.

But these ethnic islands with their positive values do not tell the whole story of the slum. Little by little, sooner or later, most of the people we are talking about leave the slum. They may leave it when they can afford to do so, and this makes all the difference. It is another story for black Americans who now inhabit so many slum neighborhoods formerly occupied by European immigrants. Their economic situation has not shown the improvement enjoyed by others and they live with the knowledge that they are not welcome in the outlying areas populated by whites. For them, the slum is a prison from which there seems no escape. So it is hard for them to maintain a healthy and nurturant sense of community, and easy to fall victim to personal and social demoralization: to crime, drug addiction, alcoholism, family disorganization, and the rest.

Scattered in slum residential areas are many of the social outcasts from polite society and the business places of some forms of vice and disreputable entertainment: criminals, prostitutes, gambling establishments, drug pushers, pornographic movies and bookstores, the unemployed and the unemployable. These and their clientele and hangers-on exact a relatively high social cost in the form of police courts, crime rates, physical and mental disease, and other social ills. Yet it would be a mistake to think of such elements as the few bad apples in the barrel of society at large. Their goods and services are often purveyed to the respectable elements in the community. And their very presence reflects conflicts of values in the community, and its failure to provide the elements of a decent life for all.

SOCIETAL RESPONSE TO SLUM PROBLEMS Over much of this century the more fortunate segments of the community have often simply ignored the zone of transition when they could. It is harder to maintain this posture today because of the increasingly active efforts of slum dwellers, particularly blacks, Mexican Americans, and Puerto Ricans, to compel city dwellers to heed their complaints, and because of the escape of such activities as drug-peddling out of the slum into middle-class neighborhoods.

Insofar as city dwellers have noticed what happens in the zone of transition, their traditional response has been moral condemnation or a well-intentioned conviction that "something should be done to help these people." The latter reaction has at least a humanitarian impulse behind it. The "something" has taken such forms as missions which furnish simple religion and cheap food and lodging to transients, secondhand clothing stores for the poor, clinics to rescue alcoholics and drug addicts, and efforts to tear down the slums and replace them with more adequate dwellings.

Yesler Terrace in Seattle, one of the earliest low-rent public housing projects, is also one of the successful ones. This is how it looks today, a generation after it was built. Note that individual yards and gardens close to apartments are available.

Housing This approach is particularly interesting because, more than anything else, it has fascinated urban reformers for half a century. Basically this view assumes that bad housing creates bad citizens. If people were given better housing they would somehow metamorphose into good (usually meaning middle-class) citizens. On this assumption the federal government, beginning in the 1930s, began a long-range investment in public housing for low income groups, acting through local bodies called housing authorities. After World War II it expanded its efforts to fit the broader notion of urban renewal, in which slum areas were demolished but not always replaced by new residences.

The story of these programs is too long to tell here. The evidence of their effectiveness is incomplete and sometimes contradictory. Schorr (1963) systematically examined studies made over several decades, showed their cumulative significance, and considerably advanced our understanding of this whole matter. He was able to show that the basic assumption (that bad housing makes bad citizens, and vice versa) is an oversimplification. It is necessary to identify the specific aspects of housing, of people and of their behavior, as well as their relationships to other factors, in order to see just what the influences of housing are. And in most research this has not been done with care. Yet Schorr concludes that the effects of housing on human behavior have probably been understated rather than exaggerated. He summarizes the possible effects of poor housing as follows.

A perception of one's self that leads to pessimism and passivity, stress to which the individual cannot adapt, poor health, and a state of dissatisfaction; pleasure in company but not in solitude, cynicism about people and organizations; a high degree of sexual stimulation without legitimate outlet, and difficulty in household management and child rearing; and relationships that tend to spread out in the neighborhood rather than deeply into the family. Most of these effects, in turn, place obstacles in the path of improving one's financial circumstances (1963:20–21).

Schorr's analysis is persuasive, yet by itself does not let us determine the effects of the slum clearance and low-rent housing construction of the past few decades; in terms of the original oversimplified assumption about housing, the effects are mixed. Some housing facilities have been too expensive for the intended residents, who have had somehow to find homes in the remaining dilapidated tenements. All too often slum clearance programs seem to have resulted merely in the physical redistribution of the poorest, and of the socially undesirable activities found in the zone of transition. One reason for this opinion is implicit in this statement.

Like the supermarket in its locus, or the central business district in its locus, the slum provides on an appropriate site a set of services called out by, produced for, delivered to, and paid for by the self-same elite whose wives are likely to adorn with their names the letterheads of committees to wipe out or "clean up" the slum. Many of the services provided by the slum are not within the monetary reach of slum people: the bulk of the bootlegging, the call-girl services, a great part of what some feel able to call "vice," the greater part of the gambling, the whole set of connections that connect the underworld with the overworld serve the latter rather than the former, and are as much a response to effective (that is, money-backed) demand as is the price of a share of A.T.&T. or General Motors (Seeley, 1959).

Slum Problems as Reflection of Society's Problems Seeley's opinion is that if the physical location of such goods and services is turned over to some other use, they will merely be provided from another location. His view suggests that many features of the zone of transition are expressions of characteristics of the entire urban community, indeed of American society as a whole. Black ghettos are what they are because race is a still unresolved problem in our national life. To the extent that this is true, solution of slum problems awaits changes in the entire culture and social structure of which these problems are mainly symptomatic expressions.

The sociological perspective shows that it is not very useful to blame problems of the cities on a few "bad guys." Mainly they are the consequences of unplanned and unforeseen interaction of technological changes, deeply imbedded cultural values and norms, specialized vested interest groups seeking their own socially respectable or disreputable ends, and the land itself with its increasingly exploited resources. All these forces have been working simultaneously, in interdependence, often in competitive struggle for advantage. *So far as the whole urban community is concerned, nearly all this complex interaction has been blind.* Individuals, groups, and organizations have often moved purposefully and effectively *within* the complex pattern, seeking to reach private and specialized goals. But human intelligence did not set out to create the pattern.

Now, at this point in history, the problems of urban society have become so costly and so dangerous that man must seek control over what has, until now, been beyond his control. We are in the early years of an effort to deal with the *whole* community in the interest of *all* its inhabitants.

The Pruitt-Igoe project in St. Louis was razed by housing officials in 1974 because of increasing crime and deterioration. Its failure, perhaps partly due to its large, impersonal character, contrasts with the success of Seattle's Yesler Terrace.

So far we have spoken of American cities. There are both parallels and differences between these and the development of European urban centers, also in the early period of the industrial revolution. But cities have also been growing explosively during recent decades in the so-called developing countries, in Africa, Latin America, many parts of the Orient, and elsewhere. The total population of these areas is increasing rapidly, mainly because of dramatic declines in the death rate. But urban growth has also been sensational because of mass migrations from rural hinterlands. At present the most rapid rates of urbanization in the world are found in these regions. Some urban pop-

URBANIZATION IN DEVELOPING COUNTRIES

ulations are doubling or even tripling in a ten-year period. These are all countries to which the industrial revolution has only come lately, and as yet only partially, and all are economically poor. For these and other reasons typical of countries now developing, the course of urban development has been quite different than in either the United States or Europe.

McElrath (1968) has summarized the distinctive features of this new urbanization. First, remember that the movement of Americans off the farm into the cities was accompanied by a technological revolution in agriculture which still continues. Astonishing gains in productivity were accomplished with a declining agricultural labor force. The expansion of the industrial economy in the cities insured that the newly arriving workers would be employed. The urban demand for labor could also readily absorb the large numbers of immigrants from abroad. Although there was much frustration and exploitation, it remained true that in the famous melting pot the new urbanites, domestic and foreign, found conditions that encouraged severing ties with their former homes and ways of life, and their full and permanent incorporation into the cities.

The dilemma of urbanization in the developing countries is apparent in the contrast between the primitive building tools of the worker in the foreground of this picture and the sophisticated construction techniques being used for the elegant buildings in the background, designed by the French architect Le Corbusier for the capital of the Punjab in India. The natives who flock to the swollen cities of the underdeveloped countries find that there is no real economic place for them.

UNDEREMPLOYMENT IN THE CITIES In the new and the newly developing nations agricultural productivity is not increasing markedly. Peasants who leave the soil for the city are not surplus agricultural labor, and their presence in urban communities merely makes the total food supply of the society more perilous. In the cities they do not find a hungry labor market, and a large proportion encounter a life of underemployment and abysmal poverty without hope of improvement. The city is unable to absorb them and they congregate in countless thousands around its margins in abominable districts variously termed *barrachi, favelas, rancheros,* or *bidonvilles.* Public services scarcely exist. Filth, disease, crime, almost every sort of personal and social demoralization are rampant. As McElrath points out, this new urban migrant often returns briefly to his village; movement is in both directions.

These cities, then, are made up of migrants who are only segmentally and temporarily involved in the urban way of life. They are not only marginally employed in the city, but they are also marginal members of a new urban community. They are not yet urban men. For a long time these future urbanites will be oriented away from the cities, sometimes to a tribal village, often to a rural community which no longer exists, to a way of life which is being displaced by industrializing agriculture, by political and social transformations stemming from the city and only partially insulated from the daily rounds of life in the peasant communities. They will see the city with peasant eyes, unaware of the requirements of time, money, and urban skills; of compromises, of accommodation, of subtle gradations and organization, which the truly urban man knows so well that it is like the air he breathes (1968:6).

THE WORLD VIEW OF VILLAGES   It is very difficult for a citizen of this country even to imagine the ancient, parochial, tribal worlds from which so many of these people come. For even a glimpse of what they are like most of us must depend on the accounts of anthropologists and other sensitive travelers. For instance, in interviews with nomadic, camel-raising Beduins of Jordan, Lerner (1964) gives fascinating insights into their primitive states of minds.

We Beduin don't need the cinema. . . . Those who go are not real men. They are useless and have lost all value of morals. Movies spoil men. . . . Those who go get a very bad character and are no more men.

Those who read are politicans and trouble seekers. If you don't read you are far away from trouble and government.

The U.S. is a very far and cold country and they sleep all winter and have lots of ice. How many days walking distance is it from here?

All I need to know is here in this tribe and that is enough. . . . My business is only what happens in the tribe. Do you expect me to worry my head over what is going on outside our camp? We have enough news and activity here and we don't like to mingle it with the outside (1964:319–21).

People with such world views are entering the cities of the developing countries by the millions. They find an unbridgeable gulf between their lives and those of the wealthy and the relatively small middle classes. Is it any wonder that disorder, violence, and rebellion are never far below the surface?

What is the meaning of community in a world steadily becoming more urban, even if at different rates and in different ways? Early in this chapter we presented one definition of community (among many possible ones). We suggest that you read it again, now. It fits perfectly the agricultural villages in which so many men have lived over so much of the past. Of them Greer says,

Each person is dependent upon the village for his status, his access to production, his share of the surplus, his social and personal security, his place in the world. Such villages tend to be largely self-sufficient and the inhabitants are consequently dependent upon the village world . . . so many functions are served by the same group in isolation from outsiders that a rich and complete symbolic flow occurs, and a corresponding wealth of primary relations characterizes the social order (Greer, 1955:45).

But what is happening to this kind of community as we move into the urban age? And what does it do the quality of life now and in the future?

THE DECLINE OF COMMUNITY IN THE CITY   Our definition of community does not apply so neatly to modern cities. While a city is a social unit with interdependent parts, its inhabitants and many of its organizations depend as much on outside structures as on those within the city. Cities depend financially and otherwise on

THE DECLINE OF COMMUNITY

Communities

How shall we find a solid basis for and sense of community in the new urbanized world. Sitting with strangers on a park bench does not replace what the elderly once had in smaller communities—a sense of belonging to a group, whether family or neighborhood, by taking care of children, getting together with neighbors for conversation or projects, giving advice based on past experience.

state and national governments. Jobs and working conditions are influenced by national corporations, labor unions, government, and other nonlocal forces. One's only hope of exerting influence on such outside enterprises is through taking active part in them. There is little that people can do within their urban communities.

If a military base is closed down as a result of a change in national policy and thousands of local people are thrown out of work, the only recourse is to work through representatives in the national legislature. A decision to close the local plant of a large corporation is not made by local people nor is it made in the interests of the city which may lose thousands of jobs. A Chamber of Commerce which persuades a manufacturer to move his plant from one city to another must convince him that the move is in his economic interest. Meanwhile as one city gains, another loses, while neither controls the process.

Population Density and Diversity There are other ways in which the modern city weakens the kind of community discussed in our definition. Among them are the concentration of large numbers in small space, the sociocultural diversity in this dense mass of people, and high mobility within and between cities. Although a person shares citizenship and other kinds of interdependence with others in his city, he can know only a few of these others, nor does he want to know them. He hasn't the time for it. Many have ways of life he dislikes. And he is likely to feel no long-term investment in the neighborhood he lives in or even in the city as a whole. As he earns more (or less) he will move with little regret from one part of town to another, or leave the city for another hundreds or thousands of miles away in order to better his situation and circumstances.

So the sense of belonging, the sense that the city's fate is one's own fate, that for better or worse it is the scene of one's life, is weakened. In our definition of community, remember, the individual willingly, almost inevitably, identifies with a place which has all or most of the essentials of his life. It is more than a place. Because it provides the conditions for his total existence he responds to it with a rich and varied sense of belonging. Few Americans living in cities feel like this about their communities viewed as wholes.

Whether a city is or is not a community (by our definition) is not easy to determine. Population clusters vary in the degree to which they have the attributes of community. Modern cities are communities in a much weaker sense than those self-contained villages in which most of mankind lived for so long. So as societies are urbanized, communities in the traditional sense are less and less the setting for people's lives. Since more than two-thirds of all Americans now live in SMSAs you can see how far the process has already gone.

THE DECLINE OF COMMUNITY IN THE SMALL TOWN The real centers of power in the United States are mostly in large cities, which means that many crucial decisions affecting countless small communities are no longer made locally. Political and economic realities which loom large within a small town may be only a small part of a larger pattern shaped and controlled in a distant city. Wherever an American lives, he listens to the same radio programs, watches the same TV shows and movies, subscribes to the same mass circulation magazines. Even if he lives in a small town he is likely to subscribe to a city newspaper. Through such channels we are all exposed to the same advertising, values, and beliefs. The people who run the mass media are urbanites, and the values and lifestyles they espouse are urban. Even small communities become less community-like as they are drawn into the orbits of the cities.

Bogue (1955) uses the term *metropolitan dominance* in speaking of this spreading influence. In *The Eclipse of Community,* Stein (1960) shows the process at work in a village in upstate New York. Notice that the residents do not recognize the degree to which urbanism has penetrated their community and come to control it.

The singles bar depicted here (a very urban social invention) may provide opportunities for meeting large numbers of young people. However, it is not a viable replacement for the sense of community that young unmarrieds once had when they participated in neighborhood social activities, civic projects, cultural events, and church groups.

Small towners still cling to the traditional image of their community as a stronghold of opposition to urbanism. Indeed, this conviction forms the central theme in their self-image. Springdale takes great pride in its "neighborliness, equality, grass roots democracy and rugged independence." This favorable self-conception is juxtaposed against a counter-image of the big city as a place steeped in corruption and devoid of human values.

Research showed that this public image had very little relationship to social reality. . . . They (the sociologists) accumulated detailed evidence of the ways in which "metropolitan dominance" manifested itself in Springdale. Every aspect of local life depended upon adjustments to mass society. But these adjustments were rarely recognized as such by the people making them.

Some sociologists feel that the eclipse of community and the growing dependence on vast, centralized, impersonal structures (big business, big government, big labor) is one main cause of the widespread alienation and restlessness in contemporary America to which so many observers have testified.

Substantive values and traditional patterns are continually being discarded or elevated to fictional status whenever they threaten the pursuit of commodities or careers. Community ties become increasingly dispensable, finally extending even into the nuclear family, and we are forced to watch children dispensing with their parents at an ever earlier age in suburbia. The process seems to have two poles. On the one hand, individuals become increasingly dependent upon centralized authorities and agencies in all areas of life. On the other, personal loyalties decrease their range with the successive weakening of national ties, regional ties, community ties, neighborhood ties, family ties and finally, ties to a coherent image of one's self. These polar processes of heightened functional dependence and diminished loyalties appear in most sociological diagnoses of our time. However, we have only recently become aware of the full extent of human vulnerability and manipulability. We live in a period when the existentialist experience, the feeling of total "shipwreck," is no longer the exclusive prerogative of extraordinarily sensitive poets and philosophers. Instead, it has become the last shared experience, touching everyone in the whole society although only a few are able to express it effectively (Stein, 1960:329).

THE SEARCH FOR COMMUNITY IN AN URBAN WORLD   If this view is essentially correct, it gives us new insight into other phenomena in contemporary America which may be efforts to rediscover community in the modern setting.   Some such efforts are contrived and self-conscious. Apartment complexes and housing projects in many suburbs now boast community centers. These and the programs developed in them are supposed to convert the apartment cluster into a real community.

The very word *community* enjoys a special vogue these days. New hospitals are sometimes called community health centers. There are brave but wistful references to community spirit. At the very time when genuine community is declining, people use the word as if to bestow something of community upon enterprises that are not and cannot be genuine communities.

In a very different way, the hippie communes of the last decade or so express an urgent search for a new, more meaningful community life (Plumb:1968). It is as though the deeply alienated young people had lost all hope for mass society and were trying to create small societies of their own which are communities in almost as pure a sense as the old agricultural village.

Other manifestations of the search for community are more indirect. According to Nisbet (1960:575):

A great deal of the character of contemporary social action has come from the efforts of men to find in large scale organizations, especially political ones, those values of status and intellectual security which were formerly acquired in church, family, and neighborhood. How else can we explain the success of such movements in the modern world as Communism, Nazism except as mass movements designed to confer upon the individual some sense of that community which has been lost under the impact of modern social changes? The horror and tragedy are that such political movements have been based upon, and dedicated to, force and terror.

These words were written at the beginning of the turbulent sixties. Since then other examples, not all political, have appeared. Among these can be cited the movement for black power, the anti–Vietnam war movement, the movement on campuses for increased student power, the antipollution movement, and the women's liberation movement. In short, many contemporary social movements, in addition to their announced goals, also offer their adherents a sense of committed belonging, of sharing worthwhile things with others. This *bonus for participation* satisfies a deep human need which has increasingly been starved with the decay of community in the traditional sense. People in these causes may not be consciously seeking community, but it is an important by-product of their activities.

Need for New Forms One of the most urgent sociological needs of advanced industrialized societies is the development of new forms of community. This is easy to say. But there are no clear, unmistakable solutions to the problem. And indeed the problem is extraordinarily difficult. If community is to be retained in new forms, these forms must be able to survive in societies much like our own. Perhaps in the societies of the future, the element of place will be less important in the idea of community. Even today place is often irrelevant to groupings that have other attributes of community. In cities, one's network of friendships is seldom based on the immediate neighborhood but on other common interests; occupational and professional associations, religious groups, and many others maintain their identity with little reference to proximity.

We cannot assume that these are very good examples of community, or that they point the way to the future. But while some of them are absurd and even dangerous, there is hope in the fact that industrial man is seeking new ways to root his life. The need for some ground for the individual life is apparently so deep that people struggle for it even when they cannot name the search. In this there is a historic irony. At the very time when urban man desperately seeks some new community to replace the defunct agricultural village, technology forces on him an extended community size, not just beyond the village to the city or even the whole society, but beyond these to the community of the world. As Minar and Greer (1969:331) have said,

Community is then an aspect of the way men relate to one another, the primary dimension of human interaction, that aspect which goes far and away beyond the coerced and the necessary, the "functional requisites." Beginning in the experiences of children in the family, it moves outward to include neighborhood and peer group, congregation and collegium, the nation, and in some cases the human race. But it attenuates as we move further from the immediate; feeling and conception are replaced by principle and abstraction. There are limits to the possible inclusiveness of community.

It is almost certain that there are limits to the inclusiveness of community in all senses of the term. Yet the technological qualities of the emerging world seem to require that all men develop some sense of community toward mankind as a whole.

The theories and the research methods for collecting evidence developed by sociologists have relevance for practical programs aimed at the solution of many urban problems. But there are also

SOCIOLOGICAL APPLICATIONS TO URBAN PROBLEMS

City planners work at the cutting edge of urban growth and development, and they do so from the perspective of the community and its residents as a whole, not just from the point of view of certain elements in the community.

limitations to the uses of sociological knowledge in this area. Implicit in most of this chapter has been the view that many urban problems are so embedded in the nature of society that their final resolution requires significant changes in society's values and their organizational expressions. Further, as a group, sociologists couldn't achieve fundamental changes in society even if they wanted to. And they don't yet know enough about urban problems to furnish precise blueprints for programs of social action with guaranteed results.

Gans (1970), distinguished as a sociologist and a city planner, points out that quite a few American sociologists involved themselves in the social reform movements of the early 1900s, especially in the cities. Many of these reforms became well established in various social welfare and civic agencies. These began to develop their own professional personnel and programs. Volunteer workers, consultants and researchers—sociologists among them—then pretty much dropped out of the picture. Gans observes that workers in public health focused their efforts on medical clinics. Practitioners of the new field of social work relied on psychoanalytical casework techniques. Another new profession, city planning, stemming from architecture and engineering, saw control and alteration of the physical community as the main avenue to the good life.

Sociologists too were becoming professional, and were more and more concentrating in the colleges and universities. For several decades, all but a few lost touch with those occupations working at first hand with city problems. Recently, sociologists and other social scientists have again become interested in urban problems. And the applied professions have turned to the social sciences for help as they saw that their own approaches were not working well. The last decade has brought new programs and proposals, many supported by federal funds, aimed at breaking the vicious circle of lack of opportunity and aspiration which afflicts so many residents of the urban slum. Gans is critical of these new programs because they fail to escape the limitations of their familiar assumptions. He feels that they are characterized by

absence of a conceptual and theoretical framework about the nature of lower-class life and accompanying processes of social deprivation and disorganization. For example, most of the proposals do not seem to be aware of the concepts of class, social stratification, or social mobility. A theoretical framework is required to allow the formulators of action programs to move from an understanding of present conditions and their causes to the setting of goals and to the development of programs that will achieve these goals (Gans, 1970:924).

Gans feels there are four ways in which sociologists are equipped to render valuable help to the planning and caretaking professions in whose hands the new programs principally lie. They can provide a theoretical framework based on knowledge of the social realities in urban communities as a guide to planning. They can help in the subtle task of determining goals. They can and should help formulate programs. Finally, they are equipped to do research to evaluate programs and so provide a basis for improvement. We recommend that you read Gans's article to see his recommendations in detail. He firmly believes that sociologists now know enough to make valuable contributions to urban programs and strongly urges sociologists to participate in such programs.

Practicing the Sociological Perspective

The chances are good that you live in or near one of the 243 SMSAs in this country. If so, there are many ways in which you can become more sensitive to the problems of urban communities. It is a curious fact that urbanites live for years in their communities yet remain almost completely oblivious to some of their most striking features.

Your city almost certainly has a planning agency with a professionally trained staff. The chances are that this agency conducts its day-to-day business in relation to a comprehensive plan for the development of the city. This plan is intended to control change and growth in harmony with certain principles of good city planning. A planning commission or board holds meetings at regular intervals. Much of the business conducted at these meetings is the hearing of petitions from individuals and groups for *exceptions* to zoning and other ordinances intended to serve planning objectives. The professional staff does the background work needed by the lay members of the commission to guide their decisions and recommendations. The purpose of all this is to correct difficulties in the physical layout of the city and to foresee and forestall future problems. The planning agency acts in the interest of the whole community. *Such agencies exemplify what American cities have been able to do thus far to take deliberate control over their development.* As we said, planning agencies so far have had only partial success, but there is urgent need for more effective controls in the future.

Try to arrange an interview of about an hour with your chief city planner or a member of his staff. To conserve his time it would be wise to do this with other interested students. Ask him to talk to you about the greatest problems he is facing. Inquire about the comprehensive plan, how often it is updated and how well the city is adhering to it. He can probably show you a copy of this significant document. Ask him what additional tools the planning agency needs in order to do a better job. If possible, attend a meeting of the planning commission after talking with the planner. You will probably find that almost no citizens attend except those with an immediate vested interest in the decisions being made that day. Yet this body is making decisions affecting every resident of the city. What do you think of the arguments made by petitioners for departures from the existing rules? What is the role of the city planner in relation to the lay members of the planning board or commission and the petitioners? After these experiences, rethink what you have learned about the need for intelligent planning and the relative absence of it.

It would be interesting to locate a person who had lived for some years in an ethnic ghetto in the zone of transition. Ask him why he moved. Does his answer suggest the typical pattern in which the physical move outward also reflects social mobility upward? What about those who because of race are blocked from this traditional social and physical movement? Can you begin to see how easily such a group, locked into poverty and hopelessness, can become bitter or defeated? Ask your informant whether there is anything he misses about life in the slum. If he now lives in a middle-class neighborhood, does he find it cold and unfriendly?

Secure a map which shows the legal boundaries of your city. Then walk or drive along several segments of this boundary. Can you tell by looking where the city ends? Along two or three axes radiating outward from the center of town, drive past the boundaries until the visible city finally unravels and disappears. You may have gone miles beyond the official city limits without ever leaving the real, sociological community. These outer areas are now occupied by former residents of the inner city. They do not pay city taxes and they don't want to, but they depend on many services paid for by city residents.

Talk to one or more officials at city hall and inquire about the financial health of the city. On what basis are taxes collected, and how equitable is the distribution of this load? Ask about typical land prices in the central business district, the zone of transition, and outer suburban areas. You may be surprised to find that the value of land in slum districts is substantially higher than in middle- and upper-class residential districts in the suburbs. How can that be? What happened to your city and SMSA according to the 1970 census? Did the central city grow at all? What about the growth rate of the urban area outside the central city?

Get in touch with the League of Women Voters in your nearest city. It is a predominantly middle-class national organization with local chapters and is concerned with problems of government at all levels. You are likely to find that it is one of the very few groups of lay citizens seriously working to improve local government with no special interests other than the community as a whole. How well informed on urban problems are the members of this group? What do they see as the most important problems locally? Perhaps they can use your help in one of their current projects.

Other questions will amost certainly occur to you. You will find that few people have anything like an adequate understanding of what is really happening in our cities, and not many care much about matters that go even a little way beyond their own personal concerns. Such ignorance and indifference may be calamitous. What will you do about it?

Part 2 / Social Units and Processes

Social Stratification

6

For centuries there have been people who dreamed, hoped, and even worked for a human society in which all would be equal. It is obvious, however, that human beings are *not* all equal in size, strength, intelligence, or in anything else that can be measured. Nor are they equal in intangibles such as happiness, character, and goodness. The plain fact is that people are *un*equal—and that the inequalities among them are more than accidental. Moreover, inequalities in some of the most important attributes are socially structured, not only in the United States but everywhere.

Some form and degree of structured social inequality is an aspect of organization in all social systems, large or small. For this reason, almost every chapter in this book touches on the topic in one way or another. Thus in Chapter 4 on microsociology, we analyzed ranking behavior in small, face-to-face groups. In Chapter 9, authority is seen as one of the principal bases on which complex organizations are differentiated. In Chapter 12, we will see that the distribution of authority among the members of a family is important in its organization.

By stratification we mean the ranking of individuals and social units (persons, activities, roles, groups, organizations, and so forth) in a way which implies superiority and inferiority. There would be general agreement for example that, as an *individual,* a Mr. John Connally (once Secretary of the Treasury in President Nixon's Cabinet) has higher social rank than a Mr. Herb Nelson who manages a small supermarket. Likewise, the *role* of physician ranks higher than that of bulldozer operator. As an *organization,* the United States Senate is accorded higher rank than the city council of Butte, Montana.

When a considerable number of people have about the same location in a stratified order we speak of a stratum. *A stratum is a cluster of people who share a pervasive subculture and common life experiences which are distinguishable from those of other strata which rank higher or lower in power, wealth, prestige, and lifestyle.* In relation to communities and whole societies, the most important kind of stratum by far is *social class.* Following some observations on the importance of stratification we shall undertake a sociological analysis of this important aspect of social behavior.

SOME CONSEQUENCES OF STRATIFICATION

For the individual, particularly in a society like that of the United States, the social stratum into which he is born, and perhaps that to which he aspires, can have profound and far-reaching consequences in practically every aspect of life.

LIFE AND HEALTH Stratification affects the medical treatment that people receive. Hollingshead and Redlich (1958) found that persons at lower levels are likely to be hospitalized longer than persons at higher levels, and those in the highest stratum receive considerably more outpatient treatment. In a study of midtown Manhattan, Srole and his associates (1962) found that about 70 percent of impaired persons in the upper stratum were either receiving care or had received care at one time, while only 1 percent of persons in the lower stratum were receiving care and another 20 percent had at one time received care. And treatment tends to be more successful in the middle and upper than in the lower stratum.

There is evidence that people in lower strata feel sick oftener than those in higher strata, but are more reluctant to consult a physician, visit doctors less often, and are more fearful of disease. Although the rate of exposure to disease is probably much the same, lower-class people are slower to seek medical aid, and so tend to have longer and more serious illnesses and a higher death rate (Kadushin, 1964). From an exhaustive survey of thirty studies in several Western countries over a long period, Antonovsky (1967) concluded that one's place in the system affects one's chances of staying alive. He reports that the death rate for all age groups in 1950 was highest for laborers. In the United States, the infant death rate in the lowest stratum is shockingly high, sometimes twice the national average.

Emotional as well as physical well-being is influenced by one's position. Faris and Dunham (1939) found that the highest rates of admission into Chicago's psychiatric hospitals came from the lower socioeconomic strata. Some twenty years later, Hollings-

The accident of birth determines our first and sometimes permanent location in the stratification system. This fact has immense consequences for every individual. If life is thought of as a race, it is a very unequal one. Some runners start with an advantage they did not earn, others with an equally unearned disadvantage. Furthermore, for most, these inequalities are maintained to the very end of the contest.

head and Redlich (1958) obtained data from clinics, private physicians, and hospitals in New Haven that generally corroborated these findings. These data, of course, are for persons who received medical treatment; they show nothing of how the total amount of emotional illness is actually distributed in any given population. But a survey made in New York City by Srole et al. (1962) does give some information on this broader question. Through intensive interviews, Srole and his colleagues learned that nearly four times as many persons in the lowest stratum were impaired by psychiatric symptoms as in the highest. The relationship between mental health and stratification is not restricted to urban areas. Leighton and his colleagues (1959) studied a rural county of maritime Canada and found that neurosis was more prevalent in the lower than in the middle and upper classes. The accident of birth has a powerful effect on vital statistics.

JUSTICE UNDER THE LAW All Americans are legally entitled to equal justice, but they do not in fact receive equal justice. Criminologists have noted that the probability of being arrested varies inversely with one's position in the stratification system. Persons at the bottom are more liable to arrest than persons in the middle and at the top. This is true despite the fact that differences between strata in the *occurrence* of criminal behavior are not as great as arrest figures would suggest. Inequality continues in the bail system, which favors the influential and the well-to-do. Indeed, our present bail system is a clear and flagrant example of discrimination against persons with low incomes. This fact, plus crowded court calendars and legal delays, result in long and unpleasant terms in jail for low-income defendants, while those of higher status remain free to carry on life much as usual. After an individual has been convicted, he has the right of appeal. But appeals are costly, and the poor and powerless cannot afford them. If an appeal is lost there is always, eventually, the possibility of parole or probation. Here too the middle and upper strata have the advantage, for the conditions of parole and probation include employment and a conventional environment.

A dramatic effect of stratum on social justice occurs in capital crimes. A group at the Stanford University Law School studied 238 separate juries, isolating two hundred factors which might influence a jury's decision. Their major conclusion was that blue-collar workers in California stand a greater chance of being sentenced to death than white-collar workers.

VALUES, BELIEFS, AND BEHAVIOR Stratification systems are not made up of clear-cut layers with fixed boundaries and totally separate ideologies. But there do appear to be values, beliefs, and attitudes recognizably associated with different social strata. For example, Stouffer's study *Communism, Conformity and Civil Liberties* (1955) revealed that in the United States over six times as many college graduates with high-status white-collar jobs held tolerant political attitudes as did persons with only a grade school education and a low-status manual occupation. Lipset (1960) holds that a type of working-class conservatism and authoritarianism can be found in a variety of countries. He further states that on economic issues such as social security the poor are more liberal or leftist, but on issues of civil liberties and internationalism are more intolerant.

One of the most comprehensive discussions of the relationship of social strata to values and orientations is *Class and Conformity* by Melvin L. Kohn (1969). This book is based on three studies, one of Washington, D.C., one of Turin, Italy, and the third of the United States as a whole. According to Kohn, persons in the lower strata are the ones most likely to think they are—and in fact to be—subject to forces and people beyond their control and comprehension. This condition promotes compliance to authority, narrow-mindedness about dissent and nonconformity, wariness of other people, and rigid adherence to rules and regulations. Yet the feeling that one is subject to forces and people beyond one's control is pretty realistic when one is indeed near the bottom of the heap in power and prestige.

STRATIFICATION AND MINORITIES   American minorities will be discussed at length in the next chapter. But their association with social strata is so striking in the United States that we must mention the matter here. In 1972, the median income of white American families was $11,500, but the median income for nonwhite families in the same year was $6,900. In 1972, the unemployment rate was 5.0 percent for white Americans and 10.0 percent for nonwhite Americans. While blacks constitute the largest racial minority in the United States it should not be supposed that they are the only such group suffering economic deprivation. This can be shown from census data on the proportions of persons whose income is below the poverty level (as calculated from an index developed in 1969 by a federal interagency committee). Among citizens of English, Scottish, and Welsh descent, for instance, only 8.6 percent had incomes below the poverty level in 1970; this proportion was typical of European groups. But in the same year 29.2 percent of Puerto Ricans, and 28 percent of Mexicans, had incomes below the poverty level. And among blacks, 25.9 percent in metropolitan areas and 51.6 percent living elsewhere had poverty incomes, while the comparable figures for whites were 8.0 and 13.2 percent.

The same relationship between minorities and stratification exists among the more fortunate in society. Lundberg in *The Rich and the Super-Rich* (1968) shows that few of the ninety thousand plus American millionaries in 1968 were black, Mexican, Oriental, Indian, or Catholic. A study of *Who's Who in America* and *The Social Register* (Baltzell, 1953) suggests the same thing. One of the most definitive studies of national and international leaders, by Keller (1963), bears directly on this point. She discovered that most of the persons she called strategic elites (persons whose judgments, decisions, and actions have determinable consequences for all or most members of society—such as leading militarists, scientists, and statesmen) were white, male, native-born of British or Northwest European descent, and of the Protestant (especially Presbyterian and Episcopalian) faiths.

TV's popular Archie Bunker is a fictional character, but—by design—he portrays some of the attitudes reported by Lipset and Kohn in their researches.

THE BASES OF SOCIAL STRATIFICATION

Since some kind of stratification is universal, it might appear that we could take the fact for granted and with no explanation needed. After all, we don't spend much time trying to understand why human beings have only one head! But there are many kinds and degrees of stratification. What accounts for these differences? Again, there are a number of fairly obvious sources of inequality among men, but this does not tell us the contribution of each source to the production of a particular kind of prestige ranking.

For example, from Aristotle on there have been those who sought to explain social inequality as a direct consequence of biological differences: those in the uppermost stratum of society are there because they are biologically superior while those at the bottom are ordained by nature to be there. This view has an obvious appeal to conservatively oriented people, for it justifies the status quo in the distribution of the world's goods. Unfortunately for the biological explanation, while physical characteristics do play a role in the achievement potential of individuals, they fail utterly to account for the wide variations in social stratification that actually exist. The evidence on this point is convincing. Take a condition like mental retardation, for example. To the extent that it is hereditary and an important cause of low social status we would expect to find it concentrated in the lower classes, but this is not the case.

If we judge theories by their influence on history, Karl Marx's explanation of the basis for social inequality is by far the most important, since he is the revered intellectual godfather of modern communism. For him, social classes are based on the distribution of control over the means of economic production. Those who control these means exploit those who do not. History is a record of struggle between classes, and this struggle is a precondition to progress. Marx believed that the outcome of the battle between classes is inevitable; it will end in the overthrow of capitalist orders by the proletariat, the abolition of private ownership of the means of production, and the disappearance of classes.

Earlier in this century an important German sociologist, Max Weber, set forth some ideas on the topic of stratification. "For Weber as for Marx, the basic condition of class lay in the unequal distribution of economic power and hence the unequal distribution of opportunity. But for Weber this economic determination did not exhaust the conditions of group formation" (Bendix, 1960:105).

He spoke of a status order in society which is based on prestige and a shared style of life. Upper-level examples would be the nobility of feudal Europe and the old families in American cities. There is much overlap between the class system and the status order, but the two are not identical. For instance, wealth does not automatically insure acceptance in the highest social circles in the United States and persons who have little money occasionally have high social prestige—the impoverished-aristocrat phenomenon. In this concept of status order Weber broadened Marx's explanation of the basis for social stratification and came closer to contemporary sociological theories, to which we now turn.

If we simply ask why stratification exists at all (disregarding the causes of its different forms), a broad sociological answer would say that stratification arises out of the *differentiation* of society into dissimilar parts, and the inevitable evaluation of these parts which accompanies differentiation. Differentiation is inherent in the nature of human societies. In even the simplest, there is considerable division of labor and a differentiation of roles. The tasks of defense, of food production, of child-rearing, and all the rest entail different skills. If they are to be done there must be some agreement as to who does what. Since some tasks are viewed as more vital than others, it follows that some activities will be more highly valued than others. Insofar as an activity is associated with a person or category of persons as well as a valuation, the person or category will come to be valued accordingly. In the American system, for example, the tasks of a judge are valued more highly than those of a housewife. So persons in the role of judge will have higher prestige and rank than those in the role of housewife. We turn now to two important and more specific explanations of stratification.

FUNCTIONALIST THEORY The functionalist position on social inequality is distilled in the following statement by one of its principal advocates (Davis, 1949:367). "Social inequality is . . . an unconsciously evolved device by which societies insure that the most important positions are conscientiously filled by the most qualified persons." Since some tasks require more ability or are more difficult than others, the most competent individuals have to be motivated to assume these, and society motivates such individuals by giving them greater rewards. The size of the rewards will therefore vary with the functional importance and difficulty of the tasks contained in roles; the more important and difficult the task, the greater the reward.

The number of competent persons available at any given time also affects the size of the rewards. For example, the roles of physician and attorney are complex and difficult. Hence physicians and attorneys receive high incomes relative to many other occupations. But in comparison to demand, there is a smaller supply of physicians than of attorneys; hence, physicians receive higher incomes on the average than attorneys do.

For the functionalists, stratification persists because of the functional requirements of the total society, not because of the problems and needs of individuals. Differences in stratification from one society to another arise out of differences in the details of their functional requirements. Thus American society contains thousands of occupations for which persons must be recruited, and an elaborate differentiation of rewards is needed to get an efficient distribution of people into these many occupational niches (see Chapter 8). In a hunting and food-gathering society, the occupational basis of stratification is very much simpler.

The functionalist view, which we have necessarily treated briefly, has had a good deal of influence in modern sociology. It stems from and is consistent with a somewhat conservative tradition. From this position one might argue that whatever system of stratification exists is the best possible one for that place and time, since it is manifestly serving the principal functions of stratification as seen by these theorists. In all fairness, we should point out that some developments of the functional theory of social inequality have opened up adjustments to this interpretation and shown that functionalism is not incompatible with change in stratification systems.

CONFLICT THEORY   The conflict theory of social inequality is allied with a more radical tradition. For such writers as Mills (1956) and Dahrendorf (1959) stratification is a result of the struggles of individuals and groups that are unequal in the amount of power at their disposal. Those with the most power hold the most favored positions, and so on. For instance, in the division of the earnings of American industry, functionalist theorists would emphasize the comparative scarcity and importance of the contributions of different parts of the work force and of the owners as the principal factor in determining income distribution. Conflict theorists, on the other hand, would stress the power struggle involving owners, managers, and organized labor. Lenski (1966:16–17) neatly summarizes the main distinctions:

> Conflict theorists, as their name suggests, see social inequality as arising out of the struggle for valued goods and services in short supply. Where the functionalists emphasize the common interests shared by the members of a society, conflict theorists emphasize the interests which divide. Where functionalists stress the common advantages which accrue from social relationships, conflict theorists emphasize the element of domination and exploitation. Where functionalists emphasize consensus as the basis of social unity, conflict theorists emphasize coercion. Where functionalists see human societies as social systems, conflict theorists see them as stages on which struggles for power and privilege take place.

A THEORETICAL SYNTHESIS   In the history of ideas it sometimes happens that out of the clash of competing views grows a synthesis more adequate than any of the original notions. This process is now taking place in sociological accounts of stratification. Ossowski (1963) was among the chief contributors to this synthesis, and Lenski's formulation (1966) reflects the functionalist and conflict orientations but makes an advance beyond both.

Cooperative Distribution Lenski's theory is essentially an answer to the question of who gets what in society and why. In other words, he is concerned with what may be called the *distributive process,* about which he makes two fundamental assumptions. First, "men will share the product of their labors to the extent required to insure the survival and continued productivity of those others whose actions are necessary or beneficial to themselves" (1966:44). This proposition is logically deducible from the assumption that some degree of cooperation in performing differentiated tasks is essential to the survival of both the individual and society. Here Lenski draws on functionalist theory, using its valid insight that all societies not only divide the work of the world, but that this division requires cooperation in main-

Among the Eskimos, hunting is essential to survival, not a form of recreation. Since theirs is a society without significant surpluses, according to Lenski's theory the spoils of the hunt portrayed here will be divided essentially on the basis of need. Power will have comparatively little to do with who gets what. In wealthy countries, power determines the distribution of surpluses.

Part 2 / Social Units and Processes

taining coordination of the differentiated parts. He is saying that men cooperate enough to permit the continued performance of differentiated tasks essential to personal and social survival.

Power Distribution A second proposition is introduced to account for the distribution of surpluses, that is, goods and services beyond what is needed to keep individuals and groups functioning. The second proposition is "that power will determine the distribution of nearly all the surplus possessed by a society" (1966:44). Power, incidentally, entails the capacity of one individual or group to compel others to behave in desired ways, even against their will. The exercise of power does not always involve open coercion, but the possibility of coercion is there, to be used if necessary.

Notice the words *nearly all* in the second proposition. Lenski concedes that altruistic motives will account for distribution of a minor portion of a society's surpluses. In 1971, for example, private philanthropy in the United States contributed funds to various causes totaling more than 21 billion dollars (*Statistical Abstract of the United States*). For Lenski, the distribution of prestige in a society is mainly determined by the distribution of power. As he says, "Empirical evidence strongly suggests that prestige is largely, though not solely, a function of power and privilege, at least in those societies where there is a substantial surplus" (1966:45).

This second proposition is derived from conflict theory. Together the two propositions exemplify Lenski's synthesis. From the base they provide he derives a number of hypotheses of which we will mention only two: "In the simplest societies, or those which are technologically most primitive, the goods and services available will be distributed wholly, or largely, on the basis of need. . . . As a second hypothesis we are led to predict that with technological advance, an increasing proportion of the goods and services available to a society will be distributed on the basis of power" (1966:46). Lenski examines the adequacy of his propositions (and hypotheses derived from them) in a wide variety of societies. At the end of the process he finds that the main components of his theory have received substantial support, though in need of revision in some particulars.

We do not suggest that Lenski's work completes the development of sociological stratification theory. Without question many modifications and developments lie ahead. But for the moment, it resolves what had seemed an unproductive impasse between functionalist and conflict interpretations. Notice that his theory (as presented here) does not deal specifically with strata including classes. Instead, it concentrates on the distributive process as a whole in total societies. Classes are aggregations of persons who share about the same amount of power and therefore prestige in a particular society. Whether they are more than this—

whether, for example, class consciousness is an important attribute of classes—is not dealt with directly in Lenski's approach.

ANALYZING AMERICAN STRATIFICATION

We are now in a position to see how sociological stratification theory sheds light on the situation in the United States. We shall focus on four interdependent factors: power, income, prestige, and style of life. Lenski would hold that the distribution of income and prestige is determined by the distribution of power in a country such as the United States, which has large surpluses of income compared with most. The relationship is not just one way, however, for there are feedback effects as well. For instance, an increase in a person's prestige may act to increase his resources of of power. And lifestyle may be seen as an expression of power, prestige, and income.

THE DISTRIBUTION OF POWER   It is difficult to say much about distribution of power in the United States in a few sentences. Tracing out the strands of power in the society as a whole presents formidable difficulties. Sociologists who have treated the subject disagree sharply with one another, because there is not enough empirical evidence to allow a clear-cut choice between interpretations. There are many fine studies of organizations and communities which encompass the power dimension, but none of the United States as a single social system. In these circumstances we shall merely introduce two contrasting views on power distribution in this country. We cannot resolve the disagreement between them on the basis of existing evidence which meets scientific standards.

One point of view, associated particularly with Mills (1956), has appealed strongly to those who are radical in social philosophy. The other, which can be illustrated by the work of Riesman (1953) among others, has a stronger appeal to those who think of themselves as liberals. Kornhauser (1966) has usefully analyzed the distinctions between these two propositions.

Power Elite   Mills believes that there is a large concentration of power in the hands of a power elite. This is a relatively small number of persons in government, industry, and the military who have common and interlocking interests. The power elite is able to control all important public policies, domestic and foreign. Kornhauser summarizes Mills's view:

By virtue of similar social origins (old-family, upperclass background), religious affiliations (Episcopal and Presbyterian), education (Ivy League college or military academy), and the like, those who head up the major institutions share codes and values as well as material interests. This makes for easy communication, especially when many of these people already know one another, or at least know many people in common. They share a common way of life, and therefore, possess both the will and the opportunity to integrate their lines of action as representatives of key institutions (1966:213).

Essentially, Mills would argue that since power is concentrated at the top, only relatively small amounts of it trickle down to lower levels where the consequences of major decisions are merely administered or where there may be struggles between groups, none of which has much power anyway. At the bottom of the power pyramid are the great bulk of the population who have no real power at all.

Power Pluralism Riesman simply does not believe that a power elite exists in the United States. Instead (quoting Kornhauser, 1966:211), he holds that there is

a diversified and balanced plurality of interest groups, each of which is primarily concerned with protecting its own jurisdiction by blocking actions of other groups which seem to threaten that jurisdiction. There is no decisive ruling group here, but rather an amorphous structure of power centering in the interplay among interest groups.
The question of who exercises power varies with the issue at stake; most groups are inoperative on most issues, and all groups are operative primarily on those issues which vitally impinge on their central interests. This is to say that there are as many power structures as there are different spheres of policy.

For Mills, there is a single power structure for the entire society, highly concentrated at the top. For Riesman, there are many power structures, no one of them dominant for very long and all of them in competition with one another as their interests conflict. In Riesman's view, the great masses of people at the bottom of the power pyramid are courted by various interest groups as allies in their conflicts with one another, rather than being dominated or exploited by a tightly cohesive group at the top of the power structure.

Aron (1966) also believes that in most Western states power is distributed among competing interest groups rather than concentrated in the hands of a small, ruling elite. He contends that "the characteristic trait of the oligarchy, within Western societies, is not the hidden power of a group of men (the heads of industry or of the army); rather it is the absence of a common will, of a common conception among the power strata who fight each other according to the rules of the democratic polity" (1966:209). He feels, however, that a sense of powerlessness which is (allegedly) engendered by these societies among ordinary citizens is expressed in myths about power elites. Here is a concise statement of his position.

Even though the leading power centers treat each other as enemies and the State is not held by a resolute minority aware of a mission, the masses will not feel the exaltation of freedom; on the contrary, they will imagine a mysterious elite which in the shadows is weaving the threads of their destiny; a few must be all powerful, if so many millions of men are powerless (1966:209).

In short, Aron appears to view the concept of a power elite as a kind of collective paranoia.

Our comments don't do justice to the fully developed views of these men, but we have gone far enough to show how much they disagree, and all three are writing about the same time period! So much disagreement is possible only because of the scarcity of critical evidence which would permit us to choose rationally between two views—or, more likely, to evolve an interpretation which would improve on both.

INCOME   In contrast to the difficulties encountered in describing power distribution in the United States, the essential facts about income distribution are readily available.   United States Census Bureau figures for 1970 show that median income was $9,867.   Of all families, 19.3 percent received incomes of $5,000 or less; 31.7 percent received incomes of from $5,000 to $10,000; 26.8 percent had incomes ranging from $10,000 to $15,000; and 22.3 percent received $15,000 or more.

Because inflation has rapidly changed the value of the dollar in recent years, these figures are not particularly revealing.   More helpful is Table 6-1 (also from the census) which gives the percentages of total private income received by each fifth of American families, and unrelated individuals, and the most affluent 5 percent.   The table shows that the bottom fifth of the population gets less than one-twentieth of the income, while the top fifth gets almost half, and the top twentieth almost one-fifth!

Reading across the table from 1950 to 1970 (a period of high prosperity) shows some improvement in the distribution of income, but it is minute compared to the massive general imbalance.   Note that the most affluent 20 percent of the population received close to eight times as much income as the least affluent 20 percent in 1970.   In fact, the highest 5 percent of the population in 1970 had an aggregate income that was two and a half times as great as the least affluent 20 percent.

TABLE 6-1   PERCENT OF AGGREGATE INCOME RECEIVED BY EACH FIFTH AND TOP 5 PERCENT OF FAMILIES: 1950 TO 1970

ITEM AND INCOME RANK	1950	1955	1960	1963	1967	1968	1969	1970
Families	100.0	100.0	100.0	100.0	100.0	100.0	100.0	100.0
Lowest fifth	4.5	4.8	4.9	5.3	5.4	5.7	5.6	5.5
Second fifth	12.0	12.2	12.0	12.1	12.2	12.4	12.3	12.0
Middle fifth	17.4	17.7	17.6	17.7	17.5	17.7	17.6	17.4
Fourth fifth	23.5	23.7	23.6	23.7	23.7	23.7	23.5	23.5
Highest fifth	42.6	41.6	42.0	41.3	41.2	40.6	41.0	41.6
Top 5 percent	17.0	16.8	16.8	15.8	15.3	14.0	14.7	14.4

Source: U.S. Bureau of the Census, *Current Population Reports*, series P-60, No. 80, and unpublished data.

Part 2 / Social Units and Processes

You may find it surprising that in 1970, a prosperous year in the richest country in the world, 12.6 percent of all Americans, about 26 million people, were living below poverty income levels. The poor are invisible to many readers of this book, because many will not have visited Indian reservations, certain remote rural areas, inner city ghettos, and places like Appalachia.

On the other hand, many will not have known anyone who is very rich. How many of the following names do you recognize: J. Paul Getty, Howard Hughes, H. L. Hunt, Dr. Edwin H. Land, Daniel K. Ludwig, Ailsa Mellon Bruce, Paul Mellon, Richard King Mellon? Each of these persons is worth from one-half to one and one-half billion dollars (*Fortune*, 1968). Only a handful of Americans command such fantastic sums of money. And the number of people with less astronomical but still large incomes also constitutes a very small proportion of the population. Only one-half of one percent of Americans are millionaires. In 1968, roughly 153 of them were worth one hundred million dollars or more.

Income and Power If Lenski's position as we outlined it is correct, income distribution should be closely associated with power. In other words, the amount of money one makes would be a rough indicator of the amount of power he commanded. We suspect that Mills would regard the data we have just presented as supporting his contention that the country is ruled by a power elite. Riesman, on the other hand, would probably feel that the connection between income and power (in a system made up of many competing power hierarchies) is not really very close. He could remind us that a university president or a high government official may wield considerable power while receiving an income which is modest by comparison with those of many persons in private industry—and, on the other hand, that some individuals of great wealth have little or no interest in wielding power.

PRESTIGE Power and income do not lend themselves as readily to a discussion of classes as aggregates of persons forming recognizable strata. Not enough is known to be sure whether we may speak of the stratification of power in any realistic sense. Income is continuously variable from top to bottom. It does not fall into neatly definable strata except by quite arbitrary statistical designations. Prestige, however, can be more directly treated in relation to a sociological conception of class. If classes exist in the United States, people will recognize the fact and be able to place individuals with some significant agreement. Further, where several classes exist, each will have its characteristic level of prestige.

Recognition of Classes Over the past generation there have been many studies of the distribution of Americans into prestige strata, mostly in towns and small cities. Some have used local persons as

Compare the town portrayed on the sign with the actual scene below. Advertising usually perpetuates the myth of an America in which everyone is prosperous and happy. In actual fact, the distribution of income is quite unequal in this country.

A part of Hamlet, North Carolina, in the Appalachian Mountains; the photo on the right was taken on the San Juan Indian reservation in New Mexico. Unless you have had personal experience of such settings, it may be hard to realize that one out of eight Americans really lives in poverty.

judges of prestige, asking them to assign other residents to class levels. Other studies have asked local people to assign themselves to class levels. A well-known example of the first type is by Warner and associates (1949), and of the second type by Centers (1949). There is considerable agreement between the two, despite the difference in method. A little more than half (53 to 58 percent) of those rated were classified as lower (or working) class, from 38 to 44 percent as middle class, and 3 to 4 percent as upper class.

This whole body of research supports the idea that Americans do recognize classes as differentiated strata, each with a typical prestige level as distinguished from higher or lower classes. We would caution, however, against assuming that Americans are divided into classes in the precise percentages the figures in the previous paragraph would seem to suggest. *All* methods for determining class membership (and there are others) are subject to criticism on one ground or another; *no* method can do the job as acceptably for all sociologists.

Defining and Measuring Class Some of the difficulties are technical, involving the suitability of techniques or research designs. Others arise from lack of clarity about the nature of social class. Finally, American society itself makes the job difficult. However class is defined, we can be sure the lines between strata in the United States are blurred. They may vary with the criteria used, and from one setting to another. For instance, the number and characteristics of classes in a small midwestern city may differ considerably from those in a large eastern metropolis, or in the nation as a whole.

The general tendency has been to construct multiple indices of class level, based on several indicators (Hodges, 1964:78–101). Such an index might include income, occupation, education, self-defined class membership, and kinds of organizations to which a person belongs. All these criteria, and others, are related to class level. Multiple indices are preferred because no single indicator serves in a society where class membership, while real and important, is not rigidly determined.

STYLE OF LIFE Loosely defined and fluid as they are, American social classes unmistakably reflect broad differences in mode of life. For the sociologist, style of life is an ambiguous concept, hard to define because it includes so many things, both obvious and subtle. We can make the concept clearer by describing some of these things, though there are so many of them that we can only suggest their great variety.

The ambiguity and the importance of the concept have made it particularly suitable to the technique of the novelist. As Hodges pointed out (1964:131), "Few have contrasted lower-middle- and upper-middle-class so well as Sinclair Lewis in *Babbitt* and *Main Street,* or middle- and upper-class so trenchantly as John P.

Marquand in *Point of No Return*." And these authors only sample the list of American novelists who have been attracted to the class theme. At the same time, sociologists too have made notable contributions to our understanding of class-linked styles of life.

Standards of Consumption One indicator of lifestyle is standard of consumption, attractive to social analysts because its components are easy to identify. In the United States, however, it is a tricky index for several reasons. For instance, swings in fashion are so rapid that an item which is highly fashionable today may quickly move beyond the pale. No one possession serves permanently as a quick easy label which says to all, "this is the class to which I belong." Mass production and advertising tend to cancel out the real status-increasing properties of any particular article as distinguished from those advertised. So what might at first seem to be easily identifiable class differences in consumption are more likely to be "subtle variations on a theme rather than differences in the themes themselves" (Barber, 1957:140).

Yet there are differences in consumption which matter. Studies of the buying habits of the American poor document some of the less obvious kinds of impoverishment in lifestyle. Poor people often have to buy necessities at once (when the welfare check arrives) and are unable to take advantage of sales. They are less able to shop for best buys. They are less able to afford insurance for repairs on major appliances. They are less able to buy in bulk, and enjoy the attendant savings, for they usually have cash only for immediate necessities. They often pay more in interest charges, since debts must be paid over longer periods. It isn't lower income alone which encumbers the poor. For them a given amount of income just doesn't go as far as it does for the more affluent.

At the opposite end of the scale, the Christmas catalog of an old and famous jewelry firm contained the following advertisement for husbands and suitors of "hopelessly romantic" women: "We'll fly you to Paris, just for dinner, just for two. We'll take care of all the delicious details to see to it your gift is in the proper place the moment you want to present it—right in the middle of her favorite hors d'oeuvre." The gift is an octagon-shaped diamond ring, perched atop a mound of Romanoff caviar, and the price is $69,950. An apex of opulence appears in the same catalog a few pages later. The gift is a sixteen-carat pink diamond which can be "secreted in her luncheon coconut" after a safari to Tiger Tops Hotel at the base of Mount Everest in Nepal. The price tag: $325,000.

Residence, Education, and Religion Some other class-linked variations in style of life are reported by Hodges (1964:130–71). Residential areas are class-related in communities of all sizes. Between the extremes of wealth and poverty are subtle gradations

Tennis has traditionally been an upper-level sport, but it is rapidly percolating downward in the stratification order.

recognized by local residents. The same is true for house furnishings, though sorting out class implications is a complex task, judging by the efforts that have been made. In spite of the numbers who now go to college, a degree still signals middle-class attainment and is also associated with many indicators of class level. Religious preference is class linked. Certain Protestant denominations, particularly the Presbyterian, Episcopalian, Unitarian, and Congregational (now United Church of Christ) churches have had large numbers of upper- and upper-middle-class members. Baptists, Lutherans, Methodists, Catholics, and fundamentalist sects have had large numbers of lower-middle- and working-class members.

Leisure Activities   The higher the social class, the less likely are persons to watch television, and class differences extend to the types of programs preferred. Plays, discussion programs, and news programs are favored by upper-middle-class viewers, while westerns are preferred by blue-collar audiences. The reading of books is closely associated with class. The higher the class the more likely that books of any kind will be read, and that they will be nonfiction. Do-it-yourself activities in crafts and home improvement are more a lower- than a middle-class enterprise.

Sports in America are related to class. At the upper levels people are more likely to participate than to watch. And when they do watch, they are more likely to watch different sports. Thus polo, tennis, and yacht racing have for obvious reasons long been associated with the upper classes, and hockey, baseball, football, bowling, and basketball with the middle and lower. Golf, long a sport for the rich and well-to-do, has become more widely popular through the increasing number of public courses, and recently as a spectator sport on television. Skiing and pleasure boating are other examples of sports once confined to the affluent which have percolated downward in the stratified order in recent years.

Our discussion of lifestyles can be only the merest sketch. But we have said enough to suggest strongly that there are broad class subcultures. These overlap and mingle at many points, to be sure. Their specific elements undergo rapid change. Yet sociologists find that to be a member of a particular class is to have one's whole social and personal experience affected in obvious and subtle ways by the pervasive presence of class subcultures.

SOCIAL MOBILITY—A DYNAMIC ASPECT OF STRATIFICATION

Social mobility refers to the fact that the location of a person within a society can change. The reference is to social, not physical or geographical, location. Since a feature of societies is hierarchical arrangement, we may speak also of *vertical mobility, which denotes movement upward or downward from one stratum to another.* Thus when a person acquires more power, income, and prestige, and makes appropriate changes in style of life, he is said to be upwardly mobile, and vice versa.

Amount of social mobility can be observed both within a generation and between generations. To assess the first, note the mobility implications of job changes made within a lifetime. Are successive jobs higher or lower in income and prestige, or is there no change? To find mobility between generations, compare the jobs or other positions held by sons with those held by their fathers.

Interest in social mobility runs high in this success-oriented country. Yet there are some popular but mistaken notions about social mobility in the United States which have been corrected by sociological research. One common myth is that America is an open society with the highest social mobility in the world. It is widely believed that any American, given the ability and motivation, can move from a log cabin or cold water walk-up tenement to the White House. This has happened only rarely in our history. While vertical mobility is comparatively high in the United States, several countries which do not have our open class ideology have comparable rates of social mobility. Lipset and Bendix (1960) surveyed rates and patterns of social mobility in different countries and found that rates for total vertical mobility both up and down ranged between 27 and 31 percent for the United States, Germany, Sweden, Japan, and France.

There is another misconception about whether opportunities for movement have increased or decreased. Some observers have held that opportunities have steadily expanded since frontier days, while others claim that American society has become more and more rigid. Bernard Barber (1957:431) in a comprehensive survey rejects both views. He concludes that comparative studies of mobility in the nineteenth, early twentieth, and mid-twentieth centuries in the United States show neither a decrease nor an increase. There appears to have been no basic change in vertical mobility in the past hundred years.

Since some other industrialized countries have comparable rates and there has been no recent change in the United States, what does the American mobility picture really look like? Several studies using occupation as an index of where the individual stands in the stratified order suggest the following conclusions: (a) sons are more likely to follow their fathers' work than any other; (b) much of our mobility tends to be horizontal, that is, sons move in different occupations but in about the same social stratum; and (c) most vertical movement is to an adjacent level (Blau and Duncan, 1967:95—105).

How difficult is it to enter the highest reaches of American society? Many studies (among them Warner and Abegglen, 1955; Miller, 1949; Newcomer, 1955) strongly indicate that it is far easier to inherit an elite position than it is to achieve it in one's own lifetime.

In a society where people believe in and hope for upward mobility, advertising has available a powerful theme. Perhaps one can raise one's status by serving "The Rich Man's Scotch"!

CONDITIONS CONDUCIVE TO SOCIAL MOBILITY   The amount of vertical social mobility in a society results from the combined effects of many factors, some encouraging mobility, others discouraging it. Lipset and Zetterberg (1956) identify some of the favorable factors. The absence of any of these would be unfavorable to social mobility.

They state that considerable upward mobility results from an enlargment of the proportion of professional, managerial, and white-collar positions when accompanied by a decrease in unskilled workers. This is just what has happened in the United States in the last half century. Historically, persons in the upper and middle strata have fewer children than persons in the lower strata. This fact, coupled with the occupational trend just mentioned, creates a situation whereby children of lower-ranked parents can move into newly created middle and upper positions.

Marriage is another avenue for social mobility, both up and down. If mate selection is not tightly restricted by family background, and it is not in the United States, it is likely to produce some vertical mobility. Educational opportunities and attainment are also associated with occupational success. Greater social mobility is likely to result when educational opportunities are available to everyone. The historical trend in this country has been toward increased equalization of educational opportunity (a matter discussed more fully in Chapter 13). Finally, it is highly unlikely that social mobility can take place unless individuals are motivated to aspire to higher position.

THE PROSPECT FOR FUTURE MOBILITY   In recent American history the factors mentioned by Lipset and Zetterberg have been mostly favorable to a high rate of social mobility, but in the future these particular conditions may well lose some of their force. Ultimately, the occupational trend of recent decades must come to an end, if only because not everyone can be in professional, managerial, and white-collar occupations. At that point, occupation will become a less vital factor in determining one's position in the stratification order than it has been thus far. There is also scattered evidence that birth rate differentials between classes are declining. If we assume that in time there will be no class differences in fertility and combine this with a cessation of the occupational trend, we have a condition in which upper-level people have enough children to fill all upper-level positions and almost none are available for upwardly mobile individuals from lower levels. In these circumstances, motivation to achieve higher position might well decline and marriages might be contracted on the basis of equal class position more than is now the case.

Thus we face the sobering possibility that traditional American mobility between strata may well decline in the future. The prospect seems likely when we look only at the factors identified by Lipset and Zetterberg. We do not predict this outcome with confidence, though, because additional factors—some not known at present—could enter the picture and change the outcome. Freely available unsettled land on the American frontier was once a powerful factor conducive to upward mobility. Toward the end of the nineteenth century the frontier disappeared and it might have been predicted then that American classes would become much more closed. That didn't happen, in substantial part because the occupational changes mentioned by Lipset and Zetterberg were just appearing. We can't assume that other new factors will not play a part in the reasonably near future.

The growing body of evidence about stratification and social classes in the United States lends considerable support to existing theory about such matters and tells us a good deal about the forms they take in technically advanced societies. But much remains to be done before these theories can be taken as adequate and detailed accounts of stratification phenomena.

One aspect of stratification which still needs to be explored is what is known as *consistency*. Any individual or group can be ranked on various criteria, such as power, income, prestige, style of life, and so on, and all these rankings contribute to overall status. A person whose rankings are uniformly high, low, or medium is said to be *status-consistent*, whereas a person who ranks high on some things and low on others is said to be *status-inconsistent*. Thus it is not infrequent in our society that a person of high income and power ranks low in education and style of life.

STATUS INCONSISTENCY AND STRESS   Jackson (1962:469–70) cites studies suggesting "that status inconsistents labor under a variety of difficulties: unsatisfactory social relationships, unstable self-images, rewards out of line with aspirations, and social ambiguity." Social ambiguity here refers to an individual's uncertainty about how his relations with others should be conducted. Jackson himself studied the relationship between status inconsistency and psychosomatic symptoms of stress, for example, sleeplessness, nervousness, dizziness, shortness of breath. He found that psychosomatic symptoms were high (a) for persons whose racial-ethnic rank was higher than their educational or occupational rank, (b) for males whose occupational rank was higher than their educational rank, and (c) for females whose educational rank was superior to their husbands' occupational rank (1962). Jackson (1962), Lenski (1967) and others have found that some persons with inconsistent status respond by politically active liberalism. Jackson found this to be a likely outcome in persons who had *achieved* high status in one sphere but were *assigned* by society to low status in another area.

The various studies of effects on the individual of status inconsistency all suggest in one way or another that this condition is psychologically disturbing. The particular symptoms of the disturb-

The ability to pay for this elaborate gangland funeral does not mean that the deceased person ranked high in other measures of status. The wealth of gangsters was one indicator of high status and was displayed on such occasions as this. But the money was not enough to buy acceptance, let alone high status in other respects.

ance vary a good deal with the particular kind of status inconsistency and with psychological differences among people. One's location in any important rank ordering of individuals has implications for the role he will play in relation to others and for his own image of himself. As Jackson says, "An individual's rank on a status dimension controls, in part, his expectations of others, his expectations of himself, and others' expectations of him" (1962:470). A person with high rank in one area and low rank in another is put into a situation of conflict, both externally and internally. Some degree of stress is inherent in any such situation.

Anyone who is status-inconsistent faces a rather complex range of possible strategies in his dealings with others, and he also confronts uncertainties in the responses of others. Should he try to maintain relations with others on the basis of his highest status? This will probably be resented by those whose rank is lower than his. On the other hand, he will probably find it unacceptable to behave everywhere in terms of his lowest status. He may, however, try to use his highest ranking as a lever to raise his ranking in other areas and thus approach status consistency. It seems likely that many people use a kind of averaged-out assessment of their inconsistent ranks as a basis for behavior.

It is probable that in slowly changing societies, status consistency is high. It is certain that in rapidly changing complex societies status inconsistency is common, particularly when there is a great deal of vertical mobility. While most persons enjoy substantially consistent ranks in the various departments of their lives, many do not. Wealth sometimes comes to persons with few other status qualifications. It may take years for the newly rich to become consistent, and it may not happen until the next generation. Often people who have moved up fast bring mannerisms, beliefs and other lifestyle components of a very different past with them.

THE NEED FOR KNOWLEDGE ABOUT STRATIFICATION

We believe that some familiarity with the sociological study of stratification can make a real contribution to one's understanding of his own and other societies. It can also help in the development of one's social philosophy. Some degree of stratification is intrinsic to all human societies; this is a basic fact of social life. One may wish for a society in which distinctions of rank are forever abolished, but wishing will not make it so.

To recognize the inevitability of stratification and to get some grasp of how it operates does not require accepting a particular stratification system in one's society as necessary and morally right. We have not been presenting a thinly veiled argument for the status quo. We wish to stress this point because occasionally sociologists who describe how things are at the moment are accused of arguing that they must or should stay that way.

Take the situation in the United States. Much important information about stratification has been gathered by sociologists and others. But it is possible to be well informed about this system yet think it disgraceful that 12.6 percent of the people in the richest country in human history are still poor. The United States has and will continue to have social stratification, but it need no longer have poor. Educational opportunities and health care are fairly widespread in America; yet in the light of democratic values, these things are still unfairly distributed among the different classes of citizens. There is nothing in the sociology of stratification which argues that educational and health facilities cannot be equally available to all. It is not possible to have a human society without stratification. It is possible to have a society in which the essentials and many of the amenities of life are not denied to anyone.

KNOWLEDGE AND PRACTICAL PROGRAMS This book is written in an era of unusually intense criticism of some aspects of American society. Many of the criticisms are directed at features of our national life which are closely linked to stratification. We have witnessed in the last few years a considerable number of private and governmental attempts to cope with such matters as the plight of minority groups and the poor in general. Sociological knowledge has useful work to do in suggesting and trying out programs to make real progress possible. It is a sociological insight, for example, which is skeptical of programs for helping the poor which are wholly conceived and administered by people who are not themselves poor and do not know the life of the poor at first hand. As Beck (1970) has pointed out, too many programs aimed at poverty are couched in terms of *we* the respectable ones doing something for *them* the disgraced and dispossessed.

It is not true that answers to the problems of stratification are lying about just waiting to be used. As in so much of sociology, we do not know as much as we should. And not all problems of stratification are even amenable to a sociological approach. Other disciplines—economics, law—have vital tools and insights. But we feel confident that if the American people really want to solve some of these problems, the existing knowledge in sociology and other disciplines could move us faster than we are going now.

Practicing the Sociological Perspective

The problem with stratification is making visible something ordinarily concealed from view; it is not simply an unfamiliarity with the sociological perspective. American ideology makes recognition of the facts about stratification distasteful. It isn't so much that Americans don't sense that we are a stratified society, but that finding the fact distasteful we would rather not think or talk about it. It is easier to take refuge in comforting myths: "Everyone gets pretty much what he deserves in this country," "There are no classes in America," or "Anyone can get to the top if he's willing to work hard enough."

Here is a short list of simple suggestions for learning how to take a clear look at one form of social reality. If you will do these things, others will come to you. First, see if you can arrange this little experiment. It will require the cooperation of a friend; call him A. Introduce A to B just as you would ordinarily introduce one friend to another. After a few moments of conversation quietly drop the comment to B that A is a cousin of the President of the United States or some other high-ranking person. Watch carefully to see if you can detect and identify any changes in B's manner toward A. Then reflect: A has not changed in any way since the offering of this fictitious information. What accounts for the change in B's behavior?

Think about the style of life of your own family. Apart from the income level which makes it possible, ask yourself where this particular style of life originated? You can be quite sure that it did not originate in any really fundamental sense with your parents. Then where did it come from? Can you see the stratification implications of this example? Your perception will be sharpened if you can do the same thing for some other family you know that has a very different style of life.

If you have access to a community with several high schools, find out from the central office of the school district what proportion of graduates from each high school enters college. Ask yourself what accounts for the difference. It would be revealing if you could visit classes in primary or high schools in very different kinds of districts and observe behavioral differences in the children. The question would be the same: how did these differences come into being?

Sensitize yourself to signs of deference. For one full day observe every contact you see between two or more people. What you are looking for is evidence, explicit or subtle, that one person or persons show deference to others. The signs may range from the use of names or titles to subtle changes in facial expression or tone of voice. Such behavior is a recognition of differences in prestige. You will be surprised at how much behavior of this kind you see. After you have learned to recognize it, you can elaborate the exercise by watching for behavior which expresses superior status. Finally, watch for evidence that the need to express deference is resented. These signs are likely to be disguised, but if you are an acute observer you can often find them in ordinary communication between people. Not all deference behavior is evidence of stratification, although all of it is evidence of rank differentiation in the broadest sense. See if you can find an example of deference which clearly does reflect stratification into social classes.

Part 2 / Social Units and Processes

Think of some matter which concerns a large number of people in your college or university, and ask yourself how the power to affect decisions on this matter is actually distributed in the campus community. If you can give a close answer to this question, you will have identified one of the bases of any system of stratification, including that on your campus. If you care to push this example further, you might consider if in this campus community power is the sole basis of stratification, or if income, prestige, and style of life also play a part.

These suggestions will not make you an expert on social stratification, and we have no wish to oversensitize you. But learning to observe such phenomena in a sociological way will, as with so many other branches of the discipline, serve as a corrective to misconceptions and consequent mistakes in judgment. Merely to recognize that some trait in another person comes primarily from his place in the stratification system and is not some quirk of body or mind can be very helpful in relating constructively to that person.

7 Minorities

The United States has shown racial, ethnic, and religious diversity for generations, and it has had accompanying problems for an equal length of time. There is nothing new to us about minorities. What is new is that black Americans, native Americans (Indians), Mexican Americans (Chicanos), Puerto Ricans, and other minorities are pushing hard for social justice, where once they suffered in silence. The marches, demonstrations, boycotts, sit-ins and outbreaks that have filled the news in recent years have made Americans very sensitive to the whole subject. In the past, the unequal treatment of minorities was buttressed by social forms and traditions which let more fortunate Americans conveniently ignore this ugly aspect of our national life. No longer is this so. Our minorities demand equality and they refuse to be ignored.

Sociology can make a major contribution to an understanding of this whole troubled area. It can help to put current events in a perspective which avoids emotional extremes.

DEFINING MINORITIES   In current usage the word *minority* is pretty ambiguous. What we need is a clear definition that also contains the meaning which is central to sociological analysis. *The American Heritage Dictionary* gives this definition first: "The smaller in number of two groups forming a whole: a group of persons or things numbering less than half of a total." Certainly this is clear. One determines a minority simply by counting. But this definition makes no reference to other meanings of the word, as in "minorities don't get a fair shake in this country."

The American Heritage Dictionary comes somewhat closer to this meaning in its second definition: "A racial, religious, political, national, or other group regarded as different from the larger group of which it is part." This statement retains the notion of smaller numerical size, and recognizes other differences. It does not, however, make any suggestions about the consequences of such differences. For example, black Americans are a minority by this definition since there are fewer of them than white Americans, and skin color is recognized as a difference between the two. But American males are also a minority by this definition, for there are slightly fewer males than females in this country.

Our purpose is not to play with words, but to suggest that in defining minority we must be careful to do so in a way which will permit us to focus the sociological perspective most usefully on the problem at hand. Thus, *a minority is a category of people who, on the basis of one or more characteristics which are difficult or impossible to conceal or eliminate, are discriminated against by others who possess greater social power*.

This statement is carefully drawn to reflect sociology's special approach (as distinguished from other valid approaches), and its full implications may not be immediately clear. For one thing, it makes no mention of numerical minority. Like the second dictionary definition, it mentions other defining characteristics, but it does not name them. And it does state (as the dictionary only implies) that they are difficult or impossible to conceal or eliminate. Finally, our definition names two factors the dictionary does not: systematic discrimination and a differential in social power.

While most cases which would meet our definition of minority are smaller than the comparable elements in the total population of which they are a part, we do not regard this as a critical characteristic. In fact, given our definition, it would be desirable to use some other word altogether so as to minimize the factor of numerical size. We have not done this only because the word *minority* has become so deeply embedded in sociological literature that it would be more confusing than helpful to use another term.

IDENTIFYING CHARACTERISTICS While it is true that most minorities have racial, religious, political, or national characteristics which help to identify them, we prefer not to include the particular characteristics in the definition itself. Hypothetically, at least, almost any characteristic could enter into the identification of a minority. People who are short (or tall), fat (or thin), stupid (or unusually intelligent) could be minorities provided they had the other characteristics mentioned in the definition.

Ecclesia

Ecclesia

Denomination

Sect

Cult

Pictured here are some American minorities that have been passive in the past but now are demanding an end to discrimination. The black civil rights movement encouraged other minorities to speak out.

We shall speak of minority but not of *minority group*, despite the prevalence of the latter term. As we defined *group* in Chapter 3, it may or may not apply to a minority. Furthermore, a single minority may contain thousands of groups, Mexican Americans, for example. On the other hand, we do no violence to concept or social reality by saying that all minorities are categories (aggregates with common characteristics). American Indians are a minority. All have a common racial ancestry, and nearly all who share this ancestry meet the other parts of our definition. Despite this, Indians are socially constituted into scores of tribes, many of which have little contact with or knowledge of one another. It violates our meaning of the word *group* to apply the term to all Indians.

Our definition requires that the identifying characteristics of minorities be difficult or impossible to conceal or eliminate. The kind of phenomenon we have in mind does not appear overnight or quickly disappear. In its fully developed form it is deeply embedded in a society and entails relatively stable values, norms, roles, and social relationships based on these cultural elements. One element of stability is the identifying characteristic(s) mentioned in the definition. One's race does not change. His religion may but is not likely to. A minority identified by national origin may ultimately disappear, but it takes many years for this to happen.

DISCRIMINATION   Discrimination is important in the definition of minority. In general use discrimination means the making of distinctions. In our context it means *a form of behavior in which some people deny to other people equal opportunities for rewards or experiences of different sorts*. For example, if two engineers of equal ability and training, one having white and the other black skin, apply for a job, and the job is given to one because he has white skin, we have an instance of discrimination.

We speak of *systematic* discrimination because it is the experience of minorities (as we define the term) that acts of discrimination occur frequently and in many different settings. We wish to set off this kind of discrimination from that which often occurs in other situations. A parent may discriminate against a particular child, or a teacher against a certain student, but this isolated event is not what we have in mind. The ability to discriminate against a whole category of people implies that those doing the discriminating have superior social power. We have made this distinction explicit in our definition.

END OF MINORITY POSITION   Over considerable periods a minority may become more or less minority-like. For as our definition makes clear, a minority is not defined by the people in it but by a relationship between them and others in the total population. If that relationship changes, the category of persons in the minority may no longer be a minority at all. Insofar as a minority is no longer thought of as separate because of some identifying characteristic, insofar as its social power becomes equal to that of people who once engaged in discrimination, it ceases to be a minority. A number of ethnic minorities in the American past have had just such a history.

WHY MINORITIES EXIST   The sociologist often observes that once we step outside our customary ways, things so commonplace that everyone takes them for granted are really quite strange and problematic. Surely this is true of minorities. Why on earth should certain people be subjected to a systematic constriction of their life opportunities merely because they have characteristics which set them off from others? Why, for example, should the color of one's skin be assumed to have anything at all to do with his worth?

The most popular explanation of minorities among persons who aren't minority members themselves is that minority people are biologically inferior in some way or other. It is not that being female or having a black skin is itself inferior. Rather, such characteristics identify a person who is somehow incapable of producing normally acceptable role performances.

Believers in this explanation can sometimes point to facts which appear to support their point of view. Black Americans, by and large, do not do as well in school as white ones. Indians do have an especially high rate of alcoholism. Women do show less interest and capability in mechanical and scientific matters than men.

Unfortunately for the view that minorities are inherently inferior, it gets no support from science. There is no evidence for the idea that the actual distribution of motives, individual skills, life opportunities, social ranking, income, and social power is caused by innate or intrinsic qualities associated with any minority. It seems not to occur to many people that blacks may not do well in school because their experience in American society gives them little reason for believing that education pays off. Or that Indians may escape into alcoholism (an extreme form of escape wherever it occurs) because life in the white man's society offers them little hope. Or that a girl who has been told from her early years that interest in mechanical and scientific subjects is for boys only may finally come to accept this as inevitable.

RACISM   The widespread but sketchy view that minorities reflect biological differences in capacity sometimes gets elaborated into fairly systematic ideologies for which the term *racist* seems appropriate. Racism, in whatever form, not only calls for discrimination but offers some sort of rationale for the necessity and inevitability of such behavior. The central assumption is that the different races of man are inherently unequal. Some forms of racism place the races in a rank order of quality. Naturally people who think this way put their own race at the top of the list. Depending on local variations a number of other assumptions follow from the basic proposition of inherent inequality. For example, it is believed that high culture can be developed and maintained only by the "best" races. For this reason biological mixtures of superior and inferior races are to be avoided at all costs. Usually the fundamental position of racism is rationalized by reference to pseudoscientific or religious authority, sometimes just to myths.

Racism is actually a fairly recent development in intellectual history. Van den Berghe (1967), in an important study of this curious ideology, traces its development in Western countries from the early nineteenth century. He feels that it reached its peak between 1880 and 1920 and currently is declining in influence. In Van den Berghe's opinion, one of the causes of Western racism was the development of ideals like freedom and equality at the very time when slavery was being practiced in the West and Africa was undergoing colonialization. How could slavery be justified by people who believed in such ideals? Why of course by showing that the slave peoples were not fully human!

There is a legitimate sphere for the study of racial characteristics by biologists and physical anthropologists. But that is not what we refer to in our comment about the popular biological explanations of minorities. These are pseudoscientific at best. Why should we even mention these mistaken views which range all the way from vague notions to elaborate, intellectually absurd rationales for bigotry? Because they are socially important. If only a few eccentrics believed this kind of biological nonsense it would have no importance. But millions believe it, and their behavior toward minorities is influenced by their beliefs. Racism, then, becomes a factor in creating and maintaining minorities. In other words, a false doctrine has important real social effects and thus becomes a topic of interest to sociology.

Believers in racism use even the term *race* in a very loose and unscientific way. Anti-Semitism, for instance, is racism directed toward Jews, who are not a separately identifiable race at all, but a religious category. Rose (1966:430) indicates that "There was little anti-Semitism in the United States until the White Russian emigrés after World War I brought the Czar's propaganda to the United States and persuaded Henry Ford of its authenticity as fact, so that he had it disseminated at his own expense." A few years later, the Nazis in Germany made racism (particularly anti-Semitism) a central part of their fascist ideology.

Apartheid in South Africa and Nazism in Germany illustrate racism as an ideological basis and justification for government programs of discrimination.

MINORITIES AND SOCIAL POWER Social power is the capacity to compel others to behave in desired ways, against their wishes if necessary. Superior social power is essential to discrimination, which can only occur when part of the population can force discrimination on others who have identifiable characteristics (race, ethnic status, sex). Systematic discrimination is at the very

White males in their middle years. Numerically a minority of the total population, they are in no way a minority as we define the term. Although the picture is slowly changing now, white males control most of the important kinds of social power in the United States.

heart of the social process which creates and maintains a minority, and differential social power makes systematic discrimination possible.

The power that makes discrimination possible is exercised because great practical advantages accrue to power holders. An employer who pays women less than men for the same work gains economically. If an occupation with a fixed number of jobs extends equality of opportunity to minorities the number of jobs available to the powerful is reduced. If minorities can be kept ignorant and apathetic in the political sphere it is easier for holders of political power both to manipulate them and to avoid the accountability to them which is supposed to be part of a democratic polity. In a broader sense, the cessation of discrimination will lead in time to a sharing of power with people who once comprised minorities. Many people who are accustomed to the exercise of power over others are very reluctant to see that power weakened.

Those who discriminate against minorities seldom want this behavior to be understood as entirely a consequence of superior power. On this point Lenski (1966:54) quotes Mosca:

Ruling classes do not justify their power exclusively by *de facto* possession of it, but try to find a moral and legal basis for it, representing it as the logical and necessary consequence of doctrines and beliefs that are generally recognized and accepted.

This is part of the attractiveness of racism. Business, governmental, or educational leaders do not need to subscribe to it fully to be influenced by its general perspective. It furnishes reasons justifying the use of power to discriminate against minorities. We characteristically find beliefs and myths about any sort of minority that legitimate a continuation of the power status quo. So it is said that women like to be dominated by men, that they are emotional and unsuited to the hard-headed world of practical affairs. They prefer things the way they are. Nature ordained that their proper destiny is to be mothers and homemakers. And so on.

Minorities and Classes There is a connection between certain minorities (racial, ethnic, and religious) and the class system we discussed in the last chapter. Most fully developed minorities are concentrated disproportionately in the lower classes. Blacks, American Indians, and Mexican Americans illustrate this fact on the current American scene. As we showed in discussing classes, one's location in the stratification system of society greatly affects one's life chances. Hence being of the lower class becomes a factor in accounting for the disadvantaged treatment received by minorities. It is a general factor, however, in the sense that class membership as such is not equivalent to minority membership. The lower class contains many individuals who do not belong to minorities. Poor whites in the Appalachians have all the handicaps of poverty, but not the additional ones visited on poor blacks.

When a minority begins to lose its character as such, to be assimilated into the general population, its linkage with social classes gradually disappears. That is, its members will eventually be found at all class levels, not concentrated in any one. Once fully developed minorities like the Italians and the Irish illustrate the point.

PSYCHOLOGICAL AND SOCIAL PSYCHOLOGICAL FACTORS There are always close connections between the social and the psychological levels of human experience. So it is no surprise to learn that minority phenomena have psychological as well as social roots. We shall deal with several of these.

Prejudice Simpson and Yinger define prejudice as "an emotional, rigid attitude toward a group of people" (1965:10). As distinct from other kinds of attitudes, prejudices involve emotionally defended negative responses to a whole category of people (the minority). A person with a prejudice toward a minority reacts as though every member of the category were alike and ignores the individual differences among members. Even though prejudices involve misjudgment and oversimplification, a prejudiced person does not easily bring his attitudes closer to reality. As Simpson and Yinger put it, "One may misjudge the speed of an approaching car, but one is anxious to correct the error. Prejudice is a misjudgment that one defends" (1965:10).

Prejudice is an attitude; discrimination is actual behavior. The two should not be confused, though they are related. Many Americans assume that prejudice causes discrimination, which makes discriminatory behavior (an aspect of the concept of minority) a rather simple result of a psychological state. But prejudice may as often be the result of discrimination as the cause. If you have treated another person unjustly by your own standards, you may find yourself easing your feelings of guilt by finding excuses in prejudiced attitudes toward the person offended. He deserved to be treated that way or you wouldn't have done it! Thus prejudice and discrimination are both cause and effect with respect to each other.

On some occasions the two may be independent of one another. For instance, a truck farmer in the Southwest may have strong prejudices against Mexican Americans, but still offers employment to them because he has no practical alternative. This kind of situation has increased markedly in recent years with the tightening up of legal proscriptions against discrimination. Sometimes a person relatively free of prejudice behaves in a discriminatory way because of the social pressures upon him. Some members of social clubs with discriminatory membership policies might not like these policies yet go along with them because they cannot (or will not) oppose them. We conclude that prejudice is a psychological accompaniment to minority phenomena. It both intensifies them and is produced by them.

Frustration and Aggression Many years ago Dollard et al. (1939), examined the relationship between frustration and aggression. Evidence was found for the idea that when strong impulses are blocked (frustration) their energy is often released in aggressive behavior. There are other responses to frustration but this is one of the important ones. Often aggression cannot be directed at the immediate causes of frustration because they are not present or because it would be too dangerous to do so. A man may be very angry toward his boss because the latter did him an injury, but feel unable to express the anger for fear of retaliation. The aggression may, however, be discharged against other persons or groups who are relatively powerless to protect themselves. Minorities, being relatively powerless, furnish ready targets for displaced hostility generated by deep-seated frustration.

Society presents its members with a wide range of frustrating situations, all the way from inability to satisfy simple impulses to long-continued ordeals such as can arise from the absence of satisfying primary group experience, inability to find gratifying work, and a sense of powerlessness in a society dominated by impersonal complex organizations. Some of this frustration gets displaced against minorities. The process is often called scapegoating. "Somebody must be to blame for our troubles. What about those strange people who don't think, or act, or look like us? What about the blacks, the Jews, the hippies, the Communists? Aren't they causing all our problems?" The psychological process involved is essentially irrational and largely unconscious, which makes it all the more difficult to control.

Authoritarian Tendencies Years ago the work of a number of psychologists, especially Adorno et al. (1950), produced evidence that prejudice toward minorities is particularly likely to appear in what they called the *authoritarian personality*. Authoritarian persons had been subjected to unusually strict parental control. As children they had learned to acquiesce in and depend on it, and yet to resent it often without knowing that they did so. They tend to express their resentment in hostility toward those they can safely attack (Newcomb et al., 1965:441).

While this theory has been very influential, it is doubtful that the existence of the authoritarian personality syndrome has been established beyond question. But it is clear that some persons do have deep-seated predispositions toward prejudice while others do not. The presence of such persons in a population containing minorities is another psychological factor in the perpetuation of prejudice and discrimination.

Learning Prejudice The fact that people learn to be prejudiced in exactly the way they learn not to be is more important. A study by Pettigrew (1958) establishes this fact. Pettigrew obtained measures of authoritarianism and of attitudes toward blacks from university students in the Union of South Africa and from adults in four southern and four northern communities in the United States. He found that prejudice against blacks was higher among the South African students but that the degree of authoritarianism did not differ between the citizens of the two countries. In the United States, southern respondents were more prejudiced toward blacks than northern respondents, but the two groups did not differ in degree of authoritarianism. There was also a moderate association between authoritarianism and prejudice in both the United States and the Union of South Africa. That is, up to a point authoritarian persons were more prejudiced than nonauthoritarian persons, but in all groups prejudice occurred in people with little or no tendency to authoritarianism.

This work is of considerable significance. Prejudice simply cannot be attributed wholly to underlying personality dispositions. Our discussion of socialization in Chapter 3 gives us a clue to what else is involved. If the values and norms of the important groups a person belongs to prescribe prejudice and discrimination toward minorities, the individual will acquire prejudice. We learn prejudice in the same process of interaction with socializing agents in which we learn to like some foods better than others, to hold education in high or low esteem, and so on. As Newcomb et al. put it:

Cultural norms alone constitute a sufficient condition for the development of prejudice on the part of most individuals who share the culture; thus authoritarianism is not a necessary condition for its development (1965:441).

Nobody is born prejudiced. One either learns or does not learn to think this way.

Decades ago, Bogardus (1925) initiated studies of the social distance Americans feel toward groups and categories including minorities. Since then, scores of other investigators have confirmed his findings, and there has been little change over the years in the order of preference Americans feel for other groups. To the sociologist, this stability in attitudes suggests the presence of norms toward out-group members which are remarkably resistant to change. Such norms, deeply embedded in the society's culture, become one of the important factors lending continuity to prejudice toward minorities.

SOME AMERICAN MINORITIES— A BRIEF OVERVIEW

The points we have made about discrimination, prejudice, and the intertwined social and psychological roots of both take on clearer meaning when we look at the situation in the United States. The identifying characteristics of most minorities are racial, ethnic, or religious, or some combination of these. We shall consider each of these types.

RACIAL MINORITIES Physical anthropologists have shown that races are rather loosely identifiable biological categories. There is much intermixture and overlapping of racial characteristics as a result of contacts over long periods. Nevertheless, persons with no scientific knowledge about race often can make racial identifications with fair accuracy. The permanence of distinguishing attributes, biologically transmitted from one generation to the next, contributes to the longevity of racial minorities. So long as they are biologically identifiable, it is more difficult for these minorities to disappear than it is for other kinds of minorities.

One out of every eight Americans (12.4 percent) is nonwhite. Blacks comprise the vast majority of all nonwhites in the United States. In 1972 there were 23,400,000 blacks, and they made up 11.1 percent of the country's total population. All other nonwhite races together furnish only 1.3 percent of the total. The largest of these are American Indians (792,730), Japanese (591,290), Chinese (435,062), and Filipinos (343,000). (These figures come from the United States Census and are reported in the *Statistical Abstract of the United States*, 1973.)

All these are true minorities by our definition. But the differences between them also illustrate that the minority concept may be manifested in varying degrees. Blacks and Indians, for instance, are fully developed minorities in every meaning of the term. Americans of Chinese and Japanese ancestry, on the other hand, suffer far less discrimination and prejudice. In income, occupation, educational attainment, and most other measures they have moved far closer to the white population than have Indians and blacks. We will document the situation of black Americans later in the chapter. Of Indians we will simply state that as a whole they suffer at least as much discrimination and prejudice as blacks, and there are as few individual Indians who have been able to transcend the minority limitations.

We learn from a report to the House Committee on Education and Labor on poverty in this country (1964) that more than half of the American Indian families have incomes below the poverty level. Five and a half years is the average length of schooling for Indian children. Ninety percent of reservation housing is classified as substandard, and unemployment for Indians is far higher than for whites, ranging from 20 to 80 percent for Indians residing on reservations (*Time* special report on American Indians, 1970).

ETHNIC AND ETHNIC-RACIAL MINORITIES   In the United States, ethnic minorities are those whose identification is based primarily on national and cultural origins. They are the familiar immigrant categories which have contributed so heavily to the peopling of this continent. A single minority sometimes has both racial and cultural identification, at least for some of its members. Such is the case with the Mexican Americans concentrated in the Southwest and the Puerto Ricans concentrated in the Northeast.

From a sociological viewpoint, the main thing that distinguishes ethnic from racial minorities is that the former tend to disappear after about three generations. This is made possible by the fact that their members cannot be reliably distinguished by physical characteristics from the majority of the white population. For a time after their movement to this country, immigrants from Ireland, Italy, Poland, and other countries were fully developed minorities. Their power and prestige were low and only the poorest jobs were available to them. They were systematically discriminated against and their styles of life were regarded with distaste by nonminority Americans.

Most ethnic categories tend to lose their minority character with the passage of time. Historically, they have been assimilated into American life, a process reviewed in detail by Gordon (1964). This does not mean that all ethnic identification is necessarily lost. Glazer and Moynihan (1963) vividly demonstrated that in New York City ethnic groups of several generations' standing are very much alive and active in the political life of that city. But such groups are now minorities in only a restricted sense.

The recent resentment of some Italian Americans at being identified with organized crime indicates that sore spots still reflect the serious wounds once inflicted on a major ethnic minority. On the other hand, millions of Americans whose ancestors a few generations ago were members of minorities have lost all sense of such identification because of the reactions of their fellow citizens.

Discrimination and Size of Minority   The degree to which ethnic categories exhibit minority characteristics reflects not only their length of time in America but also their relative numbers locally. Generally, when large numbers of immigrants arrive in a locality, discrimination and prejudice are likely to be more intense

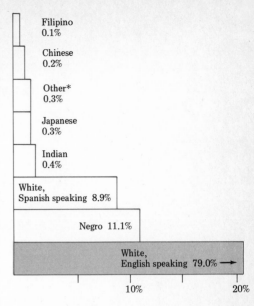

FIGURE 7-1 MINORITY GROUPS IN THE UNITED STATES

"Other" includes Aleuts, Asian Indians, Eskimos, Hawaiians, Indonesians, Koreans, Polynesians, and other races not shown separately. Percentages do not total 100 because of rounding.

[Source: *U. S. Department of Commerce, Statistical Abstract of the United States,* 1972, pp. 29, 33.]

than when only a few arrive. For example, while Mexican Americans comprise well below 1 percent of the population in most states, they were not far short of 10 percent of the 1970 population in Texas. The same was true of Cubans in Florida.

Spanish-Speaking Minorities By historical accident, the ethnic minorities of substantial size now the chief targets of discrimination and prejudice are Spanish-speaking. In 1971 there were about five million Mexican Americans, one and a half million Puerto Ricans, six hundred and fifty thousand Cubans, and more than a million people from other Latin American or Spanish-speaking countries.

The Mexican-American Legal Defense and Educational Fund (MALDEF) reports that Mexican Americans have an average of nearly four years less education than non-Mexican whites, and over one and a half years less than the average black American. Unemployment is more than 50 percent higher among Mexican Americans than among non-Mexican whites, and almost 80 percent live in substandard housing in urban ghettos often called *barrios*.

Of the Puerto Ricans, Senior (1965:40) puts it this way: "They are relegated to the worst (and most expensive) housing; they hold the lowest-paying jobs; their children attend overcrowded schools; they are exploited by unscrupulous landlords, easy-credit merchants, and racketeers; they suffer winter temperatures and even more chilling social contacts; they are deluged with the same verbal brickbats once showered on our ancestors; and, finally, teen-age groups, already in possession of their turf, are ready to kill the newcomers, if necessary, to maintain their sovereignty."

RELIGIOUS MINORITIES Until the second half of the nineteenth century, the United States was heavily Protestant. Beginning in the 1880s millions of Roman Catholics came here from Ireland, Italy, and Poland.[1] In many eastern and midwestern cities, these people became full-fledged minorities, not solely because of religious identification; along with religion were strong ethnic identity and lower-class membership.

As with purely ethnic minorities, Roman Catholics nowadays have pretty much lost the characteristics of a minority. Without losing their religious identification, they have pretty much lost their ethnic identifications, and they have moved upward in the country's stratification system. Mexican Americans are an exception to this generalization.

A dramatic symbol and reflection of this movement away from minority status was the presidency of John F. Kennedy beginning

---

[1] In 1970, according to the *Yearbook of American Churches*, Roman Catholics, with 48,215,000 members, were the largest single church body. There were 5,870,000 Jews, and Protestants of all denominations numbered 71,713,000 members. These figures are furnished by the church bodies themselves and—being based on different methods of computation—are not strictly comparable.

in 1960. Even then some Americans clung to the prejudices of a majority's orientation toward a minority. A post-election survey conducted by the University of Michigan indicated that Kennedy's religion cost him a million and a half votes.

Jews also are an interesting case. For many centuries adherents of Judaism were a minority in the full meaning of the term in numerous European countries. In fact, in many European cities Jews were forced to live in separate (often walled) sections known as ghettos, the original reference for this term (Wirth, 1928). In the Western world, no religious category has been treated as a minority so persistently and in so many societies. In our own time, the experience of the Jews in Nazi Germany testifies in extreme form to the savagery with which minorities have sometimes been treated by so-called civilized men.

Unlike some religio-ethnic minorities, Jews have not generally desired to lose their identity. It is true that many individual Jews have become fully assimilated, and have become indistinguishable from other Americans save for their religious preference. More typically, Jews have preferred to live in a state of pluralism with other groups in society. That is, they have liked to live alongside other groups, each with its own identity, without discrimination or prejudice.

In the United States, Jews like Roman Catholics have become far less a minority than they once were. Prejudice and discrimination still exist in many quarters, to be sure. According to Goldstein and Goldscheiner (1968:11), for example, anti-Semitic discrimination still exists in many country clubs, some recreational facilities, and in personal interaction.

If space permitted, other American minorities could be listed. For example, what about the aged? Read the news story "Thinking Young" and see if you think this population category meets our definition of a minority. We wish, however, to consider at some length two of our largest: black Americans and women.

A Jewish-American family observing Seder, a religious holiday, in their home. Signs of ethnic identity have survived, but these no longer mark a group as inferior in power or as subject to discrimination.

BLACK AMERICANS AS A MINORITY

Black Americans are a true minority, as we define the term. Their most critical distinguishing characteristic is skin color. This seems straightforward enough, though not quite so simple as it may at first appear. For instance, how dark does a person's skin have to be for him to be classified as black? Or, putting our question in a different way: what proportion of black ancestry must one have to be classified by society as black?

If these questions sound silly, we assure you that idiocies have often been perpetrated in the answers whites have given. Both legal and administrative definitions have often specified that a person is black if he has an indicated proportion of Negro blood, or if he has an ancestor who was black. On such a basis, people have been so classified who in appearance cannot be distinguished from whites. Furthermore, in a country where there has been much racial mixture in the past, a person may be legally black even though genetically he is much more white. From a genetic viewpoint this has the same logic as classifying as white persons with any white ancestry. Thus when we say that there are 23.4 million blacks in this country (1972) it should be understood that this many persons are *socially* classified as Negro.

Thinking Young

In Chicago, a 38-year-old man can't become a trainee fireman because he's too old. In Scottsbluff, Neb., a newspaper advertises for a sports editor, and one of the requirements is that the applicant be "youthful." In Phoenix, Ariz., lawyers for Greyhound Lines prepare to appeal an adverse Federal-court decision. The point at issue: the company's refusal to hire drivers who are over 35.

The U.S. is predominantly a nation of young people. More than half the population is under the age of 30, and many of the rest wish they were. "Both subtly and blatantly, our society has exalted youth and shrunk from what are euphemistically called the golden years," says legal director Howard Eglit of the Chicago chapter of the American Civil Liberties Union. And this pervasive attitude translates itself into widespread job discrimination against older workers. It's called age-ism, and to many employers "older" often means simply over 40.

Like racism and sexism, ageism is against the law. But legal sanctions don't seem to help much. The Labor Department investigated about 6,000 companies in 1972 and found that more than a third were violating laws against age-ism. At 45, according to chief counsel David A. Affeldt of the Senate Select Committee on Aging, the jobless rate, the length of unemployment and poverty all start to rise. Discouraged older people also begin to drop out of the work force.

"The way our system works is to force older people out of the labor force to make room for young people," notes Alice Brophy, director of New York City's Office for the Aging. It is not a conscious bias, but represents "an underlying corporate value," according to one management consultant. "The essence of age discrimination is the urge to get bright young people," sums up Frank McGowan of the Labor Department's division of equal pay and employment standards. "No one perceives of himself as being discriminatory."

Indeed, many of the reasons that companies give for not hiring older workers seem to stem from practical considerations. "Many companies refuse to hire or promote those over 30 because people are convinced that older workers have no potential," says McGowan. There is the fear that older workers are more set in their ways and, hence, more difficult to train. Once the worker has been trained, he may be ready for retirement before the company has gotten enough years out of him to justify the expense of training. In addition, older workers generally command higher salaries and boost pension and insurance costs.

Many of the disadvantages older job applicants face are more inadvertent than deliberate. Most large companies, for instance, use young, inexperienced personnel people to conduct initial job-screening interviews. "When you're faced with a younger man, there's hostility in the interview," says a 52-year-old member of the Forty Plus Club, a nationwide organization of out-of-work, middle-aged executives. "You can feel it."

There are also many organizations that deliberately exclude older job seekers. Greyhound maintains that the rigors of being a new bus driver are simply too much for men over 35; low seniority means being on call 24 hours a day for routes all over the country. Most police and fire departments feel the same way about stamina and age. And, ironically, many federally funded job-training programs limit entrance to those under 28.

An increasingly worrisome aspect of age-ism is forced early retirement. Once an optional benefit that allowed workers to retire in their mid-50's with reduced pension payments, it has now become a widely used management tool to cut costs and trim the payroll. In addition to being cruel, forced early retirement also can be a waste of skills. The ACLU cites studies showing there is little if any decline in intelligence and almost no decline in motor ability between the ages of 60 and 80.

While the situation for older workers is bad, at least it has improved somewhat from the go-go years of the late 1960s when youth was equated with ability and the whiz kid was the darling of the corporate world. "Experience is coming into its own again," reports vice president George Klein of the New York chapter of Forty Plus. Klein tells a story of a mining engineer whom the club helped get a job in South America. The man did so well that a Canadian mining firm lured him up north to a better job. The engineer was 80.

Source: Newsweek, April 29, 1974. Copyright Newsweek, Inc. 1974 reprinted by permission.

To meet our definition of a minority, a category of people must experience systematic discrimination. The evidence on this point for black Americans is all too abundant. No reasonable person who looks at the facts can have the slightest doubt that they have been systematically excluded from equal opportunity and treatment in almost every area of our national life. The facts have been heavily documented and are readily available. Here we can do no more than sample the evidence.

EDUCATION, THE MARKETPLACE AND OFFICE HOLDING A 1973 Bureau of the Census report on the social and economic status of black Americans presents figures that are all the more sobering because they were collected after the black civil rights movement of the sixties. In spite of the legislation and the court decisions which opened the way for black progress in the economy and in education, the overall impression, while mixed, is of a slower rate of gain than in the immediately preceding decade or so.

Educational Improvement The picture was brightest in education. Of all blacks between 18 and 24, 18 percent were in college in 1972, compared to 13 percent in 1967. This was a real gain and promised well for the future of these young people. Yet in the same year the proportion of whites in college (ages 18 to 24) was 26 percent. The high school drop-out rate for blacks also had declined, from 23.9 percent in 1967 to 17.8 percent in 1972. For whites the high school drop-out rate in 1972 was 10.7 percent. And there were other indications of educational improvement for blacks.

Income On the other hand, the census report was less encouraging on the marketplace. In 1972 median family income for white Americans was $11,500, while for blacks it was about $6,900. This was about the same disparity as in 1967, showing no progress in a five-year period of prosperity for the country as a whole. At the lower end of the scale, 33 percent of blacks were classified in 1972 as having low incomes, and about 9 percent of whites. A quarter of all black families received some form of public assistance compared with only 5 percent of white families.

The same census report shows 10 percent unemployment for blacks in 1972, just twice that for whites. This ratio has not changed since at least the early fifties and no real improvement is in sight.

Elective Office There is somewhat more room for encouragement in the election of blacks to public office. In 1972 there were sixteen black members of Congress, up from ten in 1968. Black state legislators increased from 172 in 1968 to 238 in 1972, and mayors increased from twenty-nine to eighty-three. Overall, twenty-six hundred blacks held elective office in 1972, twice the 1968 total. This is a real gain, yet these twenty-six hundred persons were less than one-half of one percent of all elected officials in 1972, while blacks make up 11 percent of the population.

RESIDENTIAL SEGREGATION—THE DEVELOPING PATTERN After World War I, there began a massive and continuing migration of blacks from the South into northern cities. Hauser summarizes what has happened (1966:76).

Between 1910 and 1920, the Negro population in central cities of mettropolitan areas increased by 40 percent; between 1920 and 1940, by 83 percent; and between 1940 and 1960, by 123 percent. Hence, by 1960, 51 percent of all Negroes in the United States lived in the central cities of SMSAs. Of all Negroes resident in metropolitan areas, 80 percent lived in central cities. There was a much higher concentration of Negroes in metropolitan areas and in their central cities in the North and West than in the South. In 1960, of all Negroes in the North 93 percent were in SMSAs and 79 percent in the central cities; and in the West 93 percent in SMSAs and 67 percent in central cities. In the South, however, 46 percent of all Negro residents lived in SMSAs and 34 percent in central cities.

Since 1960, the trend has continued. As a result, an increasing proportion of the total population of our large cities has become black. Between 1960 and 1970 the percentage of black residents increased in all fifty of the largest cities in the country. A presidential commission has predicted that by 1984 seven of the ten largest cities in the country will have populations that are 50 percent or more composed of black citizens. In 1965, almost two-thirds of the inhabitants of Washington, D. C., were black.

At first glance, this development may not seem to reflect discriminatory behavior, but there is more to the story. As blacks have been moving into the central cities, whites have increasingly moved out into the suburbs. The two migrations can be clearly shown in Cleveland, Ohio, where the United States Bureau of the Census conducted a special census in 1965. Between 1950 and 1965, Cleveland experienced a net *loss* of 236,000 white residents and a net *gain* of 131,000 black residents. As a consequence, blacks rose from 16.1 to 34.4 percent in the central city, and nearly all (97 percent) of the blacks in the SMSA were in the central city (United States Bureau of the Census, Reports Series P-28, No. 1390; P-23, No. 20; P-23, No. 21).

In Chapter 5 we pointed out that large American cities have grown mostly outside the corporate boundaries. Central cities have almost ceased growing, and many are declining. Now we see that it is mainly whites who have moved to the suburbs, and that they have largely been replaced by blacks. Central cities are becoming increasingly black, the segment of the population which can least afford the mounting costs of city government, costs that are escaped in considerable measure by those already more affluent persons who live in the suburbs.

Black ghettos tend to be perpetuated from generation to generation. Because residential segregation is still such a strong factor in the United States, children who grow up in these ghettos usually find it difficult to break out when they want to start a home of their own.

Part 2 / Social Units and Processes

Isolation in Central Cities In a sense, then, black citizens are increasingly segregated in central cities, and within them, they are further segregated into black ghettos. This latter kind of segregation is more directly discriminatory because it is maintained by practices which make it difficult and often impossible for blacks to rent or buy homes outside already segregated districts, although such residential segregation is not legally permissible. The Cleveland studies to which we have already referred suggest that such segregation may be increasing rather than decreasing.

In 1960, the city had twenty-seven census tracts with Negro populations of 90 percent or more. These twenty-seven tracts contained 134,142 (53.5 percent) of the city's 250,818 Negroes. The 1965 census indicates that the number of tracts with 90 percent plus Negro inhabitants had increased from twenty-seven to thirty-nine. These thirty-nine tracts now held 180,373 (64.6 percent) of the city's 279,353 nonwhites. Thus, in both absolute and relative terms, Negroes were growing in numbers and in concentrations in the dark ghettos (Masotti et al., 1969:91).

PREJUDICE Earlier we indicated that prejudice is a psychological accompaniment to discrimination. Nationwide surveys commissioned by *Newsweek* in 1963 and 1966 amply document the existence of white prejudice toward blacks. The 1963 survey showed that: (a) 68 percent of white Americans think blacks laugh a lot, (b) 66 percent say blacks tend to have less ambition, (c) 60 percent agree that blacks smell different, (d) 55 percent believe blacks have looser morals, (e) 46 percent think blacks keep untidy homes, (f) 41 percent believe blacks want to live off the handout, (g) 39 percent say blacks have less native intelligence, (h) 35 percent agree that blacks breed crime, and (i) 31 percent feel that blacks are inferior to whites and care less for family.

Many objected to various contacts with blacks: 41 percent would object to having their own child bring a black friend home to supper, 51 percent to having a black family as a next-door neighbor, 84 percent to a close friend or relative marrying a black, and 90 percent to their own teen-age daughter dating a black.

The 1966 *Newsweek* survey revealed that white prejudice had not diminished appreciably. It showed that 73 percent of the whites interviewed felt that blacks "could have done something" about slum conditions, 55 percent agreed that blacks were to blame for their unemployment, nearly 80 percent thought half the blacks on welfare could earn their way if they tried, and 75 percent did not favor further school integration.

Women as a *minority*? True, females are a slight majority of the total population in the United States, but numbers are not the criterion. Black Americans (11 percent of the total population) greatly outnumber white citizens in many southern counties, and

WOMEN AS A MINORITY

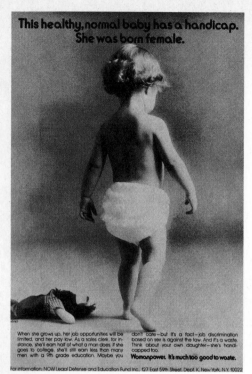

**This healthy, normal baby has a handicap.
She was born female.**

When she grows up, her job opportunities will be limited, and her pay low. As a sales clerk, for instance, she'll earn half of what a man does. If she goes to college, she'll still earn less than many men with a 9th grade education. Maybe you don't care—but it's a fact—job discrimination based on sex is against the law. And it's a waste. Think about your own daughter—she's handicapped too.
Womanpower. It's much too good to waste.

For information: NOW Legal Defense and Education Fund, Inc. 127 East 59th Street, Dept. K, New York, N.Y. 10022

Insofar as women can be persuaded that their "real" destiny is wife- and mother-hood, all other options are defined as inferior, and this strategy protects the power of males from competition of women. In addition, there is a big market (among males) for depicting women primarily as sex objects. Can you figure out how this fact relates to sex roles in the United States and to differential power between men and women?

soon will do so in many northern central cities. Perhaps you feel that women aren't a minority because they don't feel that way— more specifically, because they don't feel discriminated against. To this we would reply that while many women don't feel discriminated against, some do, and in any case a feeling of oppression is not part of our definition.

Can you think of other reasons why women are not a minority? What about the idea that women live in the closest intimacy with men? Men obviously like women very much. If so, how can it be that they treat women as a minority? We suggest that there is nothing in our definition which precludes strong personal attachments and intimate social relationships between particular members of a minority and others who are not part of the minority. Since slavery, close personal ties between blacks and whites were by no means unknown. If other arguments have occurred to you, put them aside for a while. Let us examine more closely the idea that American women are, in fact, a good example of a minority.

IDENTIFYING CHARACTERISTICS To begin with, the physical differences between women and men, we think you will agree, provide the identifying characteristics difficult or impossible to conceal or eliminate which are part of the definition of a minority. If women are a minority there must also be systematic discrimination against them by men on the basis of sex. Consider employment. A few years ago, Congresswoman Martha Griffiths (Michigan) used 1964 material from the Bureaus of the Census and Labor Statistics to state that

the median earnings of white men are $6,497, of Negro men $4,285, of white women $3,859, and of Negro women $2,674. This adverse differential exists in spite of the fact that white females in the labor force have 12.3 years of education on the average as compared to 12.2 years for white men; and nonwhite females have 11.1 years of education to 10 for the nonwhite males. . . . The same disparities exist when we examine the data for all workers, including temporary as well as full time (Reeves, 1971:280).

OCCUPATIONAL DISCRIMINATION Women are mainly employed in relatively low-status occupations, but at every occupational level tend to receive less pay than men for the same work—on the average, about 40 percent less. A large proportion of all occupations in the United States tend to be relegated largely to one sex or the other, for reasons which have little to do with the intrinsic capabilities or limitations of the two sexes. For instance, the proportion of female physicians in the United States (about 7 percent) is the lowest among advanced industrialized countries. In the Soviet Union, 80 percent of physicians are women. In spite of the increasing numbers of women attending

Part 2 / Social Units and Processes

college, the proportion of women on college faculties has declined since 1938 (Bernard, 1964).[2]

In 1964, Congress passed the Civil Rights Act, Title VII of which prohibits sex discrimination in employment.[3] This legislation came after many years of effort. The prohibition against sex discriminaion was an amendment added to the Civil Rights Act almost at the last moment by a congressman who was one of the original opponents of the entire bill, a tactic which might raise some question about his motivation. Despite this ploy, the legislation was passed with the sex discrimination amendment intact; it makes the prohibition of sex discrimination in employment official national policy. The Civil Rights Act provides for an Equal Employment Opportunity Commission to handle complaints of violations. At the end of its first year "over one-third of its processed complaints had involved charges of sex discrimination" (Reeves, 1971:284).

The Civil Rights Act and similar legislation since passed by a number of states constitutes a powerful potential weapon for women combating job discrimination. Yet much remains undone. In the 1970s we face at least a temporary surplus of workers in many high-prestige fields because the colleges are turning out more graduates than can readily be absorbed. It is just these fields which are most dominated by males. The supply-demand ratio in the immediate future by no means favors women.

OTHER FACTORS   Is it possible that the facts reflect not male discrimination but a division of labor by sex with no implication of unfair treatment? We feel that there is some measure of truth to this position. There appears to be no compelling reason why sex ratios should be precisely equal in every occupation. That would not even be possible at present, since most men are employed while only one-third of all women are in the labor market. At the same time, the evidence indicates a great deal of discrimination in the proper meaning of the term. Women do not get equal pay for equal work. There are active discriminatory practices in many occupations. A study by White (1967) documents sex discrimination in the legal profession.

Another factor behind specific acts of employment discrimination against women lends a kind of cultural legitimation to such treatment. Most American men and women appear to believe that homemaking (including motherhood) is a woman's most impor-

_____

[2] This trend probably reversed in the early seventies.

[3] In 1970, Congress also approved a constitutional amendment that decrees: "Equality of rights under the law shall not be denied or abridged by the United States or by any state on account of sex." It took nearly a half-century of agitation to secure this legislation. It must be ratified by three-fourths of the state legislatures before it becomes effective.

tant job. Hence even though a wife's job outside the home makes an important contribution to the economic well-being of the family, it will usually be seen as ancillary to her main role. With such convictions, men are more likely to discriminate and women to accept discrimination without trying effectively to oppose it.

Power Discrimination against minorities is practiced by those in positions of greater power. It hardly seems necessary to prove that in this society men have more power at their disposal than women. As of 1970, less than one percent of business executives were female; there was only one woman in the United States Senate and ten in the House of Representatives (down from nineteen in the 87th Congress). There were also fewer women than there had been in state legislatures, where women are only a tiny proportion of the total. All the traditional sentimental talk about the power of women in their positions behind men ("the hand that rocks the cradle," and so forth) is largely irrelevant to the real disposition of power in our society.

There is no question that women comprise an unusual minority in the sociological sense. Unlike many minorities, they do not fit into the overall stratification scheme of society. When Italian Americans formed a true minority they were predominantly lower class: minority and class status were closely parallel. Blacks still are predominantly of lower status in other respects besides minority designation. But this is not true of women, for their position in the class sytem of society is mostly determined by that of their fathers and husbands. When a married man is upwardly mobile, his wife goes with him, and improves her position with his.

Prolongation of Minority Status As a minority, women cut across usual class lines. In some situations (particularly employment), women of all classes can expect discriminatory behavior from men. Like blacks, they have physical characteristics which make it impossible for them to disappear as a category. Recent changes in behavior and clothing which de-emphasize sex differences do not weaken this point. Such physical identification makes it harder for women to cease being a minority.

Yet another fact makes sex discrimination resistant to change. Men and women live together in one of the closest and most durable of all social relationships, marriage. In a society still essentially patriarchal, it can be very hard to work against discrimination if the person who is closest to one believes in it. The cards are really stacked, not just behaviorally, not just in the way social systems respond to sex differences, but emotionally as well. It isn't hard to see why many women simply accept the situation and sincerely claim that they don't feel discriminated against, no matter what the facts may show.

In 1970, the American Institute of Public Opinion (Gallup Poll) questioned a national sample of women about the place of women in this country. To the question, "In your opinion, do women in the United States get as good a break as men?" 65 percent answered yes. Differences in response by educational level were not great. This is interesting in connection with another question in the poll. "If a woman has the same ability as a man, does she have as good a chance to become the executive of a company, or not?" Only 39 percent believed that a woman's chances were as good as a man's.

The difference in these two proportions suggests that many women recognize job discrimination but do not resent it. College women, incidentally, are somewhat less convinced that women get as good a break as men, and see more job discrimination. But the differences between them and their less well educated sisters are not really large.

Since World War II there has been a gathering momentum of change in the relationships between minorities and the rest of American society. Minorities have shown increasing resistance to continuing *as minorities*. They have been demanding an end to discrimination and have made some progress. The trend began with the black minority and has since spread to others. There is now evidence to indicate that behind the headlines some real social change is taking place. But why just now? Rose (1966) answered this question in considerable detail, and we give several of his reasons.

MINORITIES AND SOCIAL CHANGE

The migration of millions of blacks to the North and West somewhat improved their situation politically, for in their new locations they could vote and become significant factors in local and national elections. Over the years, national administrations became more sensitive to the plight of black Americans. World War II heightened the American conscience in these matters. The German enemy had a grossly racist government, a fact which made it harder for us to condone our own discrimination based on race. The long period of postwar prosperity also helped lay a foundation for change, because blacks participated in this prosperity (though to a much lesser degree than whites), and because when people are economically secure they are less likely to use discrimination as a tool for improving their own condition.

Beginning in 1954, the federal courts played a role in enforcing constitutional provisions which make discrimination (especially by segregation) illegal. While full compliance with the many decisions and orders of the Supreme Court has not yet been achieved, there are real changes, especially in the South. There can be little doubt that most of America has moved toward a consensus that changes are needed which would abolish at least the more obvious and official or quasi-official forms of discrimination. Congress, which often follows but seldom leads in the affirmation of new moral positions, responded with significant legislation, such as the Civil Rights Act of 1964 and the Voting Rights Bill of

Different kinds of leaders have arisen in the civil rights movement as changes in the social environment have occurred. In the top left photo, W. E. B. DuBois (center), one of the founders of the NAACP, is shown with other early black leaders, Mary McLeod Bethune and Horace Mann Bond. In the early days of the civil rights movement, the NAACP and other black groups worked within the Establishment. In the late 1950s and early 1960s, Martin Luther King (center of bottom left photo) and other leaders advocated nonviolent disobedience. To many whites at the time, nonviolent disobedience was highly deviant. To militant blacks a few years later, this strategy was also deviant—because it wasn't militant enough.

1965, both voted for by majorities of Democrats and Republicans.

The interaction between these factors and others made the structure of American society less resistant to changes affecting minorities. At the same time, Americans by and large were psychologically better prepared for change. The stage was set for the emergence of a new militancy among black citizens. The leadership of older minority organizations like the NAACP, which worked mainly through court action, was strongly challenged. From about 1960 to 1965, the Reverend Martin Luther King (head of the Southern Christian Leadership Conference) led a significant civil rights movement, mainly in the South, which used civil disobedience and public demonstrations as tools in breaking down segregation on buses, in restaurants, and elsewhere.

King stressed nonviolence, but a new younger leadership began to emerge which felt that a peaceful strategy was probably not going to be enough. Among these young leaders a conviction grew that alliance with sympathetic whites was less of a help than a hindrance (many white students and others from the North had participated in the demonstrations and voter registration drives of the early sixties). It was felt that reliance on white sympathizers delayed the development of strong black leadership and organization. Since that time, the drive for equal status has taken a number of forms, ranging from the peacefully militant strategies of the Martin Luther King persuasion to bitterly alienated programs whose participants proclaim their willingness to use violence.

As a result of the developments we have mentioned and the vigor of black Americans in pushing for equality, many real changes have taken place. Great progress has been made in eliminating legal discrimination. Some progress has been made against de facto discrimination in jobs, housing, education, religion, and other areas. But black leaders are not satisfied, and are angrily aware how much remains to be done to attain full equality. They often speak bitterly of the improvement whites have been willing to grant as tokenism. On the other hand, some whites are alarmed by the militancy of some blacks, and feel that since progress has been made, blacks should be more patient; they ought to be glad—even grateful—that there have been changes in the right direction. Let us try to understand, in sociological terms, what is now happening.

The present frustration and disappointment of blacks are a phenomenon which sociologists have observed in many other settings. In part it involves what is called *relative deprivation*. Whether or not people feel deprived depends not just on absolute deprivation, but on the amount of it in comparison to others'. Thus if only one of two deserving employees is promoted, the other will feel a strong sense of deprivation even though he is no worse off than before. Because black Americans have made some real progress here and there, and even more because they now actively aspire to equal treatment, the inequalities which remain seem even more unendurable. To whites who caution them not to expect too much too soon, they reply that blacks have already waited too long.

CONFLICT BETWEEN VALUES AND DISCRIMINATION Meanwhile in white America events of recent years have heightened what Myrdal (1944) called the American Dilemma. Essentially, the American Dilemma is a conflict between the values of freedom and equality on the one hand and the facts of discrimination and prejudice supported by white power on the other. Racism has declined as a rationalization of the conflict. Americans have become increasingly explicit in their affirmation of freedom and equality for all. But such valuations are maintained most easily and cheaply at a highly abstract level. When asked to implement them in particular cases which come close to home, whites are still slow to be consistent.

The American Dilemma is intensified because just as whites have sharpened the conflict between values and behavior, blacks have been pushing harder for a final resolution of the dilemma. It becomes more and more difficult for white Americans to take refuge in glittering generalities, or simply to ignore the conflict. Yet the trouble cannot be wholly cured without giving blacks much more real social power than they have ever had, and this the whites are reluctant to do.

Blacks too have a dilemma, which was put like this by Masotti et al. (1969:159):

> The Negro in his drive for implementation of *de facto* equality faces a choice: he can attempt to effect change through the established democratic process or he can resort to violence. In either case, the prospect is not optimistic. The dilemma is that neither road to equality is likely to produce the desired change.

This gloomy estimate is based on the inability of blacks so far to form a winning coalition with other groups seeking the same kind of change through the democratic process. Violence is also doomed, we feel: the whites have too much power. We shall not

In spite of the brave principles of freedom and equality set forth in the Declaration of Independence, discrimination violating those principles has been part of American life from the beginning. The religious persecutions of colonial New England, the seventeenth- and eighteenth-century slave trade, and the "Jim Crow" practices of the nineteenth and twentieth centuries are memorable examples of this unfortunate fact. In very recent years substantial progress has been made in bringing our practices into closer agreement with the Declaration of Independence and the Constitution, but much remains to be done.

here project the future, except to say that while further gains for the black minority are probable, they will not soon be enough to erase the minority stigma. There are painful years ahead before that happens.

New Activism   So far we have spoken only of the black minority. Our reason for this is that the present era of minority activism was initiated by blacks. Their boldness, sacrifices, and partial successes have awakened hope in other minorities that resolute challenge of white power can lessen discrimination for them too. And so we are now witnessing a new insurgency of such formerly quite passive minorities as American Indians and Mexican Americans. It is against the same background that the women's liberation movement has come into being.

The American people have recently been challenged as never before to make good their belief in their best values. Further real progress in reducing discrimination against minorities will require that minority people no longer be excluded from the councils of power throughout society. This is a hard lesson to learn. If this era ends without our learning it, the closing of options that can lead to real gains for our minorities will have very destructive results for the American people as a whole.

Sociological analysis lays bare what we feel are the deepest roots of discrimination and prejudice. The import of this analysis is that programs and policies which do not go to these roots are unlikely to bring fundamental or permanent change.

Above all, Americans must learn that members of minorities will have to be admitted to positions with enough power to make the important decisions in our society. Tokenism will be recognized and will not be enough. Many practical-minded people will say that not enough minority members are competent to wield power in many technically complex situations. That is true, but it is discrimination that has produced this state of affairs. Enlightened citizens must find ways of giving minority members the kinds of socialization experiences that produce competent leadership.

One present embarrassment is that organizations willing to make this effort often fail to find qualified people. Universities that would like to add minority faculty members often have trouble doing so. In every department of our national life, we must train minority people to enter the same pipelines that raise others to power and responsibility.

It is also consistent with the sociological position to point out that economic insecurity tends to strengthen discrimination and prejudice. Any national or local programs which reduce the objective base for economic insecurity in all citizens should help.

PRACTICAL IMPLICATIONS OF THE SOCIOLOGY OF MINORITIES

USING NORMS TO REDUCE DISCRIMINATION The social norms which legitimize and prescribe discrimination cannot be changed by wishing them away or exhorting people to give them up. Since these have their greatest effect in local groups, local efforts should be particularly appropriate here. Most groups which contain discriminatory norms have other norms which sometimes can be used to inhibit prejudice and discrimination. We recall a black family that moved into a middle-class, all-white neighborhood in a northern city. At once a neighbor of influence visited the new housewife, asked her to coffee to meet others, and invited the family to the local church. The new family was accepted into the neighborhood without incident. This behavior elicited norms of neighborliness and fair play. An ugly situation could have developed if some other resident had chosen to arouse the latent prejudice which surely was also present in the neighborhood.

Practicing the Sociological Perspective

Suppose you have a violent argument with a friend who belongs to a different racial or ethnic category. Would you be tempted to use racial or ethnic slurs if you are really mad? Try to figure out why you might use them, and how you know that they would hurt. How do you feel about jokes based on racial or ethnic stereotypes? Do they strike you as funny? Under what circumstances might such humor not cause pain to persons belonging to groups involved in such jokes?

Alone or with others pretend for a day that all blondes are superior to all brunettes or vice versa. Think up an ideology that justifies this assumption, a kind of racism, if you will. During the day watch for "evidence" that "proves" the superiority of blondes. As you act out this idea do you find that it affects your attitudes toward and relations with others?

Is it possible for a society to culturally brainwash some of its members so that they don't mind being treated as second class citizens? Can you think of any illustrations of this? If this really happens does it justify discrimination and prejudice?

About 11 percent of all Americans are black. What is the proportion of black students on your campus? How do you account for the difference between the two figures? If there is no racial discrimination on your campus the number of blacks holding positions of leadership should roughly equal their proportion in the total student body. Is this the case? If not, what does this suggest about the relationship between prejudice and discrimination?

How many women faculty members do you have? Ask professors in several fields why the number is so low. If possible, go to an establishment which employs both men and women and find the proportion of women to men at each organizational level.

Compare men's salaries with women's on each organizational level. Ask a number of men and women to explain the facts you find.

Members of a minority, we have said, share some characteristic that is hard to eradicate and that identifies the minority to others. Do you think a time might come in the United States when, say, black Americans would disappear? That is, their skin color would scarcely be noticed, or other Americans would attach no significance to it? Think carefully about this, and about what conditions would first have to exist. Do you know of any places in the world where something like this already exists?

Occupations and Professions

8

THE MEANING OF WORK

Present attitudes toward work are often very different from those of earlier times; there is good reason to predict that these attitudes will change again.

Tilgher (1931) examined the changing meaning of work from the Greeks to the middle of our century. The Greeks felt that work was a curse from the gods. To the Romans, only two occupations were honorable; agriculture and big business; otherwise, they felt much the same. The Hebrews regarded work as having some intrinsic worth and meaning; although it was distressing, it had religious overtones, since it brought atonement for original sin. The early Christians inherited this notion, and also believed men should work to share with those less fortunate. At that point work began to be regarded as a physical and spiritual necessity. Early Catholicism gave it a new spiritual dimension through the teachings and examples of the Benedictine monks in particular, who alternated between work and prayer. St. Thomas Aquinas formalized the idea of work as a natural right and duty, and as the basis for society, property, and profit.

Max Weber, in *The Protestant Ethic and the Spirit of Capitalism,* showed that with the advent of Protestantism, work assumed an even more central place in the scheme of things. He argued that the Protestant view of work's importance was a precondition for modern capitalism. To Luther, labor was a way of serving God and there was no better way. In connection with his doctrine of predestination, Calvin "taught that one must find solace solely on the basis of the true faith. Each man was duty-bound to consider himself chosen and to reject all doubt as a temptation of the devil, for a lack of self-confidence was interpreted as a sign of insufficient faith. To attain that self-confidence, *unceasing work in a calling was recommended*" (emphasis added) (Bendix, 1960:81).

Later, in colonial America, "The Puritan divines praised work as a defense against all such temptations as religious doubts, the sense of unworthiness, or sexual desires. . . . But unremitting labor was not merely a negative good; it was the way of life ordained by God in which every man must prove himself" (Bendix, 1960:83).

In America today, work still has much of the dignity it had in Calvin's time, even though the feeling that hard work is a religious duty has probably declined. Meanwhile the work ethic, so strongly buttressed by Protestant theology and multiplied many times by the industrial revolution, has produced an unprecedented flood of goods and services in the technically advanced societies. So productive are these societies that they now must devote substantial resources to persuading workers to consume more and more, an impulse that would have horrified the early Protestant theologians. As Tilgher (1931) puts it, "Thus in the very homeland of the religion of work a still later religion is growing up, the religion of large buying and of amusements, a religion of comfort, of well-being, of convenience, of cleanliness, a religion of the body."

Harvesting scene from Breviarium Grimani, late fifteenth century.

WHY PEOPLE WORK   To many Americans, work furnishes some of the central meanings of life; it is scarcely to be distinguished from play. When such people retire, what they give up is not hated drudgery but some of the most valued experiences they have known. These people work as much because of their fascination with what they are doing as for the monetary rewards they receive. While such attitudes toward work may be found in almost any occupation, they are particularly likely to occur among professionals, top executives, scholars, scientists, poets, novelists, and artists.

There also are many who hate their work and derive no satisfaction or self-fulfillment from it. Each day they must carry out tasks which may even seem degrading to them. These attitudes also occur in many different occupations, but mainly among people who work at monotonous, disagreeable, unskilled tasks. These people work in order to live and because they see no practical alternatives.

Probably most people in the United States neither love their work nor hate it. They see it as an unavoidable part of life, and their feelings about it are not strong, either positively or negatively. Most of the white-collar and blue-collar occupations in our society arouse this feeling in large proportions of their practitioners.

During the nineteenth century, in the early years of the industrial revolution, the prevailing moral valuation of hard work was used as a justification for exploitation of labor.

Berger and Berger (1972:237–38) suggest that questions about the meaning of work take different forms in the occupations where the foregoing attitudes are most likely to be found. Among high-status occupations such as the professions people ask sophisticated questions about the meaning of the work they do. Social scientists argue about whether they should be politically neutral, and business executives philosophize about the social obligations of business.

Most white- and blue-collar workers, say the Bergers, do not trouble themselves with complex questions about the meaning of their work. Instead, they are more concerned with how it affects other parts of their lives where self-fulfillment is more likely to be sought. They think about job security, working conditions, retirement, and medical insurance, for these affect their ability to carry on in more important sectors of their lives.

The meaning of work for those in the least attractive occupations is almost wholly negative. Deprived of the religious connotations once attached to any work, people in the poorer jobs simply feel a never-ending comparison with others more fortunate. Work means a daily assault on their feeling of personal worth.

A study by Morse and Weiss (1962) carries us beyond these generalizations and gives us a glimpse into the diversity of meanings that work can have. They interviewed a sample of 401 employed men and asked them: "If by some chance you inherited enough money to live comfortably without working, do you think that you would work anyway, or not?" Four out of five of these men answered that they would want to keep on working. The reasons they gave are summarized in Table 8-1. Note their variety. Actually, the reasons are of two kinds. Reasons 1, 2, 4, 6, 9, 10 and 12, making up 68 percent of the total, in one way or another all suggest that one of the most common reasons for

TABLE 8-1   REASONS FOR CONTINUING TO WORK (PERCENTAGE OF RESPONDENTS)

1. To keep occupied (interested).	32
2. Would feel lost, go crazy (if I didn't work).	13
3. It keeps an individual happy, is good for persons.	10
4. Wouldn't know what to do with my time, can't be idle.	10
5. Enjoy the kind of work.	9
6. Out of habit, inertia.	6
7. Justifies my existence.	5
8. Gives a feeling of self-respect.	5
9. Would feel bored (if I didn't work).	4
10. Would feel useless (if I didn't work).	2
11. To be associated with people.	1
12. To keep out of trouble.	1

Source: N. C. Morse and W. Weiss, "The Function and Meaning of Work and the Job," *American Sociological Review*, Vol. 20, April 1955, pp. 191–98.

work is to fill the individual's time, to keep him going. Most of us are socialized to spend large amounts of time at work (whether or not we find it pleasant and interesting). The absence of work, even if it is hated, poses the problem of what to do with oneself. And, for most of us, our society does not yet provide satisfying answers to this question.

The remaining reasons (3, 5, 7, 8 and 11), 30 percent of those given, reflect a very different attitude. These people seem to say that work is good, enjoyable, and adds positive meaning to existence.

What a person does for a living represents an important part of living itself. Work takes up a major segment of one's life space, provides a stabilizing rhythm to existence, and (potentially, at least) satisfies basic personal and social needs. Additional data from the study just cited show that work has the same degree of

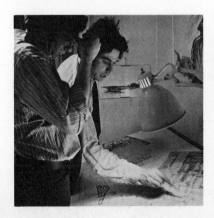

Compare the rewards that different kinds of work, such as these, can return to people. What effects are different jobs likely to have on other areas of people's lives?

importance for people regardless of occupation, though the kind of importance it has is influenced by the sort of work one does. Those in working-class occupations tend to regard work as supervised activity which occupies time. They labor to avoid boredom and restlessness. Persons in middle-class occupations are more likely to value work because it is interesting. It gives them a sense of accomplishment and contribution. To farmers, work is an especially pervasive activity, so much a part of existence that life without it is nearly inconceivable.

CHANGING OCCUPATIONS Finally, while most people would continue to work even if they did not have to, many would not continue the same line of work. Wilensky (1966:134) asked a large number of men in a wide variety of occupations the following question: "What type of work would you try to get into if you could start all over again?" At least seven out of every ten persons in each of thirteen professional categories presented in Table 8-2 indicated they would get into a similar type of work. On the other hand, with the exception of skilled printers and paper workers (52 percent each), less than half the white-collar workers and the remaining six blue-collar occupations would continue in the same kind of occupation. Plainly, the higher a job is ranked socially, the more often people are satisfied doing it.

TABLE 8-2 VARIATIONS AMONG OCCUPATIONAL GROUPS IN THE PROPORTION WHO WOULD TRY TO GET INTO A SIMILAR TYPE OF WORK IF THEY COULD START OVER AGAIN

PROFESSIONAL AND LOWER WHITE-COLLAR OCCUPATIONS	PERCENT	WORKING-CLASS OCCUPATIONS	PERCENT
Urban university professors	93	Skilled printers	52
Mathematicians	91	Paper workers	52
Physicists	89	Skilled auto workers	41
Biologists	89	Skilled steelworkers	41
Chemists	86	Textile workers	31
Firm lawyers	85	Blue-collar workers,	
School superintendents	85	age 30–55	24
Lawyers	83	Blue-collar workers,	
Journalists (Washington correspondents)	82	age 21–29	23
Church university professors	77	Unskilled steelworkers	21
Solo lawyers	75	Unskilled auto workers	16
Diversico engineers	70		
Unico engineers	70		
White-collar workers, age 21–29	46		
White-collar workers, age 30–55	43		

Source: Harold L. Wilensky, "Work as a Social Problem," in *Social Problems,* ed. Howard S. Becker (New York: John Wiley and Sons, 1966), p. 134.

Part 2 / Social Units and Processes

Gross (1958) pointed out that men and women spend most of their lives either preparing for a career, working, or thinking about their jobs. The average number of years in the working force, incidentally, varies from forty years for professional, technical and kindred workers to fifty-two years for farm laborers, foremen, and service workers (Wilensky, 1961:118). Some occupations absorb most of an individual's life. Consider how much of an astronaut's total time and energy are given over to matters relating to space exploration. His activities range from traveling on goodwill public relations tours to walking on the moon.[1]

Your work affects you in many ways, some direct, others less so. It influences the quantity and quality of your social relationships, your income, marital status, family size, leisure activities, membership in clubs, the reaction of other people toward you, and the kind of community (and the part of it) in which you live. Night custodians, lighthouse keepers, and forest rangers tend to have limited contacts with people. Waiters, salesmen, and checkers in large supermarkets have extensive but superficial contacts. If selectivity is a measure of quality, the portrait painter is well off because he can paint whom he chooses, and if he is talented enough, he will be paid for his efforts. The common house prostitute is not so fortunate. She must accommodate anyone who has the fee for her services.

INCOME Income level is closely tied to occupation. Broadly speaking, the more education, prestige, and importance associated with a kind of work, the higher the income. In 1970, self-employed male professional workers received an average annual income of $17,670. In that same year, male laborers received incomes averaging only $4,839 (*Statistical Abstract of the United States*). In 1947, and again in 1963, the National Opinion Research Center interviewed a representative sample of Americans and asked them, among a host of other things, what makes a job excellent? A high income was most frequently mentioned as the chief criterion, although almost as many people felt that a job should be judged in terms of its necessity and service to humanity (Hodge et al., 1964:286–302).

FERTILITY, MARRIAGE, AND DIVORCE Fertility is associated with occupation; persons in prestige jobs generally have fewer children. In 1969, 2,927 children were born per thousand women thirty-five to forty-five years old whose husbands were profes-

---

[1] Having given this example, it is interesting to note that Michael Collins, who remained in moon orbit while his comrades made the first moon landing, indicated shortly after returning to earth that he would not continue in space flight. "I think it's difficult to keep up year after year, to really approach the training, the living in simulators, with the zeal that you have to in order to do a good job," Collins is reported to have said on the CBS "Face the Nation" program, August 17, 1969.

sional, technical and kindred workers. But 4,607 children were born per thousand wives of farm laborers (*Current Population Reports,* 1970:10–12)

Marital status also tends to be connected to occupation. Both formal and informal norms regarding marriage attach to many occupational roles. It is just as likely, for example, for Catholic priests, airline stewardesses, and playboy bunnies to be unmarried as it is for Protestant ministers, Jewish rabbis, and high school principals to be married. Occupation also appears to be related to divorce. Goode (1956:46) found that service workers were over three and a half times as prone to divorce as professional and semiprofessional workers.

LEISURE AND ORGANIZATIONAL MEMBERSHIP   Time spent on leisure and membership in voluntary associations also varies by occupation. Wilensky has discovered that the top occupational levels are losing out in the widespread trend toward increased leisure time, and are reaching startlingly high lifetime work totals (1961). Hausknecht, in his book *The Joiners* (1962:25), reveals that 29 percent of professionals, proprietors, managers, and officials belong to two or more voluntary associations, as compared to only 5 percent of unskilled laborers.

WORK ROLES AS KEY ROLES   A person's occupation provides him with one of his key roles in life. Because these roles are culturally defined and at least partially known far beyond the bounds of the occupation itself, to know a person's job is to have many cues about how to respond to him, cues which have little or nothing to do with his personality as such. When applying for credit or considering a major purchase of some kind, one of the first questions asked is what you do. It will come as little surprise to you that an engineer would probably receive more deferential treatment from a car salesman than a gas station attendent would. In trying to convey an unusual or complicated thought, idea, or principle, it is often helpful to know something about the occupations of your audience.

PLACE OF WORK   Finally, occupation affects where one works. Much farm labor is seasonal and transitory, and workers move from one crop or harvest to another. A sociologist is likely to be found at a college or a university. Seventy-three percent of the sociologists with Ph.D.s are employed by universities and four-year colleges (Sibley, 1963:56). Nearly all architects are city dwellers. In the Great Plains, lumbermen and oceanographers are few and far between. Wheat farmers are scarce on both east and west coasts.

In view of the centrality of work in our lives, it is little wonder that many people regard the choice of a career as one of the two most important decisions an individual makes; the other involves the choice of a spouse. In many ways, when you choose a career you are betting your life.

We have already made some sociological observations about work in relation to the individual. We wish now to make a few more, to establish the sociological significance of work behavior in human societies. Keep in mind that although individuals choose to associate themselves with occupations they do not originate them. In every society the organization of work precedes the arrival of each individual on the social scene. As each child approaches maturity he confronts the way in which work is organized into occupational fields by his society. What he confronts is a very important part of the *society,* and it has fateful consequences for him personally. There are many societies in which there is no difficult choice of occupation. One simply follows the occupation ordained for him by the family into which he or she was born. In America the individual does choose, and often the choice is difficult.

OCCUPATION AS A KEY SOCIOLOGICAL VARIABLE

OCCUPATION AS A STATUS INDICATOR   Occupation is important in two other ways, in the determination of social status and in the self-concept. In their studies of status systems, sociologists use occupation as an index of prestige. In fact, occupation is the most widely accepted single measure of an individual's total position in the stratification system (Reissman, 1959:149). (You recall our lengthier discussion in Chapter 6.) The study of occupational prestige reveals some interesting facts, as shown in Table 8-3 based on a study conducted by the National Opinion Research Center. A striking fact revealed by this study is the remarkable closeness of the occupational ratings of 1963 to those of 1947. Clearly the factors in occupational prestige are slow to change.

The prestige of occupations is related to the amount of specialized training they require and the responsibility for public welfare they entail. Notice that in both 1947 and 1963 Supreme Court justice and physician ranked highest, and shoe shiner, street sweeper, and garbage collector ranked lowest. As a group, or by types of work, government positions ranked highest. Professionals and semiprofessionals ranked second. Within this category scientists were tops. The lowest rated groups were nonfarm laborers.

WORK AND THE SELF-CONCEPT   A noted sociologist, Everett C. Hughes (1951:313), said, "A man's work is one of the things by which he is judged, and certainly one of the more significant things by which he judges himself." One's identity is made up of a number of things, and the work one does is not least among them. A simple demonstration which you could conduct yourself illustrates the point nicely. Ask any number of adults who they

Table 8-3 Distribution of Occupational Prestige Ratings, United States, 1947 and 1963

| | March, 1947 | | | | | | | | June, 1963 | | | | | | | |
| | Percent | | | | | | | | Percent | | | | | | | |
Occupation	Excel-lent*	Good	Aver-age	Below Aver-age	Poor	Don't Know†	NORC Score**	Rank	Excel-lent	Good	Aver-age	Below Aver-age	Poor	Don't Know§	NORC Score	Rank
U.S. Supreme Court justice	83	15	2	II	II	3	96	1	77	18	4	1	1	1	94	1
Physician	67	30	3	II	II	1	93	2.5	71	25	4	II	II	1	93	2
Nuclear physicist	48	39	11	1	1	51	86	18	70	23	5	1	1	10	92	3.5
Scientist	53	38	8	1	II	7	89	8	68	27	5	II	II	2	92	3.5
Government scientist	51	41	7	1	II	6	88	10.5	64	30	5	II	1	2	91	5.5
State governor	71	25	4	II	II	1	93	2.5	64	30	5	II	1	1	91	5.5
Cabinet member in the federal government	66	28	5	1	II	6	92	4.5	61	32	6	1	1	2	90	8
College professor	53	40	7	II	II	1	89	8	59	35	5	II	II	1	90	8
U.S. representative in Congress	57	35	6	1	1	4	89	8	58	33	6	2	II	2	90	8
Chemist	42	48	9	1	II	7	86	18	54	38	8	II	II	3	89	11
Lawyer	44	45	9	1	1	1	86	18	53	38	8	II	II	II	89	11
Diplomat in U.S. foreign service	70	24	4	1	1	9	92	4.5	57	34	7	1	1	3	89	11
Dentist	42	48	9	1	II	II	86	18	47	47	6	II	II	II	88	14
Architect	42	48	9	1	II	6	86	18	47	45	6	II	II	2	88	14
County judge	47	43	9	1	II	1	87	13	50	40	8	1	II	1	88	14
Psychologist	38	49	12	1	II	15	85	22	49	41	8	1	II	6	87	17.5
Minister	52	35	11	1	1	1	87	13	53	33	13	1	1	1	87	17.5
Member of the board of directors of a large corporation	42	47	10	1	II	5	86	18	42	51	6	1	II	1	87	17.5
Mayor of a large city	57	36	6	1	II	1	90	6	46	44	9	1	1	II	87	17.5
Priest	51	34	11	2	2	6	86	18	52	33	12	2	1	6	86	21.5
Head of a department in a state government	47	44	8	II	1	3	87	13	44	48	6	1	1	1	86	21.5
Civil engineer	33	55	11	1	II	5	84	23	40	52	8	II	II	2	86	21.5
Airline pilot	35	48	15	1	1	3	83	24.5	41	48	11	1	II	1	86	21.5
Banker	49	43	8	II	II	1	88	10.5	39	51	10	1	1	II	85	24.5
Biologist	29	51	18	1	1	16	81	29	38	50	11	II	II	6	85	24.5
Sociologist	31	51	16	1	1	23	82	26.5	35	48	15	1	1	10	83	26
Instructor in public schools	28	45	24	2	1	1	79	34	30	53	16	1	II	II	82	27.5
Captain in the regular army	28	49	19	2	2	2	80	31.5	28	55	16	2	II	1	82	27.5
Accountant for a large business	25	57	17	1	II	3	81	29	27	55	17	1	II	II	81	29.5
Public school teacher	26	45	24	3	2	II	78	36	31	46	22	1	II	II	81	29.5
Owner of a factory that employs about 100 people	30	51	17	1	1	2	82	26.5	28	49	19	2	1	1	80	31.5
Building contractor	21	55	23	1	II	1	79	34	22	56	20	2	II	II	80	31.5
Artist who paints pictures that are exhibited in galleries	40	40	15	3	2	6	83	24.5	28	45	20	5	2	4	78	34.5
Musician in a symphony orchestra	31	46	19	3	1	5	81	29	25	45	25	3	1	3	78	34.5
Author of novels	32	44	19	3	2	9	80	31.5	26	46	22	4	2	5	78	34.5
Economist	25	48	24	2	1	22	79	34	20	53	24	2	1	12	78	34.5
Official of an international labor union	26	42	20	5	7	11	75	40.5	21	53	18	5	3	5	77	37
Railroad engineer	22	45	30	3	II	1	77	37.5	19	47	30	3	1	1	76	39
Electrician	15	38	43	4	II	1	73	45	18	45	34	2	II	II	76	39
County agricultural agent	17	53	28	2	II	5	77	37.5	13	54	30	2	1	4	76	39
Owner-operator of a printing shop	13	48	36	3	II	2	74	42.5	13	51	34	2	II	2	75	41.5
Trained machinist	14	43	38	5	II	2	73	45	15	50	32	4	II	II	75	41.5
Farm owner and operator	19	46	31	3	1	1	76	39	16	45	33	5	II	1	74	44
Undertaker	14	43	36	5	2	2	72	47	16	46	33	3	2	3	74	44

TABLE 8-3 (*Continued*)

| | MARCH, 1947 | | | | | | | | JUNE, 1963 | | | | | | | |
| | *Percent* | | | | | | | | *Percent* | | | | | | | |
Occupation	Excellent*	Good	Average	Below Average	Poor	Don't Know†	NORC Score**	Rank	Excellent	Good	Average	Below Average	Poor	Don't Know§	NORC Score	Rank
Welfare worker for a city government	16	43	35	4	2	4	73	45	17	44	32	5	2	2	74	44
Newspaper columnist	13	51	32	3	1	5	74	42.5	10	49	38	3	1	1	73	46
Policeman	11	30	46	11	2	1	67	55	16	38	37	6	2	II	72	47
Reporter on a daily newspaper	9	43	43	4	1	2	71	48	7	45	44	3	1	1	71	48
Radio announcer	17	45	35	3	II	2	75	40.5	9	42	44	5	1	1	70	49.5
Bookkeeper	8	31	55	6	II	1	68	51.5	9	40	45	5	1	II	70	49.5
Tenant farmer—one who owns livestock and machinery and manages the farm	10	37	40	11	2	1	68	51.5	11	37	42	8	3	1	69	51.5
Insurance agent	7	34	53	4	2	2	68	51.5	6	40	47	5	2	II	69	51.5
Carpenter	5	28	56	10	1	II	65	58	7	36	49	8	1	II	68	53
Manager of a small store in a city	5	40	50	4	1	1	69	49	3	40	48	7	2	II	67	54.5
A local official of a labor union	7	29	41	14	9	11	62	62	8	36	42	9	5	4	67	54.5
Mail carrier	8	26	54	10	2	II	66	57	7	29	53	10	1	II	66	57
Railroad conductor	8	30	52	9	1	1	67	55	6	33	48	10	3	II	66	57
Traveling salesman for a wholesale concern	6	35	53	5	1	2	68	51.5	4	33	54	7	3	2	66	57
Plumber	5	24	55	14	2	1	63	59.5	6	29	54	9	2	II	65	59
Automobile repairman	5	21	58	14	2	II	63	59.5	5	25	56	12	2	II	64	60
Playground director	7	33	48	10	2	4	67	55	6	29	46	15	4	3	63	62.5
Barber	3	17	56	20	4	1	59	66	4	25	56	13	2	1	63	62.5
Machine operator in a factory	4	20	53	20	3	2	60	64.5	6	24	51	15	4	1	63	62.5
Owner-operator of a lunch stand	4	24	55	14	3	1	62	62	4	25	57	11	3	1	63	62.5
Corporal in the regular army	5	21	48	20	6	3	60	64.5	6	25	47	15	6	2	62	65.5
Garage mechanic	4	21	57	17	1	II	62	62	4	22	56	15	3	II	62	65.5
Truck driver	2	11	49	29	9	II	54	71	3	18	54	19	5	II	59	67
Fisherman who owns his own boat	3	20	48	21	8	7	58	68	3	19	51	19	8	4	58	68
Clerk in a store	2	14	61	20	3	II	58	68	1	14	56	22	6	II	56	70
Milk route man	2	10	52	29	7	1	54	71	3	12	55	23	7	1	56	70
Streetcar motorman	3	16	55	21	5	2	58	68	3	16	46	27	8	2	56	70
Lumberjack	2	11	48	29	10	8	53	73	2	16	46	29	7	3	55	72.5
Restaurant cook	3	13	44	29	11	1	54	71	4	15	44	26	11	II	55	72.5
Singer in a nightclub	3	13	43	23	18	6	52	74.5	3	16	43	24	14	3	54	74
Filling station attendant	1	9	48	34	8	1	52	74.5	2	11	41	34	11	II	51	75
Dockworker	2	7	34	37	20	8	47	81.5	2	9	43	33	14	3	50	77.5
Railroad section hand	2	9	35	33	21	3	48	79.5	3	10	39	29	18	2	50	77.5
Night watchman	3	8	33	35	21	1	47	81.5	3	10	39	32	17	1	50	77.5
Coal miner	4	11	33	31	21	2	49	77.5	3	13	34	31	19	2	50	77.5
Restaurant waiter	2	8	37	36	17	1	48	79.5	2	8	42	32	16	II	49	80.5
Taxi driver	2	8	38	35	17	1	49	77.5	2	8	39	31	18	1	49	80.5
Farm hand	3	12	35	31	19	1	50	76	3	12	31	32	22	II	48	83
Janitor	1	7	30	37	25	1	44	85.5	1	9	35	35	19	1	48	83
Bartender	1	6	32	32	29	4	44	85.5	1	7	42	28	21	2	48	83
Clothes presser in a laundry	2	6	35	36	21	2	46	83	2	7	31	38	22	1	45	85
Soda fountain clerk	1	5	34	40	20	2	45	84	II	5	30	44	20	1	44	86
Sharecropper—one who owns no livestock or equipment and does not manage farm	1	6	24	28	41		40	87	1	8	26	28	37	2	42	87

Table 8-3 (*Continued*)

| | MARCH, 1947 | | | | | | | | JUNE, 1963 | | | | | | | |
| | Percent | | | | | | | | Percent | | | | | | | |
Occupation	Excel-lent*	Good	Aver-age	Below Aver-age	Poor	Don't Know†	NORC Score**	Rank	Excel-lent✔	Good	Aver-age	Below Aver-age	Poor	Don't Know§	NORC Score	Rank
Garbage collector	1	4	16	26	53	2	35	88	2	5	21	32	41	1	39	88
Street sweeper	1	3	14	29	53	1	34	89	1	4	17	31	46	1	36	89
Shoe shiner	1	2	13	28	56	2	33	90	II	3	15	30	51	2	34	90
Average	22	31	30	11	7	4	70	—	22	32	29	11	6	2	72	—

* Bases for the 1947 occupational ratings are 2,920 less "don't know" and not answered for each occupational title.
† Base is 2,920 in all cases.
✔ Bases for the 1963 occupational ratings are 651 less "don't know" and not answered for each occupational title.
§ Base is 651 in all cases.
II Less than 0.5 percent.
** Ratings were arbitrarily assigned numerical values: excellent = 100, good = 80, average = 60, somewhat below average = 40, and poor = 20. Calculating the numerical average of these assigned values over all respondents rating the occupational yields the NORC prestige score.
Source: Robert W. Hodge and others, "Occupational Prestige in the United States, 1925–63," *American Journal of Sociology,* 70, 1964, 286–302. Copyright 1964, 1965, by the University of Chicago.

are. In a majority of cases occupational role will be among the first five attributes listed (I am a housewife, I am a trainee at IBM, I am an engineer with Boeing, I am a secretary at the university).

The self-concept is profoundly influenced by social roles and membership in social categories, as we indicated in Chapter 3. I am a human being, black or white, a Catholic, Protestant, or Jew, a husband, son, parent, and so forth. Only after such attributes do most people name personality and physical traits such as being gregarious, quiet, intellectual, compassionate, affectionate, well-built, stocky, tall, and the like. And only a few persons initially think of themselves in such esoteric terms as I am a free spirit, or I am a child of nature.

Occupational Self-Image and Role Performance The development of a professional or occupational self-image is very important in the performance of role prescriptions associated with a number of lines of work. It marks a critical point in the adult socialization process. Huntington (1957:179) suggests that physicians who consistently feel and think like M.D.s perform as doctors more effectively than those who don't. She says that thinking of themselves as doctors may help them maintain confidence in coping with difficult medical tasks. This in turn leads to a reduction in personal strain. The importance of the development of an occupational or professional self-concept and the part played by schools in promoting the self-image is further documented by Lortie's study of the legal profession (1959). He says that law schools allow elements such as glamour, facility, and idealism to persist in the law student's image of the lawyer. When the young lawyer has his initial first-hand contact with actual practice he is often shocked to find that it is often mundane, laborious, and not necessarily idealistic.

When the work role has had time to become an established part of the self-concept, many other important consequences follow. Gross (1965:14) holds that the unwillingness of a group of unemployed skilled workers to accept jobs other than their usual ones is not merely a matter of wage differences, but is partly due to identification with their craft. They were reluctant to change jobs because this would mean a change in the way these men saw themselves. During the Great Depression of the thirties, many men chose to remain unemployed rather than take a job at something they had never done before.

The importance of work in self-images shows up indirectly in feelings about occupational titles, labels, or name tags. Many people are resentful if the proper distinctions are not made between occupational roles (Caplow, 1954:134–35). The rural postman, who is an independent contractor, dislikes being identified with the urban postman, whom he sees as merely an employee. A similar situation prevails with the auto mechanic and the gas station attendant, the powerhouse engineer and the janitor, the accountant and the clerk. The significance of job titles is further evidenced in the tendency for them to become more and more pretentious. Undertakers are no longer undertakers but morticians, bill collectors are credit representatives, reporters have become journalists, and street sweepers have been transformed into sanitation engineers.

To become part of the self, an occupational role must be deeply accepted and internalized. Sometimes this doesn't happen. Men drafted into the army against their will may refuse to identify their self-concept with the military work role required of them.

Almost half the labor force in the United States is engaged in manual and service work. Nearly 50 percent are classified as white-collar workers, while only 3.9 percent are in farming. The current labor force reveals some interesting trends. In 1970, there were over two and a half times more white-collar workers than there were in 1900. The sharpest increase was among clerical and kindred workers, who increased fivefold from 1900 to 1970. This dramatic increase in white-collar workers has been accompanied by a spectacular decline in farm workers, from 37.5 percent in 1900 to 3.9 percent in 1971. Manual and service workers have increased only slightly. The decrease in farm workers can be attributed to the high degree of industrialization and to changes in agricultural technology in the United States. Manufacturing, trade, transportation, the military services, and public administration have in the past recruited most of their workers from agriculture. Concurrently, mechanization in agriculture has reduced the number of workers required for farming. Now there are not enough agricultural workers left to serve as a major labor pool from which other industries can recruit.

MAJOR OCCUPATIONAL GROUPS IN THE U.S.—THE WORK PEOPLE DO

COMPLEXITY AND SPECIALIZATION Other trends in United States labor are an increasingly complex division of labor and an enormous degree of specialization. In 1965 the *Dictionary of Occupational Titles* listed twenty-three thousand different jobs in

TABLE 8-4 PERCENT DISTRIBUTION BY MAJOR OCCUPATION GROUP AND SEX FOR THE UNITED STATES: 1900–1970

MAJOR OCCUPATION GROUP AND SEX	1970	1960	1950	1940	1930	1920	1910	1900
Both Sexes								
Total	100.0	100.0	100.0	100.0	100.0	100.0	100.0	100.0
White-collar workers	48.3	43.9	36.6	31.1	29.4	29.4	21.3	17.6
Professional, technical, and kindred workers	14.2	11.8	8.6	7.5	6.8	5.4	4.7	4.3
Managers, officials, and proprietors, exc. farm	10.5	10.8	8.7	7.3	7.4	6.6	6.6	5.8
Clerical and kindred workers	17.4	14.8	12.3	9.6	8.9	8.0	5.3	3.0
Sales workers	6.2	6.5	7.0	6.7	6.3	4.9	4.7	4.5
Manual and service workers	47.7	49.5	51.6	51.5	49.4	48.1	47.7	44.9
Manual workers	35.3	36.7	41.1	39.8	39.6	40.2	38.2	35.8
Craftsmen, foremen, and kindred workers	12.9	13.0	14.1	12.0	12.8	13.0	11.6	10.5
Operatives and kindred workers	17.7	18.8	20.4	18.4	15.8	15.6	14.6	12.8
Laborers, except farm and mine	4.7	4.9	6.6	9.4	11.0	11.6	12.0	12.5
Service workers	12.4	12.8	10.5	11.7	9.8	7.8	9.6	9.0
Farm workers	4.0	6.6	11.8	17.4	21.2	27.0	30.9	37.5
Male								
Total	100.0	100.0	100.0	100.0	100.0	100.0	100.0	100.0
White-collar workers	41.0	38.4	30.5	26.6	25.2	21.4	20.2	17.6
Professional, technical, and kindred workers	14.0	11.2	7.2	5.8	4.8	3.8	3.5	3.4
Managers, officials, and proprietors, exc. farm	14.2	13.9	10.5	8.6	8.8	7.8	7.7	6.8
Clerical and kindred workers	7.1	7.2	6.4	5.8	5.5	5.3	4.4	2.8
Sales workers	5.6	6.1	6.4	6.4	6.1	4.5	4.6	4.6
Manual and service workers	53.7	52.9	54.6	51.7	50.0	48.2	45.1	40.8
Manual workers	47.0	46.2	48.4	45.6	45.2	44.5	41.3	37.6
Craftsmen, foremen, and kindred workers	20.1	18.9	19.0	15.5	16.2	16.0	14.1	12.6
Operatives and kindred workers	19.6	20.1	20.5	18.0	15.3	14.4	12.5	10.4
Laborers, except farm and mine	7.3	7.2	8.8	12.1	13.6	14.0	14.6	14.7
Service workers	6.7	6.7	6.2	6.1	4.8	3.7	3.8	3.1
Farm workers	5.3	8.7	14.9	21.7	24.8	30.4	34.7	41.7
Female								
Total	100.0	100.0	100.0	100.0	100.0	100.0	100.0	100.0
White-collar workers	60.5	55.3	52.5	44.9	44.2	38.8	26.1	17.8
Professional, technical, and kindred workers	14.5	13.1	12.2	12.8	13.8	11.7	9.8	8.2
Managers, officials, and proprietors, exc. farm	4.4	4.7	4.3	3.3	2.7	2.2	2.0	1.4
Clerical and kindred workers	34.5	30.0	27.4	21.5	20.9	18.7	9.2	4.0
Sales workers	7.0	7.2	8.6	7.4	6.8	6.3	5.1	4.3
Manual and service workers	37.7	42.3	43.9	51.0	47.3	47.6	58.1	63.2
Manual workers	16.1	17.2	22.4	21.6	19.8	23.7	25.7	27.8
Craftsmen, foremen, and kindred workers	1.1	.9	1.5	1.1	1.0	1.2	1.4	1.4
Operatives and kindred workers	14.5	16.0	20.0	19.5	17.4	20.2	22.9	23.8
Laborers, except farm and mine	.4	.3	0.8	1.1	1.5	2.3	1.4	2.6
Service workers	21.7	25.1	21.5	29.4	27.5	23.9	32.4	35.4
Farm workers	1.8	2.4	3.7	4.0	8.4	13.5	15.8	18.9

Sources: D. C. Miller and W. H. Form, *Industrial Sociology*, 2d ed. (New York: Harper and Row, 1964), pp. 62–63; *American Almanac*, p. 230.

over two hundred industries (United States Department of Labor, 1965:xv). Around 1800, there were probably only fifty to one hundred distinguishable occupational titles. Wilbert E. Moore (1962:93) dramatizes our current job specialization by listing strange occupations, such as winding clocks, tasting tea, helping out-of-town shoppers get rid of their money, smelling water, walking on mattresses (to stamp out lumps before they are sold), knocking out teeth (of animals in meatpacking companies), spooning (cleaning out holes for dynamite in coal mines), and necking (putting on sweater necks in knitting mills).[2]

Specialization is not restricted to legitimate occupations. The late E. H. Sutherland (1937) conducted intensive studies of professional thieves and identified five kinds of pickpockets depending upon which pocket they picked: the breech, prat, tail, fob, and insider. To this list we could add such illegitimate sounding, but definitely legal occupations as the chiseler head (who removes meat, glands, and organs from animal heads to make meat products or for medicinal use), the pillar robber (who removes pillars of coal, ore, or salt left to support roofs during production mining), and the heavy forger (who operates a press to shape heated metal in the forging industry).

THE EMPLOYEE SOCIETY Work in the United States usually involves working for someone else. We have been referred to as the employee society (Drucker, 1953). In the short period from 1950 to 1965 the proportion of the United States labor force classified as self-employed—which had been declining for many years—dropped from more than 17 percent to 12 percent (Bureau of the Census, 1950, and Department of Labor, 1965). The self-employed person is vanishing simply because the small businessman, farmer, and professional (for example, lawyer and medical doctor) find it increasingly hard to compete with larger businesses, farms, or firms. As we will note in Chapter 9, more and more people are going to work for the large organizations. Other trends in the labor force include the diminishing importance of child labor, earlier retirement, and the steady increase in the number and importance of women in the labor force (Fichlander, 1962:97–111).

HOW CAREERS ARE CHOSEN

Sociologists and others have done some research and developed some partial theories on occupational choice. Considering the critical importance of the subject, there is surprisingly little information available, certainly far less than is needed to provide a firm, factually based explanation of how one enters an occupation. Perhaps this state of affairs is a subtle legacy from the agrarian

_____

[2] We suggest an amusing diversion next time you are in your college library. Look up the *Dictionary of Occupational Titles* and conduct your own search for exotic and unusual jobs.

Self-employment slowly declines as we become more and more an "employee society."

past in which there was little choice of occupation for most people. The individual simply fell naturally, if not always enthusiastically, into a job identical or similar to that of his father. Today virtually all males and many females must choose. Somehow they must strike a bargain between job-related qualities they themselves may or may not have and a staggering variety of possible occupations (many thousands of them) about which they have varying amounts of accurate or grossly distorted information. Even though scientific information on occupational choice is inadequate, a number of partial explanations and some evidence exist. Ginzberg et al. (1951) have identified four broad approaches which visualize occupational choice as brought about by: (a) accident, (b) unconscious forces in the individual, (c) vocational guidance, and (d) a complex developmental process.

Accident as a cause is nearly self-explanatory. Given certain talent or potential, an individual selects an occupation because of some unplanned exposure to a powerful stimulating experience. This notion is probably reflected in the phrase "being in the right place at the right time." Accident unquestionably enters into many job choices, but taken by itself it offers far too simple an explanation. In a way, to attribute this decision to chance is merely to concede that one cannot identify the factors actually at work.

The idea of unconscious forces stems from psychoanalytical theory. It posits that over a period of time, an occupation is selected as a result of accumulating decisions all governed by some basic impulse over which one has little control. The role of unconscious impulses and defense mechanisms in choice of occupations is such that persons prefer, choose, and enter vocations which have some symbolic relationship to their inner conflicts and unrecognized desires. Vroom (1964:64) cites, for example, the work of Brill. Brill contends that sadomasochistic impulses are subli-

Part 2 / Social Units and Processes

mated in the vocational choices of physicians; unconscious guilt feelings are characteristic of lawyers and ministers; actors and lifeguards are said to sublimate infantile exhibitionism; photographers are presumed to have voyeuristic tendencies. This approach has serious limitations, not the least of which is that individuals are assumed to be passive agents, and such factors as ability, luck and conscious motivation are overlooked.

Vocational guidance is commonplace these days. Trained people are supposed to fit an individual's aptitude and interests to a particular job which then becomes his career. To be sure, this sometimes happens, but not often enough to be a common description of job selection.

Ginzberg et al. postulate that occupational choice is a developmental process which is largely irreversible, culminating in a compromise between personal characteristics and factors in the environment. There are three periods of occupational choice, with several stages in each period. Fantasy choice takes place between the ages of six and eleven. In these years, children come to realize that they must eventually work, but they think of it mostly in terms of pleasurable fantasy. They are not very objective about themselves and have little concept of time. The period of tentative choices runs from about eleven through seventeen. At first, choices are based on likes and dislikes, with the understanding that some decision must eventually be made. There gradually emerges an awareness of the need to be more realistic. Goals, values, and a host of other factors are then considered, particularly as they relate to work. The person thinks about how choice of an occupation will fit into some sort of life plan. Usually there is some fear of a premature commitment. Increasingly the person comes to view work as a means to an end.

The last period in this process, the realistic one, involves three stages: exploration, crystallization, and specification. The individual begins to have enough experience to be helpful in making his choice. He can assess many factors affecting his selection. At the end of the period he makes a final commitment. He now wants to specialize, and resists anything that would deflect him from his course.

In a similar vein, Stephenson (1957), Ford and Box (1967), Blau et al. (1956) conceive of occupational choice as a developmental process involving a series of interrelated decisions, but stress the compromise between preferences for certain jobs and the likelihood of getting them. Blau et al. suggest that to the person's choice must be added some examination of the processes by which some individuals, but not others, are selected for a certain occupation.

VALUES AND OCCUPATIONAL CHOICE Most of the research on occupational choice bears on the developmental approach, though often indirectly. Rosenberg (1955) has shown that students who want to become teachers or social workers tend to choose people-oriented values ("give me an opportunity to work with people rather than things" and "give me an opportunity to be helpful to others"). Students planning to enter business emphasize the extrinsic rewards of work ("it provides me with a chance to earn a good deal of money" and "it gives me social status and prestige"). Artists, natural scientists, and dramatists are concerned with self-expression ("it permits me to be creative and original" and "it provides me an opportunity to use my special abilities and aptitudes"). Scharzweller (1960) also sees clusters of values similar to the people-oriented, extrinsic reward-oriented, and self-expression–oriented values noted by Rosenberg.

Sociologists themselves illustrate a connection between values and occupational choice. Hopper (1963) identifies three influential value positions of persons who choose sociology as a career. First, they hold that sociology, as a humanistic study, is vital to a comprehensive liberal arts education. Second, they believe that sociology will become an instrument for needed social reform. Third, they view it as a means for scientific understanding of human behavior.

Other research (Stephenson, 1957; Bennett and Gist, 1964) shows many discrepancies between wanted and expected occupations, reflecting acceptance of compromise. For example, this happens with some students preparing for dentistry. Sherlock and Cohen (1966) found that some had wanted an occupation with high financial reward and exclusiveness. So they chose medicine. But many of them couldn't make it, and switched to an occupation not quite so high in reward, but more accessible—in this case, dentistry.

Wrong Career Choices   There is still a great deal we don't understand about the complicated interaction between individual and society that ends in job placement. As the process of choosing (or *being* chosen) now operates, many people change their minds, make the wrong choices, or are not properly prepared. A nationwide study of the aspirations and expectations of 33,982 graduates of 135 colleges and universities in 1961 showed that approximately half reported "some meaningful career shift or development during college" (Davis, 1964:61–62). Several years ago a western university publication began an article with the following inquiry: "If you were to begin all over again, would you go into the same line of work?" This same question had been put to a representative sample of workers by a Gallup poll in 1950, and one out of three answered negatively.

Other information tends to reinforce this finding. Twenty-five percent of all college graduates wish they had selected a different major. A follow-up study of a freshman class at Stanford University after nineteen years revealed that only 50 percent were in an occupation related to original vocational choice. A majority of those majoring in education in college never go into teaching. Two-thirds of a group of lawyers interviewed urged revision of the curriculum to give more training in the technical and social skills required in practice. Many of them said, "I wasn't prepared" (Lortie, 1959).

Such information clearly shows that the process of choosing an occupation does not work well from the standpoint of the individual. In view of the complexity of choice this is hardly surprising. One confronts thousands of occupations with little reliable information about most of them. His knowledge about his own qualifications with respect to this bewildering array is probably inadequate. While there are now many vocational counseling programs (and related vocational aptitude-testing instruments) in high schools and colleges, these often do not reach individuals in a useful way, and at their best are not developed enough to insure good choices in a high proportion of persons involved.

We wish to give special emphasis to a group of occupations known as the professions. These occupations have high social prestige. They have accommodated an increasing proportion of the total number of persons employed. In certain ways which we will explain, they serve as a kind of benchmark against which to measure other occupations. The readers of this book will enter professional occupations in large numbers.

PROFESSIONS: THE GLAMOROUS OCCUPATIONS

Industrialized societies are professionalizing by nature (Goode, 1969). In England, Wales, and the United States the proportion of professional workers in the labor force has been rising since 1871 (Farrag, 1964:20). In the United States the proportion of professional workers has nearly doubled in thirty-six years: from 6.8 percent in 1931 to 13.3 percent in 1967 (Bureau of Labor Statistics). It should not be supposed that all occupations will ultimately become professionalized, or that this would be desirable (Wilensky, 1964). The professions do, nevertheless, perform many of society's most important social functions, notably the pursuit of science and liberal learning and its practical application in medicine, technology, law, and teaching (Parsons, 1954:48). Furthermore, the prestige attached to the professions is widely envied. This fact is attested to by the numerous occupations which strive to become professionalized or at least to appropriate some of the appearances of professionalism in the hope that increased social standing will follow.

It is for such reasons that a number of persons have suggested using the professions as a model for a comparative perspective on all occupations (Gross, 1958; Vollmer and Mills, 1969). This involves placing occupations on a continuum ranging from nonprofessional through semiprofessional (Etzioni, 1969) to professional. No fields of work are found at the extreme polarities; all vary in the degree to which they possess professional attributes. The meaningfulness of this comparison is enhanced by the importance of the most professionalized occupations, their prestige in the society and the fact that a large number of people holding very non-professional jobs constantly seek to approximate the professional model.

THE CHARACTERISTICS OF A PROFESSION What, then, are the characteristics of a profession? While we shall not draw up a formal ideal-typical description, we shall indicate what such a description would contain, drawing on the work of sociologists who specialize in this subject. A well-developed profession, according to Greenwood (1962), has five essential attributes: a basis in systematic theory; authority recognized by the clientele; broad community sanction and approval of this authority; a code of ethics regulating the relations of professional persons with clients and colleagues; and a professional culture sustained by formal associations. Professional occupations have the maximum amount of these attributes, but countless others have them in lesser degree.

Systematic Knowledge Greenwood contends that it is not skill as such that distinguishes a profession but the systematic knowledge upon which the skill is predicated. He goes on to say that (1962:208–9)

theory serves as a base in terms of which the professional rationalizes his operations in concrete situations. Acquisition of the professional skill requires a prior or simultaneous mastery of the theory underlying that skill. Preparation for a profession, therefore, involves considerable preoccupation with systematic theory, a feature virtually absent in the training of the nonprofessional. And so treatises are written on legal theory, musical theory, social work theory, the theory of drama, and so forth; but no books appear on theory of punch-pressing or pipefitting or bricklaying. . . .

. . . On-the-job training through apprenticeship, which suffices for a nonprofessional occupation, becomes inadequate for a profession. Orientation in theory can be achieved best through formal education in an academic setting. Hence, the appearance of the professional school, more often than not university affiliated . . . as an occupation moves toward professional status, apprenticeship training yields to formalized education, because the function of theory as a groundwork for practice acquires increasing importance.

In a slightly satirical vein, one might counsel those seeking professional standing for their fields of work to first develop a theoretical rationale for occupational activities, then—above all—to secure university affiliation where a theory may be elaborated which increasingly sets off the initiate from the layman. The development of professional training programs at several universities in fields like hotel management, to name but one, shows that quite a few occupations have in fact taken just this route.

Professional Authority Professional authority expresses itself in the matter of who decides what goods and services are rendered.

Someone else decides this for the nonprofessional, but the professional makes such decisions himself.

Greenwood (1962:209–10) points out that the client of a professional (because he is presumed to be without the essential theoretical training for making judgments) cannot diagnose his own problem or choose among the various ways of dealing with it. He isn't even regarded as competent to judge the quality of the service he receives. In short, the professional has a monopoly of judgment. This subordination of the client to the professional's authority is, in fact, "a principal source of the client's faith that the relationship he is about to enter contains the potentials for meeting his needs." Imagine a physician who asked his patient to help him choose the best treatment for the patient's complaint!

If your attorney believes your best course is to plead guilty you had better follow his advice. Your barber will have achieved this degree of professionalism when he tells you that you must have a razor cut next time and let your sideburns bush out—and you meekly do as he says!

Community Sanction Community sanction usually means the granting of a virtual monopoly of certain powers and privileges to the profession. Sanction offers two major powers: control over training centers and control over admission into the profession. Schools must have accreditation, which is given or withheld by professional associations. These are regulated in terms of numbers, location, curriculum content, and caliber of instruction. The nonprofessional occupations have no such seats of power. Consent from a national beauticians' association is not necessary in order to establish and operate a local beauty salon. But a law school would find it difficult if not impossible to operate without the consent of the American Bar Association and the American Law School Association.

Admission into a profession is controlled by three means: professional title; a licensing system; and an examination. The professions determine who is to receive titles. Greenwood puts it nicely (1962:211):

Anyone can call himself a carpenter, locksmith, or metal-plater if he feels so qualified. But a person who assumes the title of physician or attorney without having earned it conventionally becomes an impostor.[3]

In many parts of the country it is necessary to be licensed to perform one's work. Through the community, the profession controls

---

[3] Interesting cases occasionally appear of someone who has, for a time, successfully passed himself off as a *bona fide* professional, perhaps as a physician, in which capacity he has routinely performed surgical operations. Public reaction ranges from malicious amusement to outrage at the notion of someone illicitly (and successfully) playing a role to which he has no right.

the licensing procedure, and thus determines who may practice the skill. Sometimes it is necessary to pass an examination before being admitted to a profession. In nearly all such cases the examiners are made up mostly of members of the profession.[4] Licensing is governed by law, and unlicensed persons who practice are subject to prosecution.

Confidentiality and immunity are the two main professional privileges, found in the most highly developed form in medicine and law. The relationship between a professional and his client requires that the latter be completely free to divulge confidences which could be damaging and to do so without fear of reprisals. Hence the community protects the professional in his refusal to share such information outside the professional relationship. Leaders in other occupations, such as journalism and law enforcement, are seeking the right of privileged communication as part of their effort to become more professional (Greenwood, 1962:211).[5]

Another one of the professional privileges is a relative immunity from community judgment on technical matters. Standards for professional performance are reached by consensus within the profession and are based on the existing body of theory. The lay community is presumed incapable of comprehending these standards and, hence, of using them to identify malpractice. It is generally conceded that a professional's performance can be evaluated only by his peers.

A Code of Ethics Every profession has a set of regulations to compel its members to behave ethically. Without such a code certain abuses could result, and indeed sometimes occur even in spite of the code. These include overpriced services, creation of a personnel scarcity through restriction of entry into the occupation, lowering of the quality of performance, and obstructing of beneficial social changes. A study in California in 1968 revealed that about 5 percent of the physicians participating in the Medicare program were either overcharging or overtreating patients. And in New York it was discovered that a few physicians were charging patients from 1,000 to 10,000 percent above cost for such laboratory tests as blood count, urinalysis, sedimentation rate, and blood sugar.

The professions seek compliance to their codes of ethics by the use of sanctions. Consultation and referral are two positive sanctions. Consultation is a request for a colleague's professional advice and help. Referral is recommending a colleague to a client. The consultation-referral system is a principal source of a professional's practice, and can be used very effectively in dealing with

---

[4] A special case of partial professional certification is the practice of the President of the United States in consulting the American Bar Association on major judicial appointments and the American Medical Association on important medical appointments in the Department of Health, Education and Welfare.

[5] In 1973, the right of journalists to privileged communication was being fought out in the courts, in Congress, and in state legislatures.

a deviant colleague. Two severe negative sanctions are public censure and disbarment from practice. Success is most unlikely for those who are not members of their professional association in good standing.

A Professional Culture Professions possess values, norms, roles, and symbols. This is what is meant by a professional culture, and each profession has its own. Values underlie such beliefs as these: without the services of the professional, society itself would be threatened; laymen, compared to professionals, are totally ignorant in matters of practice; social progress can come about only through a professional monopoly; objectivity is the watchword in all things pertaining to theory and technique; and one's profession is a calling. The notion of calling implies the view that one's work is an end in itself; it is one's life; there is total personal involvement. It has been said, not wholly in jest, that a nonprofessional works to get paid, while the professional gets paid to work.

In professional life there are norms or rules that regulate all standard interpersonal relations. Wilensky and Lebeaux (1958:303–8) identified four norms that govern relations among colleagues: (a) do what you can to maintain professional authority and professional standards of work; (b) do not air professional problems, complaints, and mistakes publicly; (c) be aware of the limited competence of your own specialty within the profession; honor the claims of other specialties; and be ready to refer clients to a more competent colleague; (d) interpret the behavior of colleagues as well as clients in professional terms.

Such things as insignia, emblems, modes of dress, professional histories, special words, heroes, and stereotypes are used as symbols by different professions—for example, academic hoods, white jackets, Albert Schweitzer, quacks, and shysters. Closely associated with heroes and stereotypes are prototypes or ideal professional types. Every profession has its notion of the ideal practitioner. It is a primary goal of professional schools to train neophytes who are as close to these prototypes as possible. This is accomplished through screening out undesirables and intensively socializing the chosen newcomers. Most of the appropriate values, norms, and symbols are acquired through the relationships—both primary and secondary—formed in schools and associated settings.

A second professionalizing agency is the unit of practice such as the firm, law office, hospital, clinic, university, or company. A third type of socializing organization is the professional association (American Medical Association, American Bar Association). The American Sociological Association, like other learned societies, has a primary commitment to the advancement of a field of knowledge. On the other hand, the American Medical Association is mainly concerned with protecting and developing the quality of highly skilled services its members furnish to the public (Bates, 1967:89).

Proposed Code of Ethics for Sociologists

Sociological inquiry is often disturbing to many persons and groups. Its results may challenge long-established beliefs and lead to change in old taboos. In consequence, such findings may create demands for the suppression or control of this inquiry or for a dilution of the findings. Similarly, the results of sociological investigation may be of significant use to individuals in power, because such findings, suitably manipulated, may facilitate the misuse of power. Knowledge is a form of power, and in a society increasingly dependent on knowledge, the control of information creates the potential for political manipulation.

For these reasons, we affirm the autonomy of sociological inquiry. The sociologist must be responsive, first and foremost, to the truth of his investigation. Sociology must not be an instrument of any person or group which seeks to suppress or misuse knowledge. The fate of sociology as a science is dependent upon the fate of free inquiry in an open society.

At the same time this search for social truths must itself operate within constraints. Its limits arise when inquiry infringes on the rights of individuals to be treated as persons, to be considered—in the renewable phrase of Kant—as ends and not as means. Just as sociologists must not distort or manipulate truth to serve untruthful ends, so too they must not manipulate persons to serve their quest for truth. The study of society, being the study of human beings, imposes the responsibility of respecting the integrity, promoting the dignity, and maintaining the autonomy of these persons.

To fulfill these responsibilities, we, the members of the American Sociological Association, affirm the following Code of Ethics:

1. *Objectivity in Research*
In his research the sociologist must maintain scientific objectivity.
2. *Integrity in Research*
The sociologist should recognize his own limitations and, when appropriate, seek more expert assistance or decline to undertake research beyond his competence. He must not misrepresent his own abilities, or the competence of his staff to conduct a particular research project.
3. *Respect of the Research Subject's Rights to Privacy and Dignity*
Every person is entitled to the right of privacy and dignity of treatment. The sociologist must respect these rights.
4. *Protection of Subjects from Personal Harm*
All research should avoid causing personal harm to subjects used in research.
5. *Preservation of Confidentiality of Research Data*
Confidential information provided by a research subject must be treated as such by the sociologist. Even though research information is not a privileged communication under the law, the sociologist must, as far as possible, protect subjects and informants. Any promises made to such persons must be honored. However, provided that he respects the assurances he has given his subjects, the sociologist has no obligation to withhold information of misconduct of individuals or organizations.

If an informant or other subject should wish, however, he can formally release the researcher of a promise of confidentiality. The provisions of this section apply to all members of research organizations (that is, interviewers, coders, clerical staff, and so forth), and it is the responsibility of the chief investigators to see that they are instructed in the necessity and importance of maintaining the confidentiality of the data. The obligation of the sociologist includes the use and storage of original data to which a subject's name is attached. When requested, the identity of an organization or subject must be adequately disguised in publication.

6. *Presentation of Research Findings*
The sociologist must present his findings honestly and without distortion. There should be no omission of data from a research report which might significantly modify the interpretation of findings.
7. *Misuse of Research Role*
The sociologist must not use his role as a cover to obtain information for other than professional purposes.
8. *Acknowledgment of Research Collaboration and Assistance*
The sociologist must acknowledge the professional contributions or assistance of all persons who collaborated in the research.
9. *Disclosure of the Sources of Financial Support*
The sociologist must report fully all sources of financial support in his research publications and any special relations to the sponsor that might affect the interpretation of the findings.
10. *Distortion of Findings by Sponsor*
The sociologist is obliged to clarify publicly any distortion by a sponsor or client of the findings of a research project in which he has participated.
11. *Disassociation from Unethical Research Arrangements*
The sociologist must not accept such grants, contracts, or research assignments as appear likely to require violation of the principles above, and must publicly terminate the work or formally disassociate himself from the research if he discovers such a violation and is unable to achieve its correction.

12. *Interpretation of Ethical Principles*
When the meaning and application of these principles are
unclear, the sociologist should seek the judgment of the
relevant agency or committee designated by the American
Sociological Association. Such consultation, however,
does not free the sociologist from his individual responsibility for decisions or from his accountability to the profession.

13. *Applicability of Principles*
In the conduct of research the principles enunciated
above should apply to research in any area either within
or outside the United States of America.

Source: proposed by a committee of the American Sociological Association and published in *The American Sociologist,* Volume 3, Number 4, November, 1968.

Degree of Professionalization Nearly all occupations possess
professional characteristics to some degree. There is considerable
agreement that physicians, lawyers, university professors, and
clergymen are among those who come closest to the professional
ideal. At the other end of the scale, such jobs as maid, usher, mes-
senger, bellman, and manual laborer boast very little professionalism. Most callings fall between these extremes, though as
we noted, many occupations are making strides toward professionalization. These have been described as semiprofessions (Etzioni, 1969), in process, or marginal (Wilensky, 1964). Among
these are the librarians, nurses, optometrists, pharmacists, school
teachers, social workers, and veterinarians.

THE PROFESSIONALIZATION PROCESS: HOW OCCUPATIONS BECOME
PROFESSIONS   The transformation of an occupation into a profession tends to follow a fairly orderly sequence; this has been described by Caplow (1954:139–40). First comes a professional association which defines who is qualified and who is not. Then
comes a change in the name of the occupation, intended to break
public identification of the occupation with its former and lesser
status. Also, the new name can sometimes be made a legal monopoly. Next comes the development of a code of ethics which both
elevates the social importance of the occupation and eliminates
the unqualified and punishes the unscrupulous. A fourth step is
political activity to get government certification for the occupation's monopoly in its area of competence. All these actions may
take years. Meanwhile training facilities are being established, as
much as possible under the control of the professional society. So
too are attempts to secure legal protection of such rights as confidentiality of the professional-client relationship, and the conduct
of foreign relations with other professions having working relationships with the newly professionalized field.

   After comparing detailed social histories of seventeen occupations,[6] Wilensky (1964:145–46) concluded that professionalization
involves a typical sequence of events.

---

[6] Accounting, architecture, civil engineering, dentistry, law, medicine, librarianship,
nursing, optometry, pharmacy, school teaching, social work, veterinary medicine, city
management, hospital administration, advertising, and funeral direction.

There is a typical process by which the established professions have arrived: men begin doing the work full time and stake out a jurisdiction; the early masters of the technique or adherents of the movement become concerned about standards of training and practice and set up a training school, which if not lodged in universities at the outset, makes academic connection within two or three decades; the teachers and activists then achieve success in promoting more effective organization, first local, then national—through the transformation of an existing occupational association or the creation of a new one. Toward the end, legal protection of the monopoly of skill appears; at the end, a formal code of ethics is adopted.

Caplow and Wilensky focus on the professionalization process from the point of view of the occupational groups themselves. For professionalization to take place, the social structure of society must be ripe for it. Hall (1969:71–72) points out that the demand for professional services and abilities increases as society becomes more human-resources oriented. The demand for more and better educational, health, and social services promotes a greater demand for professionals in these areas, and professionally skilled persons are needed in the productive and service industries which are techno-scientifically based.

WORK, LEISURE, AND
SOCIAL CHANGE

In recent decades much has been said about shortening the hours of work, technological employment, and allied topics. Many conclude that Americans now have an unprecedented amount of time away from work. The conclusion is accurate if applied only to the brief period covered by the industrial revolution. In the past century "we moved from a seventy- or seventy-two-hour workweek down to a forty-hour week—a twelve-hour-day, six-day week to an eight-hour-day, five-day week" (Wilensky, 1964:131).

But a longer view shows that "the skilled urban worker has now achieved the position of his thirteenth century counterpart, whose long workday, seasonally varied, was offset by many holidays, rest periods, and long vacations; annual hours of work now, as then, remain in the range 1,900–2,500" (Wilensky, 1964:130). And De Grazia (1971:451) says that "any primitive tribe enjoys more free time than a resident of the United States today."

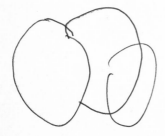

These comparisons do not show some important complexities in the present situation. Our standard forty-hour, five-day week applies to the great bulk of the blue- and white-collar occupations of working Americans, but not to other significant population categories. Wilensky and others have pointed out that professionals and higher-level executives work ten or twelve hours more per week than do those in lower-status occupations, and in fact have less leisure than in the past. Women, whether or not they work outside the home, have enjoyed no gain in free time. As Wilensky puts it:

Studies of the weekly round of women report a range of averages of fifty to eighty hours a week in housework, child care, and paid labor. If a woman

takes a job today, she has to figure on adding her work week to a forty or fifty hour "homemaking" minimum (1964:130).

And one should not overlook persons in the population who have unlimited free time: the unemployed and the retired. For the former and many of the latter free time is enforced.

THE MEANING OF NONWORK   Words like *free time, leisure, play,* and *recreation* have meaning partly in contrast with the meaning of work. Early in the industrial revolution, and in the thinking of Puritan theologians, nonwork was idleness. Idleness was bad: the Devil would find work for idle hands. Work was (and still is) good, or at least necessary, even if unpleasant in the doing. Nowadays, except for the unemployed and some retired persons, nonwork is good, and we call it leisure, recreation, or play. It is no longer a moral lapse, but a desirable alternative to work. Once it was not acceptable to work in order to have leisure; today it is.

Nonwork, then, is now desirable *if* one works to get it. The problem for the unemployed and for many of the retired is that they have unlimited free time yet are not happy with it. Why? The most obvious answer advances our thinking about modern leisure: they are short of money. Must one have money to enjoy not working? It would seem so, for most people. As we said, advanced industrial societies stress a very high level of consumption. They produce so much that workers must be induced to buy more and more and more. Important industries spring up simply to produce goods and services for leisure use. Table 8-5 gives an impression of the economic importance of recreation.

USING FREE TIME   The increases in free time in the past century have also created a problem: what shall I do with my free time? Today free time is spent in a changed environment for which pre-industrial traditions give little guidance. The worker is on his own; he can do what he likes. But what shall he do?

TABLE 8-5 PERSONAL CONSUMPTION EXPENDITURES FOR RECREATION 1950 TO 1970

[In millions of dollars. Prior to 1960, excludes Alaska and Hawaii. Represents market value of purchases of goods and services by individuals and nonprofit institutions. See also *Historical Statistics, Colonial Times to 1957*, series H 500–515]

TYPE OF PRODUCT OR SERVICE	1950	1970
Total recreation expenditures	11,147	39,049
Books and maps	674	3,441
Magazines, newspapers, and sheet music	1,495	4,097
Nondurable toys and sport supplies	1,394	5,726
Wheel goods, durable toys, sports equipment, boats, and pleasure aircraft	869	4,873
Radio and television receivers, records, and musical instruments	2,421	8,328
Radio and television repair	283	1,322
Flowers, seed, and potted plants	457	1,436
Admissions to specified amusements	1,781	2,413
Motion picture theaters	1,376	1,162
Legitimate theaters and opera, and entertainments of nonprofit institutions (except athletics)	183	735
Spectator sports	222	516
Clubs and fraternal organizations[1]	462	1,158
Commercial participant amusements[2]	448	1,819
Pari-mutuel net receipts	239	1,018
Other[3]	624	3,418

[1] Gross receipts less cash benefits of fraternal, patriotic, and women's organizations except insurance, and dues and fees of athletic, social, and luncheon clubs, and school fraternities.

[2] Billiard parlors; bowling alleys; dancing, riding, shooting, skating, and swimming places; amusement devices and parks; daily fee golf greens fees; golf instruction, club rental, and caddy fees; sightseeing buses and guides; and private flying operations.

[3] Photo developing and printing, photographic studios, collectors' net acquisitions of stamps and coins, hunting dog purchase and training, sports guide service, veterinary service, purchase of pets, camp fees, nonvending coin machine receipts minus payoff, and other commercial amusements.

Source: U.S. Bureau of Economic Analysis, *The National Income and Product Accounts of the United States, 1929–1965*, and *Survey of Current Business*, July issues. U.S. Department of Commerce, *Statistical Abstract of the United States, 1973*, p. 208.

Most suggestions come from mass media advertisements which paint glowing pictures of the pleasures that await him. But it costs more and more to play. Consider the expensive and elaborate equipment now thought necessary to go hiking and camping. Once people simply did these things with whatever was at hand. But now one hears earnest discussions of the merits of different imported hiking boots, tents, packs, trailers, and campers, some costing twice the price of a respectable automobile.

In fact, current work hours might be shorter without the pressure for money to spend on recreation. So our dilemma has its irony; we have to work more because it costs so much to play. Probably one worker in ten moonlights, that is, holds two jobs concurrently. Overtime is popular, although it is interesting to note that a key issue—and a novel one—in the UAW strike of Chrysler workers in 1973 was whether or not employers could compel workers to put in overtime. In wanting overtime to be voluntary they were saying that sometimes they want extra income, but other times freedom means more than money.

De Grazia believes that working hours will decline by about an hour and a half a week in each decade. "By the year 2000, the overall average of hours worked is to be thirty-one per week" and may go as low as twenty-one (1971:452). So there will be more free time. But most Americans don't yet know how to spend it. The first answer of our affluent society was to create demand for goods and services to keep the wheels of industry turning ever faster. But that answer is suspect, for while it helps business, it does not necessarily make sense to the individual in an urban society. He is yet to be persuaded that what's good for business is good for his leisure time. Even now, we think, millions of Americans feel cheated, that the delights promised by advertisements seem ephemeral or empty. How many TV sets, outboard motors, cameras, and stereo sound systems does one acquire before surfeit and boredom with the hardware of pleasure set in? Yet there may be hope for the development of more satisfying answers to the use of leisure time in the gradually rising level of American education.

Contemporary society, for some of its critics, is too leisure-oriented. But careful scrutiny of the facts shows that most people still have a very strong tendency to work, and that those in some occupational categories work more than they used to. Wilensky (1966:121) states that

the average man's gain in leisure has been exaggerated by selective comparison of gross daily or weekly averages in working hours with those of the "take-off" period of rapid growth in England, France, and America—a time of bloodcurdling schedules and conditions. Estimates of annual and lifetime leisure and comparisons with earlier times suggest a different picture.

UTILITY OF THE SOCIOLOGY OF OCCUPATIONS

Here, as in the other branches of sociology, we take the position that an increase in basic understanding of social phenomena will furnish a solid basis for practical efforts toward solving social problems. Even with our very incomplete present knowledge, we think that the sociology of occupations has implications that can be put to work in seeking solutions. In this chapter we shall deal only with one such implication, but it will suggest others.

THE PROBLEM OF ALIENATION   Because so much time is spent in one's occupation, the experience of prolonged alienation from work can be deeply frustrating and discouraging. If one asks an estranged person why he feels as he does, he will no doubt give some sort of answer. But it should also be possible to approach

TABLE 8-6 ATTRIBUTES OF PRIZED SELF-IMAGE AND CORRESPONDING
ATTRIBUTES OF WORK SITUATION

ATTRIBUTE OF PRIZED SELF-IMAGE (BOTH PERCEIVED AND VALUED)	ATTRIBUTE OF WORK SITUATION (BOTH PERCEIVED AND VALUED)
Sociable	Can talk sociably on the job (shoot the breeze) at least four or five times a day
Intelligent	Plenty of chance to use own judgment
Conscientious (competent, efficient): person who believes that if a thing is worth doing, it is worth doing right	Chance to do work well: do a good, careful job
	Chance to do the things you're best at: use the kinds of skills that you have
Independent: a man who won't hesitate to go it alone when he thinks he should	(For those with a boss) Boss not always breathing down your neck: not watched too closely
Ambitious: person who tries hard to get ahead	Good chance for promotion where you work

this problem from the sociological and social psychological perspective and get at least a tentative understanding useful in reducing the feeling of alienation. Wilensky (1966:140–47) throws some light on the problem.

You will recall that earlier in this chapter we took the view that occupation is significantly related to the self-concept. In his labor-leisure study, Wilensky specifically sought to relate components of the social organization of the job setting to the self-concept and to alienation from work. He got responses from 1,156 men in a wide variety of occupations varying greatly in prestige.

Wilensky defined alienation as an incongruence between important and prized aspects of the self-image and parallel aspects of job role. In Table 8-6, the left-hand column lists the aspects of self-image, and the right-hand column lists related job characteristics.

Respondents were asked to rate themselves on each of the self-image characteristics, and their job situations on the corresponding attributes. The degree of discrepancy was Wilensky's measure of job alienation. The alienation scores were then compared with various organizational conditions in order to find what conditions were likely to produce alienation. The men who had high economic, occupational, and educational status tended to be attached to their work. Alienation was twice as frequent in the lowest stratum of occupations as in the highest. More than four times as many upper-stratum workers were attached to their work. Yet alienated and attached persons were found at every level. That is to say, a good fit between self-concept and job demands was frequent in nearly all occupations, as was the opposite.

ORGANIZATIONAL CORRELATES OF WORK ALIENATION There were some interesting correlations. Nineteen percent of the workers who had low freedom and much discipline were alienated, compared to 7 percent of those who had much greater freedom and less discipline. Twenty-five percent of the workers who cannot get ahead of the work load were alienated, as opposed to only 12 percent who can get ahead of the work load. Of workers on a fixed schedule, 19 percent were alienated, compared to 11 percent of those who had some control over their work schedule.

A third organizational correlation of alienation was job mobility, that is, moving from one position to another. Twenty-four percent of immobile workers were alienated as against 14 percent of those who were mobile. Blocked mobility also accounted for alienation in 30 percent of one group of engineers (a high-level social and economic occupation), whereas only 6 percent of urban university professors are at all alienated. This group of engineers had the highest proportion of alienated men of all the groups studied.

If one sees work alienation as a problem needing solution, then several possible answers suggest themselves. Individuals choosing an occupation, as well as work organizations recruiting personnel, could consider whether an individual's desired self-concept will be compatible with the expectations of the job. This means intelligent matching of people to jobs as both exist at a given time. Another approach is to examine work settings with a view to reducing causes of alienation. Assuming that the work is reasonably interesting and that other factors are favorable, workers could have more freedom and less discipline. Work organizations could delegate more control over work pace and scheduling. Still another approach would be to lessen obstructions to occupational mobility.

"Leave it to good old G.M. to break the monotony of the assembly line!"

[Drawing by Alan Dunn © 1972 The New Yorker Magazine, Inc.]

Practicing the Sociological Perspective

You can become more familiar with the sociological approach to occupations and professions by trying it out yourself. We have spoken of the complicated process by which persons choose occupations and are (from society's point of view) recruited into them. Obviously this is a two-sided process. From the individual's point of view in our kind of society, there is a choice to be made among many possibilities. From society's point of view, enough people must be persuaded to enter needed occupations so that the society itself can survive. So the outcome in any one case reflects the individual's thought processes, preferences, view of himself, and so forth. And it reflects innumerable social pressures on him, experiences that give him small and large nudges in the direction he ultimately takes.

At what stage are you in relation to choosing an occupation? We suggest that you argue two opposing (and incomplete) points. First, make the best case you can that your choice is a purely personal matter. Then argue that your choice is solely the result of social pressures on you. Can these two views be reconciled?

Assume that you have made a definite choice of occupation. Do you know anything about the occupational associations in your field? Do you have any idea what control such associations have over conditions of employment and restrictions you will face in the occupation? A little research on this topic may tell you a lot.

Every occupation has its own culture, which provides values, norms, and roles that influence the behavior of people in the field. By knowing this culture we come to understand behavior which otherwise might seem strange. For example, the *value* placed on job seniority differs very much from one occupation to another. Railroad unions will go on strike to protect seniority rights. How is seniority regarded in your field? Again, academic freedom is a value of crucial importance to the academic world. Why? What significance does it have for railroad engineers?

Occupation and the self-concept are significantly related because the occupational role is so very important for so many. Does the strength of this tie find visible expression in the way work and professional groups talk, dress, and act? Try guessing the occupations of strangers, and—if you can do so diplomatically—find out what work they actually do in order to check your impressions.

Complex Organizations

9

Big organizations have been around for a long time. Organized armies appeared in the ancient civilization of Sumer, around 2500 B.C. In ancient Egypt (about 2613–2494 B.C.) as many as one hundred thousand people were organized to construct one of the great pyramids. Down through the centuries there have been massive, socially complex organizations in many parts of the world. Yet the present era is sometimes called the *organization age,* not because complex organizations are new, but because within the last century they have become the dominant social form in industrialized societies. No previous age has seen anything like today's many big organizations, wielding so much influence on mankind in every department of life. Large organizations are now found in every corner of society—in government, business, labor, education, religion, and entertainment. This is new. A generation ago, Peter Drucker commented:

The "giant business" of those days (1900), the huge "trust" which gave (my) grandparents nightmares, was Mr. Rockefeller's Standard Oil Company. Every one of the eleven companies into which the Supreme Court split the "octopus" in 1911 is today (1946) larger than the original Standard Oil Company ever was—in capital, in employees, in production. Yet only four of them rank among the major American, let alone the major international oil companies today (1946:viii).

Table 9-1 gives several illustrations of the way in which business in the United States is dominated by large companies. Compare the total number of companies in each industry with the percentage of all shipments accounted for by the twenty largest firms.

THE PROMINENCE AND SIGNIFICANCE OF BIG ORGANIZATIONS

TABLE 9-1 PERCENTAGE OF SHIPMENTS ACCOUNTED FOR BY LARGE
MANUFACTURING COMPANIES, SELECTED INDUSTRIES, IN 1967

INDUSTRY	NUMBER OF COMPANIES	20 LARGEST
Motor vehicles	107	99+
Motor vehicle parts and accessories	1,424	78
Petroleum refining	276	84
Aircraft engines and engine parts	205	93
Photographic equipment and supplies	505	89
Tires and inner tubes	2,430	97
Malt liquors	125	86
Telephone, telegraph apparatus	82	99
Radio and TV receiving sets	303	85
Soap and other detergents	599	86

Source: U.S. Bureau of the Census, Census of Manufactures, 1967, *Concentration Ratios in Manufacturing,* MC 671 (S)-2.1 and MC 67 (S)-2.3.

It has been estimated that 80 to 90 percent of the work force in the United States is employed by organizations (Ritzer, 1972:28). Increasing numbers of workers belong to large unions. The percentage of union members in the labor force increased by nearly tenfold between 1900 and 1970 (from 3 percent to about 28 percent). In 1970 there were forty-seven labor unions having at least one hundred thousand members and ranging upward from one hundred thousand to the Teamsters, with 1,829,000 members (*Statistical Abstract of the United States*).

Today there are twenty-three denominational church bodies in the United States with more than a million members, the largest being the Roman Catholic church with more than 48 million (*Statistical Abstract of the United States*). In 1900 there wasn't a single college in the Western world with more than ten thousand students, and the vast majority enrolled only a few hundred. Now more than a hundred four-year colleges and universities have enrollments of ten thousand or more in the United States alone, and the largest twelve each have more than forty-four thousand students. For instance, the City University of New York has one hundred and ninety thousand students on its eighteen campuses. And there are about one hundred and six thousand students on the eight campuses of the University of California.

The efficiency derived from organization can even be applied to undesirable ends. Organized crime is a case in point (Cressey, 1969). The transformation from Mafia to Cosa Nostra represents a change from relatively small face-to-face associations to large regional, national, and international combines. The present Cosa Nostra shares a number of characteristics with all complex organizations. There are specialists such as professional gunmen, runners, and executives. There is departmentalization into such illicit areas as narcotics, gambling, the rackets, prostitution, and there is an enforcement department. The hierarchical character

Complex organizations often produce imposing physical structures, and sometimes the latter endure longer than the social structures that built them. The Egyptian pyramids are evidence of a rather complex social structure, which no longer exists. Buildings can also reflect the degree of complexity of the organizations that they house. The town hall of Middleton, New Hampshire, and the city hall of Boston, Massachusetts, are both municipal office buildings, but the difference in complexity is quite evident.

of organized crime is illustrated by the Chicago Cosa Nostra, which has six levels of authority: a three-man Board of Directors, a President of the Corporation, four Vice Presidents, District Managers, Executive Assistants, and Soldiers.

Most of us who work or go to school spend about half of our waking hours in organizations. In addition to working in an organizational setting, many people engage in social activities with fellow employees (Etzioni, 1961:165–68): company-sponsored recreational groups such as bowling teams. Students in school interact with one another beyond the time devoted to formal instruction. Elementary and secondary school students are involved in a host of extracurricular activities such as athletics and student government. Pretty much the same thing is true of most college and university students, who, with the exception of community college students, engage in most of their social activities with one another.

The influence of organizations goes beyond the time spent and the activities engaged in, for they are sources of norms regulating a large number of activities both within and beyond their boundaries. Notice how members of the military services, religious organizations, fraternities, and schools, to list only a few examples, are bound by roles affecting dress, dating, drinking, personal grooming, morals, social activities in general, and voting for political candidates.

And so the story goes. Big organizations proliferate, get bigger, and control more sectors of our national life. They dwarf the single person, the small group, and the lesser organizations more characteristic of the past.

WHAT ARE COMPLEX ORGANIZATIONS?

It is appropriate to begin our analysis of complex organizations through the ideas of the German sociologist Max Weber, who greatly influenced this branch of sociology. Some, for example, Inkeles (1968), consider Weber to be the greatest of all sociologists who have studied the larger social forms. Writing in the early part of this century, Weber made seminal contributions to the sociological perspective on organizations and on many other topics as well, such as religion, law, politics, and even music. Students of sociology still study his work closely.

WEBER'S IDEAS ON BUREAUCRACY Weber held that there were three types of authority found in society: traditional, charismatic, and rational. Traditional authority (that once possessed by European kings and the nobility, for example) is based on belief in the legitimacy of ancient traditions. This generates personal loyalty to individuals who are established carriers of the right to issue

The broad scope and pervasiveness of complex organizations are characteristic of this social form, so we find it in all societies where such organizations are important. The degree to which Japanese businesses encompass the lives of their workers has often been noted.

Part 2 / Social Units and Processes

Shown here are Harold Wilson, British Prime Minister, the Shah of Iran, and Che Guevara, Latin American revolutionary hero. Which of these men illustrates traditional authority, which charismatic authority, and which rational authority?

commands. Charismatic authority is based on belief in the exceptional qualities of particular individuals which give such persons the right to have authority over others. Hitler, in the early days of the Nazi movement, had such authority. Rational authority is based on loyalty to a set of norms specifying relationships between people and giving authority to certain individuals occupying positions within social structures. This is loyalty to rules rather than to the person who temporarily occupies a position conferring authority.

Modern complex organizations are by far the most important manifestations of rational authority, and Weber spoke of such organizations as bureaucratic.

The Bureaucratic Official A full presentation of Weber's ideas on bureaucracy is not possible here, but the following quotation is central, and deals with the official in a complex organization.

The whole administrative staff . . . consists, in the purest type, of individual officials who are appointed and function according to the following criteria:

1. They are personally free and subject to authority only with respect to their impersonal official obligations.
2. They are organized in a clearly defined hierarchy of offices.
3. Each office has a clearly defined sphere of competence. . . .
4. The office is filled by a free contractual relationship. Thus, in principle, there is free selection.
5. Candidates are selected on the basis of technical qualifications. . . . They are appointed, not elected.

6. They are remunerated by fixed salaries in money. . . .
7. The office is treated as the sole, or at least the primary, occupation of the incumbent.
8. It constitutes a career. There is a system of "promotion" according to seniority or to achievement, or both. Promotion is dependent on the judgment of superiors.
9. The official works entirely separated from ownership of the means of administration and without appropriation of his position.
10. He is subject to strict and systematic discipline and control in the conduct of the office (*Wirtschaft und Gesellschaft,* 1925, quoted in Miller, 1963:68–69).

Speaking more broadly, Weber identified the following characteristics of bureaucracies:

1. Fixed and official jurisdictional areas, which are regularly ordered by rules, that is, by laws or administrative regulations.
2. Principles of hierarchy and levels of graded authority that ensure a firmly ordered system of super- and subordination in which higher offices supervise lower ones.
3. Administration based upon written documents; the body of officials engaged in handling these documents and files, along with other material apparatus, make up a "bureau" or "office."
4. Administration by full-time officials who are thoroughly and expertly trained.
5. Administration by general rules which are quite stable and comprehensive (M. Weber, *Theory of Social and Economic Organization,* trans. by A. M. Henderson and T. Parsons, New York: Oxford Univ. Press, 1947, p. 333).

Weber saw bureaucracies as adaptable to many settings, public and private. Such organizations, he said, are more efficient than alternative forms.

Precision, speed, unambiguity, knowledge of the files, continuity, discretion, unity, strict subordination, reduction of friction and of material and personal costs—these are raised to the optimum point in the strictly bureaucratic administration. . . . (*Wirtschaft und Gesellschaft,* quoted in Miller, 1963:71).

Weber also maintained that the more completely bureaucratic an organization, the more "it succeeds in eliminating from official business love, hatred, and all purely personal, irrational, and emotional elements which escape calculation. This is the specific nature of bureaucracy and it is appraised as its special virtue" (*Wirtschaft und Gesellschaft,* quoted in Miller, 1963:72–73). Weber underestimated the role of nonrational behavior and especially of informal organization rising within the formal organizational structure, as subsequent research showed. We will return to this point shortly. Yet despite modifications by later writers, Weber's early analysis of bureaucratic organization remains highly influential to this day.

COMPLEX ORGANIZATIONS DEFINED While no formal definition of complex organizations has been universally accepted, the one given here is consistent with current usage. *A complex organization is a social unit oriented mainly toward attaining one or more specific goals. It is persistent in maintaining its identity through time. It has fixed boundaries, possesses a set of norms, three or more levels of authority, a communication network, and a system of sanctions* (primarily suggested by Scott, 1964).

When you think of some of the social units that have already been discussed, you may not see how our definition distinguishes complex organizations from other social forms. Families are not complex organizations, but certainly they have goals and persist through many years of time. And as we pointed out in Chapter 4, small groups, even very informal ones, do have boundaries and develop norms which affect the behavior of their members. Communities are not complex organizations, but there are significant differences in authority in every community. Patterns of communication are found in *all* social units, of whatever kind. And sanctions (means for rewarding desired behavior and punishing disapproved behavior) are also found in all kinds of social units.

The fact is, the defining characteristics of complex organizations, taken individually, are not unique to this kind of unit. It is their combination and the high degree to which they are developed that sets them off from other familiar manifestations of social structure.

Orientation Toward Specific Goals   Max Weber was among the first to suggest that organizations are characterized by their primary orientation toward the attainment of specific goals. For Weber, an organization is "a system of continuous purposive activity of a specified kind" (1947:151). In this regard, compare a community like Kansas City with General Motors. Taken all together, the citizens of Kansas City have many goals for their community. On some there may be high agreement, on many there is not. The central goal of General Motors is to make profits for its shareholders. Manufacturing cars is a means to that end. With the attack on tobacco products in recent years, some large tobacco companies (whose goal is profits also) began to diversify their activities into other areas. It is true that complex organizations have subsidiary goals, but as a class of units they are distinguished by the degree to which everything is concentrated on the achievement of clear, concrete ends.

Maintenance of Identity   And so it is with the other items in the definition; other structures have them, but not in the same way. Thus many units other than complex organizations may survive for years, and complex organizations sometimes come to an end, as when a corporation goes out of business or a government agency is disbanded. Yet it is generally true that complex organizations are so organized as to permit their continuance over very long periods, even centuries. They always have provisions for replacing existing personnel so that the unit is never permanently dependent on a living generation of participants. College students come and go, and so too do faculties, but most colleges outlast many generations of both.

Fixed Boundaries To say that complex organizations have fixed boundaries is to indicate that more care is taken in defining who is and who is not a member than is true in many other social units. Yet many other kinds of units also set perfectly clear boundaries. With organizations, either one works for Boeing Aircraft or one does not; there is nothing in between. A person is or is not a candidate for a Bachelor of Arts degree in a certain college. On the other hand, a free university will generally admit anyone who cares to come and, if a given person leaves, the others may scarcely be aware of it.

Set of Norms The set of norms in the definition includes both formal and informal rules and regulations which are part of the complex organization. In a business firm, formal norms specify, among other things, the division of labor among employees, hours of work and rates of pay, who reports to whom about what, and so on. Informal norms, not officially recognized by management, may specify the minimum and maximum output levels which one's coworkers see as acceptable, ways of getting around some of the formal rules, loyalty to coworkers as against supervisors, and the like. The presence of both formal and informal norms, continuously supported in a system of social interaction, is particularly characteristic of complex organizations, and unusual outside them.

Levels of Authority While authority and ranking are found in all social units, they are particularly clear and specific in complex organizations. There are at least three levels, that is, differences in power over the behavior of others are distributed formally in a hierarchy of at least three ranks. The power structure of a typical university, for example, would include trustees, president, vice presidents, deans, department chairmen, professors, associate professors, assistant professors, instructors, fellows, research assistants, teaching assistants, graduate students, and finally, undergraduates. If you are an undergraduate and feel that you are sitting at the bottom of a rather large heap, you have good reason for feeling that way.

Communication Network Like all social forms, complex organizations exhibit order and pattern in the way communication flows back and forth between individuals and parts of the organization. Social interaction is as fundamental to the life of an organization —such as a giant bank—as to a group of college friends who go on a ski trip together. It is not a communication network as such that distinguishes the complex organization. What we find is that the network is large and complicated because so many different kinds

Both formal and informal communication take place in all complex organizations.

of activity by so many different persons have to be coordinated. And this leads to formalization of the network. Formal rules spell out approved channels for messages, and procedures for transmitting them (memos in so many copies, phone conversations, tape recordings, and so forth). Here too there are informal channels of communication as well as formal channels used for informal messages. People may get together at coffee breaks to talk about and even decide on courses of action in ways not provided for in the formal communication network. On other occasions, members of the organization may use formal channels (a meeting of an important committee, for instance) to discuss matters not on the agenda.

Sanctions Finally, sanctions (rewards and punishments) are, as we have said, by no means peculiar to organizations. A person may punish a friend who has displeased him by sulking, or by breaking an agreement to do something the other wanted him to do. In complex organizations sanctions are spelled out *in advance* to an unusual degree and are likely to be specific and concrete. Incentive pay systems indicate in exact detail what the reward will be for varying increments of production. In the armed forces, loss of privileges is a traditional form of negative sanction meted out for violating norms.

Informal sanctions operate with particular reference to the informal norms of an organization. In one of the classic researches in industrial sociology, it was noted that a factory work group had established an informal norm which set the right amount of work for an employee to do in a day. A man who violated this norm was subject to *binging*, that is, to being hit hard on his upper arm, a way of saying "don't do that again."

To sum up, complex organizations share individual features with many other social forms. Homans suggests that "the organization of the large formal enterprises, governmental or private, in modern society is modeled on, is a rationalization of, tendencies that exist in all human groups" (1950:186–87). Their distinctiveness lies in the way characteristics are combined and expressed, as Scott (1964:486) indicates in the following statement.

Organizations are characterized by distinctive structures which modify the form in which the generic social processes are expressed. For instance, attempts on the part of one person to control the behavior of another may be investigated profitably in any social setting. But certain forms of control (for example, an authority structure) are best studied within organizations since they appear here in their most highly developed form.

BUREAUCRACY AND INFORMAL ORGANIZATION

We have referred several times to informal organization within complex organizations, and to Weber's underestimation of its importance. You will recall that Weber saw authority in a highly bureaucratic organization as rational, that is, it is based entirely on understood and accepted rules efficiently designed to serve the organization's goals. The interests of the organization are all that matter in the development of these rules, and the formal aspects of a bureaucracy manifest these interests and rules. But Weber fails to consider factors which guarantee that any actual complex organization will be more than its purely formal aspects. The total organization includes not only the elements Weber identified but the whole arena of informal organization. Why does informal organization always develop?

The heart of the matter lies in Weber's assumption (made for analytical purposes) that people are capable of behaving in a completely rational way when being "rational" means serving the interests of large organizations. Take the notion that the rules of a bureaucracy are efficiently geared to the ends of the organization. In the first place, such rules often are not efficient and may even hinder progress toward organizational goals. We suspect that, as a student, you have sometimes been confused and angered by your inability to cope with college rules which seemed to make no sense, and which in the end were defended simply on the ground that they existed. In many business and government offices, male employees are permitted to smoke when and where they please but female employees are not. It isn't easy to argue rationally that the interests of the organization require this distinction. Sometimes people (seeking personal security within the system) develop a vested interest in maintaining bureaucratic procedures whether or not they are efficient. Also, since bureaucratic rules serve only the organization, inevitably they sometimes work against the interests of individuals, and this too becomes a source of resentment.

The large size of complex organizations coupled with their reliance on rationally developed rules serving the organization and not the individual leads to a radical depersonalization of relationships between people. They come to feel that they scarcely exist as persons, only as cases, statistics, or problems for which the rulebook provides standard answers. This is a source of alienation and unhappiness. For even though people realize that the organization encompasses only part of their lives, they still want to be treated as persons—variable, complicated, feeling.

AUTHORITY, POWER, AND ALIENATION   Weber also paid too little attention to the fact that rationally derived authority in an organization also gives power to some individuals; that is, it gives them the ability to apply sanctions for disobedience to orders. Those in authority are in a position to coerce others. Bureaucratic officials are supposed to hold their positions by virtue of their technical competence, and they often do. But because there are levels of authority in a bureaucracy, a given official also holds power over those beneath him, power to reward (promotions and pay increases) and power to punish (failure to give rewards and ability to demote or discharge).

Power, whether or not rationally derived, induces anxiety and insecurity in those who don't have it. A college professor has rationally derived authority with respect to his students, but he also has the power to give and withhold course credits and grades. Perhaps you can attest to the anxiety and insecurity this can produce in students. Relative powerlessness also leads to alienation and hostility. The individual is made receptive to efforts directed toward moderating and containing the power of others over him.

This organizational age has seen a steady and growing expression of personal estrangement from these features of the large bureaucratic organization. In literature and drama, in the escape to communal living by some young people, and in other areas too, the symptoms of resentment against the organizational imperatives of our time are everywhere. We commented on this in Chapter 5, where we suggested that the modern loss of community has some of its roots in the impersonality of organizations. And we will point to this source of alienation again in several of the chapters which follow.

The fact is that people in highly industrialized societies have not yet learned how to humanize big organizations, how to retain their undoubted efficiencies in getting work done without causing the frustrations they have too often brought to individuals.

INFORMAL ORGANIZATION AS A RESPONSE For such reasons, the formal part of any complex organization is always accompanied and modified by informal kinds of organization which never appear on charts showing how the system is supposed to work. At every level of authority, and sometimes between levels, people get together in small groups seeking advancement and protection of their own interests as against the purely rational and efficient requirements of the formal part of the organization. They do this because, as total persons, they sometimes feel threatened by the formal organizations. They do not want, as persons, to be governed solely by the interests of the organization, for it is not coterminous with their whole lives.

When we look at particular cases it is usually easy to see the protective function of informal organization in bureaucratic structures. Workers paid on incentive plans band together to establish norms limiting production to what they regard as reasonable levels. In various rather subtle ways students often collaborate in pressuring professors to moderate their demands. We need not assume that informal organization is necessarily destructive to the ends of the formal organization. Sometimes it is, sometimes not.

THE CLASSIFICATION OF COMPLEX ORGANIZATIONS

In science, schemes for the orderly classification of phenomena are useful aids to the development of knowledge. You have probably met such classifications (often called *taxonomies*) in fields like chemistry, botany, and zoology. They are often found in sociology as well. A good classification scheme helps the scholar to visualize a complicated subject matter in such a way that he can readily identify differences and similarities. Sometimes, such a scheme reveals gaps in existing knowledge and even suggests research ideas which can contribute to the development of scientific theory. The field of complex organizations has produced a number of classification schemes. We refer to two of them, because we think they will aid you in grasping a few more qualities of these units.

THE BLAU AND SCOTT CLASSIFICATION Blau and Scott (1962: 42–57) proposed a classification scheme based on the question of who is the prime beneficiary of the organization's operations. They designate four major types of organization: mutual-benefit associations, business concerns, service organizations, and commonweal organizations.

The membership is the prime beneficiary of mutual-benefit associations. Political parties, unions, fraternal associations, professional associations, and religious sects are typical examples. Owners and managers are the prime beneficiaries of all types of business firms operated for profit. Service organizations primarily benefit their clients or the "public in contact." This type of organization includes social work agencies, hospitals, schools, legal aid societies, and mental health clinics. The public-at-large is the prime beneficiary of commonweal organizations. The State Department, the Bureau of Internal Revenue, the military services, and police and fire departments are of this type.

Each of these organizations, according to Blau and Scott, faces special problems. For the mutual-benefit association, the central problem is maintaining a democratic system internally. For businesses, the major problem is maximizing operating efficiency in a competitive situation. Service organizations have problems arising from potential conflict between professional service to clients and administrative procedures. Finally, commonweal organizations are faced with the problem of developing and maintaining democratic procedures in order that they may be controlled externally by the public.

THE ETZIONI CLASSIFICATION In 1961, Etzioni published a scheme for classifying organizations which has proved useful in sociological analysis. He used two criteria, the kind of power a particular organization has over the behavior of people, and the kind of feelings participants have toward the organization. The three kinds of organizational power are: *coercive power,* which is the application or threat to apply force in order to control behavior; *utilitarian power,* which involves "control over material resources and rewards through allocation of salaries and wages, commissions and contributions, 'fringe benefits,' services and commodities" (Etzioni, 1965:651); and *normative power,* which involves control of behavior through techniques of persuasion, manipulation, or suggestions based on the allocation and manipulation of social symbolic rewards and deprivations. Organization members are seen as responding to the kind of power found in an organization with one of three kinds of involvement (feelings about the organization). *Alienative involvement* refers to a strong hostile orientation toward the organization. *Calculative involvement* denotes an emotionally neutral, slightly positive or slightly negative orientation. *Moral involvement* is a strongly favorable feeling about the organization. Etzioni's scheme is based on both criteria, power and involvement. In theory at least, his taxonomy provides subclasses for all possible combinations of the three types of organizational power with the three types of member involvement. To illustrate, organizations whose power is mainly coercive could be subclassified into those whose members' involvement is mainly (a) alienative, (b) calculative, and (c) moral.

As it turns out, the most frequent combinations of organizational power and member involvement are coercive power and alienative involvement: coercive organizations; utilitarian power and calculative involvement: utilitarian organizations; normative power and moral involvement: normative organizations.

In which of these three categories would you place a prison? Since force is used in prisons to control inmates who typically have hostile feelings toward the organization, a prison is coercive. Insurance companies are utilitarian. Control over workers' pay is

TABLE 9-2   THREE COMMON TYPES OF ORGANIZATION

COERCIVE	UTILITARIAN	NORMATIVE
Concentration camps	Blue-collar industries and blue-collar divisions in other industries	Religious organizations (including churches, orders, monasteries, convents)
Most prisons		
Most correctional "institutions"	White-collar industries and white-collar divisions	Ideological political organizations
Custodial mental hospitals		Fraternal associations
Prisoner-of-war camps	Business unions	Fund-raising and action assocs.
	Farmer organizations	Therapeutic mental hospitals
Relocation centers	Trade associations	Scholarly associations

their principal source of organizational power. Employees typically have a calculative orientation toward the organization. They give it acceptable job performance in return for income, but ordinarily their loyalty and liking for the firm have no deeper sources than this.

Typical normative organizations are the Presbyterian church, the Young Republicans, and Students for a Democratic Society (a student organization at the peak of its influence in the late sixties). Organizational control comes from appeals to the philosophical or moral values being served. Honorific recognition, including the holding of office, is a typical way of rewarding and encouraging effective performance. Members allow themselves to be influenced because they believe in the organization's goals.

Etzioni's scheme does not suggest that every organization contains *only* those characteristics which place it in a particular category. Few if any organizations are pure manifestations of their type, but all organizations have dominant characteristics and can be classified. Etzioni found that there is significant variation among these three types of organizations in a number of important properties.

Goal Differences   Compared with other types of organizations, coercive ones have goals which emphasize order and control. Thus custodial mental hospitals seek to maintain good social order by removing the so-called unfit from the larger society. Utilitarian organizations are likely to stress economic goals. Banks provide an essentially economic service and do so in order to gain an economic return for the organization and its owners. Churches and other normative organizations have goals which are defended on moral or philosophical grounds, in general on grounds which transcend the separate interests of individuals.

Where social order is defined as the dominant goal of an organization, it readily appears that force and coercion may be needed and justified to insure order. Those who threaten social order must be repressed. We saw much of this orientation in the police responses to some of the antiwar demonstrations of the sixties. On the other hand, the economic goals of utilitarian organizations seem rather naturally to imply the kinds of bargains struck in an impersonal way between employers and workers in such organizations. So much work for so much pay. And, with respect to normative organizations, the aims of a religion, a philanthropic organization or an organization supporting a worthy social cause are better supported by persuasive control techniques and by personal loyalty of participants than by the power and involvement characteristics found in the other two types of organization. One may work for a church just for salary received; and one may love a repressive, authoritarian organization, but neither seems likely.

It follows that when an organization changes its goals there are implications for the manner in which participants are controlled and for the participants' attitude toward the organization. As a case in point, many mental hospitals have changed their objectives from control and custody to more genuinely therapeutic and rehabilitative goals. These attempts at establishing therapeutic goals have been successful when the means of controlling patients have also changed from an emphasis on coercion (strait jackets, solitary confinement, sedating drugs, and the like) to less threatening forms of psychotherapy. This change in control techniques is usually accompanied by a more favorable attitude toward the hospital.

Differences in Distribution of Control   This is a complicated topic. The only aspect of it that we will treat here relates to our earlier distinction between formal and informal organization. How do these two kinds of control get along? In coercive organizations, the formal and informal elements are very clearly separated, and usually are mutually antagonistic. While prison guards and officers do exercise a great deal of control over inmates, it is also true that inmates control one another, and in a way which pits prisoners against prison officers. Inmates of prisons and prisoner-of-war camps have often held mock trials or kangaroo courts in which severe sanctions were applied to those among them who violated inmate norms while conforming to directives of the formal structure.

In utilitarian organizations the formal and informal control systems are also quite easily distinguishable from each other, but are not often as hostile as in coercive organizations. The clear division between management and labor in blue-collar industries, with a foreman to represent management and a shop steward to act in behalf of workers and their union, is an illustration. It is understood that interests may be in conflict some of the time but not all the time. At least to some extent, the interests of the entire

Admitting students to the process of faculty-administrative decision-making may reduce the extent to which students, as an informal organization, are hostile to the formal organization of faculty and administration.

organization are recognized within both control systems, and workable compromises and accommodations are acceptable.

In normative organizations, the formal and informal control systems may overlap to some extent, and this is a recognition that powerful interests are held in common and can be served collectively. Today, students often hold membership on college committees and boards, along with faculty members, administrators, and trustees. Some of the recent symptoms of strain on campuses can be attributed to the fact that the several kinds of interest (student, faculty, administration) have not in the past been very well incorporated into effective shared arrangements for making decisions.

Socialization Differences The process of socialization, discussed at length in Chapter 4, goes on continuously in all organizations, but has a quite different character in each of the three types under discussion here. We refer again to prisons, for there is no better example of coercive organizations. In the more traditionally run prisons, despite protests to the contrary, not much really serious effort is made to formally impart habits, skills, beliefs, and norms which would aid the prisoner in later adaptation to civilian life. Most of the important learning takes place within the informal organization run by the inmates themselves. McCleery (1957) indicated that the incoming prisoner is heavily dependent on experienced inmates because the official intentions of the prison are often not clear, because of the secrecy and capriciousness of much disciplinary action, and because of the unfamiliarity of prison society and its regimented character.

There is more formal concern with socializing participants in utilitarian organizations. While large businesses depend to some extent on schools and colleges to socialize their employees, all supplement this with their own training programs. People must be taught specific job skills and how to coordinate their activities with the other parts of a complex structure. The socialization efforts of utilitarian organizations, as is consistent with their utilitarian type of power and calculative member involvement, stress pragmatic, practical content: the particular accounting principles used in the financial division, the precise line of authority upward and downward from any particular employee.

Normative organizations are also heavily concerned with socialization, but, as compared with the others, are likely to place great emphasis on their values and goals rather than on the means for reaching their goals. Church organizations devote much attention to training young members in the fundamental beliefs of the religion. And even for adult members, much of the content of church programs reflects deep concern with preserving and serving the essential purposes for which the church exists.

Consensus Differences Consensus refers here to the degree of agreement among organizational participants with respect to such factors as values, goals, policies, and role prescriptions. In general, coercive organizations tend to have low consensus, utilitarian organizations moderate consensus, and normative organizations high consensus.

In a study of a tuberculosis hospital, which was quite coercive, Julian (1969) discovered that patients, aides, nurses, and physicians agreed very little on what was expected of one another. Slightly more consensus of attitudes toward management was found between foremen and workers in a study of four blue-collar industries. However, a study dealing with the attitudes of lay leaders, a group of women, and two youth groups in the Methodist church with regard to the acceptability of a prospective minister found a very high degree of agreement (Etzioni, 1961:132).

Differences in Communication Blocks All organizations require extensive communication networks, and roles and mechanisms especially devoted to the flow of communication. The number of obstacles to the flow of communication varies with the type of organization. Generally, it is true that as one moves from coercive to utilitarian to normative organizations, communication blockage decreases. This proposition was supported in a study of five hospitals by Julian (1966). The hospitals were located within the metropolitan area of a large western city. It was determined that two of them had predominantly normative power structures and their patients evinced a positive involvement toward the hospitals. Two others had custodial orientations with coercive power structures and patients who had relatively unfavorable attachments to the hospitals. The fifth hospital fell somewhere between the two extremes.

A total of 183 patients in the five hospitals were interviewed in an effort to determine the communication patterns between patients and staff. It was found that the more coercive the hospital, the greater the likelihood that patients would indicate that: (a) they are not told as much as they would like or that they are not told many important things about their illness or how they are coming along; (b) the hospital staff held back certain information about their case "very often" or "fairly often"; (c) they do not get to talk to or ask questions of their physicians "almost always" or "fairly often"; (d) new treatment, medication, tests, and so forth were "not usually" or "hardly ever" explained to them ahead of time; and (e) they "almost always" or "usually" hesitated to speak up and ask questions of the hospital staff.

Differences in Entry into the Organization Prisons must ordinarily accept all inmates assigned to them. Very little selectivity is possible. Until recently, both utilitarian and normative organizations did sometimes exclude some classes of potential members, but this has become increasingly difficult with the passage of legislation forbidding discrimination. Even with discrimination outlawed, utilitarian organizations in particular can insist that potential participants have minimum levels of competence for the tasks they will be assigned. We might point out that persons are compelled to belong to coercive organizations. Utilitarian organizations on the other hand persuade people to join them by the offer of wages and other economic incentives. Normative organizations find new members by pointing to the values they represent and asking people to join in order to support those values.

WHY PEOPLE JOIN ORGANIZATIONS

We could explain this question simply by stating that people join organizations because socialization teaches them to do so. So far as it goes this reasoning is correct, but for our purposes a bit more needs to be said. Incidentally, since we are dealing with inner states in the individual (motives) in relation to social forms outside the individual (organizations), our comments are social psychological rather than sociological in nature.

Motives sometimes have nothing to do with why people join organizations; often they are compelled to join. A child in the United States has to go to school. A young man may be drafted into the army whether or not he approves. A person becomes a member of some churches simply by being born to parents who are members. The question of motive arises only when people may choose whether or not to associate themselves with an organization.

Often a person is neither entirely free nor wholly constrained in seeking or accepting membership. What shall we say about a man who must earn his living but finds that there is only one employer

Part 2 / Social Units and Processes

Which type of organization (coercive, utilitarian, normative) would you say is illustrated by each of these photos?

in town with a suitable job opening? Is he free to accept or reject the job? A little freedom, but not much, one would probably say.

With respect to the Etzioni categories of complex organizations we have just discussed, we suggest that people are compelled to belong to coercive organizations. This no doubt has something to do with the alienation found in such organizations. The greatest contrast is found in normative organizations. Here membership is almost always completely voluntary. Most utilitarian organizations are somewhere between these extremes. Voluntary decisions to join are tempered by factors that make the choice something less than wholly free, as in the case of our man with a choice of one job or none. One characteristic of all voluntary associations, as the name suggests, is that people themselves choose to belong.

INSTRUMENTAL AND EXPRESSIVE MOTIVES In Chapter 4 we mentioned that behavior in groups is of two kinds: instrumental and expressive. Instrumental behavior is concerned with getting some necessary job done; expressive behavior serves to maintain satisfactory relationships among members. There we were speaking of behavior in groups. The instrumental-expressive distinction can also be used to distinguish some groups and organizations from each other, because they are often predominantly instrumental or predominantly expressive. For example, contrast a law firm with a country club. The instrumental-expressive distinction can also be applied to the motives people have for joining organizations.

People join some organizations for primarily instrumental reasons. They believe that membership will facilitate the performance of necessary personal or social tasks. One joins a political or religious organization because it will multiply one's effectiveness in realizing political or religious goals. Most people must make a living. So they seek employment because the income received will support them.

On other occasions people join organizations for primarily expressive reasons. Membership holds out the promise of alleviating loneliness, and of giving pleasant companionship and pleasurable activities shared with others. Such motives are prominent in bringing people into fraternal organizations like the Elks and the Masons. This distinction between instrumental and expressive motives shouldn't be allowed to obscure the fact that both kinds of motives are sometimes satisfied in a single organization. Perhaps this is the typical case. One function served by informal organization in bureaucratic structures is the satisfaction of expressive needs in members, needs which would be starved if the formal part of the structure was all there was. Yet like a high school student, the person cannot choose whether or not to belong to the total organization.

VOLUNTARY ASSOCIATIONS There is an important kind of social unit called voluntary associations. Some of these are complex organizations, others are not. Because of their significance we need to include them in our treatment of organizations.

A voluntary association develops when a small group of people, finding that they have a certain interest (or purpose) in common, agree to meet and to act together in order to try to satisfy that interest or achieve that need (Rose, 1965:390).

As Rose's words indicate, in their beginnings many voluntary associations are small groups as we used that term in Chapter 4. Some eventually become very large and evolve into fully developed complex organizations of the kind we have been discussing. Whatever their size, voluntary associations have explicit organizational features agreed upon by their members, for example, formal

The fire station is essentially an instrumental organization; civic service clubs, like the Rotary Club, are predominantly expressive.

leaders, procedural rules, and the like. This distinguishes even very small associations from other small groups which have no formal organization at all. What distinguishes the largest voluntary associations from many other complex organizations is that membership is entirely voluntary. Most normative organizations are voluntary. Voluntary associations, however, are by no means all normative. Both the YMCA and a bridge club are voluntary associations. The former is normative, the latter is not.

The instrumental-expressive distinction has been applied to the classification of voluntary associations (Jacoby and Babchuk, 1963). Some emphasize instrumental kinds of activity. Environmental protection groups such as the Sierra Club and the Wilderness Society are examples. Others stress expressive activity as illustrated by athletic clubs and amateur theater groups. Still others mix both kinds of activities to the extent that they can be called instrumental-expressive. Rose (1965:391) indicates that instrumental voluntary associations are comparatively rare outside modern democracies. The heterogeneity of such societies and the freedom of associations to pursue their private ends without hindrance from state or church probably account in large part for this fact.

Both instrumental and expressive associations are exceedingly numerous in the United States though their total number is not known. Rose (1965:395), extrapolating from fragmentary evidence, estimates that there are well over one hundred thousand. As just one example, Schmidt and Babchuk (1973:145) indicate that upwards of twenty million Americans belong to fraternal associations alone, Masons, Elks, Moose, Odd Fellows, Eagles, and others.

Evidence of the participation of Americans in voluntary associations is in some ways difficult to compare, and sometimes contradictory. One of the best studies (Babchuk and Booth, 1969) suggests that something over 80 percent of Americans belong to at least one association and almost half are members of two or more. Schmidt and Babchuk (1973:145) state that the number of persons joining associations "is increasing and probably will continue to increase in the future."

A great many studies have investigated the relationship between social class and membership in voluntary associations. There is virtually complete agreement that the higher the class level the higher the rate of participation in associations (Smith and Freedman, 1972:154). Although there is some disagreement within the available evidence, a number of studies, including the most recent known to us (Williams, Babchuk et al., 1973), indicate that black Americans are even more likely than whites to join associations. Rose (1965) summarizes studies which converge in showing that participation in associations declines in the later years of life. This occurs in spite of the greater amounts of free time available in the retirement years. Apparently most elderly persons restrict their lives to a circumscribed home and neighborhood setting, choosing not to utilize free time for wide participation in associations. The research literature on differential rates of participation in voluntary associations is very large and we have only sampled it here.

FUNCTIONS SERVED BY ASSOCIATIONS Voluntary associations would not be so numerous and popular as they are if they did not serve useful purposes. In our comments on why people join organizations we said something about the function that membership serves for individuals. In addition, as with so many social forms, associations also perform functions for society, and their members may not even be aware that this is true. Rose (1965:420–24) mentions several functions of the latter kind.

The Power Distributing Function By joining instrumental voluntary associations citizens emerge from the anonymous mass and acquire power to influence public policy. The legislative and legal victories of environmental protection associations in recent years are a dramatic example.

The Orienting Function In at least the limited sphere of a particular association's activities, members learn how society really works, and do so at first hand. They acquire a working knowledge of what strategies may be effective, what is possible and what is not.

The Social Change Function As Rose says, "Voluntary associations offer a powerful mechanism of social change; they are the organizational form of . . . reform movements" (1965:422). (We will consider social movements at some length in the next chapter.) In democratic societies, government will sooner or later be responsive to voters who have acquired some power by joining together in associations seeking change. It should be noted, though, that associations may also oppose change. In recent years, we have often seen associations opposing each other in state legislatures over proposals to change legislation dealing with abortion. Some wish to liberalize existing statutes; others wish to retain them unchanged.

The Function of Personal Identification We have commented on the sense of isolation and powerlessness felt by many persons in relation to the large and impersonal social forms and forces of our time. Voluntary associations perform a valuable function in at least moderating this feeling of alienation for their members. By their own voluntary acts of affiliation and commitment to such associations, individuals do in fact potentially increase their effectiveness in a complicated social world. Rose (1965:423) says that "many members of voluntary associations today find that their memberships and activities in the association help materially to give meaning and purpose to their lives." Insofar as this is true, voluntary associations also aid the cohesion of society at large, for they increase the individual's sense of meaningful participation in and commitment to it.

ORGANIZATIONS AND CHANGE

While sometimes the massive complex organizations of this day may seem to stand solid and impervious to change, we know that this is an illusion. The great corporations, government agencies, educational systems and other giants of our time can no more halt change than any other social unit. Change of many kinds takes place whether it is sought or not, whether it is welcomed or not. For example, in recent years many large businesses have begun to take seriously the environmental impact of their products and processes. This has come about not so much because of an inner decision that this was needed but because of external forces, for example, voluntary associations bringing pressure on government which in turn required changes of industry.

In all social units, including complex organizations, change arises both from necessary adjustments of the unit's internal parts and from relations between the entire unit and the surrounding environment. Our comments here are restricted to changes produced internally, or primarily so. While change of some kind is inevitable and will occur whether or not it is desired, our interest at present is in efforts within organizations to deliberately bring about change and control its course. We are indebted to Leavitt (1965) for a scholarly analysis of this topic. He describes a number of approaches to organizational change and we shall draw upon two important and contrasting examples.

We have seen that it is in the nature of bureaucratic organizations to place a high value on orderly, rational procedures for reaching goals. So we should not be surprised that these organizations are often interested in bringing about changes in their own structures and processes, generally in the interests of higher efficiency or productivity. But disagreements exist on just what means are most effective in enhancing organizational efficiency, and the two approaches to change reviewed in the following sections illustrate this disagreement.

THE TECHNOLOGICAL APPROACH TO CHANGE The history of modern organizations is full of instances in which new technology has made possible or forced internal changes in organizational structure. The whole field of personnel management was made possible by new techniques of personality and aptitude testing, attitude measurement, and job evaluation. More recently, computer technology is leading to important innovations in work organization and the flow of communication in bureaucratic organizations.

In the twentieth century, there has been a succession of approaches to the management of change directed toward greater organizational efficiency, all of them making use of currently new techniques. And each in its turn has been rather widely adopted by many organizational leaders. Probably the earliest was called *scientific management*. It was based on new methods of making very detailed analyses of eye-hand and muscle tasks in factory and office settings. The essential idea was to break down any job into its smallest parts, then reorganize them so as to achieve the maximum output.

More current approaches, made possible by the computer, are called *operations research* and *human engineering*. The newest of all involves what are called *simulation techniques*. The computer makes possible the simulation of alternative solutions to a given organizational problem and therefore an evaluation of alternatives without the cost of trying them out empirically. These newer approaches allow managers to grapple with far more complex problems than was possible with the old scientific management.

All these technology-based approaches are alike in certain respects. For instance, they share "a faith in the ultimate victory of their version of *better* (cheaper or more rational or more elegant) problem solutions over worse ones" (Leavitt, 1965:1150). You can see how consistent this is with Weber's emphasis on the rationality of bureaucracies.

They are also alike in concentrating entirely on the instrumental aspects of the organization. The people who belong to the organization are merely one kind of input into an organizational process. This means ignoring the fact that the role a person performs in an organization is only one among many roles, and ignoring the fact that around his many roles every individual develops complex and sometimes conflicting emotions.

Generally speaking, the people approach tries to humanize organizations. The doctor wearing a "Snoopy" smock and the Batman murals on the wall create a friendly atmosphere and help children to relax at the Cardinal Glennon Memorial Hospital for Children in St. Louis. Their parents also respond favorably to the more humanized environment.

achievement
discrimination
minority

Leaving out the full psychological reality of people may seriously interfere with the success of change programs and problem solutions based entirely on the interests of the organization, however rational these may be, and Leavitt cites significant research supporting this point. Adherents of technologically based approaches are likely to argue that people should be educated or persuaded to be more logical and rational. But since rationality is to be employed in the service of the organization, not of the individuals within it, this argument is rather likely to fall on barren ground. The tendency of the technology-based approach to leave people out was a factor in the development of people approaches to social change, to which we now turn.

THE PEOPLE APPROACH TO CHANGE There are actually several quite well developed variations of this approach. According to Leavitt:

The people approaches try to change organizations by first changing the behavior of the organization's members. By changing human behavior, it is argued, one can cause the creative invention of new tools, or one can cause modifications in structure (especially power structure). By either or both of these means, changing human behavior will cause changes in task solutions and task performance and also cause changes toward human growth and fulfillment, usually highly valued in these approaches (1965:1151).

The people approaches are an interesting and valuable example of cross-fertilization of ideas and techniques from several branches of social, scientific and psychological study. For instance, the work of Carl Rogers and his nondirective therapy in psychology has been influential. So too has the early experimental work in the small groups area, some of which concentrated on changing people's behavior in democratic ways. Finally, the variety of sensitivity training called T-groups (discussed in Chapter 7) has been extensively used as a technique for inducing change in industrial settings.

The people approaches generally appear committed to the idea that power in organizations should be as widely diffused as possible, more so than is very often the case. "Operationally, this belief was made manifest in a variety of ways: in encouraging independent decision-making, decentralization, more open communication, and participation" (Leavitt, 1965:1154).

T-Groups T-groups are frequently used in business firms and as management training devices in many business schools. Today, cross sections of the organization power structure often participate in the same T-group experience, and this is done in such a way as to minimize power differences otherwise separating these people. For example, the group might include foremen, section and division chiefs, vice presidents, and the president. Direct, full, even intimate communication is encouraged on such occasions.

We should remember that the T-group, as a tool of the people approaches for "changing people in order to change organizations," was developed first in nonorganizational settings. You will recall from our discussion in Chapter 4 that sensitivity training sessions seldom last for more than a few days; then the participants disperse. Within organizations, the circumstances are very different, and the T-group raises a kind of dilemma. As a technique it is intended to enhance personal spontaneity, openness, and personal fulfillment in general. But complex organizations have special, technical problems of their own which are quite different from the personal problems and needs of participants. Personal and organizational needs are not necessarily compatible as we have pointed out. Leavitt (1965:1158) feels that this dilemma remains unresolved in attempts to bring about organizational change via the people approaches.

The Scanlon Plan This scheme falls within the people approach orientation but does not involve the use of T-groups; it has been adopted by a number of firms. Requiring union-management cooperation, the plan has two principal features. First, all employees are paid bonuses (keyed to their base pay) for accepted improvements in operating efficiency. Second, committees are established that represent different authority levels within the company, with the objective of developing changes that will lead to greater work effectiveness. This quite simple plan appears to work well, both in increased efficiency and in better relations between people working at the same or at different levels within the company. "In general, the direction of movement is toward greater acceptance of responsibility by lower levels and greater sharing of responsibility by higher with lower groups in the hierarchy" (Leavitt, 1965:1159).

Leavitt feels that not enough research has been done on the effectiveness of people approaches to organizational change to pass judgment on the total effort. He does feel that the approach will continue to be used and that it will develop alongside others.

Sociology has made valuable contributions to the understanding of organizations, and sociological knowledge is used in many specific efforts to resolve concrete organizational problems. This is the case in some of the techniques used in people approaches to organizational change. Our comments here deal with the great need for continuing and enlarging organizational studies.

THE UTILITY OF STUDYING ORGANIZATIONS

More than ever before, more and more of us live greater proportions of our lives in today's big organizations. The situation is historically new in our experience and in that of any other people. It has come upon us unexpectedly and the evidence is overwhelming that we have not yet learned how to live well in a society dominated by massive organizations. It sometimes seems that we exist for the organization rather than the other way around. It is tempting to fall back on the conspiratorial or bad guys interpretation of events, to assume that our troubles with organizations are caused by stupid or insensitive bureaucrats.

While stupidity and insensitivity are sometimes found in organizational officials we do not think that this explanation is very helpful, for the same qualities are found everywhere. The greater truth is that people with good intentions and strategic locations in bureaucratic organizations simply *do not know* how to humanize them, to make them serve people rather than to trivialize and dehumanize them. Sometimes they think they do, or think that what is typically done in organizations today is the best that can be done.

Both suppositions are wrong. We are only at the beginning of the knowledge we need. Meanwhile, organizational leaders continue on an essentially trial-and-error basis, developing folk wisdom about their work. They have no alternative; it is simply an error to suppose that our civilization's early experiences with large organizations have taught us all we need to know.

There have been social critics who would like to wave a magic wand and abolish bureaucratic organizations, wistfully longing for a simpler age, but this is sociologically naive. In our kind of society organizations can do many things that separate individuals and small groups cannot do as well and often simply cannot do at all. Exploration, world peace, freedom and equality, the integration of all segments of society, and major industrial production are objectives sought through the use of large-scale organized efforts. Regardless of the nature and extent of one's commitment to these or other goals, it should be recognized that their attainment is determined in large measure by how well the efforts of individuals are coordinated in large-scale organizations. Consider, for example, the fact that thirty-five thousand or so people were systematically involved in the successful launching, tracking, and space capsule recovery of John Glenn's three-revolution orbital flight in 1962.

As an organization of countries seeking the maintenance of world peace, the United Nations had 132 member countries as of September 1972. Since its beginning in 1945, the United Nations has in several cases helped to prevent conflicts from developing into full-scale wars, and has provided an open forum in which nations may air their differences. Despite its failings, most observers agree that one of the requirements for world peace in our time is some organization such as the United Nations.

As we saw in Chapter 7, some parts of the American population have been disadvantaged compared to others. It is a little-appreciated fact, however, that equal participation in our society is directly related to the application of *organized* social, political, and economic influence. Whatever recent gains have been made by black Americans have followed directly from organized efforts. Furthermore, leaders as well as observers of the civil rights movement are persuaded that freedom and equality can be more effectively achieved only through organized programs (Carmichael and Hamilton, 1968; Killian, 1968). Saul Alinsky, the radical organizer, put it both bluntly and graphically when he said that "civil rights is a movement, and a movement without organization is nothing more than a bowel movement."

Racial and ethnic minorities are not the only segments of our population seeking wider participation in the good life through concerted efforts. The current women's movement parallels the early formative years of the civil rights movement. The incidence of discrimination against women is well documented. And many women have resented discrimination for decades. Their individual feelings counted for little, though, until effective organizations began to appear in the sixties. The elimination of sexism cannot possibly come about without the development and coalescence of such core organizations as the Women's Action Group (WAG), the National Organization of Women (NOW), and others.

Agism, particularly with regard to older and younger people, is a lot like racism and sexism. The elderly have been discriminated against in employment; they have been financially penalized and otherwise socially isolated. Steps have been taken to correct these inequities through such organizations as the American Association of Retired Persons and the National Retired Teachers' Association. Through the efforts of these organizations older persons increasingly may obtain specially designed auto insurance, drug service, low-cost travel, new learning experiences, new social contacts, and reinforced financial security.

The fact is that social power in our kind of society depends on effective social organization. Because this is a democratic society, those who are powerless may take this way toward the achievement of power if they wish. And we have seen a good deal of this in the past two decades. Thus an increase in reliable sociological knowledge about organizations may not only help to make all organizations better settings for human endeavor but assist those still left out to attain an equitable share of power.

Practicing the Sociological Perspective

The following suggestions should help you to become more sensitized both to the sociological perspective in this area and to the meaning of organizations in your own experience.

Make a list of the organizations to which you belong, those to which you once belonged, and those to which you can reasonably anticipate belonging in the future. Classify the organizations you have listed into the three types delineated by Etzioni: coercive, utilitarian, and normative. Which kind is most common in your experience? Do you find that there are differences in the propor-

Like so many others, elderly Americans have discovered that organization is essential if help is to be found in solving their problems. The elderly man in the left picture found work on a housing project as a result of efforts by an association of elderly people.

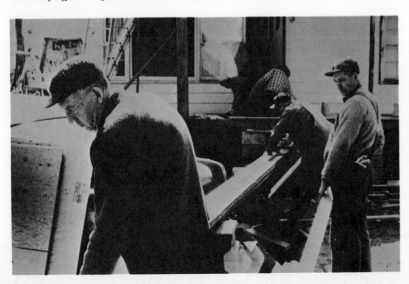

tions of the types of organization when you compare your past experience with the present and with the anticipated future?

What are your complaints about organizations with which you have been affiliated? Think carefully about this. Be specific and try to pin down exactly what you haven't liked. Be on guard here; the question is about organizations, not individuals in organizations. Avoid the temptation to attribute your bad experiences to stupid or insensitive persons. While this may be accurate sometimes, often the difficulty lies in the impact of the organization on you, and the individual who does things you dislike may be merely an instrument of the organization. Now, how would you change the organization so that its legitimate interests were protected while your objections were met?

In the matter of doing something about individual difficulties within organizations, are you familiar with the *ombudsman* idea? Does your college have an ombudsman? The concept originated in Sweden in 1809 and has spread widely since. Essentially, an ombudsman is an individual within an organization who is free to move about within it. He or she has no position in the authority structure, but can move up and down it at will, trying to solve individual grievances, trying to humanize the impact of bureaucratic rules and arrangements on persons. What do you think of this approach?

One can overstate the case against organizations. Doing so is a kind of game people play in this organizational society. It is certainly true that complex organizations can be run more efficiently and humanely than they often are, but are you really ready to get rid of them? Go back to your list of past, present, and future organizations. Imagine that you have resigned from them all or that you never joined them in the first place. What would your life be like? Just great? Better think again. Quickly make a list of your personal goals, the things you want out of life now and in the future. How many of these do you think you could realize without organizations? We can't live without them in our kind of society and sometimes it seems we can't live with them. Consequently we had better learn all we can about them so that we can make them better servants.

Collective Behavior

10

Under the colorless terms *collectivities* and *collective behavior,* sociologists study some of the most unusual and bizarre, exhilarating, frightening, and just plain fascinating, of all the forms of social behavior. These include rumor, crowds, publics, social movements, mass hyteria, riots, panics, disaster responses, and fads. We shall not have the space to treat more than a few of these at any length.

In some situations classified as collective behavior, people are elevated to peaks of exaltation and sacrifice. In some they run in mindless panic from completely imaginary dangers. In others, ordinary people have become screaming mobs which killed innocent victims with brutal savagery. Collective behavior also includes less dramatic phenomena, such as the processes by which public opinion is formulated and people are swayed by fads and fashions. What lies behind such changes?

Sociologists have crammed so many different phenomena under the heading of collectivities that no general theory has been developed which adequately treats them all. Another factor hindering the development of theory is the great difficulty of doing research in some of the most important forms of collective behavior. The occurrence of riots and panics is often so unpredictable that it is impossible to have trained observers on the spot, and we must rely on the reports of witnesses whose perceptions are typically very distorted.

However, Smelser (1963) has identified six conditions which will serve as a useful background for our more detailed consideration of several specific kinds of collective behavior.

The two women who appear to be transmitting a rumor, the great crowd before the Lincoln Memorial in Washington, D.C., the early feminist parade (when women sought the vote), and the poll taker sampling public opinion illustrate the four kinds of collective behavior analyzed in this chapter. It is hard to believe that such different kinds of behavior have anything in common, but sociological analysis indicates that this is the case.

In Smelser's view each of the following conditions is necessary if collective behavior is to appear. If all are present, collective behavior is almost certain to follow. We should caution that his analysis does not apply to a few forms of collective behavior, such as fads and fashions.

STRUCTURAL CONDUCIVENESS This term refers to those conditions in society which *make possible* some kind of collective behavior. For example, the religious riots of recent Irish experience and the race riots that sometimes occur in this country would not happen if different religious and racial groups were not living close to each other in the same society. Structurally conducive conditions by no means guarantee collective behavior; they are merely a precondition.

STRUCTURAL STRAIN The likelihood that a structurally conducive condition will lead to collective behavior is increased if people are experiencing strain as a result of social conditions and if the existing culture does not offer effective ways of reducing strain. Frustration and anxiety accumulate and people are psychologically prepared for episodes of collective behavior. Examples of situations which can produce this effect are often found in wartime (especially when things are not going well), in disasters such as earthquakes and floods, and in prolonged strikes where the outcome is very uncertain.

GROWTH OF A GENERALIZED BELIEF The experience of frustration arising from a condition of structural strain is not a sufficient condition for the appearance of collective behavior. But another step is taken if the people affected come to believe that they have an interpretation of the structural strain that will resolve it or at least make sense out of it. Such interpretations or answers may be very simple or quite complex. In 1973, several murders of white persons by blacks took place within a few days in Boston. Aware of racial tensions in the city, public authorities took great pains to play down the racial aspect of these crimes. They did so in order to forestall the emergence of mobs whose answers to the problem would be to engage in unrestrained violence toward persons of the other race. They knew that such interpretations of needed action were present in many isolated individuals, awaiting only an episode of collective behavior to make them manifest.

Social movements, which we shall discuss later, are much more elaborate examples of generalized beliefs as responses to widely shared experience of structural strain. Their ideologies offer detailed interpretations of the source of frustration and programs for dealing with it. Religious sects, for example, offer theological interpretations of the frustrating social condition and religious solutions to the stress experienced.

In a situation like this the scene is set for the appearance of a precipitating factor, for instance, a policeman who loses self-control and engages in physical violence. From a single such incident may come the violent and destructive release of the pent-up frustration of many thousands of people.

PRECIPITATING FACTORS   All the foregoing factors may be present without bringing about collective behavior. The situation is prepared, but it awaits a precipitating factor. This may be an event which, considered in isolation, is quite minor. Its importance derives from its power to sharpen and dramatize the accumulated sense of frustration and to give credence to the shared interpretation of what is causing the frustration. Later in this chapter we shall present a brief case history of the Berkeley student revolt, which was vital in initiating the student activism of the late sixties. When the Berkeley administration banned political activities at the entrance to the campus, that act triggered all that followed.

MOBILIZATION OF PARTICIPANTS FOR ACTION   At this point we have a considerable number of people suffering continuing frustration from a condition of structural strain. Sharing a common orientation toward the source of the frustration, they have witnessed or experienced one or more precipitating events. All that remains to produce an episode of collective behavior is to move the concerned persons into action. Studies of these situations show that leaders often emerge at this point who are effective in moving an otherwise unorganized mass to action.

OPERATION OF SOCIAL CONTROL   This factor is different from the others. The first five operate in a cumulative way; each developing condition increases the probability that the next will appear. Social control inhibits this cumulative process. Either deliberately or inadvertently, events may occur that interrupt or deflect the developing probability that collective behavior will ensue. That is the meaning of the response of the Boston authorities to their perception that race riots might occur as an aftermath of several brutal murders. However, efforts at social control of collective behavior may have the opposite of the intended efect.

Keeping Smelser's perspective in mind, we turn to a consideration of several specific kinds of collective behavior.

RUMOR   We start with rumor, partly because it gives interesting insight into the general nature of collective behavior. *Rumor is information, true or false, transmitted along informal, uncontrolled channels from anonymous sources.* Whether the content of rumor is true or false does not matter for purposes of definition. When we say that rumors travel along informal, uncontrolled channels we do not suggest that similar channels are not used in established social relationships, groups, and organizations, for indeed they are. And of course transmission may and often does take place between people who are otherwise complete strangers. Our point is that the transmission of rumor is not an officially, formally controlled process. It takes place *regardless* of the presence or absence of existing structures of communication. All it requires is enough contact between people so that communication can occur. When we say that the source of rumor is anonymous, we mean that it is ordinarily impossible to locate the exact point from which a rumor began to circulate. This, naturally, makes for extreme difficulty in checking back on a rumor's accuracy. The anonymity of the source rises out of the devious, informal, and subterranean nature of the channels along which rumor travels.

In the study of their transmission, one may concentrate on the content of rumors, on those who transmit and receive rumors, and on the kinds of social situation which are particularly conducive to rumors.

THE CONTENT OF RUMOR A considerable amount of research has been done in social psychology that bears on the question of the accuracy of rumors. Allport and Postman (1947), Bartlett (1954), and others have constructed ingenious experimental replications of the rumor process. The main conclusion from these studies is that the content of rumor undergoes distortion as it travels from person to person. Part of the content usually drops out and the remainder is organized about a dominant theme. Both the elimination of some content and the thematic emphasis are shown to reflect the personal and social characteristics and the special interests of the people involved in the rumor process (Allport and Postman, 1947:80f.).

However, Lang and Lang (1961:57–58) question whether or not distortion always accompanies the transmission of rumors. They point out that experimental studies which lead to this conclusion fail to duplicate the natural conditions in which rumor occurs. They also report research on armed forces rumors in World War II by Caplow (1947) and other studies which find a surprisingly high level of accuracy in the transmission process. In the absence of further and definitive research we must conclude that distortions may or may not be significant, depending on conditions which are not yet fully identified. Incidentally, distortion (or accuracy), as used here, merely applies to the question of *changes* in rumor content as it travels, and has nothing to do with the original accuracy of the information embodied in a rumor. Lang and Lang (1961:57) report one study of rumors after an earthquake in India. The investigator mentioned a tale that had come to him from several quite different channels in almost the same form, suggesting that not much distortion had taken place. The rumor was that in about six weeks everyone's sex would change!

By and large, it is probably not a good idea to rely on rumor for information if there is any other way of getting the facts. A rumor may be wholly true or wholly false, or partly true in a misleading way. Because of the way rumors are transmitted, it is very hard and often impossible to verify their accuracy by checking back along the line of transmission. Each person in the chain merely

Religion, which often appeals to the noblest in people, can also galvanize them into savage violence when religious conflict becomes extreme. One example is the notorious Bloody Sunday Riot which took place in Belfast, Ireland, on January 30, 1972. What do you think accounts for this paradox?

passes the story along; he is not responsible for its accuracy. We might also mention that rumors may be deliberately started, and often have been by persons with special purposes to serve. But the intention of the person who starts a rumor is irrelevant to the process of transmission.

RECIPIENTS AND TRANSMITTERS OF RUMOR Rumor involves social interaction, a concept introduced and discussed in Chapter 2. It is, however, a special form of interaction. Put simply and schematically, most social interaction involves a communication sent by A to B. B then responds with another message, stimulated by but different from A's message. In rumor transmission, A communicates a message to B, who then transmits the same content—or what he believes to be the same content—to C, and so on until the rumor dies. Each person in the chain is both receiver and transmitter of the same, or essentially the same, content.

There is considerable complexity to the manner in which rumor content is reproduced as it passes from one person to another in this process of *serial reproduction*. Both individual and social factors are known to be involved, that is, rumors do not spread outward in all possible directions from a point of origin. Whether they are transmitted, to whom, and whether they are believed are among the factors influenced by both psychological and social considerations. Lang and Lang state that

the chances of any person's hearing a rumor are greatly increased if the following three conditions are met: (1) the information must be perceived as *relevant* for the potential recipient, (2) by friends or persons with whom he is in frequent contact, and (3) who are themselves actively interested and involved in the matter the rumor concerns. The third condition, active interest and involvement, seems to determine the chances of anyone's becoming an active *transmitter*. Passing on a rumor involves a desire on the part of the transmitter to affect other people's behavior, to bring their perspectives into line with his own, or at the very minimum, to share a valuable bit of information (1961:65).

Credibility In this same vein, Turner (1964:399–400) reports evidence from a number of sources (some of it conflicting) that whether or not unsubstantiated rumors will be believed varies with three factors: (a) the rationality of the recipient—a number of studies show that better educated people are more likely to make independent checks of rumors; (b) consistency with preconceptions—the more a rumor supports one's preconceptions the more likely it is to be believed; and (c) utility—the more useful the rumor is in helping the individual to order his response to a situation the more likely it is to be believed.

Influence of Social Situations Both as receivers and transmitters of rumors, people are always involved in socioculturally defined situations and systems. Thus we would expect to find that discernible influences of these social situations are involved in rumor transmission. In short, we see rumor as a social process embedded in other social forms. Among other students of the subject, Turner and Killian (1972) see rumor as part of a collective decision-making process in which people must coordinate their action with respect to some significant situation facing them, and where there exists no clear-cut, established way of coming to terms with the situation. Seen in this way, rumors (whether true or false makes no essential difference) rapidly disseminate information among people who are trying to arrive at a common orientation as a basis for action. Information is important in deciding how to act.

Turner cites some interesting research by Shibutani which illustrates this principle. During World War II, Japanese Americans on the West Coast were "relocated" in special camps for the duration of the war. A series of confusing, ambiguous and anxiety-producing developments took place among those affected before the final establishment of the camps.

Rumors developed at each stage which offered guidance in decisions regarding whether to leave the area or stay, whether to send children east to school or not, whether to sell property or not, and so on. As each stage passed, the rumors relevant to the decisions which could only have been made at that stage also disappeared from the scene (1964:404).

In short, rumor helped this unhappy group come to terms with the quite desperate situation into which they had been thrust by the government, and for which experience provided no trustworthy guides.

CONDITIONS CONDUCIVE TO RUMOR FORMATION. A number of social conditions which are particularly likely to give rise to rumors are summarized by Turner (1964:405–6). The rigidity of the formal structures of society often impedes the flow of information which people need in order to decide on appropriate courses of action. Formal structures cannot adapt with sufficient speed and flexibility to the rapidly changing circumstances with which people have to cope. In the summer of 1971, President Nixon suddenly and dramatically announced a ninety-day freeze on prices and wages as an anti-inflationary measure. This had obvious and significant implications for every citizen and for hundreds of thousands of organizations, large and small. The action immediately gave rise to scores of questions to which there was no immediate official answer. But some kind of action had to be taken in thousands of situations. Rumors were widespread in the first days after the announcement.

Unfamiliar Occurrence Rumor is stimulated when something happens for which there is no familiar basis of understanding. Visualize two situations; in the first, the President of the United States dies in a hospital of natural causes; in the second, he is as-

During the oil shortage of 1973–1974, much conflicting information was passed out, as illustrated here. Because the shortage was threatening and confusing to millions of Americans, this conflict of "expert" evidence contributed to the spread of rumors.

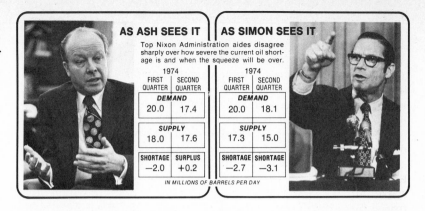

AS ASH SEES IT · AS SIMON SEES IT

Top Nixon Administration aides disagree sharply over how severe the current oil shortage is and when the squeeze will be over.

	AS ASH SEES IT 1974		AS SIMON SEES IT 1974	
	FIRST QUARTER	SECOND QUARTER	FIRST QUARTER	SECOND QUARTER
DEMAND	20.0	17.4	20.0	18.1
SUPPLY	18.0	17.6	17.3	15.0
	SHORTAGE −2.0	SURPLUS +0.2	SHORTAGE −2.7	SHORTAGE −3.1

IN MILLIONS OF BARRELS PER DAY

sassinated. Everyone knows that death comes to all in some form. Hence, while the natural death of a president may bring grief to many (and pleasure to some), its occurrence presents no mystery requiring understanding. When President Kennedy's life was ended by a sniper's bullet, the event produced an extraordinary outbreak of rumors. The biological event, death, is the same but the familiar perspective within which death is interpreted is no longer adequate. What really happened? Even after the investigation and report made by a select presidential committee headed by the Chief Justice of the Supreme Court, thousands of Americans refused to believe the official account. Rumors circulated for years about mysterious persons and events allegedly involved in President Kennedy's assassination. In a case so prominent nationally, it is probable that no conceivable investigation could have convinced all Americans that the full, knowable truth had been told.

Emotional Stress When people are highly excited, under stress, or victims of disaster, they are prone to engage in rumor. This is particularly true when legitimate news media do not provide enough information to enable people to cope with the situation. "Rumor is a substitute for news; in fact, it is news that does not develop in institutional channels" (Shibutani, 1966:62). On occasion, rumors can be distorting, divisive, and destructive. This was very much the case in the aftermath of the riots that took place in Detroit in June 1967 (Rosenthal, 1971). Due to the aftereffects of the riots and a prolonged newspaper strike, a rumor control center was established where stories could be validated. During nearly one month of operation, it received more than ten thousand calls. Fear rumors were the most common, and often involved terrifying stories of castration, infanticide and genocide. The rumors of genocide were most prevalent within the black community, and began with the notion that concentration camps were being readied for blacks. This story had many believers among responsible and thoughtful members of the black community. One reputable black leader, in referring to provisions for reactivating internment camps contained under the McCarran Act, was quoted as saying: "If it can happen in Germany with the Jews, it conceivably can happen again. . . . Camps could be used for large numbers of arrested rioters or might be operated if a Fascist spirit, like that of the radical Right, should become dominant in this country" (Rosenthal, 1971:41).

The rumors exacted a heavy toll from the city of Detroit. Fear, distrust, and ill feelings were generated, fanned throughout the community, and expressed in the formation of vigilante groups, an excessive increase in the purchase of firearms, and in written and spoken tirades. In attempting to understand the causes of the Detroit rumors two factors seem to stand out. First, the four-month-old newspaper strike seriously curtailed communication. Second, the city was still highly stimulated emotionally from the riots of the previous summer and the assassination of Martin Luther King in April.

Any social situation which provokes fear and hostility can produce rumors, provided that objective and verified information is in short supply. Allport and Postman collected one thousand rumors in 1942, during World War II, and found that 66 percent were hostility rumors and 25 percent were fear rumors. The hostility rumors dealt with the presumed shortcomings of the armed forces, the government, allies, and American minorities.

We were told that the Army wasted whole sides of beef, that the Russians greased their guns with lend-lease butter, that Negroes were saving ice-picks for a revolt, and that Jews were evading the draft (Allport and Postman, 1945:62).

During 1942, shipping losses due to enemy action were enormously exaggerated, according to these same authors, in giving examples of fear-inspired rumors.

Knapp records one instance where a collier was sunk through accident near the Cape Cod Canal. So great was the anxiety of the New England public that this incident became a fantastic tale of an American ship being torpedoed with the loss of thousands of nurses who were aboard her (Allport and Postman, 1945:62).

Diversion from Normal Life   Rumor also arises as a permanent consequence of living in society: a desire to be excused temporarily from the normal requirements of orderly social existence. This condition produces in people a more or less constant state of readiness to be diverted briefly from customary tasks by speculation about some novel event. On a college campus, a rumor that the authorities are going to excuse all classes because a great football victory has been won may spread like wildfire for a few hours. An anthropologist, Firth (1956), who studied a small Polynesian society called the Tikopia, reports an amusing example. Ships called at the island infrequently and their coming was important to all.

The people of Tikopia were prone to accept rumors that a ship had been sighted, even though they were generally skeptical of rumors. If a ship were actually coming in this would justify putting aside normal duties. The rumor furnished an occasion for a pleasant diversion.

Rumor is not only a form of collective behavior in its own right; it is an accompaniment and aspect of a number of other forms of collective behavior. We find it frequently in some kinds of crowds, in panics, in disaster phenomena, sometimes in the formation of public opinion, and sometimes in social movements. In short, we find rumor playing a prominent role as a form of communication in many situations where more usual channels of information are not functioning well, yet people face some problem situation which requires action. The news article on the toilet paper crisis tells about just such a situation.

Is Johnny Carson Behind the Toilet Paper Crisis?

"You know, we've got all sorts of shortages these days," Johnny Carson told his faithful latenight television audience. "But have you heard the latest? I'm not kidding. I saw it in the paper. There's a shortage of toilet paper."

Thus began, on the night of last Dec. 19, the second chapter in what may go down in history as one of the nation's most unusual crises—the toilet paper shortage—a phenomenon that saw millions of Americans strip every roll of bathroom tissue from thousands of grocery shelves.

It was a shortage full of humor, misunderstanding and fear. It was a shortage involving government officials, a TV personality, a well-meaning Wisconsin congressman, eager reporters, industrial executives and ordinary consumers.

And it was a shortage that need never have been. For the toilet paper shortage was a rumor run wild in a nation that recently has become geared to expect shortages in items considered absolute necessities.

Fears of a possible bathroom tissue shortage, which continue in some areas as the result of abnormal buying and hoarding, seem to have sprouted last November, when news agencies carried articles about a shortage in Japan.

Meanwhile, in Washington, Rep. Harold V. Froehlich, a 41-year-old Republican from Wisconsin's heavily forested 8th District, was getting considerable complaint from his constituents of a shortage of pulp paper, allegedly caused by companies that increased paper exports to avoid federal price controls.

On Nov. 16, Froehlich issued a news release that began, "the Government Printing Office is facing a serious shortage of paper." Like most other news releases from such sources, it was virtually ignored.

Then Froehlich discovered that the federal government's national buying center had fallen 50% short in obtaining bids to provide 182,050 boxes of toilet tissue, a four months' supply for the country's bureaucrats and soldiers.

On Dec. 11, a day now etched in the minds of Froehlich's staff, he issued another news release. It began:

"The United States may face a serious shortage of toilet paper within a few months . . . I hope we don't have to ration toilet tissue . . . a toilet paper shortage is no laughing matter. It is a problem that will touch every American."

"It got more attention than we ever dreamed of," one aide said of the release. The wire services picked it up. So did the television networks. Radio stations called to talk. German and Japanese correspondents lined up for interviews. In some reports, however, qualifying words like "potential" shortage somehow disappeared.

In Philadelphia, reporters called the headquarters of the Scott Paper Co., one of the nation's 10 largest paper manufacturers. Television crews then filmed supermarkets

Crowds are an important as well as an interesting form of collective behavior. Unfortunately, sociological theory and research remain primitive on this subject. It is not that crowds have gone without attention in social science. Long ago, a French scholar named Le Bon (1895) published a book, *The Crowd,* which was destined to influence thought on the topic for many decades. Much impressed, as many other observers have been, by the extreme behavior which can emerge in crowd situations, Le Bon argued that a kind of crowd mind comes into existence which is different from the minds of the people involved.

Whoever be the individuals that compose it, however alike or unlike be their mode of life, their occupations, their character, or their intelligence, the fact that they have been transformed into a crowd puts them in possession of a sort of collective mind which makes them feel, think, and act in a manner quite different from that in which each individual of them would feel, think, and act were he in a state of isolation (Le Bon, 1895:27).

---

and toilet paper streaming from the machines in Scott's suburban plant here.

Company officers went on television to urge calm, saying there was no shortage if people bought normally.

Some consumers may have believed those remarks—until they saw other shoppers wheeling cases of toilet tissue from some stores or signs rationing each buyer to two rolls each. "There are so many many credibility gaps today," said one paper executive, "and we fell into one."

Wire service reporters and broadcast newsmen passed the self-fulfilling shortage reports on to their readers and audiences, one of whom included Johnny Carson, a television talk show host whose nightly monologue is often geared to current events.

On Dec. 20, the day after his comments, the toilet-paper buying binge began nationally.

In the Bronx, Jimmy DeTrain, manager of the Food Cart store on Lydig Avenue, watched customers check out with $20 in toilet paper purchases.

"I heard about it on the news," said Mrs. Paul McCoy of Houston, "so I bought an extra 15 rolls."

In Seattle, one store owner ordered an extra 21 cases of toilet paper. When he received only three cases, he became worried and rationed his supply. That prompted more buying, even at increased prices.

When Mrs. Clare Clark of Jenkintown, Pa., gave a party, guests asked what they could bring, "I told them toilet paper," she said.

Here in Chester, at Scott's plant, the world's largest such facility (capable of producing 7,500 miles of tissue every day), production continued at full capacity.

Although paper industry officials say the toilet paper shortage was hard to believe, Steuart Henderson Britt, a professor of marketing at Northwestern University, regards the shortage as a classic study in rumor.

"Everybody likes to be the first to know something," he said. "It's the 'did-you-hear-that' syndrome. In the old days, a rumor took a long time to spread, enough time to let people discover its validity. Now all it takes is one TV personality to joke about it and instantly the rumor is in all 50 states."

Britt said the rumor had all the necessary elements. "It could affect everyone intimately," he said. "There was a congressman, presumably an authority, talking about it. He says there could be a problem. The next person says there probably is a problem. The next person says there is a problem."

Britt expects the shortage rumor to die as soon as shoppers discover that tissue paper supplies have been replenished.

Source: From article by Andrew H. Malcolm, *Sunday Journal and Star,* Lincoln, Nebraska, February 3, 1974. © 1974 The New York Times Company. Reprinted by permission.

This apparent crowd mentality results from the contagiousness of suggestion when many people are in a situation of physical closeness. Le Bon was living in a period when many conservative people were afraid of crowd behavior, much as they are today. His antipathy shows through in such statements as this. A man who becomes part of a crowd "descends several rungs in the ladder of civilization. Isolated, he may be a cultivated individual; in a crowd, he is a barbarian, that is, a creature acting by instinct" (Le Bon, 1895:35).

While Le Bon's conception of a collective mind did not long stand the test of critical reactions, his emphasis on suggestion as the psychological mechanism underlying crowd behavior continued to influence the thinking of social psychologists and sociologists in this country for a long time. Meanwhile, serious research into crowd behavior almost disappeared, and as a consequence, significant theoretical developments virtually came to a halt. Only quite recently have a few scholars, among them Turner (1964) and Smelser (1963), returned to the task of building a more adequate theory of crowds. In doing so, they are bringing the whole topic more firmly into sociology proper than it has ever been before. Some of our comments which follow reflect these more recent and more sociological conceptions of what is involved in crowd behavior.

In retrospect, one can see that from Le Bon forward, attempts to understand crowds uncritically accepted the assumption that what people do in these situations is somehow completely unrelated to their normal behavior. Crowd behavior was seen as having no roots in normal psychological organization and none in the ordinary operation of social structures. This assumption inhibited the development of both psychological and sociological theories because it made crowd behavior, in effect, unique, lying outside the normal boundaries of investigation in these fields. The fact that research was scanty postponed the recognition that more progress might be made if it were assumed that crowd behavior was explicable in much the same terms as any other kind of behavior.

Yet it is not difficult to understand why the assumption was made that crowd behavior is qualitatively different. Anyone who has witnessed the rampages of a destructive mob could be sympathetic to this viewpoint. Here are a large number of people, each of whom ordinarily goes more or less quietly about his business, joined together in the commission of ferocious acts of violence against persons and property. We are sure that no single one of these people would do such things acting alone. What has happened? Isn't it possible that in some strange way they have become different, temporarily capable of things which have no continuity with the rest of their lives?

CROWDS AS NORMAL BEHAVIOR However plausible the assumption behind this question, it has proved scientifically barren, and the conviction that crowd behavior can be understood better if it is

While the behavior of the people in crowds illustrated here and on the next page may seem to be completely out of control, that isn't really true. Lynch mobs were an accepted tradition in some parts of the country for many years, and the idea of a riotous celebration of victory is an old tradition in American sports.

Part 2 / Social Units and Processes

approached from the perspectives of familiar psychological and sociological theory has grown. We shall only mention here one influential example from social psychology, the frustration-aggression hypothesis of Dollard and his associates (1939). In brief, these scholars held that aggression against others arises from frustrated impulses in the individual. Aggression may be released against those who actually cause the frustration, or it may be *displaced,* that is, directed against vulnerable persons who are not the real causes of the frustration.

Dollard et al. were able to show a significant relationship between the price of cotton in southern states between 1882–1930 and the frequency of lynching mobs. When the price of cotton was high, lynching mobs were infrequent, and vice versa. Lynch mobs were predominantly composed of poor whites, those who suffered intensified frustration in bad times; aggression was displaced against the helpless blacks. Interesting and valuable as this approach has been, for our purposes it is deficient in some respects. It helps to account for only one kind of crowd—violent or destructive in its behavior—and there are many other kinds. Furthermore, this explanation would predict noncrowd kinds of aggression too. Nothing in the formulation explains why aggression should occur in crowds rather than in other kinds of settings.

There is also reason to believe that crowd behavior is more closely linked to familiar social and cultural phenomena than earlier theories supposed. Consider the fundamental insight in sociology and social psychology that the ideas and behavior of the individual are subject to social control, operating through all the agencies of society and culture. The same sociological fact of life is present in crowds, which also control individual behavior though perhaps in a somewhat different manner than in most other situations.

Traditional crowd theories have stressed "spontaneity and discontinuity from conventional norms and social structure" (Turner, 1964:383). But Turner feels that this has been overemphasized.

Careful examination of a wide range of collective behavior reveals few instances that are not specifically justified by their participants on the basis of some extant social norm and which cannot be shown to have some continuity with tradition (1964:383).

Visualize a situation in which the spectators at a college football game become an unruly but mainly good-natured mob after a victory. The goal posts are torn down, there is a good deal of milling about, a parade through the business district materializes, and a few people get roughed up before the excitement dies down. The event appears at first glance to be completely spontaneous. But is it really? Is there not a kind of informal tradition in American colleges which sanctions occasional outbreaks of this kind? Some of the students involved may even have heard parents or older friends fondly recalling the mob scene that broke out after a big game when they were in school.

In recent years many of the riots involving college students and

blacks also illustrate the point made by Turner. For example, in 1965 a serious and destructive riot took place in a black ghetto of Los Angeles called Watts. Interviews with rioting persons make it quite clear that, to the residents of Watts, the mob action was justified by long-standing grievances against the police and the white merchants in the Watts area. The *San Francisco Chronicle*, August 21, 1965, reported that burning and looting of stores was first directed at "businesses whose owners had a reputation for gouging Negroes or for foreclosing mortgages."

CHARACTERISTICS OF MAJOR AND SERIOUS DISORDERS In 1967, President Johnson established a National Advisory Commission on Civil Disorders. The commission's report revealed that 164 disorders had taken place during 1967. Of these, forty-one (25 percent) were classified as major or serious. Major disorders were characterized by: (a) many fires, intensive looting, and reports of sniping; (b) violence lasting more than two days; (c) sizable crowds; and (d) use of National Guard or federal forces as well as other control forces. Serious disorders contained the following factors: (a) isolated looting, some fires, and some rock throwing; (b) violence lasting between one and two days; (c) only one sizable crowd or many small groups; and (d) use of state police though generally not National Guard or federal forces (1968:68–77, 323–35). The commission also reported a study conducted by the Permanent Subcommittee on Investigations of the Senate Committee on Government Operations. This study investigated seventy-five disturbances in sixty-seven cities, and disclosed eighty-three deaths and 1,897 injuries. In property damage, certain cities suffered severe losses: Detroit ($40–45 million), Newark ($10.2 million), and Cincinnati (more than $1 million). The commission concluded that disorders, particularly in black communities, typically followed a pattern of events: discrimination, prejudice, disadvantaged conditions, intense and pervasive grievances, a series of incidents which heightened tension and culminated in the eruption of disorder by young, politically conscious activists.

DEFINING CROWD The very dramatic character of some crowds tends to deflect our attention from the fact that there are many sorts of crowds. What is a crowd, anyway? The following definition is broad enough to encompass a wide variety of sociological events which also have some things in common. *A crowd is a number of people temporarily in close physical proximity. The interaction rate is high and characterized by a relatively high proportion of emotional expression. Social structure is simple, rarely consisting of more than a differentiation between leader and followers.*

The characteristics of crowds identified in this definition fit many other situations besides the mobs to which we have referred. Many audiences (those which attend athletic contests, for example) are crowds by this definition. Crowds frequently develop in connection with socially organized activities such as strikes or boycotts, the visits of famous people, and patriotic or religious occasions. Crowds often develop in streets and other public places because some incident of interest such as an accident or a fire has occurred. A big sale by a large store may trigger crowd behavior. Table 10-1 classifies several kinds of crowds.

Crowds are far from being a sociological abnormality. This is true despite the fact that they sometimes engage in extreme behavior and despite the additional fact that much, but not all, crowd behavior seems to occur outside the normal, structured routines of social life. Whether or not a crowd will develop in particular circumstances, and how it will behave if it does develop, are related at innumerable points to the manner in which everyday life is organized by society and culture. We have already suggested examples of how this is true, and many other illustrations could be given. Sometimes crowd situations are deliberately created and manipulated in order to serve instrumental ends. Both politics and religion furnish many examples of leaders who are highly skilled in creating crowd-like audiences through the manipulation of slogans, symbols, and other tools. In sum, crowds are often a perfectly normal, even routine accompaniment to orderly social existence. Even when they are not an aspect of conventional societal patterns they are produced by such patterns, as when the Watts rioters expressed their desperation at the consequences of white discrimination.

TABLE 10-1 TYPES OF CROWDS

	CHARACTERISTICS	EXAMPLE
Casual	Unplanned, takes no action, usually emotionally calm.	Crowd watching a fire or a building under construction.
Conventional	Planned, behavior under normative control, hence some patterning of behavior; may be intense emotional expression.	Crowd at athletic contest.
Audience	Quite similar to conventional crowds. Behavior more inhibited by norms. Emotions may be strong but are expressed in conventional ways.	Theater audience.
Expressive	Strong (but not socially threatening) emotional release. Normative control of behavior present but not rigid. Some conventional crowds also are expressive.	Large parties, political rallies, religious revivals.
Mob	Intense emotional expression *not* under the control of norms defining suitable behavior. Temporary leaders emerge. Potentially destructive.	Riots related to racial, religious or political issues.

THE EMERGENT NORM THEORY OF CROWDS   The emergent norm theory, particularly associated with the contributions of Turner (1964), is one of several recent attempts to develop theories of crowd behavior which are more sociological in nature than those which sprang initially from Le Bon's approach. Turner holds that the homogeneity of feeling and behavior so often attributed to persons in a crowd is at most an illusion. Most persons in a crowd are really not very much involved emotionally and are not particularly active. What happens, in Turner's view, is that something like a norm (defining appropriate behavior) emerges out of the highly visible remarks and actions of a few persons. In what was initially an ambiguous situation, these persons define the kind of behavior which ought to be followed. "Because it (the norm) is so perceived, it constrains others to act in a manner consistent with it, inhibits contrary behavior, and justifies converting others to this particular line of action" (Milgram and Toch, 1969:553).

Many people present in a crowd situation will not agree with the emerging norm, but will refrain from expressing opposition. In much the same way, two loudly talking persons who blunder into what is obviously a very serious meeting will moderate their behavior to conform to the new situation. This does not mean that they share the mood or purpose of the meeting. The unwillingness of many crowd members to openly oppose the feelings and behavior called for by the emergent norm gives an illusory appearance of homogeneity to the casual observer.

We do not offer this as a fully adequate account of the mechanisms of crowd behavior. But it is a point of view amenable to empirical testing. As Milgram and Toch have observed (1969:554–55), the development of theory in this area must await the production of much more careful, empirical observation of many kinds of crowds than is now available. We concede that research in this area is almost invariably difficult and may on some occasions even be dangerous, but the need justifies the effort.

Not all members of a crowd are deeply aroused emotionally, as Turner pointed out in his emergent norm theory. The point is illustrated by this portion of a crowd scene. Note the highly visible reaction of the person on the right, as contrasted to the lack of visible reaction by the people on the far right and far left.

A social movement is a deliberately organized, persistent social response to some perceived inadequacy in society. Such a movement may last from several months to many years. Students sometimes think that sociologists see individuals as wholly passive in their relationships to the forces of society; there is a vast quantity of evidence suggesting that our behavior is controlled by groups, organizations, and culture even when we are completely unaware of the fact. But the concept of social movement reminds us that this is not the whole story. In social movements, people come together for the explicit purpose of doing something themselves about a condition in society. Social movements are people taking matters into their own hands, trying to bring about a change in a state of affairs which they disapprove; this is a far cry from passivity.

In labeling movements persistent we distinguish them from crowds, which otherwise fit our definition very well. Crowd behavior is often involved in social movements, but all crowds are temporary events, enduring only a few hours, or at most a few days. While most social movements seek some change in society, not all do, despite the suggestion in much of the literature on the topic that this is the case. The civil rights movement of the sixties is an example of a movement seeking change. There have also been religious movements—monasticism, for instance—which sought mainly to dissociate members from the larger society rather than to change it. All movements are a collective response to perceived inadequacy in society, but not all seek to change society.

CONDITIONS WHICH GIVE RISE TO SOCIAL MOVEMENTS   Societies always produce some frustration in their members; this is an inevitable aspect of the human condition. By itself this sociological fact of life cannot account for the appearance of movements at particular times and places, for it holds true in all times and places, and some people are more frustrated by societal structures than others. Evidence indicates that social movements are likely to emerge from categories of people who are subjected to unusual stress and frustration, but this tendency is not a sufficient condition for the emergence of a movement. Black Americans have been subjected to systematic discrimination for more than a century, not counting the preceding period of slavery. Why then did the vigorous civil rights movement, and later the black power movement of the 1960s, not develop much earlier? Many other examples could be given of oppressed peoples who have not managed to develop viable movements for the improvement of their lot.

Expectation of Success Students of social movements have shown that in addition to unusual deprivation or frustration, there must also be a widely shared feeling that something really can be done before a movement will develop. Sometimes an actual recent improvement in the lot of the affected population leads to such a hope or conviction. In the United States, legislative and judicial actions which began with the Supreme Court desegregation decision of 1954 placed the federal government much more firmly on the side of equal opportunity for all. This fact alone caused hope to spring up among black Americans. Once hope has appeared and some progress has been made, people become much more impatient with remaining frustrations and more determined to remove them. By these conditions the seedbed for social movements is made ready. As Milgram and Toch say (1969:590):

The recruits for social movements are individuals who not only find themselves faced with a social deficit, but who (1) experience it as such, (2) view it as remediable, and (3) feel the need to become personally involved in the achievement of the solution.

IDEOLOGIES AS AN ASPECT OF SOCIAL MOVEMENTS Every social movement encompasses a set of ideas which justifies its existence; we refer to this as its ideology. These ideas identify the people represented by the movement and the conditions in society against which the movement acts or which its members regard as enemies. In addition, the ideology expresses the frustrations felt by members of the movement and the aspirations that they share. The ideas also lend ideological support to the tactics adopted by the movement. In some cases, ideologies may be given highly intellectualized expression, while in others they may constitute only a vaguely formed though deeply felt collection of slogans, stereotypical images, and emotion-laden epithets.

Ideologies help to sharpen the distinction between the in-group (the movement) and the out-group (all others, especially those in opposition), a distinction we discussed in Chapter 4. For the committed member of a social movement there is a heightened sense that the world is divided into *us* and *them*. "If you are not for us you must be against us." Although this view is almost certainly an oversimplification, and thus a distortion, of reality, a movement's ideology provides a rationale which explains why it is required. Since social movements seek some form of change, their ideologies stress change. Whether or not they are realistic from an outsider's point of view, they give their members a platform for belief and commitment to a better future. Any current social movement will illustrate this value of an ideology. The black power movement has developed a number of articulate ideological spokesmen who give voice to the despair of black Americans, to their vision of a new pride in black identity, and to the need for more aggressive tactics in wresting fair treatment from white society. All social movements, however, do not seek goals which would seem liberal or radical to most Americans. Many whose ideologies are ultraconservative form part of the radical right. As Epstein and Forster comment (1967:21):

One does not properly toe the Radical Rightist line unless one speaks out vociferously against the United Nations, the civil rights movement,

Ideologies express many things about a social movement. This photo captures the elements common to ideologies—an identification of the people (the in-group) in the movement, the conditions that they are trying to change, and their values, aspirations, and tactics.

Part 2 / Social Units and Processes

Social movements seek change but may be diametrically opposed on what change is needed to make society better. Shown here are a left-wing organization, the SDS Women's Militia (with the Vietcong flag), and some right-wing demonstrators. There are, of course, many social movements with more moderate ideologies between these two extremes.

mental health programs, the National Council of Churches, federal aid to schools, the Anti-Defamation League, the New York Times, disarmament treaties, and the fluoridation of water.

THE STRUCTURE OF SOCIAL MOVEMENTS The ideology of a social movement formulates the movement's values. As we have seen, values have implications for behavior; they justify and help to develop norms which define roles. Roles specify the approved forms of relationships between persons engaged in some common enterprise; at this point we are talking about social structure. Social movements, like other forms of organized social behavior, have social structure. "Indeed, it is as a structure develops, with leaders and their followers being identified as peculiarly and intensively concerned with the promotion of certain values, that the members of a society recognize that a social movement has arisen" (Killian, 1964:439–40).

Leaders and Followers We shall discuss here only the most important role distinction in social movements, that between leaders and followers. Leadership in some form is a nearly universal aspect of organized social life. In social movements, leadership has unusually high social visibility. Movements are characterized by enthusiasm and excitement, especially in their early stages.

Mussolini (above) and the Rolling Stones (opposite page)—as different as they are, both illustrate charismatic leadership.

Leaders are symbols of values around which this enthusiasm can be organized; they also stimulate commitment among members and attract recruits by their personal appeal. Social movements give us some of our best examples of what Weber called charismatic leaders (Gerth and Mills, 1946). Such leaders do not get their influence from the conventional, established seats of power in society but from a relationship with their followers based on personal devotion. To the followers, a leader embodies in his person everything the movement stands for. Good examples of charismatic leaders of social movements are Jesus, Hitler (Nazism was initially a social movement), and Martin Luther King.

The followers and supporters of a social movement are by no means equally engaged in its program. As Lang and Lang state (1961:495):

The organized aspects of a social movement never entirely encompass it; they reside in a core group whose role in relation to the social movement is, in itself, never planned. There is no completely organized social movement.

A core group of followers makes major commitments to the movement. These accept responsibility and discipline and, along with the leaders, assert the claim to represent the movement as a whole, to attract new followers into it, and to carry out its strategy in moving toward its goals. Around this core group is a much larger number of adherents who support the movement in varying degrees. Some enter and leave again after only a brief flirtation. Others share sympathy with goals but contribute little to development. As a movement grows, it may pick up more and more adherents whose ideological commitment is not strong but who believe that the movement will succeed and want to be identified with its success, or perhaps simply hope to profit personally from its progress.

Several Organizations Often a social movement is comprised of several organizations, each with its own set of leaders and followers. Among the organizations actively involved in the civil rights movement of the sixties were the Congress on Racial Equality (CORE), the National Association for the Advancement of Colored People (NAACP), the Student Non-violent Coordinating Committee (SNCC) and the Southern Christian Leadership Conference, headed by Martin Luther King. In the radical right movement, organizations include the John Birch Society, the Americanism Educational League, the Liberty Lobby, Christian Crusade, and Constructive Action.

Both cooperation and competition—even outright conflict—are possible when several organizations claim to represent a social movement. Remember that there is no formal legitimation and support of movement organizations or their leaders from outside sources. This fact, together with the highly emotional commitment of core members to the organization and its charismatic leaders, sets the stage for competition. Quite commonly, social movements exhibit a kind of warfare over who has the right and duty to lead the movement. Movement organizations often co-operate, typically forming alliances which shift and change. Where there are several participating organizations, the movement may be said to consist of all these, together with the whole body of persons who support the movement's goals, many of whom may not actually belong to any formal group.

Increasing Complexity of Social Structure Social movements which persist for a long period of time eventually cease to be movements at all because of internal changes in their structure and changes in their relationship to the surrounding society. In their early stages, social movements have a very simple social structure, consisting of a comparatively small number of core members and the leadership, which may be only a single person or a small, cohesive group. At this stage, "decisions are made for the most part by the leadership group, and sometimes by a single, powerful, charismatic leader. Only in the leadership group is there sufficient continuity and coherence for decisions to be made" (Killian, 1964:447).

If the movement grows in size and achieves some success in its program, task differentiation (and hence, role differentiation) is inevitable. Specialists of different sorts must be evolved. Structure becomes increasingly complex. Furthermore, partial success means that the movement is getting some of its goals accepted by society. Insofar as this is the case, the movement loses some of its reason for remaining in opposition to those establishments in society against which its program is directed. Thus increased structural complexity and growing reconciliation with society slowly transform the movement into a more or less conventional association. It becomes respectable, so to speak, in many ways indistinguishable from other socially accepted associations. Leadership is less charismatic and emphasizes administrative skills. There is a complex organization to maintain, in whose continuation—simply as an organization—large numbers of people have a personal stake. A well-known example of this process can be seen in the history of organized labor in the United States. It began as a movement in every sense of the word. Charismatic leaders headed the early organizing drives against fierce opposition from business and government. After years of struggle, unions achieved recognition in the form of contracts with employers and legislative protection by government. Collective bargaining became the accepted mode of interaction between unions and employers. The success of the unions transformed their nature. The old battling charismatic union leader who earned his scars on the picket line was gradually replaced by the business agent, an administrative leader who met with employers as equals across the bargaining table. Members lost much of the old zeal that sustained them in prerecognition days. Unions have now become an established power center in respectable society. The same kinds of transformation have been studied in religious organizations, where movements have been changed by success into secure, highly respected denominations. (We will have more to say about religious movements in Chapter 14.)

CASE HISTORY OF A SOCIAL MOVEMENT   In the early 1960s, there was a good deal of rather unorganized ferment on American college campuses. Students were increasingly critical of colleges and their administrations. They opposed their own lack of autonomy, the use of school attendance and grades as a basis for exemption from the draft, and the university's special relationship to the Selective Service System and the so-called military-industrial complex. University officials also were perceived as being oversensitive to conservative pressures, and as inadvertently supporting the racial and ethnic status quo.

In the fall of 1964, at the University of California, Berkeley, student protests were staged that were to become the model for unprecedented student revolts and demonstrations throughout the country over the next six years. The protests at Berkeley began when the university officials prohibited the use of the campus for such political activities as recruiting and fund raising (Stern, 1965). Although this rule had been in existence for some time, it had never before been enforced. The students viewed the rule as a violation of their constitutional rights, and ignored the restrictions by continuing to recruit and collect money. The administration's response was to suspend eight students for violating restrictions on political activity.

The students countered by conducting their political activities in front of the administration building. On October 1, a violator was arrested. While he was being placed in a campus police car a group of students spontaneously threw themselves in the path of the car. In the following hour as many as a thousand students gathered around the car to form a solid wall. This incident escalated into thirty-two-hour massive sit-in and rally on that spot. The demonstrations ended when the students and the administration approved the terms of an agreement.

During the next two months the administration agreed not to press charges against the arrested student, reinstated the eight suspended students, and lifted the ban on political fund raising and recruiting. Meanwhile the students were busy organizing the various political organizations on campus into the Free Speech Movement (FSM), circulating petitions and staging rallies and demonstrations. The situation erupted again when on November 28, the chancellor initiated disciplinary action against four FSM leaders for their part in the police car demonstration. The students interpreted this as an act of bad faith because of the agreement ending the initial demonstration. So four days later, more than one thousand students occupied four floors of the administration building, and the graduate student organization and teaching assistants called a university-wide strike in support of the FSM demands. During the strike forty-eight hundred students went on the picket lines, fifty-six hundred refused to attend classes, thirty-five hundred actively opposed the strike, and the rest were passive (Kornhauser, 1968:373). The students who supported the FSM came from liberal homes, regarded themselves as liberal Democrats, were strongly pro–civil rights, opposed American policy in Vietnam, had better than average grades, and majored in the humanities and social sciences. The strike ended on December 8, six days after it had been called. The major protests ended on the day when the university faculty, by a vote of 824–115, passed a resolution calling for full freedom of speech and advocacy (Kornhauser, 1968:373).

FSM represented an organized coalition of nineteen student groups with an executive committee of fifty and a steering committee of twelve. During the course of the demonstrations a newsletter, leaflets, and reports were produced, and a central command post was established to coordinate activities. A communication network, aided by walkie-talkies, received and disseminated information faster than any other system on campus. The solidarity of FSM was reflected in the characterization of people in terms of *them* and *us*. Persons who did not support the demonstrations were referred to as stooges of the administration. Ostensibly the goal of the FSM was to change the rules governing soliciting of funds and recruiting for political activities. The real goals were to reduce student alienation and curb university bureaucratization. The principle ideology of the FSM was derived from the civil rights movement and emphasized the idea that bureaucratic organizations must be just and responsive to the needs of the people they serve. The tactics employed, sit-ins and strikes, were well suited to the goals and ideology of the FSM. While there have been social movements in every period of American history, they have been unusually frequent in the last two decades, and they have made bold challenge to the holders of established power. Movements both reflect and create social change.

PUBLICS

Publics are another kind of collectivity that plays a large role in industrialized, and especially democratic, societies. *A public consists of a substantial number of people who share a significant interest in some issue or topic, an interest important enough to arouse opinions and sometimes actions.* Members of a public do not ordinarily know one another personally, though they are likely to be aware that their interest in a particular issue is widely shared.

In the United States there are almost as many publics as there are widely known issues. Some publics engage the attention of millions of people, such as the voting, buying, and TV-viewing publics. Others are far narrower in their appeal, like the peace advocates, the anti-pollutionists, the rock star fans, the consumer protectors, and the supporters of educational television. Any one person is likely to participate in quite a number of publics.

OUT HERE,
THERE'S OIL AND GAS
TO EASE AMERICA'S
ENERGY SHORTAGE IN
YEARS TO COME.

EXPERTS SAY THAT BENEATH OUR COASTAL WATERS THERE'S ENOUGH OIL AND NATURAL GAS TO MEET A SUBSTANTIALLY LARGER PORTION OF AMERICA'S ENERGY NEEDS.	THIS IS AN IMPORTANT FIRST STEP THERE MAY STILL BE DELAYS BECAUSE OF ENVIRONMENTAL CONCERNS.
PRESIDENT NIXON HAS DIRECTED THE SECRETARY OF THE INTERIOR TO INCREASE THE RATE OF LEASING OF OUTER CONTINENTAL SHELF AREAS FOR EXPLORATORY DRILLING.	THE HISTORY OF U.S. MARINE DRILLING SUGGESTS THAT THERE WOULD BE SMALL RISK IN PROVIDING THE NATION WITH MUCH-NEEDED NEW SUPPLIES, WHICH COULD BE AVAILABLE WITHIN A FEW YEARS.

A COUNTRY THAT RUNS ON OIL CAN'T AFFORD TO RUN SHORT.
THE OIL COMPANIES OF AMERICA

Big business, like other organized components of society, seeks to influence public opinion in its own interests.

IMPORTANCE OF PUBLIC OPINION   Publics are genuine social units, but their organization is so vague and rudimentary by comparison with voluntary associations, complex organizations, and even informal small groups, that at first glance it seems that they can have little social significance. It would be a mistake to make this assumption. Modern governments, whatever their political stripe, cannot ignore *public opinion* altogether, and this is particularly true of democracies. In democracies public opinion polls are scanned by politicians with great care, for what the public thinks sets limits on what courses of action may realistically be considered.

The whole economic institution in advanced capitalist countries like the United States is sensitively tuned to consumer publics. Profit and loss, failure or success, are closely tied to whether or not a firm can ascertain what the public wants, or, increasingly, *create* a public demand for products or services. The support of public opinion is also vital to many other kinds of organizations. The ultimate success of a social movement, like women's liberation, is firmly tied to the kind of public support that can be aroused in people who are not themselves actively involved in the movement. Because the support of public opinion is so critical, billions of dollars are spent each year in this country by businesses, politicians and organizations of many kinds, all seeking to sway public opinion. Advertising, propaganda, and related techniques have become major examples of applied social psychological knowledge.

For the social scientist, analysis of public opinion by modern polling techniques can provide a sensitive indicator of value and norm conflicts in different parts of the population. To illustrate, in 1970 a Gallup Poll revealed the following opinion differences between college students and their elders (Gallup Opinion Index). Over three and a half times as many college students (29 percent) as older adults (8 percent) believed that persons refusing to be drafted should be let off without a penalty. There were over twice as many liberals (61 percent) as conservatives (26 percent) on college campuses. By contrast, there are three adult conservatives (52 percent) for every two adult liberals (34 percent). In addition, students believed that organized religion is not relevant (58 percent), marrying a virgin is not important (73 percent), and marijuana should be legalized (50 percent).

Public Opinion Polling One measure of the importance of publics and the opinions they hold is the very rapid development in recent decades of public opinion polling. There are now hundreds of analysis and polling agencies working in this area. Many continue to use primitive and outmoded techniques and some are, to put it bluntly, dishonest. But the technology of opinion polling, basically an elaboration of well-known social science research techniques, has come a long way, and there are many agencies of skill and integrity that use these techniques

Part 2 / Social Units and Processes

today. Prominent among them are Gallup's American Institute of Public Opinion, Elmo Roper and Associates, Louis Harris and Associates, A. C. Nielson Company, governmental agencies (for example, the Department of Agriculture), the Survey Research Center at the University of Michigan, and the National Opinion Research Corporation at the University of Chicago.

The legitimate value of polls is directly related to their proper execution and to the public's understanding of the polling process. Polls conducted correctly yield data that are extremely useful and informative. The polling process involves four stages: formulating the questions, selecting the respondents, asking the questions, and analyzing the answers.

Asking the right questions in the right way is very important. The specific questions asked, to be sure, coincide with the interests and aims of the particular polling agency. But advice and suggestions often come from such informed sources as newspapermen, government officials, educators, social scientists, and poll watchers. How a question is phrased influences the validity of responses. Loaded words, that is, terms that produce intense emotions ("What do you think of black power?"), should be avoided. Similarly, words with more than one meaning should not be used ("How many birthdays have you had?").

Ambiguities and verbal problems can usually be resolved by using questions in a small-scale trial run (pre-test). The way a question is structured may also bias the response. This can be remedied by offering different types of questions—for example, yes or no, multiple-choice, or discussion questions. Opinions often vary in degree of intensity as well as in kind. It is important on many issues to determine the extent to which a public is for or against a given matter. It would seem vital, for example, to ascertain how much the American public approved or disapproved of, say, a military action taken by our government. Questions may be constructed so as to reveal the strength of opinions.

Selecting respondents begins with specifying the particular publics in question. A totally accurate poll would require an interview with every single individual within a given public. Obviously, this would be prohibitively expensive and time-consuming. It has been estimated that a poll of one hundred million adults, even if it reached ten thousand persons a week, would take five hundred years!

The theory of sampling, used by all sciences, makes a total coverage unnecessary. A sufficient number of persons (Gallup samples typically include fifteen hundred civilian adults) randomly selected and representing a cross section of a given public, will generally yield results with an acceptably low margin of error. Representativeness, in terms of such factors as geographic location and community size (not the mere size of the sample itself), is the main prerequisite of a good sample. One of the largest samples in polling history, over two million persons, not only picked the wrong winner in the 1936 presidential election but was

Truman's presidential victory over Dewey in spite of an almost universal prediction of his defeat by the polls led to an improvement of polling techniques.

off by nineteen percentage points. That poll ignored what is known about scientific sampling techniques.

The third stage of polling is the interview itself. It is important for the interviewer to establish rapport with the interviewee because some issues are sensitive, and not all persons are eager to express their opinions openly. It is necessary, therefore, to select interviewers who are motivated and who relate well to people, and then to train them properly.

The polling process ends with interpretation of the answers. Prudence should be shown in not exceeding the boundaries of the data gathered. For example, opinions expressed represent the feelings of persons on that given day. This does not mean that these feelings will necessarily remain unchanged. Also, people may feel one way about something and yet behave differently. Further, it should not be assumed that the opinions of all persons are based on knowledge or information. People may feel strongly about ecology, and still know little about environmental pollution.

COMMON ELEMENTS IN COLLECTIVE BEHAVIOR

Rumor, crowds, social movements, and public opinion are four kinds of collective behavior, but there are other types which we shall not analyze here. Sociologists have grouped these various phenomena under the label *collective behavior* in the conviction that all have at least some things in common.

Simple Structure One quality found in many kinds of collective behavior is that it is relatively unstructured, in comparison to most sociological units of similar size. The structure of a crowd of ten thousand people is simplicity itself compared to that of an organization of the same size. The same may be said of publics and public opinion, even though a single public may contain several million people. Panics, crazes, and fads may be dramatic and may affect many thousands, but they are not structurally complex as the sociologist uses that term. Social movements are the most complex of collective behavior phenomena. A new movement may spring to life out of a crowd. Years later, to describe it as mature is to say that it is ceasing to be a movement at all and is becoming something else.

Short Duration   Related to the structural simplicity of collective behavior is the fact that most of it is of short duration. It does not last long enough for complicated structures to evolve. Most crowds last only a few hours. Once a public has acted on an issue (voted in a local election, for instance) it is likely to dissolve. Even social movements, some of which have a comparatively long life, either disappear or are transformed, as we have seen. When we contrast the duration of any collective behavior with that of governments, business firms, churches, and many other established structures, we see how ephemeral collectivities are.

Common Orientation   Another quality of much collective behavior is that it helps people to form a common orientation toward a situation which requires action, arouses anxiety or fear, is ambiguous, and for which conventional routines give no sure guide. This is true of rumor; many but not all crowds perform the same functions. In a more dispassionate way, publics also are a means of clarifying and deciding between alternatives on issues that really need to be acted on. Social movements give organizational expression to widespread frustrations.

Emotional Relief In speaking of rumor we pointed out how it can offer relief from the rigidities of everyday life. The same applies to such other collective forms as crazes, crowds, and social movements. Closely related is the emotional relief (*catharsis*) which many kinds of collective experience can give to participants. All human beings are creatures of emotion, and the orderly, rationalized and socially structured routines of society often constrain the free expression of feeling. Much collective behavior, whether it is socially approved and part of a cultural tradition, or an unexpected outbreak against which society reacts oppressively, gives vent to repressed emotions.

  All societies have social forms which let people temporarily break away from routines to seek emotional release. Anthropologists use the term *saturnalia*[1] to refer to such occasions, when the normal rules are briefly suspended. Can you think of any such events in our society? The emotions released in collective behav-

---

[1] In ancient Rome, the feast of Saturn, which was celebrated with feasting and revelry.

ior may be of different kinds. Fear and hatred are strong emotions, and when their expression in the individual is intensified by a mob, they may become very destructive. Emotional exaltation also may be elicited by collective behavior, directed toward a religious or patriotic value or a lofty moral or social ideal. Public expressions of feeling can also contribute to social solidarity by strengthening loyalty to important societal values.

COLLECTIVE BEHAVIOR AND SOCIAL CHANGE   Finally, many sociologists believe that collective behavior plays a significant role in social change.

A small, motley group of admirers of an itinerant heretical rabbi . . . could hardly be characterized, at the time when it was active, as the nucleus of an expanding movement which would eventually cover the Western world; a few emigrants conspiring to confirm the views of a renegade economist might never be viewed as the vanguard of revolutions to take place in their own and other countries; a few unemployed veterans congregating to listen to hysterical speeches by an illiterate corporal might not look like the potential destroyers of their generation (Milgram and Toch, 1969:585).

In this reference to Jesus, Marx, and Hitler as leaders of social movements, Milgram and Toch dramatically suggest the importance of collective behavior in social change. Some collective behavior occurs in even the most stable societies and is actually a by-product, as we have suggested, of the routine operation of social structures. However, many students of collective behavior (Lang and Lang, 1961; Lasswell, 1930; and Cantril, 1941) say that such phenomena are particularly characteristic of societies undergoing rapid social change.

It will help put the matter in perspective to remember that change is inherent in all social systems. Change is produced by tensions which arise in the relations between the parts of any social system, and in the relations between a system and its physical and social environment. Chapter 16 will show how change is also produced by the inherent tendency of culture to become more complex, especially as it deals with technology. In short, many changes in society take place whether men want them or not, and whether they foresee them or not. Such changes inhere in social systems, and individuals must adjust to the changed circumstances which result. In Chapter 5, we showed how the structure of American cities is an unplanned, unforeseen consequence of the technological developments of the industrial revolution. Yet there the city is. We must live with it if not in it, and try to cope with the problems which so bedevil it today.

When we look at social change in this light it seems that people are passive in the process. Change happens to them; they do not deliberately cause it. But this is only part of the picture, for people do make deliberate efforts to bring about change. This is true even though individuals never comprehend the entire process of change in a whole society nor ever wholly control it.

From one point of view, collective behavior is a reaction to social change, a kind of symptom. When Japan surrendered at the end of World War II, spontaneous crowds formed in many American cities, especially in the West, to celebrate the change from war to peace. There is considerable evidence that rumor tends to increase in periods of rapid change where the newly developing situation is unclear and somewhat threatening. In the United States, many of the publics which form and dissolve do so because underlying social change has brought into being new issues which need to be resolved.

But our special interest is the role of collective behavior in initiating change, not just responding to it. There can be no doubt that crowds have sometimes played a significant part in getting change started. The outbreaks of crowds on many campuses in the middle and late sixties helped to convince college administrators and faculties that student demands for a larger part in educational decision-making would have to be considered seriously. The changes that took place had many other causes, but the dramatic quality of these crowds helped to persuade authorities that they faced something more formidable than a handful of disgruntled kids.

Role of Social Movements in Initiating Change Social movements are the most effective form of collective behavior in initiating change. As we have said, most movements deliberately seek some change in the status quo, and they have enough organization over a long enough time to produce more impact than other forms of collective behavior.

Even social movements that fail and are soon forgotten (and there are many) sometimes have more impact than is realized. By promoting ideas unknown to the general public or unacceptable to the main centers of power in society, they gain a hearing and a start toward acceptance. The peace movement of the sixties mounted a strenuous compaign against the Vietnam war when this position was anathema to the main power centers of American society. This movement can be said to have failed, since it did not bring an immediate end to the war as adherents demanded. Yet it was almost certainly a factor in changing governmental policies. Sometimes movements which fail influence later movements of the same kind. You probably never heard of the Garvey movement of the twenties. It was a forerunner of the Black Muslims who came to prominence in the early sixties, and was so acknowledged by a Muslim leader (Killian, 1964:453).

How shall we define a sucessful movement? We could say it is one which survives long enough to become a respected and conventional association. But in social change, success is more meaningfully described as impact of some observable kind on society. In this sense, many long-forgotten movements have had some success. As Killian points out (1964:453), third-party move-

The vigorous peace movement of the sixties mobilized public opinion in opposition to the Vietnam war and ultimately influenced American policy in Southeast Asia.

ments in American political history are good examples, even though many quickly disappeared as such. "Although failing to win political power, (they) have at times forced the major parties to adopt modified versions of their programs."

No movement ever completely achieves the goals it began with and which are implicit or explicit in its ideology. Even political movements which eventually bring revolution do not fully succeed, for the movement then becomes a government, and

faced with the challenge of consolidating its gains, of defending a new regime rather than attacking an old one, the new government adopts many of the values and norms which it promised to replace (Killian, 1964:453).

In short, the impact of movements on society is compromise among all the forces which favor and retard change. This is not a cynical judgment; it simply records the fact that massive social change is a response to a host of interdependent factors, some beyond control or even awareness. The evidence is also convincing that social movements are among the significant forces in society that produce change. That their impact is never what was intended makes them no less significant as illustrations of how deliberate attempts to mold society do have important consequences.

SOME PRACTICAL CONSIDERATIONS   We have explained that theory and research in collective behavior have not been fully developed, certainly not on a level with the importance of the subject. Hence there is no technology for controlling collective behavior, based squarely on social scientific knowledge. There are of course practitioners: in most periods, a few people develop great skill at arousing and controlling crowds. Police manuals usually discuss ways of managing crowds and riots. The manipulation of public opinion by propaganda is a considerable art, and so too is the control of fashion and consumer demand by the advertising media. We do not belittle the talents of these agents, which are often impressive. We wish to stress that most of these techniques have grown haphazardly out of practical experience. Based on both accurate and inaccurate assessments of collective behavior, as in many applied fields, they are often supported more by tradition and individual commitment to favorite methods than by demonstrable effectiveness.

We have no doubt that if the sociology and social psychology of collective behavior were more advanced, control over all forms of collective behavior could be more effective than it is now. But we have some reservations about whether society is ready to use sophisticated knowledge of this kind responsibly. An illustration will explain our position.

In an essay dealing with TV commercials on children's programs, Morgenstern (1971:9) refers to research at the Harvard Business School, supported by the National Institute of Mental Health and the Marketing Institute. The study shows that children begin to doubt TV commercials by the second grade, and by the sixth grade have a strong distrust of all commercials except public service announcements. Often this attitude is formed by experience with the products advertised. The research also indicates that when commercials appear on the screen, there is a decline in the attention of children.

What's to be made of this? Should we be pleased with our progeny for developing such an early mistrust of hucksters and turning them off so efficiently? To the contrary, I think we should be appalled that they're being lied to, incessantly and systematically . . . (1971:9).

The viewing of commercials is not the best example of collective behavior, but Morgenstern's reaction is close to what we want to say. Collective behavior can be and often is deliberately promoted and manipulated for private ends as well as by public agencies, allegedly in the public interest. But such actions raise serious issues, especially in democratic societies. We believe that the American people have not thought through these issues or even yet fully grasped their implications for the public good. If this is so, it should not be regretted that the means for controlling collective behavior remain primitive. At this stage, do we want advertisers to be able to control children, for example, so that they become what Morgenstern calls acquisitive robots? More broadly, do we want those with the greatest power in society to have sure techniques for controlling the mind and the emotions?

LIMITS OF CONTROL In a democratic society, what should be the limits of public or private control over collective behavior? Who

Are we approaching a time when special-interest groups can control our thoughts, emotions, and behavior through the mass media? Are we subjected to too much manipulation now? Are there protections that a democratic society can devise against excesses of this kind?

A rally in Red China. In totalitarian countries collective behavior is frankly used by the government as an instrument for controlling citizens. In democracies, the manipulation of public opinion is just as important, but the means for doing so are more open to competing groups.

has the right to prevent collective behavior, to bring it into being, or otherwise to manipulate it, in the pursuit of what ends? These are among the issues unrecognized and unresolved. We in the United States are not quite without accepted guidelines. None of the main forms of collective behavior is intrinsically unlawful, though official action may be taken against them if it is deemed that their effects are or may be unlawful or otherwise destructive to the general welfare. There is undoubtedly a high degree of consensus among Americans that violence which may accompany crowd behavior is bad. But have we as a people learned to look beyond immediate violence to the social conditions which brought it about, and then sought to change those root causes?

When we condemn crowds or movements for breaking laws, do we ignore the fact that there are times when people have a moral right to disobey laws they deeply believe are bad? Civil disobedience, deliberately employed in the recent civil rights movement, helped to change many laws and weakened the legal basis of discrimination. Was this bad?

Our economic system seems to require a high and ever-increasing level of consumption. So far we seek to accomplish this by advertising, which is often subtly or blatantly deceptive, and which encourages people to buy products for which they have no real need. In politics, the manipulation of public opinion operating through the mass media increasingly displaces serious political debate. A presidential candidate these days must be professionally packaged, like a high-priced product. Millions of dollars are invested in the packaging and sale of the product.

When we ponder such matters we may seriously ask whether our society is mature enough so that its leadership can safely be trusted with much more powerful means of controlling public opinion and other collective phenomena. When atomic energy was first harnessed, scientists and laymen wondered whether the world was ready to use such power constructively—and this is still an open question. The same question applies here.

Practicing the Sociological Perspective

In the next few days, try to identify a number of rumors when you hear them. See if you can trace them back to their source. Do you feel that there has been distortion as they have been transmitted? Why do you think these rumors developed, that is, what functions beyond transmitting information may they have performed?

Jot down a list of the crowds in which you have participated. Compare them to see how they seem alike and different, not so much in the immediate situations in which they formed as in their sociological characteristics and their impact on your own mind and feelings. Have you ever felt foolish or guilty about your behavior in a crowd after it was over? Have you ever, when you were in a crowd situation, imagined how your behavior there would appear to you if you viewed it when you were alone? To the extent that your own behavior in crowds seems uncharacteristic of your usual conduct, does the discussion in this chapter help at all in understanding the difference?

Have you ever actually participated in a social movement as we have defined this term? If so, were you part of the leadership group, part of the core group of members, or one of the more marginal adherents? At what stage of the movement's evolution did you become associated with it? How did your part in it affect your relationships with outsiders? Did the movement succeed or fail? In light of this chapter, what do these terms mean? Would you join a movement today? Why, or why not? In other words, are you a potential recruit to some or any social movement?

In your opinion, can a social policy be evolved which would protect collective behavior for its desirable and valid functions, yet guard against the cynical exploitation of people's capacities for such behavior? This is a difficult question, and we don't think the components of such a policy are obvious. But what do you think? Can you formulate the elements of a policy which might be better than things are at present?

11 Social Deviance

Every individual—from birth to death—is circumscribed and directed by innumerable norms, role prescriptions, and other social directives. Neither society nor the individual could possibly survive without this framework of rules. Yet there is something in each of us that occasionally rebels at the restraints imposed on us by so many pressures to conform. In varying ways and degrees, we are both repelled and attracted by the idea of breaking rules. Some conformity to social demands is a price we have to pay in order to survive, but we do not always pay it willingly.

Sociologically speaking, it is as normal and inevitable for us to break rules as it is to obey them. In this chapter we try to understand why this is so. To this end we shall use the sociological perspective, and we shall examine specific forms of errant behavior in American society, beginning with a general discussion of the meaning of such behavior, which we call *social deviance*.

THE MEANING OF DEVIANCE The word *deviance* and its derivatives are used in many senses besides those used by sociologists. We say that the height of an unusually tall person *deviates* from the average height of males or females. Average height in this case is a point of reference from which departures are observed in particular cases. In sociology, the points of reference for deviance are social rules such as norms, role prescriptions, regulations, laws—all parts of culture.

DEVIANT BEHAVIOR AND DEVIANT MOTIVES   But what is it that deviates from social rules? First, it is behavior. Deviant behavior occurs whenever a person's actions in a particular situation are seen as violations of the social rules for that situation. Sometimes the behavior directly and obviously violates the rule. A shoplifter who steals a pair of gloves from a store is breaking a law. In other situations deviance is failure to behave as the situation calls for. When two strangers are introduced by a mutual acquaintance, convention calls for at least a formal show of cordiality. If one of the two fails to produce this behavior his conduct will be seen as deviant. Either way, whether by doing or by not doing, behavior is deviant when it is seen by interested persons as breaking an applicable social rule.

The performing of a deviant act doesn't necessarily tell us anything about the person's own attitude toward the rule that was broken. One may engage in deviant conduct without knowing it. All of us have had the experience, in new or strange situations, of breaking social rules we were not aware of. In analyzing social deviance we must distinguish clearly between deviant behavior and the motives or attitudes of persons who engage in it. Such motives may or may not be deviant.

Simple examples can be found in traffic situations. A driver may break the speed limit on an arterial street because he doesn't know it had been changed the day before. Another driver may break the rule against changing lanes without signaling in order to avoid an almost certain accident in his own lane. We can scarcely say that either driver is hostile to the rule, though their behavior, strictly speaking, must be classed as deviant. Another driver wants very much to exceed the speed limit on an interstate highway, but he doesn't do it because he sees a state patrol car in his rearview mirror. This person's desire and intention are deviant but his actual behavior is not. In short, if a person is aware of a social rule, his motives or attitudes toward it may conform or deviate. *Deviant motives and attitudes exist when a person wishes or intends to violate a social rule.* What he will actually do cannot always be predicted from what we know of his attitude toward the rule.

We emphasize that everyone engages in deviant conduct from time to time, and everyone has deviant motives. In fact, a majority of Americans occasionally do things which are crimes under the law. Of 1,678 New Yorkers representing a cross section of that city's population, 91 percent stated that they had broken at least one law, excluding juvenile offenses, for which they could have been fined or imprisoned if convicted. On the average, men had committed eighteen crimes and women eleven (Wallerstein and Wylie, 1947:107–12). Most of these lawbreakers, incidentally, would not be regarded as criminals by the community at large and certainly did not think of themselves as such, even though they knew they had broken the law.

Several examples of minor deviance. Deviance is not defined by the seriousness of the rule-breaking behavior but simply by the fact that the rules are broken. Everyone deviates to some extent under various circumstances. Can you tell whether values, norms, roles, or laws are being violated in these scenes?

SOURCES OF DEVIANCE   What we have said about the nature of deviant behavior and motives gives us clues to the sources of deviance. We need to consider these sources now, and we shall find them in the very nature of social behavior and of individuals.

DEVIANCE AS A BY-PRODUCT OF CULTURE   In Chapter 3 we treated the relation between culture and actual behavior at some length, showing why the latter always departs in some way and degree from the former. That discussion is very pertinent to our present topic and it would be helpful to read it again now. Here we shall supplement it by drawing on an influential analysis of Merton (1968), which shows how the relationship between goals (values) and means (norms) causes individuals to produce varying conforming and deviant behavior. Merton points out that the relation between parts of culture can generate deviance in individuals.

The goals we strive for are provided by society and its components. A young man who wants to be a doctor seeks a goal that society has created. A given person may accept or reject such goals. The young man who wants to be a doctor must go through college, and be admitted to a medical school. One may accept or reject society's means for achieving goals. That is, he may accept a goal as valid but not the means of achieving it. Or he may feel that the means are good but the goal is not worthy. Let us examine some possible situations.

Conformity When a person accepts both goal and means, the result is generally *conformity*. Thus a student who values higher education and thinks the college rules for earning a degree make sense conforms to the rules to get the degree. His is the typical, normal, conventional attitude and behavior.

Innovation When a person accepts the goal but not the means, he innovates: he creates his own means for achieving the goal and in this sense is deviant. There is a great deal of this kind of deviance in America, with its strong emphasis on the positive value of success, but limited and uneven access to success. The approved ways to success work much better for some than for others. Thus there is much tension between means and ends, which generates departures from approved norms. Feeling they cannot succeed by the approved routes, many resort to whatever means they can find. A public official who sells his influence or breaks laws to win an election, a businessman who misrepresents his product, a student who cheats on an exam, a poor and uneducated person who steals because he can't earn money to buy the products television tells him he should want, are all deviants of this sort for whom the end justifies the means.

Ritualism Sometimes a person gives up important social values yet does lip service to them by carefully observing the related norms of behavior. Here the deviance is in refusing to take courageous and possibly dangerous action demanded by true adherence to values, and instead taking refuge in neutral but safe behavior which looks like decent conformity. A good example is the now-famous case of Kitty Genovese, a New York woman who was stabbed to death within sight of a number of neighbors who refused to get involved. To describe the motives underlying this kind of behavior, called *ritualistic,* Merton uses phrases like "I'm not sticking my neck out." Except in extreme cases like that of Kitty Genovese, safe, ritualistic conformity to behavioral norms will not seem deviant to most people, and certainly not dramat-

The lady is trying a little innovative deviance. [Cartoon by Ross. © 1974 The New Yorker Magazine, Inc.]

ically undesirable. Ritualism is hard to criticize harshly. Indeed, it bows in the direction of another approved social value, keeping one's nose out of other people's business. Yet who has not felt a flash of irritation at the man of impeccable manners who has no real solicitude for others? Ritualism is a form of deviance because norms exist or should exist to serve values; they should not eclipse values or transcend them.

Retreatism The rejection of both values and norms is retreatism—in one way or another, dropping out of society. The person who drops out resigns, so to speak. Psychotics, vagabonds, tramps, drug addicts, alcoholics, and suicides have all resigned from society; they take no part in making the machinery go. Recently some forms of the hippie reaction to society could be included. Unlike ritualists, retreatists are likely to receive strong social disapproval. They decline to bear any share of keeping society going, yet consume at least some of its resources. They care little for the values most people live by. Frequently unconventional in dress and appearance, they trigger strong reactions, sometimes pity, more often anger or contempt.

Retreatism, like the other modes of adaptation here considered, varies in degree. Perhaps all the deviant responses Merton discusses are practiced at some time or other by nearly everyone. But when retreatism becomes a way of life, it comes close to living outside society. Yet it is not wholly so. The bona fide retreatist is, in fact, a product of society. His state of mind is often the end-product of a long series of defeats in which his efforts to come to terms with society's values and norms have gone wrong time after time; he is escaping frustration and despair.

In one way or another the retreatist gives up on society.

Rebellion Like retreatism, rebellion is produced by alienation from both values and norms. But the two behaviors differ greatly. Instead of retreating, the rebel gives active allegiance to an incompatible set of values and norms which he regards as superior to those of conventional society. He seeks some reconstruction, some change in the existing order, perhaps even its complete destruction and replacement. Like the other forms of deviation in Merton's classification, rebellion appears in both large and small social scenes. And revolution is a dramatic, large-scale case of it. In some respects, the Black Panthers illustrate this kind of deviation in their fierce rejection of the white man's values and norms and their zealous espousal of competing black values. On a smaller scale, a college student who leaves school, not because he is forced out but because he wants no more to do with the means and goals of a college education, illustrates rebellion if he then gives loyalty to another set of values, perhaps entering a religious life of poverty and self-denial.

Merton's goals-means classification is illuminating because it focuses on the way culture produces conformity as well as various forms of deviance.

Part 2 / Social Units and Processes

DEVIANCE AS A BY-PRODUCT OF SOCIAL ORGANIZATION We see that culture both gives orderliness to social behavior and insures some departure from its dictates. The same is true of social organization. True, social organization consists of regularity in the relations among men. And this orderliness, ordained by culture, is supported by power and the application of sanctions for disobedience to social rules. Nevertheless, it is also true that social organization produces some deviance. A single illustration will make our point.

Conformity, Deviation, and Social Rank Years ago, Homans (1950) showed that the ranking accorded by group members to each other is partly based on past performance in conforming to group norms. In other words, the more a member's behavior lives up to the norms, the higher his rank in the group. High rank, then, is a reward for performing well and low rank a punishment for performing poorly.

Thus far this analysis illustrates how social organization makes for conformity rather than deviation, for insofar as high rank is desirable a person will seek it by conformity to norms. But Homans goes on to show that once a group has evolved a rank ordering of members in this way, its members then act to preserve the status quo in rank distribution. This means that if members try to change their rank by conforming more fully to group norms, the group as a whole will act in such a way as to force them back to their *characteristic level* of conformity. In effect, sanctions will be employed to prevent a member from conforming to norms as much as he now would like. At this point, members are acting more in the interest of maintaining an aspect of group structure (the rank hierarchy) than of obtaining greater compliance to norms. In doing so they illustrate our point that the normal operation of social organization produces deviance as well as conformity.

DEVIANCE AS A BY-PRODUCT OF INDIVIDUAL CHARACTERISTICS Individuals are not chess pieces moved helplessly about the board by cultural and social forces. Every time a social rule is applied to an individual, his own characteristics will play an important part in determining whether his behavior will be called conformity or deviance.

Capacity Differences The norms in schools, occupations, and many other areas prescribe conduct calling for abilities that are not equally distributed. In an occupation requiring physical strength, agility, or good hand-eye coordination, some people are naturally better endowed than others, and this affects capacity for living up to norms. In other activities, ability to reason abstractly or to deal effectively with people in complex situations may be at a premium, and again variations in capacities affect ability to conform to norms.

Motives and Deviance Except in cases where conformity to norms is forced by coercive power, the motives of individuals play a part in whether behavior conforms to norms or deviates from them. The survival of society depends on its being generally true that people want to do what social norms require them to do. This broad coincidence of individual motives and social requirements is insured by the process of socialization (discussed at length in Chapter 3).

DEVIANCE AND LABELING Both deviance and conformity, then, are products of the relation between culture and actual social behavior, and of the relation between the individual and the social unit. Further insight into the sources of deviance comes from the labeling approach, a point of view associated with Goffman (1963), Becker (1963), Lemert (1967), and others. These writers agree that deviance is defined in relation to specific norms and values. They go further to probe the process by which particular acts, and especially particular persons, come to be associated with the idea of deviance. They point out that acts and persons are not deviant until they are so labeled. And successful labeling requires enough power to make the definition stick.

If Larry says, "John really is a genius," his responses to John are likely to be affected by his assumption that people called geniuses have certain traits. And he may respond more to these presumed traits than to John's other known attributes. Maybe John isn't really a genius at all (depending on what the word is supposed to mean), but his friends, having so labeled him, behave accordingly.

When the deviant label is applied to persons whose behavior or thought is or is presumed to be deviant, they are then deviant persons. Familiar among such labels are *criminal* or *hoodlum*, *delinquent* or *punk*, *psychotic* or *nut*, *alcoholic* or *drunken bum*, *drug addict* or *drug fiend*, *prostitute* or *whore*, *homosexual* or *fag*. *Whenever response to a person is governed mainly by the perception that the person acts or thinks in deviant ways, that person is a social deviant.*

For example, a person charged, tried, convicted, and sentenced to prison for committing a crime is involved in a long, complex process of social definition controlled by powerful segments of society and their agents. He is henceforth a *criminal*. In his contacts with the police, lawyers, the courts, and the officials and officers of the prison, he is deeply and effectively stigmatized (to use Goffman's term) as a deviant person. Even after he leaves prison he will continue to face reminders of this defining process. He may have to report at intervals to his parole officer. The police may keep a close watch on him. The chances are that he will have trouble getting a job, or holding one if his being a deviant becomes known.

This person, now a criminal, is likely to sense changes in the response of relatives, friends, and acquaintances. Almost certainly his conception of himself and of his alternatives for the future will be deeply affected. Goffman (1963:14) reports this statement of a criminal's experience with others after society had successfully stigmatized him.

And I always feel this with straight people—that whenever they're being nice to me, pleasant to me, all the time really, underneath they're only assessing me as a criminal and nothing else. It's too late for me to be any different now to what I am, but I still feel this keenly, that that's their only approach, and they're quite incapable of accepting me as anything else.

The process that we have illustrated with criminal behavior occurs in much the same way with many other forms of social deviance. To be an alcoholic, a homosexual, a prostitute, or mentally ill is to have had the label of deviant person successfully applied by those with power to win general acceptance for their use of the labeling process.

Such social labels get in the way of our seeing those who bear them as whole persons. Take the label *criminal*. A great deal of the behavior of any person so called is perfectly conventional and law-abiding. But labeling inhibits our realization of this fact and concentrates our attention on the deviant parts of his behavior. We think we know what criminals are like. Mr. French is a criminal, so we feel we know what Mr. French is like. Labeling converts people into special human types, somehow different from the rest.

Labeling also confuses our thinking about deviance in general. It is tempting to suppose that deviant behavior is simply the behavior of deviant persons as we have defined the term. But we now know that all persons, without exception, sometimes engage in deviant behavior and have deviant attitudes and motives, yet are not labeled deviant. Hence their conduct does not arouse in others the special, systematic social disapproval of their entire persons that is applied to those called deviant persons.

It is not hard to find examples of the difference it makes to a person whether or not he is defined by society's responses as deviant. In the Watergate scandals of the early seventies, allegations of specific serious crimes were made against some of the highest officers of the national government. While most Americans disapproved of the alleged actions, the persons claimed to have perpetrated them were not typically labeled as deviant persons in our meaning of the term. They were, so to speak, normal persons who had done wrong, not human beings of an almost special kind. Indeed, some people argued that the officials involved in the Watergate affair were only doing what most politicians do, except that they got caught at it.

Each year in the United States large sums of money are embezzled by persons of high standing in their local communities. It is not uncommon for such a theft to reach millions of dollars. While embezzlement is clearly seen as deviant behavior, local reaction seldom labels the embezzler a deviant *person*. Others are often puzzled at what led such an upstanding citizen to steal,

Having been booked by the police, this young person now runs the risk of being permanently stigmatized as a criminal, that is, deviant.

Senator Joseph McCarthy (pointing) during hearings he conducted in the Senate in 1954. His irresponsible labeling of people as political deviants finally led to his censure by the Senate.

and remind each other that Mr. Weber was always a good church member, supported local charities, and was in many ways a model citizen. By contrast, a man who is known to make his living as a burglar may steal far less than Mr. Weber, and be labeled a criminal. The labeling shuts out awareness of almost everything about the burglar except the fact that he steals.

While most persons labeled deviant have in fact violated social norms in ways that lead to their being stigmatized in this way, not all have done so. Some years ago, during the so-called McCarthy era, Senator Joseph McCarthy publicly denounced a great many people, calling them subversives and Communists, when he had no evidence to justify the use of these terms. For a time he managed to convince quite a few Americans that he was telling the truth. His victims were labeled deviant in spite of the fact that the charges were false. And many suffered all the special indignities often visited on deviant categories in the population. Much earlier, in colonial Salem, Massachusetts, girls and women were condemned to death as witches because other citizens accused them of being possessed by the devil. The absurdity of the charges didn't prevent the full operation of the labeling process (Erikson, 1966). In short, the deviant label is sometimes successfully attached to people merely by convincing others that deviant behavior has occurred whether or not it has.

THE COSTS AND BENEFITS OF DEVIANCE

To call something or someone deviant usually implies disapproval, but in sociological analysis this is often not true. When we look at the effects of behavior we find that deviance can have constructive as well as destructive consequences.

In any social unit there is a point beyond which further deviance damages the very structure and operation of the unit. It is inevitable that a few lawyers or teachers, physicians, and nurses will violate the ethics of their profession. But if this is more than a rare phenomenon the integrity of the entire profession is seri-

Part 2 / Social Units and Processes

ously threatened. The Watergate political scandals involved so many lawyers that the American Bar Association expressed grave concern at its annual meeting in 1973, and several state bar associations began investigations of prominent lawyers involved in the scandals. Figure 11-1 shows the decline of trust in the government that began even before the Watergate situation. No great damage is done if some citizens decline to honor their civic obligation to vote in elections, but if nearly all citizens deviate in this way the very meaning of representative government is destroyed.

Values, norms, and role prescriptions, it should be remembered, are guidelines for people linked together in social relationships. When these standards are too frequently or flagrantly violated, the framework of relationships within which people seek individual and collective goals is threatened. When behavior loses all predictability in relation to commonly understood rules, individuals become confused and alienated, losing the motivation to engage in joint actions with others. Social order itself breaks down.

It isn't hard to see that deviance often exacts heavy costs from society and individuals. More likely to escape attention is the fact that deviance may have good results, and actually is essential to social welfare. We follow Cohen (1966:6–11) in suggesting several of these desirable or harmless consequences.

NONDESTRUCTIVE RULE-BREAKING You will recall from Chapter 9 that complex organizations often prescribe a bewildering variety of rules and procedures, and that often these become excessively rigid, time-consuming, and generally counterproductive. Individuals show much ingenuity in evading such rules. For instance, a student who needs a particular course for graduation finds that enrollment is closed. By some illegitimate means (perhaps falsifying a dean's signature) he manages to get into the course. He reasons that his need is great and that one more student will not cause any real problem—and he is probably quite right in his assumption. Such evasions do not seriously threaten the operation of the college.

Such informal, sub rosa deviations from rules are sometimes socially developed and maintained. Williams (1972:421–30) speaks of patterned evasions of norms in these circumstances. At a football or baseball game where not all seats are taken, there may be only token resistance to boys climbing the fence and getting in free. Often those with authority in organizations are well aware of such patterned evasions and do little to eliminate them so long as they are not a major problem.

In complex societies official norms cannot always be enforced, and yet the population is not ready to abandon them. Patterned evasions are likely in these situations. Again, most divorce laws in the United States generally assume one guilty party and one innocent party in a divorce action. Furthermore, collusion to gain divorce is not allowed. Finally, perjury under oath in the court-

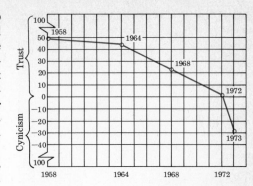

FIGURE 11-1 INDEX OF TRUST IN GOVERNMENT
Studies at the University of Michigan's Institute of Social Research, employing representative national samples, show that distrust of the government has grown steadily and at an increasing rate since 1958. The trend is shown in this graph, which is based on five questions concerning the federal government's performance (figures represent the percentage of persons in the most trusting category minus the percentage in the most cynical category). While the Watergate scandals clearly accelerated the trend, you can see that it began much earlier. And this is going on among all segments and age levels of the population. In essence, Americans express deepening cynicism about the integrity, wisdom, and responsiveness of government. It is instructive to note in connection with the Michigan findings that voter turnout in presidential elections has declined steadily since 1960, reaching its lowest level since 1948 in 1972. The evidence is sobering. It is possible to ask: is the failure of government in the eyes of citizens nearing the point where the very structure and operation of government itself is endangered?

[Source: *ISR Newsletter*, Spring-Summer 1973 and Winter 1974, Institute for Social Research, The University of Michigan.]

Nondestructive rule-breaking—or is it?

room is an actionable offense. Yet when we consider what actually happens, the assumption of complete innocence in one party and total guilt in the other is absurd; marriage is not that simple. Hence married couples seeking divorce have typically engaged in some collusion to satisfy the letter of the law. Perjury is a daily occurrence in divorce courts. Patterned evasion occurs because the immediate need to dissolve particular marriages is deemed more desirable than an attempt to change the law, a process long and uncertain of success.

DEVIANCE AS A SAFETY VALUE   Occasional deviance is also a kind of safety valve. There is always some frustration in curbing one's own desires to conform to society's rules, thus some of the deviance in all social systems, large or small, relieves and expresses the tension produced by such frustration. Often this expression is informal and peculiar to the circumstances and the person. However, all societies provide periodic and recognized occasions on which the normal rules of conduct are temporarily suspended. At such times people may behave in ways ordinarily not tolerated. Although today's Halloween is only a mild version of what it once was, it still has a little of this character. The business or professional convention in contemporary America often leads to behavior which would not occur at home. In some countries, Mardi Gras, the period just before Lent, gives license to behavior ordinarily forbidden. In some societies such occasions permit almost any kind of uninhibited behavior for a specified time. But once this time is over, people are expected once more to obey the rules.

UNREASONABLE AND CONFLICTING NORMS   Not all rules are intelligible or reasonable, and breaking them can bring clarification or change. One useful effect of the campus disruptions of the sixties (which often involved illegal behavior) was a review of outmoded academic policies on student activities, and the strengthening of the academic traditions of dissent and free speech. Deliberate civil disobedience played a major role in dramatizing and getting public attention for the civil rights and peace movements, also of the 1960s.

Widespread deviance may help to eliminate norms incompatible with other values and norms of a social system. The Eighteenth Amendment to the Constitution, which outlawed alcoholic beverages, was ultimately repealed, mainly because it was flagrantly disobeyed by millions of Americans of all classes. While they may have broken the law mainly because they wanted to drink, many argued that the law was an unwarranted intrusion by the state in the area of personal behavior.

We may now be in the midst of a parallel experience with marijuana. A Gallup poll in 1972 indicated that somewhat more than half of all college students reported having tried marijuana, up from only 5 percent in 1967. The United States Food and Drug Administration estimates that up to twenty million persons have

Patronizing the speakeasy of the twenties and early thirties was a deliberate flouting of a norm (the Eighteenth Amendment to the Constitution) that Americans felt violated more important values. The kind of safety-valve activity illustrated in the second picture may be messy, but it is a harmless way of relieving tensions.

tried it at least once and that hundreds of thousands are smoking it regularly. Pot smokers, along with some physicians, psychologists, sociologists and criminologists, contend that using marijuana should be as acceptable socially and legally as drinking alcohol. Kaplan, an internationally recognized expert on drug abuse, after two years of research on California's drug laws concluded that "the social and financial costs directly and indirectly attributable to the criminalization of marijuana far outweigh the benefits of this policy" (1971:325). To be sure, there remains formidable opposition to such a step, as there was to the repeal of the Eighteenth Amendment.

Deviant behavior also plays a significant part in the whole process of social change; while people may disagree on a particular social change, most will look with favor on some kinds of change.

DEVIANCE AND SOCIAL PROBLEMS

We now see how complex social deviance is. It is everywhere about us, as is conformity to society's dictates. There is deviance in a young child hiding to escape going to bed, as there is in a brutal murder by mugging. Deviance grows from the same matrix of social forces (and the relations of people to these forces) as conformity. Sociologically, it is as normal as conformity. While it involves behavior, attitudes, and feelings, it cannot be defined by a specific list of behaviors, attitudes, and feelings. For deviance is always relative to particular values and norms in a particular time and place, and to persons with the power to apply the stigma of deviance to others. Social deviance can be enormously destructive; it may also have highly desirable results, not only for the individual but also for society.

At a given time in a society there will be some kinds of deviance that are fairly widespread, dramatic or highly visible, and very costly to individuals and society. These are the sorts of deviance about which the public expresses concern and which are likely to be viewed as social problems. According to Julian (1973:9), "In order for a social condition to become a social problem, a significant number of people—or a number of significant people—must agree that this condition violates an accepted value or standard *and* that it should be eliminated, resolved, or remedied."

We will here consider some facts about the incidence of several social problems in the United States. In general, all these problems are products of the sources of deviance already discussed. For each there are also other contributing factors and conditions, but we shall not have space to consider those here.

LAWBREAKERS AND CRIMINALS   These are people who commit or omit acts that are prohibited or required by public law and punishable by local, state, or federal governments. Actual examples may range from such minor offenses as crossing the street against the traffic light to assault, rape, and murder.

Since innumerable crimes are undiscovered, unreported, and unrecorded, crime statistics are based on offenses known to the police, not on all crimes actually committed. Yet with all due caution we can state that crime is high and rising in the United States, and that crime in the streets is regarded as a major problem by many Americans. Over one million arrests were made in the United States in 1968 for major crimes such as larceny, burglary, auto theft, aggravated assault, robbery, forcible rape, and criminal homicide (listed in decreasing order of frequency) (*Uniform Crime Reports,* 1968:117–18). Put differently, someone in the country is murdered every thirty-nine minutes; a forcible rape is committed every seventeen minutes; and every two minutes an aggravated assault and a robbery takes place.

Many other offenses, drunkenness for example, are even more numerous. According to FBI statistics, 40 percent of all arrests in this country are for drunkenness. FBI figures also indicate that shoplifters and employees combined stole goods valued at nearly $3 billion in 1970. The criminal justice system of the country employed 852,000 persons in 1970, and the costs of the system (police, courts and correctional facilities) totaled more than $8.5 billion.

An examination of persons known to commit crimes reveals many variations. Characteristically, late adolescents and young adults have higher crime rates than any other age category. Some of this is due to the proneness to arrest of fifteen- to eighteen-year-olds. The crime rate for men far exceeds that for women at all times and in all places, with the exception of such crimes as prostitution, infanticide, and abortion.

Race and Ethnic Variations Crime rates for racial and ethnic categories vary considerably. Blacks, Puerto Ricans, Mexicans, and American Indians have especially high rates, while the rates for Orientals and Jews tend to be very low. One should take into account, however, that the high rates for blacks and other racial minorities are part of a total pattern of discrimination. The probability of being arrested is three to four times greater for blacks than for whites, and is even higher for native Americans! After being apprehended, blacks run a greater danger than whites of being jailed rather than bailed, are more likely to be convicted than acquitted, and are more liable to maximum penalties.

Status Variations Social rank, like membership in certain racial and ethnic categories, appears to be associated with rate of crime. Several studies show that the lower the position in the stratification system, the greater the likelihood of being officially designated a criminal. Many crimes are committed by respectable persons of high rank, but they are less likely to be detected, reported, or prosecuted. White-collar crime, as it is called, costs the United States more than all the more notorious and spectacular crimes. A presidential commission on law enforcement and administration of justice revealed that the annual cost of embezzlement, fraud, tax fraud, and forgery was $1,730,000,000 as compared to $614,000,000 for the annual cost of robbery, burglary, auto theft, and larceny of $50 and over (*Congressional Quarterly*, 1971: 1048).

Urban-Rural Variations Finally, the official statistics on criminal behavior indicate that crime rates are highest in urban areas (particularly inner-city areas), lowest in rural areas, and in between in the suburbs. It should be noted, however, that rural officials are more likely than their urban counterparts to deal with criminal acts in an unofficial manner.

DRUG ABUSE   In recent decades, Americans have become remarkably prone to the use of drugs for the reduction of pain, control of medical symptoms, management of mood (stimulants and depressants), and as adjuncts to personal and social pleasure. Given this national faith in the efficacy of drugs, it isn't wholly surprising that in some instances drug use has become drug abuse to the point where a serious social problem exists. The National Institute of Alcohol and Alcoholism of the Department of Health, Education and Welfare estimates that about 95 million Americans use alcohol, consuming a per capita average of 30.3 gallons of liquor, wine, and beer each year. In a report issued in 1972, this agency estimated that about 9.6 million Americans are alcoholics or al-

Americans rely heavily on drugs as both physical and emotional problem solvers, but they are ignorant of and careless about the long-term effects of many of the drugs they use. Under these circumstances how can the most vulnerable among us be guarded from excessive use of dangerous drugs? And how can this be done without creating new problems—stimulating criminal activity, for instance, as happened during Prohibition?

cohol abusers. It classifies 12 percent of American adults as heavy drinkers and estimates that about half of these have serious problems with liquor. There are about five male alcoholics for every female, though the proportion of alcoholic married women between the ages of forty and fifty-five is rapidly increasing. The costs of alcohol abuse are most severe, of course, in cases of addiction. Chronic alcoholism, which develops over years of heavy drinking, entails a growing dependence on heavy consumption and a progressive failure of role performances in the main arenas of the victim's life. A genuinely vicious circle develops in which the guilt stemming from failure in husband-father, employee, and other major roles is temporarily forgotten during intoxication which, in turn, leads to still further dislocation of personal-social interaction.

A number of other drugs have become a matter of growing concern in recent years. Among these are the hallucinogens (such as marijuana, hashish, mescaline and LSD), the amphetamines (such as Benzedrine, Dexedrine, and Methedrine) and the barbiturates (such as Luminal, Amytal, Nembutal and Seconal). Many of these drugs were only recently developed for specific medical purposes; none of them were viewed as presenting a serious abuse problem until very recent years. Narcotic alkaloids, such as heroin (a derivative of opium) and cocaine (extracted from coca leaves) have been a drug abuse problem for many decades. In the last few years, their use has increased substantially.

Each of these drugs has characteristic short-term effects. Marijuana relaxes, induces euphoria and increases appetites. It may also alter one's perception of time and impair judgment and coordination. LSD produces visual imagery, increased sensory awareness, anxiety, nausea, impaired coordination, and sometimes consciousness-expansion. Amphetamines are stimulants, and thus increase alertness, reduce fatigue, and produce loss of appetite, insomnia, and a state of euphoria. Barbiturates are depressants and induce sleep. They relieve anxiety-tension, relax muscles, and may also produce euphoria and drowsiness and impair judgment, reaction time, coordination, and emotional control.

The long-run effects of the newer drugs have not yet been fully determined by substantial research; consequently there is a great deal of public misinformation about them. The evidence already available, however, certainly suggests that there is serious cause for concern. Fort (1969:110–14) suggests that a drug is abused if its use damages an individual's health or social or vocational adjustment, or is otherwise specifically harmful to society. By this definition there is reason to believe that many of the new drugs are being abused extensively. Parry (1968:800) estimates that about one out of every four adult Americans uses, in a given year, one or more of the following drugs: one or more of the amphetamines, Nembutal, Seconal, Librium, Miltown, and phenobarbital.

The long-term effect which is best understood, because it has been studied for the longest time, is the addiction associated with opium derivatives, *hard drugs.* An American addict's life typically becomes organized around maintaining a source of supply. It is estimated that there are between one hundred eighty thousand and two hundred forty thousand addicts in the United States, but that only sixty thousand of these are known to the United States Bureau of Narcotics and Dangerous Drugs. These figures do not include the increasing numbers of addicts found in the armed forces. Estimates indicate that between 5 and 10 percent of the men in the army alone became addicted to drugs during the Vietnam war. In the first half of 1971, almost sixteen thousand military personnel voluntarily requested curative treatment for drug use.

Most drug addicts are young males between the ages of twenty-one and thirty. They tend to live in the metropolitan areas of the more populous states, especially New York, California, Illinois, and New Jersey. Some minorities are overrepresented in the addict population. In New York state's new addiction control program, for example, 38 percent of the patients are black, 34 percent are Puerto Rican, 26 percent are white and 2 percent are "other." Drug addicts are found in a wide variety of occupations ranging from personal services workers to entertainers to professionals such as physicians and nurses. Thus the problem is not restricted to any particular level of the American stratification system.

Illegal Drugs and Crime In the last half century a strange situation has arisen from the value conflict among Americans over the use of drugs. Those who have most feared certain drugs have attempted to control their use or abolish them by law in disregard of the fact that others have not shared their view. Under Prohibition, the millions who wanted alcoholic beverages had the choice of going without or breaking the law to get them since they could not be had legally. A major consequence of this situation was that organized crime took over the liquor business and prospered mightily. Much the same thing has happened in more recent years with other drugs. Americans thus have a major dilemma. When they attempt legal control of behavior in areas where there are major value conflicts, their efforts to reduce one problem increase the incidence of another: crime.

MENTAL DISORDERS In historical terms, it was not long ago that mentally ill persons were thought to be possessed by devils or at least to be strange, incomprehensible, and frightening creatures, different from the rest of mankind. In recent decades, long strides have been made in viewing and treating mental disorders as illnesses. But the remnants of old concepts and attitudes hang on tenaciously, and societal reactions to the mentally ill often still reveal the characteristic reaction to deviant behavior.

Whether mental illness is seen as a problem of deviance, a medical problem, or both, it is substantial in size. About one hundred twenty-five to one hundred fifty thousand patients are admitted to public mental hospitals each year, and another two hundred thousand are admitted to general hospitals for the treatment of mental disorders (Duhl and Leopold, 1966:277). In addition, more than twice as many other persons are being treated as outpatients at mental health clinics. These figures do not take into account those undergoing private treatment and those who need medical help but are not receiving it.

In a high proportion of cases, mental illness produces role performances which are deviant by the standards of ordinary role prescriptions. A large body of evidence summarized by Clausen (1971) and others indicates that social and cultural factors play at least some part in developing such aberrant behavior, and that social reactions to the behavior of the mentally ill typically tend to intensify the symptoms of illness rather than to relieve them. As Clausen points out, the dominant American pattern of coping with the problem has been to isolate and wall off those defined as mentally ill, almost as if other people wished to deny that they existed.

SUICIDE In the United States, suicide is the tenth largest cause of death, and 22,630 persons were reported as having taken their lives in 1970 (*Statistical Abstract of the United States*). Every year, about one hundred thousand college students threaten suicide, about ten thousand actually attempt it, and around one thousand achieve it (Whitely, 1967).

People who have once been confined to mental institutions, such as this one, are often always considered to be deviant, even when released from the institution.

Throughout most of the United States and the Western world, more women than men make suicide attempts, but nearly three times as many men actually kill themselves (*Demographic Yearbook*, 1967: Table 24). The older an American male is, the more likely he is to take his own life. A series of studies has shown that Catholics and Jews are much less likely to commit suicide than are Protestants (Gibbs, 1971: 295–96). Single people, in general, are far more likely to be suicides than married people. Finally, suicide rates vary a great deal in different occupations. Occupations with high or low income and status tend to have very high suicide rates. For example, more unskilled laborers as well as artists, professional men, and top executives commit suicide than other people, and two in every one hundred physicians do so.

While the person who takes his own life isn't likely to think of his behavior as social deviance, the fact remains that suicide is seen as deviance by most people in our society. It violates both formal norms embodied in law and many religions, and a widespread informal norm that it is wrong to kill oneself. When someone we know takes his own life, many of us not only disapprove, but find the action almost incomprehensible. Beyond the actual loss of life, the costs of suicide extend to the disruption of groups to which the suicide belonged.

SEXUAL DEVIANCE Because of the strength of the sex urge and the critical importance to society of responsible procreation and child-rearing, sexual behavior is hedged about with formal and informal restraints. Prostitution, rape, adultery, incest, indecent exposure, and homosexuality are among the types of behavior regarded as deviant and proscribed either by laws, strong informal norms, or both.

Despite the intense feeling about the social rules for sexual conduct, they are frequently violated. But reliable social statistics are almost impossible to get, and we merely cite a few facts to support our generalization. While traditional forms of prostitution have probably declined in the United States because of a generally greater sexual permissiveness, it is still a thriving business. Twenty-five years ago it was estimated that there were about six hundred thousand prostitutes in the United States (Esseltyn, 1968). The late Alfred C. Kinsey and his associates in their study of white American males found that about 70 percent of the men they sampled had had some experience with prostitutes (1948:597).

Homosexuality is a good deal more prevalent than most people realize, because of the strong taboos against public recognition of it. The Kinsey reports, which contain the best evidence on prevalence, suggest that 37 percent of all males and 19 percent of all females have had at least one homosexual episode, and that 10 percent of American men have long periods of more or less exclusive homosexuality (1948:650–51). Rough estimates indicate that there are about 2,600,000 men and 1,400,000 women who are predominantly homosexual in preference and behavior.

Pornography, the depiction of sexual stimuli in a manner calculated to arouse sexual excitement, has also become a social problem in recent years. The volume of pornographic materials offered for sale increased dramatically after a series of court decisions weakened existing legal restrictions. The issue of moral deviance involved is complicated by serious constitutional questions about freedom of expression. In 1968, the United States Commission on Obscenity and Pornography was established in order to shed some light on the effects of pornography and the extent of exposure to it. Studies conducted under the auspices of the commission showed that nearly three-fourths of the men and just over half of the women in this country have been exposed to explicit sexual material by the age of twenty-one. The proportions for both sexes rise at later ages.

Resentment in some parts of the public against the flood of easily available pornography kept the legal issue alive, and in July 1973 the Supreme Court handed down a decision which appeared to lend great encouragement to local areas which wanted to control or outlaw the public sale of such materials. The consequences of this potentially far-reaching decision are not yet evident. Perhaps the problem in sexual morality will be lessened by the Court's action, although the constitutional issue involving freedom of expression is not as likely to be settled.

The evidence of much behavioral deviation from sexual norms could readily be extended. For example, in 1971, forty-two thousand cases of forcible rape were reported to the police, and this is one of the most underreported of all crimes (*Statistical Abstract of the United States*). Obviously, the personal and social costs of sexual deviance are considerable. One need only mention such things as the brutal sexual exploitation of immature and vulnerable persons, women who make their livings by selling access to their bodies, broken homes, illegitimate children, fear of exposure and feelings of guilt.

All social units, even society itself, must have provisions that keep deviance within limits that do not threaten the survival of the unit. The mechanisms of control can be formal, informal, or latent.

FORMAL CONTROL   Complex societies develop specialized roles and even organizations mainly devoted to deviance control. "Such more or less 'functionally specific' control agents and agencies are truant officers, police, courts, correctional institutions, inspectors, auditors, now and then deans of men, and certain social agencies and youth-serving agencies" (Cohen, 1966:40). Deviance control is also built into many other roles as a secondary function. Elementary school teachers, for instance, do not see deviance control as their main job, but it is a part of it. It is also a component of most leadership roles, regardless of the type of organization.

INFORMAL CONTROL   Formal control, even backed by specialists, and power to apply sanctions to erring persons and groups alone can never get the job done. Evasion of surveillance and punishment is too easy, and the protection of informal organization too readily developed for formal controls impersonally applied to individuals to be sufficient.

Insofar as membership in a group is rewarding, as the regard of a friend is valued, as one hopes to achieve personal goals through association with others, one will be sensitive to indications that one has obeyed or broken the rules applicable to such associations. For nearly everyone, acceptance by others is important. In hundreds of settings our experience teaches us that being accepted has its price: a tolerable degree of conformity to norms. The more important a group is to us, and the more personal the relationships within it, the more effective are the informal controls.

In the end, both formal and informal controls depend on the internalization of norms by individuals. We come to require of ourselves what society demands. Otherwise even informal controls would be less effective than they are.

LATENT CONTROL   Latent control refers to the unintended and unrecognized social behavior that influences the amount and kind of deviance that occurs. For example, the level of employment may affect the volume of crime. The portrayal of crime in the mass media may suggest ways of breaking the law to persons who would not have thought of them otherwise. A child starved for

Kidnapers demand $4m more in food

United Press International

HILLSBOROUGH, Calif. — The kidnapers of Patricia Hearst today demanded another $4 million as a condition of precisely," they will threatened to hold M hostage for two men group held in San (

A family spokesman said the latest communique from the terrorist Symbionese Liberation A came in

Atlanta news editor feared kidnaped

By Carmen Fields and Seymour Linscott
Globe Staff

ATLANTA—John R. (Reg) Murphy, the editor of the Atlanta Constitution, has apparently been abducted by a group calling itself the American Revolutionary Army, the paper said today.

wanted to talk to him about a new story. He has not been heard from since.

Executive's son kidnaped in N.Y.

DIX HILLS, N.Y. — The eight-year-old son of a wealthy tire wholesaler yesterday was kidnaped by three unidentified persons as he was walking home from school or Island

Fields said he assumed that meant means other than a telephone.

Fifteen minutes later, Atlanta television station WAGA was called by a man who gave the same message.

Doug Dougherty, said the man told no use to call the FBI

a crank call. He asked the caller: "What are you going to do with him?"

There was a pause of about five seconds, and then the man hung up without saying anything else.

A few minutes after that a third call was made, to Murphy's wife, Virginia. The man told her only: "If you want to h

Hearst, "is not ill gesture.

if the family lands, the SLA nications and age according neva Conven ll not change nged for the seph Remiro

Both formal control and informal control can only work when most individuals internalize norms and, for the most part, police themselves. One unintentional latent effect of the heavy mass media coverage of the Patricia Hearst kidnaping in 1974 was a rash of subsequent kidnapings.

parental love may seek attention and admiration by behavior defined as deviant.

Almost any aspect of society may have implications for deviance and control, although sometimes the chain of cause and effect may be subtle and devious. Moreover, the process can work either to increase or decrease the volume of deviance. A strong vocational program aimed at persons having trouble getting jobs may have the ultimate effect of reducing robbery and theft. Effective counseling of troubled families may reduce the extent to which children seek undesirable substitute gratifications.

INCOMPLETENESS OF SOCIAL CONTROL Control over deviance could never be wholly effective, even if half the population were set to guarding the other half. Our earlier discussion should make the reasons for this clear. Cohen (1966:40) also points out that deviance can become a problem even in formal control agencies, citing negligence, favoritism, cruelty, and corruption; and he asks: "Who will guard the guardians?"

But it isn't necessary to wipe out all deviance. Nor is it desirable, since deviance is often socially useful. Social units survive very well in the presence of deviant behavior, feelings, and attitudes. For any given social unit it is helpful to think of an optimum level of deviance, beyond which the existence of the group or organization, community, or society is threatened. At the same time, a level much below this point may lead to stagnation and be evidence of repression.

Some years ago Homans (1950) argued that the social control of deviance in groups comes into play when members start to deviate from their customary level of deviance, for this is upsetting to the delicate interdependence of the group's parts. He assumes that all members deviate to some extent. He also pointed out that occasional deviance keeps the machinery of social control in good working order. It reminds people of the values and norms by which they live.

DEVIANCE AND SOCIAL CHANGE

Deviance and social change are intimately related, and a certain dynamic links the two. Imagine that man's earliest societies had never tolerated the slightest departures from the values and norms which then obtained. This is of course an impossible situation from the sociological point of view, but the mere suggestion gives an inkling of how necessary deviance is to change, quite apart from whether a particular change is judged to be good or bad, progress or retrogression. Presumably, if such total conformity could have been enforced, human societies could never have evolved at all. Indeed, they would have had no mechanism for adjusting to changes in the environment.

Remember that in Chapter 2 we said that culture influences behavior, and behavior also influences culture. Applied to the present subject this is like saying that while values and norms, reinforced by sanctions, influence behavior, behavior can also change values and norms. There is always a tension between culture and behavior. Most people, most of the time, do a pretty good job of conforming to the social rules. It is equally true that all people, for hundreds of reasons, tend to fall away from the rules, to evade them, to deviate. Thus sooner or later the rules become eroded and changed as actual behavior drifts away from them.

As the years pass, some social change is inevitable, arising from the normal strain between culture and actual behavior even when there is no effort to bring about change. Over the past two or three generations, the role relations between college professors and their students have slowly become far less formal. Little by little, American parents have become less authoritarian in rearing their children. Gradually it becomes easier for unhappy spouses to divorce without social disgrace. Thus the normal operation of all social systems, large and small, produces a drift of social change, even when no one consciously seeks change. Deviance is at the heart of the process.

Deviance also has a part in social behavior that is deliberately organized to bring about social change. Social movements, discussed at some length in the last chapter, are excellent examples. When a few Indians associated with AIM (American Indian Movement) illegally occupied the South Dakota hamlet of Wounded Knee in 1973, they deliberately broke the law to dramatize the plight of the Indians and to bring about improvement in their treatment.

Several recent social movements in the United States, such as the women's liberation movement and the civil rights movement (especially with racial and ethnic groups like blacks, Chicanos, and Indians), have attempted to force society to practice its values of civil rights and equal opportunity. The objective is to reduce behavioral deviation from societal values. To this end, the strategy has sometimes included deliberate, dramatic violation of laws. The movements have used visible deviant behavior as a means to increase conformity to the basic values of society.

Yet any change, however accomplished, which brings behavior closer to values and norms is a genuine social change. Thus if employers discriminate less in response to pressure from such movements, and to the new laws and court decisions the movements bring about, it is accurate to say that real change in the distribution of opportunities has been brought about. The destruction of property in some student riots in the sixties was viewed by powerful segments of the community as deviance. And the rioting students intended that their behavior be so interpreted. But we must distinguish between this immediate interpretation and the long-run consequences of the social movement. If a movement gains its objectives, even in part, then behavior once regarded as deviant may no longer be thought so.

Not so many years ago, many American restaurants and other public places refused to serve blacks. Persons who sought to violate this ban were regarded as very deviant, and severe negative sanctions were often applied. But since the civil rights movement, blacks are now served with civility where they would once have been refused admittance. Again it is not particular behavior, but the way in which behavior is related to values and norms that determines whether deviance is perceived. The service of black Americans in public places once reserved for whites is no longer defined as deviant.

The sociological perspective helps us to see that while deviance is often troublesome and expensive, it is sometimes indispensable in social change. Some such change will ultimately be seen as progress. It is hard to remember today that women who agitated for the right to vote were once regarded as troublesome shrews who deviated from the true role of woman. Whites who spoke out against slavery before the Civil War were often viewed as dangerous radicals. Take a hard look at some of today's social protest movements. Is it not possible, indeed probable, that some of their goals will someday be taken for granted as just and good behavior?

The same behavior may be defined as deviant at one time and conventional at another.

We believe that the most useful aspect of the sociology of deviance is its extension of the general sociological perspective to deviant behavior. We have used deviance in a carefully defined way, but we have spoken of things popularly referred to by other labels such as odd, peculiar, crazy, and radical. The behavior we call deviant is often viewed with suspicion, distrust, dislike, fear, and hatred. While such behavior should not necessarily be welcomed with open arms, social deviance must be removed from some limbo in which it is equated only with the repulsive antics of the "abnormal."

Within the intellectual perspective of sociology, where we try to understand and not to condemn out of hand, what is called deviance is as inevitable and socially normal as what is called conformity. The aspect of being human that we call social can no more avoid breaking rules than it can evade obeying them. When we combine this insight with the recognition that deviance is always relative to particular values and norms and to particular persons and groups with the power to enforce them, we have the basis for a liberating view of the human scene. It is another partial release from the time, place, and immediate social circumstances in which we were born and reared.

The broader view of deviance also has practical implications for programs of social control and social change. In this chapter we could not do full justice to existing sociological theories of de-

THE SOCIOLOGY OF DEVIANCE:
PRACTICAL IMPLICATIONS

viance, or to practical applications of theory to problem situations. Theory is not yet firm enough to serve as a base for programs that guarantee results—with crime, for example. But sociologists are making valuable contributions to programs to control destructive deviance in crime and delinquency, mental disease, alcoholism, drug addiction, certain kinds of sexual deviance, and other areas.

Practicing the Sociological Perspective

One of the best ways the beginner can sensitize himself to social deviance is by learning to recognize it in ordinary settings. Select several social settings familiar to you. Make yourself an observer in these settings. Try to identify behavior you think would be viewed as deviant by others present. Be as specific as you can. Exactly what action (or failure to act) qualifies as deviance? Attempt to infer the presence of deviant feelings or attitudes. You can infer these from tones of voice, facial expressions, significant glances, and the like.

Make a list of what you have observed in several social settings so that you can look it over at your leisure and ponder such questions as these: On what grounds did you decide that deviance was present? Your own familiarity with the values and norms of the group? The responses of other members to the presence of deviance? How did they respond? Was there evidence of sanctions? What was it? Remember that sanctions needn't be public or ceremonious; they may be expressions of displeasure, even a lack of normal enthusiasm in response to behavior. What do you think is the function of the deviance you observed for the deviating person, and especially for the group? Were these instances of deviance potentially damaging or potentially helpful to the group? How would you decide?

After the foregoing exercise we suggest a second which we think would be eye-opening. Try saying hello to every stranger you meet. In a situation where others expect you to talk freely, say nothing. When a good friend greets you, do not respond. Wear a garment backwards for a while. In a setting where you are seen, read a book or newspaper upside down. Do these things convincingly so that others will not know what you are up to. Carefully observe the responses. What happens inside you (even though the situation is contrived) when you are confronted with the response to deviation? These are trivial kinds of deviance. Still, do you feel the pull toward conformity arising inside you as well as from the reactions of others? Imagine how much stronger this would be for serious violations of major norms.

Perhaps you know someone who is a deviant person by our definition: deviance has been made a part of the public image of such a person. Consider what this labeling means to his view of himself and to the experiences he has.

PART 3
Social Institutions

Part Three analyzes several social institutions. *An institution is a cluster of values and associated norms and roles that together define an established way of carrying out some important set of activities in society.* Institutions are part of culture and are therefore analytically distinguished from actual social behavior. As with all culture, there is always a kind of dynamic tension between institutions as the script for social living and the actual acting and living out of that script under highly specific conditions involving particular people.

In any society there are only a few institutions, but these few institutions tell all the members of society how to behave in almost countless specific situations. Some clusters of activities or functions are so essential to the survival of society that institutions based on them are believed to be universal. These are the economic, political, educational, familial, and religious institutions. Of these we give chapter treatment to only three: the family (Chapter 12), education (Chapter 13), and religion (Chapter 14). Other activity clusters lead to the development of institutions in some but not all societies. For example, science is a full-fledged institution in the United States and we devote Chapter 15 to it, but it does not exist in many societies. Sometimes institutions extend beyond the borders of a single society. Thus Christianity as an institution crosses the borders of many societies. So do capitalism and communism as economic institutions, and monarchy and representative democracy as forms of government.

Aside from the culture of a whole society, institutions are the biggest parts of culture. A single institution may include dozens of values and thousands of norms, and may be given specific behavioral expression in millions of organizations and groups. So, for example, we may speak of *the* American family institution, but of millions of separate families. There is one institution of Christianity but many thousands of churches, which manifest the institution in organizational form. And we may speak of one American educational institution, which provides the basic pattern for many thousands of schools and colleges.

While actual social behavior in its many forms ordinarily either manifests the major institutions of society or supports them in some way, this isn't always true. Some organizations, associations, and groups may, in fact, oppose the major institutions. Thus feminism challenges those aspects of our family institution that condemn women to play inferior roles to men. In the chapters that follow we treat both institutions as such and their organizational expressions in contemporary American society.

Family

12

The family is probably the most ancient group in human experience, extending back thousands of years before the dawn of history. There have been innumerable variations in the way in which the family is organized, yet as far back as we can see, there has always been something which sociologists and anthropologists would recognize. If you, perhaps belonging to a family in American suburbia, could visit the family of a prehistoric hunter living in a cave in what is now France, you would see similarities between that group and what you think of as a family. The impressive antiquity of the family compared to most other groupings raises the question why it has been so enduring.

The family testifies to the survival capacity of groups which perform important functions for their members and for society at large, and which have built into them a means for generating new groups of the same kind. The family is vital to the individual. Most of us have a longer connection with kinship groups than with any other kind. Add the years you have spent in the family you were born into (your *family of orientation*) to the years you will probably spend in the family you establish by marriage (*family of procreation*) and see for yourself. Actually, our statement could be true for either of your families.

The psychological foundations for all later personal development are laid down in our first years. Here inherited charac-

THE INFLUENCE OF THE FAMILY

teristics receive their first modification by experience, and almost all psychologists agree that the consequences are deep and lasting. The family one is born into establishes an *initial location* in society, and that location will have much to do with the opportunities available as time goes by. It is true that the poor boy or girl can rise far higher than one might predict. But this is not usual. (Recall the research on mobility between generations cited in Chapter 6.) Who one's parents are has fateful effects on most people's chances in life. Finally, the emotions that color the social relations between husband and wife, parent and child, and among siblings are among the most powerful and lasting in all experience. Whole psychologies, such as Freud's, have been built on the idea that throughout life the individual's emotional ties reflect his bonds with parents and siblings in childhood.

The family is indispensable to society as well as to the individual. The *biological survival* of society is entrusted to it. Procreation can, of course, occur outside the family, and sometimes does. But most children in all societies are born into families. And family members, especially parents, are expected to play a key role in *socializing* the newborn. There are other socializing agents, but across the world the crucial and indispensable ones are within the family. The *social control of sex* is given more to the family than to any other agency. This doesn't mean that American views on sex are universal, but everywhere the family draws lines between approved and unacceptable sexual expression in society.

Thus it's not surprising that laymen and sociologists alike view the family as one of the critical forms of social organization. Every family unit imparts to its children society's expectation that when they are adult they too will start families of procreation. The family is not only vital in each generation, but it also perpetuates itself indefinitely into the future.

DEFINING FAMILY

Definitions of the family used by anthropologists and sociologists reflect the variety of forms the family takes. Here is a definition useful to social scientists, formulated by Zelditch (1964:681).

A family is a social group in which sexual access is permitted between certain adult members, reproduction legitimately occurs, the group is responsible to society for the care and upbringing of children, and the group is an economic unit, at least in consumption.

THE NUCLEAR FAMILY   This statement was carefully worded to include the many variants in family form in different societies. It is a broad definition of the *nuclear family,* which in the United States can be identified as *a single husband-wife pair and their natural or adopted children, ordinarily occupying a separate household.* Everywhere each nuclear family is embedded in a broad network of kinship ties. Thus separate nuclear families are linked by common recognition of actual or presumed biological

Currently there is a great deal of experimentation in new forms of family-like household arrangements, and much of it is taking place among middle-class, well-educated persons. A group of young people establish a kind of urban commune in large cities. Older people establish cooperative living arrangements. Young unmarried couples establish homes together, often as a kind of trial marriage. Some reasons: sharing expenses, sharing household tasks, companionship, sex.

relationships. You recognize such terms as uncle, aunt, cousin, grandparent, grandchild. The density of kinship links becomes clear when one considers that every uncle is a brother of a parent, and the person you call grandmother is mother-in-law to one of your parents. The chances are good that at least some of these kinship ties are active, important social relationships for you. Yet Americans put much less emphasis on kinship than do many other peoples. For example, speaking of a small Polynesian society, the Tikopia, Firth says, "Every person of ordinary competency can ultimately trace connection with every other person in the community of over twelve hundred souls . . . the whole land is a single body of kinsfolk" (Firth, 1936:234).

THE EXTENDED FAMILY In many societies, two or more nuclear families are closely affiliated in an *extended family,* which involves much more than the kinship ties we are accustomed to. The several nuclear units may share the same household, a common division of labor, economic assets, and other aspects of family activity. In many preliterate societies (those which have not developed writing) economic, political, religious, and educational activities are not carried out by specialized organizations but by kinship groups of many nuclear families (Stephens, 1963:145–57). It is common for extended families to be *generational* (Murdock, 1949:1–3). That is, a single household may be composed of a man, his wife and children, and his married sons and their wives and children. Thus two, even three generations of nuclear families may share the same household.

FORMS OF MARRIAGE The concept of marriage exists in all societies and is clearly distinguished from temporary sexual relationships which superficially resemble it. As Stephen put it (1963:5):

Marriage is a socially legitimate sexual union, begun with a public announcement and undertaken with some idea of permanence; it is assumed with a more or less explicit marriage contract, which spells out reciprocal rights and obligations between spouses, and between the spouses and their future children.

Monogamy is the marriage of one husband and one wife. Because the culture of America and of the societies we know best decree monogamy as the proper marriage form, it may surprise you to learn that the requirement of monogamy is rather unusual among the societies of the world. In his *World Ethnographic Sample,* Murdock (1957) reports this requirement in only about one out of five societies.

Plural marriages are acceptable, if not preferred or most common, in all the rest. By far the most common form is *polygyny,* in which one husband has two or more wives. *Polyandry,* where one wife has two or more husbands, is rare; Murdock reports only four societies in which it is the prevalent form. A logically possible variation is *group marriage* in which there are multiple spouses of both sexes. According to Stephen (1963:33), "There is no known society in which group marriage is clearly the dominant, or most frequent, marriage form, but . . . there are a number of doubtful borderline cases."

DISTRIBUTION OF AUTHORITY IN THE FAMILY As with all established groups, the distribution of authority (legitimated power) in the family is patterned in a way characteristic of the society in which the family is located. Such a pattern is, of course, contained in culture. Of forty-one societies compared by Stephen (1963:297–99) the patriarchal pattern (male clearly dominant) was found in twenty-one. There were six additional societies in which the husband's authority was only slightly greater than the wife's. He found five societies in which the authority of the spouses was about equal, and six others where husband and wife had different spheres of authority in which he or she was dominant. There were three cases in Stephen's sample in which the balance of power favored the wife.

In Chapter 4 we reported Zelditch's (1955) evidence that in many societies husbands are *instrumental* leaders and wives are *expressive* leaders. Since this distinction first appeared in laboratory studies of small groups, it was suggested that the division of labor involved might be widespread in groups of many kinds. We suggest here that the older terms, like *patriarchal,* primarily denote instrumental elements of leadership in the family.

Instrumental behavior has more implications of authority than expressive behavior. Hence Zelditch's evidence is consistent with Stephen's finding that the greatest authority is more often lodged with the husband than the wife. It might be worth adding Stephen's observation, based on cross-cultural comparisons, that American wives have relatively strong power positions.

THE FAMILY IN AMERICA

We now focus on the American family, which is mainly derived from European sources, although here and there we shall mention family organization in other societies. It is important to remember that the American pattern is only one among many that have stood the test of time. We shall need to make generalizations about the family system in this country which apply as broadly as possible to all individual nuclear family units. In smaller, simpler societies this would be far easier to do. In America there are many subcultural variations within the overall system, and we shall not be able to explore these as fully as we would like, significant though they are. Some of these are racial or ethnic, some religious, some spring from social class, others are regional. It is a big country, in size and population.[1] It is also culturally complex, and changing rapidly. Many changes affect families at different times and with unequal force.

Yet despite significant changes, there does exist a single family system. Nearly all family units reflect an overarching cultural concept of what family life is and should be, and this makes it easy to distinguish an American family from a Chinese or a Mexican one. It also lets us see the relationship of the American family to European family systems, and so to trace ours to its roots in Mediterranean civilizations thousands of years ago. We focus on the overall pattern, but we shall glimpse many stresses, strains,

---

[1] In 1971, the population of the United States was 207,000,000. It had doubled since 1915, a period of fifty-three years, and was predicted to double again (assuming certain birth and death rate conditions) by 2000, a period of only thirty-two years.

and alterations in the pattern produced by changes in the larger society.

MATE SELECTION The social controls that operate when nuclear families are established make a good starting point. Every society must have some arrangement for getting young adults safely married. Some societies, like ours, place no formal limitations on the free choice of marriage mates. In other societies initial choice by the potential spouses must be ratified by the parents, a custom once common in our own society. Much more common than either of these methods is some form of *arranged marriage* in which spouses are chosen by socially approved third parties, usually parents or others close of kin (Stephens, 1963:197–99). Arranged marriage is most common in societies with extended families. There, marriage is regarded as much more than a personal arrangement between young people; it is an alliance between kinship groups, with implications that extend far beyond the couple.

There is no better example of the free choice system than the American family.[2] In theory, young men and women look around until they find a good bet, and if the feeling is reciprocated, marriage follows. Of course free choice implies that there is a considerable number to choose from. There can't be much choice if you know only one eligible person of the opposite sex! But let us look a little closer.

Homogamy in the Choice of Mates There is much evidence that people tend to marry those with similar backgrounds and characteristics. The technical word for this tendency is *homogamy*. For example, a long series of studies, beginning with that of Bossard (1932), has shown that within cities, as the distance between the residences of two young people decreases, the probability that they will marry each other increases. Hollingshead (1950), Kennedy (1952), Thomas (1951), and others have shown that mates are likely to be chosen within broad religious groupings (Protestant, Catholic, Jewish). People also tend to marry within ethnic groups. Close religious and ethnic group identity has overlapping effects on mate selection (Winch, 1963:327–36). Marriage within the same social classes is also likely (Hollingshead, 1950; Centers, 1949; Winch, 1963:338–39). And there is some evidence that marriage partners are likely to resemble one another in a number of psychological characteristics (Winch, 1963:345).

---

[2] It is not strictly true that there are *no* formal controls over mate selection. States impose minimum ages at which persons can marry without consent of parents. Custom, and to a lesser degree law, proscribe marriages between persons who are closely related biologically. Finally, until recently outlawed by the Supreme Court, a number of states had antimiscegenation laws which forbade interracial marriages. Despite these exceptions, mate selection is remarkably free of explicit controls imposed either by the state or by family tradition.

It may seem odd to us, but the selection of marriage partners by socially approved third parties is far more common among the world's societies than our own system of mate selection.

Clearly, homogamous tendencies in mate selection effectively restrict choice. There is no great mystery about why this is so. Factors like race, ethnicity, religion, education and social class, *as they operate in particular localities,* markedly influence contact. We are most likely to meet people who are like us, and in social settings conducive to emotional bonds that could lead to marriage.

The evidence for homogamy is strong, but we do not wish to overstate it. Of course, there are marriages that bridge ethnic, religious, class, and other barriers. Incidentally, a particular homogamous tendency may vary with circumstances. Thomas (1951) found that intermarriage between Catholics and non-Catholics is higher in areas where Catholics are scarce, and vice versa.

Restrictions of Location While broad homogamous tendencies can be seen on a very large scale, their most immediate effects are in local areas: a high school, a college, a part of town, a place of work. One does not actually have all the people in the country with similar characteristics as a pool of potential mates. Only those with similar characteristics who are immediately present are available. In extreme cases this may reduce the local field of eligibles to close to zero; for example, think of the young person who is a college graduate and holds a professional job, but lives in a small town with few single people, almost all of whom are unskilled or semiskilled workers.

The field is usually larger than that, but it is often quite small. Coeducational colleges contain unusually large numbers of eligibles. Every local pool of potential choices is already preselected for homogamy, as we have indicated. But even within this narrow context people do not have equal access to each other.

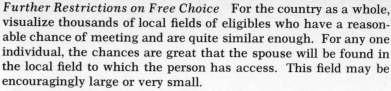

Further Restrictions on Free Choice For the country as a whole, visualize thousands of local fields of eligibles who have a reasonable chance of meeting and are quite similar enough. For any one individual, the chances are great that the spouse will be found in the local field to which the person has access. This field may be encouragingly large or very small.

Even in such local fields choice is further reduced. For instance, there is the widespread feeling in our society that a man should be as tall as his wife or taller. While there is no biological reason for it, this notion is deep-seated. Obviously it broadens the chances for the tall man and narrows them for the short man and the tall woman; no doubt you have seen this in action. You have probably also observed that there is a lot of difference in the skill and finesse people have for attracting and relating to the opposite sex. Obviously, personal style can have a good deal to do with the actual number of marriage choices a person has.

A host of factors converge to limit freedom in mate selection by reducing the number of persons who are, in any real sense, available choices. Some of these factors operate indirectly by affecting the chances of personal contact. Others act more directly, such as those already mentioned. In spite of all, as long as one has at least two persons to choose between, he has some freedom of selection. But there are other social influences on the choice one makes.

Love and Mate Selection When a person chooses among alternatives, he does so by one or more criteria. One factor common in America is that the individual marries because he or she is in love. We may seem quaintly professional for making so obvious a point. Indeed, there may seem to you *no other acceptable reason*. You may have known or heard of people who married for other reasons, and pitied or disapproved such strange behavior. Americans are likely to feel cheated if they cannot convince themselves that their marriage is a love relationship.

Remember, however, that the most common form of mate selection in the world is arranged marriage, where the individual has no choice. No doubt people in such societies experience heterosexual love, but for them being in love has nothing to do with mate selection. If we include families with all other groups and broadly question how groups are formed, we see that love between two persons is a comparatively rare basis for establishing new groups. It may seem obvious to Americans that marriage should be based on love, but sociologically and anthropologically, it is a rare phenomenon.

Society defines love as a legitimate criterion for finding a mate, and further, in socializing the individual it teaches what heterosexual love is, how to recognize it, and what part it should play in life, including the choice of a mate. We learn how to love in much the same way that we learn anything else. From our earliest years, we are subjected to a stream of material from literature, popular music, TV, motion pictures, parents, friends, and other socializing agents, all of which trains us to give to love the particular meanings embedded in the society's culture.

Much of what American society teaches about love is called romantic love, epitomized in the following passage by Waller and Hill (1951:114).

According to the prevalent mythology, the young man or young woman usually arrives at the marriageable age with his heart undamaged, and then a mysterious thing happens; he falls in love and, of course, he marries the girl and lives happily ever after, or for quite awhile. Romantic love, as Americans understand it, is an ungovernable impulse, a wholly normal and even sought-for state of grace in which one is unable to think of anything but the loved person—a great tenderness together with the most extreme delusions as to the nature of the loved person—and a striving toward her sometimes attended by extravagances of jealousy and morbid despair if one does not prosper in his suit. . . . The phenomenon of falling in love is thought of as a violent manifestation arising from unknown causal processes in the mind; it contains, if one's love is real, a mysterious and authentic message that this is one's intended mate.

Like thousands of films, the classic "Gone With the Wind" portrays romantic love as the ideal relationship between a man and a woman.

This need not be taken as an accurate description of what happens to any given individual. It is, however, a cultural model which, even if never realized in every detail, is one source of the American concept of love.

Romantic love has a long and fascinating history in Western society. It appears to have originated in medieval Europe, where it was confined to the socially elite. In the beginning, it had nothing to do with mate selection, but was an elaborate social game played mainly between high-born married women and courtly lovers who were not their husbands (Beigel, 1951; Reiss, 1960). Only in recent times, with the breakdown of arranged marriages in the emerging urban-industrial societies of the West, has romantic love spread to the masses and furnished a rationale for mate selection.

While a free choice in mate selection is significantly different from arranged marriage, there is much evidence that choice is not nearly so free as we often assume. Falling in love and getting married is an intensely personal experience, but it is socially influenced and guided in many direct and indirect ways.

Popularity of Marriage in America Marriage is very popular with Americans. According to Gendell and Zetterberg (1964:4) the proportion of persons married in this country is probably the highest in the Western world. In 1971, 74.1 percent of people eighteen years and over were married. The popularity of marriage is also reflected in the frequency of remarriage after divorce. Ratios vary by age and sex, but reach 95 percent for those divorced at under twenty-five, and about 75 percent for all ages (Carter and Plateris, 1963).

The average age at marriage has been slowly declining for many years, and Americans marry younger than people in many other industrialized countries. In 1971 the median age of

American men was twenty-three and that of women twenty-one. That is, half of all marriages were made by people younger than these ages! In 1890, the median ages were twenty-six and twenty-two. So in these years, the average age at marriage has declined, and the difference in age between bride and groom has lessened.

HUSBAND AND WIFE ROLES AND THEIR SOCIAL SETTING The American family is dominantly patriarchal, as were its ancestral family systems for several thousand years. But the authority of the husband today is much diminished and continues to erode. Within the family, women have made great strides toward equality. For example, American husbands could once control and dispose of the property brought to the marriage by their wives without the wives' consent. For many middle-class, college-educated young couples today, the equalitarian pattern seems preferred, at least in their premarital thinking.

Why has the husband's authority declined? Parsons (1955) proposed a sociological answer based on the fact that over most of their histories, Western societies have been mainly agrarian. This meant that the man's part in economic production (mainly agricultural) was typically close to that of other family members. His total role in the family included his economic activity. In an industrial society like the United States, the man's job is outside the domestic scene. Other members of the family seldom see and know little about this part of his life. Yet his economic role is extremely important; it not only provides income but mainly determines the whole family's status, not just the man's.

An important role for the man, once part of his total role in the family, is now detached and performed in a different setting. No longer is he the instrumental leader of a family which, as such, is an important unit in society's economic system. As the basis for his instrumental leadership has been removed from the family, there has been a relative gain in the importance of the wife's expressive role. In other words, expressive activities loom larger in the family, and as expressive leader the wife's influence has increased.

With the father away much of the time, even the instrumental tasks of child-rearing fall more on the mother. And there is reason to believe that the time fathers spend with their children is likely to be concentrated in the expressive rather than the instrumental area—for example, in playing with them on weekends, evenings, and vacations (Rossi, 1968), all of which further raises the wife's status within the family.

Further reduction of patriarchal authority is likely, though the actual degree may be closely related to changes in the status of women outside the family, particularly in jobs. Occupation is a sensitive determinant of social status, and only if women make more headway toward job equality with men will there be much further improvement in the status of wives in relation to hus-

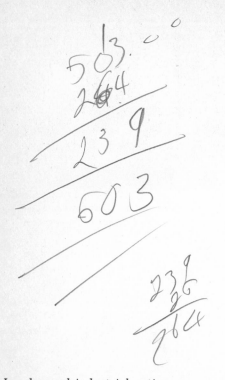

In advanced industrial nations, many are experimenting with new family roles. In this young Swedish family the wife goes off to work while her husband remains home. What do you think about this arrangement?

Part 3 / Social Institutions

bands. The American family remains patriarchal in spite of the steady decline in culture's mandate for strong patriarchal authority. Even in such a matter as the relative influence of the spouses in the choice of close friends, the husband's influence remains considerably greater than the wife's (Babchuk and Bates, 1963). Table 12-1 suggests that, while some tasks are nearly always performed by one sex or the other, the range of variation in the sexual assignment of tasks is very wide on a cross-cultural basis.

Wives and the Job Market There has long been an upward trend in the proportion of the labor force represented by women, particularly married women. Women constituted only 18 percent of the labor force in 1900, but 42.8 percent in 1971 (Dublin, 1965:276, and United States Bureau of the Census). Table 12-2 shows an increase of married women in the labor force from 23.8 percent in 1950 to 40.8 percent in 1971. The table shows another striking fact. The increases have been larger for women who have minor children than for those who do not. Having young children at home does not keep women from taking jobs as much as it used to.

These figures fail to show some other significant facts about women and jobs. The higher a husband's income, the less likely it is that his wife will be employed. So it appears that women take jobs more to enhance family income than for other reasons. Women are much less likely than men to hold jobs of high status, and at every level they receive substantially less pay than men for the same work (Dublin, 1965:279–82). The fact is that women are severely discriminated against when they take jobs outside the home.

Spouse Employment Early in the Family Life Cycle We now return to husband and wife roles in the statistically typical family life cycle in the United States. The first peak in the employment of wives comes from ages twenty to twenty-four. Income is usually small at this time, and the first child has not been born. The young husband is starting a career which is likely to claim much of his time and energy for most of his life. His family will depend on him for most of its financial support. His job will be of prime importance to his own feelings of self-regard and to the social status of his family in the community.

Statistically speaking, even the young wife is a bit more likely not to work. The 1971 rate of employment was 48.4 percent. If she does have a job it may have short-run significance—saving a nest egg, buying a car, helping the husband finish his training. But in the long run, her work is likely to be seen as much less important than his to the family as a whole. She is, so to speak, helping out until the first child is born. Since many people she meets seem to feel this way, it may be hard for her not to share the general attitudes. If she does, she aids and abets discrimination

More and more married women are in the job market. Day care centers both reflect this trend and accelerate it as they make it easier for mothers to hold jobs. Is an outside occupation frustrating or fulfilling for women? What does our analysis and your own observation of individuals suggest?

against women in the job market by being willing to work at less than her maximum skill level, and by not actively objecting when she is passed over for earned promotions and pay increases.

TABLE 12-1   COMPARATIVE DATA ON THE DIVISION OF LABOR BY SEX

	NUMBER OF SOCIETIES IN WHICH:				
ACTIVITY	MEN USUALLY DO IT	MEN ALWAYS DO IT	EITHER SEX MAY DO IT	WOMEN USUALLY DO IT	WOMEN ALWAYS DO IT
Metal working	0	78	0	0	0
Weapon making	1	121	0	0	0
Pursuit of sea mammals	1	34	0	0	0
Hunting	13	166	0	0	0
Manufacture of musical instruments	2	45	0	0	1
Boat building	4	91	4	0	1
Mining and quarrying	1	35	1	0	1
Work in wood and bark	9	113	5	1	1
Work in stone	3	68	2	0	2
Trapping or catching of small animals	13	128	4	1	2
Lumbering	4	104	3	1	6
Work in bone, horn, and shell	4	67	3	0	3
Fishing	34	98	19	3	4
Manufacture of ceremonial objects	1	37	13	0	1
Herding	8	38	4	0	5
House building	32	86	25	3	14
Clearing of land for agriculture	22	73	17	5	13
Net making	6	44	4	2	11
Trade	28	51	20	8	7
Dairy operations	4	17	3	1	13
Manufacture of ornaments	3	24	40	6	18
Agriculture: soil preparation and planting	23	31	33	20	37
Manufacture of leather products	3	29	9	3	32
Body mutilations, for example, tattooing	14	16	44	22	20
Erection and dismantling of shelter	2	14	5	6	22
Hide preparation	2	31	4	4	49
Tending of fowls and small animals	4	21	8	1	39
Agriculture: crop tending and harvesting	15	10	35	39	44
Gathering of shellfish	4	9	8	7	25
Manufacture of nontextile fabrics	0	14	9	2	32
Fire making and tending	6	18	25	22	62
Burden bearing	6	12	35	20	57
Preparation of drinks and narcotics	1	20	13	8	57
Manufacture of thread and cordage	2	23	11	10	73
Basket making	3	25	10	6	82
Mat making	2	16	6	4	61
Weaving	2	19	2	6	67
Gathering of fruits, berries, and nuts	3	12	15	13	63
Fuel gathering	1	22	10	19	89
Pottery making	2	13	6	8	77
Preservation of meat and fish	2	8	10	14	74
Manufacture and repair of clothing	3	12	8	9	95
Gathering of herbs, roots, and seeds	1	8	11	7	74
Cooking	1	5	9	28	158
Water carrying	0	7	5	7	119
Grain grinding	4	2	5	13	114

Source: From *The Family in Cross-Cultural Perspective* by William N. Stephens. Copyright © 1963 by Holt, Rinehart and Winston, Inc. Reprinted by permission of Holt, Rinehart and Winston, Inc.

Whether or not young wives are employed outside the home for a few years, they, their husbands, and society generally see their primary role as motherhood and housekeeping. We suggest that the number of married women who pursue and desire to pursue careers with the same long-term commitment as men is at present small. Jobs typically have quite a different meaning for women than for men.

The much-discussed choice, or conflict, between homemaking and career as yet has little application to most married women. Yet for a minority of wives the choice is vital, and sometimes difficult or agonizing. These are the women who want lives parallel in many ways to those of their husbands. They want marriage and careers pursued the same way that men do. Such women are mostly found in the upper income and educational levels. Orden and Bradburn's research (1969) indicates that women who are college graduates are more than twice as likely to hold down jobs by choice than women with an eighth-grade education. And such women will become more numerous in the years ahead.

TABLE 12-2 MARRIED WOMEN (HUSBAND PRESENT) IN THE LABOR FORCE, BY AGE AND PRESENCE OF CHILDREN: 1950 TO 1971

					[Prior to 1960, excludes Alaska and Hawaii]			
ITEM	1950	1955	1960	1965	1968	1969	1970	1971
Labor Force Participation Rate[1]								
Total	23.8	27.7	30.5	34.7	38.3	39.6	40.8	40.8
With no children under 18 years old	30.3	32.7	34.7	38.3	40.0	41.0	42.2	42.1
With children 6–17 years old only	28.3	34.7	39.0	42.7	46.9	48.6	49.2	49.4
With children under 6 years old	11.9	16.2	18.6	23.3	27.6	28.5	30.3	29.6
Also with children 6–17 years old	12.6	17.3	18.9	22.8	27.4	27.8	30.5	29.2

[1] Married women in the labor force as percent of married women in the population.

Source: 1950 and 1955, U.S. Bureau of the Census, *Current Population Reports,* series P-50, No. 62; thereafter U.S. Bureau of Labor Statistics, *Special Labor Force Reports.*

TABLE 12-3 OPINIONS OF AMERICAN WOMEN ON TWO QUESTIONS

IN YOUR OPINION, DO WOMEN IN THE U.S. GET AS GOOD A BREAK AS MEN?			IF A WOMAN HAS THE SAME ABILITY AS A MAN DOES SHE HAVE AS GOOD A CHANCE TO BECOME THE EXECUTIVE OF A COMPANY OR NOT?		
	Yes	*No*	*As Good*	*Not as Good*	*No Opinion*
All women	65	35	39	54	7
Women with children under 21	66	34	33	60	7
Women attended college	53	47	22	75	3
High school	68	32	39	54	7
Grade school	69	31	54	36	10

These data come from a Gallup poll conducted in July 1970. The two questions (among others) were asked of a sample of American women. They seem to support our opinion that despite male discrimination a large proportion of women are fairly well satisfied with their lot. Notice two things in particular. The differences between the categories of women are greater for the second question than the first, and, for both questions, college-educated women are the least satisfied.

THE IMPACT OF CHILDREN ON FAMILY ROLES   On the average, the first child is born one and a half to two years after marriage, and the mother will be about twenty-six when her last child arrives (Glick, (1957). On the average, there will be two children. Sociologically speaking, the nuclear family now becomes more complicated. To the original roles, husband and wife, has been added a third, that of child. The first two are thereby altered, for now they are husband-father and wife-mother. Instead of having only one social relationship to maintain, as in all dyads, the family has three pair relationships after the arrival of the first child, and ten after the third. Before the birth of the first child the husband-wife relationship may retain many features of courtship. But when the children come these earlier roles must change. They are the same persons, but even to one another they may seem to have changed because their role-defined relationships have been deeply altered by parenthood.

The wife is now less likely to hold a job, for she has the major responsibility for child and home care for years to come. If she stays home she will face a period of considerable isolation, especially if she lives in a suburb, where an increasing proportion of Americans live. Her husband is away most of each day except on weekends. The high geographical mobility of Americans means that friendships can easily be made on the basis of common interests rather than only neighborhood closeness.

KINSHIP RELATIONSHIPS OF THE NUCLEAR FAMILY   The nuclear family today probably has less direct contact and support from relatives than in our agrarian past. Yet the isolation from the larger kinship network has sometimes been exaggerated. Even in urban settings like New Haven, Cleveland, and Detroit, visiting and helping remains vigorous among relatives, especially in the form of financial and other aid from parents to children in the early years of their marriages (Sussman, 1953; Sussman and White, 1959; Sussman and Burchinal, 1962; Litwak, 1969; Reiss, 1962; Robins and Tomanec, 1962; Mirande, 1969). Many urban families have relationships with a few close friends that are kin-like in all but name, substituting in some measure for close ties with actual kinfolk (Babchuk and Bates, 1963; Williams, 1970:66).

Compared with most other cultures, the nuclear family unit in America is expected to show a great deal of independence. It is expected to occupy a private household. Man and wife are expected to forge their own economic independence. And they often must even do their family duties in isolation from each other. At the same time, the family system provides them—because of social change—with less clear role directions than once existed. Adams (1971:242) speaks of role blurring. As they begin their life together, spouses face many role choices, often not easy to make.

A young couple must face such questions as which one has the authority to make decisions, and in which areas? What decision-making, if any, will be shared with the children? Are we to be

FIGURE 12-1   THE NUCLEAR FAMILY
Rather than the extended family, in which several generations live together in one household, the nuclear family has become the predominant form in the United States. Each generation breaks off to form an independent household, often moving far away from the original family unit. As a result, a degree of close kinship caring has been traded off for a sense of independence.

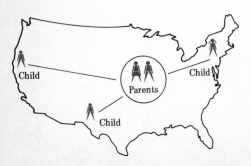

Part 3 / Social Institutions

close companions, sharing our free time and our interests, or do we go our own ways in such matters? How do we handle authority and companionship where our children are concerned? Is one of us to be the authority figure and the other a playmate, or do we share both kinds of activities, and how do we work this out when the husband is away from the home most of the time? Is the husband to be the sole financial provider and the wife the homemaker, or can these functions be divided in some way yielding greater satisfaction to both? Do we have separate friends or will friendships be on a couple basis? Because American culture does not speak with one voice to such questions, husband and wife may be in doubt as to what is possible, and may even disagree strongly because of differences in their backgrounds.

Marital Roles and Social Class There is evidence that marital roles vary by social class. For example, Rainwater (1965) classified role-defined relations between husband and wife as *joint,* in which many tasks and activities are shared; *segregated,* in which they are highly compartmentalized; and *intermediate,* or partway between. He interviewed a sample of couples from different social class levels, and found (Table 12-4) a dramatic correlation between social class and the nature of the husband-wife relationship. High-status couples tended to have a joint relationship (a newer pattern), and lower-status couples a segregated relationship (a traditional pattern). On the assumption that high-status practices gradually filter down to other levels, it is likely that the joint pattern will become more widespread.

Departure of Children After twenty or so years of child-rearing, the last child leaves the home. The mother is somewhere in her late forties, the father in his early fifties. This point marks an im-

TABLE 12-4 SOCIAL CLASS AND CONJUGAL ROLE RELATIONSHIPS

| | ROLE RELATIONSHIPS (PERCENT) | | |
	Joint	*Intermediate*	*Segregated*
Upper middle class (32)†	88	12	—
Lower middle class (31)	42	58	—
Upper lower class*			
Whites (26)	19	58	23
Negroes (25)	12	52	36
Lower lower class*			
Whites (25)	4	24	72
Negroes (29)	—	28	72

† Numbers in parentheses refer to couples interviewed.

* Whites and Negroes at each class level combined for test.

Source: Reprinted from Lee Rainwater, *Family Design* (Chicago: Aldine Publishing Company, 1965); copyright © 1965 by Social Research, Inc. Reprinted by permission of the author and Aldine Publishing Company.

There must be many ways of living well in old age, just as there are at other ages. America urgently needs more experimentation in new social roles for the aged.

portant change in the structure of the nuclear family and has vital consequences for husband and wife roles. The unit has come full circle and is once again a dyad, just as when husband and wife first married. The nest is empty. As in the beginning, there is now only one relationship to maintain within the household.

The first time man and wife were a dyad both looked ahead to the child-rearing period. Now all that is behind them. Especially in the middle and upper middle classes, the husband is at the peak of his career and will be deeply absorbed in it for about another decade. The main job of the mother apart from housekeeping is child-rearing, and it is finished perhaps thirty years before her life ends.

What is the wife to do when her task is completed while the husband goes on with his? It is no surprise to find that a second peak in the employment of married women comes at this point. While with some a job takes up an interrupted career or begins a new one, it is more likely to resemble the general picture for employed women: relatively marginal jobs and marginal pay. This may be one reason why after about age fifty-five the employment of wives drops off sharply, long before the life span nears its end. As man and wife enter the final period of the family life cycle, despite similarities to the first period, their roles as a whole are not in good balance with one another. The wife is now free to devote much more time and attention to the marriage dyad, but the husband, because of his commitment to a major role outside the family, does not share this freedom.

Statistically, we anticipate that the husband will die sometime in his late sixties and his wife eight or nine years later, for most women live somewhat longer than men, and marry men older than themselves. Despite this difference the spouses will go on together for a decade or more, entering old age before the first of the two dies. When the United States was an agrarian country, aging spouses could expect to remain at home, which was also the place of work. Just as children contributed to the work of the farm according to their abilities, so did elderly parents. Because their contribution could be adjusted to their ability, their sense of belonging and of personal participation in the real work of society was not impaired.[3]

Today, the man is likely either to have retired years before his death or (in lower-level occupations) to have lost his job with nothing equivalent to replace it. Given the importance of occupation to male self-esteem in this society, the psychological consequences are often bad. The children who have left home are

---

[3] We are reminded of an old harness maker in the city where we live. He still carries on his trade, diminished by age and the fact that if he earns more than a certain sum his Social Security income will be reduced. But he does the work he knows, is sought after by the owners of pleasure horses in the city, and has plenty of time to swap stories and gossip with old cronies who are always in his little shop.

likely to be living at some distance. Aged parents are seldom welcome to live in the small homes or apartments of their grown children. While there are vestiges in the legal system of the ancient obligation of children to support elderly and needy parents, these are weakening, and there is far from unanimous agreement in the population that children have any such obligation at all. Cohen, Robson, and Bates (1958) found that 53 percent of the people in one state felt that children should have this responsibility, while 39.8 percent believed that the government should have all or some of it.

When we consider that the elderly constitute about 10 percent of the population (and the proportion is growing), it is clear that the American family system does not yet provide adequate social roles for them, adapted to contemporary societal conditions and permitting people to live satisfying lives in their declining years.

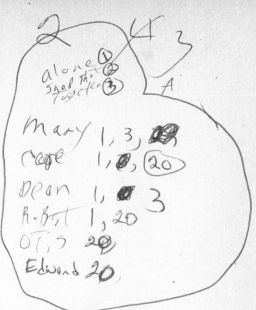

THE CHILD'S ROLE AND ITS SOCIAL CONTEXT

The American nuclear family is small, but it was once much larger. The number of births per one thousand population per year was 30.1 in 1910 and 17.3 in 1971, an all-time low. At this point it was only slightly above the level of zero population growth, assuming that existing death rates would continue. Average family size in 1971 was 3.6 persons, including childless families as well as those with children. It seems unlikely that family size will decline much further.

We have said that the American family institution does not speak with one clear voice in defining the roles of husband and wife, nor is it explicit on the roles of children and adolescents. Because people everywhere tend to take their own times and lifestyles pretty much for granted, Americans find it hard to realize that in most societies in most ages, tradition (the culture of the family) provided safe and comfortable answers to such questions as how children should behave, and how parents should bring up a child properly. These answers came easily and informally, almost without special training, simply by observing what had always been done.

Today, most American parents lack calm confidence in their ability to rear their children wisely, and so the children are not clear about the role of child. Tradition speaks in a distorted and confusing voice to parent and child alike, and sometimes seems to give no answers at all to the needs of families in an industrialized and urbanized society.

Science, however, has great prestige; the very word conveys an aura of authority. Given this state of faith, it is unfortunate that the relevant fields of science do not yet know enough to give parents and children the sure practical answers they usually want. All scientific knowledge is tentative and incomplete, and it is particularly so in the social and psychological sciences. Efforts

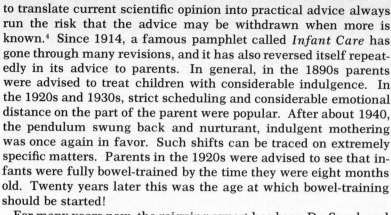

to translate current scientific opinion into practical advice always run the risk that the advice may be withdrawn when more is known.[4] Since 1914, a famous pamphlet called *Infant Care* has gone through many revisions, and it has also reversed itself repeatedly in its advice to parents. In general, in the 1890s parents were advised to treat children with considerable indulgence. In the 1920s and 1930s, strict scheduling and considerable emotional distance on the part of the parent were popular. After about 1940, the pendulum swung back and nurturant, indulgent mothering was once again in favor. Such shifts can be traced on extremely specific matters. Parents in the 1920s were advised to see that infants were fully bowel-trained by the time they were eight months old. Twenty years later this was the age at which bowel-training should be started!

For many years now, the reigning expert has been Dr. Spock and his famous book on child-rearing. Spock stresses permissiveness, and the encouragement of individual differences and developing each child's potential. We stress that parents do not necessarily act upon the conceptions of child-rearing and the child's role implicit in such materials. But their popularity suggests that many at least try to be guided by them.

Neither the older traditions of the family nor the new but changing information coming from science provide permanent authoritative models of children's roles, either for parents or for children.

THE CHILD AND SOCIALIZING AGENTS The relative isolation of the nuclear family and the frequent absence of the father have consequences for the role of the child. As in most societies, the mother has the principal responsibility for the child's socialization in the first years, but unlike children in most other societies, the American child does not have surrogate parents in the form of other adult kinfolk. Thus he is sharply focused toward the mother, especially at first. From her he receives most of his first experiences of acceptance and love and also of frustration and discipline. The father is simply not there enough to equal the mother as a socializing agent, though he is important in his own right.

This marked containment within the nuclear family, and intense concentration upon the mother-child relationship, is lessened in a few years by the child's gradual movement outside the family. First, there are occasional forays into play groups of age peers. Then come the mothers of playmates, and peers and teach-

---

[4] This very thing has happened and has been documented in a number of studies, such as those of Stendler (1950) and Wolfenstein (1953). The former analyzed changes in child-rearing advice from 1890 to 1950 in *Ladies' Home Journal, Woman's Home Companion,* and *Good Housekeeping.* Wolfenstein made a somewhat similar study of a famous pamphlet, *Infant Care,* published since 1914 by the United States Children's Bureau.

ers in nursery school, kindergarten, and elementary school. Recent decades have seen a great proliferation of organized groups for children; more and more, the child confronts a world in which nearly all his time is organized for him by adults. All these adults are earnestly trying to educate him, to train him, and to make some constructive contribution to his development. Since the adult leaders of these groups see themselves as socializing agents, they may be a kind of substitute for the part-time parents which in many societies are found among kinfolk. Certainly after the earliest years of a child's life, American parents typically surrender much of his training to a large number of other agents in the socialization process, especially schoolteachers.

It is in these many nonfamilial groups the child has his early experience with the diversity of American culture and realizes that much of it disagrees with what he has been taught at home. Amidst all this diversity, and sensing unsureness of standards, American children learn to manipulate their parents to get what they want. And they learn that parents have only limited power to affect what happens to them in outside groups. Hence the odd fact that, while the American child is at first almost totally contained within the nuclear family and stays part of it for many years, the direct control of American parents rapidly diminishes with the age of the child, and is in general slight. Williams (1970:77) puts it this way. "There seems to be little doubt that on the whole American children have extraordinary freedom in certain respects and develop, at an early age, patterns of independence that differ from the roles of children in corresponding social and economic classes in nearly all the major cultures of Europe, Asia, and Latin America."

Class Variations This reference to classes is a reminder that distinct subcultural variations exist here. Child-rearing and children's roles are not the same in all classes, or in all ethnic and religious groups. There has been much research on all this, especially on class differences, but the results conflict and conclusions can be drawn only with caution. In the spirit of withholding final judgment, Winch (1963:507) offers the following tentative statement. "Relatively speaking, the middle class tends toward indulgence and love-oriented discipline directed at the intent of the child's behavior, whereas the lower class tends toward sternness, physical punishment, and discipline directed at the consequences of the child's behavior."

Surrogate parenthood, as illustrated by this child and his grandmother, is not very common in the United States as compared with most other societies.

At the end of childhood, adolescence begins; at the end of adolescence, adulthood. That much is clear. About what lies between these points Americans are notoriously worried, confused and upset. As social roles, both childhood and adolescence are socially defined. While these roles are tied to physical characteristics and

THE ADOLESCENT'S ROLE AND ITS SOCIAL CONTEXT

Two rites of passage are the Jewish Bar Mitzvah (above) and the ceremonies that occur among the Vachokue in Angola (opposite page). Where such events are widely understood and accepted, they ease the transition into and out of adolescence because they remove all doubt as to when a person is a child, an adolescent, or an adult.

changes, they are not determined by physiology alone. Cross-cultural differences in the roles of childhood and adolescence are substantial and make this point clear.

To the sociologist, adolescence is a period in which the individual plays a social role called adolescence. While linked to the physical transition from childhood to bodily maturity, there is no necessary physical reason why this time should be as full of stress and problems as it so often is alleged to be in America. We must conclude that if there is an adolescent "problem" it springs mainly from the way the social role of adolescence is currently defined. The general truth of this observation is attested to not only by many puzzled parents and young people, but by a vast, growing body of research, commentary, and analysis (Goodman, 1956; Gottlieb and Ramsey, 1964; Musgrove, 1965; Keniston, 1965; Gottlieb, Reeves, and TenHouten, 1966; Campbell, 1969).

THE LIMITS OF ADOLESCENCE   The points at which one begins, and especially the point at which one ceases, to play the adolescent role are not well marked in American culture. In many societies, at a particular point such as the onset of puberty, every child goes through a set of personal and publicly defined *rites of passage,* from which he emerges as an adult in the eyes of the community. But in the United States the traditional and role-defining experiences vary so widely that social placement and self-definition may be highly confusing. The same individual may at the same time be regarded by different people as a child, an adolescent, and as an adult.

At the beginning, no single experience universally signals the assumption of the adolescent role. The bodily changes of puberty often serve this function, but these begin at varying ages. Thus some children assume the adolescent role considerably after these changes have begun, while others undertake it well in advance of sexual maturation.

It is even harder to pinpoint the end of adolescence. Boys may be drafted into the armed forces at eighteen. Surely we do not send boys to fight the country's wars. But, until the constitutional change in the voting age in 1971, a man (boy) of nineteen, having been in armed combat, could not vote back home. In some places he is regarded as a minor child when it comes to buying liquor. A twenty-one-year-old may be legally adult but be treated as less than an adult if he is a college student. A nineteen-year-old who does not go beyond high school, marries immediately, becomes self-supporting, has a child, and begins to buy a house may in many respects be seen as more of an adult than someone several years older who is still in school. By cultural definitions, both the beginning and the end of adolescence are ambiguously and inconsistently defined.

The adolescent role moves through a series of steps each of which relinquishes some parental and other adult control and increases the independence of adulthood. Cohen, Robson, and

Bates (1958) show that adult Americans of all classes generally see adolescence in this light. They expect their children to push forward eagerly toward the privileges of adulthood but are not prepared to give them all these privileges at one time. And parents are not in any way near complete agreement on the steps toward independence or on when each should be taken.

THE FUNCTIONS OF ADOLESCENT PEER GROUPS   In order to see the adolescent's family role in perspective, we must also look at the age peer groups which claim so much time and loyalty from young people. Their importance varies among societies and reflects structural features of a society as a whole (Eisenstadt, 1956). In the United States, unlike many societies, the roles an adult plays are not often replicas of the roles and relationships in the nuclear family. The family is a primary group; many adult groups are far more secondary in character and far more complex and specialized in structure. The adult must command a wide repertoire of social skills and appropriate emotional responses for which life in the parental family does not prepare him. Our society is simply too complex for life in the nuclear family to provide a smooth transition from childhood to adulthood.

Several years elapse from the beginning to the end of adolescence. In this time, peer groups wean the individual emotionally from dependence on the family, expose him to new social relationships and new perspectives on the adult world. These groups also accept and support the individual as the complexity and the internal contradictions of the adult world begin to dawn on him. They ease the transition to adulthood in ways which are hard if not impossible for the family to perform. There is no better place to see the adolescent peer group operate than in a large, urban high school with its complex programs and casual shifting relationships.

CONFLICT BETWEEN GENERATIONS   Many Americans and some students of the family see adolescence as a time of emotional stress and instability, and more than in most societies, a time of strain and hostility between generations. Certainly there are causes for strain. Because we are vague and inconsistent in defining adolescence and the steps by which it moves into adulthood, young people are bound to make "mistakes." They will say and do things which parents and other adults will see as unwarranted claims and demands. Adults, themselves uncertain, also react to these pressures in ways which adolescents, or some of them, will see as repressive and unsympathetic. Eisenstadt's analysis makes it clear that some adolescents see their parents as inflexible, out-of-date, and incompetent to offer good advice and control. Children move from a point in childhood where parents seemed to know everything to adolescence where it becomes all too evident that they don't. This disillusionment is accentuated by the rate of change in society, which rapidly dates some of the knowledge

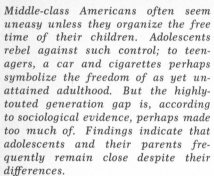

Middle-class Americans often seem uneasy unless they organize the free time of their children. Adolescents rebel against such control; to teenagers, a car and cigarettes perhaps symbolize the freedom of as yet unattained adulthood. But the highly-touted generation gap is, according to sociological evidence, perhaps made too much of. Findings indicate that adolescents and their parents frequently remain close despite their differences.

parents acquired in their own youth. But does the youth culture developed in adolescent peer groups really isolate young people from their parents and other adults and set them in opposition to the values and norms of the adult world? Among sociologists there is some disagreement on this question. Important research under Coleman (1961) lends at least qualified support to a yes answer to our question. Consider the following (Campbell, 1969:839):

Having a good time is important, particularly social activities in company with the opposite sex; there is a strong hedonistic quality. On the male side, extreme emphasis is given to athletics, and this is a measure of valued masculinity, as sexual attractiveness is a measure of valued femininity for females. Explicit acceptance of adult-sponsored interests, expectations, and discipline is negatively valued. Common human elements are emphasized among associates, such as that a person is valued humanistically for his general demeanor and attractiveness rather than instrumentally for performance as a competent specialist. Glamour and excitement are sought, and the luxuriant waste of time is virtuous.

A youth culture with such values and perspectives does seem likely to generate some conflict between the generations. For parents are likely to value such qualities as self-discipline, working toward long-range goals defined by the adult world, and competitive striving for achievement in fields other than athletics.

Yet some sociologists have argued for years that conflict, especially between parents and children, has been exaggerated. Campbell (1969:827–33), reviewing evidence from a variety of sources, says that

the research literature is almost entirely compatible with the conclusions that ties between parents and children remain close throughout the adolescent years; that the positive orientation toward parents does not diminish, and may indeed increase, during adolescence; and that parents and the parent-child relationship both are important influences on the adolescent.

The following conclusions seem tenable. Since the limits of parental control are not precisely defined in the family culture, there is a good deal of trial-and-error pushing and resisting by parents and children alike. This is well understood by the parties concerned. Parents also wish their children to do well in adolescent peer groups and recognize that it is in these groups that some of the limits are tested.

Relationships within the nuclear family are usually flexible enough to withstand reasonable stress without trauma for either generation. As Campbell says, "The special intimacies and commitments of the family bond create conditions that encourage controlled disagreement and the restoration of tolerance and affection" (1969:831). While some aspects of the youth culture may foster alienation from the adult world (including parents), this effect is limited, and adolescent peer groups perform the useful function of smoothing the transition from childhood to adulthood.

There are times, we think, when the youth culture encourages activities which parents see as countercultural—frontal attacks on deeply held adult values and norms. Such times were frequent in the sixties and early seventies. Active opposition to the Vietnam war and the widespread use of drugs are cases in point. Such behavior also clashes with what may be a common view among parents, that children should play at being adults but should not seriously attack adult viewpoints, especially those on which adults themselves have guilt feelings. On balance, we suspect that conflict between generations is more superficial than has often been thought.

THE FAMILY AND SOCIAL CHANGE

It is hard to talk about the American family without also speaking of change. When we describe typical family relationships we are keenly aware that they have been evolving steadily for decades and continue to alter as they move toward still unknown shapes which may lie just a few years ahead.

To most sociologists, the main forces producing this rate of change are the economic and technological explosions that so swiftly made an agrarian into an industrial economy and a rural into an urban society. While the major institutions and systems of the society are all interdependent, the family has been overwhelmingly on the receiving end of changes starting elsewhere. Table 12-5 recapitulates some of the changes in the American family which, directly or indirectly, flow from the urban-industrial revolution.

Table 12-5 is far from complete, but if you read it thoughtfully, remembering that Americans have made these changes in a traditional system in a few short generations—while a host of changes were occurring in the rest of society at the same time—you will get some notion of how much has been going on. No wonder there are confusions, dilemmas, and conflicts in and about the contemporary family! No doubt countless individuals are paying a high price for the rapidity of change. With this perspective, one can see how wrong it is to think of family problems in terms of praise and blame, or as manifestations of personality only. Families today are pioneering in new family forms. When clarified and supported, as they may be some day by high levels of agreement, these forms may lead to a kind of family life in an in-

TABLE 12-5 FAMILY CHANGES DERIVING FROM THE URBAN-INDUSTRIAL REVOLUTION

	THEN	NOW
Family size	Many children, high infant mortality. Many relationships to maintain.	Few children, low infant mortality. Fewer relationships to maintain.
Authority	Husband-father authority supreme.	Husband-father authority declining in relation to wife and also children.
Work	Closely related to total family activity; a division of labor involving all family members, the results visible to all.	Husband-father works outside home. Wife-mother often does so too. Housekeeping less integrated into a family division of labor. Children have little or no "work."
Child-rearing	Father and mother fairly equal in child-rearing responsibilities. Child-rearing covered most of parents' lives.	Mother plays greater role than father. Child-rearing over sooner, leaving many women "jobless."
Role consensus	High consensus; roles clearly and compatibly defined.	Low consensus, roles often ambiguous or conflicting.
Role compatibility over family life cycle	High compatibility over family life cycle.	Lower compatibility; especially in empty nest stage of family, after children leave.
Durability of nuclear family	High durability (low divorce rate).	Low durability (high divorce rate).

dustrialized society which is more satisfactory than any we have ever known.

Families in America and in other highly industrialized societies may also be pioneering for many developing societies just starting along the path toward urban-industrial evolution. If the kind of family being forged in America today indeed reflects industrialization, as we think it does, then we may find solutions which can be adapted to other contexts.

In this connection, Goode comments (1964:108-9) that "in all parts of the world and for the first time in world history all social systems are moving fast or slowly toward some form of the conjugal family system and also toward industrialization. . . . With industrialization the traditional family systems—usually, extended or joint systems, with or without lineages or clans—are breaking down."[5] In other words, industrialization everywhere tends to produce a family system much like that we now have in this country. Goode points out that extended family systems, with their stress on kinship ties which permeate life, are not well adapted to industrial societies which need to award status on the basis of competence and achievement, not of kinship. Also, our kind of nuclear family is more mobile, both socially and geographically—another important advantage in an industrial society. Goode indicates that even the affectional function in our nuclear family is functional for industrialism, since the economic enterprise has no responsibility for the emotional input-output balance of the individual.

DIVORCE, A BAROMETER OF FAMILY CHANGE   How high is the divorce rate in the United States, and is it going up or down? Figure 12-2 answers both questions. There are many ways of computing the incidence of divorce, each with advantages and disadvantages. Here we record the number of divorces in a given year per thousand marriages existing in that year. The frequency of divorce in the United States is among the highest in Western countries, though most industrialized countries have shown great increases.

Examine Figure 12-2 with care. Note that during and after World Wars I and II, particularly the latter, the rate of increase was especially high. Also note the sharp but temporary decline during the economic depression of the thirties. When such short-run fluctuations are disregarded or averaged out, it is apparent that divorce has been increasing for a century. Since 1963, the last date in Figure 12-2, there have been further increases, and the final peak has probably not been reached.

This in itself is one kind of change in the family: it has become less stable. Each new nuclear family has a somewhat smaller chance of completing the family life cycle.

---

[5] The term *conjugal family system* may be taken as essentially equivalent to the kind of American system we have been describing.

A village family in India. What will happen to the family in agrarian developing countries as they become in some ways more like ours? Will their families also come to resemble ours?

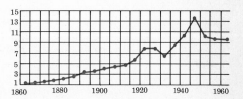

FIGURE 12-2   DIVORCE RATE PER 1,000 MARRIAGES IN THE UNITED STATES BETWEEN 1860 AND 1963 BY FIVE-YEAR INTERVALS

Unlike her ancestors when they were children, this modern urban child makes no economic contribution to her family. She consumes numerous goods and services, and that is her only economic function.

Figure 12-2 covers the era in which the United States became an industrialized country. The coincidence between industrialization and the rise in divorce is no accident. When economic production left the home it took with it a stabilizing influence on the family group. There is economic *consumption* in today's urban family, but this involves competing claims for satisfaction, not responsibilities in a common task. In yesterday's family, Johnny had his share of work regarded by all as economically essential. In today's family, the economic significance of Johnny's behavior is pretty well expressed in his demands for goods and services earned by his parents' incomes.

Also important is the rise in the employment of married women outside the home. This means that they are less dependent on the support of a male. A woman considering divorce need no longer fear a life of grinding poverty.

Family Stability and Emotional Bonds Practically all family sociologists agree that reduction in the economic function of the family has greatly increased emphasis on its affectional function. That is, the quality of the emotional bonds in a family has become much more important in judging the family's success. We have already noted that the urban family is more isolated from a larger kinship network than is true in many other societies and in our own past. The nuclear family is expected to stand on its own feet. It is also numerically smaller than a century ago. All these factors give heightened importance to the personal satisfactions given and received within the family circle. One marries for love, not for economic gain or family prestige. One judges marriage by its yield of happiness and personal fulfillment. One seeks in family relationships surcease from the competitive struggle outside. But under the stresses of modern life, happiness and personal satisfaction may be evanescent. The man and wife deliriously in love at marriage may feel little for each other a few years later. Judging marriage by how much pleasure it gives them, they may think it better to try again with another mate than to continue a marriage which seems from their view to have failed.

Social Meanings of Divorce A century ago even a very unhappy couple would have been reluctant to seek divorce, for it signaled a major personal failure and even considerable social disgrace. In many circles divorce was unthinkable. This view has not disappeared, but it has been drastically weakened. Marriage has become less a sacred bond contracted in God's presence for life, and more a human relationship—a very important one, to be sure, yet susceptible to some of the same secularized criteria for judgment as other social bonds. In other words, certain structural changes in society have led to changes in the personal and social meaning of divorce, and this in turn has tended to increase the actual incidence of divorce.

The marked increase in the frequency of divorce has led some observers to fear that the American family is in real danger. There have been a few sociologists in this group, among them Zimmerman (1949) and Moore (1958). The latter's position is particularly interesting because it uses sociological reasoning. Moore questions the effectiveness of the present-day family in performing even its residual functions, such as child-rearing and the fulfilling of affectional needs. While he does not predict what the family will become or what will replace it, he does feel that other arrangements would better fit current conditions. But he doubts that most people would accept them. Since he does not specify what these arrangements would be, it is hard to evaluate Moore's suggestions.

Those who fear or hope for the demise of the family as we know it have additional evidence in recent experiments in communal living. In many communes nuclear family units are dissolved in favor of a nonkin community which defines sex and parenthood in communal terms. These groups are highly visible because the alternatives they offer are so radical. But they include only a microscopic portion of the total population, and there is little reason to see them as the wave of the American future.

On balance, the evidence is not compelling that the American family is about to disintegrate. There is a big difference between the stability of a single family unit and the stability of the family system as a whole. The probability that any particular family unit will survive the entire family life cycle has lessened. But as Hunt puts it, the "wide use of divorce today is not a sign of a diminished desire to be married, but of an increased desire to be happily married" (1966:292).

On the whole, we are inclined to interpret present stresses in the family more as evidence that Americans are trying to adapt family life to the radically changed circumstances of industrialization and urbanization than as symptoms of decay and imminent downfall. We go along with Nye, who says that

there is little doubt that the institution of the family is here to stay, not because this basic unit of social structure is valuable per se, but because it is instrumental in maintaining life itself, in shaping the infant into the person, and in providing for the security and affectional needs of people of all ages (1967:241–48).

Family life is so personal and intimate that it may almost seem offensive to treat it in the detached, analytical manner of the sociologist. But there is another side. The ties of the family are often so deep and sometimes so painful that emotions get in the way of understanding. The perspective of the sociologist can help us to see more clearly into these very personal events, and perhaps, as a result, to be more effectively faithful to the values of family life which we most want to preserve and enhance.

While the trend is toward liberalized divorce laws in this country, many states still have strict laws. Hence, many (who can afford it) go to places like Juarez, Mexico, where easy, uncomplicated divorces are available.

THE UTILITY OF FAMILY SOCIOLOGY

Here are two examples of what we mean. One is a middle-aged student, recently widowed and experiencing great emotional trauma from her loss. She expressed a wish to examine some of the sociological literature on bereavement and subsequently insisted on writing a paper about her own experience, analyzing it from a sociological point of view. Later she confided that this work had eased her a great deal. How could this be? Certainly, she had not been given solace, in the religious sense. We submit that it helped her to be able, for a time, to detach herself from her personal loss, to step away from it and dispassionately examine the social and psychological processes involved. She put a little distance between her inner self and the event which caused her suffering. She could see her experience against the common human lot, as something we all must face, and could understand how society reacts to such experiences and channels our responses.

Or consider the common problem of sibling rivalry and jealousy. To the people most involved, it is too likely to be explained in terms of unfairness, unreasonableness, selfishness, and the like. Yet it has its roots in the nature of our family institution. Yinger (1959) makes these comments with special reference to the eldest child.

Our present family structures are ill-equipped to help him (the eldest child) struggle with the jealousy that almost inevitably hits him when a younger brother or sister arrives. Our democratic traditions even lead us to deny that it exists or to declare that it is the result of individual willfulness, deserving only censure. In fact, however, our small, child-centered families seem almost designed to create a problem of jealousy. The first child is not only much-loved but also the only loved. Then along comes a noisy competitor who manages to command a great deal of mother's time and even to be rewarded by attention for doing the very things that he, the older child, is now being punished for.

Recognizing some sources of this problem in the social structure of the family does not solve the problem. But it can aid indirectly by helping harassed parents to lower their emotional temperature and view the situation with more understanding and compassion. We suggest that there is genuine practical value to you in using the sociological point of view to examine relationships in your own family, especially when they are tense or hostile or puzzling.

Sociological findings on the family are also used in clinical fields such as social work and clinical psychology. The channels to such fields are not as good as they might be, but have been improving in recent years. A social worker whose client has a troubled marriage, we hold, is better able to help if he views that marriage not as a unique case, not only in terms of the psychodynamics involved, but also against the backdrop of what is happening to American families generally as they try to cope with a society in swift and confusing change.

Here is a perfect example of the kind of situation commented upon by Yinger—sibling rivalry. How can the sociological viewpoint help to lower the tension and the emotional temperature in relationships such as these?

Practicing the Sociological Perspective

Since most people live in the midst of family-related behavior, opportunities for practicing the sociological perspective should be easy to find. Here are a few suggestions.

On every campus mate selection is a major interest. Think of your campus as a sizable pool of people eligible to marry one another. Most of the people you see about you every day will ultimately pair off and marry. Question: what determines who marries whom?

Forget for a moment that these students are persons who act as they do for personal reasons. Think of them as units possessing characteristics in variable amounts which affect their potential for mutual attraction into a social bond called marriage. For example, some of the characteristics of the units which affect mutual attraction might be physical, psychological, or social skills. On your campus, what unit characteristics seem most important in making one unit attractive to another? When you have answered this question, pause to reflect that a unit characteristic which has high attractiveness on your campus may not work the same way in other settings. The reasons for this are largely social. For example, slenderness may be desirable in a woman in one place and time, while just the opposite may be true elsewhere.

These unit characteristics always become significant in a social situation predefined by formal and informal norms, and by local physical conditions which affect the access of units to one another. The general tendency in mate selection is toward homogamy. Your campus population is already quite homogamous, but there is still room for this tendency to operate locally. Do organizations on your campus tend to bring units together which are more like one another in one organization than another? Think about it. Does one's major field affect his access to units of the other sex? What about place of residence? Does living in one area make contact easy or hard? What informal social rules does a unit need to know and observe to attract others?

When you have answered these questions for your own locale, you will see that culture and social structure are very important in an experience which, at the time it is being lived, seems wholly personal. These things strongly influence whether a person will have a chance at marrying at all, and go a considerable way toward explaining why a particular man and woman finally choose one another.

Think about your own family of orientation, or, if married, your family of procreation. To what extent is it in touch with other kinfolk? Do such contacts have a ritual character, mostly living on the capital of earlier experiences? Or do members of your nuclear family share activities even today? If so, what kinds? Do you feel closer or less close to these kinfolk than to friends who are not related to you? Answers to such questions will help show how much your family is isolated from an extended network of kin.

Here are some questions about family roles and role-playing which may lead to new insights about your own family. Would you say that your father is the instrumental leader, seeing that the many tasks of the family group get done? Is your mother the expressive leader, concerned with the emotional aspects of family relationships, reassuring, soothing hurt feelings, reconciling members to one another? How is authority distributed between husband and wife? Don't just make an overall judgment, but ask yourself if each has more authority than the other in particular areas. What are these areas? What do they think is right in the distribution of authority? Do they agree? How do your father and mother feel about a wife's employment outside the home? What effect does (or did) this have on family relationships? Ask your parents what they know about women's liberation. Ask each (apart from the other) what they think of it, and ponder their replies.

Ask your parents separately to tell you about their philosophy of child-rearing and how it worked out in rearing you. How confident and clear-cut is each on this question? How much do they appear to agree or disagree? How much was and is there intergenerational conflict between you and your parents? In what areas does it appear to be sharpest? Try seriously to explain such conflict *without once referring to the character or personality of the parties*. Does going to college mean that you are upwardly mobile with respect to your family of orientation? If so, has this had any effect on your family relationships? Do you find it hard to be candid with your parents about your new experiences and ideas? Why?

In what stage of the family cycle is your family of orientation? Can you identify any shifts in the roles of members as the family moved from one stage to another? What do you think will happen to this family in the future? What role changes will occur? How aware of these are family members? Do you foresee specific problems? Think seriously about what life will be like for your father when he retires, and for your mother when the last child has finally left home.

These are suggestions, and may lead to others. We have designed them with your experience in mind. However, the answers you give from your own experience may become even more meaningful if you ask the same questions of a family with a different background. They will help you see social factors and forces at work despite personality differences.

Education

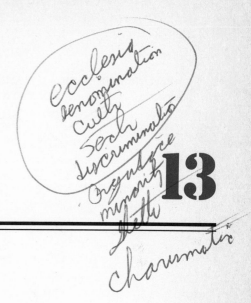

13

About ninety-five hundred infants are born in the United States every day. The stream of biological newcomers flows endlessly, confronting society with an overwhelmingly important task, for *not one of these babies knows anything at all.* Somehow they must be socialized. Otherwise these "untutored savages" would quickly overwhelm society and bring it to an end.

Since we have already devoted a chapter to socialization, it may seem redundant to add another on education. If the United States were a typical preliterate society this would be true. Educational tasks and functions are usually not organizationally differentiated in such societies. They are simply performed in a structural matrix (typically the kinship system) which is responsible for many other functions as well. In technically advanced societies, education is organizationally differentiated. It is one aspect—and a critically important one—of the total set of social arrangements whereby modern societies undertake to insure their social as well as biological continuation.

Here we shall restrict the term *education* to planned instructional programs. Even so, educational programs permeate almost every corner of modern societies, far beyond the role played by the public schools. In 1957, the President's Commission on Education Beyond the High School reported that there were as many students in business-sponsored educational programs as in all of the country's colleges and universities (1957:2). Government agencies also conduct a myriad of instructional programs. So do churches and many other organizations. And the mass media, quite apart from their entertainment function, are the source of much intentional educational material.[1] Here we shall restrict analysis to formal education in the usual sense, the primary and secondary school systems and the system of higher education.

THE FUNCTIONAL SIGNIFICANCE OF EDUCATION

As organizations, schools perform functions which serve the underlying values of the educational institution as a whole. In doing so they serve society, its smaller parts and its individual members. Our interest here is in education's overriding master functions. Like all social systems, schools frequently perform many subsidiary functions. So the kindergarten may play a baby-sitting function for Mrs. Johnson, making it easier for her to do her shopping than it was the year before. This, however, is not the level of importance at which our discussion aims.

FUNCTIONS EDUCATION PERFORMS FOR SOCIETY In Western society, education as a separate institutional complex emerged gradually. For a long time, its growth was closely tied to developments in the religious institution. The need for trained priests, for example, played a major role in the development of the medieval universities. Later, the Protestant emphasis on man's need to face God directly was in large part responsible for the emphasis on teaching everyone to read so that they could read the Bible.

The schools and universities developed over many centuries were the foundation for the extraordinary educational development brought about by the industrial revolution. The Protestant stimulus to literacy was strengthened by industry's need for literate workers. Industry depends on education more than on any other source for the manpower to conduct its research and development. Machlup (1962:159–61) indicates that the number of scientists and engineers employed in research and development in the United States increased from seven to ten thousand in 1920 to four hundred twenty-five thousand in 1962. An expanding industrial economy demands a growing supply of highly trained talents, and at the same time raises the minimum level of the talent it can effectively use.

The importance of education in industrialized countries is heightened in the many societies around the world which are seeking rapid modernization. If these countries are to have any chance at all of achieving the goals they set for themselves, they must depend heavily upon mass education of a kind they have

---

[1] In March 1970 President Nixon's message to Congress on educational reform asserted that the average high school graduate has spent eleven thousand hours in school classrooms and fifteen thousand hours watching television! It goes without saying that only a tiny portion of all this TV watching has had anything to do with education as we are treating it here. But viewed broadly, it does form part of the content of socialization.

never had in the past. This chapter could easily be devoted to an account of how education has rapidly attained unprecedented importance in the twentieth century. Political leaders today know that the stature and the fate of their countries are closely tied to the ability of the educational institution to produce enough educated people.

Two broad functions of education are the preservation of existing culture and the development of new knowledge.

The Preservation and Transmission of Culture Insofar as socialization is successful in each generation, *culture is preserved by transmission through a learning process.* In societies such as ours, the schools have grown steadily in importance, both absolutely and in relation to other socializing agents, because of the volume, the diversity, and the technical complexity of the culture

COPYRIGHT © 1958 JULES FEIFFER

America was chagrined at the fact that the first successful spacecraft, Sputnik, was produced by Russia. Many felt that American education had failed the nation in its competition with Russia for power and prestige.

The volume of culture is now so immense that the human brain cannot contain it all. Increasing amounts must be stored in books and journals and in libraries of computer tapes.

that must be transmitted. The size of the job has far outstripped the informal educational resources available in the family. And culture is far too massive to be communicated as a whole to any single individual, no matter how much training he has had. Hence an elaborate formal educational system is required which (a) gives common and essential *core* training to everyone, and (b) provides *specialized* training to smaller numbers.

Some clue to the growing importance of the schools is given by such facts as these: around 1900 the average American received only an elementary school education; now at least 80 percent of the population completes high school. At the turn of the century, only a small minority attended college. Now, about 55 percent of all high school graduates at least enter college (Figure 13-1).

Schools are responsible for transmitting knowledge, skills, and values. In all three of these areas of socialization content there is a distinction between core and specialized material. Core content is the particular responsibility of the elementary schools and, to a lesser extent, the high schools. In a way, the curricula of elementary schools define what society at a particular time views as the essential minimum of knowledge, skills, and values needed by all, so vital that their transmission must be entrusted to a formal socializing agency. Given the high proportion of the population which now graduates from high school, the same statement applies to high school curricula, though elements of specialization do appear. The elementary schools are intended to make everyone technically literate, able to use simple arithmetic, write, and use English with some approximation of good usage. Beyond that they are expected to make every citizen aware of fundamental facts about the human body, the physical world, and society. Still more, they are expected to instill value-related attitudes of loyalty to the United States, good citizenship, moral behavior, and even such subtle things as belief in the work ethic.

Higher on the educational ladder, the transmission of culture changes in two ways: it is offered to only part of the population, and its content becomes more specialized. It becomes less concerned with the transmission of basic values of the general culture and more focused on specialized knowledge and skills (Clark, 1964:745). This trend reaches its peak in the professional and graduate schools where knowledge and skills become highly differentiated and compartmentalized and the values transmitted are those of specialized disciplinary or occupational subcultures. But even at the most advanced levels education is at work in the preservation of culture.

Development of New Knowledge In many societies the development of new knowledge is not institutionalized at all. In modern industrialized countries there is a constant interaction between science and industrial technology. Science continues to grow by its very nature (see Chapter 15), and its growth constantly produces new technological applications. The rising standard of living in industrial countries provides another impetus to technological change.

Quite apart from this relation between science and technology, Western education at its higher levels inherits a long tradition of scholarship and search for new knowledge regardless of immediate practical applications. It is the institutional and organizational setting of greatest importance for science, and the traditional home of scholarship in all fields of learning.

Compared to the total population and even to the total teaching force in the schools, the number of creative scholars on university faculties is very small. But like the yeast in a batch of bread, the importance of these creators is out of all proportion to their numbers. Not only do they play a critical role in the explosion of knowledge taking place in our time, but they are also the key socializing agents in the training of their own replacements. Travel on the frontiers of knowledge requires long and arduous training. More and more people with such training are needed. In the last half century, the number of engineers in the United States has increased at a rate of five times that of the general population, and the number of scientists by ten times (Wolfle, 1954). The universities play the chief role in maintaining the flow of new knowledge and in training new recruits to keep the process going.

FUNCTIONS EDUCATION PERFORMS FOR THE INDIVIDUAL   There are about twenty-three thousand different occupations in the United States (*Dictionary of Occupational Titles*, 1965). The problem of rationally choosing one's own occupation from such a fantastic variety is overwhelming. It is doubtful whether most people could name even 1 or 2 percent of the possibilities.

If everyone really had to face such a bewildering set of choices without organized intervention and assistance the result would be chaos. The truth is that here, as in all the major decisions in life, society is ready with a set of organized influences which guide the individual even when he is not aware of it. (See the discussion of career choice in Chapter 8.) We like to think we make our own occupational choices just as we like to think we choose our own spouses. There is much truth in the view that choice is personal. But while it may seem to be free, that choice is channeled by a number of social influences, among which the schools play a leading role.

The schools make the individual aware of some choices and keep him ignorant of others. Simply by going to college, one will have opened to him a large number of desirable occupations he might scarcely have known existed. Through counseling and guidance programs the schools help the student find a suitable match between his interests and talents and the available possibilities. Finally, the schools train the individual in knowledge and skills needed to enter many occupations, and they even help in finding jobs. In the United States, formal education has become the best

Total high-school graduates: 1,221,000

1940

Those who went on to college: 418,000

Total high-school graduates: 2,688,000

1965

Those who went on to college: 1,442,000

FIGURE 13-1   NUMBER OF HIGH-SCHOOL GRADUATES IN THE UNITED STATES GOING ON TO COLLEGE, 1940–1965

[Source: *The New York Times,* March 20, 1966, p. E13. © 1966 by The New York Times Company. Reprinted by permission.]

and largest way individuals can reach a social status higher than they were born to. The schools maintain or improve status for large numbers of people.

Influence on Style of Life But the importance of education to the individual goes beyond such functions. Amount and kind of education play an important part in opening or closing doors to differing lifestyles, and in understanding and appreciating cultural values of many kinds. One's tastes in music, art, literature, and drama, one's social, political and religious ideas and ideals may be significantly shaped by educational background. So too may be the choice of a spouse, of friends, and of organizations in which time is willingly spent.

VALUES UNDERLYING AMERICAN EDUCATION

If we know the major values of important social institutions such as family, religion, or education, we are in touch with what people regard as the source and justification of many of the norms found in organizations associated with the institution. And the same goes for many of the attitudes and much of the behavior of individuals. Such major institutional values tend to last for long periods. They are more resistant to change than actual organizational practices. Furthermore, essentially the same values can be served by quite different educational procedures.

Up to a point, the expansion of the educational system in the United States can be understood as a consequence of an industrial society's manpower needs. But there is more to the matter. In most other highly industrialized countries, the average young person receives much less formal education than in the United States. Mack (1968:54) indicates that in 1959, 65 percent of young people in the United States had completed secondary school, while in France 11 percent, in the United Kingdom 7 percent and in Italy slightly under 7 percent had done so. A far higher proportion attend college in the United States than in any other nation.

We suggest that at least some of the difference in average educational attainment between the United States and other industrial nations is due to the special nature of American values on education, values deeply embedded in our culture. On balance, these values strongly favor education. The astonishing growth of educational organization largely reflects our putting these values more and more into practice. They have given American schools some of their special characteristics and special problems. What are some of these values?[2]

Education in the fine arts can broaden the student's perspective by acquainting him with other peoples and cultures. This enrichment can, in turn, affect one's style of life.

---

[2] Our list of values (though not their treatment) is similar to one offered by Williams (1970:319).

FAITH IN EDUCATION Overwhelmingly, Americans believe, with various qualifications, that education is a good thing. This faith has existed for a long time. It seems to be based on a perception that education is necessary for a democratic society, and that it is a powerful aid to the individual in the pursuit of his personal goals. Our belief in the potency of education for both collective and individual ends has fueled the dramatic expansion of both public and private schools. Each year Americans spend huge sums to finance schools. In 1972 it was $86 billion, 8.2 percent of the gross national product (*Statistical Abstract of the United States*). Parents and young people alike make painful sacrifices to get that high school diploma or college degree.

Yet there is much ambivalence in the American view. For generations there has been a vein of anti-intellectualism in our society, a suspicion of the highly educated man, a feeling that too much education renders a person impractical in dealing with the real problems of life (Hofstadter, 1963). One small clue to other manifestations of this attitude is the word *academic* used as an epithet. How many times have you heard people dismiss an idea as academic—that is, unrealistic or impractical?

The roots of anti-intellectualism in America go back to the rise of the Jacksonian, democratic, common man in the early nineteenth century and beyond that to still earlier developments in England, including the seventeenth-century development of Puritanism. The antiaristocratic elements in Jacksonian democracy became linked with anti-intellectualism. The fact that most Americans in the early nineteenth century were very poorly educated helped this fusion of the two notions. The social and political activism of college students in the late sixties and early seventies was like a hair trigger which suddenly released all these vague but strong animosities.

How can a people so devoted to the idea of education also entertain so much suspicion and even outright hostility toward educational activities? The apparent inconsistency is lessened when we realize that the greatest agreement on the goodness of education is found when the meaning of the word *education* is least specifically defined, which is to say, *when the value is expressed most indefinitely*. Almost everyone agrees that some kind of education is a good thing. But when the general value is, as it must be, translated into concrete educational programs, all the cultural diversity of the American people, and all the indigenous value conflict, comes to a focus, and sharp disagreements are visible at once.

Education is good, yes. But should there be religious instruction in the schools? Should high school students learn facts about communism? What kind of sex instruction, if any, should the schools undertake? Should schools be permitted to raise critical questions about American life? And so on, and on. On scores of

Developing countries that wish to become industrialized (and most do) must, it appears, develop educational systems patterned at least in part on Western models.

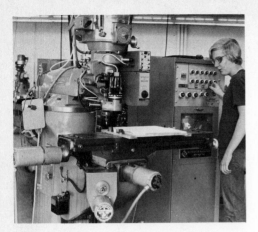

The construction of new vocational schools and the sophisticated equipment with which they are provided are evidence of the value placed on highly practical training in American education.

issues that arise when any concrete educational program is undertaken, Americans find their faith in education in general sorely tried.

BELIEF IN PRACTICAL EDUCATION   Americans are pragmatic and practical-minded. Not many understand, let alone approve, such concepts as a search for knowledge or truth for its own sake, or the notion that education may be an end in itself, simply making life more interesting and worthwhile than otherwise. Education, in their view, should do something specific and observable for the individual: make him a better citizen, perhaps enable him to get a better job, earn a higher income, live in a better neighborhood, and improve his social status. Tyler and Miller have stated (1965:117) that

as many students say they go to college in order to develop vocational skills as say they want a basic education. This corresponds to a national survey of adults; two-thirds said they wanted their sons to go to college mostly in order to get better jobs. Only 15 percent most wanted knowledge for their children; 20 percent wanted their children to get a broader view of the world.

Vocational emphasis runs like a strong thread through American education. Most citizens find it much easier to understand why a new program is needed to provide trained workers for a local industry than they do to grasp the need for an expansion of offerings in the humanities or the sciences. It may be easier to equip an expensive new shop in a high school than to do the equivalent for the music program at much less cost. We do not mean to suggest that the actual educational programs in America reflect only this pragmatic emphasis, but its influence is strongly apparent.

SUCCESS THROUGH COMPETITION   Think back over the endless classroom situations in which you have been directly or implicitly urged to strive—for what? For knowledge? For understanding? Or for high grades? You may remember times when your parents were anxious about your work in school. What reassured them most? Evidence of growth in knowledge and understanding? Or grades which showed them you were doing all right in the competitive struggle? This competitive meaning of grades is present even in classes where students are not actually in competition with each other but striving to meet the instructor's standards of performance so that a top grade comes from meeting those standards, not just from beating out other students. The emphasis is on being ahead of others, not on acquiring knowledge.

But grades are not the most important goals for which students compete. Coleman (1961) in an important study of the effects of school climate on high school education shows that competition for goals more important to students also implies devaluation of the content and objectives of education.

Coleman's research shows that student values downgrade educational objectives. Think back on your own schooling. Does it support the analysis on these pages? If not, how did your experience differ?

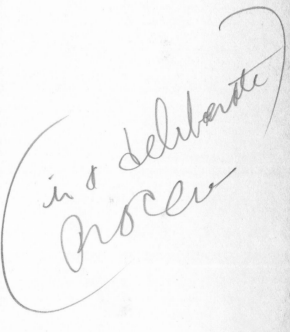

As has been evident throughout this research, the variation among schools in the status of scholastic achievement is not nearly so striking as the fact that in all of them, academic achievement did not "count" for as much as did other activities in the school. Many other attributes were more important. In every school the boys named as best athletes and those named as most popular with the girls were far more often mentioned as members of the leading crowd, and as someone to "be like" than were the boys named as best students. And the girls who were named as best dressed, and those named as most popular with boys, were in every school far more often mentioned as being in the leading crowd and as someone to be like, than were the girls named as best students.

The relative unimportance of academic achievement . . . suggests that the adolescent subcultures in these schools exert a rather strong deterrent to academic achievement (1961:265).

The Role of Peer Groups As we pointed out in discussing the family, groups of age peers are extremely important in the lives of American adolescents. Coleman shows how these powerful groups *typically downgrade the pursuit of knowledge* in favor of other goals. We suspect that in many colleges similar conditions exist, though perhaps in modified ways and to a lesser degree. Placing low status on academic goals is hardly countercultural. We have pointed out that parents too see education as a means to pragmatic ends, mainly a good job.

Given this matrix of conditions, why do students go to high school at all, and why do they compete for grades? They go to school because they must, for one reason. Remember our first value theme: *education is good,* so good that children are required by law to go through secondary school in most parts of the country.

Collective striving for a common goal is not altogether absent in American schools, especially in sports and other group activities. But competitive striving between individuals lies close to the heart of the system as it actually operates.

POSITIVE VALUE OF CONFORMITY IN EDUCATION In an educational institution that stresses individual striving for success it may seem paradoxical that there is also much emphasis on conformity to norms. The paradox disappears when we see that the object that one is supposed to strive for competitively is the goals set by the educational establishment. A student who accepts or appears to accept these goals, and successfully uses the competitive method to achieve them, is conforming.

More specifically, students confront a school atmosphere which encourages them to keep their heads down, keep an eye out for innumerable rules, and look elsewhere for joyful and spontaneous experiences. Silberman (1970), a strong critic of overemphasis on conformity in the schools, has this to say:

It is not possible to spend any prolonged period visiting public-school classrooms without being appalled by the mutilation visible everywhere— mutilation of spontaneity, of joy in learning, of pleasure in creating, of sense of self. The public schools . . . are the kind of institutions one cannot really dislike until one gets to know them well. Because adults take the schools so much for granted, they fail to appreciate what grim, joyless places most American schools are, how oppressive and petty are the rules by which they are governed, how intellectually sterile and esthetically barren the atmosphere (1970:10).

Even a hint that students and some teachers may be questioning the value of conformity is deeply disturbing to many members of the larger community. There are exceptions, but most Americans are uncomfortable at the idea that the schools may question established values and procedures. Students are in school to be *taught* things, useful things at that, not to go on voyages of exploration with unknown destinations!

DEMOCRACY AND EQUALITY OF OPPORTUNITY For decades, American schools have consistently taught democratic values in the classroom, and to a lesser extent, have carried on practices that serve democratic values. The country long ago abandoned an elitist concept of education; schools are for everyone. Teachers are not supposed to show preference for students from advantaged homes. They are officially expected to make every effort to develop the potential of each child seen as an individual, not as a representative of a class. Student organizations are encouraged to admit members on the basis of individual interest and to conduct themselves according to democratic procedures. Secret and exclusive organizations are for the most part regarded without enthusiasm.

To say that a preference for democracy and equality of opportunity is a valid and important value theme in American education is not to argue that the value is always effectively realized. Despite the relative informality of teacher-student relationships by European standards, there is more than a tinge of authoritarianism in most American schools. And anyone who has paid any attention to the struggles of black American and other minority groups for integration and equality in education must realize that the goal of true, equal opportunity has not been reached.

The landmark study of educational opportunity by Coleman et al. (1966) shows in abundant and meticulous detail how far America still falls short of equal educational opportunity. With cruel and factual clarity the study shows how much the quality of the learning environment differs with the student population served. Where the students are predominantly black, the quality is lower.

Most discouraging is that the nonschool influences on black children—classmates, home, and neighborhood—are not conducive to achievement in school, yet these children are the ones who attend the poorer schools, making a vicious circle into a downward spiral. For a more detailed discussion of this subject, see Chapter 7. One of the authors of this study (Campbell) has put the problem this way (1969:846):

Those whose nonschool environments are least equipped to provide or support meaningful educational experiences are placed in schools that provide the least stimulating interpersonal environments for learning, whereas those whose home environments most typically provide knowledge and encourage curiosity attend schools that provide interpersonal environments more appropriate to educational tasks. It should be clear that race is merely illustrative of the point; we would make the same observations if we ignored race altogether and compared classmates in suburban with those in inner city schools, or classmates in wealthy urban communities with those in rural Appalachia.

Despite these sober facts, easy cynicism toward democracy and equal opportunity is not appropriate. Such recent progress as there has been would not have been possible except that this yet unrealized value is sincerely held important by most of our people.

Those whose personal background provide the least encouragement for educational achievement are likely also to attend schools offering the poorest, least challenging learning environments.

POSITIVE VALUE OF PATRIOTISM   Indirectly, schools help integrate society by preparing children to take their places in a highly differentiated social structure. Explicit emphasis on patriotic values and attitudes is a more direct contribution to the integration of society which most Americans expect the schools to make.

By and large the schools have acted in a way consistent with this value, and your own experience probably bears this out. In recent years, more sympathy to other societies has been shown below the college level, but the student is never left in doubt as to which society is best and which deserves his loyalty.

The United States is far from alone in this patriotic emphasis. In one way or another we find much the same nationalistic theme in most modern societies. Schools make a significant contribution to the political nationalism that is one of the marks of our time.

ORGANIZATIONAL ASPECTS OF AMERICAN EDUCATION

As our guiding values took shape in the schools, the educational system, once small and simple, grew to be huge and bewilderingly complex, as the figures in Table 13-1 suggest. Yet while these figures are large, they are not complete, for there are also unknown numbers of nursery schools, academically marginal colleges of many types, and technical institutes and semiprofessional schools which train students for particular occupations but do not award diplomas comparable to ordinary college degrees.

All these types of schools, the persons who teach in them and administer them, and the people who attend them, are organized into many associations based on common interests. There are dozens of associations representing teachers in various fields, college deans, college admissions officers, administrators of school finances, and so on. In 1971, 1,755 such national associations flourished, not to mention larger numbers of regional and local ones.

Teaching is by far the largest professional occupation in the United States. In 1970, education's work force included 2,287,000 teachers in elementary and secondary schools and 559,000 in higher education (*Statistical Abstract of the United States*). Not far short of 30 percent of the entire population is in attendance at some kind of school. The actual number in 1970 was 59,628,000. Of these, 7,484,000 were attending college in that year.

It is no simple matter to make sense out of the diversity and frequent contradictions of the educational landscape. We must content ourselves with identifying several outstanding characteristics. These apply particularly to the public schools of the country, which enroll about 85 percent of our students.

LOCAL CONTROL   Public education in the United States, in contrast with many European countries, has very strong community control. This condition was foreseen by the Constitution, which did not give the federal government the power to control educa-

TABLE 13-1· UNITED STATES PUBLIC AND PRIVATE SCHOOLS, BY LEVEL; 1970

TYPE OF SCHOOL	NUMBER OF SCHOOLS
Public (total)	94,043
Combined elementary & secondary	2,310
Elementary	66,672
Secondary (includes junior highs)	23,972
Higher education	1,089
Private (total)	21,413
Elementary	15,340
Secondary (includes junior highs)	4,606
Higher education	1,467

Source: *Statistical Abstract of the United States*, 1973, p. 104.

Although American educational values have remained essentially the same, they have been given new and increasingly complex organizational expression with the passing years.

tion. The matter was left to the states, which have long been inclined to pass on most of their powers in this area to local communities, except in the area of higher education.

Recently, states have taken greater part in primary and secondary education, both in setting minimum standards and in direct financial participation. A powerful force in this direction is the growing demand for educational equality. In cost alone, differences in the tax bases of communities make it virtually impossible to have equal education without support from a larger territory.

Federal involvement in the financing of education has also been growing, and increased from $1.5 billion in 1955 to $12 billion in 1972 (*Statistical Abstract of the United States*). While even this huge sum was only 11.3 percent of total school expenditures, it had become vital to the continuation of many local programs, particularly in higher education and especially in the universities. Federal money has built and equipped buildings and laboratories, supported faculty, underwritten loans and grants to students, supported research programs in dozens of fields, and become essential to present levels of professional training, perhaps especially in medicine. The growing influx of federal dollars has come about with a careful regard to the powers of local school authorities. These funds do not have to be sought for or accepted, and most of the details of expenditure are left firmly in local hands.

Despite the growing financial presence of the federal government, and the increasing financial and standard-setting activities of state departments of education, American public schools are still largely controlled by local school boards made up of lay members often but not always elected by voters in local school districts. Since there are more than twenty-three thousand local school districts in the country it is at least a little surprising that there is any unity at all in public school programs.

In spite of the firmness of local control, school programs around the country are enough alike so that up to a point one really can speak of a national system of public education. It is not national in the sense of centralized control of policy, but in the rough similarity of programs, of graded levels, and of teaching methods. A high school junior in one part of the country can usually transfer to the same level in another part of the country without serious disruption of his progress through the system. For that matter, a similar transfer from a public to a private school, or vice versa, is also feasible in most cases. And Sirjamaki (1967:52–53) indicates that the subject matter taught in Catholic schools (the largest religiously controlled system of schools in the country) is very similar to that in the public schools.

The Sources of Similarity   One basis of the similarity in public school programs is the broad agreement on basic institutional values which we mentioned earlier. Another is the need throughout society for particular kinds of training. A school system which focused training on local community needs would not only fail to do its job from a national point of view, but would also—in a society where individuals move about a great deal—severely handicap its children. A third force making for similarity is the existence of an educational labor force aware that it transcends local boundaries. Schoolteachers and administrators are employed locally, but unlike local school board members, they can operate in a much larger labor market than any local community affords, and are much aware of interests shared with counterparts across the country. Through professional organizations, meetings, and publications, ideas quickly spread across the land. Finally, there are nationwide testing programs for college entrance, for admission to graduate and professional schools, and for other ends, and there are state and regional accrediting associations for schools at all levels. These too are important pressures toward uniformity. A college student who has tried to transfer credit from a nonaccredited to an accredited college will understand the point.

Diversity in School Programs   But it would be misleading to talk about similarity in public school education in the United States without also pointing out the equally pervasive diversity. Local control and financing create considerable diversity in the quality of programs. For instance, in 1972 expenditures per public school pupil ranged from $1,466 a year in New York to $543 in Alabama (*Statistical Abstract of the United States*). Such differences unquestionably produce variations in the quality of instruction. And there are also sizable differences within states and even within communities.

   Local control results in many variations in program content. Especially in metropolitan communities, these often reflect the influence of class, ethnic, and racial considerations (Coleman et al., 1966). The American high school, at least in theory, offers pretty much the same kind of education everywhere. In a small town the theory may be pretty well realized, since every child attends the same school. But not so in the cities, which have many high schools. As Clark indicates (1964:751), "Neighborhood of origin, an ascriptive factor for the individual, weighs ever more heavily in the educational process, wherever the internal differentiation of the metropolitan area—the slums from the suburbs—outruns the efforts of school systems to provide equal opportunity for students unequal in social origins." In other words, the actual program of the high school differs in both obvious and subtle ways between suburbs, where perhaps 85 percent of students will enter college, and the central city, where a large proportion of students will not even finish high school.

Problems of a National System Without National Control Education in the United States, like the federal government and large business, is in some ways a single social system. But unlike government and business, education has no centralized planning and control. Yet the schools are not isolated from the rest of society, and we think it likely that there will be increasing public control over some operations in the schools where it has been rare in the past.

One force pushing in this direction is the rapid rise in the cost of education. Between 1950 and 1968 the operating budget for public elementary and secondary schools increased by five and a half times. A public backlash against these rising expenditures became a serious force early in the seventies. Today, a large proportion of the public and private colleges and universities are having major financial troubles. In a December 1970 press release on its forthcoming study, the Carnegie Commission on Higher Education stated that the financial crisis in higher education "is unmatched in any previous period of history."

This financial pressure is likely to lead to more political control over education, and to more serious attempts within education for a better match between ends and means. Inherent in this situation is the real danger that legislators and other elected officials will exert undue influence on the content of education. There has always been a precarious compromise between educational autonomy and political control of the schools. The interface between the political and educational institutions will undoubtedly continue to produce much social friction.

THE BUREAUCRATIZATION OF EDUCATION Most local school systems are now large. Even in thinly populated areas the consolidation of school districts has brought this about. A steady increase in the specialization of educational tasks has come with size so that educational organization has become increasingly bureaucratic, reflecting a tendency dominant in business, government, and other sectors of society. This trend was discussed in Chapter 9.

Bureaucracy in the Lower Schools Curiously, bureaucracy has developed in somewhat different ways in elementary and secondary education than in higher education. In the former, authority within the school system travels from top to bottom, down a single

These headlines indicate something of the potential for conflict that can arise between a state university and the state legislature that provides financial support for the university. Restraints and controls could have more serious consequences than attempts at social control, however, especially in the areas of subject matter and the hiring of staff.

hierarchy. The school superintendent, responsible to a lay board, is at the top. Everyone below him has a fairly clear responsibility and clearly defined tasks. Through the superintendent, the system is unusually vulnerable to outside control (Clark, 1964:760–61; Callahan, 1962). Contrast his position to that of the president of a good-sized corporation, who is responsible to the board of directors and the stockholders. In contrast, the superintendent receives pressure from many different and often conflicting interest groups in the community, all of whom feel that they should have a voice in determining school programs.

This vulnerability encourages a play-it-safe, protective attitude through ever greater reliance upon standardized, impersonal rules and regulations, standardized course content, and vigilant maintenance of tight administrative control. Considerations of administrative efficiency come to loom large in the determination of school programs, and *the making of policies which affect the child is moved further and further away from the child.*

Bureaucracy in Higher Education The rapid growth in size, cost, and specialization which bureaucratized primary and secondary education has worked differently in the colleges, especially the universities. It is in universities that the commitment to the expansion of knowledge is mainly located. Workers at the frontiers of knowledge in dozens of fields must have considerable autonomy in the direction of their work. Officials whose main expertise is administrative are not in the best position to exercise detailed supervision. "At the same time, the differentiation and proliferation deepens the need for administrative coordination, and so the campus moves toward some bureaucratic arrangements. The modern campus is too large and complicated for col-

In a society where it is increasingly true that only the social organization of power can protect legitimate interests, teachers are becoming more militant in organizing to protect themselves in relations with employers and the public.

Part 3 / Social Institutions

legial (faculty) direction to provide the overall coordination, and this task is performed largely by bureaucracy. But bureaucracy cannot provide or adequately protect the exercise of judgment by diverse experts, and this task is performed largely by a federated professionalism" (Clark, 1964:760).

The authority of the faculty in college governance has a long history, going back to the medieval universities of Europe. This tradition has eroded somewhat under the impact of bureaucratizing forces in higher education, a fact which worries more professors than administrators! Thus bureaucracy represents an uneasy truce between a simple hierarchical chain of command and anti-bureaucratic forces to which students have recently added their weight. Sometimes the truce breaks down and there is open conflict. While the system is not free from outside community pressures, it is freer than elementary and secondary schools.

ELEMENTARY AND SECONDARY TEACHERS Women comprise just under 70 percent of all teachers in elementary and secondary schools (*Statistical Abstract of the United States*): about 85 percent of elementary and about half of secondary school teachers. In higher education only about 20 percent are women. Below the college level, the sex ratio has contributed directly and indirectly to the high turnover and comparative instability of the teaching force.

Years ago, Charters (1956) studied a decade of graduates from the University of Illinois. He found that out of those graduated with teaching qualifications, *40 percent never accepted teaching jobs,* and of every one thousand qualified to teach, only one hundred fifty were employed five years after graduation. Women have shown a high "in-and-out" pattern. Men, partly because of the relatively low pay in the field, gravitate to high-paid administrative positions. Needless to say, this is a wasteful situation.

For many years this instability seriously retarded the professionalization of the field. (See the analysis of professions in Chapter 8.) While it still exists, compared to some other professions, the last ten or fifteen years have seen a sharp growth in autonomy of one kind in the profession: teachers have become active and even militant in dealing with their employers. This has occurred mainly through the National Educational Association, long in the field but scarcely militant in representing teachers since it also includes administrators among its members, and more recently through the American Federation of Teachers, which is affiliated with the AFL-CIO. The AFT supports the use of strikes, which have become increasingly common in large cities. While these two organizations are very different in philosophy and preferred tactics, it is likely that their competition for teacher loyalty will increase the organizational aggressiveness of teachers.

The old stereotype of the teacher as a maiden lady working in the same (or nearby) small town in which she grew up, who knows the parents of her pupils, is sometimes invited for Sunday dinner but mostly lives in genteel obscurity and poverty, is long out of date. At least in large communities, teachers are increasingly drawn from the working class and varied ethnic groups as well as from the traditional middle class. Their lives are more and more isolated from those of the families in which their pupils live. If their personal values and backgrounds are similar to those of their students, teachers may experience little conflict in their jobs. But often in today's large cities, the teacher finds it hard to understand and to reach pupils whose whole lives outside the classroom are foreign and unknown. The failure of many teachers to be fully and comfortably accepted into their local communities and neighborhoods strengthens reliance on professional associations.

THE CLIENTELE—MASS EDUCATION AND ITS PROBLEMS The United States undertook a massive social experiment of momentous consequence when long ago it embarked on a program of free public education for all. This was especially true when the concept was extended to include the full high school program. The country has not yet decided between a public college education for all who are qualified, or for all who want it whether they are qualified or not. The first alternative is already rather well established. Beyond this, most states and many cities are striving to provide some higher education for all who meet minimum qualifications, often not very high.

The Open Door College The value of any ability test at all has recently been challenged. It has been argued forcefully that underprivileged groups have not had a fair opportunity to qualify for college admission, and that this fact should be considered. In theory, at least, the idea of *open door* colleges is not new. They have long existed in many states, and Ohio, Kansas, Montana, and Wyoming legally require that all high school graduates may be admitted to state colleges.

In practice, however, such colleges have not always been as open as they may seem. Sometimes poorly qualified applicants are notified that their chances of success are poor—hardly an inducement to try. Typically one-third or more of freshmen, particularly those "unqualified," simply drop out of school with little effort to overcome their handicaps. But recently, in spite of swollen enrollments, some public and private colleges have begun to feel that they should try seriously to serve students who are not good risks. In the sixties, many schools began to admit students who could not meet admission standards and came from underprivileged backgrounds. One of the most massive and thorough of these experiments began in the fall of 1970, when the City University of New York instituted an all-out open admissions policy.

Even the Great Hall at City University of New York was partitioned to provide space for the remedial sessions the university felt were essential to the success of their open admissions policy, which was launched in September 1970.

College for All

For all the current rhetoric about equal educational opportunity, the United States has yet to decide the question of whether every young man and woman who wants a college education ought to have one. But last week, New York City put the issue to its sternest test to date: the huge tuition-free City University of New York (95,000 full-time students) began the academic year under an "open admissions" policy that guarantees a college place to every city high-school graduate regardless of his academic record or the quality of his previous education.

The remedial and counseling programs will be crucial because many of the students benefiting from open admissions are Negro and Puerto Rican ghetto youngsters whose elementary and secondary preparation ranged from the barely adequate to the totally inadequate. In fact, a university study made last spring indicated that as many as one-third of all entering freshmen would need catch-up work in reading and mathematics to raise them to the level that is considered minimum for college study. Furthermore, the whole idea of college is so alien to some of these students that they will have trouble at first coping with such rudimentary challenges as registration and flexible class hours.

Each of the university's nine four-year and seven two-year colleges has made special preparations for its new students. Hunter College will staff a student center with tutors around the clock and pair older and younger students on a "buddy" system. City College has doubled its staff in psychology counseling and will operate a workshop to help students with writing problems. Lehman College will allow students to start with the courses that interest them most.

City University authorities believe that the course they have embarked upon is both essential and workable. . . . Says deputy chancellor Seymour Hyman, "Open admissions is a reflection of a revolution in our society which demands a college degree and is sensitive to the survival in school of those trying to earn it."

Since 1966 (the University) has operated a program called SEEK (Search for Education, Elevation and Knowledge) to recruit and provide compensatory education for students from families below the poverty level. "What SEEK has proved," says vice chancellor Timothy Healy, "is that some 50 percent of disadvantaged students could master college—and some do brilliantly." Healy believes that the key to the success of open admissions is the increasingly accepted theory that college need not be a four-year program. "As long as you can expand the time-sequence," he insists, "you can hold your standards. While getting in may be easier, getting out will be just as hard."

Most students and faculty have accepted open admissions, if not with enthusiasm at least with equanimity. "There is not as much gut hostility as there was earlier," says City College English professor Jerome Brooks. "I believe people are cooperating. We have no alternative. If you dump that many students back on the streets, you'll have an untenable situation." In short, CUNY's pioneering effort has raised expectations so high that it cannot be allowed to fail.

Source: Condensed from *Newsweek,* September 28, 1970, pp. 85–86. Copyright Newsweek, Inc. 1970, reprinted by permission.

PROFESSORS Assuming that you are attending a four-year college or a university, consider the professors you know on your own campus. What are their professional roles like, and how do professional roles differ in these two broad types of schools?

The four-year college is typically much smaller than the university and its student body consists entirely of undergraduates. Both characteristics have major implications for the professor. Small size makes it physically possible for him to know many students well. Often students will visit in the professor's home, and he will attend many student activities. He is expected to devote a good deal of time to students, outside as well as in class. His teaching load will be heavy compared to that in universities, for in

SOME OBSERVATIONS
ON HIGHER EDUCATION

a college teaching is the main professional obligation. He will be more of a generalist than a specialist, and this orientation may be reinforced by ease of contact with colleagues in other disciplines. In addition to teaching and counseling, he is expected to devote considerable time to committee work both inside and outside his department.

The role of the professor in the four-year college is molded by its commitment to the function of conserving and transmitting culture. We do not suggest that teachers in these schools never develop new knowledge; sometimes they do. But the organizational setting usually does not offer much encouragement for this kind of activity. The role performance rewarded is that of being a good teacher, a good counselor, a friend of students, and a person willing to carry his share of the committee work of the college.

There are striking differences in the university. While the university professor also teaches undergraduates, he is in charge of the more advanced graduate training and thus is in daily contact with two different student bodies. Since there are fewer graduate students, he is likely to know them much better than undergraduates.

The university professor is also likely to be engaged in research or other scholarly work intended to advance the state of knowledge. He is more likely than his counterparts in four-year colleges to be actively engaged with the professional community of his discipline beyond the local campus. This is partly because of his research, for which he needs financial assistance from private or government sources and close contact with other persons doing related work. (See the more extended treatment of science in Chapter 15.)

Like his colleague in the four-year college, the university professor also does committee work inside and outside the department. There is more conflict built into the university professor's role than into that of the college professor. Each major component of this role demands the full attention of a highly trained and dedicated person, and no person can give each component all it ought to have. The result is endless compromise.

STUDENTS Ever more numerous and representative of the population, source of the principal elites, the hope and sometimes the despair of older Americans, college students are an important and highly visible kind of people. Some things about their world are fairly constant; other things change very rapidly.

Flow-Through and the Structural Weakness of Students
There are three principal sorts of roles in a college: faculty, administrative, and student. Looked at as parts of a social system, the actual people who perform these roles normally remain in the system longer if they are in faculty or administrative roles than in student roles.

The three kinds of roles are permanent in the system, but the flow-through rate is drastically different. As a freshman enters the system on a four-year cycle, a senior leaves it. The turnover of people in faculty and administration is on the average much slower. Since the system is not necessarily changed radically by personnel flow-through, faculty and administration are in a better position to control it, quite apart from the fact that the college's values and norms give them this right anyway.

A perennial problem for student organization, no matter of what type, is the rapidity of flow-through. A new program or a concession wrung from the administration today may silently disappear tomorrow, or may have to be established all over again because of the lack of continuity. This is why many of the issues raised by undergraduates come up again and again. They may seem new to each generation of students, but not to persons who have observed the system longer than four years.

This structural disadvantage of students may be lessened if their activities relate to broad off-campus forces rather than to purely local issues. Such larger forces may endure longer than four years, and continue their influence despite the rapid rate of student turnover.

Purely local issues such as closing hours in the dormitories or the powers of a student senate may be fought over many times with little perceptible change. But when civil rights engage students across the country, as they did in the sixties, students may be able to use the national momentum to initiate real and permanent local changes in college programs or hiring practices.

In Loco Parentis In American colleges and universities, the faculty and administration have traditionally served *in loco parentis.* Their roles have included some of the supervision associated with parental roles. This is the source and rationale of the rules and regulations governing the social and personal life of students which have been an irritant for so many decades. The policy is based on an assumption that students are not yet ready to handle the privileges and responsibilities of adulthood. There can be little doubt that parents and the surrounding community in general have supported this view in the past. But the whole idea has come under frontal attack from students in the past few years, as you are doubtless aware.

Some faculty members and administrators have been uncomfortable with this requirement. They often feel that acting *in loco parentis* interferes with the main business of the college. They know that many of the standards represent the more conservative views found in the community, and that many highly respectable people do not live by these standards in their own homes.

Sociologically, *in loco parentis* presumes a high degree of consensus in the community on conservative norms for personal conduct—a consensus that does not exist in fact. Hence the college, whose students usually represent some of the real diversity and conflict of values in the community, is put in a dubious and constantly strained situation.

As graduates leave college, new freshmen enter. People flow through the system, changing it slightly, but the system remains.

Student Power and Its Limitations Another reason why students have less power in college than the faculty and administration is that the whole enterprise rests on the assumption that colleges and universities are centers of expert knowledge to be transmitted to a constant succession of students. The process by which knowledge is transmitted, tested, recorded, and certified excludes the student, except as the recipient of the benefits. Students are not asked to question the basic assumption or the process by which it is carried out.

In recent years students on many campuses have refused to accept this passive role. Many have actively challenged both the purposes of higher education and its means and methods. As a result, students on many campuses are admitted to membership on important college committees, and sometimes directly confront their elders on fundamental issues. This is a real and significant change in the academic scene, though it seems to have run its course at least for the time. Yet much we have said still accurately describes the situation on most campuses.

Students live together for four intense, important years in a system which controls their fates but largely excludes them from setting the criteria by which they are judged. Student peer groups hence become a refuge from the rigors of the system. In them students may find escape, rationalization of their hostility against those in authority, or even—as in the sixties—a base for attacks against the establishment. It has long been known that a considerable part of the learning in college takes place outside classrooms and laboratories, in the formal and informal group memberships of students.

EDUCATIONAL CHANGE AND ATTENDANT PROBLEMS

The values underlying American education are not changing nearly so rapidly as are the attempts to give these values organizational expression, and our discussion thus far illustrates the point.

As the nation moves haltingly yet significantly toward equality of education, new problems arise most of which had not even been visualized a few years ago. Equal opportunity in education certainly means that admission to college training should not be based on any consideration other than ability to profit from it. The record shows movement toward this goal. In 1900, only about 4 percent of college-age persons were in colleges; today more than 40 percent are.[3]

If the open door trend proves viable it will provide another push toward universal higher education. Are we moving toward the time not too far distant when nearly everyone in the United States will have a college degree? If this seems an absurd question,

[3] As of the time of writing, college enrollments seem to have peaked out. Whether the rise is resumed depends partly on the strength of the desire among disadvantaged groups for a college education.

recall that a couple of generations ago few people believed that nearly everyone would someday have a high school education.

While the strength of the American belief in education can scarcely be doubted, its continued realization at ever higher levels of formal training raises serious problems. To illustrate, consider the changing meaning of higher education as more and more people obtain it. As long as education has status implications, a society with the ideal of equal opportunity will push to gain these advantages for everyone. But the very achievement of this goal can become self-defeating, for the status advantages (occupation, income) of a college education have come from its being a gateway to social advancement for a relatively small proportion of the population.

If everyone had a college education its usefulness in maintaining or improving status would be canceled out. There would be a gain to *society* from a more highly educated citzenry, but the *individual* would lose the competitive advantage a college degree has conferred in the past. College training would simply become a standard base for placement in nearly all occupations as high school education is now. One of the deepest meanings of education has been its value in assisting upward social mobility. What will be the meaning of education for Americans when this value has disappeared? Could it be that one day—as a consequence of coming close to universal college training—higher education may be valued more for its contribution to a rounded and fulfilling life than for its use in getting an especially good job?

If college becomes universal, what then? Will everyone want a graduate degree? We don't suggest this, but there has already been dramatic growth in the number of persons seeking advanced degrees. From 1940 to 1970 the number of master's degrees earned each year in the United States rose from 27,000 to 209,000. In the same period the number of doctorates grew from 3,000 in 1940 to 30,000 in 1970 (United States Office of Education, Earned Degrees Conferred).

In 1967, Perrucci reported that more than half of the Ph.D.s earned in the United States since 1870 had been awarded in the twelve years since 1955 (1967:112). The country is now getting as many new doctorates each year as it did master's degrees thirty years ago. The same rate of increase for another thirty years will see more than three million new doctorates every year. Already in the early 1970s, the country was overproducing doctorates in most fields. Clearly, insofar as the uppermost levels of education are needed to fill rather small numbers of very highly specialized jobs, there are practical limits on the degree to which everyone can aspire to the very highest levels of formal training.

These matters suggest that Americans may be forced to reassess the meaning and value of college training. As a result we will see many organizational experiments and improvisations in the near future. As a single example, in 1970, the Carnegie Commission on Higher Education forecast and recommended a rapid expansion of two-year community colleges in the United States. This group would like to see 40 to 45 percent of undergraduates attending such colleges by the year 2000.

THE FEDERAL PRESENCE IN HIGHER EDUCATION We have mentioned the growing importance of federal funds in education, noting that local control has not been much reduced at the primary and secondary levels. In higher education the problems are more severe. Many of the problems arise from the fact that federal funds have been channeled disproportionately to the development of scientific training and research programs in the universities without regard for other priorities, and that these funds have grown and declined in response to largely political rather than educational considerations. (The implications of this situation for science will be discussed at greater length in Chapter 15.) Nonscience fields such as art, literature, music, philosophy, and the classics have received little support. An eloquent statement of the resulting strains is the following from an editorial in *Science* by Gerard Piel, publisher of *Scientific American* (1969).

The scientists were content to accept funds from whatever source was ready to supply money most generously. They thus permitted the major funding of their work to come as a by-product of mounting public expenditures for other purposes, especially for weapons. University administrators, for their part, were glad to have the scientists on their faculty take on the task of obtaining the money.

A university is a community, bound only by the common cause of the increase and diffusion of human understanding. In each of our foremost universities, the federal funding of science has exerted pressures tending to divide and dissolve that frail community. At best, it has installed and expanded scientific departments and enterprises in the universities and their medical schools without regard to the needs and priorities of the university as a whole, and often without regard to the educational process. At worst, it has established in the universities entirely inappropriate activities, motivated by the interests of the mission-oriented granting agencies and often inimical to free inquiry and to the humanity of science. Among the members of the faculty, the community has been divided on the line between the arts and sciences by the meanest issue of compensation and status, and dissolved by the transfer of the scientist's allegiance from his university to the invisible college of his field that controls his financial support in Washington. Between faculty and students, division and dissolution of the community has followed from the drafting of our scientific resources for the escalation of violence that has come to substitute for foreign policy over the past twenty-five years.

STUDENT ACTIVISM Social and political activism has long been associated with college students in many countries. Its comparative rarity in this country is unusual, not typical. There have been brief periods when the situation was different. Students today can hardly be expected to remember the considerable reformist and even revolutionary interests of some American college students during the depression of the thirties. But the broader and more complicated activism on college campuses in more recent years

STUDY THE PAST

The recent worldwide student activism reflected disenchantment at the growing discrepancies between the best ideals in society and education and the organizational means for giving expression to these values. Despite the alarm created in many countries, such protests were essentially idealistic.

has had important effects on higher education, perhaps even on secondary education. Student radicalism of the thirties ultimately had little impact either on society or on education. Recent as it is, the dramatic quality and the potential importance of recent activism has already led to a considerable literature of analysis and research (Miller and Gilmore, 1965; Lipset and Wolin, 1965; Evans, 1961; Block, Haan and Smith, 1967; Keniston, 1965). This work, still under way, will in time permit a balanced assessment of what happened in the sixties.

The new student activism is oriented both toward issues off the campus, in society at large, and toward the reform of education itself. It found its first major cause in the civil rights movement of the fifties and sixties, then in opposition to the Vietnam war, and later still in environmental pollution among other issues. It turned upon the colleges, attacking some of the traditional, and too infrequently examined, assumptions about the purposes of higher education and the organizational means by which these were put into practice. Among other things it attacked colleges and universities for not more actively criticizing established values and practices in society.[4]

In comparing radical and nonradical students, Keniston (1969:32–33) states that "student radicals are in many ways a superior group, and not the 'rabble of rejects' they have been termed. There is an impressive uniformity in the finding of a great variety of studies conducted by different researchers using different methods with different populations." Research also indicates, says Keniston, that "moral issues are central to student radicalism."

Impact of Student Activism The impact of student activism upon society as a whole may be open to question. Some educators feared that one result would be a backlash of resentment against the colleges from the general body of citizens who ultimately pay the bills for higher education. Nevertheless this change in the traditional role of student compelled more sensitivity to student opinion among professors and administrators in a few years than in many previous decades. The end result may find students sharing the power to make decisions in colleges to a greater degree than ever before in the United States.

This whole movement warns sociologists not to adopt too simple a model of socialization, in which a docile individual adapts to social demands and fits into a ready-made social niche. In complex, changing societies, such a model fits some of the facts but certainly not all of them. Many college students, having traveled for a while within the confines of this model of conformity, revolted against it. In a sense they unlearned what they had been taught. Keniston says (1969:33), "We witness today, both in America and in other nations, a phenomenon that can be called *youthful de-socialization.* Traditional roles, institutions, values, and symbols are critically scrutinized and often rejected, while new roles, institutions, values, and symbols more adequate to the modern world are desperately sought."

EDUCATION AND CHANGE IN SOCIETY Clearly the educational system of the United States is undergoing substantial change. As in the family, religion, and other institutional sectors of the society, change so profound and swift is accompanied by problems, dislocations, and dilemmas of great magnitude. Implicit in all we have said is the assumption that education is on the *receiving* end of changes in the rest of society. Like every other aspect of soci-

---

[4] These comments may recall our discussion in Chapter 10 of student protest as a social movement.

ety, the schools are attempting to adjust to the impact of the urban-industrial revolution. Does influence travel the other way as well? Do the schools become agents for change in the rest of society?

Our basic sociological assumption that the parts of social systems large and small are interdependent argues for an affirmative answer, and correctly so. Schools initiate change or help make changes in many aspects of society. We have already dealt with one of these: the key part played by university scholars and scientists in the development of new knowledge (which becomes the basis for technological innovation), and the training of the many specialists required by an industrial economy if it is to continue growing. Of all this Clark (1964:747) says that "this role is a critical change; the expansion in creation of knowledge makes education an active, intrusive force in cultural affairs, pushing scientific knowledge to the fore, and this dynamic relation to culture constitutes part of the awesomeness of the educational enterprise in modern times." Drucker (1959:87) has stated that "the highly educated man has become the central resource of today's society, the supply of such men the true measure of its economic, military, and even its political potential." It is apparent that while industrialization has transformed the schools, the latter have become essential agents in the further development and change of a technological society.

We have stated that education has played a growing role in access to occupations, which are key determiners of general social status. Thus the schools are agents in realizing the desire of Americans for upward social mobility. For decades, the proportion of Americans in the manual working class has steadily declined. The schools have been instrumental in transforming the occupational structure and modifying the class structure as well (Halsey, 1960:121).

McGee (1967) and Brogan (1961) have also called attention to the fact that the schools have contributed greatly to the cultural and ideological homogeneity of the American people out of the immense heterogeneity of its citizenry. This too is a kind of change.

Finally, Clark (1964:747) indicates that "modern education decides in some measure the fate of ideas, as well as the fate of individuals." He points out that "since values, ideas, and other aspects of culture move around horizontally from one location to another in society, and ascend or descend in prestige and influence in the structure of culture, one may speak of horizontal and vertical cultural mobility."

Schools play an important part in this movement and in the selection of important ideas; in doing so they intervene in the processes of social change in subtle ways. There are so many new and competing values and ideas in our culture that the schools confer a heightened social visibility on what they emphasize. For example, from the 1920s on, college classes in sociology, anthropology, and to some extent psychology, systematically presented scientific information on racial differences. The main burden of this evidence was antithetical to social structures based on racial discrimination. We suggest that the enlightenment of college students in this area for more than a generation helped to create the understanding which paved the way for the legal changes and the civil rights movement of the fifties and sixties.

PRACTICAL IMPLICATIONS OF THE SOCIOLOGY OF EDUCATION

The sociology of education is not confined to the study of education as an institution. It is also concerned with complex organizations in education and with microsociological levels such as those in classrooms. Practical uses of this field may occur at any or all of these levels.

In 1957, Gross, Mason, and McEachern published an important study focused on the role of the school superintendent. They were able to show how this role is enmeshed in often conflicting ways with the complementary roles played by pupils, teachers, parents, school board members, and others. Some of the difficulties faced by modern educational systems are products of this conflict. One might view their study as a powerful *social diagnosis* of a complex, confusing situation otherwise all too likely to be interpreted merely in terms of personal conflict. As a diagnosis, it forms an effective basis for programs designed to remedy some of the problems of the schools.

The sociology of education has much to offer society in this diagnostic capacity. There are so many conflicting evaluations of education today, and there is so much value conflict in society about educational ends and the means for reaching them, that dispassionate and expert analyses of what exists are very useful. The sociology of education may play a significant role in defining actual rather than imaginary problems which stand in the way of reaching desired ends. In the case of the school superintendent, local problems may not be solved simply by getting rid of the incumbent and putting someone else in his place. The same problems may continue until the structure of relationships between the superintendent's role and related roles is altered.

There is a modest body of research on social forces at work in the classroom, and this has implications for those who want to make educational practices more effective. "Of especial importance to educators is the finding that teachers appear to misperceive frequently the interpersonal relationships among students in their classrooms. They do not show high sensitivity to the way children actually react to each other, and they frequently allow their own biases toward students to hinder a correct assessment" (Gross, 1959:141). This research uncovers a basic fact familiar to all sociologists. Alongside the more formal patterns of social structure are informal ones which sometimes sabotage organizational goals, a phenomenon discussed in Chapter 9. Since it is impossible to eliminate such informal organization, strategies must be developed which encourage informal structures to support rather than hinder the formal aspects of the organization. This nearly always requires significant formal changes.

Practicing the Sociological Perspective

Most readers of this book are college students and have been in school continuously for most of their lives. If this is true of you, you are strategically located for practicing the sociological perspective in education. Here are some suggestions. Take each of the value themes in American education discussed in this chapter and see if you can identify specific manifestations of it in your own experience, first in high school and now in college. Do you find that some themes get more emphasis in high school than in college?

One measure of the structural clarity of an organization is the degree of agreement on its values (goals), norms, and principal roles. It is not hard to get an informal impression of how much agreement there is by interviewing a few people. Ask a few of your college teachers for their opinions on the purposes of college education. Then do the same with a few college students. It might be a good idea to question your parents too. Then see how much agreement there is among these categories of people, and even how much agreement there is within each category. At the same time, ask your informants to define the role of a good college teacher and a good college student. Again, check for consensus within and among categories. We suspect that you will find considerable disagreement—one source of the present problems in the educational institution.

Here are two ways in which teachers in elementary and high schools differ from teachers in colleges and universities: in the lower schools, teachers usually come from the home city or state, while teachers in higher education are recruited nationwide. A second difference is that in colleges and especially universities, teachers are often *producers* of knowledge, advancing its frontiers as well as transmitting it. For each of these differences ask yourself what the consequences are of this difference for the ways in which the lower schools function as compared with higher education.

14 Religion

In this turbulent world, religion can seem to be a rock of stability and permanence. But like all other human institutions, it is not immune to the storms of change. It is not immutable; nor—despite the predictions of some inaccurate prophets—is it about to be swept away. Depending on one's point of view, one can argue that religion is in trouble, that it is healthily adapting to the changing needs of the individual and society, or even that it does not need to adapt. To the sociologist, religion is one of the central facts of contemporary, as well as of earlier, societies. History flows through organized religion and leaves upon it the indelible marks of change. It is equally true that religion flows through history and is one of the major forces for continuity in the human story.

Whenever a rich body of symbolism permeates the life of a people, it is certain that something of great importance lies behind it. The prevalence of religious symbolism in our culture is suggested in these words of Moberg (1962:1–2).

Symbolic expressions of organized religion surround Americans. Communications are dated by the Christian calendar. Religious holidays are regularly celebrated. Coins and many postage stamps bear the slogan, "In God We Trust." Political and legal oaths are sworn upon the Bible and in the name of God. Religious and pseudoreligious music and art are a significant part of the environment. Over a thousand places bear biblical names. There is scarcely a sphere of man's life that is left untouched by the conditioning effect of religious ideas.

Religious experience is often deeply emotional and for this reason there is sometimes resistance to the objective analysis and study of religion. It is almost as though some people felt that "if you are not for my religious ideas you must be against them." But that need not be true. In the ensuing discussion we make no case either for or against religion in general, or any particular manifestation of it. Everything said here could as easily be written by other sociologists who themselves might be conservative or liberal Protestants, Catholics, or Jews, agnostics or atheists. The sociology of religion takes its stand on the firm ground that whatever religion may mean to this person or that, it involves human behavior which is social and social psychological in nature. As such it becomes fit material for study by sociologists.

Religion is so pervasive in history, it so permeates every society, and it has had such diverse manifestations, that an inclusive formal definition of it is extremely difficult. Fortunately the focus of our study is upon religious *behavior* and religious *culture*, which are more amenable to definition. There is more to religion than behavior and culture, but we shall find quite enough in them to challenge our understanding.

Here then is a definition of religion as an institution. *The religious institution is based on a set of ideas, values, beliefs, and behavioral norms concerned with ultimate issues and organized around man's relationships with entities or sources of power which are viewed as sacred, beyond the natural world, and beyond man's full understanding and control.* This definition takes no position on whether or not there are in fact entities or sources of power beyond the natural world. It refers only to men's belief in them.

Attached to the religious institution are groups and organizations which are specific behavioral manifestations of it. The First Baptist Church of Seattle, the Presbyterian denomination, the Union Theological Seminary (interdenominational), the National Council of Churches of Christ, the Archdiocese of New York, and the Catholic Church are all organizational manifestations of Christianity as a social institution. Of course, religious behavior and organizations vary immensely from one society to another and are by no means confined to the churches familiar to most Americans. In many preliterate societies, religious behavior and the religious institution (like other institutions) are difficult to distinguish from the totality of the society's culture and behavior.

ULTIMATE ISSUES What are the ultimate issues mentioned in our definition? Yinger (1957:9) describes them very well.

While there are important disagreements concerning the "ultimate" problems for man, a great many would accept the following as among the fundamental concerns of human societies and individuals: How shall we respond to the fact of death? Does life have some central meaning despite the suffering, the succession of frustrations and tragedies? How can we

A SOCIOLOGICAL DEFINITION OF RELIGION

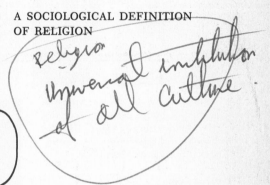

Sacred objects: above, icon from Smolensk, Russia; above center, Crocodile god, Panama; above right, Indian totem pole, Canada; right, Madonna, Sacré Coeur Church, Paris.

deal with the forces that press in on us, endangering our livelihood, our health, the survival and smooth operation of the groups in which we live—forces that our empirical knowledge is inadequate to handle? How can we bring our capacity for hostility and our egocentricity sufficiently under control that the groups within which we live, without which, indeed, life would be impossible, can be kept together?

People in religious organizations are often concerned with issues much less fateful than these. Should we allow women to become priests or ministers? How can our church meet its mortgage payments? Should parochial schools be discontinued? But at its core, religion is man's response to those overriding concerns, fears, and anxieties which are inherent in being human and living in society. To quote Yinger once more, religion "is an attempt to explain what cannot otherwise be explained; to achieve power, all other powers having failed us; to establish poise and serenity in the face of evil and suffering that other efforts have failed to eliminate" (1957:10).

THE SACRED   Moreover, in the religious view, the powers and entities that lie beyond the natural world are sacred powers and entities. The natural world includes everything that may be known to the human senses directly or indirectly, as through the use of scientific instruments to measure the temperature of distant stars. We learn about the world of nature in many ways, through everyday experience and through the more disciplined methods of science. The words *supernatural, miraculous, superempirical*, and *transcendent* describe phenomena which in some sense are beyond or outside the natural world. By definition, such phenomena are not amenable to the approaches which yield knowledge about the natural world; that is, they cannot be registered by the human sense organs. Belief, faith, prayer, and revealed truth (as in the belief that the Bible is the word of God) are typical ways of apprehending and relating to supernatural powers and entities.

Supernatural powers and entities are part of every religion, and men have believed in an enormous variety of them at different times and places, from good and evil spirits that dwell in rocks and streams to the monotheistic deities of the great religions of today. They are always seen as having fateful consequences for human affairs. Though they exist outside the natural world as we know it, their powers to influence events within the natural world are so great that men must come to terms with them. The gods are also believed to be the sources of the values and behavioral norms which deal with the ultimate issues. The norm "thou shalt not kill" is not just a good idea for human relationships; it is a commandment from God.

Our definition of religion uses the word *sacred* in relation to superempirical entities. As we employ this term, it refers to an attitude in an individual, compounded of feelings like reverence, awe, and respect (Davis, 1949:520–26). To an adherent of a particular religion, however, sacredness is a quality inherent in supernatural entities or symbols of them. Since our analysis is sociological, and thereby confined to the natural world, we cannot observe such qualities. Nevertheless, from our perspective outside any particular religion, we can see that in all religions men do act in common attitudinal ways toward powers and beings assumed to exist outside the world of common experience.

Sacred Objects   The existence of sacred objects in all or nearly all religions is a fascinating phenomenon. Familiar examples from Christianity are altars, the cross, rosaries, religious statues, and holy relics. From Judaism there are phylacteries and mezuzahs; from Buddhism, statues of Buddha and Siva, and innumerable holy places; while from Islam there is Mecca, the birthplace of Mohammed and the most holy city of Islam. In ancient pre-Hispanic Mexico, sacred objects were associated with wind, rain, corn, the moon, mountains, serpents and jaguars (Peterson, 1959:124–31). The list is endless. How is it that a piece of wood, a fragment of bone, a flask of water or a casket of wood or silver can be venerated and regarded as sacred? The answer lies in their *symbolic* relationship to still more sacred realities *which are superempirical*. Sacred objects themselves are part of the natural world. They can be touched or tasted, measured or weighed. The most knowledgeable man in the world is unable to experience supernatural reality through his senses. But the most untutored can see or touch a sacred object. It is sacred because it links him to all-important realities beyond. As Davis puts it (1949:522):

The characteristic of these (superempirical) realities is their intangibility. Since they cannot be observed directly, they can only be represented or symbolized by sensory reality. Concrete objects which happen to be sacred are not sacred because of their sensory qualities but because of their symbolic connection with the superempirical realities.[1]

Religion and Magic   The relation between religion and magic has interested anthropologists and sociologists for a long time. Like religion, magic assumes the existence of supernatural powers. But magic also assumes that man can make contact with these powers and through them achieve his own worldly purposes. There are clear differences in the goals sought through magic and those sought through religion, and differences also in the attitudes of people who take part in the two types of practices. While religion is concerned with the ultimate issues, magic is oriented toward immediate, practical goals. A religious person may make sacrifice to the rain god or pray for the salvation of his soul. He may also burn his enemy's nail parings, or wear an old felt hat when he goes fishing and refuse to walk under ladders or step on cracks in sidewalks.

As we have seen with respect to the sacred, religious beings and powers inspire deep emotional responses of reverence, respect, and inspiration. In magic, the attitude of the participant is likely to be more utilitarian and matter-of-fact. If one pronounces the appropriate words or mixes the ingredients properly, then the hoped-for results are expected to take place, almost as if magic were a form of technology. The attitude is not so very different from that of the average person toward a TV set. He does not understand how the mechanism operates much more clearly than he understands how tea leaves in the bottom of a cup can reveal his

---

[1] From Kingsley Davis, *Human Society* (New York: The Macmillan Company). © Copyright, The Macmillan Company, 1948 and 1949.

fortune. He simply believes that if you do certain things in certain ways, the results will be as predicted. One can even pay a magician to cast a spell, just as one can hire a technician to make the TV work again.

Magic flourishes in troubled times, when the world seems to be shifting, uncertain, and threatening to established ways of living. We live today in such a time, and one indicator of that fact is the astonishing growth in the popularity of magical practices in the midst of our highly materialistic society. Remember that it is happening in a society which is scientifically, technologically, and educationally the most advanced in the history of the world!

THE FUNCTIONS OF RELIGION

Why is it that in all times and places men have had some concept of supernatural powers and beings? Why do they offer obeisance and sacrifices to such powers? Why do they feel it so important to relate themselves in proper ways to this unseen realm? Why, in other words, do we have religions at all? Each religion has its own theological answers to such questions, but here it is a sociological kind of answer that we seek. One such answer is that religions exist because they perform important functions for the individual and for society.

THE FUNCTIONAL IMPORTANCE OF RELIGION FOR THE INDIVIDUAL
Religion may help a person cope with his problems and make his life seem more worth living in several ways. Everyone knows that life in society is occasionally irritating and frustrating. A deeper insight reveals that by its very nature society frustrates the individual as often as it gratifies him. Because frustration cannot be eradicated from life we learn to somehow live with it. We learn that this is a price exacted from us for society's support in attaining things we want for ourselves.

But there are times in every life when the habitual ways of responding to frustration are not adequate. The violation of deeply felt personal values is too painful to be accepted philosophically. In religious circles, evil is the term used to describe such experiences. The sociologist talks about the difference between the real and the ideal.

Bad things really do happen. People suffer injustice. The good is not always victorious. Men cry out in anguish at the destruction of their best hopes and at the spectacle of good and innocent lives crippled and destroyed. They watch as evil is not only left unpunished, but rewarded. Countless human stories do not have happy endings. How can such things happen? Religion brings solace for the deep hurts people suffer by the very fact of being human, and which are often irremediable in the natural world. It offers interpretations of good and evil which make it easier to live in the real world and not be crushed by it.

Human Mortality Everyone faces death, his own certainly, and often that of a loved one whose life comes finally to its end. Few men want to die, but there is no escaping death. How can we accept this awful fate? Most people need emotional support and reassurance to help them face it. Medical and biological sciences give us an intellectual explanation, but do little to reconcile us. Death is the extreme frustration, life's greatest crisis. Religion interprets this supreme event and helps the individual accept it with fortitude, resignation, and even hope. Many religions do this by assuring the individual that the soul will survive death and continue existence in an afterlife.

That New Black Magic

Westerners laugh at the benighted superstitions of their Asian and African brothers. How amusing it is to learn that Burmans refuse to wash their hair on Saturdays, that Zambians believe eggs cause sterility, that Chinese voyagers never turn over the fish on their plates for fear of capsizing their ships. In fact, Westerners themselves seem to be on the way to becoming the most superstitious people on earth. For all his faith in scientific reason, Western man is so baffled by complex social and economic problems that he is increasingly attracted to irrational solutions—to all kinds of new black magic.

Superstition is a natural human reaction to overwhelming dangers or baffling situations. The word stems from the Latin *superstitio*, meaning "a standing still over," and connotes amazement or dread of supernatural forces beyond one's control. Rationalists scorn superstition as a hangover of primitive man's obsolete interpretations of the world. Indeed, nothing seems sillier nowadays than rituals like knocking on wood or chanting "God bless you!" (to prevent the sneezer's soul from flying away). Even so, modern behavioral scientists respect superstition as an enduring expression of the human need to master the inexplicable. "One man's superstitution is another's religion," contends Anthropologist Sol Tax. Says Margaret Mead: "Superstitions reflect the keenness of our wish to have something come true or to prevent something bad from happening. The half acceptance and half denial accorded superstitions give us the best of both worlds."

In the second half of the twentieth century, the gap between wish and denial has often been widened by the very institutions that should provide certainty. Science has bared the mysteries of subatomic particles, and in the process has almost turned into a new metaphysics groping for evidence of things unseen. As organized religion loses its appeal through stuffiness or sterility, people seeking faith increasingly turn to mystical religions, such as Zen and Zoroastrianism.

To be sure, modern life is already rife with ancient superstitions that will probably never go out of style. But the new phenomenon is the upsurge in new superstitions—the faith in flying saucers, the theory that H-bomb tests caused rain and that the test ban has since caused droughts. Even scientists are highly susceptible to superstitious beliefs. One California physicist who flies to Washington once a month eases his fear of a crash by carrying a special amulet: a copy of *Time,* a magazine he otherwise dislikes.

Nothing so demonstrates modern man's need for myth as the superstitions created by "rational" technology itself. Hardly anyone is more superstitious these days than the supposedly no-nonsense men who fly huge jetliners at multimile altitudes. Aviators frequently cross unused seat belts prior to takeoff, or spit on a wheel after their preflight inspection—thus indulging the old belief that saliva is an offering of the spirit to the gods. Some auto racers don't like peanuts or women in their pits. In keeping with the belief that new machines cause sterility, United States servicemen blithely took sexual advantage of British girl radar operators in World War II. A similar male myth has it that airline hostesses are incapable of conception because their cross-country flights confuse their menstrual cycles. (Not so.)

Computer technology is bewitched with superstition. For one thing, today's young cyberneticists tend to anthropomorphize their tools. Tom Allison, 25, a Coca-Cola ex-

Affirmation of Life's Value It may appear that the functions religion performs for the individual relate only to sorrow, frustration, and defeat. But that is by no means true. Many religions play a more positive role in the lives of their adherents. As Williams (1970:361) puts it, religion

can also represent a positive affirmation of the value of living, a faith in objective truth and goodness, a belief in the ultimate balancing of the cosmic scales. For many persons in all ages, this affirmation has sustained hope and energy not only in crises but in the "quiet desperation" so often confronted in daily life.

---

ecutive in Atlanta, is convinced that his computer is feminine. "She keeps cutting me off at the most inopportune times," he complains. A programmer in Los Angeles will not feed blue cards into his computer—he feels she deserves pink. Seymour Greenfield, a research manager for the military DRC-44 computer program at Dynamics Research Corp. near Boston, complicates the matter further. "I hired everyone building the computer by the zodiac signs under which they were born," he says. As a Leo, he has prejudices. "I hired two Cancer men and they both ended up with ulcers."

Apollo Flight Director Gene Kranz disclaims any superstition, yet regularly dons a white vest during launches, a red vest during long flights, and a flashy gold-brocaded vest immediately after a safe splashdown. At California's Hughes Aircraft Co., any unmanned space probe, like Surveyor, is accompanied in the control room by more crossed fingers, arms and legs than a contortionists' convention. Most space scientists believe in Murphy's Law: "If something can go wrong, it will go wrong, and at the worst possible time." Is there really a Professor Murphy? Answers one California scientist: "Sure, just like there's a Santa Claus."

All sorts of old superstitions have re-emerged in a new era, sometimes in new guises. One Chicago dealer in magical objects reports that "crystal balls are selling like popcorn" for as much as $23 apiece. New York's TBS Computer Centers Corp. now cranks out twenty-page personal horoscopes for a mere $15, the electronic brain taking only a minute to compute a life history that flesh-and-blood astrologers need a week to prepare. Necromancy, the art of communication with the dead, has undergone a rebirth, abetted by California's Episcopal Bishop James

Pike, who engaged in a seance at which he claims to have talked with his suicide son.

A mystical renaissance is evident everywhere, from television to department stores. This year three TV series will deal with witches and ghosts. The movie *Rosemary's Baby* is both demonological and box-office. Miniskirted suburban matrons cast the *I Ching* or shuffle tarot cards before setting dates for dinner parties. Hippies, with their drug-sensitized yen for magic, are perhaps the prime movers behind the phenomenon. Not only do they sport beads and amulets that have supposed magical powers; they also believe firmly and frighteningly in witchcraft. Some of the hippie mysticism is a calculated put-on—as when Abbie Hoffman and his crew attempted to levitate the Pentagon last October—but much of the new concern with the arcane is a genuine attempt to find enrichment for arid lives.

The danger of overindulgence in superstition is that it breeds a kind of shortcut thinking. Already, TV commercials verge on magic: how does a deodorant differ from a love potion? Already, the incantations of New Left and New Right extremists echo the irrational chants of sinister shamans. No one has ever been hurt by tossing salt over his left shoulder; many have felt a vibration of personal peace by crying "Om!" The trouble is that superstitions, like Occam's razor, cut both ways. Before Western man gets any more mystical, perhaps he should distinguish between superstitions that destroy tranquility and those that enhance it. If he succeeds, the rest of the world will not have to keep its fingers crossed.

There is abundant evidence, too, that religion can release and channel creative impulses ranging from great art to noble behavior. To say that religion performs highly useful functions for people is not to deny that it may also cause them problems. It may reinforce feelings of guilt and personal inadequacy that already exist. Over the centuries countless thousands have suffered religious persecution. But if we ask why religion persists we must concede that one reason is that it gives answers for some of the deepest problems everyone must face.

THE FUNCTIONAL IMPORTANCE OF RELIGION FOR SOCIETY Insofar as religion helps individuals solve personal problems, it makes them more effective members of society. As we have pointed out in many ways, while man lives in society, society also lives in the minds of men. Hence, when people are freed from harassing and crippling personal problems, their energies are released to act in ways that are socially beneficial. A person who is constantly depressed and anxious about himself is less capable of constructive and creative relationships with others.

One function of religion which sociologists stress is its contribution to the solidarity of society. When we consider that there is nothing in the human biological makeup that impels men to social cooperation and self-denial, it is a wonder that societies exist at all. The wonder is increased when we realize the immense hostility generated by the competitive struggles and frustrations of life. How are people persuaded to restrain their own self-seeking enough to make society possible, and to control their hostilities enough to keep society from being torn apart?

Socialization is the main answer to this question. And religion's contribution to socialization comes from its guardianship over values and norms essential to social cohesion and solidarity. We turn to Kingsley Davis (1949:519–20) for an excellent statement of the sociological position on this matter.

One of the functions of religion is to justify, rationalize, and support the sentiments that give cohesion to society. Certain observations bear out this interpretation. In the first place, religion is a part of society. It is common to the group; its beliefs and practices are acquired by each individual as a member of the group. The relationships of people to the gods and the relations between the gods parallel those in the society itself.[2] The worship of the gods is a public matter, supported by the community and performed for communal purposes. The priest has a recognized status, and in complex societies the priesthood forms a recognized class. Finally, the communicants or adherents of the religion are united by other bonds as well, so that community and church often include the same persons. In the second place, the expression of common beliefs through collective ritual seems to enhance the individual's devotion to group ends. It strengthens

---

[2] To clarify this sentence, you may recall such familiar usages as God the *Father*, men as the *children* of God, and men as being *brothers* in the eyes of God.

his determination to observe the group norms and to rise above purely private interests. It reinforces his identification with his fellows and sharpens his separateness from members of other tribes, communities, or nations.[3]

The existence of society requires that most members accept a number of central values and associated behavioral norms. Some of these values and norms are incorporated in a society's religion. By lending supernatural support to such values and norms, religion increases individual acceptance of them and so helps hold society together. This is particularly true of religions high in ethical content, such as Judaism and Christianity, both of which emphasize man's responsibility to his fellow man in the eyes of God.

What happens to a society containing two or more seriously conflicting religious institutions? Rather than integrating the society, religion would then weaken its cohesion. We have seen this divisive process at work many times in Protestant-Catholic struggles of the past, the Huguenots in France, for instance. Today the religious strife in Northern Ireland and in Belgium has the same destructive effect on social cohesion.

Religion and the State In Western civilization there has been an alliance for mutual support between the political and the religious institutions for centuries. Sometimes there has been an outright struggle for power between the two. More typically in recent times, the government has supported the church in one way or another while the church has lent its unifying influence to the government in power. Some unusual features of government and religious organization in the United States have made this relationship unusually complex.

The Constitution strictly requires the separation of church and state; how absolute this separation is remains open to some question. Churches derive great financial advantage from their tax-exempt status, and in recent years there have been efforts to tap public funds for the support of church school systems. The whole matter is much discussed and argued, and the Supreme Court has often been called upon to reinterpret the constitutional provision. It is nevertheless true that there can be no official alliance between the state and organized religion. The state cannot speak for organized religion as a whole.

Yet there is a tenuous and shadowy but important relationship of mutual support. It shows up in numerous statements supporting religion made by public officials from the president on down, in the existence of chaplains for the two houses of Congress and for the military services, and in many other ways. But if you look closely you will find that while politicians support religion,

---

[3] From Kingsley Davis, *Human Society* (New York: The Macmillan Company). © Copyright, The Macmillan Company, 1948 and 1949.

A famous historical example of the divisiveness that religious conflict can bring to a society is the struggle between French Protestants, known as Huguenots, and Roman Catholics. It led eventually to civil war and to what became known as the Massacre of Saint Bartholomew's Day in 1572, shown here, in which many Huguenots were murdered.

they also seek to harness its integrative capacity to favorite political programs. Likewise religious leaders exhort their followers to obey civil authority, to trust the officers and policies of government, and to be good and patriotic citizens.

The term *civil religion* is sometimes attached to this somewhat vague, safe, and conventional religiosity (Herberg, 1962). *Newsweek* (1970:55) speaks of the "God of civil religion" as follows: "In His name, preachers today still glorify America, condemn disorder and counsel oppressed spirits to place their hopes in the hereafter. Not surprisingly, He is the kind of God lawyers appreciate and to whom politicians pay homage."

Yet in maintaining an operative level of societal integration, religion need not blindly support the status quo. It may indeed sometimes become a vantage point for severe criticism of society. We shall return to this topic in our discussion of religion and social change.

A COMPARATIVE VIEW OF RELIGION

Adherence to one's own religion is often so much a matter of deep conviction, faith, and belief that it is hard to take seriously the fact that the followers of other religions feel the same way. Nevertheless the observations we have made about religion in general apply just as much to religions that are strange and exotic to most Americans as to those associated with the familiar Judeo-Christian tradition. As students of sociology it is important to get some sense of the great diversity of religion in human experience.

At least as long ago as Neanderthal man (from one hundred thousand to twenty-five thousand years ago)—and perhaps much longer—religion was a part of human experience. The burial of food, clothing, and tools with the dead, and other evidence such as

Above left, portion of the ancient initiation rites of a Dionysiac mystery cult, as depicted in a frieze discovered in a villa outside Pompeii. Above right, voodoo ceremony being performed in Haiti.

that indicating reverence for certain animals, strongly suggest at least the beginning of recognizable religious ideas; in many parts of the world there endure prehistoric stone monuments such as Stonehenge in England which clearly were associated with religious beliefs and practices.

Turning to primitive societies that have survived into modern times, beneath the bewildering variety of their religions Noss (1969:10–21) finds such recurrent features as awe before the sacred, expression of anxiety in ritual, myth, the bipolarity of religion and magic (which we have already noted), divination (ability to know what is hidden to most people about present and future), mana ("belief in indwelling supernatural power as such, independent of either persons or spirits") (1969:15), animism (belief in spirits inhabiting both animate and inanimate objects), veneration and worship of spirits, recognition of high gods (contrary to many opinions, belief in a remote high god or supreme being or force is not rare among primitive peoples), taboos (prohibitions against touching or approaching specified objects or persons, or acting in certain ways), purification rites (ridding a person or community of some pollution), sacrifice (offerings to gods or impersonal spiritual powers), and totemism (recognition "of a more or less intimate relationship between certain human groups and particular classes or species of animal, plant, or inanimate object in nature") (1969:21).

Civilizations, the oldest of which emerged only six to seven thousand years ago, built on the far older foundations of prehistoric religion. Here and there arose and evolved the great world religions we know today. From what we now call India came Hinduism and Buddhism; from China, Confucianism and Taoism; and from Japan, Shinto. In the Near East appeared Judaism,

Christianity, Islam, and Zoroastrianism. Scores of other religions exist, but these are the ones that have held the world stage for a long time. Estimates of their present memberships are presented in Table 14-1.

Christianity is the largest religion in the world, but the total membership of the other religions greatly exceeds the number of Christians. Judaism is probably the most familiar religion to Americans after Christianity. Yet it is one of the smallest of the world religions, as Table 14-1 shows, and not much less than half of all its adherents live in the United States. Americans who unknowingly project on the world their impression of the relative numbers of Protestants and Roman Catholics in this country may be surprised to note that worldwide there are almost 2.7 times as many Catholics as Protestants.

DIFFICULTIES OF COMPARISON All the high religions are so complex and have changed so much over the centuries that it is impossible to compare them in a few sentences without gross distortion. We shall not try to do so. Shall we, for example, "explain" Christianity to someone who doesn't know of it by the surviving words of its founder or by the history of what it has become in nearly two thousand years? Noss (1969:147) tells us that "there ultimately developed within Buddhism so many forms of religious organization, cults, and belief, such great changes even in the fundamentals of the faith, that one must say that Buddhism as a whole is really, like Hinduism, a family of religions rather than a single religion."

Each of the great religions grew out of a particular culture and history, and in turn helped mold that culture and history. Some of

TABLE 14-1 MAJOR WORLD RELIGIONS AND THEIR ESTIMATED MEMBERSHIP

RELIGION	NORTH AMERICA	SOUTH AMERICA	EUROPE	ASIA	AFRICA	OCEANIA	TOTAL WORLD
Christian	214,258,000	150,426,000	442,006,000	61,473,000	42,056,000	14,055,000	924,274,000
Roman Catholic	126,468,000	147,219,000	226,303,000	47,622,000	28,751,000	4,107,000	580,470,000
Eastern Orthodox	3,675,000	47,000	114,103,000	2,819,000	4,956,000	84,000	125,684,000
Protestant	84,115,000	3,160,000	101,600,000	11,032,000	8,349,000	9,864,000	218,120,000
Moslem	166,000	416,000	13,848,000	374,167,000	104,297,000	118,000	493,012,000
Hindu	55,000	660,000	160,000	434,447,000	1,205,000	218,000	436,745,000
Confucian	96,000	109,000	55,000	371,261,000	9,000	57,000	371,587,000
Buddhist	187,000	157,000	8,000	176,568,000	–	–	176,920,000
Shinto	31,000	116,000	2,000	69,513,000	–	–	69,662,000
Taoist	16,000	19,000	12,000	54,277,000	–	–	54,324,000
Jewish	6,035,000	705,000	4,025,000	2,460,000	238,000	74,000	13,537,000
Zoroastrian	–	–	12,000	126,000	–	–	138,000

Source: *Britannica Book of the Year 1971* (Chicago: Encyclopaedia Britannica, Inc., 1971), p. 652.

the parallels and differences in their development are interesting and enlightening. The founder of Buddhism, Gautama Buddha, born in 563 B.C. in northern India, said this:

As a mother, even at the risk of her own life, protects her son, her only son, so let him (a disciple) cultivate love without measure toward all beings. Let him cultivate toward the whole world—above, below, around—a heart of love unstinted, unmixed with the sense of differing or opposing interests (Noss, 1969:142).

No Christian should find this statement alien and the same could be said of many morally lofty statements embedded in otherwise different religions.

Or take the orientation of a religion toward the material world of everyday experience. In its earliest years, Christianity rejected the world because it was believed that the end of that world was near. When the world did not end the religion ceased to reject it and considered instead how to come to terms with it. Buddhism too turns away from the world but for a different reason, because it preaches that what is essential in life can be sought only by an inward process such as meditation. A person who successfully travels Buddhism's Noble Eightfold Path becomes an *arahat,* one who has conquered all earthly desires, whose energy is only spiritual, and who calmly awaits entrance into Nirvana at death. And yet, within this tradition which places little emphasis on making the world a better place, individuals and sects have risen which have sought social reform. Thus two great religious traditions have at different times and for different reasons substantially varied the emphasis given to both personal redemption and the creation of a better world.

Americans and Oriental Religion In recent years many Americans have been attracted to some aspects of Eastern religions such as Buddhism. An interesting example is Zen, which is an offshoot in Japan of the Mahayana school of Buddhist thought. "Zen is primarily an attempt to experience . . . the unitary character of reality. 'I' and 'not-I' are one ('not-two'); both are aspects of Buddha-reality. This becomes clear when one 'sees into one's own nature,' in a moment of awakening'" (Noss, 1969:174). Such experience of reality cannot be arrived at intellectually; it can come only in a flash of intuition. Japanese Zen masters have a variety of techniques for helping a person to give up thinking of the world as separate from oneself, something that can be approached by the use of reason. Disciplined meditation is important, but a master may kick or slap a learner who persists in clinging to the use of reason and asking questions about reality and experience; a kind of shock treatment, one could say. Or the master may pose the learner a *mondo.* Here is an example: "A monk who saw Yao-shan meditating asked: 'In this motionless position what are you thinking?' 'Thinking that which is beyond thinking.' 'How do you go about thinking that which is beyond thinking?' 'By an act of not-thinking'" (quoted in Noss, 1969:175).

According to Noss such devices say to the learner, in effect: "Stop clinging to objects, the self included; cease asking dualistic questions; instead, know in yourself the undifferentiated Void that is at the same time the ground of all discrete being" (1969:175).

It may seem very strange that Zen, with its negation of striving to control fate through rational effort, should appeal to anyone reared in this country. Our mature industrial society puts such stress on the use of reason in understanding and on technological mastery of problems, and it so strongly advocates the pursuit of worldly goals by competitive means, that the conceptions of Zen Buddhism seem remote and almost incomprehensible. But remember that at many points we have called attention to the alienation of many Americans from their own society. We have pointed out the decline in the authority of traditional values, the presence of conflicting values, the depersonalization associated with bureaucratic dominance, and the loss of a sense of community. All these associated conditions prepare at least some Americans for attraction to Zen, precisely because it offers a radically different way of making sense out of experience, different from the familiar one which for some Americans is discredited.

RELIGIOUS ORGANIZATIONS IN THE UNITED STATES

Religion in America is close in many ways to religion in Western cultures generally. Jews, Catholics, and Protestants are not only historically related but continue to share many characteristics, particularly compared to other religions of the world. Still, organized religion in this country does have distinctive characteristics.

ORGANIZATIONAL DIVERSITY According to the *Yearbook of American Churches* (1968) there are 241 distinct religious bodies in the United States with a total membership of 126 million.

Most of the 241 denominations are quite small. Twenty-one denominations contain 90 percent of all church members. Eighty-one religious bodies having 50,000 or more members account for 98 percent of church memberships, whereas the remaining 1 percent is scattered through 160 groupings. The largest single organized church, the Roman Catholic, reported about 47 million members of a total reported church membership of 126 million, whereas the Protestant groupings accounted for somewhat more than another 70 million; and the number of Jewish persons was roughly estimated at 5.7 million. However, the social importance of the smaller bodies is not adequately represented by their numerical standing, since the presence of so much diversity unquestionably strongly influences the total religious scene (Williams, 1970:377).

Table 14-2 gives slightly more recent and much more detailed information on religious membership and gives a vivid impression of how fragmented American religion is—far more so than most societies. Even in its colonial period America had a variety of religious groups, and this diversity was increased by a long succession of immigrant groups bringing their different faiths with them. The competition between these many religious organizations in the freedom of the new country produced endless doctrinal battles. Often what seemed to outsiders like minor points of disagreement led splinter groups to break away and form new churches. The end product was the amazing diversity of the present time.

Sects and Churches Many years ago, building on the work of the German sociologist Max Weber, another German scholar, Ernest Troeltsch (1931), distinguished between *sects* and *churches* as types of church organizations.[4] Other sociologists have found the distinction useful, particularly in the study of American Protestantism. Building on Weber and Troeltsch and on later work by Pope (1941) and Wilson (1959), Salisbury offers the following on sect and church (1964:96–97):

1. The sect is hostile or indifferent to the values of secular society and the state, while the church accepts and reinforces them.
2. The sect stresses a literal Biblical interpretation of life and is otherwordly in its orientation and emphasis. The church accepts some degree of scientific and humanistic thinking in its interpretation of life and of doctrine, and worldly success as an appropriate goal and norm for behavior.
3. In the sect personal perfection is the standard, exclusiveness is emphasized, and unworthy members are expelled. The church admits to membership all who are socially compatible with it; it accepts the standards, values, and conventional morality of the prevailing culture. It is easy to get in the church, and even the apathetic and wayward are seldom expelled.
4. The sect emphasizes congregational participation and a lay ministry, while the church delegates religious responsibility to a professionally trained ministry.
5. The sect shows a principal concern for adult membership, and its worship and ethic are adult-centered. The church is concerned that religion and religious education be adapted to the needs and interests of the child.
6. The self-conception in the sect is definitive and clear: that of an elect—a gathered remnant—that possesses special enlightenment. In the church self-conception is diffuse and unfocused; doctrinal positions are not stressed.
7. The sect is suspicious of or hostile to rival sects and is characterized by a psychology of persecution. The church, characterized by a psychology of dominance and success, exhibits disdainful pity.
8. Commitment tends to be total and the religious role pivotal and central in the sect. Commitment in the church is less intense for most members and the religious role is more marginal or peripheral.

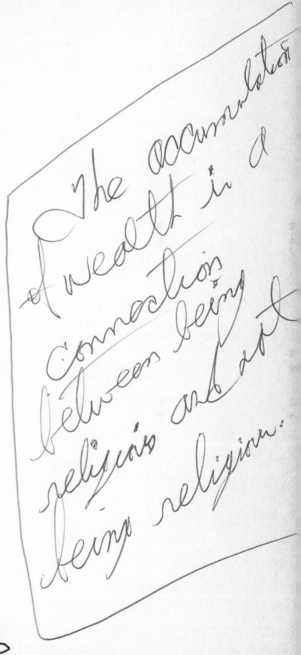

The accumulation of wealth in a connection between being religious and not being religious.

----

[4] *Cults* resemble sects in some ways. The main distinction is that sects reflect disillusion with existing churches while cults disavow even the tradition out of which both sect and church grow. The Black Muslims are a recent example of a cult in this country but they are significant in many other parts of the world. The cult organizes around charismatic leaders and—because charisma is hard to pass along—many cults do not last long. Jesus was a charismatic leader of a cult which did survive to become something else.

Table 14-2 Religious Bodies United States—Membership

[Represents latest information available from religious bodies with memberships of 50,000 or more; excludes a few groups giving no data. Not all groups follow same calendar year nor count membership in same way; some groups give only approximate figures. Roman Catholics count all baptized persons, including infants; Jews regard as members all Jews in communities having congregations; Eastern Orthodox Churches include all persons in their nationality or cultural groups; most Protestant bodies count only persons who have attained full membership, and previous estimates have indicated that all but a small minority of these are over 13 years of age; however, many Lutheran bodies and The Episcopal Church now report all baptized persons, and not only those confirmed. Data which appear in italics are "noncurrent," i.e., they are reported for 1969 or earlier. All other data are "current" and were reported in 1970 or 1971]

RELIGIOUS BODY	YEAR	CHURCHES REPORTED	MEMBER-SHIP (1,000)	PASTORS WITH CHARGES	SUNDAY SCHOOL ENROLLMENT (1,000)
Total	(X)	328,657	131,046	235,189	(NA)
Bodies with membership of 50,000 or more	(X)	314,083	129,470	222,734	(NA)
Current data	(X)	238,575	114,591	172,334	(NA)
Noncurrent data	(X)	*75,508*	*14,879*	*50,400*	(NA)
African Methodist Episcopal Church	*1951*	*5,878*	*1,166*	*5,878*	(NA)
African Methodist Episcopal Zion Church	1970	4,500	940	5,000	162
Albanian Orthodox Archdiocese in America	1971	13	62	18	1
American Baptist Association	1971	3,295	790	3,280	453
American Baptist Convention	1970	6,090	1,472	4,317	742
American Carpatho-Russian Orthodox Greek Catholic Church	1971	69	107	58	5
American Lutheran Church, The	1970	4,822	2,543	4,046	753
The Antiochian Orthodox Christian Archdiocese of New York and All North America	1970	92	100	96	(NA)
Apostolic Overcoming Holy Church of God	*1956*	*300*	*75*	*300*	(NA)
Armenian Apostolic Church of America	1970	34	125	25	3
Armenian Church of North America, Diocese of The (incl. Diocese of California)	1971	58	300	62	8
Assemblies of God	1971	8,734	1,065	8,140	1,065
Baptist General Conference	1970	677	104	673	119
Baptist Missionary Association of America	1970	1,408	187	1,500	107
Buddhist Churches of America	1970	60	100	74	12
Bulgarian Eastern Orthodox Church	*1962*	*23*	*86*	*10*	(NA)
Christian and Missionary Alliance, The	1970	1,112	113	861	165
Christian Church (Disciples of Christ)	1970	5,114	1,424	4,590	671
Christian Churches and Churches of Christ	1970	4,688	1,020	(NA)	1,071
Christian Methodist Episcopal Church	*1965*	*2,598*	*467*	*2,214*	(NA)
Christian Reformed Church	1970	660	286	154	(NA)
The Church of God	1971	2,025	76	1,910	97
Church of God (Anderson, Ind.)	1970	2,282	150	1,779	239
Church of God (Cleveland, Tenn.)	1970	4,024	272	6,700	316
The Church of God in Christ	*1965*	*4,500*	*425*	*4,000*	(NA)
The Church of God in Christ, International (Evanston, Ill.)	1970	1,006	500	(NA)	(NA)
The Church of God of Prophecy	1970	1,561	51	1,561	84,417
Church of Jesus Christ of Latter-day Saints, The	1970	4,828	2,073	14,484	2,136
Church of the Brethren	1970	1,038	183	705	86
Church of the Nazarene	1970	4,636	383	3,404	840
Churches of Christ	*1968*	*18,000*	*2,400*	(NA)	(NA)
Congregational Christian Churches, National Association of	1970	327	85	305	(NA)
Conservative Baptist Association of America, The	1970	1,127	300	(NA)	(NA)
Cumberland Presbyterian Church	1970	901	92	516	58
Episcopal Church, The	1970	7,069	3,286	6,786	738
Evangelical Covenant Church of America	1970	527	67	405	68
Evangelical Free Church of America	1971	562	70	(NA)	(NA)
Free Methodist Church of North America	1970	1,095	65	977	124

TABLE 14-2 (*continued*)

RELIGIOUS BODY	YEAR	CHURCHES REPORTED	MEMBER-SHIP (1,000)	PASTORS WITH CHARGES	SUNDAY SCHOOL ENROLLMENT (1,000)
Free Will Baptists (National Association of)	1970	2,163	186	2,100	152
Friends United Meeting	1970	517	68	323	36
General Association of Regular Baptist Churches	1971	1,426	210	(NA)	(NA)
General Baptists	1971	854	65	1,000	81
Greek Orthodox Archdiocese of North and South America	1971	482	1,950	530	73
Independent Fundamental Churches of America	1970	901	112	649	161
International Church of the Foursquare Gospel	1963	741	89	741	(NA)
International General Assembly of Spiritualists	1966	209	164	221	(NA)
Jehovah's Witnesses	1970	5,492	389	(X)	(NA)
Jewish Congregations	1970	5,000	5,870	5,100	(NA)
Lutheran Church in America	1970	5,812	3,107	4,789	931
Lutheran Church, Missouri Synod	1970	5,690	2,789	4,581	857
Mennonite Church	1970	1,181	89	2,090	110
Moravian Church in America (Unitas Fratrum)	1970–71	157	59	143	22
National Baptist Convention of America	1956	11,398	2,669	7,598	(NA)
National Baptist Convention, U.S.A., Inc.	1958	26,000	5,500	26,000	(NA)
National Baptist Evangelical Life and Soul Saving Assembly of the U.S.A.	1951	264	58	128	(NA)
National Primitive Baptist Convention, Inc.	1970	2,196	1,523	597	33
North American Baptist General Conference	1971	343	55	333	50
North American Old Roman Catholic Church	1971	117	59	78	8
The Orthodox Church in America	1970	312	1,000	(NA)	(NA)
Pentecostal Church of God of America, Inc.	1967	975	115	975	(NA)
Pentecostal Holiness Church, Inc.	1970	1,318	67	(NA)	140
Polish National Catholic Church of America	1960	162	282	151	(NA)
Presbyterian Church in the U.S.	1970	4,063	958	2,791	587
Primitive Baptists	1950	1,000	72	(NA)	(NA)
Progressive National Baptist Convention, The	1967	655	522	(NA)	(NA)
Reformed Church in America	1970	923	368	851	133
Reorganized Church of Jesus Christ of Latter-Day Saints	1970	1,025	153	(NA)	59
Roman Catholic Church	1970	23,708	48,215	(NA)	10,374
Romanian Orthodox Episcopate of America, The	1970	45	50	42	2
Russian Orthodox Church in the U.S.A., Patriarchal Parishes of the	1965	67	153	61	(NA)
The Russian Orthodox Church Outside Russia	1955	81	55	92	(NA)
Salvation Army	1970	1,115	327	3,812	112
Serbian Eastern Orthodox Diocese for the U.S.A. and Canada	1967	52	65	56	(NA)
Seventh-day Adventists	1970	3,218	420	1,504	369
Southern Baptist Convention	1970	34,340	11,628	31,000	7,288
Triumph the Church and Kingdom of God in Christ	1971	498	55	900	51
Ukrainian Orthodox Church in America	1966	107	87	107	(NA)
Unitarian Universalist Association	1969	1,076	265	538	(NA)
United Baptist Church	1955	586	64	415	(NA)
United Church of Christ	1970	6,727	1,961	6,019	766
United Free Will Baptist Church	1952	836	100	915	(NA)
The United Methodist Church	1970	40,653	10,672	20,619	5,924
United Pentecostal Church, Inc.	1971	2,400	250	(NA)	(NA)
The United Presbyterian Church in the U.S.A.	1970	8,610	3,087	7,406	1,303
The Wesleyan Church	1970	1,898	84	1,918	212
Wisconsin Evangelical Lutheran Synod	1970	967	381	733	60
Bodies with membership of less than 50,000	(X)	14,574	1,576	12,455	(NA)

NA Not available.   X Not applicable.   [1] Includes pupils, officers, and teachers.

Source: *Statistical Abstract of the United States*, 1972, Table 59, pp. 44–45.

Sects tend to follow a growth pattern which eventually transforms them, if they survive, into church-type organizations. Originally formed by less advantaged people, and alienated from some aspects of the larger society, the sect typically makes its peace with secular society as it grows and its members win status and acceptance. Baptists and Methodists have traversed this route, beginning in the late colonial and early national period. It is hard for a sect to maintain its sense of separateness (and its other characteristics) in a pluralistic and materialistic society. Since members live in society at large as well as within the sect, they are constantly exposed to influences counter to its values. Hence even the most scrupulous efforts to weed out dissent seldom succeed in the long run. Yet there are exceptions such as the Amish, several Mennonite groups, and a few others which have maintained sect-like characteristics for long periods. At any given moment in the United States, religious bodies can be found which represent points all along the pathway from newly formed sect to established denomination. New sects appear constantly. Most of them soon disappear, but a few grow and begin to evolve in the direction of churchhood.

If we look back over generations we can see tendencies to develop new sects in part as an outgrowth of the nature of Protestant Christianity, which encourages each individual to establish his own relationship with God. This emphasis on the individual, when coupled with the tendency for church bodies to evolve into complex organizations dominated by priestly hierarchies, produces a continuing source of strain.

It is hard to say whether the multiplication of Protestant sects, which has played so large a part in the religious life of the United States, will continue. Immigration from now on is unlikely to produce as many sects as it has in the past. Many American churches have recently been strongly influenced by the worldwide ecumenical movement, the coming together organizationally of formerly separate Protestant churches. Yet schismatic tendencies are certainly not dead. We live in troubled times, and turmoil has generally been associated with the appearance of sects. On balance, the evidence seems to suggest some decline in the rate at which new sects will be formed from now on.

CHURCH POLITY Although the specific organizational forms found in American religious life vary widely, most churches can be classified as predominantly *episcopal, presbyterian,* or *congregational*.[5] In the first of these (*espiscopus* = bishop) a hierarchy of authority and control proceeds from the center or top level downward. A number of denominations have this form, though the Roman Catholic Church is perhaps the most familiar. In the presbyterian form, priestly authority (*presbyter* = priest)

---

[5] As used here these words do not refer to particular denominations, despite the fact that there are churches with these names. We speak of types of church organization, and each type has several representatives in American religion.

The Hare Krishna, the Mennonites, and the Process are some examples of the rich diversity of American religious sects. Sects have been based on so many different things it is not inconceivable that even the recent therapeutic technique sometimes referred to as the "primal scream" might become the basis of one. [Cartoon, top right: drawing by H. Martin; © 1974, The New Yorker Magazine, Inc.]

may be modified considerably by the presence of laymen at decision-making points. Individual churches compose district organizations (which may be known as synods), but there is no single person as head, like the Pope, or the Primate of the Church of England. Churches with the congregational form, or some modification of it, stress the freedom of local church bodies in making decisions. Centralized control is weak or nonexistent, and laymen are influential in all important decision making.

The Ecclesia and the Universal Church

These two forms of religious organization are not found in the United States, but are or have been important elsewhere. According to Becker (1932:624–25):

The ecclesia is a predominantly conservative body, not in open conflict with the secular aspects of social life, and professedly universal in its aims. . . . The fully developed ecclesia attempts to amalgamate with the state and the dominant classes, and strives to exercise control over every person in the population. Members are *born into* the ecclesia; they do not have to *join* it. . . . The ecclesia naturally attaches a high importance to the means of grace which it administers, to the system of doctrine which it has formulated, and to the official administration of sacraments and teaching by official clergy.

Established national churches are examples of ecclesia. Yinger (1970:263) holds that ecclesia-like circumstances apply to Hinduism and Buddhism in parts of the East, citing Thailand as a particularly clear example.

The universal church includes all types of religious organizations and may cut across national boundaries. "It combines both church and sect tendencies in a systematic and effective way. It is thus universal both in the sense that it includes all the members of a society and in the fact that the major functions of religion are closely interrelated. It also tends to be characterized by a complex ecclesiastical structure" (Yinger, 1970:257).

Yinger believes that the Roman Catholic Church in the thirteenth century best illustrates the universal church in European civilization. He suggests that the same tendencies which led to sects in Protestantism produced the monastic orders in Catholicism. But in the latter case the individualizing tendencies were contained within the overall structure. At certain times and places, Islam also produced something like a universal church.

THE LOCAL CHURCH[6]   Despite the doctrinal and organizational differences between America's churches, there is no more important unit in any of them than the local parish church. Here sweeping changes which eventually affect all of organized religion come most directly into play. It is here that religion is most immediately embedded in the complex cross pressures of a changing society. We shall discuss the two chief roles in the local church: clergyman and lay member.

The Role of the Clergyman   Every experienced priest, minister, and rabbi is personally acquainted with the facts mentioned here but they are far less known to others. To a sociologist, the main feature of the role of the American clergyman today is the extraordinary complexity of the demands made upon him. As Glock and Stark (1965:124) put it:

The minister is at once pastor and preacher, administrator and organizer, counselor and educator. His multi-faceted role poses a number of problems to him. One is the problem of acquiring the competence to perform these many functions, another the problem of judging the relative importance of each function and dividing his time accordingly, and a third the related problem of resolving the cross pressures which inevitably arise where there is more to be done than can effectively be done.

---

[6] This section is based on an important treatise written by C. Y. Glock and R. Stark, entitled *Religion and Society in Tension*.

The minister is expected to be a theologically trained preacher, but also an applied sociologist and psychologist, an administrator, and an educator. In a short period of time he may preside at weddings, births, and funerals, visit the sick, act as the administrative head of his church, allocate scarce resources, mediate conflicts, and raise money; he may be an ambassador from the church to the larger community, devise educational programs for different age groups, attend meetings of interest groups attached to the church, manage the church's physical plant, counsel couples with marital difficulties, read, study, and preach. Even this does not exhaust the variety of his tasks. Since many of these activities call for considerable training and skill, it is manifestly impossible, especially in the typical church where there is only one clergyman, to do all these tasks well. Hence every clergyman must make difficult choices, and his choices will be reflected in the character of the programs of his church.

Blizzard (1957) studied the manner in which Protestant ministers actually allocate their time. Some of his results are reported by Glock and Stark (1965:125–26) as follows:

The average minister spends most of his time, about 40 percent of it, in performing the administrative duties of the parish—attending staff meetings, handling publicity, supervising and actually doing clerical and stenographic work, and administering the church's finances. About a quarter of his time, on the average, is devoted to pastoral duties—visiting, ministering to the sick and distressed, and counseling. The functions of preacher and priest take up about 10 percent of his time, including the time devoted to sermon preparation. The remaining 15 percent is divided between organizational work and parish education.

Koval (1971) has presented evidence indicating that both Catholic priests and Protestant clergymen presently experience serious occupational stress. He finds that one out of four Roman Catholic priests in this country have given thought to resigning from the clergy, and one out of eight Protestant clergymen. The potentially disaffected are especially likely to be in the younger age groups. Loss of faith is not frequently given as a reason for giving up the priesthood or ministry. The problems arise out of clerical frustration and impatience with aspects of church structure, policy, and program; Koval indicates that these are greater for Catholic than for Protestant clergymen.

Role conflict is built into the minister's task in at least two ways. First, the role makes superhuman demands. Second, parishioners' conceptions of the role are inaccurate and may be in outright conflict with the minister's own view of it (Ringer and Glock, 1954; Glock and Stark, 1965). As local churches are now organized there are no obvious or easy solutions to this problem.

The Role of the Lay Member We are plagued by a dearth of solid information out of which to form a composite picture of the relationships between church members and the local church. How-

The social activism of clergymen like the Berrigan brothers (above), well known because of their radical protests against the Vietnam war, and the modification of such traditional rituals as the mass (opposite page) are symptomatic of the desire for role modification among some of the clergy and the desire to make the traditional church organization and church ritual more meaningful, to young people especially.

ever, an important study of the Protestant Episcopal denomination was conducted by Glock, Ringer, and Babbie (1967), who developed a composite index of involvement in the church. Some of their findings are summarized here:

1. More church members are women than men, and women (overall) are more active in the program of the church than men.

2. Involvement in the church is related to the life cycle of the individual and to the family cycle. It declines for both men and women when marriage occurs and is reduced again when the first child is born. When the children get older participation increases, but more for women than for men. The level of female participation continues to increase into the later years of life. It increases for men also, as they get older, but less so, so that the discrepancy between male and female involvement becomes greater. Glock and Stark (1965:141) point out that this tendency for participation to be highest in the older age categories may have something to do with the conservatism of many churches.

3. After the age of thirty, the highest level of involvement is found among those members who are neither married nor parents. It is lowest among those who are married and have children. Given the emphasis on the family found in most churches this is an interesting finding, and would seem to have implications for churches trying to reevaluate their programs.

4. The social status of members is not as significantly related to involvement as the factors mentioned above. There is some suggestion that upper-class persons are less involved than those at middle and lower class levels.

In commenting on the findings above, Glock and Stark (1965:142) point out that "characteristics associated with low involvement are all more highly valued by the society-at-large than the characteristics associated with high involvement." While cautioning that the data do not establish causal sequences, they say, "What these observations suggest is that a strong factor affecting deep involvement in the church may be a feeling of being rejected by general society."

Local churches, and religion in general, face many serious dilemmas as they try to define, redefine, and work toward their goals under the rapidly shifting conditions found in a complex society like the United States. This leads us to a consideration of religion in relation to social change.

RELIGION AND SOCIAL CHANGE

Religionists sometimes disagree on doctrinal grounds as to whether the church should exist apart from the world or be fully engaged in its concerns. From your earlier reading in this book, you will realize that sociologically speaking, religious organizations are completely interdependent with the rest of society, as is almost every other kind of organization. It is possible to maintain in a theological context that the Christian message has not changed, but it is not possible to argue successfully that the *church* has not changed. Signs of strain and tension (breeding points for change) are everywhere. Like all other groups and organizations, the church is having to come to terms with the manifold and unsettling social consequences of the urban-industrial revolution. So much is happening, in fact, that it will be necessary to restrict ourselves here to only a few aspects of the subject.

For some years following World War II there was much talk in religious circles and elsewhere about a return to religion in American life. What the phrase implies is not always clear, but presumably it suggests a growth in the role of religion for the individual and perhaps for the whole society. We shall consider several kinds of evidence which bear directly or indirectly on the question whether or not this is happening.

The Bureau of Research and Survey of the National Council of Churches of Christ in the United States publishes the *Yearbook of American Churches*. Table 14-3 presents figures on the proportion of the total United States population that also constituted church membership over the period from 1940 to 1965.

Insofar as church membership is a measure of religious influence, these figures taken at face value suggest that there was an increase in influence after World War II which leveled off toward the end of the fifties. American church membership is at the highest point in history. For instance, it is estimated that only 36 percent of the population were church communicants in 1900, and that the percentages were still lower at earlier periods. Furthermore, 95 percent of all Americans identify themselves with some religious body, even though—as Table 14-3 shows—a much lower proportion actually hold membership (Herberg, 1955).

Figures like these have strengthened the belief in a current return to religion. Unfortunately, data on church membership in this country are notoriously unreliable. For example, much of the apparent gain in membership over a century comes from church bodies which formerly did not report at all but now do so. There have been drastic differences in the way churches define the word *member*. Many Protestant churches which formerly excluded children from membership figures (whereas Catholics and Jews did not) are now including children, a change which obviously leads to a spurious gain in overall membership (Demerath and Hammond, 1969:120).

The American Institute of Public Opinion (commonly known as the Gallup Poll) has frequently sought information on the proportion of Americans who had attended church in the week before being interviewed. Between 1939 and 1964, these figures ranged from 37 to 49 percent of the adult population. The higher figure occurred in 1955 and 1958. After 1958 there was a very slow decline, to 42 percent by 1970. While there was an increase from 1950 through 1955, it was not a very large one, and the subsequent declines do not suggest any strong religious revival. In short, neither church membership nor church attendance can be viewed as certain evidence of a remarkable growth in religious vitality in recent years.

TABLE 14-3   CHURCH MEMBERSHIP AS A PROPORTION OF TOTAL UNITED STATES POPULATION

1940	49
1950	57
1955	60.9
1956	62
1957	61
1958	63
1959	63.6
1960	63.6
1961	63.4
1962	63.4
1965	64

(In 1971, the proportion had declined slightly, to 62.4.)

Source: *Yearbook of American Churches*, 1968.

Beyond the inadequacies of the figures themselves is the important question of what they mean. How much does membership in a denominational body or even attendance at church services tell us about depth of religious commitment, either in those who go or in those who do not? Perhaps the best information we have on this matter is found in an important study by Lenski (1961). Although his data indicate that religious orientation does indeed affect ideas and behavior, there is no comparable earlier information to tell us whether there has been any change in this regard.

"At the present time, do you think religion as a whole is increasing its influence on American life or losing its influence?" In 1957, 14 percent of respondents to this Gallup Poll thought religion was losing influence. In 1962, 31 percent thought so, and in 1968, 67 percent. In commenting on this trend, Demerath and Hammond (1969:129) state, "Gallup himself cited this as 'one of the most dramatic shifts in surveys of American life,' one that characterizes Catholics as well as Protestants, old as well as young, women as well as men, college graduates as well as the uneducated." This is a change all right, and a dramatic one. But it is not direct evidence of a decline in the influence of religion, though it is direct evidence of American opinions on the matter.

Thus while there was much talk of a major religious revival in the United States after World War II, we are forced to conclude that sociologists, on the kinds of evidence they can consider, cannot resolve the issue.

THE DEVELOPMENT OF PENTECOSTALISM One related development is of considerable significance: in general, the established, mainline (and often relatively liberal) denominations have ceased to grow or even lost ground, while doctrinally and often socially conservative groups have made relative gains. This latter group includes both well-organized and securely established groups, and many sect-like bodies.

We may get some insight into the forces underlying this broad trend by examining a loosely organized movement called Pentecostalism. A native American development which began around 1900, it has recently made rapid gains not only in this country but in many other parts of the world as well. A fascinating recent study by Gerlach and Hine (1970) is our primary source on this movement.

Most organized Pentecostal groups resemble other fundamentalist sects in many ways. They stress the subjective experience of knowing the "Baptism of the Holy Spirit" at first hand. This is often accompanied by a kind of behavior which sets these groups apart from others: *glossolalia*, for which the ordinary phrase is "speaking with tongues." "Glossolalia is the utterance of streams and sounds which are unintelligible to both speaker and listener but which Pentecostals call a 'heavenly language' and consider to be the Holy Spirit acting through them. Its practice is usually accompanied by a sense of emotional release, joy, and closeness to God. It may or may not be associated with 'trances,' 'automatisms,' or other apparently involuntary motor activity" (Gerlach and Hine, 1970:2).

Despite the inadequacy of church membership statistics (especially inadequate in this case) it is almost certain that Pentecostal churches now have over two million members in the United States. An unknown but substantial number of them do not belong to established churches. These make up large numbers of independent groups not recorded in church statistics available to outsiders. Others are and remain members of churches in the major denominations, including Roman Catholicism.

Even more curious to the sociologist is that Pentecostalism draws its members not only from the lower class (as have most sects) but from a wide socioeconomic spectrum. In fact, it is among the relatively affluent, newer members in independent groups (and "hidden" members in older denominations) that the least church-like behavior is found. Gerlach and Hine state that "these bodies which are most 'church-like' within the Pentecostal movement as a whole represent the relatively lower socioeconomic groups participating. The higher socioeconomic groups most recently drawn in are among those which exhibit the most 'sect-like' behavior" (1970:5).

Why have the conservative churches gained while the main-line Protestant and the Roman Catholic churches are only holding their own? It looks as if Pentecostalism is not a sect typical of the kind so familiar to sociologists of religion, but a manifestation of a significant change in American religious life. Its numerical growth, its multitude of newly formed independent groups, its penetration of older churches while remaining outside of their official organizations and its appeal to persons of higher status, all say that something is happening to American religion of greater significance than the numbers of people involved.

There are wholly religious explanations for Pentecostalism. Like other sects, Pentecostals can claim to have found the true religious experience and can cite biblical sources as support. As always, we seek understanding in sociological terms. Provisionally, we suggest that the marked growth of Pentecostalism had two causes. One is the same social soil which has produced so many other religious sects in the past: poverty, frustration, and the sense of being dispossessed. The other is a feeling that conventional churches have lost much of their commitment to the religious life and have become too concerned with organizational problems.

The first of these causes links Pentecostalism with other sects. Early in this century the movement did appeal predominantly to the same comparatively disadvantaged segments of the population from which most new sects arise. These people are still very much part of the movement, more likely to be found in the established, older Pentecostal churches than are the persons of relatively high status who have come into the movement recently. Up

Along with Pentecostalism, the "Jesus Movement" is a contemporary expression (concentrated among the young) of the revival of interest in doctrinally and often socially conservative religion.

to this point, we see the growth of Pentecostalism as quite typical of the history of religious sects. One would predict that in time surviving Pentecostal churches will move along the usual line of change from sect to church. Wilson (1959) and Kendrick (1966) have observed this kind of change in older churches in the movement.

The second cause for the spread of Pentecostalism—distrust in the commitment of other churches—has mainly brought in the more affluent and educated converts of recent years. Most broadly, the sect's attraction for these people reflects the widespread alienation from traditional values and establishment social structures seen in so many other parts of society. Gerlach and Hine hold that many people feel that their conventional churches lack vitality. "Like the Pentecostals, they read the accounts of the era when the early church was bursting with religious zeal, when lives were being changed, and when, in spite of persecution, the church was growing by leaps and bounds. Yet their contemporary efforts to revitalize, either from the top of the religious bureaucracy down or from the bottom of the local church up, have resulted in remarkably little lasting change in the overall picture" (1970:207).

Gerlach and Hine (1970:203) see Pentecostalism in the established churches as one of many efforts to change organized religion from within. In particular, it brings with it the element of emotional and ecstatic experience, often characteristic of sects, and indeed of religious experience around the world.

At this point no one can say whether Pentecostalism (or some other effort to revitalize the church) will survive long enough to bring about enduring change. But the persistence of such efforts suggests that the present dissatisfaction with existing religious organizations has deep roots. Like the family, education, and other social institutions, the church is struggling to come to terms with the social consequences of the industrial revolution. It seems unlikely that this can be done without much more change in the familiar patterns developed in earlier and different times.

THE ECUMENICAL TREND IN THE UNITED STATES In light of Christianity's historic tendency to split off and develop new forms, it is interesting to note the reverse in recent years: a coming together in cooperation and unity. We shall use the word *ecumenism* to refer broadly to efforts intended to bring different denominations closer together, whether or not through actual organizational union. We can say at once that a significant social change is actually taking place. The ecumenical movement is not just a gleam in the eye of some religious people; it is a social fact.

Nondenominational Ecumenical Organizations The modern movement had its roots in several relatively independent movements which developed in the early years of this century. We mention specifically the Federal Council of the Churches of Christ

Pope John XXIII encouraged the ecumeni-cally minded among both Roman Catholics and Protestants by calling for a worldwide church council, Vatican II, which met from 1962 to 1965. As a result of this council, many liberal reforms were instituted within the church.

in America, which was established in 1908. In 1950, this body merged with others to form the National Council of the Churches of Christ in the United States of America. This is a loose federation with no organizational control over its members. Nevertheless it coordinates many specific activities among most of the main-line Protestant denominations; for example, some years ago it supported a group of ministers who carried on a radical civil rights program in Mississippi.

There are many other interdenominational agencies, though none so large and influential. The American Council of Christian Churches (ACC), made up of militant fundamentalist groups, is firmly opposed to much that the NCC stands for and may be an organizational response to the very existence of the NCC.

The Roman Catholic Church is a special case, apart from ecumenical tendencies in Protestantism. It has followed very limited policies of cooperation with other churches in this country in such organizations as the National Conference of Christians and Jews. But Vatican II, with its ecumenical emphasis under the leadership of Pope John XXIII, revitalized those forces within the Catholic Church in America which would like to see a greater coming together of all Christian bodies. We do not suggest, however, that there is any serious possibility of organizational union in the sense discussed in the next section.

Denominational Mergers Perhaps the most striking evidence of the ecumenical movement is the number of denominations that have actually merged in recent years.

American groups resulting from the merger of two or more denominations include the Five Years Meeting of Friends (1902), United Church of Canada (1925), Congregational-Christian Churches (1931), Evangelical and Reformed Church (1934), Methodist Church (1939), Evangelical United Brethren Church (1946), Evangelical Free Church of America (1950), United Presbyterian Church in the U.S.A. (1958), American Lutheran Church (1961), and United Church of Christ (1957), a merger of the Congregational-Christian and Evangelical and Reformed Churches which was not fully consummated until 1961 (Moberg, 1962:256).

This list was compiled some years ago and since that time discussions have continued among many denominations, large and small, some of which will probably lead to further mergers or, in some cases, to less complete levels of affiliation. For instance, in 1969 the Lutheran Church, Missouri Synod, voted to enter into "altar and pulpit fellowship" with the American Lutheran Church. Sometimes these partial affiliations are a prelude to later union.

Why should this important change in religious organization have come about when it did? Here is Moberg (1962:259) on the subject.

Many recent conditions have stimulated the ecumenical movement. These include student Christian movements, attempts to relate religion to ethical and social problems, experiences in modern missionary enterprises, growing recognition of the social nature of divisions of Protestantism, the spread of theologies which do not follow denominational lines, the growth among Christians of a sense of world-wide community, and, above all, the Scriptural emphasis upon the church as the "body of Christ" transcending the ethnic, national, class, and racial barriers that divide men.

Such mundane considerations as the growing costs of church programs (which in many respects are parallel in different churches) have also played a part. So too has the relatively rapid growth of the Roman Catholic Church in recent decades. Now the largest single church body in the country, it has aroused many Protestants to compete more effectively. The high rate of geographical mobility of Americans, and the lessening of local isolation by mass communications, have affected the trend. When people move, they may not find a church of their own kind in the new location, and may find that another church is not so different as they had assumed. Thus in general, the ecumenical movement is a product of forces in the larger society which have an impact on religion, and of developments within religion, theological, organizational, and other.

But like all important social trends, ecumenism meets determined resistance. To many Christians it is neither inevitable nor desirable. Again, we turn to Moberg for a concise statement of some of the factors at work (1962:261).

Theological differences are stressed by non-cooperators who promote denominational particularisms, regard religion as purely individualistic, or fear centralized control. But various sociological factors appear to be more significant hindrances to ecumenism. These include institutionalism and resistance to change because of loyalties to outmoded traditions; real or imagined threats to institutional independence; ethnocentric belief that one's own church alone has truly Christian doctrine or polity, hence cooperation compromises the truth; denominational bureaucracies which are blind to or have a vested interest in maintaining the status quo; and the desires of churches in missionary fields to assert complete independence.

A major instance of resistance to ecumenism took place in 1973. Nine Protestant denominations had been working toward union over a period of ten years through an organization called the Consultation on Church Union. The effort to achieve formal unity at the denominational level was given up in 1973, because many local congregations grew disenchanted with the idea. At about the same time a new and formal schism occurred in the southern branch of American Presbyterianism, called the Presbyterian Church in the United States. Some seventy conservative congregations broke away altogether rather than follow the denomination's decision to rejoin the more liberal United Presbyterian Church in the United States of America.

The Limits of Ecumenism Carried to the logical extreme, ecumenism ultimately would unite all Christians in a single church. If this ever happens, it will be in a future too distant to predict at this time. But there are a few things that can be said about the reasonably near future, and with special reference to the United States.

It is reasonable to assume that the more alike Protestant Americans become in social characteristics and particularly in religious beliefs, the further ecumenism is likely to go. There is some disagreement among sociologists, however, on the degree to which Protestants really are moving toward similar religious positions. Herberg (1955) thinks they are. But substantial research reported by Glock and Stark (1965), on a wide variety of theological beliefs in different denominations, throws a good deal of doubt on Herberg's thesis. Table 14-4 makes it abundantly clear that on a wide variety of doctrinal issues, great differences still exist between churches.

Glock and Stark came to the conclusion that denominations can be grouped in four or five categories on a doctrinal basis. Their summary is so relevant to the future of the ecumenical movement that we quote it here.

At least four and probably five generic theological camps can be clearly identified among the American denominations. The first, the *Liberals,* comprises the Congregationalists, Methodists, and Episcopalians, and is characterized by having a majority of its members who reject firm belief in central tenets of Christian orthodoxy. It is likely that the changes that have gone on in these bodies, since they are among the highest status and most visible Protestant groups, have largely produced the impressions that Protestantism in general has shifted toward a secular and modernized world view.

The second group, the *Moderates,* is composed of the Disciples of Christ and the Presbyterians. This group is less secularized than the Liberals, but more so than the *Conservatives,* who are made up of the American Lutheran group and the American Baptists. The *Fundamentalists* include the Missouri Synod Lutherans, the Southern Baptists, and the host of small sects.

Because of historic differences with Protestantism, the Roman Catholics are perhaps properly left to form a fifth distinct group by themselves. But on most theological issues, both those presented here and many more, the Roman Catholics consistently resemble the Conservatives. Only on

	Congregationalists	Methodists	Episcopalians	Disciples of Christ	Presbyterians	American Lutherans	American Baptists	Missouri Lutherans	Southern Baptists	Sects	Total Protestants	Catholics
"I know God really exists and I have no doubts about it."	41	60	63	76	75	73	78	81	99	96	71	81
"Jesus is the Divine Son of God and I have no doubts about it."	40	54	59	74	72	74	76	93	99	97	69	86
"Jesus was born of a virgin."	21	34	39	62	57	66	69	92	99	96	57	81
"There is life beyond death."	36	49	53	64	69	70	72	84	97	94	65	75
"Belief in Jesus Christ as 'Saviour.'" (absolutely necessary)	38	45	47	78	66	77	78	97	97	96	65	51
"Doing good for others." (absolutely necessary)	58	57	54	64	48	47	45	38	29	61	52	57

* The percentages indicated are those holding the strongest conviction about the particular doctrine. Respondents could, if they wished, report lesser degrees of conviction.
Selected and condensed from C. Y. Clock and R. Stark, "Is There an American Protestantism?" *Trans-Action* 13 (November–December 1965), pp. 8–13, 48–49.

special Protestant-Catholic issues such as Papal infallibility (accepted by 66 percent of the Roman Catholics and only 2 percent of the Protestants) were the Catholics and the Conservatives in any extensive disagreement.

Merging the denominations to form these five major groups is the greatest degree of clustering that is statistically permissible. *It seems very unlikely that ecumenical clustering could result in fewer* (emphasis added) (Glock and Stark, 1965).

THE IMPACT OF RELIGIOUS CHANGE ON SOCIETY We have been discussing change *within* American religious organizations. In the process it has become pretty clear that organized religion has felt the impact of changes occurring elsewhere in society. But does the church in turn change society? If we believe in the basic sociological postulate, that change in one major institution brings about changes in others, then there must be effects upon society at large. It may be true, as with the family, that religion has been more on the receiving than the originating end in the enormous matrix of change known as the urban-industrial revolution. Yet the influence cannot be just one way.

Effects of Religion on Behavior We start with a reminder of our basic position that while the individual and society are not identical, they are so interdependent that together they may be seen as different aspects of one totality, the human experience. It necessarily follows that if religion plays a major role in the lives of most individuals in a society, it also influences the unit we call society. We have already said that most Americans belong to some church and an overwhelming majority at least identify themselves with some religious persuasion. Since religion is one of the major sources and supports of the important values and norms found in society, it enters, at least indirectly, into the whole process of socialization by which people acquire their personalities and learn how to live in the world society has made for them.

There is interesting empirical evidence in Lenski's landmark study of religious beliefs and behavior subtitled *A Sociological Study of Religion's Impact on Politics, Economics and Family Life* (1961:326). After an exhaustive analysis in which socioreligious group membership was tested for its relationship with thirty-five different behavioral variables, Lenski comes to the following conclusion (among others). "Socioreligious group membership is a variable comparable in importance to class, both with respect to its potency and with respect to the range, or extent, of its influence" (1961:326). This statement takes on added importance when one realizes that few variables studied by sociologists are comparable to class in the range of influence.

In short, religion does indeed play a major role, at least indirectly, in the nonreligious parts of the lives of Americans. But this is not the same as demonstrating a connection between some aspect of religion and some specific change in society. In this connection, Lenski feels that the influence of religion upon behavior is probably increasing. If so, this would argue in very general terms that societal effects of religious commitment will also increase, at least relatively, in relation to other sociological causes of change. Looking back over a long sweep of history, Parsons (1957) has concluded that Christianity has been a source of creative innovation in Western society because of its "activism," its tendency to overcome obstacles rather than to retreat inwardly from an imperfect world.

The Prophetic Function of Religion   Before leaving this subject, we shall take a look at what Demerath and Hammond (1969) call the prophetic function of the church. They discuss this in relation to the integrative function of religion, treated earlier. Whereas the integrative function of religion is to hold society together, and may be seen as inherently conservative, the prophetic function is to sit in judgment upon society, calling upon men to do better than they are doing now. Insofar as the church is prophetic in this sense, it is potentially an active agent in bringing about social change.

After a carefully reasoned analysis, Demerath and Hammond conclude that the powerful pressure for performing the integrative function within local parishes

militates against vigorous pursuit of the second major religious function, that of religious prophecy in the interests of social change. There is a very real sense in which the functions of integration and prophecy are hostile to one another within the contemporary church. This is a major reason why the source of religious prophecy itself has shifted to nonparish personnel and to officials high in the church bureaucracies who have no specific parish flock to bind together.

However, one must distinguish between prophetic ventures and prophetic impact, and here a major irony is discernible. On the one hand, nonparish personnel are allowed to make prophetic pronouncements precisely because so few members of either their differentiated church or the differentiated society are affected; in a word, they are able to shout because so few are listening. On the other hand, the parish personnel are in the opposite situation. Because they are concerned over who will be listening, to the detriment of the parish's stability and membership, they are reluctant to shout and are confined to whispering (1969:230–31).

It is our opinion that the church does not at present intervene directly and deliberately to bring about changes in society, despite an occasional dramatic instance to the contrary. As Demerath and Hammond put it, "One can expect churches to be conservative more often than they are innovative, to follow society more often than they try to lead it" (1969:214).

Two events of 1973 which we have already mentioned, the difficulties of the Consultation on Church Union and the schism within the (southern) Presbyterian Church in the United States, seem to illustrate and support the view of Demerath and Hammond. In the 1960s, many of the main-line Protestant denominations engaged in liberal social action: civil rights work, anti–Vietnam war and anti-poverty programs, and the like. These programs were initiated by national leaders at the denominational level and were resented by members of many local churches. Many church leaders attributed the two incidents in 1973 to accumulating resistance at the local level.

Left, visiting a sharecropper's cottage in the South. Right, demonstrating against the Vietnam war (William Sloane Coffin, Jr., Episcopal chaplain of Yale University).

Part 3 / Social Institutions

A few years ago, Fukuyama (1963) published a survey of the uses of sociology made by religious bodies in this country. He noted scattered instances at the beginning of the century and even a bit earlier. This is a period roughly equal to the entire history of sociology as a separate discipline in the United States. Actually, this influence is not especially surprising in view of the fact that many early American sociologists of note were also ordained ministers.

Through the 1920s and 1930s, sociologists made many useful descriptive studies of rural churches and of churches in changing or decaying urban neighborhoods. Sociological research method was used to help locate new churches in expanding cities and neighborhoods. In 1921, the Institute of Social and Religious Research, with financial help from John D. Rockefeller, Jr., was organized to continue part of the work begun by the Interchurch World Movement. "Organized 'to apply scientific method to the study of socioreligious phenomena,' it made over fifty surveys and published over ninety volumes in its thirteen-year history from 1921 to 1934. . . . Perhaps the most lasting of its contributions to sociological literature were the Institute's financing of Lynd and Lynd's classic study of *Middletown* and the collaboration of the Institute's staff with President Hoover's Research Committee in the study of *Recent Social Trends in the United States*" (Fukuyama, 1963).

Since World War II, according to Fukuyama, sociological research and researchers have been incorporated into the organizational apparatus of a number of major denominations. Yet he seems to feel that the best work is being done in academic rather than officially religious settings, and he cites examples of faculty and graduate student research which have made notable contributions. In his view, this is true mainly because church bodies are defensive about research which might uncover weaknesses in programs and administrative practices.

This, of course, is a problem in any research involving action-oriented organizations, religious, business, government, or other. If research is to deal with significant problems and do so scientifically, powerful interests may indeed be offended; there is no easy way around that. At the risk of oversimplifying, we can say that one condition for effective use of sociological knowledge and research in religion is the courage of religious leaders to run risks and to let the chips fall where they may. Meanwhile, studies of great theoretical and practical potential are occasionally done with the official collaboration of religious organizations or even under their sponsorship. One such is the research we have cited by Glock and Stark, which was financed by the Anti-Defamation League of B'nai B'rith, a Jewish organization.

There is a broader sense in which the sociological viewpoint on religion has practical value. We refer to the benefit of being able to view important phenomena from the *outside*, so to speak, as well as from the inside. This of course applies to nearly the whole of sociology. A religious person who sees the vast field of

Religion 401

When religious leaders and professionals or certain religious sects challenge conservative secular values in the interest of what they feel are superior religious values, resistance develops among lay members in local churches. In this way an organizational dilemma raises serious problems for the religious institution and also for the personal faith of individuals.

religion *only* from his own perspective as a devout communicant misses a very great deal. Having little understanding of religion in general, and its social sources and consequences, he is ignorant of much about his own religion. Intellectual knowledge of the sociological kind is certainly not incompatible with faith and belief. On the contrary, a religious person may understand and appreciate his own faith better if he can place it in a context of secular understanding. In so doing, he will be better able to use sociological knowledge in pragmatic ways to make religious organization more effective in achieving religious goals.

Practicing the Sociological Perspective

At the beginning of this chapter a quotation from Moberg listed a number of symbolic representations of religion which appear in the nonreligious aspects of our national life. See if you can extend this list; a little thought will bring many other examples to mind. Attend a religious service in a church as different as possible from the one you know best. Try to be an observer rather than a participant. Compare the ritual aspects of the service with what you are accustomed to. What differences do you see? How do you suppose these differences came into being? Compare a historical or sociological answer to this question with a theological one.

If you are acquainted with a minister, rabbi, or priest, ask him why religion exists. Compare what he tells you with the functional answer presented in this chapter. Must one of these answers be wrong and the other right? You may also discuss with this person—or with any well-informed religious person—the role of the church in social change. Think carefully about what you are told and compare it with the discussion of the topic in this chapter.

Suppose you are commissioned to do a major piece of research on the question of whether or not the United States is becoming more religious with the passage of time. You have ample financial resources to carry out this study. What would you accept as evidence of any trend? In other words, what does being religious mean in the life of an individual or a nation? Assuming that you can be clear in your own mind about what being religious means, into what kinds of obtainable information would you translate this conception?

Part 3 / Social Institutions

Science

15

Is science a sort of Frankenstein's monster turning on its creator and threatening to destroy him? Or is it a wonderful force for good in human affairs, promising fruitful control of nature and ultimate prosperity and happiness for all? Both views have advocates today. In this chapter we shall examine science from a sociological perspective, and we shall find that it is neither an arch villain nor the savior of man. It is a troubled and troublesome aspect of society, playing a key role in the evolution of industrial nations and certain to be a prime mover in future social change across the world.

Two assumptions underly science: that the universe is orderly, and that its nature is discoverable by reason and empirical exploration. The first assumption does not argue that every event in the physical universe is predetermined. It does mean that by and large, order—and thus predictability—prevails. The second assumption means that the nature of this order—the laws which govern the universe—can be identified insofar as they may be apprehended by the logical-empirical method. If there are aspects of the universe which do not reveal their nature through this method, they lie outside the realm of science. Hence, science is restricted to the physical universe as knowable by its characteristic (and quite possibly, limiting) approach to reality. Related to these assumptions is a fundamental value: knowledge is good, and therefore should

DEFINING SCIENCE

The glittering magnificence of the technologies based on modern science, perhaps best represented by the computer, has in no way released man from full responsibility for the products of his own intelligence.

be enlarged. The centrality of this value suggests why science has long appealed to the curious and creative.

SCIENTIFIC NORMS   Norms, as we know, are standards of behavior. Here are some of the norms which have operated within the scientific community, as formulated by Merton (1957:550–61) and Barber (1962:122–42).

Universalism   Essentially, the norm of universalism specifies that truth in science has nothing to do with the personal or social characteristics of scientists. Truth can be established only by the impersonal empirical and logical procedures of scientific method and in relation to existing scientific knowledge. *All* persons who conform to these requirements may contribute to scientific growth. This norm holds that the race, religion, social class, and nationality of a scientist are irrelevant to determining the truth of scientific knowledge.

Knowledge Belongs to All   This norm specifies that scientific knowledge is not subject to property rights. It is produced through direct and indirect social contacts. Even an individual scientist working alone builds on the work of thousands of predecessors. Likewise the work of every scientist belongs freely to everyone. As Merton states: "Property rights in science are whittled down to a bare minimum by the rationale of the scientific ethic. The scientist's claim to 'his' intellectual 'property' is limited to that of recognition and esteem" (1957:556).[1]

---

[1] The process whereby the government confers property rights via the patenting process may appear to conflict with this statement, and perhaps does to a degree. Patents are granted, however, not so often for contributions to basic scientific knowledge, as for technological applications of such knowledge.

The idea that knowledge belongs to all is incompatible with secrecy in scientific work. If there are no property rights in science, there is no reason within science itself why any individual, organization, or nation should withhold scientific findings from others. There is, in fact, a strongly felt injunction to communicate new findings to other members of the scientific community.

Disinterestedness Disinterestedness denotes behavior free from self-interest and partiality. In effect, this norm says that whatever personal reasons one may have for being a scientist, one's work must be judged by the publicly shared standards of the scientific community and these standards do not take account of individual motives. Merton notes the rarity of fraud in scientific work, observing that many people think it is because science recruits people of high integrity. He thinks a more plausible explanation is the vitality of the norm of disinterestedness, the public nature of scientific knowledge, and the probability that any claim of new knowledge will be carefully checked. In other words, the institutional norm supported by actual practice is a powerful force in "keeping scientists honest."

Organized Skepticism Applied to science, organized skepticism refers to "the suspension of judgment until 'the facts are at hand,' and the detached scrutiny of beliefs in terms of empirical and logical criteria" (Merton, 1957:560). Skepticism in the scientific community is organized in the sense that it is built into the scientific method which is binding on all scientific workers who must be skeptical about both their own work and that of others. Chances are that you have read one or more descriptions of scientific method. Every working scientist knows that his research seldom fits exactly the sequence outlined in textbook discussions of this method. Nevertheless, such descriptions do give the nonscientist a general idea of "doing science," the working procedures followed by scientific personnel.

Scientific skepticism is anything but cynical. It seeks to extend knowledge, not to destroy existing beliefs. The procedures by which scientists extend knowledge do, however, prohibit them from accepting any kind of nonscientific authority as the arbiter of truth about the natural world. This fact can, and in the history of science frequently did, bring conflict with groups who *do* accept nonscientific standards of truth supported by other institutions.

Emotional Neutrality Since scientists are as human as anyone else, it isn't reasonable to expect them not to have emotional investments in their work. But the scientist should "avoid so much emotional involvement in his work that he cannot adopt a new approach or reject an old answer when his findings suggest that this is necessary, or that he unintentionally distorts his findings in order to support a particular hypothesis" (Storer, 1966:80).

There are many sciences, but these assumptions, values, and norms permeate all of them. They are part of the culture of what

The idea of keeping scientific knowledge locked away from "unauthorized" people is basically opposed to one of the fundamental values of science. Yet scientists are often overruled in this matter by their employers in government and industry.

Storer (1966) calls the social system of science. They are the things which let us speak of a scientific community or even an institution of science, despite the diversity of fields and organizational settings (many of them predominantly nonscientific) in which scientists work. Whatever science may mean to the general public, and we will consider this later, there is great consensus among scientists on the subject. Such assumptions, values, and norms as these contain the philosophical underpinnings of science, specify the broad procedures for expanding knowledge, and go a long way toward defining the scientist's social role.

It would be a mistake to assume that every scientist behaves at all times by the code. As with the values and norms in all social systems, there is a gap between what people agree they ought to do and what they actually do. There are scientists who are intellectually dishonest. There are others who, without knowing it, let their feelings distort their work. Even so, the conduct of scientists is influenced by the values and norms we have listed.

SCIENCE AS VERIFIED KNOWLEDGE   These norms tell us something of the broad social imperatives that govern scientists as they go about expanding knowledge. Science is not only the process, but also the product of the endeavor; it is the accumulation of empirically verified knowledge in every scientific field. What we know about the world as a result of scientific research is as much a part of society's culture as any other component.

In Chapter 16 we shall speak about the tendency of some parts of culture to accumulate at an increasing rate. This appears to have been true of scientific knowledge in recent centuries. You can get some inkling of this growth by a glance at the growth of scientific publication. The first, still surviving, journal which began publication in 1665, is the *Philosophical Transactions of the Royal Society of London.* The total of such journals, for the entire world, is now rapidly approaching one hundred thousand (de Solla Price, 1966:51). Since 1665, the number of scientific publications has doubled nearly every fifteen years with astonishing regularity, and the rate has been greater in the United States. The resultant increase, projected to the year 2000, is portrayed in Figure 15-1.

Kaplan (1964:857) quotes a government report as follows:

Chemical Abstracts in 1930 contained 54,000 abstracts; a private subscription cost $7.50 per year, an institutional subscription cost $12 per year. In 1962, *Chemical Abstracts* published 165,000 abstracts and the 1963 price will be $500 to American Chemical Society members and to colleges and universities, and $1000 per year to all others (President's Science Advisory Committee, 1963, p. 18). Some have estimated the total number of papers published annually in the sciences in the early 1960s as over 2 million. In addition to published papers it was estimated that in the United States alone some 100,000 informal government reports are published annually, of which 75,000 are "unclassified" (President's Science Advisory Committee, p. 19).

FIGURE 15-1   GROWTH IN NUMBER OF SCIENTIFIC JOURNALS

[Source: From *Science Since Babylon,* by Derek J. de Solla Price, p. 97. Copyright © 1961 by Derek J. de Solla Price. Reprinted by permission of Yale University Press.]

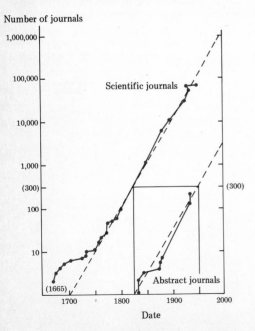

Another measure of recent growth is that from 1955 to 1972, expenditures for basic and applied research in the United States rose from slightly over $2 billion to $10.5 billion (*Statistical Abstract of the United States*, 1973).

We do not believe that this growth rate can be indefinitely maintained, and it is becoming a factor in an increasing number of significant problems.

To be a scientist is to play a social role having this name. Within the scientific community, this role is deducible in broad outline from the norms previously considered. It is given specific content in each field and setting where scientists are employed. The role is also defined in different ways by nonscientists, but we shall ignore that for the moment.

Table 15-1 presents the number of scientists in the United States in 1970.[2] It is not complete but it gives the best enumeration we have. The total number of scientists given is 312,644, or about one and a half out of every thousand Americans. This may strike you as quite a small number considering the profound impact of science on the rest of society.

Look more closely. The table classifies scientists by the principal type of work done. These categories are arbitrary, however, and can lead to misinterpretation. Many scientists, for instance, are both teachers and researchers. Still, the figures do serve in a rough way to point out a surprising fact: only 44,544 people are engaged full-time in basic research in all scientific fields combined. Most scientists, it appears, are mainly teachers, or are doing applied research, or managerial-administrative tasks, or other ancillary activities.

Basic research is the accumulation of knowledge for its own sake, without immediate regard to its practical application. In the scientific community, it is viewed as the indispensable basis for progress in applied research and technology. According to Table 15-1 then, only about 14 percent of all scientists are carrying out this critical function full-time. By far the largest employer of scientists is education, mostly higher education. Industry and business is second, followed by government. These facts have implications which we shall shortly examine.

Table 15-2 gives an idea of how scientists are distributed by field. It is obvious that physical scientists far outnumber social scientists.

While the total number of scientists is small in relation to the whole population, there have been dramatic increases in recent

SCIENTISTS

---

[2] This information is compiled by the National Register of Scientific and Technical Personnel of the National Science Foundation, a federal agency. The National Register secures its figures in cooperation with the professional organizations of scientists.

decades. A few years ago, de Solla Price estimated that about 90 percent of all scientists the world has ever known are living today. As he put it, "We might miss Newton and Aristotle, but happily most of the contributors are with us still" (1966:58). Incidentally, about 90 percent of all American scientists are men. Recent increases in the numbers of women in graduate training, laws against discrimination in employment, and the activities of women themselves in the past few years should change this picture fairly soon.

THE MOTIVATION OF SCIENTISTS We may analyze science without speaking of scientists but obviously one would not exist without the other. An important question is why they choose scientific careers, undergoing long, arduous socialization in order to enter them. And why do scientists work hard through their careers, often with little public recognition? Money is no doubt the most widely understood incentive for hard work in this society. But incomes of scientists are far from impressive compared to those in many occupations requiring much less extensive training.

TABLE 15-1 SCIENTISTS IN THE UNITED STATES BY TYPE OF EMPLOYER AND WORK ACTIVITY, 1970

| | | WORK ACTIVITY | | | | | | | |
| | | Research and development | | | Management or administration | | | | |
TYPE OF EMPLOYER	Total	Total	Basic research	Applied research	Total	R and D	Teaching	Production and inspection	Other
Total scientists	312,644	97,078	44,544	40,704	68,708	29,723	72,408	16,086	58,364
Educational institutions	130,389	39,843	28,764	10,543	11,938	3,997	70,302	203	8,103
Federal Government	31,118	12,860	5,538	6,643	11,417	4,794	355	952	5,534
Other government	11,741	3,016	1,062	1,789	4,829	1,433	361	556	2,979
Military	7,285	1,422	630	699	2,635	692	404	254	2,570
Nonprofit organizations	10,911	4,601	2,173	2,231	3,051	1,520	265	231	2,763
Industry and business	97,542	33,803	5,655	18,155	33,321	16,779	274	13,437	16,707
Self-employed	6,314	535	147	312	857	265	65	257	4,600
Other	2,116	668	366	232	482	175	214	166	586
No report of employer	15,228	330	209	100	178	68	168	30	14,522

Source: U.S. National Science Foundation.

TABLE 15-2 SCIENTISTS IN THE UNITED STATES BY SCIENTIFIC FIELDS 1970

| | | | | SCIENTIFIC FIELD | | | | | |
Total	Agricultural Sciences	Biological Sciences	Psychology	Atmospheric and Earth Sciences	Mathematics and Statistics	Physics	Chemistry	Economics	Other Social Sciences
312,644	15,730	47,493	26,271	30,393	38,677	36,336	86,980	13,386	17,378

Source: U.S. National Science Foundation

Part 3 / Social Institutions

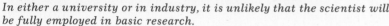

In either a university or in industry, it is unlikely that the scientist will be fully employed in basic research.

It is true that scientists have high social status. In 1947, North and Hatt showed that scientist was the eighth most prestigious occupation in the United States, and newer data in 1963 showed it tied for third (Hodge et al., 1964:286–302). Certainly high status is a reward which people will work hard to achieve. On the other hand there are numerically larger occupations with high social status *and* higher incomes, medicine and law, for example.

Another clue comes from recognition of the fact that scientific work is inherently creative, that is, it is concerned with creating knowledge. Insofar as this element is understood it will attract (and hold) persons who desire to be creative in this way. Storer speaks of "a fairly widespread motivation to be creative on the part of those individuals who become scientists, even before this motivation is shaped and channeled by the social system of science" (1966:59). The opportunity to do creative work is crucial, Storer holds, to the attraction of people into science, for other motives like the desire for high status can be as well satisfied by other kinds of careers.

How does the social system of science make use of the creativity motive in the individual? Merton (1962), Storer (1966), and others indicate that *professional recognition* is a major part of the answer. Professional recognition may take such forms as "eponymy,[3] prizes, awards, fellowships, scholarships, honorary memberships and committee work in scientific organizations, editorships, honorary degrees, professorships, chairs, lectureships, consultantships, mention by historians of science, publication,

---

[3] This word applies to the derivation of the name of something, such as a scientific discovery, from the name of a person, as in Einstein's theory of relativity.

Einstein was very probably attracted to the field of science at least partly because of the encouragement and recognition of creativity within that field.

acknowledgments in others' work, and evaluations by colleagues" (Glaser, 1964:2).

Professional recognition comes to a person from within the social system of science. It is recognition by one's professional peers that one has contributed to the advancement of knowledge. In this way the individual's behavior simultaneously satisfies his creative motive and receives social reward from a social system which highly values creativity. This interaction between individual motive and social reward is reflected in the importance of priority in scientific discovery. As Storer says, "The *second* man to arrive at a particular discovery, even if his work was entirely independent of the original discoverer, has lost virtually all opportunity for recognition and for immortality via the literature of science" (1966:21). The history of science records many bitter disputes over priority in discovery.

SCIENCE AND SOCIAL ORGANIZATION   The main goal of science, and thus of scientists, is the extension of verified knowledge. So scientists have created organizations designed to serve this purpose. Yet like everyone else, they must receive incomes from somewhere. The interaction between the nature of science and the need for the financial support of *scientists* (as distinct from scientific *research*) has helped to shape the social organization of science in the United States.

Limits of Employment   Unlike those in such service professions as medicine and law, scientists do not often sell their expert knowledge to buyers.

It is for this reason that there are so few scientists whose entire activity is devoted to basic research; the products of basic research are, almost by definition, not of immediate value to the layman, and so society is less willing to support this activity. (The fact that basic research is supported rather handsomely now by the federal government does not contradict this argument; this support is premised on the government's assumption that the products of basic research will eventually be of practical value, even though this possibility is not the basic researcher's goal in most cases.) (Storer, 1966:18.)

A physician is self-employed, a businessman works for a firm, a teacher for a school, a social worker for an agency. A scientist is rarely self-employed (about 2 percent in America), for there are few paying clients for his expertise. He is rarely employed in a purely scientific organization. The places where scientists make their livings are typically parts of larger organizational settings with predominantly nonscientific goals. Scientific research in the United States is highly concentrated in the economic institution (industry), the political institution (government), and the educational institution (universities, particularly).

While science has grown immensely, society has produced few organizations devoted solely to scientific ends and employing scientists on a large scale. This is quite unlike the situation in many occupations which expanded rapidly with industrialization. Instead, basic sciencing is an auxiliary function in many kinds of organizations with quite different goals. This not only dilutes the manpower available for scientific research, but also gives scientists much less than complete control over the conditions of their employment.

Scientists have two weapons in dealing with employers. First, they can refuse to work. Because of their sophisticated and non-transferable expertise this could be a more powerful weapon than it has traditionally been with organized labor. On the other hand, because scientific work is auxiliary in many organizations, stopping it may pose no immediate threat. In any case, scientists have rarely gone this route.

A second weapon of scientists is the power to certify persons as competent, using their control over university graduate training as a means to this end. As it happens, they have not much exercised the power to restrict entry into scientific careers (hence to increase economic bargaining power) as have many other occupations from craft unions to service professions such as medicine.[4] This situation has generated serious tensions within science, and between science and the rest of society.

Increased Size and Complexity The enormous growth of scientific work in recent decades has generated a cluster of organizational problems. Sheer growth in size raises such questions as how the large financial burden of modern research should be handled; what the most appropriate institutional shelter for science is—universities, industry, or government; and who should be responsible for determining short- and long-run programs of research development. Until World War II, in most advanced countries "science continued to expand mainly as a result of a series of individual decisions made in the universities and other laboratories and by individuals attracted to pursue science" (Kaplan, 1964:869).

The breakdown of this laissez-faire system, as Kaplan calls it, was most rapid in the United States. Such questions as those above have been provisionally answered by locating and supporting science in government, industry, and the universities. And this has been done largely by hasty responses to national emergencies, large and small. These answers may well not be good ones. One consequence is that science is no longer a small, self-contained, autonomous, self-governing community" (Kaplan, 1964:870).

But whether good or bad, what has happened in this country is a response to the growth in size, complexity, and cost of modern sci-

---

[4] Many of these characteristics of science as a field of employment are shared with most scholarly fields. But the consequences for the relationships between science and the rest of society are quite different, and follow the nature of science.

entific endeavor. Kaplan (1964:867–68) thinks the greater speed of this development here than in Europe has led to a relative decline in European science; witness the migration of European scientists to the United States. And he cites several analyses of European science which seem to agree that the persistence of laissez faire in Europe contributed to the comparative decline of European science.

Scientific Organizations Like other interest groups, including scholarly disciplines, scientists have formed many associations to represent their common interests. The number and size of these associations have grown dramatically with science itself. A century ago there was a small handful of them. Today there are several hundred, with more appearing almost every year. While there are several national associations, the most inclusive is the American Association for the Advancement of Science. When the AAAS held its first meeting in Philadelphia in 1848 (Bates, 1958:75), it provided only two internal divisions for different areas in science, and there were no independent societies affiliated with it.

Subsequent developments faithfully mirror the growth of scientific specialization. Until about 1900, the AAAS strove to represent all of science, even in the sense of directly sponsoring research, though a few groups such as the chemists and geologists did split off and form separate associations. But after 1900, there were many divisions and independent specialized associations developed rapidly. As a consequence, the AAAS adopted the strategy of affiliating independent societies with the most appropriate division in the larger association. In this way it achieved some unification of the interests of science as a whole without standing in the way of independent organizational developments. By 1919, forty-three societies were affiliated in this way. As Bates reports,

By 1955, the American Association for the Advancement of Science, with 265 affiliated and associated societies included forty-two academies of science, had an aggregate membership of more than 2,000,000 and was by far the largest and most important scientific organization in the world (1958:193).

The magazine *Science,* published by the AAAS, is one of the most widely read, authoritative, general magazines devoted to science in the world.

Few scientific societies have made serious efforts to represent the interests of their members as *employees* in marked contrast to organizations like the American Medical Association and the American Bar Association. This is probably because so many scientists are employed by colleges and universities. As professors scientists look to organizations like the American Association of University Professors to represent them in their jobs.

Instead, scientific associations have focused mainly on promoting specific scientific disciplines. In this capacity they hold meetings at which new work is reported on and informal relationships can be cemented. They sponsor journals which disseminate the results of research, and sponsor data centers and information retrieval procedures made possible by computer technology. In addition, they maintain contact with other sections of the scientific community, and especially in recent years with private foundations and government agencies which are sources of funds for scientific research.

Science is in increasing trouble in the United States. Angry denunciations are hurled against it for its collaboration in destructive activities like war, its alleged trivialization of modern life, and its indifference to fundamental problems of human welfare. In recent years, fewer young people are being attracted to careers in the older sciences. What is wrong? Sociologically, the answer lies in the kind of relationship recently developed between science and the rest of society. Considerable insight can be gained from viewing this relationship sociologically.

SCIENCE AND SOCIETY:
A TROUBLED RELATIONSHIP

How would the scientific community operate if social circumstances permitted it to be a highly autonomous, self-governing community relatively free of unwanted influences from the rest of society? This is, of course, an imaginary situation; science never was so independent. Yet if we consider only the values and norms of science, the social arrangement we sketch below might be attractive to many scientists. We speak primarily of basic science, not applied. In this ideal scheme scientists would be completely free to pursue knowledge in any way they saw fit; society would support their work financially and would place no limitations on the direction it took. Research priorities would be set solely by scientists using purely rational judgments as to which strategies would best and soonest lead to an increase in knowledge about all aspects of the natural world, including man.

Technological spin-offs would be of no concern to scientists; others in society would deal with such problems. Society would reward scientists with good incomes and high social status; otherwise, it would leave them alone. Politicians, businessmen, educators, and citizens at large would say, in effect, "We don't know what the scientists are doing; it's too technical for us. But we believe in it. We must not interfere with them in any way because they tell us that would make good science impossible."

SOME SOCIAL CONSEQUENCES OF SCIENCE This is certainly no description of the existing relationship between science and society in the United States. To come closer to the facts as they are, we shall first examine some effects of science on society, then some effects of society on science.

Relation to Technological Change Probably the most widely recognized effect of science on society is its role as a generator of

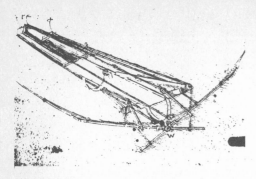

Despite Leonardo da Vinci's great technological ingenuity, as shown by the drawing above, a successful airship, such as the glider on the opposite page, could not be designed until the growth of science made possible the solution of fundamental aerodynamic and other engineering problems.

technological advancement. "In the broadest terms, we may say that man's increasing control of his natural environment, made possible by advance in scientific knowledge and made real by technology, has been primarily responsible for the accelerating rate of social change that we have experienced since the end of the last century" (Storer, 1966:3).

Notice that Storer's time reference is only to the last seventy-five years or so. Until about a century ago there was little relation between the growth of scientific knowledge and of technology. As Storer puts it:

Before that time, and in some areas to this day, technological change was almost entirely independent of progress in science. Probably the first important application of scientific knowledge to practical problems occurred in the mid-nineteenth century when aniline dyes were discovered and their manufacture formed the basis of the great German dye industry. Before that time developments in architecture, navigation, industrial processes, and armaments had come not from scientists but from men interested in solving immediate practical problems rather than in building a body of generalized knowledge (1966:2).

Particularly in this century "it has been increasingly the case that scientific advances are directly responsible for technological advances" (Storer, 1966:3). Can we expect this to continue indefinitely? Given enough time, the answer is certainly no, and the saturation point may be much nearer than is generally realized. What may happen can be crudely likened to the speed of a jet plane taking off from the ground. At first a jet moves very slowly, then it picks up speed at an increasing rate. But once it is in the air, its speed does not increase indefinitely; it cannot exceed a certain air speed. De Solla Price (1966) points out that if the growth rates of scientific manpower for the past few decades continued, then "if every school and college were turned to the exclusive production of physicists, ignoring all else in science and in the humanities, there would still necessarily be a manpower shortage in physics before the passage of another century" (1966:61). Nothing like this is actually going to happen, of course. As de Solla Price indicates:

The normal expansion of science that we have grown up with is such that it demands each year a larger place in our lives, a larger share of our resources. Eventually, that demand must reach a state where it cannot be satisfied, a state where the civilization is saturated with science. This may be regarded as an ultimate end of the completed industrial revolution (1966:62).

He cautions Americans against expecting this indefinite rate of expansion.

In particular, it cannot be worthwhile sacrificing all else that humanity holds dear to allow science to grow unchecked. . . . It would seem more useful to employ our efforts in anticipating the requirements of the new situation in which science has become, in some ways, a saturated activity of mankind, taking as high a proportion of our expenditure in brains and money as it can attain. We have not reached that stage quite yet, but it is only a very short time before we will—less than a human generation (1966:64).

Increasingly, de Solla Price thinks, the tactics and strategy for the employment of scientific resources cannot be left in the hands of scientists alone, but require a more rational and responsible societal policy than yet exists.

Corrosion of Traditional World Views Most men are not very curious or intellectually venturesome about the nature of the world, and this has apparently always been true. By and large, men like to have the main outlines of the universe and their place in it firmly in place; after that, they take these things for granted. Almost from its beginnings, however, science has subverted this orientation. People long thought of man as the summit and center of creation, and earth as the point around which the universe revolved. All cultures contained myths which explained these matters to everyone's satisfaction, but science showed them to be incorrect. It reduced man and his planet to a speck in the immensity of space, and traced out the unmistakable relations between human and other forms of life, erasing the impassable boundary between men and animals.

The challenge of science to ancient world views was first felt by religion, the official repository for many traditional beliefs. Since the mid-nineteenth century, there has been a sporadic struggle by organized religion to combat the newer scientific view of the universe. Though most larger religious bodies have yielded to science on the natural world, not all have done so. As recently as 1971, there was a vigorous effort in Colorado to pass a state law requiring that if evolutionary theory was to be taught in the schools, the biblical version of creation should also be taught as an alternative. Some of the arguments showed a profound misunderstanding of the differences between science and religion.

But the influence of science in this area has a subtler and probably more pervasive consequence. Older world views were based on tradition and on faith in religious authority. The views of science are based on reason and empirical research. Its picture of reality is never complete and is constantly changing. Insofar as laymen grasp the modern scientific picture of the universe, they realize that instead of substituting a new, simple certainty for an old one, it offers a prospect of flux and change. And it formulates the new pictures of reality in symbols and language so abstruse that most people cannot understand them. To laymen, scientists seem to be saying, "Trust us; through reason and empirical investigation we will come to understand reality more and more adequately." The dilemma lies in the fact that people once had clear and simple notions of what the world is like, and now science has largely destroyed these notions, offering something less satisfying to most people. It is too complex, too provisional and shifting, and too barren of familiar symbols around which people can organize their emotional as well as their intellectual responses to life.

Science appears to have made life uncertain and complicated not only in its effects on technology, but also through its effects on ideas and beliefs, on the intellectual framework in which people try to make sense of their lives.

Response to Rationalism Quite apart from science, the value system of American society puts considerable stress on mastery of the environment through individual, pragmatic efforts. Science is fundamentally in harmony with this value. Williams has stated that "science is at root fully compatible with a culture orientation that attempts to deny frustration and refuses to accept the idea of a fundamentally unreasonable and capricious world" (1970:488).

Yet can it be that one effect of science on society has been to overstress the rational component in human life? The method of science is rational, and the business of science is to use it. But may not scientists unwittingly argue that rationality and facts should characterize all of life? The prestige of science has been so great through the middle of our century that this message may have come through as part of the popular image and stereotype of science and the scientist. Americans may have come to accept an overrationalized and faulty version of life's meanings and possibilities partly because science is consonant with values which already exist in our society.

All this is pretty much conjecture, though some current social phenomena are consistent with this view. We believe that the popularity of existentialist philosophy in the past generation may be a reaction to a world which science helped to create.

The existentialist might say to the scientist, "In your field, reason and empirical method may be supreme, but you have made possible a society which depersonalizes and fragments us. Partly because of you we have forgotten how to be whole men. You haven't really made us rational, and you have oversold rationality, forgetting that we are creatures of emotion as well as thought. You are not helping us learn how to live decently in a world with no fixed meanings or guideposts."

We wonder also whether the remarkable growth of Pentecostalism (see Chapter 14), with its emphasis on immediate and emotional religious experience, may not be another reaction against overrationality in science. If so it is actively anti-intellectual in a way that existentialism is not. It seems to say that feeling and experience is all, and rational thought is nothing.

Many young people are reacting very strongly against the establishments of society today. The anti-intellectual tone of much of the counterculture, the drugs, the interest in Eastern religions, and the taste for communal living, among other things, may derive in part from rejection of the rationalism of science, technology, and American culture in general. The remarkable revival of occultism, magic, astrology and the like may also be signs of the same disillusionment and frustration.

For many decades and through the sixties, science and its dependent technologies (and most laymen do not clearly distinguish the two) seemed to be steadily disseminating a rationalistic orientation toward the world and human experience. Now in the seventies, a many-sided reaction has set in. The very success of science has caused the pendulum to swing the other way.

Generally, and in sociological terms, science and its products have introduced so much strain into traditional values and social arrangements that countervailing resistances have been aroused. For a time irrationality will often seem more attractive than rationality, and everything science stands for will be rejected. But we do not foresee the destruction of science; indeed the current atmosphere may play a part in reassessing the proper role of science in a mature industrial society.

We can now see that the picture of science as an autonomous community isolated from society can only be fiction. Indeed the influence of science has been so great that the rest of society cannot remain passive and disengaged in the face of it.

SOCIETAL INFLUENCES ON SCIENCE Earlier we pointed out that society does support science. It pays the costs (today very large ones) of scientific research, and it gives employment to individual scientists. Society exacts a price for its support. Increasingly, science and scientists have been employed directly or indirectly by the main power centers of society, government and industry, to serve their own purposes, not those of science. Here as elsewhere he who pays the piper gets to call the tune.

Political Control In the United States the federal government controls scientific priorities more than does any other center of influence. The chief instrument of this control is money for research. In 1972, 54.3 percent of all such funds in the United States came from federal sources. And this was the lowest proportion for many years. Basic research in particular is done in the universities. In 1972, the federal government was by far the largest supporter of this research, furnishing 58 percent of funds.

Congress appropriates money for research in a political process reflecting many factors—including powerful pressure groups—that have little to do with the priorities which scientists would set in the development of knowledge. Thus political control is felt not only in the amount of money appropriated for scientific work but in the specific fields where the money must be spent. No more important example can be found than recent allotments to national defense and the exploration of space. In 1972, the federal government spent $16 billion for research and development, of which nearly $9.5 billion went to defense and over $3 billion to space. Something over $2 billion was spent for a wide variety of pro-

The current interest in astrology is one example of rejection of scientific and technological rationalism. Some "back-to-nature" groups found in the counterculture might also be said to share this attitude. What is your view of the technological emphasis in our society?

grams under the heading human resources. Again this was the lowest proportion going to defense and to space in many years.[5]

Government and industry not only set research priorities by controlling funds, they may also attempt more direct control over what kinds of problems may be investigated. This is a challenge to the integrity of science difficult to ignore. A recent case is the 1970 legislation which would have given the federal Department of Justice broad new controls over drugs, promulgated at a time when public and political concern over drug abuse were high. The bill was opposed by important elements in the medical and scientific communities. A Committee for Effective Drug Abuse Legislation was formed, numbering fifty distinguished scientists, including Nobel Laureates Salvador Luria of MIT and Joshua Lederberg of Stanford. These critics strongly objected to provisions in the bill which would give the Department of Justice what they considered dangerous and unwarranted control over research in drugs and medical practice. While the scientists won this particular battle it is only one of many that confront them.

The strategies and priorities reflected in such direct and indirect control over research hardly reflect the interests of the scientific community. They reflect the government's preoccupation with the use of the military in foreign policy, the space race, and the influence of pressure groups. This has probably done more to stimulate the growing disenchantment with science than anything else. It certainly led to the attempts by college students in the late sixties to make universities cancel contracts for military research. As one critic put it:

Why is it that the science most readily supported by Congress is either a science for death or a science for leaving the planet, when in fact there is so much to be done in developing our own planet? We do not yet understand the processes of physical and mental disease. We have not solved problems of water and air pollution. Most of the world is impoverished, although for the first time in human history we have the means to eradicate poverty. . . .

Yet plans to realize these possibilities awake fears of socialism, despite the fact that they would create a higher standard of living and help solve the problems of the underdeveloped world; while the investment in destruction and space, involving at least as much government control, is rationalized as national security (Maccoby, 1970:265).

Science and scientists have let themselves be caught in a powerful social trap. The size and cost of the scientific enterprise have far outstripped the supportive capacity of scientists and of their traditional home, the universities. Government, and to a lesser extent industry, have picked up the tab, but in doing so have deprived science of its independence. As a result science has largely lost control of the direction of its own development.

---

[5] The information here and in the preceding paragraph is compiled and presented in the *Statistical Abstract of the United States* for 1973.

The same processes are at work in applied science. Businesses are established for profit, not for the advancement of scientific knowledge. Thus in spite of the slaughter on the highways, the automobile industry would not invest in research on auto safety until critics like Ralph Nader organized enough public pressure to persuade government to force safety improvements. In view of this fact, how important is it that applied scientists be put to work developing still another toothpaste that will make teeth whiter?

Ambivalence in the Scientific Community Our account of the increasing control over science by political and economic powers may suggest that science is a helpless and protesting victim. There is a modicum of truth in this. Many scientists have spoken out against the trend, and the atomic physicists were among the first to do so. Here is the last stanza of a ballad they sang at a meeting shortly after the end of World War II (Piehl, 1964: 105):

Take away your billion dollars, take away your tainted gold,
You can keep your damn ten billion volts, my soul will not be sold.
Take away your Army generals; their kiss is death, I'm sure.
Everything I build is mine, and every volt I make is pure.
Oh, dammit! Engineering isn't physics, is that plain?
Take, oh take, your billion dollars, let's be physicists again.

Scientists have spoken on this topic in such widely respected periodicals as *Science* and *Scientific American,* and have testified before congressional committees. Orlans reported that 70 percent of the many scientists he interviewed thought the federal presence in research not in the long-run national interest (1962:103).

Yet much of the scientific community has, knowingly or not, collaborated in subordinating scientific to political priorities. Maccoby (1970:262), after reviewing considerable evidence, accuses American scientists of "a reluctance to risk power, prestige, and support by clashing with priorities set in advance by the interplay of political forces." Reflecting Price (1962), who studied the relationship between government and science, he suggests that "generally, American science goes along with fixed political goals rather than trying to influence society toward better goals (1970:261). Maccoby also holds that scientists in the United States have more power at the highest levels of government than in most other countries, but have not used this power at all effectively "to oppose pressures which could reduce their community to a technical bureau" (1970:259).

Scientists are not a breed apart. They are ordinary men for the most part, as vulnerable to the pressures of society, as easily blinded by ambition and opportunism in a society which rewards these qualities, as most men are. This has always been true. But today's pressures may have led scientists further from the path defined by scientific goals than in earlier times. Certainly what we have sketched here is far removed from the picture implicit in our description of the values and norms of science.

Government Security Consciousness There is still another area of friction between science and government. For more than a generation, numbers of scientists have been employed by the government directly or indirectly in universities and industrial firms upon research which government classifies as secret. This means that the product of a scientist's work cannot be communicated freely to colleagues everywhere. Government security restrictions in these circumstances are thus a direct challenge to the norm that knowledge belongs to all. During World War II, while scientists chafed under these restrictions, they accepted them as unavoidable. Since then, they have resisted such measures more strongly. The problem continues, of course. Government has its own imperatives, which these days include the assumption that scientific knowledge is power, and the more of it we have and can keep from actual or potential enemies the better. And science has its fundamental beliefs, among them that science is a worldwide

Is It a Science World Again?

Perhaps it is necessary to examine first the process that has propelled our scientific and technological enterprise. That process has been a combination, on the one hand, of responding to the needs of society at various stages of its development and, on the other, of taking advantage of new knowledge that grew independently from our support of the freedom of inquiry. Scientists have long supported such inquiry in the belief that increasing knowledge was inherently a good thing, and society has supported it on the faith that eventually all knowledge becomes applicable to the fulfillment of some human endeavor. That belief and faith still exist, but it would be foolish not to recognize how they have been strained by the crisis approach that has grown in our use of science and technology to meet national needs.

It was somewhat inevitable that that crisis approach would develop, and that science would play a role in it. Early in our history, science responded to our national needs by exploration and survey, it helped advance our agriculture, improve our public health and increase the productivity of our industry. In the process of doing this, it helped make possible a system—an urbanized, technologically based society—of growing complexity and pressures to which we responded in somewhat piecemeal fashion while remaining rather oblivious to the direction it was taking and the potential problems it was building.

During this period, and in our lifetime, we further proved the power of science and technology to respond to crisis demands—once by meeting a wartime challenge and again by winning a race into space. But now we have turned our eyes and attention back to ordinary Earth only to realize that we face a whole new range of challenges and crises that were rising, as it were, directly out of our past achievements. For the first time, we seemed to see our world in a new light as a system, a series of systems—natural, technological, social, economic, and political—all in a symbiotic relationship, all needing to be better understood and dealt with as such, all raising a whole range of new questions we have to face.

Let me pose a few of those questions. They are the kind of questions that should concern the entire science community and, further, all involved in public policy, or its little sister, science policy.

The first relates to our need to release ourselves from the trap of having to use science on a crisis-to-crisis basis. In the recent past, the pace of change and the problems it has created have far outstripped our ability to bring science—long-range, comprehensive scientific thinking—to the point of acceptance and action by the political system. Most of our past experience has shown that the system will not respond to mere information, however persuasive, but requires a social crisis to trigger it. Our current energy situation is a case in point. As is now being revealed, enterprise and there should be no barriers to the communication of knowledge.

Public Images of Science In a democratic society, an indirect but vital influence on science proceeds from the images, values, and attitudes current among citizens at large. Withey (1959) published some interesting facts on this subject, based on a study by the Survey Research Center of the University of Michigan. He states that:

Probably not more than 12 percent of the adult population really understands what is meant by the scientific approach. For about two-thirds science is simply thorough and intensive study, which is, in a way, an adequate label. But the sensitive reader of interviews is aware, in the responses of most people with this point of view, of a lack of insight and understanding. It seems as though these people see a stage set facade, a house front without a house. What happens backstage is only surmised (1959:382).

---

for decades all the urgings of science advisers in the White House, all the scientific advisory bodies and individual scientific, technological, and business experts testifying before Congress and writing in the papers in past years were unable to head off the current situation— although within the past several years, a program of medium and long-range energy research had begun to emerge. Then, today's short-term crisis set in motion the comprehensive energy R&D program now being initiated.

This poses a vital question: Is the energy situation a turning point that will affect our policy making on other issues we are being warned about or will we wait for further crisis? Admonitions have also long been coming forth concerning our critical materials, our land and water resources, food production, the viability of our urban systems, and a whole range of environmental problems to which we have only begun to react. Will the lesson of the energy crisis improve our reaction time in these other vital areas?

The science community faces two major responsibilities in regard to this matter. The first is producing the right information—and in this we should excel, since it is what we have been trained to do. The second may be more difficult because it often takes us afield of our specialities— that is, getting that information in a meaningful and timely way into the social and political system so that policymakers will promote the formulation of laws, regu-

lations, and policies that the information indicates we need.

This seems to be one of our greatest problems and may continue to be so for a time—the problem of matching the impedance between our scientific-technological system and our socio-political system. We have a desperate need now to fine-tune these systems, and especially to interrelate them. . . .

In bringing our scientific and technological information to the social and political systems, we must confront them with the possible outcomes of what we have to offer. For we present not only technological options but potentially very significant choices in human values. As you well know, the elucidation of the human consequences of a systems change, whether it involves a decision as to how we change our transportation system or if we should go to a four-day work week, is a very important aspect of technology assessment. The known implications and consequences of such decisions must be examined and laid before the people and their representatives. Following this point, fact must give way to value and the final decisions must be made on a social basis.

Source: Remarks of Dr. H. Guyford Stever, Director, National Science Foundation, at the Annual Meeting of the American Association for the Advancement of Science, San Francisco, California, February 27, 1974.

Table 15-3, responses of Americans to evaluative statements about science and scientists, discloses some of our ambivalence on both topics. The highest agreement is on the belief that science leads to progress in making life more comfortable for all, and that the desire to do this is what motivates scientists.

It is interesting to contrast these sentiments with the figures on military and space research in the federal research budget, and with the description of science as seeking knowledge above all other goals. Notice that 65 percent of the respondents disagreed that most scientists are mainly interested in knowledge for its own sake. On most of the items in this table, Americans are considerably divided. Observe in particular that 40 percent agree that "the growth of science means that a few people could control our lives," while 52 percent disagree.

On the whole we suspect that doubt about the value of science and disapproval of what scientists are doing have increased. At the very least, articulate minorities have voiced their disapproval of some aspects of science more forcefully than people did when Withey's study was done. It seems likely that while ambivalence toward science continues in the total population, the balance has swung more toward the negative side.

TABLE 15-3   REACTIONS TO STATEMENTS ABOUT SCIENCE AND SCIENTISTS

ABOUT SCIENCE	Percent Agree	Percent Disagree	ABOUT SCIENTISTS	Percent Agree	Percent Disagree
Science is making our lives healthier, easier, and more comfortable.	92	4	Most scientists want to work on things that will make life better for the average person.	88	7
One of the best things about science is that it is the main reason for our rapid progress.	87	6	Scientists work harder than the average person.	68	25
One trouble with science is that it makes our way of life change too fast.	47	46	Scientists are apt to be odd and peculiar people.	40	52
Science will solve our social problems, like crime and mental illness.	44	49	Scientists are not likely to be very religious people.	32	53
The growth of science means that a few people could control our lives.	40	52	Most scientists are mainly interested in knowledge for its own sake; they don't care much about its practical value.	26	65
One of the bad effects of science is that it breaks down people's ideas of right and wrong.	25	64	Scientists always seem to be prying into things they really ought to stay out of.	25	66

Source: S. B. Withey, "Public Opinion About Science and Scientists," *Public Opinion Quarterly*, 23, 1959, pp. 328–88.

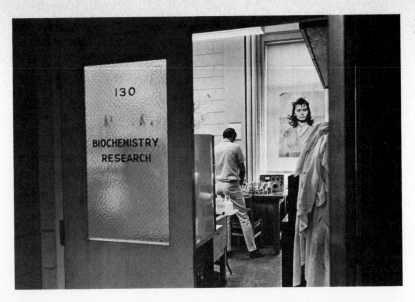

Many think of scientists as "eggheads," dull people who do not share the normal interests and emotions of the rest of society. But, in fact, scientists are human!

Citizens at large do not appropriate or withhold money for scientific research and do not have any other direct vital connection with the scientific enterprise. It may seem, therefore, that the nature of public opinion about science has little importance. In a democratic society this is not so. The positive components in the attitude toward science are a factor in the almost explosive growth of science and its support by agencies of government. If the negative components become strong enough politicians will pay heed and science will be affected. In the long run, it is of vital importance to both science and society that citizens know well enough what science is and have enough information to relate scientific work to the public welfare.

It is difficult to talk about science and society at all without also talking about change. One unusual feature of science has a bearing of great importance on change in society: while most social units, large or small, tend to be culturally and organizationally conservative, science has a built-in search for one kind of change. The body of scientific knowledge is never regarded as complete, and the main purpose of basic science is to change the state of knowledge, that is, to make it a more effective representation of the knowable universe.

Individual scientists may have an emotional investment in a particular theory which impels them to cling to it against

SCIENCE AND SOCIAL CHANGE

mounting, contrary evidence. But the culture of the scientific community firmly holds that empirical evidence is the only test of scientific truth. As contrary evidence accumulates, existing theories must be modified or abandoned. Hence science as a culturally defined social enterprise is constantly generating change in science as a body of existing knowledge.

Modern technologies are built mainly on the growing body of scientific knowledge. In turn, technologies produce dynamic and unending sequences of effects which we experience as social change. Research produces changes in knowledge which stimulate technological innovations. These in turn, and in interaction with other factors in society, have social consequences which may seem far removed from the beginning of the sequence. For example, a tax increase may result from the need to buy more land to enlarge a local airport to accommodate supersonic transports—in turn made possible by technology derived from gains in scientific knowledge.

Indeed, it can be argued that in modern societies science has become the single most important long-run source of change, though as we have seen this may soon be less true. Yet this effect is easily overlooked in face of the more socially visible, immediate, and often dramatic manifestations of social change. The social movements and countermovements, confrontations, battles, and campaigns that fill the daily news capture our attention and engage our emotions. But if we stand off a little, it is not hard to show that science and science-based technology have played a major role, direct or indirect, in setting the stage for many of the struggles which mark new or impending changes in the social forms of this turbulent age. Consider these illustrations.

Medical science, including public health, has virtually doubled life expectancy in many advanced countries and drastically cut death rates almost everywhere. One consequence is the threatening population explosion. Human societies are just beginning to organize the social responses which will reduce birth rates throughout the world.

In a few countries, technology makes it possible for the first time in history to abolish poverty, and this makes the continuing existence of poverty something that is intolerable to more and more people.

While technologies based on science have enabled man to exploit the resources of nature more effectively than ever before, they have also created a frightening crisis in the pollution of the environment. As yet, only a few societies have begun to make needed changes in the social structures which control resource-using technologies.

In undermining traditional myths about racial superiority and inferiority, science has helped to weaken social arrangements based on such myths. It has thus helped produce current struggles to eliminate racism.

Part 3 / Social Institutions

Too many people and too much pollution of air, land, and water are all made possible by science-based technologies. What are the responsibilities of science and scientists for such problems? What controls may society legitimately place on science in its own interest?

Finally, industrial civilization, made possible by science, has produced widespread alienation and rebellion against its dominant values significantly expressed in the counterculture that has sprung up among young people in recent years.

It is hardly surprising, then, that scientists have lost much of their cloistered seclusion in the academic world. Society, directly through government and industry, and more generally in rising concern among laymen, is insisting that in return for support, science bear some responsibility for social ends not inherent in science.

We must expect this trend to continue, and many scientists recognize and welcome it. New areas of contact are developing between science and the rest of society, and both scientists and nonscientists have much to learn about each other. While it has long been seen that science influences society, it is only recently felt that society also influences science. Either way, the influence can do good or harm, and more than purely scientific values and norms are at stake. Once it was asked if science can save us (Lundberg, 1947). There are some who might now ask if science can be saved. We think it can but that it may be altered by future changes in its relation with society.

PRACTICAL IMPLICATIONS OF THE SOCIOLOGY OF SCIENCE

Although the sociology of science remains relatively undeveloped, it has important things to say to other scientific fields. Most scientists still see little of the great importance for their own work of the social structure of the organizations which employ them and of the relation between science and the society around it. From traditional sociological fields like stratification, social power analysis, social change, and the structure of organizations come insights and research of high relevance for scientists today.

For example, in a large government organization working in basic medical research, Pelz (1956) found that scientists' performance, motivation, and sense of progress benefited from "(a) close colleagues who represent a variety of values, experiences, and disciplines, and (b) supervisors who avoid both isolation and domination and who provide frequent stimulation combined with autonomy of action." Information from the sociology of science, if used in the training of young scientists, would pay its way in the kind of world they will work in during the years ahead.

SOCIAL ORGANIZATION AND CREATIVITY Creativity is obviously of first importance in scientific work. The ability to do creative work is not, as some believe, solely a product of psychological characteristics, but may be enhanced or inhibited by one's social setting. The point was brilliantly demonstrated by Ben-David (1960), who sought to account for the marked differences in the advancement of medical science from 1800 to 1926 in France, Britain, Germany, and the United States (Figure 15-2).

By skillful analysis of historical materials, Ben-David was able to show that the differences arose from a number of interrelated factors of social organization. Decentralization of scientific work into many autonomous universities with a high degree of competition seemed to be crucial in the creation of scientific facilities, social roles for scientists, and the training of research personnel beyond society's immediate practical needs. In the middle of the nineteenth century, these conditions were best developed in Germany, corresponding with German leadership in this kind of science. In the 1880s, the same conditions evolved still more fully in the United States, where scientific productivity surpassed that in the other countries.

INTERSCIENCE COMMUNICATION While scientists in all disciplines share scientific values and norms, in other respects those in each field tend to be isolated from others. Most physical scientists know little of the behavioral sciences such as sociology and psychology, and the reverse is true too. This is unavoidable to a considerable extent, but it is unfortunate. All scientists, especially under modern conditions, stand to profit by some exposure to those who focus on human behavior. At present, almost no progress has been made in this potentially very fruitful area of interscience communication.

Practicing the Sociological Perspective

The chances are that you have already taken courses in one or more of the sciences and also in such fields as literature and foreign languages. Ask a science teacher about the meaning of knowledge in his field, and how new knowledge is ordinarily come by. Then ask the same question of teachers of English literature and foreign languages. Compare the answers you get. In the answers about science can you see reflections of the norms of the scientific institution discussed in this chapter? How do these answers differ from those given by people in the humanities?

This exercise may sharpen your awareness that a college or university is home to many kinds of learning, reflecting more than a variety of subject matters. Also involved are basic assumptions about the nature of reality, knowledge about reality, and means of achieving knowledge. College teachers in fields like accounting, music, or education live in different intellectual worlds than those of physicists, biochemists, or zoologists. But in each of the scientific disciplines, the local professors are representative of the same scientific institution that we have been discussing. A brief and stimulating bit of reading in this connection is C. P. Snow's *The Two Cultures and the Scientific Revolution;* it is a noted analysis of the tensions between the scientific and humanistic worlds of scholarship represented on any campus.

We have shown that Americans are ambivalent about science and are not very well informed about it. The combination of high prestige and considerable ignorance leads to some curious results which, if you are observant, can be identified quite frequently in actions and comments reported in the press by nonscientists. Check your local newspaper or a news magazine for uses of the words *science* and *scientific* in ways which would make any scientist shudder.

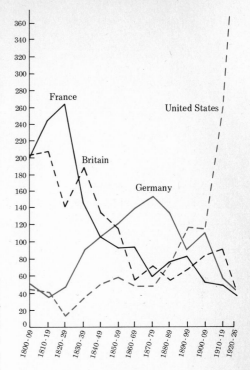

FIGURE 15-2 CHANGES IN THE RELATIVE SHARE OF MEDICAL DISCOVERIES IN SELECTED COUNTRIES, 1800–1926

[Source: J. Ben-David, "Scientific Productivity and Academic Organization in Nineteenth Century Medicine," *American Sociological Review* 25, 1960, pp. 828–43.]

Sometimes deliberately, but often not, people co-opt these words to lend authority to findings or statements they wish to have accepted. Advertising has been notorious for this misuse, but you can find it almost everywhere. When the word *scientific* is used in this way, it is usually intended to convey the notion that the idea or product is true or superior. Very recently, as we have pointed out, there has been intensified criticism of science in the United States. It will be interesting to see if, during the seventies, the man in a white jacket peering through a microscope will be less frequently invoked in the marketing of products and services.

PART 4
The Sociological Perspective

We come at last to the final social unit treated in this book—the largest, most inclusive, the least understood yet most vital of all: the society. Everybody knows the word and uses it often, but with how little comprehension of all that the familiar word denotes! Absorbed in the details of our own experience, we rarely think of the mighty stage of society and the infinitely complex sociocultural drama played out on that stage. Yet that stage and drama define who we are and the limits of what we may become.

Everything that we have discussed thus far is part of society, and so also is much that we have not talked about. But society is more than the sum of these things. It is more than all the people who make it possible, more than all the knowledge, art, wisdom, technology, institutions, organizations, and groups that its inhabitants have created. We do not mean that society is *better* than these things. It is, simply, inclusive of them all and something yet more. It is an aspect of the human potential at an organizational level so vast that it can incorporate parts of hundreds of millions of people.

Neither in sociology nor in any other discipline do we yet have intellectual tools for adequately penetrating the mysteries of society considered as a whole, for comprehending the incredibly complex interdependencies that enable a society to survive through centuries, and understanding how a society grows and changes in relation to its environment. In Chapter 16 we introduce some of the partial understandings of these matters now available from sociology.

Societies

16

All of us live in a society, and all of us are familiar with the word *society.* Yet it is probable that most people, even in the United States, have nothing more than a rudimentary notion of what inclusion in a particular society means in almost every aspect of their lives.

It is certain that people today have a much better idea of the significance of society than ever before. For thousands of years it was possible to live an entire lifetime with only a dim awareness that other societies even existed. The framework of all meanings, including even the definitions of such concepts as *nature, world,* and *reality,* was provided by the society in which one had been born. It was hard even to imagine that there might be different human worlds in which men's relationships to other men and nature were understood in very different ways. In such circumstances one did not ponder the significance of society, but took it completely for granted. Nowadays it is hard to imagine such an extremely provincial view. In sociological terms, the world has shrunk enormously as a result of modern improvements in communication and transportation. From an early age, American children learn about other societies, and a high proportion of Americans sooner or later visit one or more societies besides their own.

In a deeper sense, though, even the most modern peoples have only begun to learn what societies really are and why and how they are significant. In most parts of the world people persist in the naive belief that most things in their society were invented there, and that their own society is superior to all others. Even when we travel abroad it is impossible not to take our own perspectives along with us in our encounters with strange lifestyles. And almost certainly, only a few people really conceive of a society as a single, enormously complex social unit—which is the way we view it here. Everything in this book, and in every other introductory text in sociology, is "about society," in a way. This is true in the sense that every social form we have discussed is a part of society. A short-lived two-member group that lasts for only an hour and then is forgotten is for that time a part of society, as is the stratification system, the economic institution, and a community. But we do not adequately describe any complex whole by even the most exhaustive separate treatment of its parts, as is apparent from a description of the whole human body as distinct from descriptions of its components. Partly because the parts of society, like those of the human body, are highly interdependent, it is impossible to infer all the properties of the whole from knowledge only of the parts considered separately. Just as an interact, a role, a group, a community, and an institution have properties worth careful study, each at its own level, so too a society is a single unit or system, with properties that need careful examination at its level of social organization.

DEFINING SOCIETY

We begin with a definition. "A society is the most inclusive social organization. It incorporates all of the individuals and . . . societal subsystems . . . and combines them in their various . . . interdependencies. . . . It is the largest relatively permanent grouping whose members share a common physical setting, common interests and goals, a common mode of life, and a common destiny" (Hertzler, 1961:10).

This definition tells us that a society is people and social organizations of many kinds occupying a territory for a long period of time. More than that, a society is itself an organization. There is some similarity between this concept and the definition of community we gave in Chapter 5. Both incorporate the idea of territorial location, and in both the major social institutions are fully represented. Furthermore, in fully developed examples of the community, the life of the individual is pretty much bounded by the community, and this is true of the society as well. But there are differences between the two kinds of units. Societies are much larger, not only in the geographical sense but also in the sense that they contain many communities, sometimes thousands of them. And, unlike any single community, a society contains *all* the social institutions and *all* their organizational manifestations.

Shils (1968:287) says that "a social system is a society if it is predominantly not part of a larger society." Concerning the society and its parts he continues:

Part 4 / The Sociological Perspective

The entire Bedouin society contains only a comparatively small number of such isolated nomadic communities as this one. Yet, sociologically, the Bedouin society is as complete as our own.

But what is contained within them? We have already said that the more differentiated among them contain not only families and lineages but also associations, unions, firms and farms, schools and universities, armies, churches and sects, parties, and numerous other corporate bodies and organizations, and these too have boundaries which define the membership over which their respective corporate authorities—parents, managers, presidents, and the like—exercise some measure of control. There are also systems organized formally and informally around a territorial focus—neighborhoods, villages, districts, cities, regions—and these too have some of the features of societies. Then there are those unorganized aggregates of human beings within societies—social classes or strata, occupations and professions, religions, and linguistic groups—which have a culture more common to those who possess certain statuses or occupy certain positions than it is to those who do not. Why are all or any of these not societies? We have already answered that question, but we will now formulate the answer somewhat differently. Each of them exercises such authority as it does exercise within the framework of or in subordination to a *common* authority which is outside themselves and which is the authority of the whole society (1968:288–89).

Notice that there is no mention of size in Hertzler's definition or Shils's remarks. Some (preliterate) societies may contain only a few hundred people, while others include hundreds of millions. Perhaps we should also point out that while all nations are societies, not all societies are nations. Many societies have existed in which nothing closely resembling the nation-state had yet evolved.

SUBHUMAN SOCIETIES Man is not the only creature to develop societies. Lenski (1970:9) states that "a society exists to the degree that a territorially bounded population of animals of a single species maintains ties of association and interdependence and enjoys autonomy." This broad definition includes not only human societies but examples in a wide range of animal species, including many below the mammalian level of evolution, such as the social insects. In the long story of life on this planet societies have appeared frequently, a fact which seems to testify to the survival value of this kind of adaptation. As Davis puts it:

The emergence of society may be viewed as one of the great steps in evolution—a step that some species have taken and others not. It ranks with the emergence of the cell, with the emergence of the multicellular organism, and with the emergence of the vertebrate system as one of the crucial advances in living development. Like the other steps it represents a new synthesis of old materials, possessing unique qualities not to be found in the old materials considered separately. It is thus a true example of what is called emergent evolution (1949:27).[1]

As one moves up the evolutionary scale, more and more of the behavior found in societies is learned. This tendency is so sharply accentuated at the human level that a radical difference is found between all human and all nonhuman societies. Below the human level, the socially necessary responses of individual animals appear to be mainly, and in many species almost completely, under the control of genetic characteristics which produce appropriate behavior instinctively when the right cues are presented. Within a species, individuals are often even anatomically specialized for the tasks they must perform in their society's division of labor. Statements such as these cannot be made about even a single one of the hundreds of known human societies. All human societies *train* individuals to play the specialized roles required for the society's continuation.

There is only one species of man, *homo sapiens,* but this solitary species has developed a wide variety of different kinds of societies because, thanks to his culture-building capacity, he is not genetically locked into just one sort of social organization. Subhuman societies, by contrast, are extremely similar within a single species, even though they differ widely between species.

NECESSARY SOCIETAL FUNCTIONS   To say that societies are a successful form of species adaptation is to indicate that they perform certain functions required for survival which otherwise the individual organism would have to manage by itself. The provision of a food supply and some degree of protection against danger are the best examples of individual needs which become societal functions. The sexual drive is another important individual need, though the life of the separate organism does not depend on its gratification. However, it is absolutely necessary from the standpoint of species survival that this need be met.

If a society cannot provide stable patterns for the satisfaction of such needs in its individual members the *organic survival* of the

---

[1] From Kingsley Davis, *Human Society* (New York: The Macmillan Company). © Copyright, The Macmillan Company, 1948 and 1949.

The technology of the Ethiopian farmer contrasts sharply with that of the American farmer, as does that of the modern and primitive warrior. Nevertheless, in all societies, regardless of their technological level, functions necessary to the society's survival are carried out successfully.

entire species is threatened. It is headed for extinction because society-building creatures, as we have indicated, cannot turn backward to a solitary way of life. Hence an important aspect of every society is a set of social arrangements for the satisfaction of individual needs. But there is more to the matter than this. If a society is to take care of the elemental requirements of individuals it must also arrange for its own survival. What social needs must be met if a society is to continue in existence?

SURVIVAL   Since no society could exist without a population of individual members the basic requirements of the latter must be satisfied. In other words, the satisfaction of the individual needs we have just mentioned is also the first necessity of a society. To this end every society must have means for providing food and other organic essentials. In human societies the economic institution is responsible for the production of material necessities and, equally important, their orderly distribution among the society's members. It is also essential to the survival of both individual and society that the latter protect the former against dangers from within and without. From society's viewpoint, an adequate number of individuals must be kept alive and in sufficiently good health. This protective function includes not only defense against external enemies but also against disease and other forms of organic injury. In human societies, protection is concentrated in the political institution (including its military and policing activities) and in practices that affect health. The latter are not necessarily assigned to a specialized class, as in the United States, but may be carried out by religious, familial or other agencies.

In performing its protective function the society cares not only for individuals but also directly for its own social fabric. You can grasp this by imagining that one society invades another. It kills only a few individuals in doing so, but, over a period of years, it succeeds in imposing its own, different form of society on the conquered people. In this case the population of organic individuals remains essentially intact but the original society crumbles. Something like this has taken place many times in human history. The results can be tragic when, as sometimes has happened, the old society is destroyed but its population is not admitted to full membership in the conquering society. We need go no further than the United States to find examples—among American Indian tribes and in the fate of black people whose ancestors were torn from their tribal societies in Africa to become slaves in a foreign land.

Some years ago Alan Paton wrote movingly of this kind of tragedy in his novel *Cry, The Beloved Country* (1948). It deals with the human consequences of the destruction of Bantu society by the white man in South Africa and the refusal of the latter to admit the Bantu people, except marginally, into his own society.

MEMBER REPLACEMENT   All individuals ultimately die; if the society is to survive there must be a set of social arrangements compensating for this biological loss. The family institution provides the necessary social machinery in human societies. Sexual reproduction furnishes the biological means for the member-replacement function. The organic capacity of the species for bearing offspring is not enough, however. The important thing is that once children are born they must be adequately socialized for the performance of essential social roles. No society leaves these vital tasks to the vagaries of isolated individuals.

Part 4 / The Sociological Perspective

SOCIAL CONTROL Finally, a society must see to it that the errant impulses and actions of individual members do not result in the destruction of the social fabric upon which every member depends for his existence. This is often called the *social control* function. In subhuman societies the mechanisms of such control are primarily hereditary. The genetic makeup of man, however, contains no imperatives that force him to act in the interests of society. What he does inherit is the ability to learn to behave in accordance with social requirements. Society provides the values, the norms, the roles and the knowledge which must be transmitted through the generations in order to ensure its continuity. It also provides countless socialization settings in which each individual is taught the things that society must have him know.

In our highly differentiated society we are likely to think of social control as being entrusted to the political institution. While this is true in part, it is an oversimplification. Actually, social control is inherent in all organized social experience. There are rules and there are rewards and punishments to aid in the motivation of the individual. Ultimately, socialization produces in each in-

Broken Societies Mean Broken Lives

(A Bantu priest has come from his rural home to a Mission House in Johannesburg, and is having his first meal with a group of black and white priests.)

He sat next to a young rosy-cheeked priest from England, who asked him where he came from, and what it was like there. And another black priest cried out—I am also from Ixopo. My father and mother are still alive there, in the valley of the Lufafa. How is it there?

And he told them all about these places, of the great hills and valleys of that far country. And the love of them must have been in his voice, for they were all silent and listened to him. He told them too of the sickness of the land, and how the grass had disappeared, and of the dongas that ran from hill to valley, and valley to hill; how it was a land of old men and women, and mothers and children; how the maize grew barely to the height of a man; how the tribe was broken, and the man broken; how when they went away, many never came back, many never wrote any more. How this was true not only in Ndotsheni, but also in the Lufafa, and the Imhlavini, and the Unkomaas, and the Umzimkulu. . . .

So they all talked of the sickness of the land, of the broken tribe and the broken house, of young men and young girls that went away and forgot their customs, and lived loose and idle lives. They talked of young criminal children, and older and more dangerous criminals, of how white Johannesburg was afraid of black crime. . . .

(Later in the evening his host, Reverend Msimangu, is speaking with the visitor.)

My friend, I am a Christian. It is not in my heart to hate a white man. It was a white man who brought my father out of darkness. But you will pardon me if I talk frankly to you. The tragedy is not that things are broken. The tragedy is that they are not mended again. The white man has broken the tribe. And it is my belief—and again I ask your pardon—that it cannot be mended again. But the house that is broken, and the man that falls apart when the house is broken, these are the tragic things. That is why children break the law, and old white people are robbed and beaten. . . .

It suited the white man to break the tribe, he continued gravely. But it has not suited him to build something in the place of what is broken. I have pondered this for many hours and I must speak it, for it is the truth for me. They are not all so. There are some white men who give their lives to build up what is broken.

But they are not enough, he said. They are afraid, that is the truth. It is fear that rules this land.

dividual a state of development in which most of the social rules applicable to him are self-enforced most of the time. If this were not true, the job of securing the minimum necessary amount of social control through outside pressure would overwhelm every society.

SOCIETIES AS SOCIAL SYSTEMS In this country more than two hundred million people are living out their allotted years. Each day some die and others are born. Not one of them can have a personal acquaintance with anything more than an infinitesimally small proportion of his fellow citizens. How on earth can such an enormous multitude of strangers, each pursuing his or her own destiny, get along without destroying one another? They belong to innumerable groups, many of which are in competition or conflict with one another. Why is it that these groups do not tear apart the thing we call society? The more we learn about complex modern societies the more incredible is the fact that they exist at all.

We say that societies are single entities, things in their own right. But how can that be? Think what is involved; to do so requires a strenuous effort of the imagination. Remember the interacts we discussed in Chapter 2? In a year's time, American society somehow spawns and organizes trillions of these tiny units of social behavior. And there are billions of instances in which the behavior of a person affects others without the latter's personal knowledge, as when the purchase of a car by a rancher in Montana helps an auto worker in Detroit to have a steady job.

In just one year there are hundreds of millions of role performances, each single one of which forms a part of a group, and groups number in the scores of millions. There are many thousands of communities, complex organizations, occupations, and the many other sorts of units studied by sociologists. In every hour of every day, obedient to cyclical patterns of darkness and light, of days of the week and changes in season, and of the many other patterns ordained by culture, this mighty river of organized social behavior flows ceaselessly on. Each person, each unit of social behavior, large or small, takes its place in an immense design which includes all.

We call a society a social system, which puts it in the same class of things as the many smaller social systems already discussed in this book. It differs from the others in being more inclusive of other social systems than any other type we have discussed. Like any other social system, society is simultaneously an organization of social action and an organized culture.

SOCIETY AS AN ACTION SYSTEM Ed Simpson, a stockbroker, gets into his car and drives to work. Because his office is in downtown Chicago and hundreds of thousands of other people are also going to work in the Loop, there is fantastic congestion of traffic (and several dozen accidents) on the highways leading into the center of the city. And the same pattern is being repeated in every city throughout the country.

It is the day of the presidential election and Linda Edwards pulls the levers on the voting machine in her precinct. On the same day millions of other citizens do the same thing, and many politicans are voted out of office and others are voted in. As a result there are major changes in government policy.

As an action system, society includes the small social acts of these two persons and the cumulative patterned consequences of millions of similar acts. To George Berger, his job as a lathe operator is just that, a job. But the intricately interrelated actions of millions of Georges, in all their diversity, make up something vastly larger: the whole organization of economic production in American society. At one level, private ownership of the means of production is simply an intellectual concept that is part of the system we call capitalism. In society as an action system, this concept becomes the buying and selling of millions of shares of stocks and bonds by thousands of people, groups, and organizations on markets arranged specifically to facilitate the social behavior of exchange.

Notice that viewed as a gigantic action system, no specific reference need be made to the personalities of Ed Simpson, Linda Edwards, and George Berger. The only required assumption about them as individuals is that they are capable of playing their parts (role performances) in social patterns which build upward from very small units to very large and inclusive ones.

SOCIETY AS A CULTURAL SYSTEM Imagine that we have a sort of sociological lens which permits us to observe patterns of social behavior taking place at the same time over the entire society. We notice that from Monday through Friday of each week there is a massive movement of persons from the edges of cities into the central areas in the morning. In the late afternoon this movement is reversed as the people flow back outward again. But this pattern is weaker on Saturday, and not there at all on Sunday. Then, we observe millions of people moving toward concentration points, not just in the center of cities, but throughout cities. This movement takes place particularly in the morning. By noon or early afternoon most of these people have returned to the places they started from.

So described, we have two patterns of society as an action system, patterns which are highly predictable, for they occur over and over with monotonous regularity. We can actually see parts of society as an action system, as in this case. But we can't see society as a cultural system, for culture, you now know, is essentially ideas shared by people in contact with each other. Yet, without reference to culture, these familiar patterns make no sense and would not even exist. Actually, almost without conscious effort, you recognize these patterns of social action and understand them because you are familiar with the culture which lies behind them. You know that the tidal flow of people into and out of city centers, morning and afternoon, represents people playing out their occupational roles. And you know that the different pattern on Sundays reflects the performance of religious roles by those Americans who are active members of churches.

Although it can't be seen, society as a cultural system is parallel to the action system and in touch with it at every point from the smallest to the largest units. Just as every unit of social behavior is part, however small, of the action system of society, so is every unit of social structure partly shaped and molded "by reason of common orientation to knowledge, beliefs, values, and norms drawn from a shared culture" (Williams, 1970:585).

We see a tiny fragment of society as an action system when a student hands in an examination paper and gets it back graded by his instructor. We see another, larger fragment when the Supreme Court of the United States interprets the Constitution in a way that affects every citizen. In both units the appropriate parts of society's culture provide blueprints for action which always affect what actually takes place. All social systems have these two components: the action system and the cultural system.

SOCIETY AS A SINGLE SOCIAL SYSTEM

We have just touched on the relationship between society as an action system and as a cultural system, just as we have dealt with the relationship between culture and social action at many points in this book, beginning in Chapter 2. We have indicated that actual social behavior is always partly controlled by culture, and that culture itself is changed and sustained by its realization in social action.

CULTURE AS AN INTEGRATIVE FACTOR Here we add that in every society there is a central cluster of values, which are of course parts of culture. (See Chapter 2 for a treatment of values and value hierarchies.) These are values which rank very high in the value hierarchy of the given society. This means that they apply very broadly, which is to say that they subsume innumerable lesser values and will be given many kinds of definite expression at all levels of social organization. Insofar as there is agreement within a society on these master values, they constitute an important force toward unity for social systems, and subsystems are generally oriented toward the realization of master values. This will occur everywhere in the social system of a society.

Williams (1970:452–95) delineated the major value orientations of the United States, and found that the most significant clusters are an emphasis on achievement and success, the value of activity and work, tendencies to evaluate experiences in moral terms and to support humanitarian norms, a liking for efficiency

These pictures illustrate several basic American values—emphasis on material comfort, conformity to conventional norms, patriotism, and morality. The fundamental values of a society are important, for they are the measure of what a people considers desirable and good.

and practicality, a belief in progress, an emphasis on material comfort, a belief in equality and freedom, a concern for external conformity, approval of applied science, emphasis on nationalism-patriotism, approval of democracy, a high valuation of the individual, and group-superiority themes, including racism.

We shall not take the space to discuss these value clusters which their importance deserves, but taken together they constitute the central value system of American society. As Americans go about their daily lives they encounter these values expressed in a thousand specific settings. And these values help to tie together those thousand settings into a meaningful whole. Many of the values found in American society, of course, also occur in other societies. But in the American scene their totality, the way they relate to each other, and the comparative emphasis Americans put on each of them, distinguish American society from all others.

If you study the list you can see that most of these values are reasonably consistent with one another. That is, to support one of them is consistent with supporting most of the others. For example, belief in personal achievement and success is consistent with belief in progress. However, the internal consistency of these central values is not complete. Note the stresses implicit in simultaneously valuing freedom and equality on the one hand, and supporting racism on the other.

In summary, culture as exemplified by clusters of master values is a predominantly integrative factor in a society. But in complex and rapidly changing societies such as the United States, this is not completely true. In certain instances cultural values lessen integration, as in the conflict cited above.

INTERDEPENDENCE AS AN INTEGRATIVE FACTOR   All social systems, large or small, are made up of interdependent parts, and this interdependence operates as an integrative force. Let us see what this statement means. For a comparatively simple case, consider a family group composed of husband-father, wife-mother, and one child. When we think of this group in terms of roles, the interdependence jumps out at us. To be a husband means to have certain rights and obligations in a relationship with someone who is a wife (and vice versa). To be a father means to have certain rights and obligations in a relationship with someone who is a child (and vice versa). Each role exists and can only be maintained in interdependent ties with the other roles.

The principle illustrated in this small social system is the same in the vast social system of the total society, except that there the interdependencies are enormously more detailed and complex. The normal operation of one part of a society depends upon and contributes to the normal operation of other parts. And the whole unit that is a society is held together by these interrelationships. It may be helpful to look at interdependence both *vertically* and *horizontally*.

Vertical interdependence. Thousands of service stations depend on the presence of many automobiles if they are to survive. The automobile dealer helps distribute the cars that use gas, and, in turn, he depends on the assembly line in automobile plants, which itself is a component in the large corporation that produces several lines of cars. Each unit depends upon and is depended on by all the others up and down the chain.

Vertical Interdependence By vertical interdependence we mean that which exists between social units of varying size and inclusiveness. As one goes up the ladder of social systems, from small units to larger and still larger ones, one finds interdependence between these different levels. For example, visualize a big state university, with perhaps twenty-five thousand resident students. On its campus during a given semester, forty or fifty students are taking an introductory sociology course. When the semester is over these students will never again assemble as a group. Here are a few of the ways in which this particular class is tied by interdependence to other levels of organization: the course they are taking is required as the first step in a pattern of courses required to earn a major in sociology; it is given by the Sociology Department, which is one of thirty departments comprising the College of Arts and Sciences; the college requires its students to select a major and meet the requirements set by the department in which the major is given; the College of Arts and Sciences is itself part of the university, which contains perhaps a dozen or more colleges; the university sets conditions for the operation of all its colleges, including their coordination into the total university program; this university is a member of the Association of State Universities and also the Association of American Universities—these organizations are part of the total pattern of higher education in the country, including all colleges and universities, public and private, and higher education itself is but a part of the complete system of education in the country and depends on the lower schools to prepare students for college work.

We could start with the same sociology class and illustrate vertical interdependence in several other ways. For instance, the teacher of the class is a sociologist. He depends on the students as a key factor in his occupation, just as they depend on him for introducing them to sociology and preparing them for the next stage of learning in this field. He belongs to the regional association of sociologists, and to the American Sociological Association, a national group with which regional societies are affiliated. The teacher depends on these organizations for certain services such as the publication of professional journals which disseminate new knowledge. The American Sociological Association is a member of the American Association for the Advancement of Science, which links all scientific fields. The AAAS, which is financially supported by its member societies, in turn does such things as represent the interests of science before congressional committees.

Even these sketchy descriptions may convey the idea that these chains of vertical interdependence are both numerous and complex when we think of the society as a whole. They tie together the activities of millions of people who will never know one another. A student in our sociology class may never realize that he is linked in this way with great national educational and scientific associations, but he is, nevertheless.

Horizontal Interdependence This term refers to the interdependence between social units of roughly the same size and complexity, and of the same general type: for example, interdependence between different small groups; communities; social classes; complex organizations; and institutions. It is as though we are thinking across society instead of up and down it. For example, the notion that government and business should carry on their affairs independently of each other is part of the traditional ideology of American capitalism. Yet even the most casual observer knows that the facts depart drastically from this idea. The growth of immense and powerful business enterprises beginning in the late nineteenth century inevitably led to the formation of large and powerful labor unions in the early twentieth century.

These clusters of opposed economic power have such grave consequences for the entire society that government has done more and more in the economic arena to limit the exercise of this power. Recent decades have seen a rapid and continuing growth of legislation, regulatory commissions and other devices of government all intended to protect the public from the unreasonable exercise of organized and conflicting economic power. In other words, the governmental institution at all levels, but particularly at the federal level, has itself been enlarged and altered in form by extending its operation into economic affairs.

At the same time, events in the political institution have important repercussions in the economic institution. For example, the government controls the country's monetary system. The monetary system contains a set of controls over inflation and deflation in the economy, located in the Federal Reserve Board. The economic institution has to adjust itself to the continuing effects of government upon economic organizations. It is simply impossible today for a business firm to carry on as though the government did not exist.

These reciprocal influences and adjustments take place in American society with little reference to the fortunes of the two major political parties. Campaign rhetoric aside, the basic sociological process goes its way, not much affected by the differences which divide, or seem to divide, Democrats and Republicans. Part of the American governmental institution is a value, with its related institutional norms, which holds that government must operate in the interests of all the people, not just those of particular organized segments of the population. Given this value, it is almost inevitable that when economic developments threaten or appear to threaten the welfare of society's members, the resultant

Horizontal interdependence. Home builders depend on buyers for survival and buyers depend on builders. Both builders and buyers usually need loans in order to deal with one another and therefore depend on banks for capital and mortgage loans. Banks depend on both for their own business, but in order to have money to lend they must pay interest to people who save their money in the bank, thus making it available for loans. Individual depositors depend on the banks for safekeeping of their funds and also for the income that the bank pays them for using their money.

strains lead to government intervention in economic affairs and consequent changes in the political institution. It is equally inevitable that the presence of government in economic activities produces strains that lead to institutional changes in the business world intended to help business enterprises survive and still meet the demands of government.

Incomplete Interdependence Vertical and horizontal interdependence create a vast network of ties linking countless millions of societal parts into a single articulated whole. But in very large, highly differentiated societies, interdependence need not be as fully developed at the society level as at some lower levels. In a nation like the United States, there is greater interdependence between and within some parts than others. The point has been well stated by Williams (1970:585–86).

In a fully interdependent social system every set of acts between any set of actors affects, and is affected by, every other set of acts; and all sets are influenced by the total system. Such a completely articulated system is a limiting case, closely approximated only in relatively small-scale segmental networks of interaction. Total societies are partially articulated systems in which some subsystems may be highly interdependent (a tightly linked economy or a centralized and bureaucratized polity), whereas others are only loosely connected by low rates of interaction, with many discontinuities or gaps.

Mass public education arose in this country largely because industrialization required great numbers of highly trained workers. This development removed from the family a traditional task it was no longer equipped to perform. Here we have a major instance of close interdependence between large sectors of the society; education, economy, family. On the other hand, the recent development of the Pentecostal movement in American religion seems not to have any very close or significant interdependence with economic or political institutions.

There is, in other words, a considerable amount of slippage among the parts of a society. The whole does not control all the relationships of the parts; all the same, the whole exists.

POWER AS AN INTEGRATIVE FACTOR   Social power exists whenever a person or group is able to control another person or group even if the latter resists. There are several kinds of social power, but the one of most interest to us here is what is called coercive power (French and Raven, 1959). It is based on the ability to apply specific penalties and punishments, such as fines, imprisonment, suspension of licenses and the like. Coercive power can be a dangerous commodity, if individuals and groups feel free to exercise it in their own interest whenever they like. Societies therefore define the limits within which coercive power may legitimately be used, and these limits normally serve the major values of the society.

When we think of modern societies as wholes, the most important location of legitimized coercive power is in the political institution. Williams (1970:233) defines the state as "the structure that successfully claims a monopoly over the legitimate use of coercion and physical force within a territory." For instance, in the United States coercive power is used by government to require school attendance through the secondary level, to build the network of roads and highways that ties the country together, to maintain military forces which protect territorial integrity, to support police forces which enforce laws, to require use of a particular system of weights and measures, and to control the society's monetary system. All these activities (among many others) have at least partly integrative consequences. And all are supported by taxes which citizens must pay.

We have now identified three factors which serve to integrate even very large, complicated societies into single entities: culture; the interdependence of a society's parts; and power, particularly as employed by the state. Usually these integrative factors work together to get at least the minimum solidarity needed for a society to survive. It is most unlikely that any of them could do the job alone, at least in a modern industrial-urban society.

In Chapter 2 we pointed out that stability and change are inseparable. To talk about either without the other is merely to practice selective emphasis. Throughout this book we first focused on structure (stability), then on change. Thus since the entire book deals with aspects of society, we have talked about change in societies in every chapter. Yet there are important aspects of change in societies viewed as wholes which we have not so far discussed; this we do now.[2]

INTERDEPENDENCE TENSION MANAGEMENT AND CHANGE We have said that interdependence tends to integrate a society and hold it together as a unit. So it may seem paradoxical to say now that interdependence is also a source of change in society. And yet it is, as is the relationship of a whole society to its environment, including other societies.

One reason why interdependence is a source of change is that the articulation of society's parts is never complete. Consequently there are always strains in the relations between societal parts and efforts to reduce these strains alter the system itself. Moore (1963) speaks of society as a tension-management system, with change as an outcome of reactions to tension.

---

[2] A recent, authoritative and much fuller account of our subject can be found in Gerhard Lenski, *Human Societies* (New York: McGraw-Hill, 1970). A more condensed and technical review of theories of social change is contained in Richard P. Appelbaum, *Theories of Social Change* (Chicago: Markham, 1970).

More concretely, what does this abstraction mean? For one example, in many religious denominations the social protest movements of the last two decades led to vigorous social action programs. This induced tensions within churches between social liberals and conservatives, and one consequence was a reduction of church funds flowing into social programs. Another was a slowing up of the ecumenical trend. Again, the growing size and bureaucratization of school systems, including big universities, reduced the bargaining power of teachers and professors in dealing with their employers. And one consequence of the strain produced by this change was the growth of unionization among teachers.

Recent concern about protecting our natural environment has led to significant new federal and local legislation (the political sphere) and to changed practices in manufacturing (the economic). The emergence of the women's liberation movement was partly a consequence of the successes achieved by the civil rights movement and the anti–Vietnam war movement. Having appeared, feminism became a factor in bringing about new legislation (including a new proposed amendment to the Constitution) giving women equal rights with men. Other good examples of change produced by strain are to be found in the social effects of major technological innovations such as the automobile, the airplane, and television. Many years ago, Ogburn (1922) showed in detail how technological changes have ramifications throughout the social fabric, finally reaching points far removed from the original effects. It is a bit like a stone dropped into a pool of water, that sends waves out in all directions.

Consider the automobile. We are likely to think mostly of its benefits, and it is often said that Americans have a continuing love affair with the automobile. Yet, its long-run effects—and they are still occurring—include social stress at hundreds of points, and many of these strains have themselves led to further social change. In the beginning, the auto put several traditional industires (carriage and harness making, for example) effectively out of business and altered the balance of grain crops. It changed and is still changing the shape of the American city (see Chapter 5). It produced massive air pollution. In 1973 the federal government issued proposed actions which would drastically limit the use of the automobile in central cities. If these are adopted, even in modified form, they will bring significant changes to the transportation patterns of American cities, as well as social and cultural patterns within cities and metropolitan areas.

Changes in one part of the total system that makes up a society cannot be fully or permanently isolated from other parts, since all parts are in some degree interdependent. A change introduces tension in the total system which ultimately travels throughout society and instigates other changes.

Airports and cities are highly interdependent. As cities and air transportation grow, tensions arise over safety factors, air and noise pollution, and conflicting land-use needs. These strains have been relieved in some cities by new kinds and locations of airports and by joint private and governmental funding of sophisticated safety and pollution-control devices.

Value Conflict as a Change-Inducing Strain   Strains may and do appear at any particular point in a society, viewed as a social system or as a cultural system. Conflict between values is another cause of strain and change. As we said earlier, Americans tend to believe in equality and fair play for the individual; yet they also believe in racism. The dominant value system of the society contains both these conflicting elements. Values are part of the national culture, and as such they influence actual social arrangements all the way down the organizational ladder. These two value clusters are obviously inconsistent; one cannot logically believe in both. More important, personal or social action which supports one cluster obviously conflicts with action supporting the other. The presence of both values in the same society introduces strain into that society at every level of organization. Years ago Myrdal (1944), who did extensive research on the consequences of this conflict, called it the American dilemma. It has been one of the most divisive points of stress in the United States since African slaves were introduced into the country.

If you were from a foreign country and learning for the first time about this severe value contradiction in American society, you might suppose that some Americans believe in equality of opportunity and fair play and others believe in racism. It doesn't seem reasonable that the same people could sincerely support both. You would be wrong. A great many Americans do in fact believe both. They have been taught to do so by socialization in a society which contains this value conflict.

The conflict is often argued away in rationalizations supported by group norms. Or people may compartmentalize both their belief and their behavior, acting by one set of values in some circumstances and the other set in other circumstances. There are many ways in which people can deny the conflict for a time, but it is hard to maintain for long the position that it doesn't exist; it keeps breaking through the defenses erected to hold it at bay. Speaking more technically, we say that social arrangements intended to contain the strain generated by the conflict are always threatening to break down. We have seen this happen many times in recent years. As a result there have been real changes in American society which are bringing social organization into somewhat closer agreement with the values of fair play and equality at the expense of racist values. Needless to say the conflict is far from over, and so long as it continues it will be a potential source of change.

In modern societies there are millions of stress points in the relationships between subsystems. By no means will all of these lead to actual change, but all are at least potential sources of change. It is not hard to see why when one realizes that the first impact of social strain is felt by individuals. This impact is felt as conflict, frustration, and sometimes as damage to what are thought to be legitimate interests.

DISCOVERY, INVENTION, AND DIFFUSION   Social change often, but not always, involves the appearance of really new kinds of knowledge, technique, and social action. There are just three ways in which new elements are added to the existing culture of a society: discovery, invention, and diffusion.

Discovery   As we use the term, discovery involves *social recognition that new information is related to and an extension of existing knowledge*. What is meant by social recognition in this definition is illustrated by Storer's remarks about discovery in science. As he says, judgment about whether or not a contribution of a scientist is a legitimate discovery "must be made on the basis of how well the new contribution 'fits' current knowledge as a refinement or extension of it." And he continues, "If the terms in which a contribution represents an extension of current knowledge cannot be perceived by those evaluating it, by definition it cannot be accepted as creative" (1966:118–19). What is true of science is equally true elsewhere. In other words, a process of social recognition and validation is necessary if something is to be called a discovery.

Some discoveries are accidental, others are not. Accident played a part in Sir Alexander Fleming's discovery of penicillin in London in 1928. However, years of painstaking work went into the discoveries about the planet Jupiter that resulted from the journey of the spacecraft Pioneer 10 in 1973. While all inventions have some significant social result this may or may not be the case with discoveries. The discovery of penicillin had the immediate and important consequence of ushering in the age of antibiotic therapy in medicine. By contrast, Pioneer 10's discovery that night and day temperatures on Jupiter are identical, something that was not expected by scientists, has no discernible practical significance at this time.

Invention An invention is a recombination of existing elements of culture into something new. The social aspects of the invention process have been studied in detail by Ogburn (1922), Chapin (1928), and many others. Only a few points about it need to be made here. Contrary to what many people think, inventions do not spring by some mysterious and effortless process out of the minds of a special type of persons called inventors. Individuals are indispensable in the process, of course, and some are much better at it than others. But all inventions entail the use of existing elements of culture. The inventor conceives of a new combination of these elements, which is in itself an innovation. Figure 16-1 represents in schematic form some of the existing elements which went into the invention of the automobile.

Three consequences of the part played by recombination in inventions have special significance here. First, no matter how brilliant the individual inventor, he cannot bring forth new inventions for which the culture does not already provide the essential elements. In rare cases, a particularly creative individual may conceive inventions to which his society is unable to give practical technological expression. History's best example of this is probably Leonardo da Vinci, whose netbooks are full of ideas for inventions which society could not make use of in his time, but which were later recognized to be technologically sound. In short, the kinds of inventions which appear, and the rate at which they appear, are closely tied to what is called the *culture base.*

Second, since inventions are produced from new combinations of old elements, it follows that the larger the culture base the more combinations are possible, and the higher will be the rate at which new inventions appear. This means that new elements will be added to a society's culture not at a constant rate but at an increasing rate. Considerable evidence supports this generalization, especially for physical processes and objects. Some interesting examples of this evidence were assembled by Hart (1959:202–3). (Note Figure 16-2, pages 454–455.)

Third, it seems logical to predict that if the culture base in two different locations has about the same size and characteristics, some of the same new inventions might appear independently at about the same time; this has happened many times. Years ago Ogburn (1922) found 148 examples of important multiple inven-

[Source: Adapted and redrawn from F. S. Chapin, *Cultural
Change,* The Century Company, 1928, p. 366, by C. C.
Shrag, O. N. Larsen, and W. R. Catton, Jr., *Sociology* (4th
Ed.), (New York: Harper and Row, 1968), p. 594.]

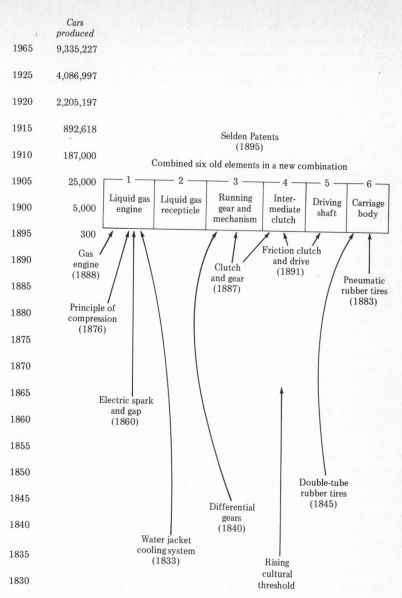

	Cars produced
1965	9,335,227
1925	4,086,997
1920	2,205,197
1915	892,618
1910	187,000
1905	25,000
1900	5,000
1895	300
1890	
1885	
1880	
1875	
1870	
1865	
1860	
1855	
1850	
1845	
1840	
1835	
1830	

tions covering several centuries of development in the sciences
and applied mechanics. This tendency for similar culture bases to
bring forth similar inventions has sometimes resulted in protracted controversy. There have been times when one inventor
sued another for stealing his idea when evidence showed that this
could not have happened; one is also reminded of the patriotic
claims by two or more countries to have been first in producing
this or that crucial invention of the modern age.

Most people think of inventions only as new ideas involving mechanical or chemical entities. Sociologists also apply the term to new social structures. With these as with all inventions, components that already exist are combined in a novel way to produce a new whole which is an addition to the culture base. Social inventions do not accumulate as rapidly or as simply as material inventions, mainly because they are likely to be seen as threats to established and emotionally supported ways of life.

Some modern social inventions include the two-year junior college, the city manager form of government, the corporation, the graduated income tax, the insurance method of covering risks, a balanced tripartite government structure including judicial, legislative, and executive components, and city planning.

Referring again to the notion of society as a tension-management system, it is easy to see that a society such as ours, which has a large, complex culture base and a high rate of invention, is constantly producing new elements capable of causing stress. The strains caused by many new elements—a new way of packaging beer—are of course trivial. But many others—the chain of events set in motion by the automobile—have profound effects which travel throughout a society and change it permanently.

Diffusion Invention and discovery are the only means by which man makes new additions to the culture base. In any relatively small area an invention or discovery appearing in one locality may spread to other localities. Diffusion is the term sociologists and anthropologists apply to this process.

As a result of intersocietal contacts over thousands of years, the cultures of all societies contain large proportions of elements that were not locally invented or discovered. People in comparatively isolated societies may have no idea at all that this is true. Even in countries like the United States most people grossly underestimate the extent to which familiar American ways of life have actually been borrowed at various times from other places of origin. When culture elements diffuse into a new area they may produce the same strains and change as if they had been locally invented.

SOCIAL EVOLUTION Many early theoretical formulations in sociology were evolutionary. The works of nineteenth-century European scholars such as Comte (coiner of the word *sociology*), Maine, Morgan, Tönnies, and Spencer are important examples. In the twentieth century, evolutionary theories fell into disrepute; they generally argued that all societies proceed through a fixed set of evolutionary stages. For this reason these are called *unilinear* theories.

As information about many societies accumulated it became clear that the facts did not all fit the existing theory. Moreover some early formulations, strongly influenced by contemporary evolutionary thought in biology, made the mistake of drawing too

FIGURE 16-2 SIX EXAMPLES OF CULTURAL ACCELERATION

Man's technological competence in the cutting and shaping of materials has increased as much in the last 3,000 years as it did in the previous million years (Chart A).

As to speed of travel, improvements in the locomotive added more in the years between 1829 and 1910 than had been achieved in all the previous million, while during the years since 1910, twenty times as much speed has been added as the locomotive contributed during its time of leadership (Chart B).

As to diffusion—the spreading of new inventions and discoveries from their place of origin—it took 400 years for the use of pottery to spread 100 miles, when it first was developed in Egypt, about 16,000 B.C. But the use of insulin spread clear around the world within one year (Chart C).

As to man's power to kill and to destroy, the most useful index for our purposes is the killing area, defined as meaning, for any given date, the maximum area within which lives and property may be destroyed by projectiles which travel through a nonstop flight from a single base. Leaving out the details, the basic facts can be summarized in the following table:

Date	Killing Area in Square Miles
1400	*1*
1900	*125*
1954	*197,000,000*

The trend is shown in Chart D.

Two thousand years ago, in ancient Rome, the average baby lived about twenty-two years. In 1840, the average expectation of life at birth, in seven Euro-American countries, was just over forty-one years. By 1940, in those same countries it was sixty-two years. Thus, one century of modern civilization extended human life more than had been achieved in the previous twenty centuries. This gain has gone on. Expectation of life in the United States increased from 64.2 in 1940 to 69.6 in 1955. The long-run trend is shown in Chart E. Cultural acceleration in scientific knowledge (Chart F) was discussed in Chapter 15.

[Source: Hornell Hart, "Social Theory and Social Change," in Llewellyn Gross, *Symposium on Sociological Theory* (Evanston, Ill.: Row, Peterson, 1959.]

close an analogy between biological organisms and societies, and between the processes of organic evolution and social evolution. Finally, some of these writers appeared to assume that nineteenth-century European society was the final goal of social evolution, and that other societies as they evolved would eventually reach the same state of perfection. A century later this unconscious cultural imperialism is much easier to recognize than it was at the time.

Despite the inadequacies of this early work there is today a renewed interest in evolutionary theory. Improvements in our understanding of how society works and in the amount and quality

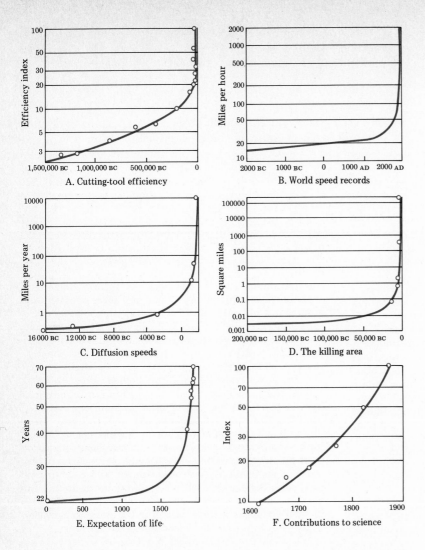

A. Cutting-tool efficiency

B. World speed records

C. Diffusion speeds

D. The killing area

E. Expectation of life

F. Contributions to science

of factual evidence make possible a more adequate consideration of long-run change in societies. In the preceding pages we have said that the interdependence of the parts of society, the appearance of new elements by invention, discovery, and diffusion, and the relation between a society and its environment constantly produce tension points, many of which become the starting points of social change. Attention to the specific details of these processes in particular localities can produce much understanding of the rate of change and its direction.

The accumulation of this kind of work in recent decades permits at least a tentative approach to the question of what directions social change may be taking in human societies over long periods of time.

We may state with due caution that the direction of human social evolution takes two broad forms: toward greater and greater diversification, and toward improvement or progress.

Diversification By diversification we mean that with the passage of time, the parts of societies become more and more elaborately specialized. In earlier chapters we cited many examples of this process, especially of changes associated with the indus-

---

The Diffusion of Culture

Our solid American citizen awakens in a bed built on a pattern which originated in the Near East but which was modified in Northern Europe before it was transmitted to America. He throws back covers made from cotton, domesticated in India, or linen, domesticated in the Near East, or wool from sheep, also domesticated in the Near East, or silk, the use of which was discovered in China. All of these materials have been spun and woven by processes invented in the Near East. He slips into his moccasins, invented by the Indians of the Eastern woodlands, and goes to the bathroom, whose fixtures are a mixture of European and American inventions, both of recent date. He takes off his pajamas, a garment invented in India, and washes with soap invented by the ancient Gauls. He then shaves, a masochistic rite which seems to have been derived from either Sumer or ancient Egypt.

Returning to the bedroom, he removes his clothes from a chair of southern European type and proceeds to dress. He puts on garments whose form originally derived from the skin clothing of the nomads of the Asiatic steppes, puts on shoes made from skins tanned by a process invented in ancient Egypt and cut to a pattern derived from the classical civilizations of the Mediterranean, and ties around his neck a strip of bright-colored cloth which is a vestigial survival of the shoulder shawls worn by the seventeenth-century Croatians. Before going out for breakfast he glances through the window, made of glass invented in Egypt, and if it is raining puts on overshoes made of rubber discovered by the Central American Indians and takes an umbrella, invented in southeastern Asia. Upon his head he puts a hat made of felt, a material invented in the Asiatic steppes.

On his way to breakfast he stops to buy a paper, paying for it with coins, an ancient Lydian invention. At the restaurant a whole new series of borrowed elements confronts him. His plate is made of a form of pottery invented in China. His knife is of steel, an alloy first made in southern India, his fork a medieval Italian invention, and his spoon a derivation of a Roman original. He begins breakfast with an orange, from the eastern Mediterranean, and a canteloupe from Persia, or perhaps a piece of African watermelon. With this he has coffee, an Abyssinian plant, with cream and sugar. Both the domestication of cows and the idea of milking them originated in the Near East, while sugar was first made in India. After his fruit and first coffee he goes on to waffles, cakes made by a Scandinavian technique from wheat domesticated in Asia Minor. Over these he pours maple syrup, invented by the Indians of the Eastern woodlands. As a side dish he may have the egg of a species of bird domesticated in Indochina, or thin strips of the flesh of an animal domesticated in Eastern Asia which have been salted and smoked by a process developed in Northern Europe.

When our friend has finished eating he settles back to smoke, an American Indian habit, consuming a plant domesticated in Brazil in either a pipe, derived from the Indians of Virginia, or a cigarette, derived from Mexico. If he is hardy enough he may even attempt a cigar, transmitted to us from the Antilles by way of Spain. While smoking he reads the news of the day, imprinted in characters invented by the ancient Semites upon a material invented in China by a process invented in Germany. As he absorbs the accounts of foreign troubles he will, if he is a good conservative citizen, thank a a Hebrew deity in an Indo-European language that he is 100 percent American.

Source: Ralph Linton, *The Study of Man* (1936).

trial revolution. By progress we mean "the raising of the upper level of the capacity of human societies to mobilize energy and information in the adaptive process" (Lenski, 1970:70).

Progress Many scholars have criticized the idea that social evolution has been progressive. There are ample grounds for such criticism if by progress one means demonstrable gains in happiness or the moral quality of human behavior. As yet we know of no way to compare objectively two societies or two historical eras for such qualities as these.

There can be no doubt that social evolution has been progressive in the restricted sense used by Lenski. Notice that progress conceived in this sense makes no assumptions about the final goals of societal evolution, as did nineteenth-century thinking on the subject. We do not know what the final states of human societies will be. We cannot even be sure that the trend toward diversification and improvement will continue indefinitely in the long future as they have done in the long past.

Since societies have developed in different kinds of environments and with varying amounts and kinds of isolation, it is hardly surprising that they differ a great deal and that some have undergone more evolutionary change than others. Considerable scholarly effort has been devoted to analysis and classification of these differences. Figure 16-3 presents a classification of societies developed by Goldschmidt (1959). We do not intend to discuss societal variation in detail and only point out that the arrows in the diagram are intended to represent the main lines of evolutionary development. For example, industrial, urban-dominated societies have evolved most recently and have passed through earlier stages of development. Herding tribal societies are believed by Goldschmidt to have developed from agricultural-state societies. And today there still are societies in much earlier developmental stages such as nomadic hunting and food-gathering.

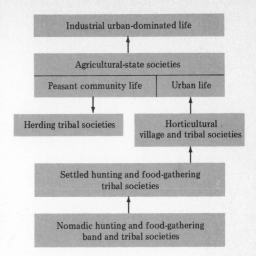

FIGURE 16-3 GOLDSCHMIDT'S CLASSIFICATION OF SOCIETIES

[Source: From *Human Societies* by Gerhard Lenski. Copyright © 1970 by McGraw-Hill, Inc. Used with permission of McGraw-Hill Book Company.]

THE PRACTICAL VALUE OF STUDYING TOTAL SOCIETIES

Is there any practical use for the study of whole societies? A simple yes or no answer to this question is not appropriate. It is hard to think of a specific action program deliberately based on a concept of total society with any resemblance to the picture we have drawn here. On the other hand, it is not hard at all to think of action programs which involve whole societies; the examples which come most readily to mind originate in the political institutions of modern states. The comments that follow represent our opinions perhaps more than they reflect sociological knowledge.

When a government makes war on another country, the whole society is involved. The far-flung Social Security program initiated by the federal government in the thirties involved the whole society within a few years. But such programs are based on quite primitive notions of the complex nature of a whole society and of the consequences of such programs in and between societies. Social scientists, including sociologists, have not devoted as much attention to the study of whole societies as their increasing importance requires.[3] So the stock of reliable knowledge specifically focused on societies as wholes which might be used for practical applications is disappointingly small.

We believe there is an urgent need for action programs involving whole societies to be based on sociologically more realistic conceptions of what a society really is. The social shrinkage and growing interdependence of the world due to technological changes has made programs at the society and intersociety levels more feasible, more necessary, and their consequences more fateful than ever before. Mankind is being forced into developing more and more programs at the highest levels of social organization.

Entirely apart from the political goals sought by the United States in the Vietnamese war, it appears that that war (an action program on the society level) was based on a serious misunderstanding of the nature of Vietnamese society. Secondarily, it involved a miscalculation of the effects of such a war upon American society. There is reason to believe that many failures of American foreign policy have stemmed from too narrowly political a view of other societies.

We are beginning to realize that the land, air, and water of the United States are the priceless heritage of all, and are in danger of destruction because we have permitted each individual, each business, each neighborhood, town, and city to exploit them almost at will. Recognition is at last growing that a society-wide approach is needed to deal with the problems of environmental quality. As yet only piecemeal, tentative beginnings of such a program exist or are even in the works.

As things are now, every total-society program is a high-risk venture whose actual effects may nullify or even contravene its intentions. And some problems go beyond a single society. We make some progress if one nation stops destroying our terrestrial home, but if the destruction goes on in the rest of the world how much will be gained in the long run? It helps if one country brings population growth under control, but how much good will that do if expansion continues unchecked elsewhere?

Many of today's most urgent problems require action organized at the level of whole societies, and interrelated groups of societies. But while societies are entities they are not living organisms. They have no intelligence, no conscience, no ability of their own to direct their destinies. The big, technologically advanced states may be likened to immensely powerful giants, blind, deaf, and

---

[3] Anthropologists have done better in this regard, but they have mostly been concerned with small, preliterate societies.

dumb, yet able to destroy each other and themselves. Only human individuals can see, hear and speak, and have intelligence and conscience. What is needed is that the minds and consciences of individuals become realistically aware of, be focused on, and in a sense be intelligently lent to the collectivities we call societies.

INCREASED LOYALTY AND UNDERSTANDING   The need for dealing with human problems of a society-wide and worldwide scope has outrun the development and organization of the qualities needed to deal with these problems. Within and between societies our world remains a place of narrow, parochial understandings and loyalties. There are at least two ways in which we need to catch up to the organizational imperatives of our time. There is a need for people to develop broader loyalties, beyond self, family, occupation, community—beyond the single society to the community of man, recognizing that to do so is a form of enlightened self-interest. History shows that men can identify strongly with collectivities of increasing size. It is only in quite recent times that great masses of individuals have demonstrated passionate loyalty to the nation-state. This kind of feeling is now needed for units larger than a single nation.

But devotion alone is not enough. Action programs based on the loftiest motives but on inaccurate concepts of society can lead to disaster. As Simpson (1949:181) puts it, "The present chaotic stage of humanity is not, as some wishfully maintain, caused by lack of faith but by too much unreasoning faith and too many conflicting faiths within these boundaries where such faith should have no place. The chaos is one that only responsible human knowledge can reduce to order." We now live in a world polarized into groups of competing, hostile, giant societies. In such a world, for mankind to react only on the basis of blind faith in parochial myths and dreams may be to collaborate in bringing the human story to its end.

Along with enlarging our loyalties, we need also to increase our understanding. The social sciences have a role to play in enlarging our stock of the knowledge that applies to macrosociological problems.

Even as we say these things we realize that the process of translating knowledge into rational social action is a complicated one. In democratic societies government and other policies must be based in the long run on the consent of the governed. And there are always real and legitimate conflicts of interest among the governed that complicate the process. Perhaps one of the most practical contributions that sociologists could make at this point would be to carry out careful, extensive research on the whole process of effectively channeling social scientific knowledge into action programs in democratic societies. Better understanding of what is involved here might help very much in making use of existing and forthcoming social scientific knowledge.

We don't know very much about the society of the future, but here and there serious efforts are made to shape that future by intelligent decisions made today. In the town-planning area, for instance, the United States Department of Housing and Urban Development has financed a study by R. Buckminster Fuller for a floating town (above) that would include its own modular schools, stores, and apartments and be anchored along the shoreline of an existing city. Columbia, Maryland (right), is an already existing city in which planners attempted to design a better urban environment than had been produced by chance in our past experience.

All this may seem remote and unrealistic to you. How, for example, can practical men of affairs who stand at the policy-making points in modern societies take seriously the point of view we have been expressing? Before answering this question it might be well to ponder one or two events of recent years. Only about fifteen years ago, the American pattern of race relations seemed to be pretty well frozen into one supported by tradition. Few practical men of affairs took seriously the early exploits of the freedom riders in Mississippi and elsewhere. But it turned out that we were witnessing the beginning of a transformation in race relations which is now reaching into every corner of society.

Only a few years ago, concern about overpopulation and about the destruction of the natural environment was confined to a few scholars in several scientific disciplines and to few others. At this moment, the accumulation of knowledge in these areas has at last begun to break through to some of the hard-headed makers of the big decisions, especially when the breakthrough is pushed hard by the power of organized population control and environmental protection groups. Growing numbers of such leaders have enlarged their conception of what is practical when confronted by effectively organized demands that they do so. Resistance to birth control programs has substantially lessened, the American birth rate

has come down, and many legal and legislative battles to protect the environment have been won.[4]

As we have learned from sociological studies of leadership, it is difficult, indeed usually impossible, for leaders to get very far ahead of their followers. Thus what leaders conclude they can do by using intelligence and knowledge in society-wide programs must depend on the enlightenment of their constituencies. Every reader of this book could become a small but ultimately vital part of a demand for leadership with a better grasp of what it takes to deal with today's grand-scale social problems.

Practicing the Sociological Perspective

Here is a simple exercise which may help to sharpen your grasp of what a society is. As you read the following lines, have two maps of the United States before you. One should portray only physical features, the other should include boundaries, highways, cities, and other human modifications of the land. First, take a good look at the physical map. Notice how the western mountain chains extend both north and south of the national boundaries, as does the great central plain. What you now see is a segment of the earth's surface with no intrinsic relationship to any society. Depending on the map you are using, there may be nothing whatever

---

[4] The severe energy crisis which surfaced in 1973 slowed the progress of the environmental protection movement. Yet it is extremely unlikely that all the gains made will be wiped out. Most likely is a "two steps forward, one step backward" kind of situation.

that suggests *society*. In fact, the mountain ranges might be read as possible natural boundaries between societies with borders running north and south.

Now look at the map which shows cultural features. Even though only in symbolic form, it depicts something of the interaction between a society and its territory. Yet this society has occupied that land only a few centuries, before which the society did not exist though other societies did inhabit the same territory. Archeological evidence suggests that Indian societies may have existed in this area for sixteen to eighteen thousand years, an enormously longer time than the entire history of the present occupant. None of those earlier societies controlled more than a small proportion of the total land area; today it is entirely occupied by one.

The boundaries with Mexico and Canada are not only lines enforced by political sovereignty. They are places where one whole way of life gives way to another. Despite the dozens of subcultures reflecting differences among citizens of the United States, all these citizens are alike in fundamental ways produced by the society to which they belong. There is even a sense in which American society lives beyond its geographical boundaries. Hundreds of thousands of citizens live abroad, and take with them some of the sociological aspects of the home society.

Next, imagine that everything used for human life had to be procured in the town or city where you live. What goods and services that are a part of your present life would have to go? How much of the total population would have to go too? How many of these things that would be lost are now available because a total society makes them possible? To start you off, consider the society's monetary system. Because of it, local economic activity is smoothly geared into not just a local or regional economy but a national economy linking all parts of the total society.

Do you recall the supersonic transport controversy of 1970–1971? The issue culminated in Congress over whether or not the federal government should continue the high cost of subsidizing production of two prototype SSTs. The supporters of federal subsidy argued that the plane should be constructed in order to make more jobs in the ailing airplane industry and to keep the United States competitive with Russian and European versions of the SST. Opponents argued that such a plane might damage the environment and perhaps, by a chain of cause and effect, even human health. They also argued that the plane wasn't needed and that the funds could be better used to combat domestic social problems.

We cite this case as one among many which illustrate the interdependence throughout society of actions taken on a large scale in only one segment. It also illustrates the fact that, little by little, responsible people are beginning to ask serious questions about all the effects that a large-scale action will have, not just those toward which a program is most directly pointed. What is needed is much more thinking of this kind. Finally, the SST case illustrates the need for reliable information about the social effects of large-scale programs as a basis for intelligent evaluation and choice. Neither on the SST nor on other cases do we yet have enough tested knowledge about societies as social systems to meet these increasingly pressing needs.

You may clarify these points perhaps by imagining that Congress, or some other source, initiates some specific large-scale program which its sponsors believe will solve a pressing problem. While you cannot have all the complex information actually needed to evaluate such a program, we suggest that once you choose your example, try to give provisional answers to such questions as what the chances are that the program really will have the effects the sponsors intend; and what some possible effects are that are not intended or even imagined, which would come about because society is a single system made up of interdependent parts. Can you specify any of the kinds of information which would be needed to develop answers to such questions as these?

In pressing the point that much more social scientific knowledge is needed for use in the social engineering that goes on in total societies today, we are not arguing that all such programs should be halted until adequate knowledge is produced. That would be folly indeed; we have no alternative but to cope with society-wide problems now. Rather, we are arguing that every attempt should be made to hasten the development of appropriate knowledge as rapidly as possible. In the meantime, it is possible at least to press for a more realistic orientation in policy makers and program builders. By realistic, we mean an orientation that recognizes the interdependence of society's parts, and that within the limits of existing knowledge tries to predict and make allowances for all the significant consequences of actions taken at a society-wide level, not just those of particular interest to this or that segment of the population.

References

CHAPTER ONE

Burgess, E. W., and H. J. Locke. 1945. *The Family.* New York: American Book Company.

de Rougement, Denis. 1940. *Love in the Western World.* New York: Harcourt.

Gibbs, J. P. 1966. "Suicide." Pp. 281–321 in Merton, R. K., and R. A. Nisbet, eds., *Contemporary Social Problems,* 2d ed. New York: Harcourt, Brace & World.

Gouldner, A. W., and S. M. Miller, eds. 1965. *Applied Sociology: Opportunities and Problems.* New York: Free Press.

Hall, C. S., and G. Lindzey. 1968. "The Relevance of Freudian Psychology and Related Viewpoints for the Social Sciences." Pp. 245–319 in Lindzey, G., and E. Aronson, eds., *The Handbook of Social Psychology,* 2d ed. Reading, Mass.: Addison-Wesley.

Hoffman, B. 1964. *The Tyranny of Testing.* New York: Collier Books.

Inkeles, A. 1964. *What is Sociology?* Englewood Cliffs, N. J.: Prentice-Hall.

McDougall, W. 1908. *Introduction to Social Psychology.* London: Methuen.

Ross, E. A. 1908. *Social Psychology: An Outline and Sourcebook.* New York: Macmillan.

CHAPTER TWO

Bates, A. P. 1967. *The Sociological Enterprise.* Boston: Houghton Mifflin.

Bates, A. P., and J. S. Cloyd. 1956. "Toward the Development of Operations for Defining Group Norms and Member Roles." *Sociometry* 19:26–39.

Beatty, J., Jr. 1969. "Trade Winds." *Saturday Review* 52(July 19).

Biddle, B. J., and E. J. Thomas. 1966. *Role Theory, Concepts and Research.* New York: John Wiley and Sons.

Kluckhohn, C., and W. H. Kelly. 1944. "The Concept of Culture." Pp. 78–107 in Linton, R., ed., *The Science of Man in the World Crisis.* New York: Columbia University Press.

Linton, R. 1936. *The Study of Man.* New York: Appleton-Century.

Moore, W. E. 1963. *Social Change.* Englewood Cliffs, N.J.: Prentice-Hall.

Roper, E. 1969. "One Helluva Way to Run a Railroad." *Saturday Review,* 28 June:18–19.

Schulman, P. Shaver; R. Colman; B. Emrich; and R. Christie. 1973. "Recipe for a Jury." *Psychology Today,* May.

Taylor, E. 1871. *Primitive Culture.* London: J. Murray.

Williams, R. M., Jr. 1970. *American Society: A Sociological Interpretation,* 3d ed. New York: Knopf. © Alfred A. Knopf, Inc., 1970. Reprinted by permission.

Yinger, J. M. 1965. *Toward a Field Theory of Behavior.* New York: McGraw-Hill.

Young, L. 1966. *Life Among the Giants.* New York: McGraw-Hill.

Chapter Three

Aberle, D. F. 1961. "Culture and Socialization." Pp. 381–97 in Hsu, F. K., ed., *Psychological Anthropology: Approaches to Culture and Personality*. Homewood, Ill.: Dorsey Press.

Berger, P. 1963. *Invitation to Sociology*. Garden City, N.Y.: Doubleday Anchor.

Clausen, J. A. 1968. "Introduction." Pp. 1–17 in Clausen, J. A., ed., *Socialization and Society*. Boston: Little, Brown.

Cohen, A. K. 1966. *Deviance and Control*. Englewood Cliffs, N.J.: Prentice-Hall.

Cooley, C. H. 1902. *Human Nature and the Social Order*. Boston: Scribner Press.

Cottrell, L. S., Jr. 1969. "Interpersonal Interaction and the Development of the Self." Pp. 543–70 in Goslin, D. A., ed., *Handbook of Socialization Theory and Research*. Chicago: Rand McNally.

Davis, K. 1949. *Human Society*. New York: Macmillan.

Elkin, F. 1960. *The Child and Society*. New York: Random House.

Homans, G. C. 1950. *The Human Group*. New York: Harcourt, Brace & World.

Inkeles, A. 1969. "Social Structure and Socialization." Pp. 615–32 in Goslin, D. A., ed., *Handbook of Socialization Theory and Research*. Chicago: Rand McNally.

James, W. 1890. *Principles of Psychology*. New York: Holt.

Kuhn, M. H., and T. S. McPartland. 1954. "An Empirical Investigation of Self-Attitudes." *American Sociological Review* 19:68–78.

LeVine, R. A. 1969. "Culture, Personality and Socialization: An Evolutionary View." Pp. 503–41 in Goslin, D. A., ed., *Handbook of Socialization Theory and Research*. Chicago: Rand McNally.

McClelland, D. C. 1961. *The Achieving Society*. New York: Van Nostrand.

McClelland, D. C., et al. 1953. *The Achievement Motive*. New York: Appleton-Century-Crofts.

Mead, G. H. 1934. *Mind, Self, and Society*. Chicago: Univ. of Chicago Press.

Munn, N. I., et al. 1969. *Introduction to Psychology*, 2d ed. Boston: Houghton Mifflin.

Newcomb, T. M. 1950. *Social Psychology*. New York: Dryden.

Piaget, J. 1952. *The Origins of Intelligence in Children*. New York: International Universities Press.

Rosen, B. C. 1959. "Race, Ethnicity and the Achievement Syndrome." *American Sociological Review* 24:47–60.

Roszak, Betty, and Theodore Roszak. 1970. *Masculine and Feminine*. New York: Harper and Row. Reprinted by permission.

Schwartz, M.; F. N. Fearn; and S. Stryker. 1966. "A Note on Self Conception and the Emotionally Disturbed Role." *Sociometry* 29:300–5.

Weber, M. 1930. *The Protestant Ethic and the Spirit of Capitalism*, Parsons, T., trans. London: G. Allen.

Whiting, J. W., and B. B. Whiting. 1960. "Contributions of Anthropology to Methods of Studying Child Rearing." In Mussen, P., ed., *Handbook of Research Methods in Child Development*. New York: Wiley.

Zigler, E., and I. L. Child. 1969. "Socialization." Pp. 450–589 in Lindzey, G., and E. Aronson, eds., *Handbook of Social Psychology*, 2d ed., vol. 3. Reading, Mass.: Addison-Wesley.

Chapter Four

Back, K. W. 1971. "Varieties of Sensitivity Training." *Sociological Inquiry* 41:133–37.

Bales, R. F. 1950. *Interaction Process Analysis*. Cambridge, Mass.: Addison-Wesley.

———. 1965. "The Equilibrium Problem in Small Groups." Pp. 444–76 in Hare, A. P.; E. F. Borgatta; and R. F. Bales, eds., *Small Groups, Studies in Social Interaction*, rev. ed. New York: Knopf.

Bales, R. F., and E. F. Borgatta. 1965. "Size of Group as a Factor in the Interaction Profile." Pp. 495–512 in Hare, A. P.; E. F. Borgatta; and R. F. Bales, eds., *Small Groups, Studies in Social Interaction*, rev. ed. New York: Knopf.

Batchelor, J. P., and G. R. Goethals. 1972. "Spatial Arrangements in Freely Formed Groups." *Sociometry* 35:270–79.

Bates, A. P., and N. Babchuk. 1961. "The Primary Group: A Reappraisal." *Sociological Quarterly* 2:181–91.

Baxter, J. C. 1970. "Interpersonal Space in Natural Settings." *Sociometry* 33:444–56.

Blumer, H. 1962. "Society as Symbolic Interaction." Pp. 179–92 in Rose, A. M., ed., *Human Behavior and Social Processes*. Boston: Houghton Mifflin.

Collins, B. E., and B. H. Raven. 1969. "Group Structure: Attraction, Coalitions, Communications, and Power." Pp. 102–204 in Lindzey, G., and E. Aronson, eds., *The Handbook of Social Psychology*, 2d ed., vol. 4. Reading, Mass.: Addison-Wesley.

Cooley, C. H. 1909. *Social Organization*. New York: Scribners.

Gibb, C. A. 1969. "Leadership." Pp. 205–82 in Lindzey, G., and E. Aronson, eds., *The Handbook of Social Psychology*, 2d ed., vol. 4. Reading, Mass.: Addison-Wesley.

Goffman, E. 1967. *Interaction Ritual*. Garden City, N.Y.: Anchor Books.

Gross, N.; W. S. Mason; and A. W. McEachern. 1957. *Explorations in Role Analysis: Studies of the School Superintendency Role*. New York: Wiley.

Hall, E. T. 1966. *The Hidden Dimension*. Garden City, N.Y.: Doubleday.

Hammer, R. 1969. "Role Playing: A Judge is a Cop, A Cop is a Judge." *New York Times Magazine*, 14 Sept.

Hare, A. P., and R. F. Bales. 1963. "Seating Position and Small Group Interaction." *Sociometry* 26:485–6.

Levinger, G. 1964. "Task and Social Behavior in Marriage." *Sociometry* 27:433–48.

Moreno, J. L. 1953. *Who Shall Survive?* Boston: Beacon Press.

Moskos, C. C., Jr. 1967. "A Sociologist Appraises the G.I." *New York Times Magazine*, 24 Sept, 33 ff.

Shils, E. A., and M. Janowitz. 1948. "Cohesion and Disintegration in the Wehrmacht in World War II." *Public Opinion Quarterly* 12:280–315.

Slater, P. E. 1955. "Role Differentiation in Small Groups." *American Sociological Review* 20:300–10.

Sommer, R. 1961. "Leadership and Group Geography." *Sociometry* 24:99–110.

——. 1962. "The Distance for Comfortable Conversation: A Further Study." *Sociometry* 25:111–16.

Thomas, E. J., and F. F. Fink. 1963. "Effects of Group Size." *Psychological Bulletin* 60:371–84.

Wieck, E. E. 1968. "Systematic Observational Methods." Pp. 357–451 in Lindzey, G., and E. Aronson, eds., *The Handbook of Social Psychology*, 2d ed., vol. 2. Reading, Mass.: Addison-Wesley.

Wolfe, T. 1968. *The Electric Kool-Aid Acid Test*. New York: Farrar, Straus, & Giroux.

Yablonsky, L. 1962. "The Anticriminal Society: Synanon." *Federal Probation* 26(Sept.):50–57.

Zelditch, M., Jr. 1955. "Role Differentiation in the Nuclear Family: A Comparative Study." Pp. 307–52 in Parsons, T., and R. F. Bales, eds., *Family, Socialization and Interaction Process*. New York: Free Press.

CHAPTER FIVE

Bogue, D. J. 1955. "Urbanism in the United States, 1950." *American Journal of Sociology* 60(March):438–45.

Davis K. 1955. "The Origin and Growth of Urbanization in the World." *American Journal of Sociology* 60(March):431–33.

Firey, W. 1947. *Land Use in Central Boston*. Cambridge: Harvard Univ. Press.

Fried, M., and P. Gleicher. 1961. "Some Sources of Residential Satisfaction in an Urban Slum." *Journal of the American Institute of Planners* 27(November):305–15.

Gans, H. 1970. "Social Planning; A New Role For Sociology." Pp. 920–32 in Gutman, R., and D. P. Poponoe, eds., *Neighborhood, City and Metropolis*. New York: Random House.

Greer, S. 1955. *Social Organization*. New York: Random House.

——. 1961. "Traffic, Transportation, and Problems of the Metropolis." Pp. 605–50 in Merton, R. K., and R. A. Nisbet, eds., *Contemporary Social Problems*. New York: Harcourt, Brace & World.

Hauser, P. M. 1969. *The Population Dilemma*, 2d ed. Englewood Cliffs, N.J.: Prentice-Hall.

Hoyt, H. 1939. *The Structure and Growth of Residential Neighborhoods in American Cities*. Washington, D.C.: Federal Housing Authority.

Lerner, D. 1964. *The Passing of Traditional Society*. New York: Free Press.

Matras, J. 1973. *Populations and Societies*. Englewood Cliffs, N.J.: Prentice-Hall.

McElrath, D. 1968. "The New Urbanization." Pp. 3–12 in Greer, S.; D. L. McElrath; D. W. Minar; and P. Orleans, eds., *The New Urbanization*. New York: St. Martin's.

Minar, D. W., and S. Greer. 1969. *The Concept of Community*. Chicago: Aldine.

Nisbet, R. A. 1960. "Moral Values and Community." *International Review of Community Development* 5:574–82.

Park, R. E.; E. W. Burgess; and R. D. McKenzie. 1925. *The City*. Chicago: Univ. of Chicago Press.

Plumb, J. H. 1968. "The Secular Heretics." *Horizon* 10(Spring):9–12.

Schorr, A. L. 1963. *Slums and Social Insecurity: An Appraisal of the Effectiveness of Housing Policies in Helping to Eliminate Poverty in the United States*. Washington, D.C.: U.S. Government Printing Office.

Seeley, J. R. 1959. "The Slum: Its Nature, Use and Users." *Journal of the American Institute of Planners* 25(February):7–14.

Statistical Abstract of the United States. 1973. Washington, D.C.: U.S. Government Printing Office.

Stein, Maurice R. 1972. *The Eclipse of Community: An Interpretation of American Studies*, Expanded edition. Princeton: Princeton Univ. Press. Copyright © 1972 by Princeton University Press. Reprinted by permission of Princeton University Press.

Taeuber, I. B. 1964. "Population and Society." Pp. 83–126 in Faris, R. E. L., ed., *Handbook of Modern Sociology*. Chicago: Rand McNally.

Tönnies, F. 1887. *Gemeinschaft und Gesellschaft*. Loomis, C. P., trans. and ed., *Fundamental Concepts of Sociology*. New York: American Book Company.

Vidich, A. J., and J. Bensman. 1958. *Small Town in Mass Society*. Princeton, N.J.: Princeton Univ. Press.

CHAPTER SIX

Antonovsky, A. 1967. "Social Class, Life Expectancy, and Overall Mortality." *Milbank Memorial Fund Quarterly* 45:31–73.

Aron, R. 1966. "Social Class, Political Class, Ruling Class." Pp. 201–10 in Bendix, R. and S. M. Lipset, eds., *Class, Status, and Power*, 2d ed. New York: Free Press.

Baltzell, E. D. 1953. "Social Mobility and Fertility Within an Elite Group." *Milbank Memorial Fund Quarterly* 31:411–20.

Barber, B. 1957. *Social Stratification*. New York: Harcourt, Brace & World.

Beck, B. 1970. "Bedbugs, Stench, Dampness, and Immorality: A Review Essay on Recent Literature About Poverty." Pp. 53–69 in Skolnick, J., and E. Currie, eds., *Crisis in American Institutions*. Boston: Little, Brown.

Bendix, R. 1960. *Max Weber, An Intellectual Portrait*. Garden City, N.Y.: Doubleday.

Blau, P. M., and O. D. Duncan. 1967. *American Occupational Structure*. New York: Wiley.

Centers, R. 1949. *The Psychology of Social Classes*. Princeton, N.J.: Princeton Univ. Press.

Dahrendorf, R. 1959. *Class and Class Conflict in Industrial Society*. Stanford, Cal.: Stanford Univ. Press.

David, K. 1949. *Human Society*. New York: Macmillan.

Faris, R. E. L., and H. W. Dunham. 1939. *Mental Disorders in Urban Areas*. Chicago: Univ. of Chicago Press.

Hodges, H. M., Jr. 1964. *Social Stratification*. Cambridge, Mass.: Schenkman.

Hollingshead, A. B., and F. Redlich. 1958. *Social Class and Mental Illness*. New York: Wiley.

Jackson, E. F., and H. J. Crockett, Jr. 1962. "Status Consistency and Symptoms of Stress." *American Sociological Review* 27:469–80.

———. 1964. "Occupational Mobility in the United States: A Point Estimate and Trend Comparison." *American Sociological Review* 29:5–15.

Kadushin, C. 1964. "Social Class and the Experience of Ill Health." *Sociological Inquiry* 34:67–80.

Keller, S. 1963. *Beyond the Ruling Class*. New York: Random House.

Kohn, M. L. 1969. *Class and Conformity: A Study in Values*. Homewood, Ill.: Dorsey Press.

Kornhauser, W. 1966. "'Power Elite' of 'Veto Groups.'" Pp. 210–18 in Bendix, R., and S. M.

Lipset, eds., *Class, Status, and Power,* 2d ed. New York: Free Press.

Leighton, A. J. 1959. *My Name is Legion.* New York: Basic Books.

Lenski, G. 1966. *Power and Privilege.* New York: McGraw-Hill.

————. 1967. "Status Inconsistency and the Vote: A Four Nation Test." *American Sociological Review* 32:298–301.

Lipset, S. M. 1960. *Political Man.* New York: Doubleday.

Lipset, S. M., and R. Bendix. 1960. *Social Mobility in Industrial Society.* Los Angeles: Univ. of California Press.

Lipset, S. M., and H. L. Zetterberg. 1956. "A Theory of Social Mobility." *Transactions of the Third World Congress of Sociology* 3:155–77.

Lundberg, F. 1968. *The Rich and the Super-Rich.* New York: Lyle Stuart.

Miller, W. 1949. "American Historians and the Business Elite." *Journal of Economic History* 9:184–208.

Mills, C. W. 1956. *The Power Elite.* New York: Oxford Univ. Press.

Newcomer, M. 1955. *The Big Business Executive: The Factors that Made Him.* New York: Columbia Univ. Press.

Ossowski, S. 1963. "Dialectic and Functionalism: Toward a Theoretical Synthesis." *American Sociological Review* 28:695–705.

Riesman, D. 1953. *The Lonely Crowd.* New York: Doubleday.

Rogoff, N. 1953. *Recent Trends in Occupational Mobility.* Glencoe, Ill.: Free Press.

Srole, L. et al. 1962. *Mental Health in the Metropolis,* vol. 1. New York: McGraw-Hill.

Statistical Abstract of the United States. 1973. Washington, D.C.: U.S. Government Printing Office.

Stouffer, S. A. 1955. *Communism, Conformity and Civil Liberties: A Cross-Section of the Nation Speaks Its Mind.* New York: Doubleday.

Warner, W. L., and J. C. Abegglen. 1955. *Big Business Leaders in America.* New York: Harper & Row.

Warner, W. L.; M. Meeker; and K. Lells. 1949. *Social Class in America.* Chicago: Science Research Assoc.

CHAPTER SEVEN

Adorno, T. W.; E. Frenkel-Brunswik; D. J. Levinson; and R. N. Sanford. 1950. *The Authoritarian Personality.* New York: Harper.

Bernard, J. 1964. *Academic Women.* University Park, Penn.: Pennsylvania State Univ. Press.

Bogardus, E. S. 1925. "Measuring Social Distance." *Journal of Applied Sociology* 9:299–308.

Changes in Economic Level in Nine Neighborhoods in Cleveland. 1966. Series P-43, No. 20. Washington, D.C.: U.S. Government Printing Office.

Characteristics of Selected Neighborhoods in Cleveland, Ohio. 1967. Series P-23, No. 21. Washington, D.C.: U.S. Government Printing Office.

Dollard, J.; N. E. Miller; L. Doob; O. H. Mowrer; and R. R. Sears. 1939. *Frustration and Aggression.* New Haven: Yale Univ. Press.

Glazer, N., and D. P. Moynihan. 1963. *Beyond the Melting Pot.* Cambridge, Mass.: M.I.T. Press.

Goldstein, S., and C. Goldscheider. 1968. *Jewish Americans.* Englewood Cliffs, N.J.: Prentice-Hall.

Gordon, M. M. 1964. *Assimilation in American Life: The Role of Race, Religion, and National Origins.* New York: Oxford Univ. Press.

Hauser, P. M. 1966. "Demographic Factors in the Integration of the Negro." In Parsons, T., and K. B. Clark, eds., *The American Negro.* Boston: Houghton Mifflin.

Lenski, G. 1966. *Power and Privilege, A Theory of Social Stratification.* New York: McGraw-Hill.

Masotti, L. H.; J. K. Hadden; K. F. Seminatore; and J. R. Corsi. 1969. *A Time to Burn?* Chicago: Rand McNally.

Myrdal, G. 1944. *An American Dilemma.* New York: Harper.

Newcomb, T. M.; R. H. Turner; and P. E. Converse. 1965. *Social Psychology.* New York: Holt, Rinehart & Winston.

Pettigrew, T. F. 1958. "Personality and Socio-Cultural Factors in Intergroup Attitudes; a Cross-National Comparison." *Journal of Conflict Resolution* 2:29–42.

Reeves, N. 1971. *Womankind; Beyond the Stereotypes.* Chicago: Aldine, Atherton.

Rose, A. M. 1966. "Race and Ethnic Relations." Pp. 409–78 in Merton, R. K., and R. A. Nisbet, eds., *Contemporary Social Problems*, 2d ed. New York: Harcourt, Brace & World.

Senior, C. 1965. *The Puerto Ricans*. Chicago: Quadrangle Books.

Simpson, G. E., and J. M. Yinger. 1965. *Racial and Cultural Minorities*, 3d ed. New York: Harper & Row.

Special Census of Cleveland, Ohio, April 1, 1965. 1965. Series P-28, No. 1390. Washington, D.C.: U.S. Government Printing Office.

Statistical Abstract of the United States. 1973. Washington, D.C.: U.S. Government Printing Office.

van den Berghe, P. L. 1967. *Race and Racism*. New York: Wiley.

White, A. 1967. "Women in the Law." *Michigan Law Review* 1051:1070–87.

Wirth, L. 1928. *The Ghetto*. Chicago: Univ. of Chicago Press.

CHAPTER EIGHT

The American Sociological Association. 1968. "Toward a Code of Ethics for Sociologists." *The American Sociologist*(November):318. Reprinted by permission.

Bates, A. P. 1967. *The Sociological Enterprise*. Boston: Houghton Mifflin.

Bendix, R. 1960. *Max Weber; An Intellectual Portrait*. Garden City, N.Y.: Doubleday.

Bennett, S., Jr., and Noel P. Gist. 1964. "Class and Family Influences on Student Aspirations." *Social Forces* 43(December):167–73.

Berger, P. L., and B. Berger. 1972. *Sociology; A Biographical Approach*. New York: Basic Books.

Blau, P. M., et al. 1956. "Occupational Choice: A Conceptual Framework." *Industrial and Labor Relations Review* 9(July, no. 4):531–43.

Caplow, T. 1954. *The Sociology of Work*. Minneapolis: Univ. of Minnesota Press.

Current Population Reports, 1970. Series P-27, no. 42. U.S. Bureau of the Census, Washington, D.C.: U.S. Government Printing Office.

Davis, J. A. 1964. *Great Aspirations*. Chicago: Aldine.

DeGrazia, S. 1971. "The Problems and Promise of Leisure." In Schuler, E. A., et al., eds., *Readings in Sociology*. New York: Crowell.

Department of Labor. 1965. Reported in *Statistical Abstract of the United States*. 1973. Washington, D.C.: U.S. Government Printing Office.

Drucker, P. F. 1953. "The Employee Society." *American Journal of Sociology* 58(March):358–63.

Etzioni, A., ed. 1969. *The Semi-Professions and Their Organization*. New York: Free Press.

Fichandler, T. C. 1962. "The American Labor Force." Pp. 97–111 in Nosow, S., and W. H. Form, eds., *Man, Work, and Society*. New York: Basic Books.

Ford, J., and S. Box. 1967. "Sociological Theory and Occupational Choice." *Sociological Review* 15:287–99.

Ginzberg, E., et al. 1951. *Occupational Choice*. New York: Columbia Univ. Pres.

Goode, W. J. 1956. *After Divorce*. New York: Free Press.

——. 1969. "The Theoretical Limits of Professionalization." Pp. 266–313 in Etzioni, A., ed., *The Semi-Professions and Their Organization*. New York: Free Press.

Greenwood, E. 1962. "Attributes of a Profession." Pp. 207–18 in Nosow, S., and W. H. Form, eds., *Man, Work, and Society*. New York: Basic Books. Reprinted with permission of the National Association of Social Workers, From *Social Work*, vol. 2, no. 3, (July 1957), Pp. 45–55.

Gross, E. 1958. *Work and Society*. New York: Crowell.

Gross, E. 1965. *Industry and Social Life*. Dubuque, Iowa: Wm. C Brown.

Hall, R. H. 1969. *Occupations and the Social Structure*. Englewood Cliffs, N.J.: Prentice-Hall.

Hausknecht, M. 1962. *The Joiners: A Sociological Description of Voluntary Association Membership in the United States*. New York: The Bedminister Press.

Hodge, R. W., et al. 1964. "Occupational Prestige in the United States: 1925–1963." *American Journal of Sociology* 70(November):286–302.

Hooper, J. H. 1963. "To Be a Sociologist." Pp. 452–65 in Ross, H. L., ed., *Perspectives on the Social Order*. New York: McGraw-Hill.

Hughes, E. C. 1951. "Work and the Self." Pp. 313–23 in Rohrer, J. H., and M. Sherif, eds.,

Social Psychology at the Crossroads. New York: Harper.

Huntington, M. J. 1957. "The Development of a Professional Self-Image." Pp. 179–87 in Merton, R. K., et al., eds., *The Student Physician.* Cambridge: Harvard Univ. Press.

Lortie, D. C. 1959. "Laymen to Lawmen: Law School, Careers, and Professional Socialization." *Harvard Educational Review* 29(Fall):363–67.

Moore, W. E. 1962. "The Attributes of an Industrial Order." Pp. 91–97 in Nosow, S., and W. H. Form, eds., *Man, Work, and Society.* New York: Basic Books.

Morse, N. C., and S. Weiss. 1962. "The Function and Meaning of Work and the Job." Pp. 29–35 in Nosow, S., and W. H. Form, eds., *Man, Work, and Society.* New York: Basic Books.

Parsons, T. 1954. "The Professions and Social Structure." Pp. 34–49 in Parsons, T., ed., *Essays in Sociological Theory,* rev. ed. New York: Free Press.

Reissman, L. 1959. *Class in American Society.* Glencoe, Ill.: Free Press.

Rosenberg, M. 1955. "Factors Influencing Change of Occupational Choice." Pp. 258–59 in Lazarsfeld, P. F., and M. Rosenberg, eds., *The Language of Social Research.* New York: Free Press.

Schwarzeller, H. K. 1960. "Values and Occupational Choice." *Social Forces* 38(December):126–35.

Sherlock, B., and A. Cohen. 1966. "The Strategy of Occupational Choice." *Social Forces* 45(December):303–13.

Sibley, E. 1963. *The Education of Sociologists in the United States.* New York: Russell Sage Foundation.

Stephenson, R. M. 1957. "Mobility Orientation and Stratification of 1,000 Ninth Graders." *American Sociological Review* 22:(April)204–12.

Sutherland, E. H. 1937. *The Professional Thief.* Chicago: Univ. of Chicago Press.

Tilgher, A. 1931. *Work: What It Has Meant Through the Ages.* London: George G. Harrap & Co.

U.S. Bureau of the Census. 1950. Reported in *Statistical Abstract of the United States.* 1973. Washington, D.C.: U.S. Government Printing Office.

Vollmer, H. M., and D. L. Mills. 1966. *Professionalization.* Englewood Cliffs, N.J.: Prentice-Hall.

Vroom, V. 1964. *Work and Motivation.* New York: Wiley.

Wilensky, H. L. 1961. "Trends in Amount of Time Worked." *Social Problems (Summer)*32–56.

———. 1964. "The Professionalization of Everyone?" *American Journal of Sociology* 70(Sept.):137–58.

———. 1966. "Work as a Social Problem." Pp. 117–66 in Becker, H. S., ed., *Social Problems: A Modern Approach.* New York: Wiley. Reprinted by permission of John Wiley and Sons, Inc.

Wilensky, H. L., and C. N. Lebeaux. 1958. *Industrial Society and Social Welfare.* New York: Russell Sage Foundation.

CHAPTER NINE

Babchuk, N., and A. Booth. 1969. "Voluntary Association Membership: A Longitudinal Analysis." *American Sociological Review* 34(Feb.):31–45.

Blau, P. M., and R. W. Scott. 1962. *Formal Organizations: A Comparative Approach.* San Francisco: Chandler.

Carmichael, S., and C. V. Hamilton. 1967. *Black Power.* New York: Vintage Books.

Cressey, D. R. 1969. *The Theft of the Nation: The Structure and Operations of Organized Crime in America.* New York: Harper & Row.

Drucker, P. F. 1946. *The Concept of the Corporation.* New York: New American Library.

Etzioni, A. 1961. *A Comparative Analysis of Complex Organizations.* New York: Free Press.

Homans, G. 1950. *The Human Group.* New York: Harcourt, Brace & Company.

Inkeles, A. 1968. "Personality and Social Structure." Pp. 3–18 in Parsons, T., ed., *American Sociology: Perspectives, Problems, Methods.* New York: Basic Books.

Jacoby, A., and N. Babchuk. 1963. "Instrumental and Expressive Voluntary Associations." *Sociology and Social Research* 47(July):461–71.

Julian, J. 1966. "Compliance Patterns and Communication blocks in Complex Organizations." *American Sociological Review* 31(June):289–382.

———. 1969. "Some Determinants of Dissensus on Role Prescriptions Within and Between Four Organizational Positions." *Sociological Quarterly* 10(Spring):177–89.

Killian, L. M. 1968. *The Impossible Revolution.* New York: Random House.

Leavitt, H. J. 1965. "Applied Organizational Change in Industry: Structural, Technological, and Humanistic Approaches." Pp. 1144–70 in March, J. G., ed., *Handbook of Organizations.* Chicago: Rand McNally.

McCleery, R. H. 1957. *Policy Change in Prison Management.* East Lansing, Mich.: Governmental Research Bureau, Michigan State Univ.

Miller, S. M. 1963. *Max Weber.* New York: Crowell.

Ritzer, G. 1972. *Man and His Work: Conflict and Change.* New York: Appleton-Century-Crofts.

Rose, A. M. 1965. *Sociology, the Study of Human Relations.* New York: Knopf.

Schmidt, A., and N. Babchuk. 1972. "Formal Voluntary Groups and Change Over Time: A Study of Fraternal Associations." *Journal of Voluntary Action Research* 1(Jan.):46–55.

Scott, W. 1964. "Theory of Organizations." Pp. 485–530 in Faris, R. E. L., ed., *Handbook of Modern Sociology.* Chicago: Rand McNally.

Smith, C., and A. Freedman. 1972. *Voluntary Associations, Perspectives on the Literature.* Cambridge, Mass.: Harvard Univ. Press.

Weber, M. 1947. *The Theory of Social and Economic Organization.* New York: Oxford Univ. Press.

Williams, J. A., Jr.; N. Babchuk; and D. Johnson. 1973. "Voluntary Associations and Minority Status: A Comparative Analysis of Anglo, Black, and Mexican Americans." *American Sociological Review* 38:637–46.

CHAPTER TEN

Allport, G., and L. Postman. 1945. "The Basic Psychology of Rumor." *Transactions of the New York Academy of Science* Series II, pp. 61–81.

———. 1947. *The Psychology of Rumor.* New York: Holt.

Bartlett, F. C. 1932. *Remembering.* Cambridge, England: Cambridge Univ. Press.

Cantril, H. 1941. *The Psychology of Social Movements.* New York: Wiley.

Caplow, T. 1947. "Rumors in War." *Social Forces* 25(March):298–302.

Dollard, J. L.; N. E. Doob; N. E. Miller; O. H. Mowrer; and R. Sears. 1939. *Frustration and Aggression.* New Haven: Yale Univ. Press.

Epstein, B. R., and A. Forster. 1967. *The Radical Right.* New York: Random House (Vintage Books).

Firth, R. 1956. "Rumor in a Primitive Society." *Journal of Abnormal and Social Psychology* 53:122–32.

Gerth, H., and C. W. Mills. 1946. *From Max Weber: Essays in Sociology.* New York: Oxford Univ. Press.

Killian, L. M. 1964. "Social Movements." Pp. 426–55 in Faris, R. E. L., ed., *Handbook of Modern Sociology.* Chicago: Rand McNally.

Kornhauser, W. 1968. "Student Protest: Berkeley, 1964." Pp. 370–75 in Broom, L., and P. Selznick, *Sociology.* New York: Harper & Row.

Lang, K., and G. E. Lang. 1961. *Collective Dynamics.* New York: Crowell.

Lasswell, H. 1930. *The Psychopathology of Politics.* Chicago: Univ. of Chicago Press.

Le Bon, G. 1895. *Psychologie des Foules* (trans. *The Crowd*). London: Unwin (1903).

Malcolm, Andrew H. "Is Johnny Carson Behind the Toilet Paper Crisis?" *The New York Times,* February 3, 1974. © 1974 by the New York Times Company. Reprinted by permission.

Milgram, S., and H. Toch. 1969. "Collective Behavior: Crowds and Social Movements." Pp. 507–610 in Lindzey, G., and E. Aronson, eds., *Handbook of Social Psychology,* 2d ed. Reading, Mass.: Addison-Wesley.

Morgenstern, J. 1971. "Children's Hour." *Newsweek* 16 August, p. 9.

Report of the National Advisory Commission on Civil Disorders. 1968. Washington, D.C.: U.S. Government Printing Office.

Rosenthal, M. 1971. "Where Rumor Raged." *Transaction* 8(Feb.):34–43.

Shibutani, T. 1966. *Improvised News: A Sociological Study of Rumor.* Indianapolis: Bobbs-Merrill.

Smelser, N. J. 1963. *Theory of Collective Behavior*. New York: Free Press.

Stern, S. 1965. "A Deeper Disenchantment." *Liberation* 9(No. 11):15–40.

Turner, R. H. 1964. "Collective Behavior." Pp. 382–425 in Faris, R. E. L., ed., *Handbook of Modern Sociology*. Chicago: Rand McNally.

Turner, R. H., and L. M. Killian. 1972. *Collective Behavior*, 2d ed. Englewood Cliffs, N.J.: Prentice-Hall.

Chapter Eleven

Becker, H. S. 1963. *Outsiders: Studies in the Sociology of Deviance*. New York: Free Press.

Clausen, J. A. 1971a. "Mental Disorders." Pp. 29–87 in Merton, R. K., and R. Nisbet, eds., *Contemporary Social Problems*. New York: Harcourt, Brace, Jovanovich.

———. 1971b. "Drug Use." Pp. 185–226 in Merton, R. K., and R. Nisbet, eds., *Contemporary Social Problems*. New York: Harcourt, Brace, Jovanovich.

Cohen, A. K. 1966. *Deviance and Control*. Englewood Cliffs, N.J.: Prentice-Hall.

Congressional Quarterly Weekly Report. 1971. "White Collar Crime" 7 May, Pp. 1047–49.

Duhl, L. J., and R. L. Leopold. 1966. "Mental Illness." Pp. 277–313 in Becker, H. S., ed., *Social Problems*. New York: Wiley.

Erikson, K. T. 1966. *Wayward Puritans; A Study in the Sociology of Deviance*. New York: Wiley.

Esselstyn, T. C. 1968. "Prostitution in the United States." *The Annals of the American Academy of Political and Social Science* 376(March):123–35.

Fort, J. 1969. "Comparison Chart of Major Substances for Mind-Alteration." Pp. 110–14 in Nowlis, H. H., *Drugs on the College Campus*. Garden City, N.Y.: Doubleday.

Gibbs, J. P. 1971. "Suicide." Pp. 271–312 in Merton, R. K., and R. Nisbet, eds., *Contemporary Social Problems*. New York: Harcourt, Brace, Jovanovich.

Goffman, E. 1963. *Stigma: Notes in the Management of Spoiled Identity*. Englewood Cliffs, N.J.: Prentice-Hall.

Homans, G. 1950. *The Human Group*. New York: Harcourt, Brace & World.

Julian, J. 1973. *Social Problems*. New York: Appleton-Century-Crofts.

Kaplan, J. 1971. *Marijuana: The New Prohibition*. New York: Pocket Books.

Kinsey, A. C.; W. B. Pomeroy; and C. E. Martin. 1948. *Sexual Behavior in the Human Male*. Philadelphia: W. B. Saunders.

Lemert, E. M. 1967. *Human Deviance; Social Problems and Social Control*. New York: Prentice-Hall.

Merton, R. K. 1968. *Social Theory and Social Structure*. New York: Free Press.

Merton, R. K., and R. Nisbet, eds. 1971. *Contemporary Social Problems*, 3d ed. New York: Harcourt, Brace, Jovanovich.

Parry, H. S. 1968. "Use of Psychotropic Drugs by U.S. Adults." *Public Health Reports* 83(Oct.).

Statistical Abstract of the U.S. 1973. Washington, D.C.: U.S. Government Printing Office.

Uniform Crime Reports. 1968. Washington, D.C.: U.S. Government Printing Office.

United Nations. 1968. *Demographic Yearbook, 1967*. New York.

U.S. Department of Justice. 1968. *F.B.I. Uniform Crime Reports for the U.S.* Washington, D.C.

Wallerstein, J. S., and C. J. Wyle. 1947. "Our Law-Abiding Lawbreakers." *Probation* 25(March-April):107–12.

Whitely, J. N. 1967. "Student Stress, Suicide and the Role of the University." *Journal of the National Association of Women's Deans and Counselors*. (Spring).

Williams, R. 1970. *American Society*, 3d ed. New York: Knopf.

Chapter Twelve

Adams, B. N. 1971. *The American Family*. Chicago: Markham.

Babchuk, N., and A. P. Bates. 1963. "The Primary Relations of Middle-Class Couples: A Study in Male Dominance." *American Sociological Review* 28:377–84.

Biegel, H. G. 1951. "Romantic Love." *American Sociological Review* 16:326–34.

Bossard, J. H. S. 1932. "Residential Propinquity as

a Factor in Marriage Selection." *American Journal of Sociology* 38(Sept.)No. 2:219–24.

Campbell, E. Q. 1969. "Adolescent Socialization." Pp. 821–59 in Goslin, D. A., ed., *Handbook of Socialization Theory and Research*. Chicago: Rand McNally.

Carter, H., and A. Plateris. 1963. "Trends in Divorce and Family Disruption." *Health, Education, and Welfare Indicators, National Vital Statistics Division, Public Health Service* (Sept.).

Centers, R. 1949. "Marital Selection and Occupational Strata." *American Journal of Sociology* 44:530–35.

Cohen, J.; R. Robson; and A. P. Bates. 1958. *Parental Authority: The Community and the Law*. New Brunswick, N.J.: Rutgers Univ. Press.

Coleman, J. S. 1961. *The Adolescent Society*. New York: Free Press.

Dublin, L. I. 1965. *Factbook on Man—From Birth to Death*, 2d ed. New York: Macmillan.

Eisenstadt, S. N. 1956. *From Generation to Generation*. Glencoe, Ill.: Free Press.

Firth R. 1936. *We, The Tikopia*. New York: American Book Company.

Gendell, M. and H. L. Zetterberg. 1964. *A Sociological Almanac for the United States*, 2d ed. Totowa, N.J.: The Bedminister Press.

Glick, P. C. 1957. *American Families*. New York: Wiley.

Goode, W. J. 1964. *The Family*. Englewood Cliffs, N.J.: Prentice-Hall.

Goodman, P. 1956. *Growing Up Absurd*. New York: Random House.

Gottlieb, D., and C. Ramsey. 1964. *The American Adolescent*. Homewood, Ill.: Dorsey Press.

Gottlieb, D.; J. Reeves; and W. TenHouten. 1966. *The Emergence of Youth Societies: A Cross-Cultural Approach*. New York: Free Press.

Hollingshead, A. B. 1950. "Cultural Factors in the Selection of Marriage Mates." *American Sociological Review* 15:619–27.

Hunt, M. M. 1966. *The World of the Formerly Married*. New York: McGraw-Hill.

Keniston, K. 1965. *The Uncommitted; Alienated Youth in American Society*. New York: Harcourt, Brace, & World.

Kennedy, R. J. R. 1952. "Single or Triple Melting Pot? Intermarriage in New Haven, 1870–1950." *American Journal of Sociology* 58(July):56–59.

Litwak, E. 1960. "Geographic Mobility and Extended Family Cohesion." *American Sociological Review* 25:385–94.

Mirande, A. M. 1969. "The Isolated Nuclear Family Hypothesis: A Reanalysis." Pp. 153–63 in Edwards, J. N., ed., *The Family and Change*. New York: Knopf.

Moore, B., Jr. 1958. *Political Power and Social Theory*. Cambridge, Mass.: Harvard Univ. Press.

Murdock, G. P. 1949. *Social Structure*. New York: Macmillan.

———. 1957. "World Ethnographic Sample." *American Anthropologist* 59:664–87.

Musgrove, F. 1965. *Youth and the Social Order*. Bloomington: Indiana Univ. Press.

Nye, F. I. 1967. "Values, Family and a Changing Society." *Journal of Marriage and the Family* 29:241–48.

Orden, S. R., and N. M. Bradburn. 1969. "Working Wives and Marital Happiness." *American Journal of Sociology* 74(Jan.):392–407.

Parsons, T., and R. F. Bales, eds. 1955. *Family, Socialization and Interaction Process*. New York: Free Press.

Rainwater, L. 1965. *Family Design: Marital Sexuality, Family Size, and Contraception*. Chicago: Aldine. Reprinted from Lee Rainwater, FAMILY DESIGN (Chicago: Aldine Publishing Company, 1965); copyright © 1965 by Social Research, Inc. Reprinted by permission of the author and Aldine Publishing Company.

Reiss, I. L. 1960. *Premarital Sexual Standards in America: A Sociological Investigation of the Relative Social and Cultural Integration of American Sexual Standards*. New York: Free Press.

Reiss, P. J. 1962. "The Extended Kinship System: Correlates of and Attitudes on Frequency of Interaction." *Marriage and Family Living* 24:333–39.

Robins, L. N., and M. Tomanec. 1962. "Closeness to Blood Relatives Outside the Immediate Family." *Marriage and Family Living* 24:340–46.

Rossi, A. S. 1968. "Transition to Parenthood." *Journal of Marriage and the Family* 30:26–39.

Statistical Abstract of the United States. 1967. Washington, D.C.: U.S. Government Printing Office.

Stendler, C. B. 1950. "Sixty Years of Child Training Practices." *Journal of Pediatrics* 36:219–24.

Stephens, W. N. 1963. *The Family in Cross-Cultural Perspective.* New York: Holt, Rinehart & Winston.

Sussman, M. B. 1953. "The Help Pattern in the Middle-Class Family." *American Sociological Review* 18:22–28.

_____. 1959. "The Isolated Nuclear Family, Fact or Fiction?" *Social Problems.* Pp. 333–40.

Sussman, M. B., and L. Burchinal. 1962. "Parental Aid to Married Children: Implications for Family Functioning." *Marriage and Family Living* 24:320–32.

Thomas, J. L. 1951. "The Factor of Religion in the Selection of Marriage Mates." *American Sociological Review* 16:487–92.

U.S. Bureau of the Census. 1949. *Historical Statistics of the United States, 1789–1945.* Washington, D.C.: U.S. Government Printing Office.

U. S. Bureau of the Census. 1960. *Current Population Reports—Population Characteristics,* Series P-20, No. 100 (13 April). Washington, D.C.: U.S. Government Printing Office.

U.S. Bureau of the Census. 1962. *Current Population Reports—Population Characteristics.* Series P-20, No. 114 (31 January). Washington, D.C.: U.S. Government Printing Office.

Waller, W., and R. Hill. 1951. *The Family: A Dynamic Interpretation.* New York: Holt, Rinehart & Winston.

Williams, R. M., Jr. 1970. *American Society: A Sociological Interpretation,* 3d ed. New York: Knopf. © Alfred A. Knopf, Inc., 1970. Reprinted by permission.

Winch, R. F. 1963. *The Modern Family,* rev. ed. New York: Holt, Rinehart & Winston.

Wolfenstein, M. 1953. "Trends in Infant Care." *American Journal of Orthopsychiatry* 23:120–30.

Yinger, J. M. 1959. "The Changing Family in a Changing Society." *Social Casework* 40:419–28.

Zelditch, M., Jr. 1955. "Role Differentiation in the Nuclear Family: A Comparative Study." Pp. 307–51 in Parsons, T., and R. F. Bales, eds., *Family, Socialization and Interaction Process.* New York: Free Press.

_____. 1964. "Cross-Cultural Analysis of Family Structure." Pp. 462–500 in Christensen, H. T., ed. *Handbook of Marriage and the Family.* Skokie, Ill.: Rand McNally.

Zimmerman, C. C. 1949. *The Family of Tomorrow.* New York: Harper.

CHAPTER THIRTEEN

Block, J. H.; N. Haan; and M. B. Smith. 1967. "Activism and Apathy in Contemporary Adolescents." In Adams, J. F., ed., *Contributions to the Understanding of Adolescence.* New York: Macmillan.

Brogan, D. W. 1961. *The American Character.* New York: Random House.

Callahan, R. E. 1962. *Education and the Cult of Efficiency.* Chicago: Univ. of Chicago Press.

Campbell, E. Q. 1969. "Adolescent Socialization." Pp. 821–59 in Goslin, D. A., ed., *Handbook of Socialization Theory and Research.* Chicago: Rand McNally.

Charters, W. W., Jr. 1956. "Survival in the Profession: A Criterion for Selecting Teacher Trainees." *Journal of Teacher Education* 7:253–55.

Clark, B. R. 1964. "Sociology of Education." Pp. 734–69 in Faris, R. E. L., *Handbook of Modern Sociology.* Chicago: Rand McNally.

Coleman, J. S. 1961. *The Adolescent Society.* New York: Doubleday.

Coleman, J. S., et al. 1966. *Equality of Educational Opportunity.* Washington D.C.: U.S. Government Printing Office.

Dictionary of Occupational Titles, 3d ed. 1965. Washington, D.C.: U.S. Department of Labor.

Drucker, P. F. 1959. *The Landmarks of Tomorrow.* London: Heinemann.

Earned Degrees Conferred, 1970. Washington, D.C.: U.S. Office of Education.

Evans, S. M. 1961. *Revolt on Campus.* Chicago: Regnery.

Gross, N. 1959. "The Sociology of Education." Pp. 128–52 in Merton, R. K.; L. Broom; and L. S. Cottrell, Jr., eds., *Sociology Today.* New York: Basic Books.

Gross, N.; W. S. Mason; and A. W. McEachern. 1958. *Explorations in Role Analysis: Studies of the School Superintendency Role.* New York: Wiley.

Halsey, A. H. 1960. "The Changing Functions of Universities in Advanced Industrial Societies." *Harvard Educational Review* 30, No. 2 (Spring):118–27.

Hofstadter, R. 1963. *Anti-Intellectualism in American Life.* New York: Knopf.

Keniston, K. 1965. *The Uncommitted.* New York: Dell.

_____. 1969. "Notes on Young Radicals." *Change in Higher Education* (Nov.–Dec.):23–33.

Lipset, S. M., and S. Wolin, eds. 1965. *The Berkeley Student Revolt.* New York: Doubleday.

Machlup, F. 1962. *The Production and Distribution of Knowledge in the United States.* Princeton, N.J.: Princeton Univ. Press.

Mack, R. W. 1968. *Transforming America.* New York: Random House.

McGee, R. 1967. "Education and Social Change." Pp. 69–104 in Hansen, D. A., and J. E. Gerstl, eds., *On Education—Sociological Perspectives.* New York: Wiley.

Miller, M. V., and S. Gilmore, eds. 1965. *Revolution at Berkeley.* New York: Dial Press.

Newsweek. 1970. 28 Sept.:85–86.

Perrucci, R. 1967. "Education, Stratification, and Mobility." Pp. 105–55 in Hansen, D. S., and J. D. Gerstl, eds., *On Education—Sociological Perspectives.* New York: Wiley.

Piel, G. 1969. "Support of Science on the University's own Terms." *Science* 166(28 Nov. 1969): 1101. Copyright 1969 by the American Association for the Advancement of Science. Reprinted by permission.

President's Commission on Education Beyond High School. 1957. *Second Report to the President.* Washington, D.C.: Government Printing Office.

Silberman, C. E. 1970. *Crisis in the Classroom.* New York: Random House.

Sirjamaki, J. 1967. "Education as a Social Institution." Pp. 36–68 in Hansen, D. S., and J. Gerstl, eds., *On Education—Sociological Perspectives.* New York: Wiley.

Statistical Abstract of the United States. 1973. Washington, D.C.: U.S. Government Printing Office.

Tyler, R. W., and R. I. Miller. 1962. "Social Forces and Trends." *National Education Association Journal* 51(Sept.).

Williams, R. M., Jr. 1970. *American Society,* 3d ed. New York: Knopf.

Wolfle, D. 1954. *America's Resources of Specialized Talent.* New York: Harper & Row.

CHAPTER FOURTEEN

Becker, H. 1932. *Systematic Sociology,* on the basis of the *Beziehungslehre and Gebildelehre* of L. von Wiese. New York: Wiley.

Blizzard, S. 1957. "The Minister's Dilemma." *Christian Century* 73(April):508–10.

Britannica Book of the Year. 1971. Reprinted with permission from the 1971 *Britannica Book of the Year,* copyright 1971 by Encyclopaedia Britannica Inc., Chicago.

Davis, K. 1949. *Human Society.* New York: Macmillan.

Demerath, N. J., III, and P. Hammond. 1969. *Religion in Social Context.* New York: Random House.

Fukuyama. 1963. "The Uses of Sociology by Religious Bodies." *Journal for the Scientific Study of Religion* 2(Spring):195–203.

Gerlach, L. P., and V. H. Hine. 1970. *People, Power, Change: Movements of Social Transformation.* Indianapolis: Bobbs-Merrill.

Glock, C. Y.; B. Ringer; and E. R. Babbie. 1967. *To Comfort and To Challenge: A Dilemma of the Contemporary Church.* Berkeley and Los Angeles: Univ. of California Press.

Glock, C. Y., and Stark, R. 1965. "Is There an American Protestantism?" Table published by permission of Transaction, Inc., from TRANSACTION, Vol. 3, No. 1, November, 1965. Copyright © 1965 by Transaction, Inc.

Glock, C. Y., and R. Stark. 1965. *Religion and Society in Tension.* Chicago: Rand McNally.

Herberg, W. 1955. *Protestant, Catholic, Jew.* Garden City, N.Y.: Doubleday.

_____. 1962. "Religion in a Secularized Society: The New Shape of Religion in America." *The Review of Religious Research,* vol. 3, no. 4.

Kendrick, C. 1966. "The Pentecostal Movement: Hopes and Hazards." *Christian Century* 80:608–10.

Koval, J. 1971. Paper presented to the Society for the Scientific Study of Religion, reported in *Newsweek,* 25 January.

Lenski, G. 1961. *The Religious Factor: A Sociological Study of Religion's Impact on Politics, Economics, and Family Life.* New York: Doubleday.

Moberg, D. O. 1962. *The Church as a Social Institution.* Englewood Cliffs, N.J.: Prentice-Hall.

Newsweek. 1970. "The Preaching and the Power." 20 July:50–55.

Noss, J. B. 1969. *Man's Religions,* 4th ed. London: Collier-Macmillan.

Parsons, T. 1957. "Religion as a Source of Creative Innovation." Pp. 558–63 in Yinger, J. M., ed., *Religion, Society and the Individual.* New York: Macmillan.

Peterson, F. 1959. *Ancient Mexico.* New York: Capricorn Books.

Pope, L. 1941. *Millhands and Preachers.* New Haven: Yale Univ. Press.

Ringer, B. B., and C. Y. Glock. 1954. "The Political Role of the Church as Defined by Its Parishioners." *Public Opinion Quarterly* 18(Winter):337–47.

Salisbury, W. S. 1964. *Religion in American Culture.* Homewood, Ill.: Dorsey Press.

Time. 1968. "The New Black Magic." *Time* (September 27, 1968). Reprinted by permission from TIME, The Weekly Newsmagazine; Copyright Time Inc.

Troeltsch, E. 1931. *The Social Teaching of the Christian Churches.* New York: Macmillan.

Whitman, L. B., ed. 1968. *Yearbook of American Churches for 1968,* 36th issue. New York: Council Press.

Williams, R. M., Jr. 1970. *American Society,* 3d ed. New York: Knopf. © Alfred A. Knopf, Inc., 1970. Reprinted by permission.

Wilson, B. R. 1959. "An Analysis of Sect Development." *American Sociological Review* 24(Feb.):3–15.

———. 1959. "Role Conflicts and Status Contradictions of the Pentecostal Minister." *American Journal of Sociology* 64(March):494–504.

Yinger, J. M. 1970. *Religion, Society and the Individual.* New York: Macmillan.

CHAPTER FIFTEEN

Barber, B. 1962. *Science and the Social Order.* New York: Collier Books; Crowell, Collier & Macmillan.

Bates, R. S. 1958. *Scientific Societies in the United States,* 2d ed. New York: Columbia Univ. Press.

Ben-David, J. 1960. "Scientific Productivity and Academic Organization in Nineteenth Century Medicine." *American Sociological Review* 25:828–43.

de Solla Price, D. J. 1966. "Diseases of Science." Pp. 49–68 in Moore, W. E., and R. M. Cook, eds., *Readings on Social Change.* Englewood Cliffs, N.J.: Prentice-Hall.

Glaser, B. G. 1964. *Organizational Scientists: Their Professional Careers.* Indianapolis: Bobbs-Merrill.

Hodge, R. W.; P. M. Seigal; and P. H. Rossi. 1964. "Occupational Prestige in the United States, 1925–1963. *American Journal of Sociology* 70(Nov.):286–302.

Kaplan, N. 1964. "Sociology of Science." Pp. 852–81 in Faris, R. E. L., ed., *Handbook of American Sociology.* Chicago: Rand McNally.

Lundberg, G. A. 1947. *Can Science Save Us?* New York: Longmans, Green.

Maccoby, M. 1970. "Government, Scientists, and the Priorities of Science." Pp. 257–66 in Skolnick, J. H., and E. Currie, eds., *Crisis in American Institutions.* Boston: Little, Brown.

Merton, R. K. 1957. *Social Theory and Social Structure,* rev. ed. Glencoe, Ill.: Free Press.

———. 1962. "Priorities in Scientific Discovery." In Barber, B., and Hirsch, W., eds. *The Sociology of Science.* New York: Free Press.

North, C. C., and P. K. Hatt. 1947. "Jobs and Occupations: A Popular Evaluation." *Opinion News* 9:3–13.

Orlans, H. 1962. *The Effects of Federal Progress on Higher Education.* Washington, D.C.: The Brookings Institute.

Piel, G. 1964. *Science in the Cause of Man.* New York: Random House. Reprinted by permission of Random House, Inc.

President's Science Advisory Committee. 1963. *Science, Government, and Information.* Washington, D.C.: U.S. Government Printing Office.

Price, D. K. 1962. "The Scientific Establishment." *Science* 29(June).

Snow, C. P. 1959. *The Two Cultures and the Scientific Revolution.* Cambridge: Cambridge Univ. Press.

Statistical Abstract of the United States 1973. Washington, D.C.: U.S. Government Printing Office.

Storer, N. J. 1966. *The Social System of Science.* New York: Holt, Rinehart & Winston.

Williams, R. M., Jr. 1970. *American Society: A Sociological Interpretation,* 3d ed. New York: Knopf. © Alfred A. Knopf, Inc., 1970. Reprinted by permission.

Withey, S. B. 1959. "Public Opinion About Science and Scientists." *Public Opinion Quarterly* 23:328–88. Reprinted by permission.

CHAPTER SIXTEEN

Appelbaum, R. P. 1970. *Theories of Social Change.* Chicago: Markham.

Chapin, F. S. 1928. *Cultural Change.* New York: Appleton-Century-Crofts.

Davis, K. 1949. *Human Society.* New York: Macmillan.

French, J. R. P., Jr., and B. H. Raven. 1959. "The Bases of Social Power." Pp. 150–67 in Cartwright, D., ed., *Studies in Social Power.* Ann Arbor: Univ. of Michigan Press.

Goldschmidt, W. 1959. *Man's Way: A Preface to the Understanding of Human Society.* New York: Holt.

Hart, H. 1959. "Social Theory and Social Change." Pp. in Gross, L., ed., *Symposium on Sociological Theory.* Evanston, Ill.: Row, Peterson.

Hertzler, J. O. 1961. *American Social Institutions.* Boston: Allyn and Bacon.

Lenski, G. 1970. *Human Societies.* New York: McGraw-Hill.

Linton, R. 1936. *The Study of Man.* New York: Appleton-Century-Crofts.

Moore, W. E. 1963. *Social Change.* Englewood Cliffs, N.J.: Prentice-Hall.

Myrdal, G. 1944. *An American Dilemma.* New York: Harper & Row.

Ogburn, W. F. 1922. *Social Change.* New York: B. W. Heubsch.

Paton, A. 1948. *Cry, The Beloved Country.* New York: Scribners.

Shils, E. 1968. "Society and Societies: The Macro-Sociological View." Pp. 287–303 in Parsons, T., ed., *American Sociology.* New York: Basic Books.

Simpson, G. G. 1949. *The Meaning of Evolution.* New York: New American Library.

Storer, N. W. 1966. *The Social System of Science.* New York: Holt, Rinehart & Winston.

Williams, R. M., Jr. 1970. *American Society, A Sociological Interpretation,* 3d ed. New York: Knopf. © Alfred A. Knopf, Inc., 1970. Reprinted by permission.

Art Credits

111, courtesy United Nations 115, *top left,* Magnum, Elliott Erwitt; *top right,* Stock/Boston, Nicholas Sapieha; *bottom left,* Bettmann Archive; *bottom right,* Photo Researchers, Joe Rychetnik 118, *clockwise,* Bill Finch; Stock/Boston, Bill Finch; Magnum, Elliott Erwitt; Magnum, Elliott Erwitt; George Gardner 124, *top left,* Black Star, David Margolin; *top right,* Black Star, Dan Moody; *bottom left,* Design Photographers International, James Karales; *bottom right,* Charles Gatewood 126, courtesy Seattle Housing Authority 127, George Gardner 128, Magnum, Marc Riboud 130, Design Photographers International, Arnold Kapp 131, Black Star, Dennis Brack 134, Stock/Boston, Donald Dietz

CHAPTER SIX
PAGE 139, *Top left,* Black Star, Michael Abramson; *bottom left,* George Gardner; *right,* Magnum, Charles Harbutt 141, Donald Dietz 144, Alaska Pictorial Service, Steve McCutcheon 149, Stock/Boston, Patricia Hollander Gross 150, Black Star, Billy E. Barnes 151, Stock/Boston, Nicholas Sapieha 152, Stock/Boston, Harry Wilks 153, courtesy General Wine and Spirits Co. 155, Brown Brothers

CHAPTER SEVEN
PAGE 162, *Clockwise,* Stock/Boston, Donald Wright Patterson Jr.; Black Star, Beuford Smith; Stock/Boston, Jeff Albertson; Black Star, Bob Fitch; Black Star, Krystyna Neuman 165, United Press International 166, Stock/Boston, Ellis Herwig 169, *left,* Magnum, Henri Cartier Bresson; *right,* Black Star, Bob Fitch 173, Design Photographers International, Grete Manheim 176, Stock/Boston, Jeff Albertson 178, courtesy National Organization for Women, Legal Defense and Education Fund 179, courtesy Heublein, Inc. 182, *top left,* Bettmann Archive; *bottom left,* Magnum, Bruce Davidson; *right,* Magnum, Charles Harbutt 184, *left to right,* Brown Brothers; courtesy Library of Congress; Black Star, Bern Keating

CHAPTER EIGHT
PAGE 189, The Bettmann Archive 190, The Bettmann Archive 191, *left,* Black Star, David Margolin; *right,* Stock/Boston, Cliff Garboden 199, Black Star, Richard Lawrence Stack 202, *left,* courtesy the Travellers Insurance Group; *right,* Stock/Boston, Ellis Herwig 213, Stock/Boston, Patricia Hollander Gross

CHAPTER NINE
PAGE 221, *Top left,* Black Star, Fred Ward; *bottom left,* Stock/Boston, Daniel S. Brody; *right,* Stephen T. Whitney 222, Black Star, Pana Feature 223, *left to right,* United Press International; United Press International; Black Star, Osvaldo Salas 227, *left,* George Gardner 234, courtesy Simmons College 237, *top left,* Black Star, Joffre T. Clark; *bottom left,* Patricia Chock; *right,* Frank Siteman 239, *left,* Monkmeyer Press Photo Service; *right,* Monkmeyer Press Photo Service, Charlotte Brooks 243, courtesy Armand E. Brodeur, M.D., Pediatric Radiologist, Cardinal Glennon Memorial Hospital for Children, Professor of Radiology, St. Louis University School of Medicine 247, photos courtesy The National Council on the Aging

CHAPTER TEN
PAGE 250, *Top,* Brown Brothers; *left,* Black Star, Flip Schulke; *center right,* Stock/Boston, Patricia Hollander Gross; *bottom right,* Charles Gatewood 252, Stock/Boston, Ellis Herwig 253, United Press International 256, *Newsweek Magazine* 260, The Bettmann Archive 261, United Press International 264, Magnum, Kubota 266, Stock/Boston, Patricia Hollander Gross 267, *left,* Black Star, East Street Gallery; *right,* Black Star, Jean-Claude LeJeune 268, Brown Brothers 269, Black Star, J. Collier 272, courtesy American Petroleum Industry 274, Wide World Photos 278, *left,* Steve Eagle; *right,* Stock/Boston, Ellis Herwig 279, Black Star, Declan Haun 280, Eastfoto

CHAPTER ELEVEN
PAGE 284, *Left,* Stock/Boston, Ellis Herwig; *top right,* Stock/Boston, Photographic Work; *bottom right,* Frank Siteman 286, Black Star, Wally Arrington 289, Magnum, Wayne Miller 290, Brown Brothers 292, Elizabeth Hamlin 293, *left,* The Bettmann Archive; *right,* Stock/Boston, Peter Menzel 296, *left,* Stock/Boston, Cary S. Wolinsky;

top right, Stock/Boston, Franklin Wing; *bottom right,* Stock/Boston, Daniel S. Brody 299, Derrick TePaske 302, *left,* Frank Siteman; *top right,* The *Boston Globe; bottom right,* Magnum, Leonard Freed 305, courtesy Philip Morris Co.

CHAPTER TWELVE
PAGE 311, *Bottom left,* Frank Siteman 315, Black Star 317, The Bettmann Archive 318, courtesy Swedish Information Service 319, Donald Dietz 324, Magnum, Leonard Freed, Stock/Boston 327, Frank Siteman 328, Magnum, Ian Berry 329, Field Museum of Natural History 330, *left,* Paul Conklin; *top right,* Charles Gatewood; *bottom right,* Magnum, Charles Gatewood 333, Editorial Photo Archives, Berne Greene 334, Stock/Boston, Frank Siteman 335, United Press International 336, Design Photographers International, Francis Laping

CHAPTER THIRTEEN
PAGE 342, Black Star, Dennis Brack 344, Elizabeth Hamlin 345, Paul Conklin 346, courtesy Southeastern Regional Vocational School, South Easton, Mass. 347, Stock/Boston, Ellis Herwig 349, Magnum, Ron Benvenisti 351, Stock/Boston, Peter Vandermark, Stock/Boston, T. D. Lovering 353, courtesy *Manchester Union Leader,* Manchester, N.H. 354, Charles Gatewood 356, courtesy City University of New York 359, Photo Researchers, Richard Frear 363, *top left,* Stock/Boston, Owen Franken; *bottom left,* Wide World Photos; *right,* George Gardner

CHAPTER FOURTEEN
PAGE 369, Stock/Boston, John T. Urban 370, *left to right,* Scala; Museum of the American Indian;

Marjorie Vlass; Photo Researchers, Mario Rossi 372, Stock/Boston, Daniel S. Brody 378, The Bettmann Archive 379, *left,* Alinari; *right,* Photo Researchers, Odette Mennesson-Rigaud 387, *top left,* Magnum, Charles Gatewood; *bottom left,* Mark Chester; *bottom right,* Stock/Boston, Frank Siteman 390, Wide World Photos 391, Stock/Boston, Cliff Garboden 393, Stock/Boston, Owen Franken 395, Magnum, Elliott Erwitt 400, *left,* Paul Conklin; *right,* Derrick TePaske 402, Donald Dietz

CHAPTER FIFTEEN
PAGE 404, Magnum, Cornell Capa 405, Silvio Bichisecchi 409, *left,* courtesy E. I. duPont de Nemours & Co.; *right,* Arthur Furst 410, Brown Brothers 414, The Bettmann Archive 415, Stock/Boston, Ellis Herwig 417, Magnum, stock photo 423, Magnum, Charles Gatewood 425, *top left,* Design Photographers International, Harold F. Fay; *top right,* Black Star, Don Rutledge; *bottom left,* Paul Conklin; *bottom right,* Black Star, Robert La Rouch

CHAPTER SIXTEEN
PAGE 433, Stock/Boston, Owen Franken; *top right,* Paul Conklin; *bottom left,* Magnum, Cornell Capa; *bottom right,* Stock/Boston, Nicholas Sapieha 441, *top left,* George Gardner; *top right,* Black Star, Michael Abramson; *bottom left,* Magnum, Bruce Davidson; *bottom right,* Design Photographers International, Syd Greenberg 443, *left,* Magnum, Cornell Capa; *top and bottom right,* Magnum, Burk Uzzle 445, *top,* Black Star, Werner Wolf; *left,* Magnum, Hiroshi Hamaya; *right,* courtesy Coolidge Bank and Trust Co. 449, Stock/Boston, Ellis Herwig 460, Fuller, Sadao, Inc. 461, courtesy Maryland Division of Tourism

Index

Brill, 202
Britt, Stewart Henderson, 259
Brogan, D. W., 365
Bruce, Alisa Mellon, 149
Buddhism, 371, 379, 380, 381
Bunker, Archie, 141
Burchinal, L., 322
Bureaucracy, 12, 13 (fig.)
  characteristics of, 224
  in education, 353–355
  and informal organization, 228–230
  officials of, 223–224
  Weber on, 222–224
Bureau of Internal Revenue, U.S., 231
Bureau of Narcotics and Dangerous Drugs, U.S., 297
Bureau of the Census, U.S., 113, 148, 175, 178
Burgess, E. W., 6
Buses, 121
Business, big, 131, 272
Business district, 126
Busing, practice of, 31
Bus systems, failure of, 122

California, University of, 220
  at Berkeley, 252, 270
Callahan, R. E., 354
Calvin, John, 188
Campbell, E. Q., 328, 330, 331, 349
  rumor on, 257
  see also Students
Cantril, H., 276
Capitalism, 308, 439
  American, 444
Capital punishment, 31
Caplow, T., 199, 211, 212, 253
Careers, 193
  choosing of, 194, 201–205
  see also Occupation
Carmichael, S., 246
Carnegie Commission on Higher Education, 353, 361
Carson, Johnny, 258–259
Carter, H., 317
Cartharsis, 275
Catholicism, 188
Catholics, 172, 173, 194, 378 (fig.), 382, 391
  marriage of, 315
  and suicide, 299
  see also Roman Catholic Church
Celibacy, 67

Census Bureau. *See* Bureau of the Census, U.S.
Centers, R., 150, 314
Central city, 119
  blacks in, 121–122
  density in, 114
  residents of, 121
Change, 100
  agents of, 72
  cultural, 27–28
  educational, 360
  initiating, 277–278
  interdependence and, 447
  and organizations, 241–245
  people approach to, 243–245
  religious, 398–400
  roles and, 98
  and social movements, 266
  societies and, 447
  sociocultural, 43
  and stability, 41–45
  technological, 127, 242–243, 413–415
  and tension, 44–45
  urban structural, 120–127
  and value conflict, 449–450
  see also Social change
Chaos, 459
Chapin, F. S., 451
Charisma
  and authority, 223
  of leader, 268
Charters, W. W., Jr., 355
Chemical Abstracts, 406
Chemistry, scientists in, 408
Chicago, growth of, 120 (fig.)
Chicanos, 304
Childhood, 61
Child-rearing, 15, 327, 332, 335
  patterns of, 14
Children, 50, 94, 101
  and child-centered family, 15
  departure of, 323–325
  disturbed, 65
  and family roles, 322
  role of, 325–331
  and socializing agents, 326–327
  socializing of, 56
China, 170
  collective behavior in, 280
Christian Crusade, 268
Christianity, 308, 377, 380, 384
Christians, 188, 398
Churches, 235, 383–384
  in America, 386

Churches:
  goals of, 232
  lay members, 389
  local, 388–390
  memberships of, 380 (fig.), 384–385 (fig.), 391
Church-goers, 390
Cincinnati, Ohio, riot in, 262
Cities, 75, 107, 109, 123
  ancient, 111
  automobiles in, 119
  boundaries of, 119
  city centers, 114–115
  community in, 129–132
  concentric zonal structure of, 116–117
  decentralization of, 119
  dependence of, 129–130
  development of, 111–112
  employees of, 123
  financial crisis of, 121–123
  growth of, 111–112
  and metropolitan community, 119
  physical structure of, 116–119
  sector structure of, 117–119
  structural changes of, 120–127
  study of, 16
  transportation in, 122
  underemployment in, 128–129
  U.S., 112
  see also Ghettos
City planning, 114, 134, 135
Civil disobedience, 280, 292
Civilization, 379
Civil liberties, 140
Civil Liberties Union, 174
Civil Rights Act, 179, 181
Civil rights movement, 162, 265, 280, 292, 304, 366, 448
  students in, 359
Clark, B. R., 342, 352, 354, 355, 365
Class, 145
  and conjugal role-relationships, 323
  consciousness, 146
  indicators of, 152
  and marital roles, 323
  Marxian theory of, 142
  measuring, 150
  middle, 129, 192
  and motivation, 59
  recognition of, 149
  variations in, 327
  working, 192

Marriage:
   arranged, 314, 316
   and divorce, 333–335
   forms of, 312
   group, 312
   minimum ages for, 67
   plural, 312
   popularity of, 317
   and work, 193–194
   see also Divorce; Family; Husbands; Wives
Marx, Karl, 15, 142, 276
Masculinity, 63
   measure of, 330–331
Mason, W. S., 366
Masons (fraternal order), 238, 239
Masotti, L. H., 177, 184
Massacre of Saint Bartholomew's Day (1572), 378 (fig.)
Mass media, 131, 214, 279
   and education, 339
Master's degrees, 361
Mate, selection of, 314–318, 337. *See also* Marriage
Mathematics, scientists in, 408
Mating, biological, 6
Matras, J., 111
Mead, G. H., 61
Mead, Margaret, 374
Meanings, 27
   interpretation and, 79. *See also* Ideologies; Symbolic systems
Medicare, 208
Medicine, 6, 374, 427 (fig.)
Megalopolis, 119
Mellon, Paul, 149
Mellon, Richard King, 149
Member-replacement, in societies, 436–437
Mennonites, 384, 387 (fig.)
Mental disorders, 298–299. *See also* Deviance
Mergers, denominational, 395–397
Merton, R. K., 285, 286, 399, 404, 405, 409
Methodists, 384, 397
Metropolitan district, boundaries of, 119
Mexican American Legal Defense and Educational Fund (MALDEF), 172
Mexican-Americans, 125, 160, 172
   education of, 172
Mexico, 141, 295

Mexico:
   prehispanic, 372
Michigan, University of, 173, 273, 421
Microecology, 96
Middle class, 152, 192. *See also* Class
Migration
   of blacks, 176, 181
   mass, 127
   rural-urban, 113
   white, 176
Milgram, S., 264, 266, 276
Military-industrial complex, 270
Miller, M. V., 346, 363
Miller, S. M., 12, 17, 224
Miller, W., 153
Millionaires, 149
Mills, C. W., 144, 146, 149, 268
Mills, D. L., 205
Minar, D. W., 133
Minister, role of, 389
Minorities, 246
   American, 162, 170–173
   blacks, 173–177
   defining, 160–164
   ethnic, 164, 171–172
   explanation of, 164
   racial, 170–171
   religious, 172–173
   and social change, 181–185
   and social power, 165–167
   sociology of, 185–186
   Spanish-speaking, 172
   and stratification, 141–143
Mirande, A. M., 322
Moberg, D. C., 368, 395, 396, 402
Mobility, 310
   geographical, 322, 396
   job, 217
   residential, 124
   social, 152–155
   upward, 153
   vertical, 152, 153, 154
   see also Social change
Mobs, 251
   lynch, 260, 261
   see also Crowds
Model Cities, 123
Moderates, religious, 397
Monarchy, 308
Monasticism, 265
Money, 128
Monogamy, 312. *See also* Marriage

Moore, B., Jr., 335
Moore, Wilbert E., 44, 201
Moose (fraternal order), 239
Morality, perspectives on, 8
   sexual, 300
   see also Norms; Values
Moreno, J. L., 101
Morgenstern, J., 279
Morse, N. C., 190
Mortality, human, 374, 441 (fig.)
Moskos, C. C., Jr., 85
Mothers, 93, 94, 101, 321
   role of, 64
   as socializing agents, 326
   see also Women
Motivation, 57, 58, 238
   achievement, 57, 58–60, 68
   and deviance, 283, 288
Movements. *See* Social movements
Moynihan, D. P., 171
Murders, 251
Murdock, G. P., 312
Musgrove, F., 328
Music, 362
Mussolini, Benito, 268
Myrdal, G., 449
Myths, 25, 158, 379, 415
   American, 149, 153

Nader, Ralph, 419
National Advisory Commission on Civil Disorders, 262
National Association for the Advancement of Colored People (NAACP), 182, 268
National Conference of Christians and Jews, 395
National Council of Churches of Christ, 369, 391, 394
National Educational Association, 355
National Guard, 262
National Institute of Alcohol and Alcoholism, 295
National Institute of Mental Health, 279
National Opinion Research Center, 193, 195
National Opinion Research Corporation, at University of Chicago, 273
National Organization of Women (NOW), 246
National Retired Teachers Association, 246

National Training Laboratory (NTL), 102
Nature, 431
Nazism, 132, 165, 268
Needs, 57
Negroes. *See* Blacks
Neighborhoods, 76. *See also* Cities
Neophyte
  role of, 54–55
  and social change, 69
Network
  communications, 11 (fig.), 95, 226–228
  of friendships, 133
  group interaction, 88
  kinship, 310, 334
Neurosis, 139
Newark, New Jersey, riot in, 262
Newcomb, T. M., 61, 168, 169
Newcomer, M., 153
Newsweek (magazine), 177
New York, City University of, 220, 356–357
  population of, 110, 113
Nielson, A. C., Company, 273
Nisbet, R. A., 132
Nixon, Richard M., 122, 255
Nomads, 129, 457
Nonconformity, 140
Nonviolence, 182
Norms, 28, 32–36, 64, 81, 291
  alienation from, 286
  appropriateness of, 36
  characteristics of, 34–36
  common orientation to, 440
  of complex organizations, 226
  conflict in, 35–36, 74, 292–293
  conformity to, 287, 301
  definition of, 33
  and discrimination, 186
  of disinterestedness, 405
  emergence of, 33–34
  and group size, 96
  patterned evasions of, 291
  professional, 209
  rejection of, 286
  and religion, 399
  and roles, 39
  in school systems, 352
  of science, 404–406, 413
  sexual, 300
  in two-person group, 39 (fig.)
  of universalism, 404
  and values, 36, 267, 285

North, C. C., 409
North America, cities of, 112
Noss, J. B., 379, 380, 381, 382
Nouveau riche, 156
Nye, F. I., 335

Occupation, 70, 154, 189, 343
  changing, 192–193
  choosing, 201–205
  and divorce, 194
  high status, 190
  and income, 193
  major groups of, 199, 200
  middle-class, 192
  prestige of, 195, 196–198
  professional, 206, 211–212
  and self concept, 218
  sociology of, 215–217
  as status indicator, 195
  and values, 203
  working-class, 192
  see also Careers; Training; Work
Odd Fellows (fraternal organization), 239
Ogburn, W. F., 448, 451, 452
Oligarchy, 147
Ombudsman, 248
O'Neill, Eugene, 80
Open-door trend, in education, 356, 360
Operations research, 242
Opportunity
  equality of, 36, 348–349, 449
  value of, 33
Orden, S. R., 321
Orderliness, 88
  in social behavior, 14
Organization, degree of, 24
Organization age, 219
Organization chart, 12, 13 (fig.)
Organizations
  in American education, 350
  big, 219–222
  bureaucratic, 242
  and change, 241–245
  classification of, 231
  complex, 222–228
  dependence on, 248
  entry into, 236
  goals of, 225, 232
  informal, 224, 228–230
  instrumental aspects of, 242
  joining of, 236–241
  nondenominational ecumenical, 394

Organizations:
  normative, 234, 236, 237
  officials of, 245
  religious, 382–390
  scientific, 412–413
  in social movement, 268–269
  stratification of, 138
  structure of, 274, 367
  student, 359
  studying, 245–247
  technical problems of, 244
  types of, 230, 232, 247
  utilitarian, 235, 236, 237
Orientals, 296
Ossowski, S., 144
Overpopulation, 460

Panics, 258
Parents, 61, 71, 99, 303, 310, 326
  adolescents and, 329
  American, 327
  conflict with, 338
  control by, 331
  socializing of, 56
  support of, 325
  see also Family; Fathers; Mothers
Parole, 140
  officers, 288
Parry, H. S., 297
Parsons, T., 93, 205, 318, 399
Paton, Alan, 436, 437
Patriotism, 87, 350, 441 (fig.). *See also* Values
Pattern, 11, 14, 97
  and change, 43–44
  of communication flow, 20
  recognition of, 12 (fig.)
  search for, 13
  social, 78, 82, 88
  sociocultural, 43
  of urbanization, 115–118
  see also Behavior
Peace movement, 277, 278, 292. *See also* Anti-Vietnam war movement
Peasants, 111, 128
Peer groups, 85
  adolescent, 329, 330
  role of, 347
Pelz, D. C., 426
Pentecostalism, 392, 393, 416, 446. *See also* Religion
Perception, 5

Rainwater, L., 323
Ramsey, C., 328
Rank
  and conformity, 55
  distinctions of, 156
  see also Status
Rape, 299, 300
Rationalism, response to, 416–417
Raven, B. H., 97, 446
Reality, 431
  alternative concepts of, 10
  and ideal, 373
  perspectives on, 5, 6
  sociological, 11–13, 113
Reason, stress on, 382
Rebellion, 129, 286
Reciprocity, 94
Recognition, professional, 409–410
Recreation, 213, 214
Redlich, F., 138, 139
Reeves, J., 328
Reeves, N., 179, 180
Referral, 208
Reform, social, 15, 134
Reinforcement, of values, 30–31
Reiss, I. L., 317
Reissman, L., 195
Relationships, 22, 75, 84, 85
  pair, 96
  role-defined, 66
  social, 110, 124
  and work, 193
  see also Groups; Society
Religion, 3, 36, 53, 151, 163, 253, 380
  and change, 398–400
  civil, 378
  and class, 152
  comparative view of, 378–382
  and crowds, 263
  and culture, 48, 369, 380
  denominational mergers, 395
  divisiveness of conflict, 378 (fig.)
  and education, 340
  estimated membership, 380 (fig.),
    384–385 (fig.)
  functions of, 373–378
  and magic, 372–373, 379
  and norms, 399
  organizational diversity of, 232,
    382–384
  Oriental, 381–382
  sacred objects, 370 (fig.)
  and social activism, 390 (fig.), 400
    (fig.)

Religion:
  and social change, 390–400
  sociological definition of, 369–373
  sociological perspective on, 48
  sociology of, 401–402
  and state, 377
  and status quo, 378, 396
  symbolism of, 368–369, 402
  in U.S., 384–385
  of work, 189
  world, 380
Religious behavior, 369, 398
Religious sects. *See* Sects
Rembrandt, self-portrait of, 60
Republican Party, 182
Research, 210
  government support of, 418
  scientific, 410
  see also Science
Residence, 151
Residential areas, 117
Restlessness, 131
Retired, 213. *See also* Elderly
Retreatism, 286
Revolutionary, 73
Rewards, 55
Riesman, D., 146, 147, 149
Rights, 94
Ringer, B. B., 389, 390
Riots
  of college students, 261–262
  in Detroit, 256
  Watts, 262
Rites of passage, 328
Ritual, 285–286, 379. *See also*
    Symbolic systems
Ritzer, G., 220
Robins, L. N., 322
Robson, R., 325–328
Rockefeller, John D., Jr., 401
Rockefeller, Nelson J., Jr., 21
Rogers, Carl, 243
Roles, 22, 28, 36–41, 82 (fig.)
  adolescent, 327–332
  and change, 98
  child's, 325–331
  cluster of, 66, 82
  conflict in, 98–99
  and culture, 38
  evolution of, 93
  family, 322, 332
  feminine, 63, 70
  as group structure, 94
  independence of, 40–41

Roles:
  invisibility of, 39–40
  learning of, 50–52
  marital, 323
  masculine, 63, 70
  as microsociological units, 81–82
  of neophyte, 54
  new, 364
  norms and, 39
  occupational, 198
  performance of, 38, 39, 41, 62–64,
    82 (fig.), 94 (fig.)
  prescriptions for, 40, 291
  and primary groups, 85, 86
  research, 210
  sex, 62, 63
  social, 41
  and social change, 67
  stratification of, 137
  suspension of, 292
  in two-person group, 39 (fig.)
  value of, 143, 267
  work, 194
Role-taking, 62–64
Rolling Stones, 269
Roman Catholic Church, 53, 220,
    369, 380, 388, 393
Rome, 111, 188
Roper, Elmo, 36
Rose, A. M., 165, 181, 238, 239, 240,
    241
Rosen, B. C., 59
Rosenberg, M., 203
Rosenhan, David L., 42
Rosenthal, M., 256, 257
Ross, E. A., 19
Rossi, A. S., 318
Roszak, Betty, 63
Roszak, Theodore, 63
Row houses, 114, 118. *See also*
    Housing
Rule-breaking, nondestructive, 291–
    292
Rules, professional, 209
  social, 282
Rumor, 249, 252–259, 274
  and assassination, 256
  and communication, 253
  content of, 253–254
  credibility of, 254
  definition of, 252
  and disaster, 256
  formation of, 255–262
  in social movements, 258

Rumor:
transmitters of, 254–255
during World War II, 253, 255, 257

Sacred, 371–373
Sacred objects, 371
Sacrifice, 379
Sails, 24 (fig.)
St. Louis, Missouri, 113
Pruitt-Iqoe project in, 126
Salisbury, W. S., 383
Sampling, theory of, 273
Sanctions, 55, 306
community, 207
in complex organizations, 227
informal, 227
in professions, 208–209
San Francisco Chronicle, 262
Sanity, judgment of, 42
Saturnalia, 275
Scanlon plan, 244–245
Scharzweller, H. K., 204
Schizophrenia, 7, 73
Scholarly associations, 232
Schools, 340
Catholic, 352
diversity of, 352
drop-outs from, 356
expansion of, 345
importance of, 342
lower, 353, 367
private, 351
public, 350, 351
secondary, 342
and social change, 365
socialization in, 71
see also Education
Schorr, A. L., 126
Schulman, P., 47
Schwartz, M., 64
Schweitzer, Albert, 209
Science (magazine), 412, 419
Science, 3, 7, 405
attitudes toward, 422
growth of, 342
history of, 410
norms of, 404–406, 413
public images of, 421
and public opinion, 423
and religion, 415
and social change, 423–426
social consequences of, 413–417
and social organization, 410–413
social system of, 406

Science:
and society, 413–423
sociology of, 426–427
values and, 417
as verified knowledge, 406–407
see also Knowledge
Scientific American (magazine), 419
Scientific journals, growth in number of, 406 (fig.)
Scientists, 343, 407–413, 419
and employers, 408 (fig.), 411
and responsibility, 425 (fig.)
by scientific field, 408 (fig.)
work of, 408
Scott, R. W., 230–231
Scott, W., 225, 228
Seattle, Washington, Yesler Terrace housing in, 126
Sector theory, 116, 117 (fig.)
Sects, 251, 383–384, 387 (fig.)
SEEK (Search for Education, Elevation, and Knowledge), 357
Seeley, J. R., 127
Segregation, 177
residential, 176–177
see also Discrimination
Selective Service System. *See* Draft, (Selective Service)
Self, 60–66
awareness of, 3, 56, 62
and behavior, 65 (fig.)
definitions of, 61
role-taking and, 61–62
Self-concept, 197–198
Self-consciousness, 60
Self-employment, 201
Selfhood, acquisition of, 66
nature of, 61
Self-image
occupational, 198
and work, 216
see also Identity; Individual
Semiprofessions, 211. *See also* Professions
Senate, U.S. Permanent Subcommittee on Investigations, 262
Senior, C., 172
Senses, 5
Sensitivity training, 102, 244
Serial reproduction, 253
Service organizations, 230
Sex, 36, 88, 165
and crime, 295
and discrimination, 319, 321
division of labor by, 320

Sex:
and occupational distribution, 200
roles, 62, 63
social control of, 310
taboos, 67
Sexism, 174
Sherlock, B., 204
Shils, E. A., 85, 432, 433
Shintoism, 379, 380
Shipwreck, feeling of, 132
Sibling rivalry, 336
Sierra Club, 239
Silberman, C. E., 348
Simmel, Georg, 15
Simpson, G. E., 167
Simpson, G. G., 459
Simulation techniques, 242
Singles bars, 130
Sirjamaki, J., 352
Sit-ins, 271
Skepticism, organized, 405
Skid row, 117
Skills, 128, 143
distribution of, 164
transmission of, 342
Skyscrapers, 110, 115, 118
Slater, P. E., 92, 94
Slavery, 178, 304
Slums, 116, 117
clearance programs, 126
housing in, 125
problems of, 127
and social costs, 123–125
societal response to, 125–128
see also Ghettos
Smelser, N. J., 249, 251, 252, 260
Smith, C., 240
Smith, M. B., 363
SMSA. *See* Standard Metropolitan Statistical Area
Snow, C. P., 427
Social categories, 82
Social change
collective behavior and, 276–278
and conflict, 44
consequences of, 71
creation of, 271
and crowds, 277
deviance and, 293, 303–305
and family, 310, 332–335
groups and, 97–101
and industrialization, 101
minorities and, 181–185
and population density, 110
rapid, 75

Transportation:
   urban, 120, 122
Tribes, American Indian, 163. *See also* Indians
Troeltsch, Ernest, 383
Truman, Harry S., 274
Truth
   revealed, 371
   value of, 33
Turner, R. H., 254, 255, 260, 261, 262, 264
Twenty Statements Test (Kuhn), 62
Tyler, R. W., 346
Tylor, E. B., 23

Ultimate issues, 369–371
Underdeveloped nations, urbanization in, 112. *See also* Developing countries
Underworld, 127. *See also* Crime
Unemployment, 125, 213
   black, 177
   in cities, 128–129
Unionization, 123
Unions, 44, 130, 220, 230, 232
   recognition of, 269
Union Theological Seminary, 369
Unit, of aggregate, 83
United Nations Organization, 246
United Presbyterian Church, 397
United States
   budget of, 29 (fig.)
   intellectual life of, 8
   religions in, 384–390
   see also America
Universalism, 404
Universals, neophyte role, 54
Universities, 220, 340, 357
   role of, 343
   see also Colleges
Urban centers, 115
   development of, 114
   growth of, 112–113, 117
   see also Cities
Urbanites, 131
Urbanization, 14, 15, 16, 111
   of America, 113
   consequences of, 124
   in developing countries, 127–129
   dilemma of, 128
   and industrialization, 118
   new, 128
   problems of, 133
   trend toward, 113

Urbanization:
   urban physical structure of, 116–119
   in U.S., 112
   see also Cities; Industrialization
Urban renewal, 126
Urban studies, 16
Utilities, public, 119

Values, 28–32, 59, 64, 81, 291
   alienation from, 286
   in American education, 344–350
   and behavior, 267
   common orientation to, 440
   conflict of, 74, 449–450
   definition of, 29
   and discrimination, 183–185
   hidden, 31
   hierarchy of, 29–30
   implications of, 32
   life, 375–376
   new, 31–32, 364
   and norms, 36, 267, 285
   and occupational choice, 203–205
   positive, 125
   and primary groups, 86
   reinforcement of, 30–31
   rejection of, 286
   religion and, 399
   and schools, 348, 352, 365–366
   of science, 413
   sharing of, 146
   and social behavior, 30–32
   and social strata, 140
   traditional, 68–70
   transmission of, 342
   in two-person group, 39 (fig.)
   urban, 131
Van den Berghe, P. L., 165
Vatican II, 395
Vehicles, explosion of, 122. *See also* Transportation
Vice, 127
Vietnam war, 277, 278, 298, 331, 458
   opposition to, 132, 363, 400, 448
Villages, 109
   agriculture and, 110–111
   Eskimo, 108
   fishing, 110
   world view of, 129
Violence, 9, 129, 184, 251, 280
Vollmer, H. M., 205
Voluntary associations, 238, 239
   function of, 241
   membership in, 194

Voluntary associations:
   and social change, 240
Voting Rights Bill (1965), 181
Vroom, V., 202

Waller, W., 317
Wallerstein, J. S., 283
Ward, Lester, 15
Warehouses, 114, 117
Warner, W. L., 150, 153
Washington, D.C., growth of, (fig.)
Watergate scandals, 289, 291
Water power, 115 (fig.)
Weber, Max, 15, 68, 142, 188, 225, 228, 229, 268, 383
   on education, 222–224
Weiss, S., 190
Welfare, 123
White, A., 179, 322
Whiting, Beatrice B., 64
Whiting, John W., 64
Wieck, E. E., 77, 96
Wilderness Society, 239
Wilensky, H. L., 193, 194, 205, 209, 211, 212, 215, 216
Williams, R. M., Jr., 240, 291, 322, 327, 375, 382, 440, 446, 447
Wilson, B. R., 383, 394
Winch, R. F., 314, 327
Withey, S. B., 421
Wives, 93, 94, 99, 101, 180, 318, 324
   authority of, 338
   and job market, 319
   roles of, 318–321
   see also Women
Wolfe, T., 103
Wolfle, D., 343
Women, 173
   competition of, 178
   and discrimination, 321
   in labor force, 200, 201, 212–213, 319, 320, 321, 334
   as minority, 177, 181
   power of, 180
   and religion, 390
   in science, 408
   as teachers, 355
Women's Action Group (WAG), 246
Women's liberation movement, 132, 246, 304, 448
Work
   and alienation, 216–217
   attitudes toward, 189, 190–191, 192, 193
   importance of, 189

Work:
   meaning of, 188
   nonwork, 213
   place of, 194–195
   and self-concept, 195
   and self-image, 216
   and social change, 212–215
   status of, 195
   see also Labor; Occupation
Workers, 193
   alienation of, 217
   blue-collar, 190
   farm, 199, 200
   income of, 193
   manual, 200
   norms of, 230

Workers:
   professional, 205
   service, 200
   white-collar, 200
Workweek, 212
World view, 6
   traditional, 415–416
   of villages, 129
World War II, 87, 181
   rumors during, 253, 255, 257
Wounded Knee, conflict at, 47, 304
Wylie, C. J., 283

Yablonsky, L., 101
Yesler Terrace, Seattle, Washington, 126

Yinger, J. M., 167, 336, 369, 371, 388
YMCA, 239
Young, Leontine, 28
Young Republicans, 232

Zelditch, M., Jr., 93, 310, 313
Zen, 374, 381, 382
Zetterberg, H. L., 154, 155, 317
Zigler, E., 50
Zimmerman, C. C., 335
Zones, urban, 116, 117, 125, 126, 136
Zoroastrianism, 374, 380

Index